JEWISH SELF-HATRED

SANDER L. GILMAN

JEWISH SELF-HATRED

ANTI-SEMITISM AND
THE HIDDEN LANGUAGE
OF THE JEWS

The Johns Hopkins University Press
BALTIMORE AND LONDON

This book has been brought to publication with the generous assistance of the Publications Program of the National Endowment for the Humanities, an independent federal agency.

The Johns Hopkins University Press
701 West 40th Street
Baltimore, Maryland 21211
The Johns Hopkins Press Ltd, London

The paper in this book is acid-free and meets the guidelines for permanence and durability of the Committee on Production Guidelines for Book Longevity of the Council on Library Resources.

Library of Congress Cataloging-in-Publication Data
Gilman, Sander L.
  Jewish self-hatred.

  Includes index.
    1. Jews—Germany—Psychology. 2. Antisemitism—
Germany—Psychological aspects. 3. Self-hate (Psychology)
4. Germany—Ethnic relations.   I. Title.
DS135.G3G55 1986   305.8'924'043   85-45050
ISBN 0-8018-3276-4 (alk. paper)

SAMUEL FRIEDRICH
His Book

Contents

Preface

The origin of this study lies in a seminar I taught on stereotypes of woman in nineteenth-century thought. During the seminar one of the students approached me with a very straightforward question: How did women respond to this masculine stereotyping of woman? My answer was that they had an entire range of responses, from the internalization of these images to their outward rejection. Yet, the student answered, they all *did* respond, didn't they? The inexorable response of the stereotyped to their image in society seemed to me self-evident. Yet when writing my study of the image of the insane, it struck me that relatively little interest had been given to how those labeled with the stigma of insanity responded to the image of "madness" in society.

This present study examines how a group defined as different by society as well as by itself responds to one very specific stereotype, the image of its language and discourse. I have examined the history of anti-Jewish attitudes in Germany from this relatively narrow perspective and have autopsied the resultant acceptance (or rejection) of this perception. The label "self-hatred" has been used to characterize the response of writers to the charge of being unable to command the language, discourse, or both, of the world that they inhabit. I have not confused language and discourse. Rather, it is evident that the myth building that surrounds the concept of a "hidden" language of the Jews links both language and discourse in the stereotype of the Jew. This study is therefore limited to those who use language as their means of shaping their identity, who are identified or identify themselves as Jewish, and who comment on the special nature of the language of the Jews. Since this still leaves us with an overwhelming number of writers and their texts, I have further limited the present study to a representative sample of writers, texts, and contexts in order to elucidate the reasons for "self-hatred" and the gradual awareness of Jews of the function of this label and its implications for Jewish identity formation. This study is not meant to be exhaustive in either documentation or the typologies of the Jews' language. What I have shown is that this concept permeates all of the Western images of the Jews (as well as all other images of outsiders). It is pernicious since though it rarely forms the focus of the image of the Jews, it is still ubiquitous.

In dealing with the historiography of self-hatred, it became evident to me that the periodization of anti-Jewish attitudes was inherently false. Speaking of Christian anti-Judaism, scientific anti-Semitism, or popular anti-Semitism meant examining the surface rhetoric in which universal attitudes toward the Other were clothed. Indeed, by tracing the continuity of a single attribute ascribed to the Jews, the deep structure of attitudes toward difference can be seen. I have therefore ignored the labels evolved by historians of anti-Semitism to describe their taxonomy of anti-Jewish images. Since I was not dealing with the political history of the use of these images, the historical terminology seemed to me to obfuscate rather than clarify the patterns I found. Each chapter in the present study deals with a central image of the discourse and/or language of the Jews but also points up the continuity of older images and their relationship to the newer images of the language of the Jews. Thus, while the arrangement of each chapter is approximately chronological, each should also be read tropologically. In most cases, I have given a relatively greater emphasis to the individual reception of the images of the Jews' language so as to show the possible range of responses to stereotypes. I have also traced one of the major sources of the rhetoric of "self-hatred," the medicalization of Jewish discourse, since it provides a context for that very concept of "self-hatred" that forms the key to this present study. Indeed, the medicalization of Jewish discourse from the late Middle Ages, as well as the appearance of "Jewish self-hatred" in the same period, gives the lie to the commonplaces that medicalization of the outsider occurred only with the rise of science in the nineteenth century and that "Jewish self-hatred" was a product of civil emancipation in the eighteenth century.

For their aid in the acquisition of material for this study I wish to thank Ezra Kahn, librarian at Jews' College, London; Geoffrey Hampson and Wendy Buckle, librarians at the Parkes Library, University of Southhampton; librarians at the Wiener Library,

London, the Olin Library, Cornell, the National Library of Medicine, Washington, D.C., and the Wellcome Library of the History of Medicine, London; and David Paisey, senior librarian at the British Library, for his special attention to detail and his friendship. For their unceasing help in ferreting out material unavailable elsewhere I wish to thank Professor Hartmut Steinecke, of the University of Paderborn, and Professor U. H. Peters and his assistant Beate Felten, of the University of Cologne. My special appreciation must be expressed to Kate Bloodgood, who edited and prepared the manuscript, and to Joanne Allen, its copy editor, as well as to Eric Halpern, my editor at The Johns Hopkins University Press. The index was prepared by Jane Marsh Dieckmann. In addition, I wish to thank the students at Cornell who helped shape the arguments in this study. Earlier drafts of parts of this study appeared in the *Lessing Yearbook, Modern Judaism, Psychoanalysis and Contemporary Thought*, and the *Journal of the History of the Behavioral Sciences*.

JEWISH SELF-HATRED

CHAPTER ONE

What Is Self-hatred?

Of all the strange phenomena produced by society, certainly one of the most puzzling is self-hatred.[1] Indeed, when the history of Western attitudes toward those perceived as different, whether black or Jew or homosexual, is studied, the very idea of black, Jewish, or homosexual self-hatred seems a mordant oxymoron. Why hate yourself when there are so many willing to do it for you! But the ubiquitousness of self-hatred cannot be denied. And it has shaped the self-awareness of those treated as different perhaps more than they themselves have been aware.

But what is self-hatred? What forms does it take? How can it be studied? Does it assume different forms within different groups? Does it alter its external manifestations according to when and where it appears? The present study is an attempt to examine one manifestation of self-hatred, Jewish anti-Semitism, in a comparative manner. While evident parallels can be made to other manifestations of self-hatred in the West, Jewish anti-Semitism does provide a self-contained problem which in turn reflects certain basic structures inherent in all manifestations of self-hatred. Thus Jewish self-hatred is both unique, following the fortunes of the treatment of the Jews within both Jewish and non-Jewish communities in the West, and representative, since its deep structure is universal.

"Jewish self-hatred" (a term interchangeable with "Jewish anti-Judaism" or "Jewish anti-Semitism") is valid as a label for a specific mode of self-abnegation that has existed among Jews throughout their history. Yet, as a label it has a very specific history and ideology. The history of its development is one with the concept itself and will form part of the narrative of this book. Now, the fact that it is part of this discourse does not deny its validity; it does, however, demand that the concept be understood in terms of a specific context, and I shall show how when that context is altered the rhetoric but not the structure of the concept is altered. As in the case of the supposed difference between "anti-Judaism" and "anti-Semitism" in the history of the treatment of Jews in Europe, we are dealing with shifts in the articulation of perception, not in the basic perception itself.

Self-hatred results from outsiders' acceptance of the mirage of themselves generated by their reference group—that group in society which they see as defining them—as a reality. This acceptance provides the criteria for the myth making that is the basis of any communal identity. This illusionary definition of the self, the identification with the reference group's mirage of the Other, is contaminated by the protean variables existing within what seems to the outsider to be the homogeneous group in power. This illusion contains an inherent, polar opposition. On the one hand is the liberal fantasy that anyone is welcome to share in the power of the reference group *if* he abides by the rules that define that group. But these rules are the very definition of the Other. The Other comprises precisely those who are not permitted to share power within the society. Thus outsiders hear an answer from their fantasy: Become like us—abandon your difference—and you may be one with us. On the other hand is the hidden qualification of the internalized reference group, the conservative curse: The more you are like me, the more I know the true value of my power, which you wish to share, and the more I am aware that you are but a shoddy counterfeit, an outsider. All of this plays itself out within the fantasy of the outsider. And yet it is not merely an artifact of marginality, for the privileged group, that group defined by the outsider as a reference for his or her own identity, wishes both to integrate the outsider (and remove the image of its own potential loss of power) and to distance him or her (and preserve the reification of its power through the presence of the powerless). Thus the liberal promise and the conservative curse exist on both sides of the abyss that divides the outsider from the world of privilege.

Those labeled as different react in the classic double bind situation.[2] Anyone faced with a set of such conflicting, inherently irreconcilable signs represses this conflict, saying, in effect, The contradiction must be within me, since that which I wish to become cannot be flawed. Perhaps I truly am different, a parody of that which I wish to be. The first sign—be like us, and you will become one of us—implies accepting one's own difference. But the more one attempts to identify with those who have labeled one as different, the more one accepts the values, social structures, and attitudes of this determining group, the farther away from true acceptability one seems to be. For as one approaches the norms set by the reference group, the approbation of the group recedes. In one's own eyes, one becomes identical with the definition of acceptability and yet one is still not accepted. For the ideal state is never to have been the Other, a state that cannot be achieved.

We might assume that perceiving the fault as lying within themselves, outsiders would acknowledge their difference and cease striving for identification with that group which has labeled them as Other. On the contrary, however, while the unconscious sense of rejection is present, this rejection is projected by the outsider onto the world. Now the mechanism of stereotyping is brought full circle, for the group defining the Other has projected its own insecurities concerning its potential loss of power onto the world in the shape of that Other through which it imagines itself threatened. This projection of Otherness, with its implied definition of what is or is not acceptable within the reference group, is accepted by the outsiders as the definition of both what they should not be and what they should become. In subconsciously integrating their rejection into their definition of themselves, they, too, proceed to project their sense of the unresolvable dichotomy of the double bind, but they project it onto an extension of themselves. For if the power group is correct in defining their Otherness—and by definition it must be, or all attempts at identification with it are pointless—then there truly must be something within them that is inherently different. In projecting this Otherness onto the world, they select some fragment of that category in which they have been included and see in that the essence of Otherness, an essence that is separate from their own definition of themselves and embodies all of the qualities projected onto them by the power group.

The central problem with this secondary level of projection is that it is almost always impossible to create a complete break with the new Other. For even as one distances oneself from this aspect of oneself, there is always the voice of the power group saying, Under the skin you are really like them anyhow. The fragmentation of identity that results is the articulation of self-hatred.

The form that this self-hatred takes is not arbitrary. If the goal of the outsiders is to escape the cloak of Otherness in which they are enclosed through their perception of the reference group's values, and their means is to accept and adopt those qualities designated as acceptable and necessary, then the form of their own projection of Otherness is determined by the stereotypical perception of the privileged group. The secondary projection is thus as protean as the primary one. It follows the needs and demands of historical accident and social change; it mirrors alterations in the basic paradigms of Otherness held by any society. The image projected onto the world of the Other by outsiders is simply an extension of that projected onto them by the group that defined them as Other. The mechanism by which this is achieved is extraordinarily simple. Every stereotype is Janus-faced. It has a positive and a negative element, neither of which bears any resemblance to the complexity or diversity of the world as it is. The positive element is taken by the outsiders as their new definition. This is the quality ascribed to them as the potential members of the group in power. The antithesis to this, the quality ascribed to them as the Other, is then transferred to the new Other found within the group that those in power have designated as Other. For every "noble savage" seen through colonial power a parallel "ignoble savage" exists. Within the world of the Other, a world seen as homogeneous by the reference group, with its presumed privilege, the same dichotomy exists. There are nobler savages and yet ignobler ones.

Self-hatred arises when the mirages of stereotypes are confused with realities within the world, when the desire for acceptance forces the acknowledgment of one's difference. It is therefore one of the universal products of the way we are forced to see the world. On one level or another we are all Others to some group. But it is the pernicious existence of culturally determined patterns of Otherness, applied not to individuals but to groups, that is most interesting. The shifting implication of roles within the society, the change from dependence to dominance in the development of any given individual, tends to blur under the pressure of the stereotyping of a group. While one can outgrow the stereotype of adolescence, with its implied lack of power and its potential for self-hatred, one cannot escape one's ethnic, religious, or class identity. One cannot escape these labels because of the privileged group's myth that these categories are immutable. The reference group distinguishes between categories of difference that are mutable, which depend on specific aspects of age or geography, and those that are perceived as inherent and inalterable, such as ethnic identity or race. These are simply myths about the nature of difference that are spun about realities, such as skin color or age. The myths are, however, powerful enough to substitute for realities. Outsiders view themselves as marginal and are thus dependent on such real or imagined categories to define the borders of acceptability, which must be crossed into the world of privilege ascribed to the reference group. This movement can be understood to take place in reality or merely in the fantasy of the Other. The former takes the place of "enacted daydreams," fantasies of power and acceptability played out on the stage of the real world. In this way outsiders assume many of the characteristics of the privileged group, especially with regard to themselves. Such "denial in word and act" is merely the living out of those "denial[s] in fantasy" that every member of a group defined as marginal experiences.[3]

The labeling of the categories of difference is not random. The structure of Otherness is relatively homogeneous. It reflects the myths of society as applied to the basic structures of humanity. Thus, external references such as language, clothing, and social and hygienic codes are as important to the construction of the myth of Otherness as are so-called internal aspects, such as gender, skin color, or physiognomy. What is stressed within the coding of Otherness at any given moment in history or in any given context is dependent on the reference group's needs and the outsider's perception of those needs at that moment or in that context. What appears to be a shifting of the mirage of Otherness is merely a change in emphasis. All the qualities in the vocabulary of Otherness are present at all times. The Other thus responds to both the overt and the covert coding of its difference, projecting those qualities perceived as negative on a subgroup within the general category of the Other.

The sense that there are "good" qualities as well as "bad" ones in the projections that are concretized into the Other means that these qualities will also be found within the newly formed self-definition of the Other. If I am "good," I will be accepted; those who are "bad" deserve being rejected. The qualities ascribed to the "good" and "bad" aspects of the Other are perceived as real. They are, of course, only chimerical. The protean nature of this coding means that any quality can become another quality, even its antithesis, instantly. Just as James Joyce tabulated "who was who when everybody was somebody else" in *Finnegans Wake*, so, too, the qualities of Otherness, even within the most rigid antitheses, are interchangeable. To see this in operation and to judge the power of such a constantly shifting set of qualities, one can turn to one of the seemingly immutable qualities of Otherness, skin color. It is a truism that skin color has mythic qualities. Frantz Fanon summarized the attitude of the West toward Blackness, which is but the projection of Western anxiety concerning the Other in terms of skin color:

In Europe, the Black man is the symbol of Evil. . . . The torturer
is the Black man, Satan is Black, one talks of shadows, when
one is dirty one is black—whether one is thinking of physical
dirtiness or moral dirtiness. It would be astonishing, if the trouble were taken to bring them all together, to see the vast
number of expressions that make the Black man the equivalent
of sin. In Europe, whether concretely or symbolically, the Black
man stands for the bad side of the character. As long as one
cannot understand this fact, one is doomed to talk in circles
about the "black problem." Blackness, darkness, shadow,
shades, night, the labyrinths of the earth, abysmal depths,
blacken someone's reputation; and on the other side, the bright
look of innocence, the white dove of peace, magical, heavenly
light.[4]

That blacks are black, that they are the antithesis of the mirage of
whiteness, the ideal of European aesthetic values, strikes the reader
as an extension of some "real," perceived difference to which the
qualities of "good" and "bad" have been erroneously applied. But
the very concept of color is a quality of Otherness, not of reality.
For not only blacks are black in this amorphous world of projection;
so, too, are Jews.

Prosper Mérimée, in his novella *Carmen* (1845), records the
meeting of his narrator, a French antiquarian, with the protagonist
on a parapet above the river in Cordova. Carmen is the quintessential Other—female, a gypsy possessing all languages and yet
native only in her hidden tongue, proletarian, and black. For as
Mérimée notes later in the tale, the gypsies are "the black ones."
But when Carmen is first introduced to the reader, it is not at all
clear who she is. The narrator hazards a guess that she "might be
Moorish or . . . (I stopped short, not daring to say Jewish)."[5] It is
Carmen's appearance that leads the narrator astray. But this over-
lapping of images of Otherness—the Moor, the Jew, the Gypsy—
is possible only from the perspective of the French narrator, for
whom Otherness in Spain is an amalgam of all of these projections.
Now, Mérimée's image of his narrator's confusion of Others is quite
blatant and has little polemical value outside the world of the
fiction that is his tale of Carmen. There is a considerable shift in
the implications of the coalescing of structures or codes of Otherness when one moves to a later text in a quite different cultural
context.

Within the late-nineteenth-century racist tractates published
in Germany, the image of the black Jew appears with specific polit-

ical implications. In his *Foundations of the Nineteenth Century* (1899), Houston Stewart Chamberlain, Richard Wagner's son-in-law, categorizes the Jews as "a mongrel race which always retains this mongrel character."[6] This is not merely a gratuitous insult, for Chamberlain, like many of the thinkers of the late nineteenth century, stressed the centrality of racial purity. The Jews are the least pure race, the inferior product of a "crossing of absolutely different types." While Chamberlain does see some value in "racial mixture" as a means of strengthening racial types, he uses the Jews as the prime example of the negative results of such interbreeding. For Chamberlain the most recent "hybridization" of the Jews was the "admixture of Negro blood with Jewish in the Diaspora of Alexandria—of which many a man of Jewish persuasion at this day offers living proof." Chamberlain's choice of the Jews was not a random one. He wished to document the biological basis of the "Jewish Question" as perceived by racist thinkers at the turn of the century. He sought out the idea of Blackness, a myth that had even stronger implications within the German tradition than elsewhere because of the almost total absence of blacks in the German experience of the world.

By the time Chamberlain wrote his infamous tractate, Germany had been a colonial power for little less than two decades, and the Germans were applying their myth of Otherness to the paternalistic treatment of blacks in their colonies. In the German-speaking countries of central Europe the black was powerless. This myth of Blackness was then applied to the political reality of the Jews, who were assuming a promised status in Europe. The Jews became the "white Negroes," as Otto von Bismarck's friend Hermann Wagener observed in 1862, because the demands of the Jews for political and social equality created in the privileged group, the Germans, the need to see the Jews as politically subservient and immutably different.[7] This image of the Jews as black is, however, not merely the product of the racist biology of the late nineteenth century, even though the examples that have been cited to this point reflect the rhetoric of this pseudoscience. For the association of the Jews with Blackness is as old as Christian tradition. Medieval iconography always juxtaposed the black image of the synagogue, of the Old Law, with the white of the church.[8] The association is an artifact of the Christian perception of the Jews which has been simply incorporated into the rhetoric of race. But it is incorporated, not merely as an intellectual abstraction, but as the model through which Jews are perceived, treated, and thus respond as if confronted with the reflection of their own reality. Adam Gurowski, a Polish noble, observed in his 1857 memoirs that "numbers of Jews have the greatest resemblance to the American mulattoes. Sallow carnation complexion, thick lips, crisped black hair. Of all the Jewish population scattered over the globe one-fourth lives in Poland. I am, therefore, well acquainted with their features. On my arrival in this country (the United States) I took every light-colored mulatto for a Jew."[9] In the eyes of the non-Jew who defined them in Western society the Jews became the blacks.

If the Blackness of the Jew is the synthesis of two projections of Otherness within the same code, then how did the Other, the Jews, respond to being labeled as black? Erik Homburger Erikson's first work, *Childhood and Society* (1950), contains a detailed analysis of Adolf Hitler's development based on a reading of Hitler's *Mein Kampf* (1923). He presents Hitler's racial typology as "a simple racial dichotomy of cosmic dimension: the German (soldier) versus the Jew," and he goes on to characterize this typology:

> The Jew is described as small, black, and hairy all over; his back is bent, his feet are flat; his eyes squint, and his lips smack; he has an evil smell, is promiscuous, and loves to deflower, impregnate, and infect blond girls. The Aryan is tall, erect, light, without hair on chest and limbs; his glance, walk and talk are *stramm*, his greeting the out-stretched arm. He is passionately clean in his habits. He would not knowingly touch a Jewish girl—except in a brothel. This antithesis is clearly one of ape man and superman.[10]

Erikson, who fled Austria to escape the Nazis and who earlier had fled his own identity as a Homburger to become an Erikson, presents very much his own reading of Hitler's racial theory. For what strikes a reader of *Mein Kampf* is that Hitler did not accept Chamberlain's hybrid theory of Jewish racial identity; rather he relied on a much more primitive conspiracy theory.[11] For Hitler the linkage between the Jew and the black was a political one. It was the Jews who inspired the French to station black troops along the Rhine following the 1919 armistice, and it was therefore the intent of the Jews to loose these "barbarians belonging to a race inspired by Nature ... with a tremendous sexual instinct into the heart of Europe."[12] Erikson simply recreates the image of the Jew as black with which he himself grew up. Erikson's image of the "black" Jew is a hyperbolic summary of the Nazi image of the Jew. For the Aryan "superman" had been destroyed, and his perfection had been shown to be chimerical. But Erikson's image of the Jew, his integration and projection of his own inner anxiety about his own identity, is present in his parody of Nazi racial theory.

Erikson begins his discussion of the nature of the Jew by dismissing Oswald Spengler's argument that anti-Semitism is merely "a matter of projection." Erikson argues that while such projections are distortions, there is always a "kernel of profound meaning," not in terms of the group projecting the stereotype but in terms of that group onto which it is projected. He then tabulates three qualities of the "Jew" which trigger the projections of the anti-Semites. First is the ritual of circumcision, which is the Jew's way of "asking for it." For Erikson, it is a symbol of the fear of castration. Second are the two models of the Jew, "dogmatic orthodoxy and opportunistic adaptability, the living caricatures of the bearded Jew in his kaftan, and Sammy Glick." This dichotomy of Jewish identity is postulated as the radical split in the identity of the Jew that gives rise to the third quality, "cynical relativism" or the adherence to dogma, whatever its nature.

Erikson's rejection of the Blackness of the Jew present in nineteenth- and early twentieth-century racial theory seems absolute. And yet when he turns to his own anatomy of the Jew, he simply adapts, in terms of his own projection of that which he sees himself not to be, other aspects of these same theories. Indeed, it is in Hitler's *Mein Kampf* that the rootlessness of the Jews, their support of all destructive dogmas, from the Talmud to Marxism, is stressed. And what is most important, Erikson selects the two images of the Jew that dominate the anti-Semitic texts of his adopted home, Vienna. The Jew is either the dogmatic, illogical Eastern Jew, "the bearded Jew in his Kaftan," or the *Luftmensch*, the wheeler-dealer, rootless, without morals or goals. The latter catgory is represented for him by the title character of Budd Schulberg's 1941 novel, *What Makes Sammy Run?* It is thus in fictions, in the world of texts and discourse, that Erikson places the "bad" Jew. While Erikson does point out that these are the extremes of what he perceives Jewish identity to be, seeing the Jewish mediation of culture within the relativity of a Jewish perception of the world, he also outlines what he is not. He is clearly not the racial stereotype of Jewish physiognomy, for that is to be like the American image of the powerless black as victim, a subject to which he devotes an entire chapter in *Childhood and Society;* nor is he the rootless Jew, without goals or morals. He sees himself as a creator of a new Jewish discourse, like his triumvirate of ideal Jews, "Marx, Freud, and Einstein," all of whom *"personify* these redefinitions of the very ground man thought he stood on." Erikson sees himself within the model of this image of the Jew; he projects his inner anxiety concerning his potential weakness, that weakness ascribed to him by the Germans as a Jew, onto the Jewish Other. One need not repeat the Nazi image of the Jew as revolutionary and destructive. Within the entire panoply of the Nazi rhetoric about the Jew, the revolutionary triad of Marx, Freud, and Einstein, the creators of Jewish class struggle, Jewish psychology, and Jewish physics, dominates. Alfred Rosenberg, the Nazi party ideologist, makes this point quite tellingly in his continuation of Chamberlain's argument in *The Myth of the Twentieth Century* (1930). Erikson has shaped his image of the Jew within the confines of the anti-Semitic rhetoric which categorizes the nature of the Jew, including the labeling of the Jew as black. No longer concerned with this superficial categorization, he includes within his image of the Jew other aspects of the code of Otherness applied to the Jew, selecting some aspects as positive and applicable to himself and others as negative, and these negative images are projected onto real Jews in the real world. Erikson's "kernel of profound meaning" found within the "Jews" turns out to be nothing more than his projection of his inner anxieties about his self-definition onto the nature of the Jew, in a rhetoric framed by his own time and place in the world.

The image of the black Jew was not simply the private fantasy of one who saw himself as different. The status of the black within Weimar Germany was extraordinarily parallel to that of the Jew under the Nazis. Much public discussion revolved about the question of what should be done with the offspring of "black" (i.e., non-European) soldiers, especially in the occupied Rhineland. The proposals were all cast in the rhetoric of "eugenics," a pseudoscience that in Germany became closely allied with the suppression of Jewish identity. What was suggested most often was sterilization.[13] Erikson's sense that the Jews were tempting fate through their public avowal of circumcision was evoked by the threat to sterilize all "blacks." Thus Jewish "self-castration" (circumcision as a sign of difference) called forth, and was called forth by, the threat of the public rhetoric about the black. Seeing oneself as outside of this circle became a necessity in order to retain any sense of control over one's own person.

Erikson's claim to have written a new, uncontaminated discourse, the discourse of the European intelligentsia, of Marx, Freud, and Einstein, who transcended being Yiddish-speaking Eastern Jews or Jewish social climbers speaking the language of business, is also rooted to some degree in this image of the blackness of the Jew. For the language, and by analogy the discourse, of the

Jew was perceived as parallel to that of the black. Julius Streicher, one of the most notorious anti-Semites of the Weimar Republic and the Third Reich, understood this when he published a long, pseudoscientific essay in 1928 in which the language of the Jew was directly equated with that of the black: "The swollen lips remind us again of the close relationship between the Jews and the Blacks. Speech takes place with a racially determined intonation."[14] Thus Erikson, who is quite sensitive to the question of the prejudice directed against American blacks and its effect on them, distances himself within his new English-speaking persona from the charge of speaking like the black and therefore calling down upon himself the punishment directed at the black in the United States. Erikson's images stem from his upbringing in the German-speaking world. He translates these into a post-Holocaust American vocabulary about difference, but one that retains traces of the imagery of European anti-Semitism. Part of his proof of his difference from this image of the Jew as black lies in the very fact that he can write about the "Black Question" as he writes about the "Jewish Question," in a distanced, scientific tone. Yet the initial fears and their association with difference are maintained even with this shift in discourse.

Now if the Jew can be seen as black, the Other can possess whatever negative qualities we perceive within ourselves. But given any historical tradition of perceiving the Other, whether as Jew, black, homosexual, or woman, there are variations in emphasis and structure in the code of Otherness. The projections concerning the Jew are different because they occur in different contexts, but they consist of the the same raw material as do all other codes of Otherness. In examining the projections of the dominant society concerning the Jews, in seeing the Jews as society has perceived them, one has the first key to the structure of self-hatred. For what we shall be interested in examining is how Jews see the dominant society seeing them and how they project their anxiety about this manner of being seen onto other Jews as a means of externalizing their own status anxiety. The Jew as black also counters one of the major objections to what will be our working definition of the Jew. The Jew is one perceived and treated as a Jew. This version of Jean-Paul Sartre's well-known definition of the Jew as one seen as a Jew was suggested by Albert Memmi, who realized that in order to respond to being categorized as different, one must experience being treated as different.[15] Emil Fackenheim objected to Sartre's definition, since it placed anti-Semitism on the same plane as all other group prejudices.[16]

Sartre's definition, departing as it does from the question of the nature of anti-Semitism, does not reflect any internal continuity of Jewish identity, only the reaction of the Jew (or any outsider) to the world in which he or she is found. This does not deny an internal group identity; it only places this identity, whether strong or weak, in a greater social context. In Sartre, Fackenheim missed the special position that anti-Jewish feeling has within the history of Europe and the Americas. Seeing the Jew as black reflects the protean nature of all perceptions of difference.

Fackenheim criticized the equation of these perceptions, and yet it is to this very equation that Jews as outsiders respond. However, it is not an abstract equation but its being acted out in the world that is the key to the response of Jews. For the power of this equation lies in the fact that Europeans begin to act out their image of the black in their actions toward Jews. When Jews do not respond to this model of treatment, a backlash occurs. Jews, responding to being treated as "black," strive evermore to escape this category. European society sees this response as a "typically Jewish" one, in which the Jew, by trying to change, denies the truth of the category of perception as well as treatment. In altering their sense of self Jews reify the reference group's treatment of them as lacking "true" character (like their analogue, the black). Jews respond by projecting this image onto the world and creating a Jew who possesses all of the negative qualities ascribed to the image of the Jew as black.

The structures by which Jews attempt this type of externalization of inner fear are not autonomous. They follow patterns of the historical perception of Otherness. They stress the marginality of the Other, but as one of the qualities ascribed to Otherness. Thus the central paradigm of self-hatred is but a carbon copy of the nature of stereotyping itself. In its dynamic reaction to shifts in perception, it is a constantly fluctuating series of self-images. Thus a study of self-hatred can provide a history of the myth building within a group, such as the Jews, as to the essence of their own identity. For in discovering what the Jew is supposed *not* to be, some sense of the constantly changing definition of the "true" Jew can be evolved. As Jews react to the world by altering their sense of identity, what they wish themselves to be, so they become what the group labeling them as Other had determined them to be. The group labeling the Other is able successfully to elude their stereotype and the reality to which it is supposed to relate, since the Other reacts to the stereotyping as if it were a valid set of descriptive categories of its identity. Nineteenth-century Austrian playwright Johannes Nestroy presented a case study of this mechanism in the alteration of the character of his red-headed hero in *The Talisman* (1840) through finding a black wig. The fiery-tempered, irresponsible, shiftless redhead (all qualities ascribed by German mythmaking to persons having red hair) is treated as a serious, accountable member of society once his hair color changes. More than a century later Max Frisch, in his *Andorra* (1961), presented a counterexample in the central character, whose assumed Jewish parentage causes his neighbors to treat him like their image of the Jew and who responds by becoming the reification of this mirage of the Jew. Erik Erikson's response to his labeling as the Other, the intellectual, the psychoanalyst (a synonym to the Nazis for *Jew*), is to project those qualities unacceptable in his own self-image onto the marginal Jews in Viennese (and American) society, the Eastern Jew and the *Luftmensch*. Erikson's case can serve as a paradigm of how images are transferred from one outsider to another and how the outsider responds in a dynamic manner.

The idea of Jewish self-hatred presupposes access to some inner image of the Jew. A study such as this one, with its historical dimensions, would be impossible if it were not for the concretions of such images within cultural artifacts—the books, newspapers, tractates, works of science and medicine, art, theater—of any society. These sources reveal the preoccupation of Jews in the West with their Otherness and provide a paradigm for the understanding of any group through its cultural record. To paraphrase the title of one of Alfred Weber's works, cultural history can become cultural psychology as well as cultural sociology. The written word provides the historian of stereotypes with the raw material with which to recreate the evolving sense of Jewish identity in response to the rhetoric of the Western world. Thus it is not merely the use of the cultural artifact as an example illustrating the progress (or decay) of any society but the very language or code inherent in the work itself that is of interest. This code provides the raw material for an understanding of some of the inner workings of a society's perception of its worlds, its mentality. The language of the Other, the mirror of the world it perceives about it, is permeated with the rhetoric of self-hatred. It takes its discourse, its mode of self-description, from the world about it, and that language is saturated with the imagined projection of the Other—not merely in the sense that *to jew* is an acceptable verb at certain times and in certain places or that "nigger in the woodpile" still is the proverbial manner of describing a potential difficulty in American rural usage. These are the crude excrescences of Otherness inherent in any language. Even more basic are the norms contained within language which are then applied to the world, as if the metaphors and metonymies were realities.

As Fanon has shown, the extensions of images of Otherness reach into the very recesses of our consciousness, so that we cannot perceive the world, and its inhabitants, outside of this filter. Our sense of the world is structured by the code of marginality that we generate out of elements in the world. We give value to value-neutral aspects of experience. We do this in applying the values to the amorphous, protean sense of anxiety that we all possess, an anxiety produced by the sense that we will lose our imagined "power."[17] This sense of the Other as undermining the power that we wish we had over the world is captured in the language that we use, either directly or indirectly, to speak about the Other. We may allude to their presence directly and thus react with language that is specifically coded to deal with differences. We may speak of them in terms that are racist or idealized, or we may simply react to the structuring of the world into "good" and "bad," into white hats and black hats, which introduces the vocabulary of Otherness into areas where its presence alters our acceptance of the world. For why are "good" cowboys identified with white hats, and "bad" cowboys with black hats? This code is one of the Other applied to an area that would seem inappropriate. And yet it carries with it the strength of all of our associations with Otherness.

Language, therefore, in codified systems of representation, traps the outsider as the source of our potential loss of power. This language is ubiquitous. When those who are labeled as marginal are forced to function within the same discourse as that which labels them as different, conflict arises that may not be consciously noted by outsiders, for they are forced to speak using the polluted language that designates them as Other. Caliban, Shakespeare's ultimate Other—deformed, hypersexual, black, son of the devil and a witch—curses Prospero for having taught him a language in which all he can do is curse. It is, of course, Prospero's language that Caliban now commands, a language that brands him as a "poisonous slave."[18] Adapting to a new language, as did African blacks in slavery, the Irish following Cromwell, or the Jews in the Diaspora, means at least a period in which the novelty of the language makes a sensitive speaker aware of the hidden agenda of Otherness present in the language to be adopted. Such a moment of conscious disparity is also present in the tensions that exist between class-determined linguistic differences. One can hear the code of Otherness better when one is able to stand outside the language, if but imperfectly. It is in language, then, that the tensions of Otherness and thus eventually of self-hatred can best be examined.

The role of a "civilized" language in defining the Other is central to the articulation of the identity of the Jew in the West. John Murray Cuddihy has tried to explain the conflicts within modern Jewish identity as the result of an Enlightenment ideal of "civilized" behavior.[19] All of modern Jewish identity, according to Cuddihy, is the result of the drive to accept "civilized" behavior and the need to reject "uncivilized" behavior. The latter is, for Cuddihy, posited by Western Jewry in the image of the Eastern Jew; the former, in the ideals of a Western, enlightened society. What Cuddihy, and indeed any student of the development of Jewish identity, is dealing with, however, are written documents, texts in the most limited sense of the word, in which the authors articulate their identity. In reading books by Freud, Marx, or Lévi-Strauss (the subjects of Cuddihy's book) we are dealing with texts written within a major, Western literary tradition in which supposedly inarticulate Others are proving their literacy and providing even more complicated models of language for the privileged group, models that by definition are nonsectarian and apply to all human conduct.

Writing plays a central role in defining Jews against the preconceptions of the world in which they find themselves. The importance of writing antedates the Enlightenment and is a general model for the articulation of Jewish identity in the West. In Western society the people of the Book meet the people of the books. Western society stresses the centrality of the written word as the icon of "civilization," or "culture," and believes that the Other does not—cannot—share in this most holy and civil of acts, the act of writing (and the parallel acts of reading and interpretation). The Other cannot ever truly possess "true" language and is so treated. They therefore are at pains to constantly stress their ability to understand, to write, on levels more complex, more esoteric, more general, and more true than do those treating them as "inarticulate Jews." The reference group sees them as inarticulate because while they use the language of their environment, they can never possess it. Why? Because they have their own hidden language, the language that is the true articulation of their Jewishness, the language of Otherness. When Al-Jahiz, in the early Middle Ages, comments on Jews who speak Hebrew and Arabic that "when the two languages meet on a single tongue, one usually hurts the other," he is giving voice to the sense that the Jew, in possessing Hebrew, can never master Arabic as does a true follower of the Prophet. There is some truth in his statement, for from the earliest days of the Diaspora the Jews were bilingual; they possessed their religious tongue as well as their secular one.[20] They spoke Hebrew as well as Arabic, some with greater facility, some with less.

Maimonides, a thousand years before Moses Mendelssohn's Bible translation (written in German but printed in Hebrew characters), wrote his works in Arabic but printed them in Hebrew characters. For, like Mendelssohn, he could assume that his *readers* knew at least the Hebrew alphabet (the minimum standard of Hebrew literacy) but understood Arabic much better than Hebrew. The existence of this "fact," the implied bilingualism of the Jews, was, of course, limited to those Jews who learned to read the Hebrew alphabet. Assuming that there was a higher level of literacy among Jews (defining literacy in the most minimal manner, i.e., as having the command of the alphabet) gives an aura of verisimilitude to the legend of the hidden language of the Jews. But it is clear that the fable of this hidden language, and how it was defined, may have drawn its external structure from the fact of Jewish bilingualism but drew its substance from the quality of language always ascribed to the Other. The Other's language is hidden, dark, magical, dangerous, private. So, too, is the language of the Jews. That language is associated with "culture" is of little surprise. In the West language is the hallmark of civilization. To be accepted in society means acquiring the reference group's discourse. This problem did not suddenly appear with the emancipation of the Jews in the eighteenth century. It is a problem inherent in the existence of the Jews in the Diaspora, a problem of exile, a problem felt as well by Africans ripped from their native land and language and transported to the Americas. These blacks, too, had their native tongues, which, like the language ascribed to the Jews, were perceived as part of their inherent nature, of the magical, dark side of the African. In myth, it has been replaced by a series of "black" discourses, the languages of the writers consciously labeled by Western society as well as themselves as black.

There is a difference between the "natural" evolution of the language of an oppressed or subjugated people in response to linguistic colonialism and the mythopoesis of this process. When a dominant culture is superimposed upon another culture, it is normal for the suppressed cultural tradition to evolve a pidginized form of the dominant culture's language. At first this language is heavily marked by the suppressed language; later, the suppressed language is retained only in the accent or the intonation, perhaps in some vocabulary items. In the final stage this slight difference becomes a positive sign; the speakers use this slight difference to stress their necessary separateness, a separateness initially imposed upon them by their reference group and now a sign of their identity. Frantz Fanon ascribed "a basic importance to the phenomenon of language. . . . To speak means above all to assume a culture, to support the weight of a civilization. . . . Every dialect is a way of thinking. . . . And the fact that the newly returned [from white schools] Negro adopts a language different from that of the group into which he was born is evidence of a dislocation, a separation."[21] This separation from the original group is bridged in Fanon's mind by the evolution of group-specific dialects, "all of it, of course, tricked out with the appropriate accent." The problem is that in order to evolve a group language that is both individual and acceptable to the dominant group, one must resolve an inherent, perhaps irreconcilable, conflict. For the dominant group sees the language of the repressed group as inferior and corrupt, both in its original form and in its adaptation to the language of the dominant group. Indeed, the more the original language vanishes and the outsider assumes the language of the privileged group, the more the values of this reference group are reified. The stages of pidgin are thus perceived by the dominant group as comic adaptation, since they mask the repression of hostility in the form of the partial acceptance of the dominant language, an acceptance that reveals again the inferiority of the repressed culture (at least in the eyes of the dominant one). Speakers of the repressed language, a language that is the primary sign of the inferiority of the culture being suppressed, are labeled as inferior, as are speakers of the various gradations of pidgin.

It is only at the moment when the value of the original group is recognized that the idea of a special language and its qualities are reversed. If belonging to a group is "good" rather than "bad," then the language of that group likewise must be "good." By then, however, the linguistic sign of that group is not the original language or even pidgin (in either its initial or later phase) but merely the shadow of the language, the intonation which can be put on or off at will, and the conscious use of specific items from the vocabulary of the language.

This is true in general of all suppressed languages and their speakers, as Richard Rodriguez observes.[22] What is interesting about the hidden language of the Jews is that while the pattern maintained itself, it did so on the level of a mythologizing of the nature of language. And I would suspect that the same is true of the development of all repressed languages. The Middle Ages posited Hebrew as the "secret language of the Jews" not only because Jews used Hebrew as their religious language but because certain magical qualities were ascribed to this tongue that complemented the idea of the Jew. As the Jew became less and less the medieval magician and more and more the object of Christian economic interest, the focus shifted from Hebrew to Yiddish, a tongue that European Jews spoke long before it became the "secret language of the Jews" in the seventeenth century.

Yiddish was perceived as a form of pidgin. It was seen as German in which were embedded shards of the original magical Hebrew. With the civil emancipation of the Jews, the demonstrable fact that Jews spoke German, but with a marked accent, created the basis for the next level of the perception of the language of the Jews. Jews spoke German, and in a comprehensible manner, but with an identifiable accent and with certain unique phrases (many of which would be intelligible to a non-Jewish listener). By the middle of the nineteenth century this comic Jewish dialect began to be replaced by an ideological parallel. For even if Jews could speak perfect grammatical, syntactic, and semantic German, their rhetoric revealed them as Jews. Sometimes this rhetoric was clothed in the intonation ascribed to the Jew, but more often than not it was the mode of discourse that was important. Whether revolutionary or conservative, journalistic or philosophic, it could always be seen as a specific language of the Jews. This was the case through the Holocaust. With the decimation of the community of European Jews a new discourse was ascribed to them that was as contradictory as the earlier tongues: it was the silence of the Jews that followed Auschwitz. Jews were thus always forced to show that they could both speak an acceptable language and speak it better than their non-Jewish contemporaries. Thus in the course of the nineteenth century, as the values of a Jewish language were perceived, it became clear that a positive value was given by Jews to their difference, but a difference as defined and perceived by the non-Jew. The renaissance in interest in Eastern European Jewry was an indicator of this shift, since it was articulated in the rhetoric and style of German belles lettres. Jews were constantly being forced to define who they were in a language that they were understood not to command. Here the world of myth led to certain basic conflicts within Jewish writers and thinkers, conflicts that served as the basis for self-hatred. This self-hatred was projected onto other images of the Jews.

When Jews attempt to "identify with the aggressor," to use Anna Freud's phrase, in order to deal with their real fear of being treated as a Jew, they accept the qualities ascribed by the reference group to their own language. George Eliot presents a remarkable image of this aspect of Jewish self-hatred in Lapidoth, the father of Mirah Cohen, the Jewish heroine of her *Daniel Deronda*. He is portrayed as a failed actor by his daughter, who

> would even ridicule our own people; and once when he had been imitating their movements and their tones in praying, only to make others laugh, I could not restrain myself—for I always had an anger in my heart about my mother—and when we were alone, I said, "Father, you ought not to mimic our own people before Christians who mock them: would it not be bad if I mimicked you, that they might mock you?" But he only shrugged his shoulders and laughed and pinched my chin, and said, "You couldn't do it, my dear."[23]

Eliot, who elsewhere in the novel stressed the natural predisposition of her eponymous "Jewish" hero for the magic language of the Jews, Hebrew, is reacting against the image of the Jew attempting to ingratiate himself into European society through self-hatred. Mirah does not have the same self-loathing that Eliot ascribes to her father. She identifies her language with the Hebrew prayers of her mother. Self-hatred is linked by Eliot to the Jews' consciousness of the myth of the difference of their language—but, of course, in a very special context. For Eliot's self-hating Jew is an actor, one who relies on a command of the tool of a European language. Similarly, those self-hating Jews whom we shall be examining in this study are all writers who rely on language for their status (and thus their power) in society. No matter what their discourse, whether literary or scientific, when they use language it is always with the anxiety that they use language differently than their reference group, in a way that is understood by it as "Jewish." Self-hating Jews respond either by claiming special abilities in the discourse of the reference group or by rejecting it completely and creating a new discourse, uncontaminated, they believe, by their exclusion from it. Thus writers perceived and treated as "Jews" tend to be in the forefront of both traditional and avant-garde movements in Germany. This provides at least one partial explanation for their visibility in this area, an area of status accessible to the "Jew" but denied him or her by the very fact of the presuppositions of the reference group about the hidden language of the Jews. George Eliot places the source of Jewish self-hatred in the position of the Jew in the West. She sees those "who must walk among the nations and be known as Jews, and with words on their lips which mean, 'I wish I had not been born a Jew, I disown any bond with the long travail of

my race, I will outdo the Gentiles in mocking at our separateness' "
as the product of Christian society. The self-hating Jew, for Eliot,
is one who "sharing in no love, sharing in no subjection of the soul
. . . mocks all" (2:380–81). It is the mockery by self-hating Jews,
the reflection of the reference group's image of their own discourse,
that marks the self-hating Jew. Mockery brings forth mockery, but
mockery directed at a projection of the self rather than at the self.

This model for the rise of self-hatred out of the myth of a
hidden language of the Jews can be examined only in very specific
contexts. For if the anxiety felt by Jews as writers centers about
their internalization of this myth and their projection of it in the
world, then only in those moments in their writings when they
choose (or are forced) to deal with "Jewish" topics will this sense
of anxiety surface. Suddenly they are dealing with that category
which they have successfully repressed through the very act of
writing and which now draws this success into question. The Jew
as writer reasons, I write for an audience that recognizes my ability
as a master of a specific discourse. Once I deal with the "Jewish
Question," I raise the specter of the hidden language of the Jews
and thus draw my own mastery into question. At such moments
the text reveals its inner fabric, enabling the reader to examine
self-hatred and its projection into the fiction of the text. For within
the text is played out the sense of the loss of control, of the rending
of the mask that enables the Other to function in spite of being
rejected by the group that defines them. They become one with
their ability to control their language, to show their difference from
the image of the Other that they have internalized.

This myth of the hidden language of the Jews can exist only
if there is an antithesis between the idea of the nature of national
language and that of the language of the Jews. Such a polarity is
itself mythic. But in societies such as the German-speaking ones
there is a strong tradition of the myth of a homogeneous language
that defines the Other as possessing a different tongue. In a more
heterogeneous society (or at least one in which the myth of heterogeneity dominates the definition of the reference group) such a
simple reduction does not work. The outsider may be defined, in
one aspect, by the hidden nature of language, but this definition
does not assume the centrality that it does in societies that see
themselves as homogeneous. The existence of such internalized
myths of difference following the Holocaust in Europe and the
United States provides a touchstone for an altered perception of
the Jew as different and for a multivalent understanding of Jewish
self-hatred. In this study I shall examine a series of examples of

Jewish self-hatred. I shall use the written words of Jews about the Jews in a number of historical and cultural contexts to examine the articulation and implication of self-hatred for Jewish identity. These texts will be read as part of the response of the writer to specific models of the "hidden language of the Jews" extrapolated from writings and statements about the Jews. These texts must be read as responses to the treatment of the act of writing by Jews as different. In examining a series of themes and case studies, figures of interest and/or of historical importance, we shall evolve a pattern of continuity and change. These cases are representative only for those Jewish males who defined themselves in the public arena as writers. Because of the discontinuity of texts by women and because of their essentially private nature (at least through the eighteenth century), Jewish women generally have been excluded in the selection of examples.[24] The double-double bind of being Jewish and being female would be a parallel study well worth undertaking. The study concludes with a study of the thematization of "self-hatred" following the Holocaust. In this sense the history of the concept of self-hatred, but not its existence in reality, however, is brought to a close. In becoming the stuff of texts, self-hatred becomes defused as the motivating factor for the production of texts. If writers can examine the problem of self-hatred, they no longer project their own insecurities onto other groups of Jews. This level of awareness, however, is not universal, even though such texts can serve as paradigms. An awareness that the language of the writer does not reveal its contamination when the author chooses specific topics is linked to the conscious use of this theme. But self-hatred continues on, part of the human condition.

CHAPTER TWO

The Drive for Conversion

I

The Special Language of the Jews

The story had evolved into a legend little over a generation after it took place. The good Gentile who rescued the Jews and their books from the vengeance of the malevolent convert to Christianity seems indeed to be stuff from which legends are made. In a posthumously published essay on ethics, Jewish commentator Haim ben Bezalel, who died in 1588, first recounted in print the legend as it was handed down among the Jews:

> I have heard from the elders that in earlier times a few baptized Jews appeared, who strove with word and deed against the divine vessel [i.e., the Talmud] and who tried to have it committed to the fire because of their mockery and hatred of that contained within it, a mockery and hatred that sprang from the smallness of their understanding. And they almost succeeded in fulfilling their evil plan when God awoke the spirit of a wise Christian, who came before the princes and their people and taught respect for this holy book. He said: "The curious tales that are found in this work are like bitter herbs and deadly poisons sold in pharmacies together with precious spices. They too are used to heal illnesses . . . but their value is known only to famous doctors, who know where and when to apply them. Thus the precious words of our wise scholars and their hidden meanings can be known only by the knowledgeable, but for the fools who wander in darkness they are death and destruction." This speech defending the Talmud held by this wise Christian pleased the kings and the princes; the calumniators went away confounded.[1]

Legends such as this are staples among all oppressed peoples. Suddenly a defender appears from the ranks of their oppressors who is divinely inspired to see the value of that which they themselves prize most. But the stuff from which this legend was shaped was history, and the deformation of the historical record reveals a response to one of the first modern examples of Jewish self-hatred, a self-hatred that derived from the Christian drive for the conversion of the Jews and the implications of this striving for Jew, Christian, and convert alike.

Within Haim ben Bezalel's retelling of the persecution of the Jews' books is hidden a key to legend itself. The "few baptized Jews" strive to destroy the Talmud because of "the smallness of their understanding." (The Talmud is the summary of Jewish laws and rituals compiled after the fall of the Temple. There are two versions, a Palestinian Talmud, which is fragmentary, and a Babylonian Talmud, which is usually seen as the central compilation of biblical interpretation. The Talmud contains two types of text, the Mishna, commentaries on biblical laws, and the Gemora, commentaries on the Mishna. The language in which the Talmud is written is Hebrew, but it also contains extensive passages in Aramaic.) The ignorance of the converts results in their attack on the holy commentaries of the Jews. Ignorance of what? The blindness of the converts is the result of their inability to understand the Talmud. They do not know enough to understand the complex mix of languages, and they are unable to follow the complex logic demanded of a reader of legal texts and commentaries.

And yet it was the possession of a secret or hidden language that the medieval Christian world attributed to all Jews.[2] For the Jews possessed Hebrew, and this set them apart from the Christians. Indeed, it was the language of the Jews, and the books written in this language, that mythically defined the boundary between Christian and Jew. Hebrew had been all but lost in Europe during the Middle Ages. Even though a Church council in 1312 had mandated the teaching of Hebrew in the centers of knowledge of the time—Oxford, Paris, Salamanca, and Bologna—in order to facilitate the conversion of the Jews, little formal knowledge of Hebrew existed in Christian Europe during the following two centuries.[3]

By the close of the fifteenth century Hebrew had acquired a mythic quality, and books written in Hebrew a magical one. Hebrew was one of the most evident external signs of the difference of the Jew and assumed a special role in defining Jewishness. For while Hebrew had been lost by the medieval Christian world, it had not been lost by medieval Jewry. The rabbinic prohibition against teaching non-Jews the "sacred tongue" was one of the factors in creating the myth of the hidden language; it also reenforced the association of Hebrew with the essence of what was understood as Jewish. Hebrew became the magical language *par excellence*. When Benvenuto Cellini described the actions of a magician holding secret rites in the Colosseum, he had him calling on the devil "in phrases of the Hebrew."[4] Whenever Jews appear in medieval Christian religious drama, they are shown conjuring up the spirits of darkness with mock Hebrew oaths. These nonsense passages are both fearful and comic, throwing the anxiety of those in the audience who believe in the power of witchcraft into comic relief, which at least temporarily relieves this anxiety. The mock Hebrew has the ring of children's rhyming songs:

> chodus, chados, adonai sebaos, sesim, sossim, chochun yochun or nor yochun or nor gun yinbrahei et ysmahel ly ly lancze lare uczerando ate lahu dilando, sicut vir melior yesse ceuia ceuca ceu capiasse amel.

So the Jews address Pilate in a medieval mystery play. But the association is even stronger. When late medieval dramatists wished to conjure up the magician, they needed only to have him speak a mock, "abracadabra" Hebrew. And it worked, whether in the popular Faust plays or in Rutebuf's religious dramas.[5]

The fear that the Jews' books generated among the Christians was not merely the result of the magical language in which they were written. Medieval commentators saw the refusal of the Jews to acknowledge the role of Christ in the redemption of humanity as the result of the reading of these selfsame books. Not only do Jews speak differently from Christians but they think differently. The Talmud is taken over and over again as the exemplary text in which the blindness of the Jews is manifest. The Talmud presents a manner of understanding divine revelation that is inherently different, at least in the perception of the Christian divines, from Christian biblical exegesis. Bartholomew, bishop of Exeter, wrote in his twelfth-century *Dialogue against the Jews*:

> The chief cause of disagreement between ourselves and the Jews seems to me to be this: they take all the Old Testament literally, whenever they can find a literal sense, unless it gives manifest witness to Christ. Then they repudiate it, saying that it is not in the Hebrew truth, that is in their books, or they refer it to some fable, as they are still awaiting its fulfillment,

or they escape by some other serpentine wile, when they feel themselves hard pressed. They will never accept allegory, except when they have no other way out.[6]

Jews argue differently—deceptively, blindly. They eschew allegory if it permits them to see prefigurations of Christianity in the Old Testament. It is this manner of seeing, embodied in the "Hebrew Truth, that is in their books," that closes their eyes to the truth of Christ.

But it is also clear that if one of the roles of the Church is to propagate the faith, then the Jews must hear the truth. This necessitates speaking their language and understanding their discourse in order to combat it. In order to learn the language one could turn to the fragmentary grammars or to converts. When, however, Johannes Reuchlin, the German jurist-scholar and hero of Haim ben Bezalel's tale, wished to learn Hebrew, he turned to the Jewish community. For Reuchlin had no interest in using his knowledge of Hebrew for the purpose of Christian missionary work, at least not overtly, and he turned to a very special section of the Jewish community.

Johannes Reuchlin had been introduced to the Jews' books while on a trip to Italy. It was, however, not the Talmud to which he was introduced but the Cabala, not by Jews but by the Italian Humanists such as Pico della Mirandola. The Cabala is the codification of Jewish mysticism, which claims to reveal the hidden meaning of the universe. Especially in the *Sepher Yezira*, the book of the Creation, it uses language, the Hebrew alphabet, as a system of thaumaturgic divination. The Humanists, both in Italy and in Germany, fell upon this magic book written in a magic language as a means to escape the dry rationalism that dominated the late Middle Ages. But their intent in reading the Cabala was clear. Pico della Mirandola, in his essay *On the Dignity of Man*, cites the Cabala when he makes reference to those who transcend the worldly and are "unaware of the body and [are] confined to the inner reaches of the mind. [They are] neither . . . earthly or heavenly beings." The study of the Cabala leads to an overcoming of this world, the purpose of which Pico states without hesitation. "The ancient mysteries of the Hebrews . . . [are] cited for the confirmation of the inviolable Catholic faith."[7] The occult books of the Jews provide further proof of the innate truth of Christianity.

The authority of the convert rested on a knowledge of Hebrew. One of Pico della Mirandola's major sources was the fabulous Flavius Mithridates, originally called Samuel ben Nissim ibn Faraj, who was converted in 1467.[8] Born in Sicily, he was active throughout Italy and into Germany, taking part in religious disputes with Jews. He lectured on Hebrew and Arabic and was able to hold his intellectual audience enthralled for hours while he expounded on topics about which he knew nothing. He was able to command the aura of authority because of his command of Hebrew. He was accused numerous times of Judaizing and was banished from Palermo as well as Rome for this. Our last glimpse of him is as a prisoner in Rome in 1489. The very fact that an adventurer such as Mithridates could command the attention and respect of his Christian audience simply by having (or claiming to have) a knowledge of Hebrew is an indicator of the power that the language commanded. But that he had converted and that his conversion was constantly questioned because of his claim to the special knowledge held by the Jews are further indicators of how dangerous it was to claim such authority. The purity of Hebrew was to be achieved by the removal of Hebrew from the world of the Jews. Immanuel Tremellius (1510–80), converted by Alessandro Farnese, later Pope Paul III, observed in his handbook of Hebrew for the missionaries to the Jews, "I have been extremely careful not to draw words and phrases from the rabbis' dirt, but I have adhered to that kind of speech in which the divine oracles were written."[9] The Talmud contains "bad" language; the Bible, "good" language. This did not prevent the university at Lausanne from refusing to appoint Tremellius to a chair of Hebrew because he was a Jew. The linkage between the Jews' language and Judaizing was felt to be very close, especially by advocates of the study of Hebrew. Reuchlin himself wrote to Wolfgang Fabricius Capito that "with the rebirth of Hebrew letters an effort might be made to revive Judaism, which is the most unfortunate offensive pestilence that might befall the Christian doctrine."[10] And Tremellius, in his last will and testament, mocked those who expected this baptized Jew, now a leading scholar of the Reformation, to recant his belief and return to the Jews.

Reuchlin subscribed to the Italian Humanists' view of the importance of the occult texts of the Jews. And like them, he was quite able to distinguish between the Jews' books and the Jews themselves. In 1505, long after he had begun his intense study of the Jews' books, he was approached by a nobleman who inquired whether he should admit Jews into his realm. Reuchlin answered him in the form of a pamphlet, directed as much at the German reading public as at the nobleman. The pamphlet, entitled *Doctor Johannes Reuchlin's German Letter on Why the Jews Have Been in Misery for Such a Long Time*, repeats all of the medieval calumnies against the Jews.[11] Their sins are a measure of their denial of Christ. They cannot be persuaded to abandon their errors. They mock and blaspheme against Christ in their books and prayers. While the intent of Reuchlin's view was that the Jews should be converted, the actual result was that the Jews were not admitted to the noble's lands. But it also put the leading Humanist in Germany on public record, a record written in German and published in broadside form, opposing the Jews and their blasphemous books. This fact must be balanced against Reuchlin's own study of Hebrew. For when Reuchlin went to learn Hebrew, he was forced to turn to a Jew. At the court of Emperor Frederick III, Reuchlin met the court physician Jacob ben Jehiel Loans. Loans became Reuchlin's master in the Hebrew tongue. That meeting, which took place in 1492, long before Reuchlin's statement on the Jews, and Reuchlin's lifelong acknowledgment of his debt and respect for Loans must be understood with his condemnation of the Jews.

Reuchlin found in Loans a Jewish intellectual who could function on his own level. He commanded the discourse of the court, had the status of a member of the court, and knew Hebrew. He was also willing to share his knowledge with Reuchlin. But there is much more to the role of Loans and the model of the Jew that he provided for Reuchlin. Jewish physicians had a very high status in late medieval Europe. Marie de Medici brought her physician, Elijah Montalto, to Paris, where he became the court physician of Louis XIII during a period when Jews were banned from France. In 1519, when the Jews were exiled from Rothenburg, the town doctor, Isaac Oeringer, was asked to remain, which he refused to do. Case after case of the status of the Jewish physician can be presented, but all illustrate the linkage between Jews and magic.[12] For the status of the medieval doctor was to no little extent owing to his access to arcane knowledge. While in the abstract it is true that Jewish physicians had access to Hebrew medical tracts, which in turn presented much of what was known of Jewish, Arab, and Greek medicine, it was the association of these books, written in Hebrew, with hidden knowledge that gave the Jewish physician his reputation. Indeed, Francis I of France refused to be treated by any doctor who was not a "pure Jew," that is, he would not be treated by a convert, even though the convert might have the same knowledge. For Francis and most of late medieval Europe associated healing with magic, and only "pure Jews" would have an unencumbered relationship to the magic books.

But for Reuchlin, Loans was not simply a magician. He was also an intellectual who through his gift of languages had access to knowledge, much of it occult, that Reuchlin, too, wished to obtain. Loans became identified in Reuchlin's image of the Jew with the Cabala, since he was his means of acquiring this knowledge. His interest in Loans was not as an individual, as a Jew, but rather as a means to an end, the study of Hebrew. Reuchlin was quite able to separate the Jews from their writings in most cases, much as the Italian Humanists were able to isolate their daily interaction with penurious Byzantine Greeks from their image of the glories of classical Greece. Both Jew and Greek were needed to provide access to the greater, mystic tradition that the Humanists sought, and both became subsumed under the greater force of the myth of the Cabala or Gnostic mysticism. In general, the individual as teacher became one with the books he taught. There was confusion in distinguishing between a specific individual and the group with which he or she would usually be identified. Reuchlin had little interest in the Jews. He wanted them as a group to bow to the greater truth of Christianity and convert, but this had no effect on his desire to possess their books. Indeed, their blindness to the value of their own books made them a hindrance to the study of their works. One had to use them to acquire knowledge that was closed to them. This knowledge was the hidden truth of Christianity, a truth that was present within the Jews' books but to which they did not have access.

Thus the stage is set for the legendary confrontation between the "wise Christian," Johannes Reuchlin, and those "few baptized Jews" who sought to destroy the Talmud and the other books of the Jews. Reuchlin's ambiguous relationship to the Jews and to their books, his focus on the Christian implications of Jewish mystical tradition, his fusing of the idea of the magical language with a specific type of "good Jew," leads to a redefinition of the image of the Jew as seen through the attitudes of those "few baptized Jews."

II

The Converts and the Jews' Books

The converts to whom Haim ben Bezalel referred were voluntary converts to Christianity. Through the Middle Ages into the sixteenth century there had been a series of organized attempts forcibly to baptize and thus convert the Jews. While the question of the reaction of forcibly baptized Jews in both Spain and Germany to their new religion is a complex one, the focus of the conflict that surrounded Johannes Reuchlin was Jews who, for whatever reason, converted to Christianity without overt force and thus saw themselves as Christians.[13]

From as early as the twelfth century there exists a detailed account of such a voluntary conversion, which is of interest because of the paucity of such material throughout the Middle Ages. Indeed, the *Letter on My Conversion*, written by the German monk Hermann, known before his conversion as Judah ben David ha-Levi, seems to be the first autobiographical account of a conversion written after St. Augustine's fourth-century *Confessions*.[14] Hermann explains the reasons for his conversion to his new Christian coreligionists in terms that they would have found extremely easy to comprehend. Upon finding himself in Mainz, he attended a series of sermons held by his debtor Ekbert, the bishop of Mainz. His attendance had been caused by his desire to keep an eye on this debtor to whom he had lent money without sufficient collateral. Hermann became fascinated by Ekbert's mode of biblical exegesis, his ability to relate the teachings of the Old Testament to the coming of Christ. Hermann's road to conversion, according to his own account, was difficult. He had to overcome the anger and threats of his coreligionists, and he had to overcome the hesitancy of the Christian world. A monk, for example, to whom Hermann confessed his inability to see his way clear to conversion damned him as innately unable to see the truth of Christ. Hermann recounts his own inner doubts at this moment, for if, indeed, Jews were unable to see the truth, as they once had refused to see it at the time of Moses, then all of his inner turmoil was without purpose, as he would never be able to acknowledge the truth of Christ.

These two strands—the monk's charge that Jews were unable to understand the truth and Hermann's fear of his coreligionists—reveal a Christian preconception of the nature of the Jew. Hermann's *Letter on My Conversion* was a text aimed at Christians by one who perceived himself as a Christian. It reflected all of the Christian attitudes toward the Jew, perceived by someone who was attempting to disassociate himself from seeing himself as Jewish. For Hermann was a most successful Christian: in later life he was the founding abbot of the monastery at Scheda. He presented in his text an image of the Jew from which he felt himself freed. First, Jews are closed-minded. They refuse to see the natural path from the Old Testament to the revelations of Christianity. They are captives of the letter, rather than the spirit, of the Bible. This is also echoed in Hermann's need for a visionary experience, a mystical moment of union with God, before he felt that his path to conversion was truly open. Such moments are impossible for Jews, at least in the image of the Jew held by the medieval Christian, since the Jews are bound to the world by the nature of their perception of revealed text. Second, Jews are vindictive and dangerous. They will turn on and attempt to destroy anyone who they feel threatens them. If they feel betrayed by a coreligionist, they will attempt to take vengeance. These two qualities are, of course, related. Hermann argues in his letter that both of these innate qualities of the Jew can be overcome and that the Jew can become a Christian, indeed a better Christian than most if his example is taken, but only through a complete metamorphosis.

The two models of the Jew in Hermann's confession are the "blind" Jew and the "seeing" Jew, or to choose two even simpler categories, the "bad" Jew and the "good" Jew. This split in the Christian perception of the Jew reflects both Church policy and community practice. The "blind" Jews, according to Paul, refuse to acknowledge Christ. They are "blind" because they are inherently unable to see the truth of Christ as prefigured in the Old Testament and act as if that prophecy were not fulfilled. Their blindness lies within the limitations of their reading and comprehension of the divine text. It is tied to their materialistic nature, for in being unable to see the allegorical truth of the Old Testament, they remain mired in this world. One must stress that this blindness is viewed by the church, at least after Bernard of Clairvaux, in the eleventh century, as the present state of the Jews. Jews can overcome this state of blindness through inspiration. Knowledge, learning, insight, doubt, are not sufficient for the illumination of the Jew. Only the flash of divine inspiration, the sudden acknowledgment of Christ's divinity (and thus the instantaneous perception of the Old Testament as prefiguring his coming), frees the Jew from blindness. In this moment, the Jew "sees" for the first time and becomes the "good" Jew.

Hermann's autobiography presents a model of the split perceived by voluntary converts between their converted self and their image of themselves as Jews. On the surface, Hermann's text, aimed at a Christian audience, teaches his audience that inner weakness and doubt can be overcome. But this text is also an exorcism of the dangerous, blind Jew hidden within Hermann, his rejection of the older persona of Judah ben David ha-Levi. The text documents not only the difficulty but also the possibility of stripping away this persona, with all its doubts and limitations, to permit the new persona, Hermann, to appear. As the central image for the shedding of this old persona, Hermann uses the difficulties imposed upon him through the Jews' interpretation of Scripture. Since the Bible is divinely inspired, misreading it reveals the nature of the Jews' blindness. It serves as an armor plating around the soul that does not permit the soul to seek after higher truths, the truths of Christianity. Christianity is symbolized, for Hermann, by the new means of interpretation, the ability to see the world and its signs as transparent, revealing God through an allegorical reading of Scripture. The Jews, limited to the tawdriness of this world, do not have this ability. Therefore, they strike out against those, such as converts, who wish to acquire it. Hermann uses standard, Christian criteria to classify his former self and thus to exorcise it within the terms understood by his audience. His text on the surface wishes to teach that inner doubts and weakness can be overcome through faith. His subtext is much more complex.

For Hermann, secure in the protective structure of the monastic orders, wishes to prove his membership within this privileged and powerful group. This group provides him with status and power, qualities lacking in his incarnation as Judah ben David ha-Levi. To prove that this power is not ephemeral, to show that his status is not transitory, Hermann must provide, in his text, the antithetical model demanded by the Church. He must bear testimony not only to his own initial weakness but to the perfidy of his coreligionists. He must show the difficulty of conversion because of the innate doubting nature of the Jew. He must reify the abyss demanded by the Church between the Christian and the Jew. Such a demand places Hermann, or any other convert, in an untenable position. For the dichotomy between Christian and Jew does not provide for a true identification with the persona of the former. There remains always the stigma of being the convert. (Indeed, this seems to be one of the demons that Hermann is exorcising in his letter.) In order that the "seeing" Jew may be an even better Christian than his coreligionists, the convert must turn this stigma into a sign of higher status. Hermann shows this by using his own autobiography as a paradigm for the ultimate insight that can be had into the nature of the self and thus into the truths of Christianity. He becomes his own text, and his allegorical reading of his conversion becomes the proof for his abandonment of the blindness of his former self, his perception of the world and its signs as transparent, revealing the glory of Christ and his ability to see in his present state the pattern for the future.

The fear of the way the Jews interpret Scripture is easily transformed into a fear of the books possessed by "the people of the Book." The Jews' books become the embodiment of the blindness and dangerousness of the Jews. In these concrete objects, the religious books of the Jews, written in the magical language of Hebrew, is seen all of the evil of the Jews. And it is the Talmud that becomes, in the Christian mind, representative of these dangerous texts. In 1239 Pope Gregory IX received a bill of particulars against the Talmud from a Dominican brother of La Rochelle, Nicholas Donin.[15] Donin, a convert, described the Talmud as a work that mocked Christianity and presented a false image of Christ. Donin, in his appeal to the pope, based his claims on the special knowledge that only a Jew could have of these books as well as on the insight that only a convert could bring to this knowledge. This pattern is one that Hermann claims obliquely in his discussion of the Jews' blindness. The pope ordered both the secular and the religious powers within Europe to seize and examine the Talmud. The result was a public debate held in Paris between representatives of the Church and of the French Jewish community, the outcome of which was preordained. In June of 1244 the "heretical Talmud," to use the Franciscan preacher Bertolt von Regensburg's phrase, was burned publicly in Paris and Rome.[16] This identification of the Jews with their books and the attempt to purge the Jews through the destruction of their books are linked closely with the attitude and special claims of the convert. Donin wished to purge the Jewishness of the Jews, to cleanse them from that stigma that made them Jews, the stigma of blindness. This could be accomplished by destroying the source of the intransigence, the Talmud.

The role of the Jewish convert in attacking the Jews in the public forum cannot be underrated. The function that a Nicholas Donin had in the Paris Disputation in 1240 is paralleled by that allotted to other Jewish converts over the centuries. Indeed, one of the flukes of history is that three detailed accounts of Jewish-Christian disputations have been preserved, either in Hebrew or in Latin. The oldest is of the debate between Donin and Rabbi Yehiel ben Joseph, concerning the nature of the Talmud and its presentation of accounts of Christianity. In 1263 there was a disputation in Barcelona in which the Jews were defended by one of the greatest Jewish theologians of the Middle Ages, Nahmanides. The Christian side of the debate was to have been led by the sage Raymund de Penforte, but he turned his role over to convert Pablo Christiani. In 1413 a debate was held in Tortosa, Spain, in which the Christian side was represented by Hieronymus de Santa Fe, born Joshua Halorki. The function of the Jewish convert in these debates was central to the purpose of the public confrontation, for if public confrontation was to illustrate the inherent blindness of the Jews, the presence of converted Jews on the side of the Church provided documentation for the fact that Jews could be made to confess their own blindness. In the debates between the Church—represented by the convert—and the Jews, this fact became part of the rhetorical proof of the Church's argument. For the defender of the Jews saw a clear difference between their attitude toward the Christian world and their attitude toward the convert. The Church, of course, never officially shared this split view. Thus, while the Jews argued that the Christians only had to respect the Ten Commandments, Jews, such as Donin, were bound to respect all of the laws of the Old Testament. This claim to an inviolate bond between the converts and their coreligionists must have heightened the converts' anxiety about their own station.[17]

The association of the false perspective of the Jews with the Talmud became universal in the following centuries. When the troubadour Konrad von Würzburg sang of the Jews in a poem written in 1268, he referred to their blindness as the result of the Talmud:

> Woe to the cowardly Jews, deaf
> and wicked, who have no care
> to save themselves
> from the sufferings of hell.
> The Talmud has corrupted them
> and made them lose their honor.[18]

Indeed, when Louis X finally allowed Jews to return to France in 1315 one of the sole demands that he made on them was that they not bring their Talmud back with them. The Talmud is representative of those magic, evil books in which the blindness of the Jews is contained. Remove it, and perhaps the Jews will be able to see the truth. This is important, more important than the conversions of the Turks or the Chinese, for the conversion of the Jews is one of the signs for the Second Coming according to Revelation.

By the beginning of the sixteenth century, the association of the Jews with their books was absolute. The conflict surrounding these books recorded in Haim ben Bezalel's account brought together the Christian's image of the Jew with the image of the Christian held by Jewish converts to Christianity. It resulted in an explosive redefinition of the idea of the Jew within the German context. It began in 1504 when Josef Pfefferkorn, a Jew born in Nuremberg, was baptized together with his wife Anna, his son Laurentius, and his mother-in-law.[19] He received the baptismal name Johannes. Pfefferkorn was soon employed by the Cologne Dominican monks as a factotum. Under their influence or inspiration he began to write a series of pamphlets. These pamphlets reflect Pfefferkorn's ardor in his conversion, a conversion that was voluntary to the extent that Pfefferkorn evidently chose Christianity without any overt physical threats having been lodged against him. The first pamphlets, written within three years of his conversion, rest upon the standard claims of the special knowledge of the convert. The central thrust of Pfefferkorn's pamphlets seems to have been directed against the Jews. Based on his claims of a knowledge of Hebrew and the Talmud, his pamphlets were taken by his contemporaries as having special status in informing them about the inner workings of the Jewish mind.

One major aside is necessary before a more detailed examination of the first Pfefferkorn pamphlets is undertaken. There have been many claims and counterclaims as to the knowledge or ignorance of matters Jewish by Pfefferkorn. He was attacked by his contemporaries for being an illiterate whose works were composed by the Cologne Dominicans and simply published under his name. While it is true that the leading intellectual among the Cologne Dominicans, Ortwin Gratius, did translate Pfefferkorn's German pamphlets into Latin, the very nature of the German text precludes its authorship by one as well educated as Ortwin Gratius. The text, as well as those of the later pamphlets, is full of the sort of popular language that the intellectuals of the time, such as Erasmus, found attractive. They catalogued such language in numerous proverb collections, but they could not generate it themselves.[20] The contrary is also true. Pfefferkorn's claim of a scholarly knowledge of Hebrew, of having translated the New Testament into Hebrew for the purpose of proselytizing his former coreligionists, is highly unlikely. Most probably Pfefferkorn possessed a rudimentary knowledge of Hebrew, sufficient to translate and transliterate the passages presented in the pamphlets. He certainly had learned passages of the Talmud by heart and knew the order of service in the synagogue. But his actual level of knowledge was not, at the beginning of the sixteenth century, nor should it be today, of any real importance. Central to Pfefferkorn's effectiveness is the simple fact that he was able to draw on the double claim of special knowledge and Christian insight. He did not have to claim more to be perceived as having special status. Here was a Jew privy to the secret books of the Jews, written in their magical language, who had been converted to the truth and was now willing to reveal the Jews' secret mysteries to the world. Thus Pfefferkorn's pamphlets are all addressed to the Christian world, of which he saw himself to be a part. They were not directed toward the Jewish communities in the Rhineland. They were written to be read by those whom Pfefferkorn perceived as fellow Christians, who were then to act based on the knowledge presented to them against the perfidious Jews.

Johannes Pfefferkorn's first pamphlet, *The Mirror of the Jews* (1507), reveals his program in its very title. Harking back to the long medieval traditions of literary "mirrors" which reflected the errors of humanity for the reader to see, Pfefferkorn's *Mirror* reflects the image of the Jews that Pfefferkorn had acquired from living in a society that was inimical to them. Pfefferkorn's program is on the surface quite clear. Stop the Jews' usury, reform them or convert them by forcing them to attend Christian sermons (such as those held by his patrons, the Dominicans), and remove them from the source of their intransigency, their books, especially the Talmud. Like most late medieval Christians, he sees in the conversion of the Jews the necessary first step in preparing the way for the millennium.[21] But Pfefferkorn's perception of himself as the mediator in this process is important. For he is also directing his critique of the Jews at a Christian society that he portrays as flawed. He criticizes the Christian world for having based its attacks on the Jews, not on the source of their blindness and false doctrine, but on fantasies about them such as the calumny of Jewish ritual murder. He further attacks the state for having based its attitudes toward the Jews on economic rather than ideological grounds. Being a convert, he sees himself in the vanguard of those bringing about the eventual purification of the world and the Second Coming of Christ. His special status provides him with greater insight into the Christian world than the Christians themselves have.

Further, Pfefferkorn sees in the blindness of the Jews a model for the errors that beset his "beloved Christians," as he addresses them in almost every paragraph of the text. They are beset by fictions that they take as the realities of this world and act from base rather than higher motives. The standard attack on usury is coupled with the charge that the Jew has a limited understanding of the Holy Bible, because both are seen as part of the Jews' fixation on the worldly. Money and the literal letter of the text are both base, since they deny the higher truths. Central to this view is the idea that the Jews can be reformed, indeed must be reformed, if history is to take its correct course. But Pfefferkorn offers himself as an even stronger example. For the Jews when they are converted will make exemplary Christians, far better than his Christian contemporaries. Thus the pamphlet has a double edge. First, it makes claims as to special knowledge about the Jews from the standpoint of the convert with the intent of encouraging the Christian reform of the Jews; second, it makes claims as to the necessary improvement of contemporary Christianity, also as seen from the special perspective of the convert.

Standing between the role that the Jews will eventually play as exemplary Christians and their miserable state are their books. Pfefferkorn addresses his Christian audience toward the close of *The Mirror*:

> My dearest Christians, you should understand and appreciate the great value and bounty that the Jews will bring to the Christian Church. And the following is true: Since the Jews are so attached to the five books of Moses, their experience of the sweetness of Holy Scripture through the gift of the Holy Spirit will make them even more zealous in their adherence to the five books of Moses. Much as a hungry bear who has broken open a beehive will not be driven away because of the attraction of the sweets, so, too, will it occur with the Jews. When they taste the honey, they will say, This is a feast above all feasts, and I believe, as true as it is within me, that all of the worldly feasts are not to be compared with one who has understood the Old Testament in the light of the New.[22]

Here Pfefferkorn uses a Jewish image, the sweetness of the letters, to present the eventual conversion of the Jews' blindness into insight. For when the Hebrew alphabet is first taught, the letters on the first page are daubed with honey, so that the child will experience the sweetness of learning. Pfefferkorn takes this image of the sweetness of truth and superimposes it upon a proverbial image. Yet his audience would not have been aware of this double level of meaning. A Christian reader would only have read the surface meaning of the text, the proverb about the bear, and would have been blind to the second level of meaning, which only the Jewish convert could possess. Here the act of writing replicates the special role of the clarity of the convert's mode of interpretation and exegesis. But Pfefferkorn goes on to condemn all books that attempt to offer explanations of divine order outside of the Christian canon. He argues that "heathen works, such as those which reveal the workings of heaven," evidently by the Arabic astronomers, are superfluous, since their truths must be found within the Bible. Similarly, "all Hebrew books should be examined and brought onto the level of faith." Not just the Talmud, though this is the major danger, but *all* books held by the Jews, written in their magic language, must be examined. Pfefferkorn's authority as an interpreter of these books rests on his insight as a convert, an insight that has made him into a more competent Christian reader than the Christians themselves. It is this role that he follows in his flood of pamphlets.

In 1508 and 1509 Pfefferkorn produced three pamphlets, *The Jews' Confession* (1508), *The Easter Book* (1508), and *The Enemy of the Jews* (1509). The first two are exposés of the major Jewish holidays, the High Holy Days in the fall and the Passover celebration in the spring. But Pfefferkorn does not merely set out to mock these celebrations. Throughout the first two pamphlets he shows how the Jewish celebrations have meaning only when seen in the light of a more symbolic, more spiritual, and thus less materialistic interpretation of their significance. It is in *The Enemy of the Jews* that the application of Pfefferkorn's critique of Judaism (and its implied criticism of the Christianity of his day) is carried to its fullest.

The Enemy of the Jews, dedicated to Pfefferkorn's patrons, the Cologne Dominicans, is the first of his pamphlets to show the overt influence of contemporary Christian polemic against the Jews. In it Pfefferkorn undertakes to document the nature of Jewish intransigency by showing the Jews' daily mockery of Christ. His text reads like a bilingual dictionary of curses. He lists term after term of opprobrium aimed at Christ, the Virgin Mary, or Christianity in general. He brings to his investigation of this vocabulary the authority of one knowledgeable in Hebrew, showing this by providing the Hebrew term, its transliteration, and then its meaning and implication. One must remember that it was precisely such blasphemy that Johannes Reuchlin noted in the prayers of the Jews and in some of their books in his public letter of 1505 on the misery of the Jews. Reuchlin, too, drew on his reputation as a Hebraist in documenting his claims. When Pfefferkorn makes reference to the hidden conspiracy of blasphemy present within the Jews' language and their texts, he is following a major figure, Reuchlin, who has set the tone of what to seek in examining the demonic language of the Jews.

In this pamphlet of 1509, Pfefferkorn also touches on two issues reflecting the effect on their daily lives of the blindness of the Jews to the truth of Christ. After condemning the usurers, he warns that the Jewish doctors are quacks who use the practice of medicine to poison Christians. The function and status of the medical profession is not being drawn into question. It is only the Jewish doctor that Pfefferkorn is attacking. The association of the hidden language of the Jews, not as white magic but as black magic, with treating the ill parallels the beginning of systematic persecution of witches in northern Europe. The fear that that which can cure can also kill is associated with the view that the healer has powers from some supernatural force, a force that is most probably malevolent. Illness was God's visitation on humanity. If cure is needed, God will send it without the intercession of a non-Christian. Now, this view is quite opposite to Reuchlin's attitude toward the language of the Jewish physicians. Reuchlin saw in the court physician the status of the emperor reflected in the image of the doctor; Pfefferkorn sees only his Jewishness reflected in his image. For Pfefferkorn, the predominant association is that between the evilness of the Jews and all of their worldly dealings. Their blindness to Christ's truth makes all of their actions suspect. Thus the doctor becomes the poisoner. He becomes one who causes death rather than one who halts it. Like the charges of well-poisoning lodged against the Jews in the times of the Plague, the association of the Jews' language and illness becomes an extraordinarily strong one.

The other issue raised by Pfefferkorn in *The Enemy of the Jews* is the immorality of the Jewesses. He condemns them as seductresses whose sole interest is in having bastards by Christian men whom they can then raise as Jews. The gross immorality of the Jews seduces and captures the souls of Christians. The evident parallel to the myth of the succuba, who seduces men in order to steal their seed, is introduced. But the malevolence is even more basic. For the evident reverse of this charge is to label the husbands of these women, as far as they have them, as cuckolds. This would be drawing the argument much too close to home. For while Pfefferkorn may repress the fact that his wife Anna was a Jewess and therefore, according to Pfefferkorn, a seductress, he cannot make the analogy without drawing his own masculine identity into question. He may have been a Jew—which can be overcome through baptism and insight—but he was never a cuckold, a state for which there is no cure. How heavily invested this charge is for Pfefferkorn can be seen in the passage itself:

> Where Jews live, there is much heresy. One finds that Christians lie with Jewesses, and if a child is produced, it remains with the Jews. This is clearly a remarkable and sinful evil which puts Christian blood in eternal damnation. As I said at the beginning of my booklet, there is no sect nor people that hates the Christians more than the Jews. And they especially hate me and those others who had been Jews and are now Christians. And I know that if I came among them, they would rend me like the wolf rends the sheep, for I have been secretly warned by letter how Jews from various lands have contracted

to have me killed. But they know that if I were to be killed,
they would not be spared, so they and some false Christians
say: "Yes, Pfefferkorn, you can't believe him. He plays at the
Christian as long as he can get money for it."[23]

The associations in this passage reveal much of Pfefferkorn's subtext.
The sexuality of the Other, here the Jew and the woman, is threatening to him as a male and a Christian. Yet behind this overt
heretical threat, the threat of the seduction by the succuba, is the
potential for his own prior cuckoldry. This would put him in as
great a danger as do the threats lodged against him by the Jews.
They want to kill him but, being weak, are afraid to do so. Thus
they lodge a campaign of slander against him on the grounds of his
conversion, a conversion that they label as merely a Jewish trick
to exploit the Christian. Thus we return to the reversal of the
opening seduction. There it is the Jewess who seduces the Christian
in order to steal his offspring. At the conclusion of this passage it
is the putative Jew who seduces the Christians to obtain their gold.
Pfefferkorn links these two moments, since they reflect on his
inner definition of self as a man and a newly baptized Christian.
He sees in his conversion the final stripping away of the essence
of his Jewishness, which has made him now the butt of the Jews'
attacks. He concludes *The Enemy of the Jews* shortly after this
passage with a reprise of his call that the Jews must be freed from
their blindness through the removal of "the Talmud which will
leave them only with the text of the Bible. Without a doubt after
such an action they will have a different spirit and they will
acknowledge the falsity of their ways and the truth of our faith."
The operative word in this passage is our, for Pfefferkorn signs
himself in the colophon to this pamphlet, as he did in the earlier
ones, "Johannes Pfefferkorn, formerly a Jew, and now a Christian."
While the overt level of this text is that of Christian preaching to
Christian on the theme of perfidious Jews, the subtext indicates
an inner questioning of Pfefferkorn's new definition. He rejects the
charges of the Jews and "false Christians" that he is not a true
Christian and yet. . . .

Pfefferkorn is not the only convert writing in the Rhineland
at this time. Victor of Karben, "formerly a Rabbi among the Jews
and now a poor, miserable priest," as he labels himself on the title
page of his pamphlet published in 1508, is clearly better educated
and more highly placed in the Jewish community than Pfefferkorn.[24] He has a good working knowledge of Latin, and his pamphlet
is filled with quotations from the Vulgate, even though the language

in which it is written is colloquial German. His audience, like Pfefferkorn's, is a Christian one. Indeed, the pamphlet is addressed quite directly to Victor's patron, Ludwig, the Count Palatinate. As with Pfefferkorn, Victor's conversion was voluntary. He defended his new faith in a debate with Jews—a favorite device of the late Middle Ages to prove to the Jews their errors—held before the Elector of Cologne in which he accused the Jews of madness in that they held to their old belief and said that this madness was caused by their devotion to the Talmud.[25] The bulk of Victor's argument reappears in his pamphlet of 1508, again in dialogue form. The Christian in this debate endeavors to show the Jews that the evil of their ways is caused by an incorrect interpretation of the Scripture. Even in Pfefferkorn's early pamphlets, written before the publication of Reuchlin's attack on him in 1511, there is mention of the insecurity felt by the convert, as can be seen in the passage from *The Enemy of the Jews* quoted above. Pfefferkorn was unable to repress his status anxiety even in his special position in the Dominican community in Cologne (a position analogous to that of Hermann). As with Pfefferkorn, many of the personal references in Victor's pamphlet deal with his own personal difficulties as a convert. The long preface to the dialogue, a dialogue presented to a Christian audience as proof of their correct interpretation of the Bible, is devoted to documenting the Christian mistreatment of the author because of his Jewish origins. Victor's tone is quite bitter, especially in the light of his audience, and reflects a tone and attitude rarely found in Pfefferkorn's pamphlets:

> And thus, says the Psalmist, one spends the entire day like a poor dog that has spent its day running and returns home at night hungry. For there are many uncharitable and ignorant Christians who will not give to you but will rather show you from their doors with mockery, saying, "Look, there goes a baptized Jew." And then others answer, "Yes, anything that is done for you is a waste. You will never become a good Christian." And thus they are mocked and insulted by the Christians from whom they expect help and solace. And they are also hated by the Jews from whom they have come. Whatever joy or pleasure that one or the other may have had is turned to unhappiness and displeasure.

Victor of Karben shows a moment in the life of the convert, suspended between two faiths, seen neither as Jew nor as Christian, that is only hinted at in Pfefferkorn's pamphlets. For Victor, these are the acts of Christian society, a society that should be more receptive to the convert exactly because it sees the truth. But this society does not acknowledge the validity of the conversion of Jews. It sees the Jew remaining a Jew even after baptism:

> And some come to me and ask craftily, "Were you a Jew?" When I answer in the affirmative, they mock me and say, "Go to St. Andrew's Church in Cologne. A cat and a mouse. A dog and a rabbit." This means that as little as a cat and a mouse, as little as a dog and a rabbit can be friends, so little could I become a good Christian. And they said with satisfaction, "Though you may act like a Christian, you are still a Jew at heart."[26]

The Church of St. Andrew in Cologne had carved on one of its doors the figure of a convert, by legend one of the former deans of the church, who held a cat in one hand and a dog in the other. This proverbial manner of seeing the convert as merely a disingenuous Jew reflects the reality of daily life for a Jewish convert in the small village of Karben on the Rhine. Such direct attacks would not have been experienced directly by one under the protection of the Dominican order in the much larger city of Cologne. Pfefferkorn would have been spared much of the direct confrontation concerning his conversion. His world, while containing threatening Jews and bad Christians, as did Victor of Karben's, would not have reflected the radical dichotomy between the official attitude of the Church, an attitude reflected in much of Pfefferkorn's presuppositions concerning the role that he was to play in the improvement of the Church, and Victor's reflection of the pain and disbelief faced by the Jew as convert in the Christian world.

Pfefferkorn, acting on his sense of mission, a mission supported by his Dominican patrons, undertook, as had Nicolas Donin before him, to translate his words into actions. He would show both Jews and Christians his function in shaping the new world, a world in which the Second Coming would be at hand. Through the Dominicans, whose interest in the conversion of the Jews was second only to their role in the Inquisition, Pfefferkorn was presented to Kunigunde, the sister of Emperor Maximilian I, the last of the great medieval rulers of Europe. In August of 1509, Maximilian entrusted Pfefferkorn with the collection of the Jews' books. The emperor ordered Jews to turn over "all untrue, useless books or writings" to "Johannes Pfefferkorn from Cologne, one who is knowledgeable and experienced in your faith and in the books of Moses and the Prophets." Pfefferkorn had achieved status within the court because of his special role as a convert. When Pfefferkorn began to carry out his program, however, objections were raised both within and without the Jewish community. Uriel von Gemmingen, the archbishop of Mainz, demanded greater theological authority than that of a Pfefferkorn for the confiscation of the Jews' books, and he called for a series of recommendations from the theological faculties of Mainz, Cologne, Heidelberg, and Erfurt as well as from three leading specialists in the writings of the Jews—the Grand Inquisitor of Cologne, the Dominican Jakob Hochstraten; the convert Victor of Karben; and the preeminent Hebraist of his day, Johannes Reuchlin. It was clear from the writings of these three prior to the archbishop of Mainz's request that they would almost automatically provide positive recommendations in support of Pfefferkorn's position.

III
*The Christian Reaction and
the Origin of Jewish Self-hatred*

As the letters of support were collected, it became clear that Pfefferkorn's position was to be upheld. The theological faculties of the universities of Mainz and Cologne supported his views wholeheartedly, while the theologians at Heidelberg and Erfurt presented minor reservations. Needless to say, both Jakob Hochstraten and Victor of Karben supported his mandate from the emperor without reservation. On October 6, 1510, Johannes Reuchlin finished his letter of support. In it he divided the Jews' books into two categories, those that attacked Christianity directly and all others. In the first he placed by name two minor post-Talmudic tractates. The other vast category encompassed the Talmud as well as the Cabala. The study of these books would, according to Reuchlin, lead to a greater understanding of the Bible and, therefore, of the truth of Christianity. Reuchlin defended the Jews' possession of such books, since they provided, for the Christian world, a means of greater knowledge. It is clear from Reuchlin's letter that he is defending the Cabala, in which he saw himself as an adept, as well as the Talmud. He defends both books directly, condemning only those few tractates that attempt to counter Christian theology as heretical. It is the latter texts that have been taken by the converts such as Pfefferkorn as typical of the inner nature of all the Jews' books. Thus Reuchlin's dichotomy presented a clear break with the unanimity of all those solicited for their views on the future of the Jews' books.

The implication of Reuchlin's defense of the Jews' books is that he is defending the Jews. Reuchlin himself is certain about this distinction. He argues on a level that transfers the value of the human being to the inanimate object, the book:

> For this may be understood: that one should not take their
> books from them against their will, for books are as dear to
> some as a child. And as one says about the poets: They hold
> the books they create for their children. Thus one must also be
> reminded that taking the books of the Jews in order to make
> them convert to Christianity is a type of forcible action.[27]

This confusion of people and books makes the printed word as dear as a child and takes literally the figurative role of the poet as the father of his work. This association of people with their books is a subtle variation on Pfefferkorn's claim, following Church tradition, that books make people what they are. Both views give a central role to the written word as the means by which the nature of humanity should be judged.

Reuchlin sees in those who attack his children, his books, as both dangerous and ignorant. He condemns Pfefferkorn, whom he addresses as "the newly baptized" by name in the letter to the emperor, labeling him as ignorant of the Talmud. Indeed, he states that "in my entire life no Jew has ever been baptized who has understood the Talmud or has even been able to read it." Reuchlin thus divides the Jews into two classes: the educated, intelligent Jews, who remain with their religion and are knowledgeable of the Talmud; and the ignorant, crude converts. The first are devoted to their children, the books; the latter wish to destroy them. Reuchlin also condemns as "buffalos and asses" those who attack the scientific books of the Jews, such as their alchemical and medical treatises, without being able to understand them. All of these attacks are based on a single premise, that a Jew, like a leopard, can never change its spots. Jews convert to Christianity "out of jealousy, hatred, fear of punishment, poverty, revenge, love of honor, love of the world, evil simplicity, and other similar reasons. And if this does not work out, they run off to Turkey and again become Jews."[28] The blindness of the Jews is universal. They are a positive force only when they serve as a vessel enclosing and protecting their books. This attitude may well explain Reuchlin's extremely positive attitude toward his tutor in Hebrew, the court physician Loans. Loans served as the means by which he was able to achieve a higher knowledge than his teacher, a level of understanding to which his teacher would never have access. Thus he encapsulated the Jews in their role as protector of the Book. They can be no more and no less. But they can never be interpreters of the Book. This is left to the Christian exegete. Even more so in regard to the Jews' thaumaturgic books, such as the Cabala. For in the hands of the Christian adept the Cabala can lead to greater insights into the truths of Christ, insights impossible for the blind Jews.

Indeed, Reuchlin would have found his view of the separation of the Jews from their language supported in a perverse way by his reading of Cabalistic texts. In the *Sohar* (vol. 1, fols. 76a-b) there is a detailed discussion of the purity of language and the creation of languages. Rabbi Hiaya is quoted in interpreting the passage from Deuteronomy concerning Babel. He states that when the Jews went to build the Tower of Babel, they drew on an antediluvial source, a source "of the secret wisdom of the primeval age." And God could not stop them because "they were one people and one language." The only way he could confound their actions was to confuse their language. With this confusion came the scattering of the peoples of the Earth across the globe. Thus the original Diaspora was the result of God's confusion of language, a deed that had to be undertaken in order for God to achieve dominion over the unity of man. From the standpoint of the Christian Cabalists, the secret from before the flood was the Cabala itself, stemming from before the Christian age, and the confusion of tongues was the expulsion of the Jews as a result of the Crucifixion. The Jews may still harbor the holy language, Hebrew, but they are merely a vessel for it. For it is in the new language, the language of exegesis taught by the Church, that the original, unified vision incorporated in the language before the Tower of Babel is to be found. Christian interpretation is thus given, in the reading of the *Sohar*, a primacy over the confusion of the Jews, a confusion exemplified by their existence in the Diaspora. Thus a clear distinction between the corrupt nature of the Jews and the potential purity of their tongue can be found in an interpretation of the very words of the *Sohar*.[29]

Pfefferkorn, acting as the agent of the emperor, read Reuchlin's letter and was offended by it. Not only did the letter dispute his claim to possess the knowledge to evaluate the Jews' books but it presented a personal attack on him by a Christian scholar whose public pronouncements had seemed to support his position on the confiscation of the Talmud. Pfefferkorn's response is direct and personal. Indeed, it is so personal that Pfefferkorn's Dominican sponsor Ortwin Gratius denied as late as 1518 that he had had any knowledge of Pfefferkorn's answer, the pamphlet entitled *The Hand*

Mirror, until its publication in 1511. Pfefferkorn labels Reuchlin a Judaizer, a tool of the Jews, and a sympathizer of their manner of seeing the world. He attacks him directly, claiming that his putative knowledge of Hebrew is the result of having had his works on Hebrew written for him by Jews. Reuchlin has become one of those "false Christians" who are but Jews in Christian guise. The Jews glory in Reuchlin's reputation, since they created him as their weapon against the Christians:

> What does it mean that the Jews praise Dr. Reuchlin's knowledge of Hebrew, which he does not know well. They say: "Dr. Reuchlin is knowledgeable in our writings." This does not surprise me about the Jews. For those who praise them will be praised by them, and those who serve them will be served by them, especially if this is directed against the Christian Church or to its detriment.[30]

The Jews, through their tool Reuchlin, have attacked the defenders of the truth. For they wish to maintain their blindness and have thus recruited or seduced scholars such as Reuchlin into their services through these scholars' vanity. The correct attitude toward such attacks on Christianity, observes Pfefferkorn, is presented in the following example:

> It is not clear in their [the Jews'] word and deeds how they hurt and mock the Christian Church. As, for example, in the previous year in Berlin, in the Mark, when they insulted and dishonored the Holy Sacrament. As a result the Christian Prince and Lord, Margrave Joachim, the Elector [of Brandenburg] roasted 38 of the selfsame Jews over a fire as punishment for their evil deeds.[31]

Jews, and by analogy those who aid the Jews, who undermine the Christian faith, who indulge in magical acts against Christians, who "hurt and mock" the truths of the Christian faith, should be roasted over a slow fire. This is not metaphor, not hyperbole; this reflects the reality of the relationship between the Jew and Christian society in the sixteenth century. The blindness of the Jews must be treated harshly so that they will learn to see correctly, as have the converts:

> After I converted together with my wife and children from the Jewish error to the Christian faith, I looked within myself to understand why the Jews continue to hold and disseminate their evil, destructive, perverted ways.

They see with their worldly eyes and cannot notice nor understand the completion and fulfillment of the Law. This having been done through Christ the Messiah, which is denied by the false books of the Talmud, created only to counter the teaching of Christ. The Talmud mocks, insults, and curses the teaching of Christ and makes into a fiction the natural order as well as the law of Moses and the prophets.[32]

Reuchlin's letter has blocked the Christian attempt to free the Jews from the blindness caused by their books. It is Reuchlin who is the secret convert to the Jews' manner of seeing the world. It is he who now holds "evil, destructive, perverted" attitudes toward the Christian truth. It is this Reuchlin against whom Pfefferkorn cites the early pamphlet on the misery of the Jews, a pamphlet that had seemed to give succor to Pfefferkorn's position. Reuchlin is hypocritical, subverting his earlier understanding of the reason for the misery of the Jews because of his vanity in being praised by these selfsame Jews.

Reuchlin's reaction was intense and bitter. The letter that he had been requested to submit to the emperor was now the subject of what appeared to him to be a public attack by a Jew in Christian clothing. He answered Pfefferkorn with his pamphlet entitled *The Eye Glasses* (1511), in which his correspondence with the emperor is printed for the first time, together with his commentary. Reuchlin lists thirty-four errors inherent in Pfefferkorn's *The Hand Mirror*, errors that reveal the limitations of Pfefferkorn's understanding of Hebrew and the Jews' book. But more than that, he refers to Pfefferkorn over and over, indeed every time his name occurs, which is several times on every page of the commentary, as "Pfefferkorn, the baptized Jew." Reuchlin is defending his children, the Hebrew books, against the onslaught of this "baptized Jew," who wishes to destroy them. He is in no way defending the Jews; rather he labels their attacker as merely a Jew, and a renegade at that. He wishes to rescue his own honor as a scholar and reveal the ignorance of his attacker. Reuchlin is not the hidden Jew; Pfefferkorn is:

Finally, I wish to reveal that the baptized Jew Pfefferkorn has written untruthfully about me and against the honor of God. He has insulted a great many as a result of his unnecessary and petulant vengeance. This is the result of his spirit, which he inherited from his parents. He accuses me of having made money from my books, in books which he sells behind my back. He made more money from me than Judas made from selling Christ. One has seen into his soul, and this has taken away his boldness. One is now tired of his Jews' pamphlets, and since he cannot write anything else except that which an uneducated author writes about the Jews, so he tries to continue to reap his money as before. Thus he wants to argue with Christians because he knows that he will get more money because of this. If one sees this and he still succeeds, then he will soon attack someone else. For he has, up to now, fed himself with his insults and won his food like a raven in a cage who learns to insult men and women in human speech. What one does to such birds, according to Apuleius, is to cut their tongues out of their throats. Therefore, one should be fore-warned that such an individual who tends to insult does get in the habit of doing so. Others learn from him, so that they earn more for their lies than does a pious individual from the truth. He has, in my case, made untrue charges as is shown by the following 34 untruths or lies.[33]

Reuchlin's litany presents the classical double bind situation, a paradox after the model of the lying Cretan, for Jews lie, no matter what they say. Their blindness is reflected in their words, their language, their discourse, their mode of speech. And this quality is immutable, inherited from their parents, grandparents, back through all generations to the Jews who condemned Christ. The special language of the Jews is not Hebrew, for that is the language of the Scripture, a language that they know but cannot truly under-stand. The special, hidden, demonic language of the Jews is the lie, the verbal equivalent of usury and poisoning. Reuchlin's equation of Pfefferkorn with Judas is but another way of saying, Here is another Jew betraying a Christian! What does one do with such liars? Well, Reuchlin's suggestion that their tongues be cut from their throats may sound metaphoric, but as will be seen, it was not.

Pfefferkorn was able to have the sale of *The Eye Glasses* halted through the intercession of the archbishop of Mainz, who had, of course, not expected Reuchlin both to seem to defend the Jews' books and to attack the spokesman of Church and emperor, Johan-nes Pfefferkorn. The pamphlet was brought before the Cologne inquisitors, the Dominicans, to be examined for heresy. Reuchlin was forced to answer the charges and in his defense argued, among other points, that in no way had he wished to leave the Talmud to the Jews. Rather, he did not want the Jews' books destroyed indiscriminately without copies of them first being deposited with

Christians for safekeeping, since for Christians, these books would have value.[34] Here the cult of the book became one of Reuchlin's central means of defense.

In 1513 this struggle was laid before the emperor. It had become a war between the old order, symbolized by Pfefferkorn and the Cologne Dominicans, and the new Humanism, represented by Reuchlin. After a series of public trials the issue became the cause célèbre of European intellectuals. It was no longer a question of the Jews and their books; rather, Reuchlin had become the symbol of the right freely to pursue all intellectual endeavors without overt limitation. Even though the emperor and the pope attempted to still this squabble among the learned, numerous intellectuals expressed their support of Reuchlin against the "force of darkness."

In 1514 Reuchlin permitted these statements of support to be published, which provided the model for some of his younger supporters among the German Humanists, especially Crotus Rubianus and Ulrich von Hutten, to create a series of letters from obscure men directed at Ortwin Gratius. These *Letters of Obscure Men*, published in two segments in 1516, form one of the world's great works of polemic. Cast in the form of letters of support for the Cologne Dominicans, the letters reflect, down to the pidgin Latin in which they are composed, the ignorance and stupidity attributed to the schoolmen by the Humanists. One of the strongest threads throughout the *Letters* is the Humanists' image of Pfefferkorn.

The Humanists present Pfefferkorn, as perceived through their fictional supporters of the Dominicans, as the quintessential renegade. He is Judas incarnate, Jew and criminal at the same time. His conversion was but a sham, brought about because of threats of prosecution for earlier criminal acts. But what is more, these satirized supporters of Pfefferkorn themselves doubt the possibility that Jews can ever truly become Christians, and they explain this doubt using the identical image employed by Victor of Karben reflecting the doubts with which he was faced about his own conversion:

> You ask me, in the third place, whether I think Johannes Pfefferkorn will persevere in the Christian faith. I answer that, by the Lord, I know not what to say. It is a mighty ticklish point. You will call to mind that the precedent, at St. Andrew's in Cologne—how a Dean of that Church, who was a baptized Jew, abided long in the Christian faith, and lived an upright life. But upon his death-bed he ordered a hare and a hound brought to him and enlarged, whereupon the hound in a trice seized the

hare. Then he ordered a cat and a mouse to be brought and the cat pounced on the mouse. Then he said to many who were standing around, "You see how that these animals cannot cast off their natures; and a Jew can never cast off his faith. Wherefore today I would fain to die a true Israelite," and so speaking he died. Thereupon the citizens of Cologne in memory of this event set up the brazen images which still stand on the wall before the cemetery.[35]

Jews remain Jews no matter what they publicly profess. "Take the case of a Jew baptized with the water of baptism: if the Holy Spirit be absent, the water profiteth nothing, and he is still a Jew. So it is with those bastards who are the sons of priests and whores—for priests cannot lawfully enter into wedlock with whores, and therefore a dispensation profiteth their children nothing" (227). The Jew remains a Jew, just as a bastard remains a bastard, because of birth, not because of belief. Conversion demands the inner conviction of the individual as well as the outer signs of baptism. And the Jew is congenitally unable to express this inner conviction.

But the blindness of the Jews is linked through the figure of Pfefferkorn in the *Letters of Obscure Men* to their sexualization. For even as Pfefferkorn had refused to carry the charge of the Jewesses' promiscuity through to the cuckoldry of the Jews, so, too, do the Humanists complete this loop. One of the primary references in all of the discussions of Pfefferkorn throughout the text is to his wife and her promiscuity. One must remember that Anna Pfefferkorn, like her husband and sons, converted to Christianity. Indeed, even her mother joined in the family's conversion. She was, therefore, not a Jewess but a Christian. And yet throughout the text reference is made to how many of the good schoolmen are "intimate with Johannes Pfefferkorn's wife" (29). One of the central passages links the total falsity of Pfefferkorn with his cuckoldry:

> You [the writer is reporting a discussion] must admit that Pfefferkorn does not know the Latin alphabet, much less can he read. And if he cannot read, much less can he understand. And if he cannot understand, much less can he write and compose. And if he can neither read, nor understand, nor write—much less can he discuss questions that none but a deeply learned man can deal with. Therefore how is it possible that he put together that material, either in Latin, or German, or Hebrew?
>
> I replied that I supposed that Pfefferkorn had such an enlightened intellect that, by God's help and the inspiration of the Holy Spirit, he was well able to dispute concerning it.

> The matter is such an easy one that Reuchlin could be
> vanquished therein by Pfefferkorn's wife. Then said the priest:
> That is very doubtful. I do not believe that five sturdy young
> Westphalian boors could vanquish Johannes Pfefferkorn's wife,
> much less could Johannes Reuchlin, who is an old man and
> feeble, and impotent withal. (140)

The Humanists have created the ultimate marginal man. He is
ignorant, foolish, and sexually incapable of dealing with his wife.
In mocking the idea of a Jew's possible conversion through the
Holy Spirit, the authors hold that the Jewess, like her husband,
remains unchanged by baptism. She is as promiscuous now as she
was before her baptism. Pfefferkorn's claim to authorship, like his
claim to fatherhood, is here drawn into question. Such charges are
standard fare when brought against the Jews, as indicated by Pfefferkorn's own use of these charges in his earlier pamphlets. Here,
however, they are lodged against a Jew seen as masquerading as a
Christian, who is cuckolding his Christian supporters through his
own falsity.

The reduction of Pfefferkorn to a marginal man has one further
aspect. Pfefferkorn is accused of having become a Christian to avoid
punishment for his crimes. "That Johannes Pfefferkorn of yours,"
mock two Jews in Worms,

> is a vile braggart; he knoweth no Hebrew, and he became a
> Christian to hide his crimes. When he was a Jew, in Moravia,
> seeing a woman standing at a money-changer's counter, he
> smote her in the face, so that she was blinded, and seizing more
> than two hundred florins, he made off with them. Elsewhere a
> gallows was set up so that he might be hanged thereon for
> theft. (74)

Not only is he a criminal but he is from Moravia. Placing Pfefferkorn at the margin of the German-speaking world, the authors of
the *Letters of Obscure Men* associate him with the fears of the
barbarians from the East, whether Slav, Mongol, or Turk. His
marginality is geographic as well as social. He is an Eastern Jew as
well as a thief.

What does one do with such a villain in the world of satire?
Why, one kills him or at least reduces him to the status of a dead
man. Leon Poliakov, in his history of anti-Semitism, discussed the
trauma of European Jewry at the first break with their status as a
people among other people, during their exposure to the wrath of
their neighbors in the course of the First Crusade, in the eleventh
century.[36] By the sixteenth century the trauma had become rein-

forced as a matter of daily experience. Pfefferkorn's own example of the thirty-eight Jews burned in Berlin provides some sense of what was potentially in store for any Jew on the whim of his Christian neighbors. One does not have to argue that the Jews possessed a memory or tradition of the martyrdom of the First Crusade and the resultant loss of social stability as part of their perception of the world. The vagaries of daily life in sixteenth-century Germany certainly created a world in which it would have been impossible to judge from day to day any action's result in the world. This basic, inherent insecurity of such a life would have provided more than an adequate reason for conversion if conversion promised that one would be identical to those who had created the instability of the Jews' world. One could act without being burnt. One could speak without having one's tongue cut out. One could imagine that one's children would live and raise children of their own. All of this, in idealized form, must have been some Jews' perception of life within the Christian community. The true instability of Christian life, the role of the Inquisition for Christian as well as for Jew, the inability of dogmatically rigid groups to accept an outsider—these facts would have been repressed or glossed over. And still within this sanctuary, the Christian world, there were specific signposts of the danger of conversion. For in 1267 Pope Clement IV had made it a crime, to be punished by the pyre, for converted Jews to relapse into their prior faith. The punishment awaiting the false convert was direct and terrible. For the convert lived *in* rather than, as the Jews, *under* the Church.[37]

Thus when the *Letters of Obscure Men* turn to considering the appropriate manner of dealing with Johannes Pfefferkorn, they draw on the inherent instability that Pfefferkorn had wished to escape and create a double for him. This double exists in flashes in the text, mentioned to qualify the true nature of the fictionalized Pfefferkorn. In one longer passage, from a fictitious priest in Halle, this double appears in some detail:

> Gentlemen, that you may understand the true nature of this
> suit against Johannes Pfefferkorn, who resembleth in name, and
> in all else, that Johannes Pfefferkorn who was in this very place
> torn with red-hot pincers, and who in like manner had become
> a pervert from his faith, by reason of the wickedness that he
> had committed. If Pfefferkorn were safe here in jail, and the
> executioners were to put the question to him as to what he had
> committed, he would make confession of not a whit less than
> his namesake. (118)

Pfefferkorn is here supplied with a double, a double called Johannes Pfefferkorn, described as a convert and as "having been burnt by the Margrave at Halle—though this was not true concerning him, but true enough of another man of the same name" (102).

This creation of a double is not merely part of the fantasy of the authors of the *Letters of Obscure Men*. In September 1514, Ulrich von Hutten, one of the authors of the *Letters of Obscure Men*, served as the official representative of the archbishop of Mainz at the torture and burning at Halle of a Jew called variously Pastor Rapp or Johannes Pfefferkorn. As punishment for having falsely claimed to have been a priest and a doctor, Rapp was roasted over a slow fire while his skin was ripped from his body. Under torture he admitted to the entire catalogue of charges lodged against Jews: He played the role of priest in order to steal and defile the host. He used his disguise as a doctor to poison those who came to his aid. He accepted money to assassinate the bishop of Magdeburg as well as the Elector of the Mark, and this money came from the Jews. He created false miracles in order to claim that he was the Messiah, a charge lodged against the Jews by Petrus Nigri at the end of the fifteenth century.[38] He mocked and insulted Christ and the Virgin. Hutten, in a Latin panegyric of 119 hexameters, glories in the death of Rapp, congratulating his readers that such a monster could only have been born to Jewish parents and that he was, therefore, no true German.[39]

Hutten seems to have been the first to call Rapp Johannes Pfefferkorn, that is, to have turned him into a double for that Johannes Pfefferkorn of Cologne who was leading the struggle against Reuchlin. And it is from Hutten that this doubling is most probably introduced into the *Letters of Obscure Men*. This doubling had existed in one other source. In the *Triumph of Reuchlin*, a long mock epic that first appeared in 1514 and was revised by Hutten in 1517, there is a long description of the maiming and torture of the Cologne Pfefferkorn, of his body being used as a bloody broom on the streets of Pforzheim, Reuchlin's hometown.[40] This is fiction. It is the wish of the poet to dismember his adversary. With the torture and execution of Rapp, a real double was found in the world rather than merely in fiction.

The primary charge lodged against Rapp was that he was a liar. He lied when he claimed to be a priest and a doctor, and he lied in order to carry out evil and destructive acts. He is thus the double of the Cologne Pfefferkorn, who lies when he claims to be a Christian, for "as men suspect baptized Jews [are] botched Christians—

therefore Pfefferkorn is a botched Christian!" (157). He bears all of the stigmas associated with being a convert, as well as the negative image associated with the Jewish physician.

Rapp's punishment, as David Friedrich Strauss has pointed out, was well within the terms of contemporary justice.[41] His torture and death were not unexpected in light of the charges lodged against him. Hutten, and the Humanists, seemingly out of character in their general objections to such actions on the part of the Church and the state, relished the death of Rapp. It provided for them a lesson of what can be done to such Jews, especially Jews who mask themselves as Christians. The literary fantasies of the group in power—and that would include both the supporters of the Church and the Humanists—had a frightening way of turning into reality when the Jews were concerned. This movement from fiction to reality through the creation of a double must have had extraordinary force for the Cologne Pfefferkorn, especially in the light of the great public acceptance of the *Letters of Obscure Men*.

IV

The Self-hatred of the Convert

On the surface Pfefferkorn's campaign against the Jews' books seemed quite successful. His approach to the emperor, the actual confiscation of the books, and the support of the theological establishment throughout Europe showed him that. Even the eventual condemnation of Reuchlin's *The Eye Glasses* by the pope proved it. When Reuchlin published *The Eye Glasses*, Pfefferkorn's response, unlike *The Hand Mirror*, which had simply tried to counter Reuchlin's recommendation, was directed not against Reuchlin but against the Jews. And yet the complicated interrelationship among Pfefferkorn the convert, his former coreligionists, and his new coreligionists' image of the Jews played a major role in shaping his argument. Pfefferkorn must respond to the charges against him *as if* they came from the Jews but is constantly aware that his enemies lie within the Christian camp.

Reuchlin has become the attacker of "us Christians," as Pfefferkorn refers to himself throughout *The Burning Mirror*. "We Christians" must defend ourselves against the lies of the Jews:

> Now I wish to inform all pious Christians about one specific doctor born of a Christian family, I mean Johannes Reuchlin, called the doctor of worldly laws. He has, without reason, ille-

gally, and untruthfully written an insulting and libelous work against me out of a sense of pride. It is called *The Eye Glasses.* This work had the purpose of defending the Jews and their false books and to mock me, to defend the Jews and repress me. I had thought better of the doctor as a Christian thinks of a Christian. . . . He has sold his booklet far and wide, but more among the Jews than among us Christians. . . . I was not the cause of the argument between him and me. He was the one who began it and broke his Christian troth to me.[42]

Just as Pfefferkorn was attacked as a Jew from a Jewish family by Reuchlin, just as he had been attacked for selling his books for gain, so, too, he counters in his attack on Reuchlin. Christians do not act like this. They do not act like Jews. For just as Reuchlin has betrayed the inheritance of his Christian family in becoming a supporter of the Jews, so, too, has Pfefferkorn abandoned the errors of his family's tradition and become a Christian. Not only can the leopard change his spots but he can do so through being seduced by the enemy.

Reuchlin's basic charge, however, is not answered by claiming solidarity with the Christians. For if Jews lie, then all this can be but a sham. To counter this, Pfefferkorn attacks not the supporters of the Jews, such as Reuchlin, but the Jews themselves. The angry, distraught tone of *The Burning Mirror* presents a new program, more radical and, on the surface, more hostile toward the Jews. Reeducating is no longer sufficient for Pfefferkorn; they must be destroyed:

> The Jews must be made to hear the word. Where this is not done nor wished to be done, it is perhaps because of the deeds of a few Christians who look through their fingers rather than see. These take presents and bribes from the Jews. . . . Thus one must reform and punish the Jews for the greater glory of God and the community. Not that one should murder them nor destroy their goods. Rather one must treat them legally and take their goods and give them to those to whom they belong and from whom they have been taken. Or give them to a hospital or church where one is obligated to repay such wrong. One must drive the old Jews out like dirty dogs and baptize the young children as one has already done with them in many places. And one should not wait for today, tomorrow, or the day after tomorrow, but rather it must take place this very hour. And the children must be taken and baptized for the glory of God and the benefit of their souls.[43]

Pfefferkorn advocates that the Jews be exiled from the major cities of Germany—Worms, Frankfurt, and Regensburg—and that their children be forcibly baptized. Here, Reuchlin's claim that one should no more take the Jews' books away from them than one should forcibly baptize their children should be remembered. For in advocating the banning of the Jews and the baptism of their children, Pfefferkorn is completing the program condemned by Reuchlin. He is treating people in the way that books should not be treated. But even more than that, he has created in Reuchlin his negative double, his antithesis. Just as their two "conversions" are mirror images of one another, one becoming a Judaizer and the other a Christian, so, too, are their programs inverted copies of one another. The major difference between the two is that if Reuchlin is not believed, he is fined; if Pfefferkorn is not believed, he is tortured and roasted over a slow fire. Thus the new program is itself quite problematical, for Pfefferkorn, contrary to much of the discussion of this pamphlet, does not advocate the destruction of the Jews.[44] He carefully repeats his earlier admonitions against harming the Jews, because the danger that he faces is real. Without much hesitation on the part of his judges, he can become like Rapp. He does not—nor can he—so identify with the Christians, his reference group, as to repress this central fact. He advocates stripping the Jews of their worldly possessions and banishing them. While these acts are surely radical ones, they do not raise the same fears as does a roasting while having one's skin ripped off with red-hot pincers.

The next series of pamphlets written by Pfefferkorn has the same major subtext. It is perhaps best summarized in the title of his pamphlet of 1516: *A Defence of Johannes Pfefferkorn, Whom They Did Not Burn*. In these later pamphlets Pfefferkorn repeats the attacks on Reuchlin as the defender of the Jews but always returns to the same focus, as in the *Booklet of Argument* (1516), in which he writes, almost in despair:

> Now Ulrich von Hutten has written falsely about me, using many falsities in the *Letters of Obscure Men*, saying that I am one who was burnt, and later, that he was my brother. Now, it is clear that I am the only son of my parents. Since this is the case, they write that he was my cousin, but I have no Christian cousin named Johannes Pfefferkorn.[45]

Pfefferkorn wishes to free himself from his double, the double burnt for playacting the Christian. In an apotropaic gesture aimed at warding off his double's fate, he projects onto Reuchlin all of the evils that have been associated with himself and with Rapp, that is, those evils traditionally associated with the Jew. His projection is an attempt to save his image as one fully within the Christian camp. But of course the dichotomies in what must seem to an outsider a monolithic structure, the Church, make such a resolution impossible. Pfefferkorn will also remain the Jew to some elements in the Christian community. His only hope is to persuade himself that these elements are but an extension of his former self, that Reuchlin truly sees in the same blind manner as do the Jews. In turning Reuchlin into the "bad" Jew, Pfefferkorn is able to save the structure through which he is able to perceive himself as the "good" Christian. But Reuchlin remains the Christian, no matter how often he is accused of being unable to see the truth. Pfefferkorn can all too easily become Rapp, even if he continues to cling to his newly perceived Christian truth.

When, on June 23, 1520, the pope finally bowed to the Dominicans and declared Reuchlin's *The Eye Glasses* to be heretical, Reuchlin was fined. The victory was a hollow one, for Reuchlin had gathered behind him most of the intellectuals of Europe, who had now begun to focus on a new controversy within the Church, this time dealing with the German monk Martin Luther. Pfefferkorn saw his position in Christian society vindicated by the pope's decision. He saw himself freed of the charge of apostasy. In his final pamphlet, after which he vanished from the historical landscape, he addressed Reuchlin and his contemporaries: "Yes, Reuchlin, had the pope done this to you eight years ago, Martin Luther and the writers of *Letters of Obscure Men* would not today be doing publicly what they are doing to the detriment of the Church."[46] What Pfefferkorn was not able to see in 1521, when this charge was lodged, was that the model of Jewish self-hatred that he supplied became central to the formulation of German anti-Semitism through its assimilation into Martin Luther's thoughts and observations concerning the Jews. Pfefferkorn necessarily modified the distance between himself and the Jews, advocating the isolation but expressly condemning their destruction. Luther's views were built on Pfefferkorn's dichotomy of the "good" Jew, who has true insight when he accepts Christ, and the "bad" Jew, whose blindness leads him to evil and destructive acts. It was with Martin Luther that the projections of Jewish converts concerning their own Jewishness were reified and provided a detailed system of perceiving the Jew as Other.

V

Luther's Judaeophobia and the Jewish Convert

It is usual to divide Martin Luther's interest in the Jews into three phases, roughly coinciding with the main biographical periods in his life: the young Catholic Luther, for whom the Jews played little or no role, except as figures within biblical commentary; the Luther in rebellion against the Church, who assumed that his cleansing of Christianity from the evils of the Church would persuade the Jews to convert; and the established Luther, embittered by the Jews' refusal to convert to the newly purged doctrine and violent in his language and attitude toward them.[47] It is this last period that is of the most interest to anyone who wishes to examine the function of the model of Jewish self-hatred in the reformulation of German anti-Judaism. Part of the reason for this is that while Luther's late texts against the Jews were viewed by a small number of his supporters as anomalies, they reappear throughout the history of German attitudes toward the Jews.[48] They serve for the Protestants as major texts upon which to draw for the correctness of their position concerning the Jews. Some scholars wished to rescue Luther from the charge of founding German anti-Judaism by seeing his development as discontinuous. These scholars were eventually forced to argue that the late texts of Luther, with their obsessive concern about the Jews, were the products of an organic brain dysfunction.[49] In his vicious attacks on the Jews, then, Luther is not even permitted to have undergone a dynamic development; rather, his late pamphlets and sermons are seen as the anomalous products of a rapid physical deterioration.

In Luther's late works concerning the Jews one major factor ties the young Luther's attitudes toward the Jews with those views held by the aged Reformer: the function of works by Jewish converts and his attitude toward converts and conversion in general in shaping his views of the Jews.[50] To understand the development of Luther's attitudes as focused through the prism of Jewish self-hatred, one must begin with the struggle between Reuchlin and Pfefferkorn.

To examine Luther's attitudes toward this argument between the Church and the Humanists, one can most easily turn to Luther's correspondence. Throughout the decade 1510–20, Luther identifies strongly with the cause of the Humanists. In a letter written to his friend Spalatin in 1514 he mocks Ortwin Gratius, and as late as 1520 he asks Martin Bucer to keep him informed of the progress of the case against Reuchlin.[51] But this is more than mere interest in the political fate of another intellectual who has gone against Church order: Luther identifies strongly with Reuchlin. In one letter to Spalatin, written in 1518, he literally sees himself as Reuchlin.[52] In identifying himself as the double of Reuchlin, he was hoping for the type of support for his own position that Reuchlin had been able to call forth. But even more so, it was an identification with the attitude that Reuchlin maintained toward his opponents, especially toward Pfefferkorn. If one begins a reading of the late pamphlets of Luther with the understanding that Luther has accepted Reuchlin's mode of treating his opponent, certain continuities in Luther's rhetoric become evident. What changes throughout Luther's life is the object to which this rhetoric is attached. In the middle period of Luther's life, Reuchlin's attitude toward the convert as enemy is applied to the "whore of Babylon," the Roman Catholic Church. All of the qualities of Otherness, the evil, poisoning, sexualized nature of the Other, are discovered by Luther in his prime opponent, the Church—so much so that in his pamphlet of 1533, directed against the Church ordination of priests and their manner of holding the Mass, he attacks the Church for its inhumane actions.[53] He compares them to those who are simply frauds and use the Mass to earn money, frauds like "that poor Jew who was burned at Halle on the Moritzburg." Luther condemns the burning of Rapp in 1533 as a sign of the evil of the Church. The power of Pfefferkorn's double, whose importance as a symbolic figure was limited to the struggle of Reuchlin and Hutten versus Pfefferkorn during the period from 1514 to 1520, kept this incident in Luther's mind for almost twenty years. The burning is given a positive role in condemning the Church in 1533, as opposed to the negative quality it had in Hutten's poem or in the *Letters of Obscure Men*. This can be attributed to the context in which Luther places the burning of Rapp. He has freed Rapp from his functioning as a double within the fiction of the *Letters of Obscure Men* and perceives him as one of the victims of the Church, a victim whose crime was no greater than those actions perpetuated every day within the Church itself.

In the late pamphlets, clearly the context in which the Jews are discussed has shifted. Luther is no longer struggling with the Church for his own existence. No longer does the fear of the Church dominate his manner of seeing the world. Rather, the Church has become but one of the chief evils of this world. And the Jews are the Other.

In the 1540s Luther authored three major pamphlets directed

against the Jews. Their rhetoric is harsh, and their program is summarized in the first and most extensive of these texts, *Against the Jews and Their Lies* (1543). Jews lie. "From their youth they have been so nurtured with venom and rancor against our Lord that there is no hope until they reach the point where their misery makes them pliable. . . . Jews lie shamefully."[54] And in their lying is their danger to the new social and moral order. For they undermine it with their way of seeing the world. They deny value where value exists. They lie in the legalism of their books, a legalism that is identical to that of the Church. They are incorrigible. They poison, defile, and whore. And they do this under the guise of the religion of the Old Testament:

> Or let us suppose that somewhere a pretty girl came along, adorned with a wreath, and observed all manners, the duties, the deportment, and discipline of a chaste virgin, but underneath was a vile, shameful whore, violating the Ten Commandments. What good would her fine obedience in observing outwardly all the duties and customs of a virgin's station do her? It would help her this much—that one would be seven times more hostile to her than to the impudent, public whore. (170)

Here is, of course, Reuchlin and Hutten's view of Pfefferkorn as the false convert, even more destructive because of his false claim to truth than a Jew who is evidently a Jew. One can compare Erasmus's comment to Wilibald Pirkheimer in a letter of November 2, 1517, to the effect that "he [Judas] attacked Christ only, whereas he [Pfefferkorn] has attacked many worthy and eminent men. He could render no better service to his coreligionists than betraying Christendom, hypocritically claiming to have become a Christian. . . . This half-Jew has done more harm to Christendom than all the Jews together."[55] Luther simply reverses this, using the image of the Jewish whore found in Pfefferkorn and the *Letters of Obscure Men* to reveal the inherent duplicity of all Jews.

Luther's program is straightforward. Burn their synagogues, destroy their homes, confiscate the Talmud and all other Hebrew books, including the Bible, forbid the rabbis from teaching, ban them from carrying out trade, stop them from moving from place to place, demand that their children learn trades, and if all else fails, ban them from the country. This is Pfefferkorn's program raised to a higher power. But it is a program that could not have come directly from Pfefferkorn, who would have seen his own status potentially endangered by the radical nature of Luther's proposals. The basis for Luther's program is the radical difference in the Jews' manner of understanding the divine order. In his second pamphlet, *On Shem Hamphoras* [the Ineffable Name] *and the Descent of Christ* (1543), Luther presents a polemic on the nature and origin of the Jews' misreading of Holy Scripture:

> I, a damned *goy*, cannot understand where they have their great skill in interpreting, except, perhaps, that when Judas Iscariot hung himself, his bladder burst and his gut split. Perhaps the Jews had their servants there with golden pots and silver bowls to catch Judas's piss and other reliques (as they are called). Then they ate and drank the shit mixed with piss to become so sharp-eyed in interpreting the Scripture. They see things in Scripture that neither Isaiah nor Matthew, nor all the angels saw, and that we damned *goys* can never hope to see.[56]

Luther uses the "insiders' " language, Yiddish, to mock the special knowledge claimed by the Jew. He sets the same claim to a knowledge of their hidden discourse as does the convert. He knows the special language of the Jews, recognizes their blindness and its source, and can thus better interpret their text, the Bible, than can the Jews themselves. Luther thus denies the Jews any insight into the Bible because they lack true command of the hidden language of that text, Hebrew. Luther's rhetoric centers about the claim that the Jews made concerning their ability to read Scripture; it is a claim that he perceives as one with their identity. In the *Tabletalk* of this period, Luther denied the special insight of the Jews into Scripture. In the *Tabletalk* for November 1540 he stated:

> If we did not have the Greek and Latin Bible, we would not understand a single word of the Hebrew. The Jews lost the sense of the language, including the tropes and figures. Thus none today understand anything. It is as if a Greek studied for years the German proverb: He can turn his coat to the wind. He can understand *wind*, *coat* has a case that he can learn, but he could never understand the complex meaning of the entire phrase. He would have to guess. So it goes with Hebrew.[57]

The Jews are here denied their claim to any of the mythic quality that had been associated with Hebrew. They are no longer perceived as having special, magical powers. The reversal of the positive sense of their divine role into the negative antithesis of their demonic possession is here turned into a worldly evil, an evil that has material rather than divine manifestation. For in denying the Jews any special quality, except stubbornness and blindness, Luther strips from them any special role in contemporary life. Their blindness is the result of their refusal to accept Christ (and therefore, according to Luther, their adherence to Judas). But a closer reading of this passage, as well as later passages in the same text, reveals a subtle shift in Luther's understanding of the roots of the Jews' misreading of Scripture. Luther suggests that "our Hebraists . . . have the obligation to cleanse the Holy Bible from the piss of Judas" (646). Or, as in the last pamphlet written against the Jews, *On the Last Words of David* (1543), that "God wills that our theologians study Hebrew well so that they restore to us the Bible from the wanton thieves who stole it. And that they do everything better, as I have done it, so that they are not captured by the torturous grammars of the Rabbis and their false interpretation. . . ."[58] This refusal to give the claims of the "blind" Jews credence mirrored and reified his reception of the convert, of the "seeing" Jews. For to deny any special knowledge to the Jews, to deny them any insight at all into the mysteries of Scripture, undermines their ability to understand themselves, to read their own texts, which was central to proving their own conversion. Luther's reaction to converts—in the flesh rather than in their textual incarnation—illustrates this refusal.

When one examines Luther's own dealings with the Jews in the 1540s, one is struck by the banality of his attitudes toward Jews, especially toward Jewish converts. One striking exception is the episode in which he perceived in the convert Michael of Posen the threatening assassin. Michael, who had come to Luther in 1540, triggered a longstanding fear of the Jews as poisoners, a fear that can be traced to the episode in January 1525 that Luther recounted in a letter to Amsdorf.[59] Luther believed that a Polish Jew disguised as a doctor had been bribed by the Jews to murder him. This fear itself can be traced to Luther's firm belief that doctors, especially Jewish doctors, were magicians. As early as 1520 there is mention in Luther's correspondence of a doctor-magician from Halberstadt who presents a danger to his life.[60] Jews, doctors, and converts are all dangerous, but they present a danger of this world, a danger that serves as a substitute for Luther's earlier sense of the magical nature of the Jews (and their language). For it is in the true text, in the Bible as written by the finger of God in Hebrew, that the evils of the Church will be dispelled. Luther's views seem to be close to those of both Reuchlin, with his stress on the special nature of the Jews' language, and Pfefferkorn, whose fears of the Jews' books reflected his own fear of becoming once again a Jew. Indeed, Luther, in the writings of the 1540s, seems to deny the Jews any special place in Christian teleology. Not only does he seem to reject the view that the conversion of the Jews is a necessary prelude to the Second Coming but he expresses real doubts about whether Jews can be converted at all. Luther recounts the same anecdote about the figure of the convert sculpted in the door of St. Andrew's at Cologne as that recounted by Victor of Karben and the Humanists to establish the intransigence of the Jews, but Luther's retelling of this tale stresses the this-worldly aspects of the depraved nature of the Jew.[61]

While it is evident that Luther used elements from Pfefferkorn's and Reuchlin's images of the Jew, one further mitigating text should be mentioned, a text that helped Luther focus his image of the Jew, an image of the Jew that was reified, since it came in part from the most authentic source, the Jews themselves. In conversations held during the winter of 1542/43, while Luther was formulating his final broadside against the Jews, he discussed a book he was reading. *The Entire Jewish Faith*, published in 1530, was written by Antonius Margaritha, a convert from Judaism who became a reader of Hebrew at the University of Vienna.[62] What strikes any reader who compares Margaritha's text with any of the Pfefferkorn pamphlets is the totally different tone. Rather than polemic, the text appears to be a detailed account of the festivals and practices of the Jews, written as a handbook for Christian missionaries. Yet one must ask oneself what the importance of such a shift of tone is, a shift that takes place within the generation in which Hebrew begins to lose its magical qualities as it is disseminated throughout the German educational institutions. Margaritha's program was not different from that of Pfefferkorn, but in the wake of Pfefferkorn's authority as a seeing Jew having been undermined by Reuchlin and the Humanists, it was necessary to create a new level of scholarship upon which to base the status of the "seeing" Jew. Thus Margaritha's claim to serious scholarship about the Jews is simply based on much the same prejudices and presuppositions as those found in Pfefferkorn's program, cast in less polemical language and possessing more details, some accurate and some spurious.

Antonius Margaritha was the grandson of the famed Nuremberg Talmudist Jacob Margolis and the son of a rabbi. Unlike Pfefferkorn, whose proletarian background was the subject of much comment among the Humanists, Margaritha could claim a good Hebrew education. His conversion to Christianity in 1522, like that of his fellow voluntary converts, is ascribed to a sudden awareness of the blindness of his coreligionists and of the truth of Christianity. In 1530 Margaritha published his work on the nature of

Judaism. Not merely seen as a tool for the enlightenment of the Christian reading public and the reification of his new status as a "seeing" Jew, *The Entire Jewish Faith* was perceived by Margaritha as a challenge to the blindness of the Jews. Its author demanded, and got, a public disputation with the leader, or parnas, of the German Jewish community, Josel of Rosheim. At the Augsburg Diet of 1530, called to solidify the emperor's power, a public disputation was held between Margaritha and Josel of Rosheim on the nature of the Jews' prayers, on their desire to make converts, and on their attacks on the emperor and the state. Present were Emperor Charles V, princes of the Holy Roman Empire, and representatives of both the Church and the Reformation (including Melanchton). Josel of Rosheim was able to refute Margaritha point by point, showing how Jewish law and ritual expressly forbade the actions and beliefs attributed to the Jews by the convert.

Charles V had been raised in a historical tradition of disputations between the now exiled Jews and Christian converts as they had been held in Spain.[63] There these debates were held to show the inherent truth of the Christian faith, and there could only be one victor, the Church. In the debate between the "blind" Jew, Josel of Rosheim, and the "seeing" Jew, Antonius Margaritha, the victor was not clear until the debate was over, and then the victory fell to the "blind" Jew. Margaritha was arrested by imperial order as a danger to the social structure. Banished from Augsburg, in 1531 he reappeared in Leipzig, where he taught Hebrew at the university. Also in 1531, the third edition of his work appeared. He had concluded the first edition (and the second) with the formulaic statement that he knew that once his book appeared, the Jews would curse him. The third edition, published after the debacle in Augsburg, turned that formulaic statement into an outcry against the perfidious Jews: "What has happened to me because of this book shall not long be suppressed. Still I pray to God, my creator, and Jesus Christ, that he save me from the stubborn and deceitful Jews. Amen."[64] Some time after the publication of this third edition of *The Entire Jewish Faith*, Margaritha converted for a second time and became a follower of Luther.

Margaritha's text presents, through its mode of interpretation, an image of the "seeing" Jew that is in contrast to the image of the blindness of the Jews described. Central to Margaritha's argument is the lack of originality of the Jews. The Talmud, that focus of Pfefferkorn's fury, is subdivided. The original parts are the more modern ones and are the result of the revelations of Christ; the older segments, antedating the coming of Christ, are unoriginal.

This view, which first appeared in the debate between Nahmanides and the convert Hieronymus de Santa Fe, is vital, since it stresses the centrality of the coming of Christ to any truthful revelation outside of Holy Scripture. The seeming insight of the Jews, as documented by the Talmud, is merely a reflection of the truth of Christianity. The Jews cannot make any claim to an independent revelation or tradition of interpretation. This view suspends the special status of the Jews after the destruction of the Temple and draws the distinction—which Luther needs and uses—between the Jews of the Bible (with their prefiguration of the events of the New Testament) and the present-day Jews with whom he must deal. Indeed, the lesson that Luther cites as having learned from *The Entire Jewish Faith* is that Jews are just like Catholics: both believe that they can achieve salvation by actions in this world rather than by faith alone. Both Catholic and Jew live in this world; they have no sense of the relationship between the material and the spiritual. And the blindness of both is made concrete by their mode of reading. The limited nature of the non-Protestant's understanding of the totality of the world is illustrated by Margaritha's presentation of Jewish ritual, a ritual that Luther immediately parallels to the Mass. For the Jews, like the Catholics, are corrupters of the True Word, untouched by insight. The lack of originality of the Jews in their mode of interpretation is further shown by their blindness to the true interpretation of Scripture. For just as the Jews stole from the Christians after the revelation of Christ made their blindness overt, so, too, does the new revelation make the blindness of both Jew and Catholic evident.

The tradition of the convert's public attack on the Jews becomes almost a commonplace in the sixteenth century. The dialogues of Samuel Maroccanus, a North African convert to Christianity, are translated into German from the Latin translations of the Arabic and introduced by a major Lutheran preacher.[65] In 1536, shortly after the publication of the third edition of Margaritha's *The Entire Jewish Faith*, Paulus Staffelsteiner, "born of Jewish seed from the generation of Aaron" and converted to the evangelical faith in Nuremberg, published his own explanation of the "Jews' Hebrew babbling."[66] In 1577 Paul of Prague, converted in 1556 in Nuremberg, published his own account of his conversion through the force of the new exegesis.[67] As with Staffelsteiner, his major claim was his knowledge of the "hidden language of the Jews," Hebrew. Yet another Paul of Prague, a rabbi, baptized in the Polish city of Chelm, published an exposition of the Cabala in 1582.[68] Again, his claim to status was his special knowledge of the text and its hidden tongue, seen through the eyes of the convert. This pattern underlies all of the special claims of these converts and provides the context for the projection of their self-hatred. For they distance themselves from their own identification as Jews, attributing all manner of evil deeds and horrors to their former coreligionists to show their own transcendence of this category. They also claim a special position within Christianity because of their knowledge of the special language, discourse, and ritual of the Jews.[69] But this claim to status only works when the audience, real or implied, is Christian. When Paul Weidner, the reader for Hebrew at the University of Vienna, baptized in 1568, addressed a Jewish audience (which was required to hear him), he could make no such claims of status, for his audience may well have possessed greater knowledge than he himself claimed. His sermon is a very straightforward call for conversion on the basis of the greater truthfulness of Christianity. He does not use his own conversion or status as an exemplum within the text.

Martin Luther based his reading of the nature of the Jews and their lack of originality on the revelation of a "seeing" Jew, Antonius Margaritha, whose status as an expert had been severely undermined by the disputation at Augsburg, of which Luther must have had detailed, if indirect, knowledge. Margaritha's new status as the Protestant's "seeing" Jew would have countered some of Luther's doubt. For here was the ultimate proof of what revelation could accomplish. First, the "blind" Jew is made to see through divine intercession, and he converts to a faulty model of Christianity. And then, when the institution of the Church abandons him, he receives true insight and becomes a "truly seeing" Jew, a follower of the Reformation. And yet this shifting could also be understood in the light of the Pfefferkorn model as evolved by the Humanists. For if the Jew can never be truly converted, if he remains eternally the Jew, as the dog remains the dog, and the hare, the hare, then Margaritha's shift from Judaism to Catholicism to Protestantism is living proof of this blindness. Seen from the standpoint of the Protestant, especially Luther, Margaritha's own biography gives substance to the charge that Jews are base and untrustworthy. Margaritha's striving for what Peter Gay perceives in twentieth-century German Jewry as "wholeness hunger" is silently understood as proof of the inherent, immutable nature of the Jew.[70] Margaritha becomes the living reification of both models of the Jew. The ambiguity felt by Luther in regard to his person is countered by his text, and yet text and person are perceived as one. The Jew is his own text, and it is a contradictory text.

In his pamphlet *The Jews and Their Lies* Luther presented this dichotomy in all its confused fullness. Drawing heavily on Margaritha for the substance of his charges against the Jews, Luther nevertheless doubts the ability of the Jew to convert:

> No doubt it is necessary for the Jews to lie and to misinterpret in order to maintain their error ever against such a clear and powerful text. Their previous lies broke down under their own weight. But even if they were to lie for a hundred thousand years and call the devils in to aid them, they would still come to nought. For it is impossible to name a Messiah at the time of the seventy weeks, as Gabriel's revelation would necessitate, other than our Lord Jesus Christ. We are certain, sure, and cheerful about this, as we snap our fingers at all the gates of hell and defy them, together with all the gates of the world and everything that wants to be or might be exalted, smart, or wise against us. I, a plain insignificant saint in Christ, venture to oppose all of them single-handedly and to defend this viewpoint easily, comfortably, and gladly. However, it is impossible to convert the devil and his own, nor are we commanded to attempt this. It suffices to uncover their lies and to reveal the truth. Whoever is not actuated to believe the truth for the sake of his own soul will surely not believe it for my sake.[71]

The inability of the Jews to be converted is not a tenet found in Luther's Christian sources on the Jews, at least not those cited in the opening of this pamphlet. Both Nicolas of Lyra and Paul of Burgos saw their expositions of Jewish law and ritual as means through which to achieve the eventual conversion of the Jews. Neither Margaritha nor Victor of Karben, whom Luther also read, provided this model. Indeed, they sought to undermine any notion of the inability of the Jews to be converted, as this view placed their own conversion in question. Luther saw in the model of the intractable Jew the figure of Pfefferkorn, and perhaps also one aspect of Margaritha. But Luther did not ignore the potential presented by the other aspect of Margaritha's presence in his world. He concludes the pamphlet *The Jews and Their Lies* with the formulaic statement: "May Christ, our dear Lord, convert them mercifully and preserve us steadfastly and immovably in the knowledge of him, which is eternal life. Amen."[72] This formula, with its promise of eventual conversion, was weakened somewhat in *On Shem Hamphoras*, where Luther prays for the potential conversion of "at least some" of the Jews, but still remained part of the ritual rhetoric with which the Jews were addressed.[73]

Luther's views on the nature of the Jews are reified by the presence of converts to Christianity in his world. The complex self-definition of these converts, their need to establish themselves as better Christians than the Christians themselves, their public attitudes toward their former coreligionists, and their use of their biographies and texts as exempla all play a role in shaping the attitude of the Christian world toward the Jew. Since the initial model chosen by the convert is a model of the Jew viewed through the eyes of the Christian world, it is of little wonder that the Christian community found their attitude toward the Jew substantiated by the converts' testimony. Yet, within the converts' texts, a sense of the ambiguous position of the "seeing" Jew—neither "blind" Jew nor true Christian—can be found. When Luther initially confronts this contradiction, it is to give the image of the convert a negative quality. In desiring the conversion of the Jews to his own brand of Christianity, he swings to the other pole present within the model and sees the potential for conversion as possible. When, in May 1542, he is again confronted with the claims of the Jews in the form of a Jewish apologetic pamphlet representing a Jew speaking with a Christian, attacking the Christian exegesis of the Old Testament, the entire model reverts to its original negative quality, as the public function of the pamphlet calls forth the negative associations held with Pfefferkorn and his exegesis.[74] It is once again the claim of a hidden language by a stubborn Jew who draws Christianity into question. It is clear that Luther has sufficient ideological reasons for his attitudes toward the Jews, reasons buttressed by theologians as diverse as Martin Bucer and Johannes Eck in their attacks on the Jews' books, but it is through the model of the Jew as perceived and presented by Jewish converts that Luther finds the reification of his perception of the Jew, a reification replete with contradictions and ambiguities present in these Jews' understanding of their status and definition within the Christian world. Luther's own presentation of the hidden language of the Jews, shaped by the writings of self-hating Jews, becomes part of a German tradition that generates further negative self-images within German Jews. In an inexorable dialectic each self-hating text generates new anti-Jewish texts which draw for their proof on the older negative self-image, and this new generation of texts becomes the matrix in which Jewish writers shape their new literary persona.

CHAPTER THREE

The Spirit of Toleration

I

The Language of Thieves

In denying the Jews' claim to Hebrew as a language over which they possessed control and through which they were able magically to affect the world, Martin Luther continued the inexorable process of dehumanizing the Jews. In destroying the Jews' special status as that people who held the hidden knowledge of their own books, a claim that presented the convert with his artificial sense of status within the Christian world, Luther debased them. If they were not magicians, able to deal with black or white powers through their magic books, then they were merely confidence tricksters who played on the gullibility of their Christian victims. Thus Luther joined a Renaissance tradition that saw in the language of the Jews the language of the most marginal elements of European society— beggars, thieves, and wandering murderers.

In 1528 Luther republished a little volume that had first appeared anonymously in 1512 in Augsburg. Entitled *Liber vagatorum* [Book of Thieves], it was reputed to be a catalogue of the various orders of thieves and tricksters who infested the German countryside.[1] Luther's introduction is one of the first claims that this thieves' jargon "has come from the Jews, for many Hebrew words occur in the vocabulary, as anyone who understands that language may perceive." The language of the thief is the language of the Jews. Indeed, in the enumeration of the various classes of tricksters is a group called by the author of *Liber vagatorum* "venererins," "women who say they are baptized Jewesses and have turned Christians, and can tell people whether their fathers or mothers are in hell or not."[2] Here the confidence woman is portrayed as drawing on the magic of the Jews and the insight of the convert. But as Luther points out in his introduction, these figures are but "liars and tricksters," whose aim is to deceive and whose model is the begging friar. Luther's denigration of the Jews' language as the language of thieves is not unique in the Renaissance. Sebastian Brant, himself a noted jurist, had incorporated elements of the thieves' cant into his *Ship of Fools* in 1494. But Luther, from his newly won position as one knowledgeable in the hidden language of the Jews, is the first to point out in print that Hebrew functions as a major element in the secret language of the criminal. Just as Hebrew letters were used on amulets in the late Middle Ages for their magical effect, so, too, were versions of this alphabet employed to provide a hidden code for criminals.

That there were criminals in the late fifteenth and sixteenth centuries, that among these marginal figures were Jews, relegated to the fringes of European society, and that these elements used a thieves' cant laced with Hebrew and created maps employing Hebrew characters is beyond doubt.[3] That Luther and his contemporaries saw the language of the thieves as the natural expression of the Jewish spirit, replacing the healing magic of Hebrew, is also beyond doubt. But for Luther and his contemporaries, the line between Hebrew, which they had now claimed for themselves, and the language of the Jews had become absolute. For the Jews spoke the thieves' cant, a mixture of German and Hebrew written in Hebrew characters. Jews spoke Yiddish.

The history of Yiddish in the West antedates the Renaissance by hundreds of years.[4] Depending on how one defines the line between Germanic dialects and proto-Yiddish, Yiddish existed as an independent language at least two to three hundred years before Luther's comments. By the sixteenth century Yiddish had produced a respectable body of texts, mainly of a popular religious nature, and was spoken widely in both Western and Eastern Europe. It was an anomalous language, one that could easily be overlooked in the categories of Christian perception. Hebrew was a religious language with its analogue in Latin. The vernacular languages were spoken by individuals who existed in a more or less homogenous geographical area. But Yiddish was a secular language spoken by a religious group scattered over a wide geographical area. In addition, it was written in a script that was not easily deciphered by readers of the Latin alphabet.

Jews and thieves were both worldly dangers to Christian order. They both spoke related (if not identical) languages, at least as perceived by the Christian world. By the end of the seventeenth century there was considerable interest in documenting the languages spoken by these dangerous outsiders. Writers such as Wenzel Scherffer, in the mid-seventeenth century, incorporated thieves' cant into their poetry, poetry that reflected the daily life in their age. When the thief Andreas Hempel and his gang were arrested in Saxony in 1687, in the investigation that followed a glossary of thieves' jargon was compiled for the first time.[5] What Scherffer had seen in the fictive world of the thief was mirrored in the reality presented by Hempel. Such lists became more and more common in the beginning of the eighteenth century, until a virtual lexicon of thieves' cant, often with the Hebrew originals, had been compiled. The basic language of the thieves' cant was German. The Hebrew words provided a secret code for the thief within the world of German speakers. The essence of Yiddish as the marker for the marginality of the Jew in the eyes of the Germans is stressed by the authorities who wrote on the nature of Yiddish. Johann Christoph Adelung, surely the most important and most prolific writer on the German language during the eighteenth century, saw Yiddish as the product of an Eastern—specifically, a Polish—corruption of German.[6] Calling Yiddish an "adventurous mix," he commented that no other language had been so massacred by the Jews as German, to the extent that the Jews seemed to have forgotten their "original" language, Hebrew. Adelung's comments place the language of the Jews on the cultural fringes of German consciousness, in the East, among the wild and barbaric Slavs. But he also points out the specificity of Yiddish as *the* language of the Jews in Europe. The Jews' marginality is thus connected to their language.

The interest in Yiddish as a means of converting the Jew appears in the seventeenth century.[7] It was evident that Hebrew was not the appropriate medium through which to approach the Jews. Their language of daily life, Yiddish, was the means by which to give them access to Christianity. The shift from using Hebrew as a means to convert the Jews, which had been the moving force behind Petrus Nigri's fifteenth-century Hebrew grammar, to using Yiddish was further proof of the new Christian claim to primacy in the use of Hebrew. Both Yiddish and Hebrew existed in the late fifteenth century in the European Jewish communities from northern Italy to Poland, but of the two, Hebrew had been more closely associated with the magical nature of the Jews. Yiddish became important to the Christian community only after the complete expropriation of Hebrew by the world of Protestant theology.

In 1699 Johann Christoph Wagenseil published his *Instruction in the Jewish-German Manner of Reading and Writing*.[8] While the beginnings of a systematic Christian interest in Yiddish can be traced back to 1609, in an appendix to Johannes Buxtorf's Hebrew grammar dealing with "Hebrew-German," it was Wagenseil who first presented Yiddish in its supposed cultural context. Wagenseil was one of the leaders of the Protestant attempt to convert the Jews at the beginning of the eighteenth century. To prove the perfidy of the Jews, he translated into Latin and German those books attacked by both Pfefferkorn and Reuchlin as insults to Christianity. He also led the attempt to reach the Jews through their own language, Yiddish. But Wagenseil's grammar is much more than a simple tool by which to teach Christian missionaries the secret language of the Jews so that they would be well armed in their attempts to proselytize among the Jews. It is a handbook on the nature of the Jews as perceived through their language.

Johann Christoph Wagenseil stands within an important Christian tradition of seeing the Jews and their evils as embodied within their writings and their language. Without a doubt the most influential writer in this tradition was Johann Andreas Eisenmenger, professor of Oriental languages at Heidelberg, whose *Discovered Judaism* (1700), which was translated into a number of European languages, presented the fanciful evils of the Talmud as the root of the conspiracy of the Jews.[9] At the conclusion of his book, Eisenmenger provided a Yiddish glossary to enable the reader to have some limited access to the secret language of the Jews. Wagenseil's volume, written at the same time as that of Eisenmenger, has the same aims, including the exposition of those aspects of the hidden texts of the Jews that reveal their true nature, which must be known in order to be challenged by the Christian missionary.

Wagenseil provides the Christian reader with his own definition of Yiddish. In the introduction he focuses on the nature of Yiddish as perceived by a Christian listener or reader:

> The Jews have dealt with no language as "sinfully," as one says, as with our German language. They have given it a totally foreign intonation and pronunciation. They have mutilated good German words, they have tortured them, they have inverted their meaning as well as invented new words unknown to us. They have mixed innumerable Hebrew words and turns of phrase into German, so that if one heard them speaking German, one would believe that they spoke pure Hebrew, since the listener could understand almost none of the words. Also, they have published not a small number of books in this gibberish in Hebrew letters, and everyday even more are printed. (B1r)

Wagenseil sees the existence of Yiddish as a sinful act committed by the Jews against the German tongue. The choice of the word *sinfully* is purposeful, for it reflects the popular view that anything that the Jews do is an attack on the innate truths within Christianity. For Wagenseil, Yiddish is a form of purposefully mangled German, German altered to look and sound like Hebrew. The calumny of the Jewish defiling of the Host is here altered to the Jews' torturing and mutilation of the German tongue. During the seventeenth century a cult of German had arisen in the innumerable German states, warring among themselves, whose sole common bond was their language.[10] It was, of course, a language divided and subdivided into innumerable dialects and quite independent (and often mutually incomprehensible) language groups running from the low German of the northern Hansa city-states to the Bavarian of the south and the Prague German of the east. But the need for a common political denominator forced at least the intelligentsia to seek it in language, for language transcended the religious differences that destroyed much of Germany during this period. So the drive for a purification of German from foreign (especially French and other Latinate) influences typified the Germans' emphasis on language. Language became—even more than religion or geography—the means by which the Germans defined themselves, a definition that clearly excluded the Jews.

The Germans saw themselves as speaking good German. Differences in dialect (or even language) were merely regional, that is, geographical, variants. The Germans evolved a literary German which transcended these differences. The Jews had done much the same thing: they had ignored their geographical isolation and evolved a written and spoken language that was more or less comprehensible to all Jews. But just as the Germans used their newly evolved sense of language purity as a means of defining themselves, so, too, did they perceive the existence of the Jews' language, Yiddish, as the means of distinguishing themselves from yet another group seen as non-German. They denied Yiddish the same value that they ascribed to the community of German speakers. There was, for the Christian, an unbridgeable gap between the good Germans and the language they spoke and the evil Jews and the language they spoke. If the former could be purified and cleansed, the latter must be impure and corrupting.

Where does this corruption of language and thought most evidence itself? Primarily, of course, in dealings with non-Jews in institutional settings, in the courts. Wagenseil presents an anecdote to illustrate this type of misuse of language:

It has not been long since in one of the leading cities of the
Empire a Jew was arrested on suspicion of having conducted an
illegal exchange of letters [in regard to financial matters]. After
the courts confiscated his correspondence, it was sent to a theologian, who was asked to translate it into German. There is no
doubt that if the letters had been written in a pure Hebrew, this
would have been accomplished. But none of the theologians
knew the German-Hebrew language, so that it was necessary to
send the letters to a university and request an interpretation
from a professor of the Hebrew language. What difficulties had
not the Jews' oath caused until one found a convention and the
ritual, so that Jews would be forced to tell the truth before a
Christian court? And do you believe that this has been achieved
in every case? (B2v)

Wagenseil goes on to describe the problems with administering the
Jews' oath, which was required of all Jews before their testimony
could be taken in court. The linkage between the Jews who hide
their evil deeds in a language that is not understandable to the
powers that be and the idea that Jews lie when confronted by these
powers gives Yiddish, perceived not as a language but as the means
for conspiracy, its own hidden power. Hebrew, as Wagenseil observes,
is now the province of even the most rural pastor, but Yiddish is
the tool of the Jewish conspiracy.

If one accepts the basic criminal nature of the Jew and the
function of Yiddish as the conspiratorial language, then one must
somehow force the Jew to tell the truth. This can be accomplished
only through the same magical language that they employ in their
conspiracy. Neither Hebrew nor German can be effective:

It is more often evident that the Jewish-German [Yiddish] translation of the words and the explanation of the oath is more
effective than any substitute. I hold that one must translate
[the oath] word for word as clearly as one can without caring
how good or bad it sounds in German. (E4v)

In forcing the Jews to take the oath, what is of the greatest value
is the use of that medium of communication which requires the
Jews to tell the truth. For if their natural state predisposes them
to lying, then the only effective countermeasure is to force them
to tell the truth in the language of their deception.

But it is not merely within the court that the Jews' secret
language evidences its conspiratorial, criminal actions against the
Christian social fabric. Wagenseil's book is looked upon by many
modern historians of Yiddish as a confused and meandering work,

only partly devoted to the description of Yiddish.[11] It is on this area that the historians of Yiddish have concentrated. But Wagenseil's book is directed, as its long subtitle notes, at "lawyers, theologians, doctors, merchants, and generally everyone" who deals with Jews. It is the function of this primary introduction to Yiddish to provide the institutions of society with the means to understand the Jews in spite of their hidden language. Thus Wagenseil provides a chrestomathy of important texts, texts that are drawn from the Jewish interpretive tradition and function as guideposts to a Christian understanding of the inner nature of the Jew. Some thirty years after Wagenseil's Yiddish grammar appeared, Wilhelm Christian Just Chrysander authored a little pamphlet in which he outlined the reasons for studying Yiddish.[12] Primary among them is, of course, the ability to convert the Jews using their own hidden tongue, but he begins his tabulation with a list of the useful texts written in Yiddish. Wagenseil had already provided a sample of what texts were viewed as important, in 1699. He had translated and annotated two major Hebrew tractates in his book: the Talmudic tractate on leprosy and a discussion of whether a man can marry the sister of his wife after her death. These two tractates form a major component of Wagenseil's long study of the Jews' discourse.

Illness and sexual rules, together with legal responsibility, determine the Christian perception of the Jew. The function of Jews as physicians in the late Middle Ages and Renaissance is counterbalanced by their image as poisoners. One means of undercutting the Jews' image as healers is to reveal their hidden sources. Thus Wagenseil provides a detailed translation of the tractate on leprosy, which deals as much with the social function of the patient and the healer as it does with medical information. The sexual sphere is revealed by both the discussion of biblical limitations on marriage and Wagenseil's discussion of the primarily female songs written and sung in Yiddish. But Wagenseil presents this sexual aspect of the Jews as a means of undercutting the sexual specificity of the Jews, their sexual selection from within their own group, a selectivity reversed in the Christian image of the promiscuous Jewess. Wagenseil is drawing on a long tradition, represented in the sixteenth century by Margaritha's comments, that characterizes the Jew as diseased.

The disease to which Wagenseil alludes is a specific form of sexual pathology that is part of a Christian iconography seeing the Jew as inherently different: Jewish male menstruation. Thomas de Cantimpré, the thirteenth-century anatomist, presented the first "scientific" statement of this phenomenon (calling upon St. Augustine as his authority). Male Jews menstruated as a mark of the "Father's curse"—their pathological difference is the result of their original denial of Christ. This image of the Jewish male as female was first introduced to link the Jew with the corrupt nature of the woman, since both are marked as different by the sign that signified Eve's mortal nature after her fall from grace. This sign also stressed the intransigence of the Jews. Thomas de Cantimpré recounted the nature of the Jews' attempt to cure themselves. They were told by one of their prophets that they could be rid of this curse by "Christiano sanguine," the blood of a Christian, when in fact it was "Christi sanguine," the blood of Christ in the sacrament accepted by the convert, that was required. Thus the medieval libel of blood guilt, the charge that Jews sacrificed Christian children to obtain their blood for whatever purpose, was the result of the intransigence of the Jews in light of the truth of Christianity. It was intimately tied to the sign of Jewish male menstruation. The persistence of Jewish male menstruation was thus understood as a sign not only of the initial "curse of the Father" but of the inherent inability of the Jews to hear the truth of the Son. For it was the intrinsic "deafness" of the Jews that did not let them hear the truth that would cure them. The belief in Jewish male menstruation continued into the seventeenth century. Heinrich Kormann repeats it in Germany in 1614, as does Thomas Calvert in England in 1649. Franco da Piacenza, a Jewish convert to Christianity, included it in his catalogue of "Jewish maladies," published in 1630 and translated into German by 1634. He claimed that the males (as well as the females) of the lost tribe of Simeon menstruated four days a year! Thus, a self-hating Jew was able to create a category of impairment that was distanced from his own reality (and new insight). In placing the menstruating male Jew in the exotic world of the lost tribes (the New World), he substantiated the charge of Jewish difference while freeing himself from the stigma of difference.[13]

Wagenseil's views are thus very much in the context of the revelations of the "knowledgeable" Jews about the true nature of the Jews. But for him it was much more clearly related to their language. In presenting this discussion of sexual rules and gender-specific behavior among the Jews, Wagenseil was careful to explode the theory put forward by Buxtorf that "Hebrew-German" was merely a woman's language. This view (a view not uncommon among early-twentieth-century Western European historians of Yiddish) placed Yiddish in the same sphere as other "kitchen" languages, languages whose main function was defined by the gender of the speaker (and in turn defined it). Wagenseil wished to destroy this contention completely. For him Yiddish was the primary language of all Jews, not merely of women and "simple men." However, in expanding the function of Yiddish, he applied many of the negative associations of Yiddish as a "woman's language" to the entire group. For him, all Jews spoke like women.

By the beginning of the eighteenth century the idea that the Jews possessed a language in which they were able to conceal their evils had come to refer to Yiddish. Yiddish was the means by which Jews were able to undermine the authority of the Christian state. Thus the language of the Jews and the thieves' cant, both made up of German with elements of Hebrew and Aramaic, both written in Hebrew (or pseudo-Hebrew) characters, had come to be identical. The language of the Jews was the language of thieves, for the Jews were quintessential thieves. Even if the criminals were themselves neither Jewish nor even Yiddish-speaking, their social function as outsiders beyond the pale of the rules and order of the state turned them into mock Jews. The Jews, on the other hand, were seen to employ the language of the thieves, Yiddish, as a means of hiding their actions from the state, since their actions were always inimical to the state's best interest. The image of the evil, hidden language of the Jews as Yiddish dominates the language of the Jew portrayed on the German popular stage in the late sixteenth century. It was on the stage that the hidden language of the Jews could be exposed, and the danger inherent in it mitigated. While Hans Folz, in a late-fifteenth-century Shrovetide play, used Hebrew to characterize this language (a Hebrew prayer cribbed from a thirteenth-century anti-Talmudic tractate by the monk Theobaldus), by the late sixteenth century the language of the stage Jew had become a mock Yiddish, quite often an invention of the playwright.[14] In Renward Cysat's 1583 reworking of the Lucerne passion play the Jews speak a nonsense language that is an evident corruption of German:

> We poor Jews complain of the pain of hunger
> and must die, have no bread
> oime give compassio
> cullis mullis lassio
> Egypt was a good land
> wau wau wau wau wiriwau[15]

The Jews' muddled German, mixed with bits of Italian, Latin, and *dog*gerel (*wau* is the sound that German dogs make), illustrates the subhuman nature of the Jews' language, a language of marginality. But it also defuses any sense of anxiety about this marginality by turning this language into the language of the comic. The Jews become comic figures as a means of reducing the anxiety of the non-Jewish viewers about their own sense of marginality.

The centrality of the special language of the Jews in defining their nature can be seen by contrasting two texts that portray Jews, texts that were written literally centuries apart but provide the two poles of understanding the Jews and their language in the eighteenth century. In 1462, a charge of ritual murder was lodged against the Jews of the village of Endingen in southwestern Germany.[16] In 1470 several Jews of the village were arrested and burnt. The events became immortalized in a public presentation that was repeated yearly within the town. The *Endingen Jews' Play* became one of the central documents in understanding the Christian image of the Jews in the early modern period. On one level this play is an image of the Jew uncontaminated by reality, for as a result of the accusation of ritual murder, the Jews were driven out of the entire area surrounding Endingen in the 1470s and were first readmitted in 1785. The text of the drama that has been preserved is a seventeenth-century one and is therefore late enough to preserve a shadow image of the Jews. The play is itself unremarkable in its presentation of the evil conspiracy of the Jews to murder Christian children for their blood, which is to be used in their ritual acts to preserve them from illnesses such as leprosy. The play begins, however, with the conspiracy among the Jews, and the audience is presented with Jews who speak, as in the Lucerne passion play, a "Hebrew-German," more German than Hebrew. In this drama what is preserved as typical of the language of the Jews is an altered pattern of intonation, indicated by the rhythm of the lines and smatterings of Hebrew. Since the audience was Christian, the language of the Jewish figures in this seventeenth-century version of the play was the equivalent of mock Yiddish. It is the comic language of conspiracy and of evil deeds. This attempt at creating a German equivalent to Yiddish in order to supply the Jewish figures with an identifiable language becomes a commonplace during the seventeenth and eighteenth centuries.

The image of the Jew as the speaker of Yiddish, the language of marginality, had a great influence on Jewish identity formation in the seventeenth and early eighteenth centuries. It is in the writings of those Jewish converts wishing to establish their own status and the power of their language and insight with a Christian, German-speaking audience that the best echo of these views can be found. In 1621 a "converted rabbi" recounted his sudden insight into the truths of Christianity in a long poem written in German doggerel; the poem used a popular literary form to show how an insightful

Jew could employ the literary means of his reference group to explore the true nature of the Jew.[17] Christian Gerson, baptized in 1605, explained the hidden mysteries of the Talmud and dismissed all of the earlier work on the secret books of the Jews written by converts, since their work was based on versions of the Jews' books "written in the German language with Hebrew letters."[18] Gerson uses his claim that he has command of "real" Hebrew, as opposed to the Yiddish of other converts, to uncover the Jews' perfidy. Like Luther, Gerson denies all Jews (converts as well as nonconverts) any true knowledge of Hebrew. All they know is the alphabet, which, of course, is also used for Yiddish. Placing himself in a privileged position, he condemns the terrible German that these Jews speak, which he attributes to their innate inability to speak German (215). This he implicitly contrasts with his own German, the language of his text, which he shows that he commands to the same degree as he claims to command Hebrew.

The special nature of the Jews' discourse as mirrored in this language of marginality is stressed in Johann Christoph Gottfried's book of 1714 simply entitled *Jewish Lies*.[19] Gottfried, a "converted rabbi from Langen-Schwalbach," presents the "lies" of the Talmud, as does Gerson, as if he were translating from the Hebrew. He rejects the "blindness" of the Jews which is masked in their misuse of German. These texts all attempt to achieve status for the author by presenting the truth about the hidden books of the Jews, but all of them also refer, directly or indirectly, to the "new" language of the Jews, Yiddish.

Similarly, handbooks by converts such as Johann Friederich Mentes, Christoph Gustav Christian, Paul Christian Kirchner, and Moritz Wilhelm Christian, all from the 1720s, echo the image of the Jew as a speaker of Yiddish, the language of thieves.[20] The most detailed autobiographical texts from this period, the accounts of the conversions of Samuel Jacob, "a former rabbi now called Adam Librecht," and Moses Levi, "a merchant now called Christian Gottlieb Hamburger," stress the linguistic conversion of the Jew.[21] Samuel Jacob is taught German by a tutor, and since he is able to abandon his Yiddish, he reads the New Testament and attains insight. This insight he communicates to Moses Levi, who has a similar conversion experience.

All of these texts written by converts stress the corrupting nature of the Jews' language. One, however, centers specifically on this image and creates, as does the drama of the period, the image of speaking Jews and their hidden language. Written by "J.W.," who describes himself on the title page as "one who has spent much time among the Jews but now loves God with his whole heart and who wishes to serve his neighbor," this text presents a series of dialogues between two speakers of Yiddish. Entitled *Jewish Language Master*, its structure is much like the colloquia of the medieval schoolmasters which were used to train children in Latin.[22] J.W. provides a parallel translation in German of the Yiddish discourse, as well as a theoretical introduction.

J.W. sees his reader's primary response to Yiddish as laughter. It creates in the hearer a sense of absurdity. But following Horace's dictum, J.W. also sees the utility of knowing the language of the Jews, for by knowing their language, one can avoid their traps. For J.W., Yiddish is the hidden language of Jewish commerce; it is the tongue through which the Jews mask their exploitation of the world about them. The exposure of this hidden language is the standard claim of the convert, but transferred from Hebrew to Yiddish. To illustrate this claim, J.W. tells an anecdote of a Christian who through his dishonest trade as a merchant of counterfeit jewels comes to know the language of the Jews. After the death of his father-in-law he comes into an inheritance, a collection of false jewels, which he tries to sell to the Jews. In Yiddish they discuss the fact among themselves that there is a real ruby hidden among the false stones. The jeweler understands them and thus manages to identify the real stone. This tale, which stresses the need to know the Jews' language in order to defend oneself when dealing with Jews, is recounted in the same mode as the dialogues. J.W. cites a line in Yiddish (using the standard Western Yiddish of his day) and provides a translation. The Yiddish line is set in roman characters, the translation in gothic ones. Gothic characters are used for the author's own commentary; thus it is visually set apart from the Yiddish. But, as was the practice in the eighteenth century, J.W. also sprinkles his German with fragments of French, which are set in roman characters. This use of the high literary language of the time, a mix of German and French as the matrix for a discussion of Yiddish, which is seen as a jumble of German and Hebrew, contrasts the acceptable with the unacceptable nature of language. The typography of the page draws the visual analogy between the two mixes of language. The very page points out to the Christian reader that he must learn bits of Yiddish and Hebrew in order to deal with the hidden language of the Jew just as he has learned bits of French to deal with the hidden language of culture, the language of the French court. The juxtaposition of higher language (German mixed with French) and lower language (German mixed with Hebrew) is made in the introduction. Thus J.W. places himself in the privileged position of one who commands both the higher and lower discourses, both hidden languages.

The topics discussed by J.W. echo the older literature on the language and nature of the Jew. The first discourse, held for the benefit of "we Christians," concerns the very nature of discourse, of proper and improper argument; the second concerns prostitutes. Among the other topics discussed are Jewish rituals and celebrations (echoing the entire literature from Pfefferkorn on), as well as sexual practices and ritual cleanliness. The subjects touched on reflect the image of the Jew in the literature of the age. The language exposed here by the convert for his Protestant reading public reflects the image of the marginal man with his hidden, destructive language. J.W.'s tract, like others written by converts in the late seventeenth and eighteenth centuries, reflects upon the nature of the Jews' language as a reflex of their marginality.

Their marginality is a direct result of their internalization of the image of the Jew held by those who wish to convert them. In an anonymous pamphlet of 1749 a convert to Protestantism echoes in detail Eisenmenger's charges against the Jews.[23] But unlike Eisenmenger, who is, according to his own account, explaining the hidden books of the Jews, the author of this pamphlet, much like J.W., provides a running glossary of the "Judeo-German" in which these ideas are disguised:

> As soon as a Jewish child can speak, the following *Principia* and teachings are taught him: he should protect himself from the *Goyem Erelem*, or from the uncircumcised, as from the devil; he should not touch a *Trefe posel*, an impure book; he should not learn the *Laschen hatuma*, Latin, nor eat nor drink with Christians, neither with a *Scheketzle*, a Christian boy, nor with a *Schicksel*, a Christian girl. (5)

Thus the entire text serves as a manual in the training of the Christian reader in Yiddish. The anonymous author concludes his pamphlet with an address to "you dear Jews" in which he calls upon them to acknowledge their blindness and convert. He does this, of course, in German in a pamphlet addressed to and for the benefit of a Christian readership. It is thus not so much a call for conversion as it is a further sign of the difference between the converted author and his subject, the Jews. It is written in good German without any of the hidden discourse attributed to the Jews. The author of this pamphlet uses his text to illustrate both the hidden nature of the Jews' language and his transcendence of this limitation. He has completely incorporated the image of the Jews and their language from the anti-Jewish tracts of the period into his own sense of self.

By the mid-eighteenth century, Yiddish had come to represent the corruption of the Jews, a corruption that could be eliminated, if at all, through the act of conversion. In 1728 Johann Heinrich Callenberg had institutionalized the study of Yiddish as the means of converting the Jews in his establishment of an *Institutum Judaicum* and by holding the first university lectures on Yiddish in 1729 at Halle. These lectures, like the earlier discussions of the nature of the Jews' language, were in no way unpolemical. Callenberg saw Yiddish as the best means of converting the Jews, since the language was representative of their blindness.[24] Through conversion they could be purged of both their false religion and their degenerate discourse. Yiddish was seen as the appropriate language of the Jews, since it was understood as a language of corruption. This view was later adopted by the German Enlightenment as a sign of the inherent corruption of the Jews. But the thinkers of the Enlightenment desired the Jews to convert, not to Christianity, but to the new religion of rationalism. This conversion was also represented by the abandonment of the Jews' language, which, as with the converts in the early eighteenth century, was conflated with the discourse of the Jews. For Yiddish was understood not merely as "language" but also as the reflection of the innate falsity of the "discourse" of the Jews. This confusion dominates the Enlightenment's image of the Jews, as well as the self-image of the Jews of the Jewish Enlightenment, the Haskalah.

By the middle of the eighteenth century German attitudes toward the Jews seemed, on the surface, to have begun to shift. The strength of the concept of toleration, which did not extend, at least in the German-speaking lands, to cultural and linguistic differences, had grown. Toleration, of course, has its limits. In the basic document of Jewish emancipation, Joseph II of Austria's 1781 Edict of Toleration, both Hebrew and Yiddish were banned from use in commerce: the secret language of the Jews gave them too great an economic edge. The Jews were directed to send their children to German-language schools or to establish such schools for them.[25] In this regard the Jews were treated no worse or better than other minorities in the Hapsburg Empire, but in no other case was the religious language of any group proscribed as was Hebrew.

This happened again when in 1812 the Prussian Edict of emancipation required the Jews to use German or French for business and for the promulgation of legal documents.[26] When the popular philosopher J. J. Engel adapted the French drama *The Diamond* into

German, in 1772, he made sure that his sympathetic Jew Israel spoke a version of this "Hebrew-German" to characterize him as a Jew.[27] He was able to play the usual negative implications of this characterization off against the positive figure but did this by introducing an altered quality of language missing from the French original. In the original French drama the Jew speaks French identical to that of all the other characters. But it was not Engel nor any of the other minor late-eighteenth-century authors who first presented a positive image of the Jew as a model for human behavior.

It was the paradigmatic German enlightener Gotthold Ephraim Lessing who undertook this in his 1749 drama entitled *The Jews*. This drama has long been understood as the first German attempt to present the Jews in a positive light.[28] The plot, concerning the rescue of a German baron by an anonymous "traveler," is inconsequential. What makes this "traveler" unique is a version of the same device used by Engel later in the century, the dissonance of language and discourse. The audience is never prepared for the revelation at the end that the "traveler" is a Jew. He travels with a servant, he is dressed correctly, his behavior is genteel, and what is most important for Lessing's audience, he speaks perfect, unflawed German. There is no possibility of identifying him as a Jew, since the hallmark of the Jew, the Jews' language, is missing.

What is more important, Lessing uses the absence of this hallmark—the Yiddish accent or Yiddish itself—as a means of presenting an individual who possesses all of the virtues of Western civilization. The thieves in the drama are revealed to be Christians who have disguised themselves as Jews but are revealed by their use of local dialect. It is language that functions for Lessing as the key to distinguishing the good from the evil. The traveler, himself a Jew, speaks perfect German; it is the criminal who reveals himself by speaking dialect. It has been remarked that the only thing that is Jewish about Lessing's traveler is his occupation as a merchant.[29] It is vital to understand the shift that the image of the Jew underwent in Germany. If earlier anti-Semitic (or even philo-Semitic) images of the Jew are examined and then contrasted with Lessing's presentation of the good Jew as wandering traveler, it is evident that the primary quality altered in identifying the nature of the Jew for the Christian audience is the Jew's language. Once the difference in language is removed, then all other differences, including that of physiognomy, fall. For the Jew looks different, according to a figure in Lessing's drama, only when he is identified as a Jew by his language. Unable to see this difference in physiognomy in the traveler, whom he is addressing, he sees before him only the noble (i.e., Christian) stranger. It is in the alteration of the language of the Jew that the disguise of the traveler is made perfect.

The question of the Jews' language is omnipresent throughout the Enlightenment. It takes various and sundry forms, however, all returning to the question of the unreliability or shifting nature of the Jews' language. If one turns to the first major attempt to articulate the demand of the Jews for emancipation, the now classic work by the Prussian official Christian Wilhelm von Dohm on the civil improvement of the Jews, it is striking that little attention is paid to the special nature of the Jews' language.[30] This failing was evidently seen by Dohm's contemporaries, for in the second volume of his work he supplied a fifty-page essay on the question of the lying of the Jews and whether Jews could be made to take binding oaths. The butt of Dohm's attack, the authority upon which his critics evidently called, was the century-old compilation of passages from the Talmud by Johannes Andreas Eisenmenger which paraded a variety of calumnies against the Jews under the guise of explication of the Talmud.[31] Eisenmenger, like Luther, had claimed the special knowledge of the Hebraist in uncovering the "true" nature of the Jew. In fact, his work stands in the direct line of works from Pfefferkorn to the late-nineteenth-century *Protocols of the Elders of Zion*. The difference is, of course, that Eisenmenger was not a Jew. Dohm, in rebutting Eisenmenger's contention that Jews lie, even when under oath, was supporting the general view that Jews, like all humans bound by natural law, will not dissemble if made to give a binding oath. His proof for this contention is drawn from the same sources that Eisenmenger used, Talmudic commentaries on oath taking and truth telling. To refute claims based on the special knowledge of the Jews, one must also have claim to this special knowledge. And this is, of course, what Dohm undertakes to gain.

The idea that Jews lie, even when bound by oaths given before a Christian court, that their nature is to dissemble, is also reflected in the legal practice of the day. For Jews were required to take specifically "Jewish" oaths if they were to be heard before a court at all. If one examines the oaths required of Jews in Prussia from the beginning of the eighteenth century to the elimination of the Jews' oaths in 1869, a strange pattern emerges that emphasizes the existence, within the non-Jews' perception of the Jews, of the idea that the Jews possessed a secret, hidden language.[32] For the oaths written in 1712, well before the beginning of the civil emancipation of the Berlin Jews, were composed for the most part in German with a few Hebrew words, such as *Adonay*, substituted for the

Christian *Jesus*. The later into the age of emancipation, the more Hebrew appears in the oath, until the end of the eighteenth century, when the oath appears to have German syntax but comprises primarily Hebrew words. It is this queer mixture of German syntax and Hebrew words that later Moses Mendelssohn consciously confuses with Yiddish. But it is, of course, not Yiddish but the fictive reconstruction of a Christian court of the special language of the Jews. But why Hebrew words embedded in a German syntax, and why an increase in the amount of Hebrew as civil emancipation progressed?

The more the Jews became like the Germans, the better their command of German, the more their existence within the body politic paralleled the existence of the non-Jew, the greater the need of some means to distinguish them from the non-Jew. This was accomplished by calling on the hidden language of the Jews. Hebrew thus served the legal system as the key to that hidden nature of the Jew, who could be forced to speak truthfully only by employing the correct magical formula. This attitude was contrary to the views of the Enlightenment. When one asks what language Lessing's eponymous hero speaks in his drama *Nathan the Wise* (1779), which presents the Enlightenment's ideal image of the Jew, the answer is, of course, that he speaks the language of reason. For what language could Lessing's idealized German represent other than this essential, nonparticularized mode of discourse? We have a Christian European, Arabs, and Jews (in terms of education, if not origin) all speaking fluent and rational German; no accent or faulty grammar mars their language. Lessing knew (and used) the technique of a distorted language in the world of the comic (e.g., in representing the German spoken by the French in *Minna von Barnhelm*), where flawed language would evoke laughter. In the world of enlightened ideas such comic representations are false, evoking precisely those stereotypes of difference which Lessing (at least in the case of the Jews) wished to counter. Pure, literary German becomes the model for the language spoken by Jews within the Enlightenment tradition, especially in those works written by enlightened Jews such as Marcus Herz and David Arnstein that portray Jews speaking.[33] This is, of course, clearly the opposite of the reality in which most Jews found themselves in the first generation after emancipation. They spoke German with a noticeable accent. They often consciously or unconsciously used false Yiddish-German cognates or Yiddish rather than German sentence structure. Certainly some Jews had a better command of German than did others (or perhaps even perfect command). But the greatest number of German-speaking Jews did not speak a German such as that of Lessing's Nathan.

The irony is that as German Jews began, at least in their idealized image on the stage, to speak perfect German, in England the perfect English spoken by Shylock during the course of the late eighteenth century "degenerated and its decay was marked by the definite appearance of Jewish gibberish in the dialogue."[34] For when Jews began to speak an idealized German on the German stage, in contrast to their generally faulty spoken German in the real world, the Jews in Britain, readmitted to British society by the Protector, had already attained a native command of English. Their literary shadow showed the faults of the Jews' language by the introduction of exactly that type of gibberish present in German images of the Jew from the Middle Ages through the early eighteenth century.

Toleration draws the line at language difference. The German Enlightenment demanded that the Jews accept the majority's language of economic and social intercourse and abandon their language of deception. This is not far from the demands of the seventeenth-century writers who saw in the linguistic unification of the Germans a substitute for political chaos. But by the mid-eighteenth century this view had become completely confused with the essence rather than the politics of German self-definition. Johann Georg Hamann, the Magus of the North, one of the most important and most articulate of the German eighteenth-century popular philosophers, wrote in 1760:

> General history as well as the histories of specific nations, societies, sects, and individuals, a comparison of many languages and a single one in relationship to time, place, and object, provide an ocean of observations which a learned philosopher can reduce to specific laws and general classes. If our concept is directed at the soul, and this (according to general opinions) is determined by the nature of its body, we can extrapolate from this onto the body of an entire nation. The lineaments of its language will correspond to the direction of its thought processes; every nation reveals itself through the nature, form, laws, and customs of its language as well as through its external configuration and the play of public actions.[35]

The devious and corrupt language of the Jews reflects and is reflected by their criminal actions against the Christian world. Remove the barrier of language, and one will have reached the first level in civilizing the Jew.

Hamann was echoing Leibniz's view that language is the determining medium of thought, a view that had specific, political implications for Leibniz and had been articulated in his 1697 tract on the improvement of German. Drawing on the works of the British anatomist Thomas Willis, in his essay of 1760 Hamann continued this argument that the relationship between national character and language is reflected in specific physiological variations in the organs of speech. Thus the Jew does not speak a "hidden" language merely by historical accident; biology so determines it.[36] Hebrew is thus tied to the special nature of the physiology of the Jew and—although Hamann does not continue his argument to this point—is responsible for the Jews' inability to speak German (or any other language except Hebrew) without some specific sign of Jewishness.

How complex this relationship between the Jews and their language becomes in the world of the Enlightenment can be seen in the very late (1802) essay by the arch-German enlightener Johann Gottfried Herder, "The Political Conversion of the Jews in Europe to Honor."[37] Herder refuses to accept the idea of forced religious toleration, but he also rejects the suggestion of the British philosopher David Hartley that they be given their own land in Palestine, where "their common Rabbinic-Hebrew language would simplify their return." Herder rejects the idea that the Jews should return to biblical lands, arguing that they should instead abandon their national pride and their inappropriate moral and ethical codes and integrate themselves into the lands in which they are now settled. Hartley's contention that the Jews have a natural and universal language in Hebrew is ignored by the Protestant theologian Herder, who sees the retention of the Jews' language, Yiddish, as one of the reasons why their integration has been foiled. The Jews have no appropriate language, for they are not a people in the sense that the Germans are. Rather, like other sects, they should accept being tolerated and integrate themselves into the body politic and linguistic. This also means accepting the values of the society, which in eighteenth-century Germany meant becoming a member of the consuming and producing public and abandoning those activities that sapped the strength of society.[38] The old image of the Jew as usurer, as a negative factor in the economic life of the state, continues its linkage with the language of the Jews.[39] As Hamann had observed, public actions and language mirror innate realities.

II

The Discourse of the Jews

Lessing's play *The Jews* was not merely an abstract work crafted out of the philosophy of the French Enlightenment. A year before he penned the play, Lessing had met Moses Mendelssohn in Berlin. Mendelssohn had come to Berlin from Dessau in order to continue his studies of German philosophy at the center of the German Enlightenment. He had learned German and Latin and had obtained employment in a manufacturing company in Berlin. Mendelssohn was clearly not the first German (or Western European) Jew to seek out the life and learning of the Christian world. Not only had the converts undertaken this but the small number of court Jews had adopted the language, dress, and outward customs of their Christian protectors.[40] But Mendelssohn served quite a different purpose for Berlin society. He was adopted as the court Jew not of a political clique but of an intellectual one that defined itself as tolerant. The traveler was in many ways the ideal Jew, whose difference was evident to no one and therefore was tolerated by all. Lessing's play aroused a furor when it was published in 1754. Johann David Michaelis, professor of Oriental languages at Göttingen and therefore one who as a specialist in their language and works "knew" the Jews, attacked Lessing's play as presenting a totally unreal image of the Jew. He saw the image as one that Lessing wished were true but one that in no way represented the Jews' lack of virtue and honesty.[41] The dishonesty of the Jews was their hallmark. Lessing answered Michaelis both in print (attacking his generalities about all Jews) and in a personal letter in which he called upon the figure of Moses Mendelssohn as proof for his image of the Jew. Lessing's play, and later his *Nathan the Wise*, became much more than fictional images of the Jew on the stage and in print.[42] They were constantly referred to as models for the potential improvement of the Jew. They were understood as reflections of a future reality for all Jews, for behind them lay a present reality, the figure of Moses Mendelssohn.

Since Mendelssohn stood as the image and model for the good Jew both for the Enlightened Christian world and for the first generation of emancipated Jews, an insight into his understanding of the nature and function of the Jews' language and discourse is essential. How did Mendelssohn perceive the Jew, the liminal man standing centerstage in Mendelssohn's perception of the world, and, therefore, how did Mendelssohn understand himself? There was one moment in Mendelssohn's life in which he was forced to define himself. It was in what was considered by his contemporaries, both Christian and Jewish, and by contemporary scholars as Mendelssohn's *confessio Judaica,* the published letter to the Zurich pastor Johann Caspar Lavater, dated December 12, 1769.[43] This letter, its genesis, and its wide-reaching influence represent for the dean of contemporary Mendelssohn scholars, Alexander Altmann, the turning point not only of Mendelssohn's public life but also of the history of Western Jewry.[44]

What was the Lavater affair? Johann Caspar Lavater was a younger contemporary—by some fifteen years—of Mendelssohn's. A Protestant clergyman of unredoubtable energy and wide publication, Lavater authored a chiliastic broadside in 1768 in which he prophesied the Second Coming as resulting from, among other things, the conversion of the Jews. Prior to this he had met Mendelssohn in Berlin, and that meeting evidently played a role in forming Lavater's own image of the Jew and the Jews' role in Christian history. During April 1763, Lavater visited Mendelssohn twice. His impression was radiantly positive, as he recorded in his diary. Mendelssohn appeared to him to be a man of discernment, taste, and knowledge, indeed one of the chief theoreticians of the European Enlightenment, a movement with which Lavater then closely identified himself.[45] For Lavater the goals of the Enlightenment and those of Christianity were not antagonistic.

Lavater's conversation with Mendelssohn touched on topics appropriate for the salon: the king's entry into Berlin after the Seven Years' War and an ode written on the occasion by a "Jew," indeed, Mendelssohn himself; Lessing's play *Miss Sara Sampson* and the idea of tragedy; the incalculable harm that present-day methods of education were inflicting on youth—topics that with slight alterations in proper names could have been discussed at Plato's dining table. They were intellectual pleasantries, charming, interesting, but not crucial to either participant.

Behind the facade of these visits a debate was raging among the enlightened theologians in Berlin, a debate to which Lavater was certainly privy. Johann Joachim Spalding, Lavater's mentor in Berlin, commented that the Berlin Christians wondered why Mendelssohn was avoiding any mention of Christianity, since he certainly must find it a rational alternative to Judaism.[46] In a later trip to Berlin, in February 1764, Lavater once again visited Mendelssohn and at this point raised Mendelssohn's refusal to discuss Christianity. This discussion, into which Mendelssohn felt himself pressured, revolved around Mendelssohn's understanding of the historical Jesus. What is more important than the substance of the discussion is that Mendelssohn clearly felt himself trapped into a debate of a problem that was polemical in nature, a debate that, given the Christian image of the Jew, Mendelssohn could not win. Mendelssohn bitterly complains in his later public letters to Lavater that he had understood that any discussion of such matters was to be held as a private matter between himself and Lavater.

The discussion with Mendelssohn about the nature of Christianity helped crystallize Lavater's thinking about the conversion of the Jews, their integration into the body religious, and the implication of their role in his chiliastic system. He felt that he was able to relate the Jewish expectation of the coming Messiah to his own concept of the Second Coming. Lavater's view of eternity, at least as articulated in the preface to the second segment of his pamphlet, written in 1769, was based on the coming of the millennial kingdom of Christ through the conversion of the Jews. Conversion would not have to be forced; it would come naturally once a golden bridge could be found that would enable the Jews to break with their rabbis. For Lavater, Mendelssohn was that bridge.

In 1769 Lavater undertook an abridgment of Charles Bonnet's *Philosophical Palingenesis* for the German-speaking Enlightenment. Bonnet, like Lavater, was one of that strange breed of Swiss savants who were half enlighteners, half enthusiasts. While Bonnet's book initially claimed to be a discussion of what can be called Christian psychology, that is, an account of the relationship between the mind and the soul, the central argument rested on his discussion of the role played by the revelation of Christ in the proof of the existence of God. For Bonnet, true revelation was proven in the miraculous act, and Bonnet wished to rest the documentation for the idea of the miracle on a scientific basis. Chief among the proofs for the existence of miracles is the function of testimony, of a correct perception of reality. This quasi-scientific approach to the primacy of Christian interpretation provided Lavater with just the device he needed to approach Mendelssohn.

On September 4, 1769, Lavater dispatched a copy of his translation of sections of Bonnet's book to Berlin. Mendelssohn opened the volume to find a preface dedicated to him, a dedication intended for Mendelssohn and not for Lavater's home audience, since it was not included in the volumes of Bonnet offered for sale in Switzerland. In this preface Lavater challenged Mendelssohn to read Bonnet, recalling his discussions with Mendelssohn concerning the moral character of Christianity's founder, discussions that Mendelssohn had believed were being held in the strictest privacy. Lavater concluded this semipublic confrontation of Mendelssohn with the challenge to examine Bonnet's arguments and either refute them or convert. Lavater's challenge was greater than even he himself could have imagined, for in confronting Mendelssohn with such a public disputation, he drew into question Mendelssohn's understanding of himself as a Jew and forced Mendelssohn to define his own image of the Jew in a public forum.

Mendelssohn's reaction to Lavater's dedicatory letter is of considerable interest. He received it during or immediately after the High Holy Days, in October, the moment when Jewish communal and religious identity is at its height. With the same mail coach, Mendelssohn received another gift, two volumes of commentary on the Mishna by the dean of the Orthodox rabbinate in Germany, Jakob Emden. Before turning to Lavater's challenge, Mendelssohn read through Emden's work and responded to it with a critique of Emden's discussion of purification by immersion in water. Mendelssohn responded to this commentary on the Mishna within the traditional Talmudic mode of argument, the *pilpul shel hevel*, an argument based on analogy and approximation and not on the syllogism, the basis of classical logic. The *pilpul* is the quintessentially Jewish mode of argument. It is the basis for all Talmudic discourse. Suspending time and space, it confronts the opinions of all authority, seeking the moment of resolution hidden within seemingly contradictory positions. Before Mendelssohn turned to Lavater's challenge, he reverted to the traditional Jewish form of argument, a mode of discourse foreign to his speculative writings from 1755 up to that moment.

How should he begin his answer to Lavater? Silence would be impossible; Lavater's challenge to refute or convert had been presented within the public arena. Silence would indicate an implicit inability to counter Bonnet. So Mendelssohn began to compose an answer. His first draft began:

> What moved him to take this step? Not friendship. Among all
> the heretics known to him personally, I cannot be said to be
> his one and only friend. Not the best interest of his religion.
> A Christian who undergoes circumcision proves more for
> Judaism than a hundred Jews who submit to baptism prove for
> Christianity.[47]

The radical tone of this beginning is not merely a sign of Mendelssohn's anger and hesitancy. It also connects two seemingly antithetical moments in Jewish self-definition. First, it reflects the polemical style of the Talmudic disputation, the *pilpul*, in its mode of proof. Since it was the fashion among enlightened intellectuals to refer to the Jews as "the circumcised ones"—Hamann, for example, could speak of Mendelssohn as "my friend Moses, the circumcised philosopher"[48]—Mendelssohn begins the first draft of his letter with an argument from analogy. All the world is divided into two types of people, the circumcised and the uncircumcised. But this division leads to the second level of Mendelssohn's presentation. The division of the world into "Christians" and "heretics," into the "circumcised" and the "uncircumcised," into "true converts" and "false converts," must be shown at some point in the course of such a presentation as specious. Conversion is, for Mendelssohn, the most evident fallacy to prove the strength of any religion. Mendelssohn's argument from analogy is therefore cast in an ironic tone. It vitiates Lavater's claim through the tone of its presentation. Yet the radical tone of such a beginning, drawing into question the entire nature and purpose of Lavater's demands, was felt by Mendelssohn to be inappropriate. The published response to Lavater, a pamphlet directed at the Christian, enlightened reading public, begins with a simple summary of Lavater's challenge.

A reading of the published letter to Lavater provides a paradigm for the split that occurs in Mendelssohn's self-definition as a Jew. He sees in Lavater's challenge a call to debate the relative merits of Judaism and Christianity. He stresses that he has long examined the nature of both religions and has been convinced by his studies of the truths of his own religion: "Thus you see that but for a sincere conviction of my religion, the result of my theological investigations would have been sealed by a public act of mine. Whereas, on the contrary, they have strengthened me in the faith of my fathers; still I could wish to move on quietly without rendering the public an account of the state of my mind." The rejection of public disputation becomes the crux of the letter to Lavater. In the draft letter Mendelssohn states this quite directly: "I hate all religious disputes, especially those conducted before the eyes of the public. Experience teaches that they are useless. They produce hatred rather than clarification." Indeed, the entire history of public debates between Christians and Jews, debates arranged by Christian authorities to show the primacy of Christianity, shows the truth of Mendelssohn's statement. His sense of the futility of such debates, whose purpose is not rational understanding but polemical proselytizing, becomes associated in his argument with all polemical disputes. Argument that cannot have a rational conclusion is, by definition, useless and, to the Jew, dangerous. And rational argument for the eighteenth century means argument according to the inexorable rules of classical logic.

Mendelssohn, however, admits that Judaism, like contemporary Christianity, is not free from human error. The errors of Christianity are implicitly seen in the striving for converts; the errors in Judaism are more complex and more human:

> I do not mean to deny that I have detected in my religion
> human additions and abuses, which, alas, but too much tarnish
> its pristine luster. But where is the friend of truth that can
> boast of having found his religion free from similar corruptions?
> All of us who go in search of truth are annoyed by the pestilen-
> tial vapor of hypocrisy and superstition and wish we could wipe
> it off without defacing what is really good and true. (3:41–42)

The human failings, abuses, and superstitions in Judaism are those texts and means of interpretation that deface the purity of the Bible. This mask articulates itself through specific structures of argument: "Anyone even slightly familiar with rabbinics from the pamphlets no sensible Jew reads or knows of could have amused the public with the most fantastic ideas of Judaism. This would not have elicited a single critical comment from me. I mean to change the world's despicable image of the Jew not by writing disputatious essays but by leading an exemplary life." Mendelssohn juxtaposes the writings of authors such as Eisenmenger and Wagenseil and, by implication, others who seek to convert the Jews such as Lavater with the image of the nondisputatious Jew, who proves the value of his religion by living a good and pure life.

Disputation is closely allied to the negative image of the Jew, who is the butt of the anti-Semite. The anti-Semite sees the Jew as argumentative but not as having any accepted mode of discourse. His mode of argumentation, like his mode of interpretation, is faulty, since it rejects the basic truths of Western, Christian rhetoric and logic. The Jew employs argument for the same reasons that he circulates debased coins, to undermine the Christian state. He is the purveyor of what Mendelssohn describes as the "pestilential vapor of hypocrisy and superstition" defacing Judaism. Mendelssohn's refusal to perceive himself as a disputant, with all the implications of that designation, remained a fixed attribute of his personality. Friedrich Wilhelm Schütz, in the first biography of Mendelssohn, commented on this reticence, as did Mendelssohn's Christian friend Maurus Winkopp, who noted that "it was unusual that he never discussed religion with me during the Sabbath. If I began to raise the subject, as I did on other days, he did not interrupt me, but brought the conversation around to other topics."[49] The association of the Sabbath, with its primary function of delin-

eating the Jewish from the non-Jewish world, with religious disputation was more than Mendelssohn could accept. The Sabbath, like
the Jews, was to be nondisputatious. And this, of course, goes
against the traditional function of the Sabbath as the day when
time could be spent in religious disputation and discussion.

Mendelssohn's rejection of such argumentation is the rejection
of Talmudic discourse, which he perceived to have obscured the
inner truths of the Bible. But this discourse is not only contained
in specific books. It also has a specific geographic locus for Mendelssohn. Some sense of this can be gotten in an unattributed anecdote
in Moses Samuel's 1827 English biography of Mendelssohn:

> The Polish rabbis usually call their learned conversations a
> dispute because they immediately interpose objections and
> subtleties before the question is fairly stated. This Mendelssohn
> disliked above all things. One day, one of these gentry tumbled
> into his room, then full of company, and in their unceremo-
> nious way accosted him with, "I am come to have a dispute, a
> *pilpul*, with you, Rabbi Moses." "I protest, before this
> company," said Mendelssohn, good-humouredly, "that we are
> at peace with each other, and that it shall not be broken."[50]

The uncouth, ill-mannered Jew is categorized by Samuel as standing in a Polish tradition. By the beginning of the nineteenth century
a tradition had been clearly established that such Jews could only
exist on the limits of Western civilization, much as Pfefferkorn
had been seen as an Eastern Jew. The *pilpul*, as representative of
Talmudic aggressiveness, becomes the crux of Mendelssohn's critique
of those elements that obscure and defile modern Judaism.

The *pilpul* is the source of all error among modern Jews. By
its manner of understanding and presentation, its faulty logic, and
its superficial analysis, it corrupts Jews, and at such an early age
that their entire lives are warped. Naphtali Herz Wessely, whose
pamphlet *Words of Peace and Truth* (1782) presented the program
of the Haskalah, the Jewish Enlightenment, for the new training
of the Jewish intellect, reflected Mendelssohn's condemnation of
the Jewish manner of interpretation and argumentation when he
wrote, "We enroll our son in school at five or six, and begin to
teach him Gemara. And as if this regrettable act were not enough,
we immediately accustom him to *pilpul*, and every week we impose
upon him the explanation of Talmudic problems, things which
quite confuse the young child's mind."[51] Mendelssohn carried this
view out to its evident conclusion when, at the close of his life,
he wrote to the tutor of his son Josef: "As you know, a very special

kind of education is required to find this exercise of the mind [the *pilpul*] to one's tastes; and though both of us received this education, we nevertheless agree that we would prefer to see Josef remain rather somewhat dull than be trained in such a sterile kind of acumen."[52] Here the split widens. For not only is Talmudic discourse the source of the perversion of the young, the source of their later disputatiousness, but it is also the antithesis of that discourse which is to be desired within the German context, dullness. Friedrich Nicolai, Mendelssohn's closest ally among members of the German Enlightenment, called the *pilpul* a "deplorable training [which] increases the mind's subtlety but not sustained thinking."[53] German dullness, manifested in the mode of eighteenth-century philosophical discourse, is much to be preferred to the aggressive superficiality of Jewish thought.

If the bad Jew is aggressive, disputatious, and superficial, the result of the bad training he had as a child, what, then, is the good Jew? In his answer to Lavater, Mendelssohn reflects on this question. He compares Judaism's refusal to accept even voluntary converts with Christianity's need to seek out and convert the heathen. Mendelssohn seems to understand that there can be no voluntary conversion when Christianity is tied to the political power of the state to punish and destroy: "We are not being urged to send missionaries to the Two Indies or to Greenland in order to preach the precepts of our religion to those distant peoples. If we take these precepts seriously, we actually should envy the inhabitants of Greenland; for, alas, as far as we can tell from all available reports, they apparently find it easier than we to live in accordance with natural law" (3:44). The good Jew, as opposed to the Christian, does not attempt to disrupt the balance of nature by indulging in polemical religious proselytizing. And Mendelssohn sees himself as the exemplary good Jew: "Moreover, my religion and philosophy as well as my station in life make it mandatory that I avoid all religious controversies and deal in my published writings only with those insights or fundamental issues that are of equal significance to all religions" (3:42). Mendelssohn rejects the substance as well as the nature of rabbinic discourse for the dull philosophical generalities that, however, do not place him in the dangerous situation of perceiving himself as a bad Jew, the Jew against whom authors such as Eisenmenger directed their barbs.[54] It is religious polemic such as that forced on him by Lavater that he views as the corruption of Judaism, as one of the major sources of the negative image of the Jew in the West. Mendelssohn accepts this image as valid, as the point of departure in his creation of the good Jew.

How clearly Mendelssohn connected the debate that Lavater forced upon him with the religious disputation of superstition and hypocrisy can be seen in Mendelssohn's initial reaction to Bonnet. Karl Gotthelf Lessing wrote of his discussion with Mendelssohn about the conflict with Lavater to his more famous brother, the playwright, who was then living in Hamburg:

> Moses has had a strange encounter with Lavater, who was here some years ago. Then they had a conversation on matters concerning religion. Harking back to it, the epic poet of the future life [Lavater] takes the opportunity to challenge Moses either to refute Bonnet's argument for the Christian religion or to profess it publicly. This printed challenge annoys the good man Moses not a little, and as he told me, he is going to prove to Lavater with arguments taken from Bonnet's own text that he is nothing but a Jew and that the fanciful imaginings of a Polish Jew [Jakob Frank] who, some years ago, pretended to be the Messiah could be defended with the same reasons. He will, at the same time, make clear that he is not going to enter into religious disputes.[55]

Mendelssohn sees in Bonnet's arguments the same weakness of argumentation that he senses in rabbinic disputation. Thus he associates the Messianic proofs of Bonnet not with any false Messiah among Western Jews but with Jakob Frank and the enthusiasm of the non-Western Jew. In that same letter Karl Lessing was also struck by Mendelssohn's strange lack of desire to engage the clearly inferior intellect of Lavater in debate: "To me it seems that Moses could, once and for all, declare his creed in the clearest terms, straight to the point." Mendelssohn's wish to avoid polemic and his careful recasting of his public letter to Lavater point toward a redefinition of the good Jew as the neutral observer.

The need to create the illusion that the Jew is the neutral observer has political grounds. Mendelssohn is quite aware of the tenuous position of the Jew in the Christian state. In the answer to Lavater he states: "I am a member of an oppressed people that finds itself compelled to appeal to the good will of the authorities for protection and shelter" (3:46–47). Silence, or at least the use of neutral speech within the accepted norms of rhetoric and logic, and concern with greater rather than parochial issues may assure the survival of the individual.[56]

Silence is the result of fear, but so can be a restructured sense of what acceptable discourse is in a society. Mendelssohn senses the tenuous nature of the German toleration of the Jew and the

Jew's marginal status in the dominant society. Even the Jews' acceptance of the outward norms of decorum may not save them. Here Mendelssohn's abandonment by Gotthold Ephraim Lessing in 1760 would have served him as a model for his own vulnerability. Lessing had been involved in a literary polemic with Reverend Johann Andreas Cramer in a periodical to which Mendelssohn was a regular contributor.[57] Following a rather scathing anonymous attack on Cramer, Mendelssohn, a Jew without official protection or permission to be in Berlin, was hauled before the court to account for his action. Upon hearing of Mendelssohn's summons, Lessing, the epitome of toleration and friendship, fled Berlin, leaving his friend Mendelssohn to accept responsibility for Lessing's political action. Public polemic leads to punishment, but not always of the guilty party. While Mendelssohn was spared the wrath of the state at this time, he was made aware of the power of the state, as well as the potential weakness of those who advocated his case within that society.

The anxiety generated by this sense of marginality had to be reduced through some form of sublimation in order for the individual to function within society. Mendelssohn identified with the very powers who could either punish or abandon him. He was forced to accept their values, to see in their world true value, for it was only within this acceptance that his own existence could be preserved. But once he accepted their values, the values of a nonpolemical, nonaggressive, nonpolitical discourse carried out according to the rules of Western rhetorical tradition, he was forced to split his image of the Jew. There are good Jews—and Mendelssohn is exemplary for them—and there are bad Jews. But the bad Jews bear a striking resemblance to figures such as Lavater and Lessing. This dichotomy is thus a manner of seeing the world, a world in which the Jews function as better citizens than do the Christians who dominate it. The Jews have the inner potential to become truly rational if they are able to shed the externals that limit their potential.

Lavater challenges Mendelssohn in the world of the German printed book. Mendelssohn replies in kind. Mendelssohn had entered into this arena earlier when he had begun publishing his works on philosophy, but it was an arena full of hazards. For the audience he addressed was not a sympathetic one. Jews do not write books, or if they do, they write them for a Jewish audience. Writing books is an activity that is carried out in the public arena, that is, in the Christian world. When Mendelssohn wrote his answer to Lavater, it was aimed specifically at this world. Like the pamphlets of the converts, it was directed, not at his coreligionists, but at his adversaries. Unlike the pamphlets of the converts, it was preaching not to an audience of supporters but to one of doubters. On his side he had the power of Enlightenment rhetoric. For whatever the reality of daily life brought to the relationship between German, enlightened or not, and Jew, in the realm of the written word the highest value was given to the idea of toleration. Within the world of the word this idea was inviolate. This strengthened Mendelssohn's position to the degree that he can be said to have won the public debate with Lavater, at least in the eyes of his Berlin supporters.

Mendelssohn, no matter what the strengths of his case within the protective world of philosophical rhetoric, never confused this world with the cold and hard realities of the Prussia of his day, a world that destroyed as well as supported those who accepted its theories of human equality. Mendelssohn's letter to Lavater concludes with what seems, on the surface, to be philological nitpicking. He notes that he has read Bonnet and observes to Lavater that

> it does not appear to possess the merit which you attach to it. I know Mr. Bonnet from other works as an excellent author; but I have read many vindications of the same religion, I will not say by English writers, but by our own German countrymen, which I thought more recondite and philosophical, than that by Bonnet, which you are recommending for my conversion. If I am not mistaken, most of your friend's hypotheses are even of German growth; for the author of the "Essay on Psychology," to whom Mr. Bonnet cleaves so firmly, owes almost everything to German philosophers. (3:47–48)

Bonnet's source is his own work on psychology, published anonymously, and Mendelssohn later found himself constrained to retract this implicit charge of plagiarism. But the central problem posited in the conclusion to the letter to Lavater is the preeminence of German philosophic dispute, even within the area of Christian apologetics. Mendelssohn so completely identifies with the *German* mode of philosophical argumentation that he sees it as the product of "our own German countrymen." For like it or not, Mendelssohn may have been tolerated by the Germans, written in their language, and employed their mode of discourse, but he was in no manner conceived as being one of them. Mendelssohn comments that "in the matter of philosophical principles, a German has seldom occasion to borrow from his neighbors." And yet it is not merely the content of his argument that he has borrowed from his German neighbors; Mendelssohn has incorporated their image of him, down to the nature and function of his language, within his definition of self.

III
Language and Identity

Mendelssohn spoke Yiddish. This was the language in which he was raised and in which his initial impressions of the world were articulated. German became his language of philosophical speculation. German and Hebrew were the two languages that he praised and furthered. His concerns with the revitalization of Hebrew and with the promulgation of a clear and direct German style helped define his sense of self. And so he served as the model not only for the Christian image of the good Jew but also for those Jews who saw his path as a means of escaping their tangential existence within European life. How did this latter group see their goals? Commenting on the group of Hebrew writers who contributed to the first modern Hebrew periodical, *The Collector*, founded in 1783, Selma Stern-Taeubler summarized the program of the Jewish Enlightenment, the Haskalah: "They wanted a purified classical Hebrew in order to replace Yiddish, which Mendelssohn, too, had considered the root cause of cultural degradation; they wanted to seek a 'rational interpretation of Holy Scripture from its own sources' in order to break the authority of the Orthodox rabbinate and to put an end to the exclusive preeminence of Talmud study; they wanted to translate or imitate German poets and to review philosophical writings in order to acquaint the Jewish youth with the contemporary secular culture."[58] This entire program demanded a basic shift in the language identity of the German Jews. From Yiddish they had to move to German and Hebrew.

Yiddish is, for the Maskilim, the followers of the Jewish Enlightenment, the "corrupted [and corrupting] language." So wrote Isaac Satanow in 1788.[59] But to understand the subtle shift in the perception of the Jews' language and discourse among German Jews, it is necessary to examine the negative image of both in seemingly neutral as well as polemical contexts. To do this we can turn to a grammar of Yiddish written in 1767 by Gottfried Selig, a converted Jew who died in 1795, which seems to be a direct, unpolemical handbook of Yiddish. Selig's introduction is intended to provide his German-speaking readers with the key to reading and understanding Yiddish, a language that they will need because of the commercial transactions they will have with Jews:

For the Jewish-German language is the property of a nation that from the most ancient times to the present has had a great role in trade and manufacture and with whom those who are in commerce have the most dealings. Thus I felt that I would perform a service to such men if I attempted to simplify the rules and basis of this language, its spoken and written speech, of this nation for them.[60]

Selig goes on to define the nature of the language of this nation. He notes that it is a language composed of German with elements of Hebrew, all spoken in a different sentence rhythm and intonation than German. This causes it to "sound corrupt," but, in fact, it follows its own rules for vowel sounds.

Such a description of Yiddish seems different from those of Christian Yiddishists such as Wagenseil and the earlier Jewish polemicists against Yiddish. It represents a view that sees Yiddish as the spoken language of a "nation," not in the geographical sense but rather in the sense of a definable subgroup. When Selig republished his textbook in 1792, the tone of the volume had shifted. While his audience remained the same, he now called, in the opening sentence of his new introduction, on the new aura of "toleration," and his program was quite different. For he advocated learning Yiddish to understand a people "who lives among and with us . . . in order to benefit from [this language] and to avoid harm [by knowing it]."[61] Here the convert's image of the thieves' cant is echoed. But even in detail, Selig's tone has shifted. When he speaks about the use of Hebrew words in Yiddish, he notes that they are often so deformed that they appear to be bits of the Hottentot language. For eighteenth-century Europe, the Hottentots were the most primitive of all races, defining the "great chain of being" by establishing its nadir. Their language (and their discourse) was perceived as the crudest and most barbaric. Thus in the eyes of the formerly Yiddish-speaking convert, Yiddish moved from being a language of a "nation within nations" to a language of the "barbarian."[62] But for the Jew, convert or not, these barbarians must be localized, like the Hottentot, in some remote geographic place to separate them from the image of the German Jew. Their locus is the East, specifically Poland, and the Yiddish-speaking Jew becomes identified with the Polish Jew.

As early as 1786 Elias Ackord published a German translation of a Polish polemical pamphlet on the nature and future of the Polish Jews.[63] This pamphlet presents a strongly anti-Jewish image of the Polish Jews, which Ackord mitigates with a series of interpretive footnotes. The translation was aimed at an audience quite different from its Polish original. The original audience would have been the Polish-speaking Catholic readership (middle-class or noble), who needed little encouragement to view the Jews among them as inherently different and corrupt. Ackord's translation into German, as one can see from his commentary, is aimed as much at a German-speaking Jewish audience as at a non-Jewish one. The anonymous author demands that Yiddish be legally banned in Poland. He sees the corruption of the Jews' language as a result of their alphabet and demands that the Hebrew alphabet be banned, and all Jewish publishing houses closed. The Jew would be forced to learn the language of the country. All foreign books would be banned, and all books published by the Jews would have to be published in Polish in order to reveal the trickeries of the Jews. This program is not that much removed from the suggestions made concerning the Jews' books in the Middle Ages. Ackord appends a long note to this section of the pamphlet, suggesting that the Jews' books need not be barred, that the same purpose would be accomplished by implementing the Josephine Edict of Toleration and introducing secular schools for the Jews. The result of this would be twofold: "First, the youth would learn the language of the country, and second, the children, as soon as they achieved any taste in the pursuit of knowledge, would abandon Talmudic teaching themselves" (41–42). The linkage between language and discourse, of Yiddish and *pilpul*, is one made over and over again by both proponents and opponents of Jewish emancipation.

David Friedländer, one of Mendelssohn's staunchest supporters and the individual seen by his contemporaries as his natural successor, published a study localizing the meeting place of the corrupt language and the corrupt discourse. His pamphlet *On the Improvement of the Jews in the Kingdom of Poland* was a report commissioned from this Maskil, who had already presented a program for the reform of the institutional structure of Prussian Jewry.[64] Friedländer, who was responsible for the secular school in Berlin that Ackord cites as his model for Jewish linguistic assimilation, turns to the Jews in Poland with quite a different eye than that which he cast on his Berlin contemporaries. The Jews in Poland, including their rabbinate, are corrupt. This corruption is manifest in their language (12). It is also manifest in their "scholastic" means of exegesis, the *pilpul*. Friedländer sees in the very language of the Talmud simply another type of Yiddish, a "mix of rabbinic Hebrew, Aramaic, Chaldean, strewn with Arabic and Greek words and artificial turns of phrase, which can be captured in no grammatical system. In this the subtlest investigations are undertaken, which consist of disputations, which devolve into questions and answers" (22). Talmudic language and Talmudic discourse are one; they are the sign of the corruption of the Jews of Poland. But what is most important, they are a sign of the results of such corruption, the rise of anti-rationalism, of enthusiasm, of the Chasidic movement, with its mystical language: "[The Chasids'] teaching is an incomprehensible mix of Cabalistic, mystic, and Neoplatonic ideas, which evidently has its origin in the Talmud" (39). The language and discourse of the Jews may be different, but only in a distanced sphere, the world of the East. They are different because of their "impurity," as opposed to the "purity" of German.

Ackord's and Friedländer's views reflect a projection of the image of the impure language of the Jews into the world of the East. But it must be understood that they are responding to a reading of their own language, a reading that culminates in the young Johann Gottlieb Fichte's view of the irredeemable nature of the Jew. Fichte's solution is not merely to ban or burn books but to "cut off their heads on the same night in order to replace them with those containing no Jewish ideas."[65] It is the biology of the Jews that determines both their language and their discourse. Fichte's views were paralleled by other calls for the "physiological transformation" of the Jews, to use Jacob Katz's felicitous phrase.

Karl Wilhelm Friedrich Grattenauer, in a pamphlet entitled *Concerning the Physical and Moral Characteristics of Contemporary Jews* (1791), argued that the mentality of the Jew was unalterable, even through the act of baptism.[66] Grattenauer, like many contemporary anti-Jewish pamphleteers, saw in the movement toward Jewish emancipation a threat to their means of distancing themselves from the powerless Jews. For with emancipation came the Jews' claim on German, the language of their own polemics. Thus he was forced to argue for the immutability of the Jews' hidden discourse as the reason for their inability to learn German (2). But Grattenauer was also reacting to the claims by proponents of emancipation, such as Abbé Grégoire, that the negative aspects of Jewish life, language, and mentality were merely artifacts of the repression of the Jews.[67] Grattenauer reverses this. He labels the advocates of Jewish emancipation as ill, consumed by the disease of equality (131)! Both, however, relate the Jews' special nature to their sexuality. Grégoire sees the sexual selectivity of the Jews as one of the reasons for their illness; Grattenauer sees their "whoredom and shamelessness" (3) as a sign of their moral corruption. Both relate sexuality to disease, and disease to the special nature of the Jews and their corrupt discourse.

Grattenauer needed to distance the Jews and show that they had always possessed an inherently different language. This task was one of the first that he undertook as a polemicist against the Jews. In his 1788 pamphlet *Notes on the Teaching of Jesus with Respect to Jewish Language and Thought*, Grattenauer expounded on Jesus's rejection of the language of the Jews, his development of a mode of discourse that was not merely different but antithetical to that of the Jews of his time.[68] The language of the Jews was the language of deceit, of corruption—of lies. Christ purified it and created a new language. In this long, polemical text, Grattenauer attempts to rescue Jesus from the charge of being but a Jew, a Jew who used the language of his time. The power of the image of the hidden language of the Jews is such that not even divinity could purify the discourse of the Jews. How much less could conversion accomplish this?

Jews such as Ackord and Friedländer saw their own distancing of the malevolent qualities of the Jews living in the East, qualities seen as universal by many of their Christian contemporaries, as an acceptable means of localizing charges about the hidden language of the Jews. Similarly, Moses Mendelssohn saw in language the key to social acceptability. Unlike themselves as youths, good Jews spoke good German rather than the sign of immutable corruption, Yiddish. Good Jews were the sum of their language and rhetoric. Indeed one of the strongest reasons given by Mendelssohn for undertaking a translation of the Pentateuch into German (printed in Hebrew characters) was the abysmal state of Yiddish translations or abridgments of the Bible. In the prolegomenon to his translation Mendelssohn refers to these translations, describing the language in which they were written as "a language of stammerers, corrupt and deformed, repulsive to those who are able to speak in a correct and orderly manner."[69] Language corrupts by creating a people who cannot think clearly. In 1782 Ernst Ferdinand Klein, a jurist in Breslau, was asked to suggest revisions of the Jews' oath, the oath demanded of every Jew before his or her testimony was heard before a German court. It was this oath that Wagenseil almost eight decades before had advocated being read in Yiddish rather than a mangled and incomprehensible Hebrew. Klein turned to Mendelssohn for advice as to the form of this oath. Mendelssohn's primary comment concerned the language in which the oath was to be administered:

On the contrary I would not at all like to see a legal authorization of the Jewish German dialect, nor a mixture of Hebrew and German as suggested by [Rabbi] Fraenkel. I am afraid that this jargon has contributed more than a little to the uncivilized bearing of the common man. In contrast, it seems to be that the recent usage of pure German among my brethren promises to have a most salutory effect on them. It would vex me greatly, therefore, if even the law of the land were to promote, so to speak, the abuse of either language. It would be much better if Mr. Fraenkel tried to put the entire admonition into pure Hebrew so that it could be read in either pure German or pure Hebrew, or possibly both, whichever might be best under the circumstances. Anything at all rather than a mish-mash of language![70]

Here one further link in the creation of the Enlightenment's image of the bad Jew is forged. For the degeneracy of the Jews, evident in their criminality and antisocial behavior, is the result of their language. This is clearly within the definition of the nature of language provided by Hamann, but it is here applied to that language which Mendelssohn himself spoke before coming to Berlin. Yiddish, the Talmud, the *pilpul*, the geographic focus of the disputatious Jew in the East—all are links in the image of the bad Jew, the Jew whose existence has the potential to call forth the wrath of philo- and anti-Semite alike. Such Jews lie and must be required to take the oath.

Mendelssohn evolved a systematic view of the nature of language that was quite different from the views of many of his contemporaries. In a series of comments on Rousseau's second *Discourse*, written in 1755, Mendelssohn stressed that language leads to the creation of reason.[71] With the innate ability to create language, one can acquire the tools for the expression of reason. Mendelssohn goes so far as to doubt the findings concerning feral children, a subject of continuing fascination in the Enlightenment. For Mendelssohn, such children have not evolved the ability to speak and therefore cannot think rationally because they have had no opportunity to do so. He continues his argument to show that language prefigures logical thought in its very categories. If one extrapolates from this early essay, which remained unpublished during his lifetime, one can see that Mendelssohn's later argument concerning the degeneracy of the Jews and their language is based on a more elaborate sense of the close relationship between logical (in the sense of Western philosophy) discourse and the quality of language. For the most evident analogy is to the feral children that Mendelssohn describes. The Jews have evolved a crude and primitive language because of their life as outcasts in Western society. This language permits them only the wildest and crudest modes of expression. Parallel to the feral children, they have not had the opportunity to express more complicated (and correct) ideas because of the limitations of their language. While the situation of the Jews is not quite as bad as that of the feral children—the Jews at least have some system of signs with which to express themselves—it is analogous. Remedy the situation in which the feral children or the Jews live, and they will then learn "human" speech and live as normal individuals in society. Allow them to continue to live among animals or like animals, and they will not. And without language they cannot become full human beings, that is, human beings who argue rationally.

Mendelssohn's creation of an image of the nondisputive, rational, German-speaking Jew using tools of Western rhetoric and logic was in fulfillment of the cultural demands of Christian, capitalistic society. This society even provided a model for Mendelssohn, just as Mendelssohn served as a model for his contemporaries. For Mendelssohn was seen as a second Spinoza. As early as the 1750s Mendelssohn began quite consciously to shape himself after the myth of Spinoza the rationalist. Mendelssohn was attracted to the figure of Spinoza not only because of the function of this philosopher in eighteenth-century speculative thought but also because those about him saw in Spinoza the image of the good Jew. Lessing, in answering Michaelis's comments that a Jew such as the traveler in *The Jews* could never exist in reality, calls upon his newly found friend Mendelssohn as living proof: "I foresee in him the glory of his nation, provided his coreligionists permit him to mature, even though they have usually persecuted individuals like him. His honesty and philosophical mind make me think of a second Spinoza, equal to the first in everything but his errors."[72] Mendelssohn is thus the extraordinary Jew, the exception, the good Jew, like Spinoza for Lessing. Lessing stresses the Jews' usual blindness to truth and their dishonesty. Mendelssohn may become an exception to his rule.

Baruch de Spinoza was for the German Enlightenment the good Jew because of his persecution by his coreligionists. But Mendelssohn would have seen even more. For Spinoza was an integral part of seventeenth-century European intellectual life. He wrote his philosophical works in Latin, the language of philosophy in his day, and in Dutch, the language of his abode. He was certainly not the first Jewish thinker to write for a non-Jewish audience in a Western European language. In addition to the converts in the Middle Ages and the Renaissance, Helia Hebraeus Cretensis wrote his *Three Questions* in an elegant Renaissance Latin. That Spinoza had some command of Hebrew is evident. Spinoza had the command of the language and rhetoric of the West, speaking three languages, none of them his own. For like Mendelssohn, Spinoza spoke a language of the European Jew, Ladino, which he referred to as "Spanish" in his correspondence with Blyenbergh, just as Mendelssohn refers to Yiddish as the "Jewish-German dialect."[73] For Mendelssohn, Spinoza's acceptance into the mainstream of Western philosophy is tied to his mode of argumentation and to the language and tone of that argumentation. It was not merely that Spinoza provided Mendelssohn with a model of the Jew who was able to reject the modes of thought and expression of the Jewish exile, of the Diaspora, but that Spinoza functioned for his contemporaries as their model of the acceptable Jew.

But Mendelssohn also felt that he had to be accepted within the Jewish community. Unlike Spinoza, who was excommunicated by the Dutch Jews, Mendelssohn wished to restructure the very definition of the Jew so as to make his new splitting of the good Jew from the bad Jew the norm rather than the exception. To do this he had to strip away from the image of the Jew the identification of Jewish identity with either Yiddish or Talmudic Hebrew. Mendelssohn encouraged his coreligionists to use either German or the newly purified Hebrew of the Maskilim. German and Hebrew became interchangeable concepts for the Haskalah. Not only did Mendelssohn translate the Bible into German and publish it in Hebrew characters but essays were written in this strange hybrid in *The Collector*. Translations and adaptations of the Hebrew liturgy appeared in German. Indeed, the knowledge of German became a prerequisite for an understanding of Hebrew, as one essayist wrote in 1786: "For who will know the clarity of the holy tongue [Hebrew] and will understand the Bible and Mishnah if he does not possess a complete mastery of another language."[74] Hebrew was to be restored to the Jews in a new and purified form, freed from the neologisms and grammatical errors of the post-biblical rabbinic writings. The Hebrew that the Haskalah advocated is the antithesis of Talmudic language. It is rather the Hebrew of the Christian Orientalists and grammarians, such as Michaelis.[75] But more than that, it is the language of Christian theology as expounded in the mid-eighteenth century by Christians whose interest focused on the conversion of the Jews. German already had undergone such a purgation. Indeed, within the living memory of the Maskilim, German had established itself as a unified language able to express the highest forms of philosophical and literary expression. Where did this leave Yiddish, the language spoken by most of the Jews in Europe? Exiled at the margin of discourse. The new language of the German Jews was to be German, and fulfilling the model of European linguistic expectation, Hebrew was to be their Latin. Their text was to be the Bible, and their mode of interpretation and argumentation that of philosophical discourse. This was the idealized model; the reality was much more complex than the paradigm permitted.

The German Enlightenment denied the Jews even the role of a nation among nations. Michaelis, following his comments on Lessing's play, formulated a view of the Jew that denied the Jew even the status of having a religion.[76] Since Mosaic law promulgated not a system of beliefs but rather a system of laws, it was not even to be considered a religion. The absence of a system of belief led the Jews to be dishonest, vicious, without honor, and useless as soldiers. This rejection of Judaism as a basis for honorable action permeates Immanuel Kant's thought. Kant defines religion on the model of Christianity and sees in the worldliness, exclusivity, and legalism of the Jews the reason to deny them any claim to the status of religion.[77] Since it was Kant's views on the nature of humanity and society that were constantly cited by the Maskilim, this negative attitude toward the Jews began to permeate German-Jewish self-definition. But Kant provided a safety valve for this critique of the Jews, which not he but his Jewish supporters sorely needed. In his *Anthropology* Kant describes the mendacious Jews as "a nation of usurers: . . . Now this cannot be otherwise with a whole nature of pure merchants who are non-productive members of society (e.g., the Jews of Poland)."[78] It is not the German Jews who are the archetypal bad Jews, but the Polish Jews, the Eastern Jews.

This fear of the stranger who has come from the East has a long history in Germany, reaching back past the Turkish threat in the seventeenth century to the invasion of the Huns. The East has long been the source of anxiety for the Germans, to no little degree because of their expansion into Slavic territories during the Middle Ages. Kant, on the fringe of Germany in Königsberg, saw the potential salvation of the Jews if they were able to shed their "Judaic spirit," a spirit manifested in their books and language, a spirit that determined their attitudes and actions. Thus the followers of the Enlightenment had a natural locus for their fears, the East, and a potential to be freed of the charge of inherent difference through the philosophy of toleration. The identification of the East as the source of the corruption of the Jews was a concept shared by German Jews. Naphtali Herz Wessely, born in Hamburg in 1725 to a family of Polish Jews, called upon Jews to support the opening of German-language schools for their children following the Edict of Toleration of Joseph II. In his call he strongly condemned Yiddish not only as a "corrupt tongue" but as an artifact of the East. He described the Yiddish speaker as "Polish-ized" and contrasted the corruption of Yiddish, of "Jargon," with the language of the "Portuguese" Jews. Ladino, the language of the exiled Jews from the Iberian peninsula, was considered to possess a higher cultural value than Yiddish. This passage is of such importance that Samuel Hochheimer quotes it for pages in his 1786 necrology of Moses Mendelssohn.[79] For the Enlightenment, for Christian and Jew alike, Yiddish becomes the sign of the corruption following from the East. And this, of course, is in a world in which those Jews who condemn Yiddish speak Yiddish as their native language, as that tongue which identifies them with the world of the Jews in the West. The condemnation of Yiddish is written in either German or Hebrew, two tongues identified by the intelligentsia as possessing the quality of culture, a quality denied to Yiddish as well as to the traditional discourse of the Jew.

IV

The Creation of the Schlemiel

If the Enlightenment as a European phenomenon is scrutinized, one major factor differentiates it from the literature of the age of absolutism. The writers of the Enlightenment took their roles as reformers quite seriously and, following the classical dictum, believed that they should educate through amusement. Voltaire, Diderot, and the other writers of the French Enlightenment, and following them Lessing, Nicolai, and writers of the German tradition, discovered that one specific literary mode provided a structure that both educated and amused: satire.[80]

Satire has a long and checkered career in European letters. In the eighteenth century, however, satire's powers became recognized within the institutions against which it was directed. Satire was perceived in the Enlightenment as the force to create the common good; therefore, it was directed against those structures in society that interfered with the creation of the common good. Those institutions that saw themselves endangered—the state, the nobility, the church—exempted themselves from being the subject of satire. Indeed, Gottlieb Wilhelm Rabener, one of the most productive of the German satirists of the mid-eighteenth century, in his little booklet *On the Misuse of Satire* (1751) excluded these areas as being inappropriate subjects of satire.[81] In enlightened Germany the author saw himself as a servant of the state, since the state became for the author the embodiment of the spirit of the Enlightenment. Rabener and others limit not only the subject of satire but also its function. One can satirize the foibles of the middle and lower classes but not their sins. Only human failing, not evil, is the subject of satire. Here the German concept of satire is clearly different from that of other European traditions. Unlike Swift's or, indeed, even Voltaire's, German satire is benign, and the satirist's favorite theme becomes the servility of letters, which the satirist embodies by focusing on this very theme.

When one examines the attitude of the Haskalah toward satire, a rather different image of the function of this means of education emerges. In a short essay entitled "Should One Counter the Rising Enthusiasm through Satire or through External Means?" which appeared in the *Berlin Monthly* in 1785, Mendelssohn presents a view of the function of satire in regard to irrationalism or enthusiasm that other writers of the Haskalah, such as Solomon Maimon, repeat.[82] Mendelssohn begins his essay by equating *enthusiasm* and *superstition*, quoting Shaftesbury. *Enthusiasm* is a key word from the Enlightenment referring to pietistic excesses, the emphasis being on the irrational and the mystical. In the course of the very late eighteenth and early nineteenth centuries, it is a term that, within German Jewish usage refers almost exclusively to the rise of Jewish mysticism in Eastern Europe, the Chasidic movement. *Superstition* is another key word of the Enlightenment. Its reference is almost always organized religion, usually organized religion that is viewed by the critic as heavily ritualistic. It is, therefore, usually applied in northern, Protestant Germany to Catholicism and Judaism. This very beginning provides a key to Mendelssohn's sense of the function of satire in dealing with those "man-made evils" that he, in his letter to Lavater, sees polluting Judaism.

Mendelssohn criticizes the use of satire without its primary function, education. "True enlightenment," he writes, "is not when people change their folly out of a fear of being mocked. They wear the mask of healthy reason at best, mock along with the rest, where this fashion dominates, but in their private bedrooms they are enthusiastic, seduced and seducing enthusiasts." The conflict between inner self and outer self is the product of the fashion of satire. Mendelssohn sees the product of this hidden enthusiasm as being fanaticism, a fanaticism that is the result of the fashionableness of superficial philosophy. For Mendelssohn this philosophy is the French tradition, which is accepted as valid in Germany even though it is pernicious. Only German philosophy, which is at the same time popular enlightenment, can cure this flight into childhood fancy, for the sole cure of both superficial philosophy and enthusiasm is true enlightenment.

Mendelssohn sees in satire an effective means of revealing the fanaticism of the enthusiasts. He concludes his essay with the sentence, "The intention of mankind is: not to suppress prejudices, but to examine them." And this examination can be undertaken through the vehicle of satire. But the meandering nature of Mendelssohn's text, with its multilevel comment on the nature of sterile philosophizing and pointless, destructive enthusiasm, concludes with a statement that has very specific implications. Nowhere in the essay except in the closing line does Mendelssohn make reference to the question of prejudice. This reference returns to Mendelssohn's central focus, the definition of self in the light of contemporary German concepts of the Jew. Satire, part of education, becomes a means of liberating any group, but especially the Jews, from the double yoke of scholasticism and enthusiasm.

The first generation of Berlin Jews who viewed themselves as emancipated employed the contemporary understanding of the nature and function of satire in their striving for self-definition. A series of satiric texts primarily dramatic in form was produced during the closing decades of the eighteenth century. The purpose of these texts was the creation of a double for the negative image of the Jew found in Germany, a double onto which all of the negative qualities of this image could be heaped. The nature and quality of this anti-image of the enlightened Jew function as a means by which the nature of the projections concerning the negative self-image of the Jew can be measured. But these images must be understood within the context in which they were written, which was consciously German and enlightened. It was from that context that the quintessential Jewish literary persona, the schlemiel, appeared.

The texts that best reveal the tensions generated by the attempt to create a new sense of identity, as well as the incorporation of the status accorded to specific institutions during the Enlightenment, are to be found in a very special theater, the theater of satire, the theater of the mind. For plays such as Aaron Halle-Wolfsohn's *Foolishness and Mock Piety* (1796) clearly were not written for any theater. Wolfsohn's play, first written in Hebrew and then translated into Yiddish, had as its audience the Maskilim, the enlightened Jews of Berlin, who were to be amused by the antics of the unenlightened Jews.[83] But Wolfsohn's play itself is derivative. Its central character is patterned after the titular hero of the first major comedy of the Haskalah, Isaac Euchel's *Reb Hennoch, or What Can One Do about It?*, written in the mid-1790s. Euchel's play is of central importance, not so much as a document that itself had direct influence—it most probably did not—but as an indicator of an approach to the institution of language and its concomitant home, the theater.

Much has been made of Euchel's drama in the past few years.[84] It has been seen as the most scathing attack on Yiddish to come out of the Berlin circle or as a continuation of the Jewish tradition of the Purim play, itself an adaptation of the Catholic Shrovetide drama. Written by one of the major authors of the Berlin Haskalah, this play has often been examined, but almost always with some polemical rationale. It is, however, like Wolfsohn's, a play written for a theater that could not exist, a Yiddish-language theater. It is a drama that uses the two central themes of the German satire of the eighteenth century—the function of language and the struggle between generations—as means of avoiding conflict with the major force of the state. It is a satire quite within the limits of Rabener's critique of German satire, as well as Mendelssohn's critique of the function of satire, in correcting the evils of enthusiasm as well as orthodoxy. Through all of this it generates the one possible central character, the schlemiel, as the answer to all of these crosscurrents.

Jewish fiction and romance, as well as epic, written in Yiddish from the fifteenth century through the seventeenth, can be little differentiated from their Christian counterparts. Not only do these texts often share heros, story lines, and narrative modes and structures but these elements are literally borrowed without alteration. Thus the figure of Bovis of Hampton in the 1541 *Bovo-Book*, written in Yiddish by the Italian scholar Elia Levita (himself a convert to Christianity), differs only in the most superficial manner from his French, Italian, English, Welsh, Irish, Russian, or Rumanian cousins.[85] The reason for this is that the function of literature among the Jews in sixteenth-century Italy was basically the same as that among their non-Jewish neighbors.

In eighteenth-century Germany, however, the concept of the function of the written word among the Jews and the institutions in which it was embedded was substantially different, even though the external structures were identical. Lessing attempted to create a German theater in Hamburg as the central cultural institution linking the various German mini-states. The theater was seen as a means of establishing identity, political as well as cultural. In this theater were to be played the dramas of the Enlightenment, dramas whose intent was to reform the viewer through either catharsis or satire. And the reformed viewer was to be the new citizen of the new state, a state that existed *in nuce* in the Prussia of Frederick the Great but that for Lessing was more a state of mind than a political reality.

Maskilim who adapted this model had certain major shifts in emphasis with which to contend. First, the idea of a "Jewish" theater in the neoclassical sense of the Enlightenment was anathema to the Jews, who permitted theater only within the strict limits of the carnivalesque atmosphere of Purim. Like Shrovetide, it was permitted within this sphere so that it could be strictly limited and controlled. To permit it to establish itself as an institution within the Jewish community was unthinkable. And even the Maskilim never thought of it. And yet they wrote comedies. Second, these comedies were written as satires, but satires of internal Jewish conflicts that were articulated within the models of eighteenth-century drama. The central model adapted by the Maskilim was the image of the Enlightenment as the conflict between generations. Ruth Angress has shown how Lessing adapted this motif in his tragedies, showing how criticism of the state is supplanted by a criticism of the internal struggles within the family.[86] What should be a criticism of the world outside of the home turns quickly and ferociously into a criticism of the blindness of the father. Peter L. Berger refers to this drive to achieve a sense of social mobility in the society at large as necessitating a "moral parricide" on the part of children. The father begins to represent the stifling demands of the society at large, demands that can never be answered completely. Euchel plays out this type of debasement of the father, and the language, style, manners, and morals of the father, in the drama.[87]

Reb Hennoch, Euchel's play, is a typical eighteenth-century drama that revolves around the stubbornness of the father, his evil effects on his son and daughter, and his inability to see the need to adapt to the new world in which his children now reside.[88] Like the earlier figures of the Jew on the German stage, Euchel's characters speak languages that reveal their inner nature. The Orthodox camp speaks Yiddish, the children speak German, and various visitors speak with a French or an English accent. Here, too, Lessing provided a model, but not in his plays about Jews. Lessing's Jews all speak beautiful, flowing German, but in his satire *Minna von Barnhelm* (1763), which presents the inner world of Lessing's youth, the Seven Years' War, it is not a Jew but a Frenchman whose broken German reveals his inner nature; it is not Yiddish but the dialect of the servant that tells the audience that it is to laugh.[89] In Euchel's play this external system of language signs is given internal significance. The struggle between generations is played out between two groups of figures, each group speaking a different language.

Reb Hennoch is the patriarch of a family whose younger members are fully within Mendelssohn's image of those who flee into sterile philosophy or into enthusiasm because of limited vision. Surrounded by conspiracies led by his supporters, he can only see them in those who are not at all conspiring against him. His blindness is total until at the conclusion of the play he is made to see his errors. He is revealed to be a fool who has hidden behind the authority traditionally given to the father. The children, even though spoiled by his blindness, are shown to have been right in rejecting his life. The young man whose attentions he wished to distract from his daughter is revealed to be the only honest suitor, and his reformist tendencies are revealed as proof for his morality. The Yiddish-speaking cronies of Reb Hennoch are shown to be the actual seducers of his children.

Schlemiels are fools who believe themselves to be in control of the world but are shown to the reader/audience to be in control of nothing, not even themselves.[90] Schlemiels are fools who are branded with the external sign of a damaged language, a language that entraps them. Schlemiels are the creation of the Enlightenment. It is the Jewish enlightener's attempt to use satire to cajole the reader into not being a fool. And yet Euchel and, indeed, Wolfsohn both undertake this reform in Yiddish.

Here is a double bind that leaves its mark on the inner nature of the schlemiel and makes it a touchstone for numerous later attempts by Westernized Jews to articulate their inner sense of insufficiency. For in writing in Yiddish, Euchel is saying that the message of being damaged can be contained within a damaged medium. Liars who say they are lying can be believed. For Euchel, there appeared to be no problem. One preaches to those one wishes to convert in the medium that can reach them. This is, of course, what the missionaries to the Jews had always done. When they believed that Hebrew was more efficacious, they used Hebrew; when it appeared that Yiddish would reach the greatest audience, they used Yiddish. The Maskilim were to reach the same audience, and they used Yiddish, but it was a Yiddish against which the tenor of the play's message was directed.

For Yiddish within the world of *Reb Hennoch* was the sign of false status, status within the world of orthodoxy. It was not real status; real status could only be found within the world of the political state. And here the reformers were not wrong. The transient nature of the Jews' role within the German state stressed the importance of the status that they were able to maintain within the inner world of the Jewish community. Status became the single most important quality that Jewish self-definition claimed for itself. The schlemiel thus relied for his sense of self on this false status, status within the group rather than within the broader context. The schlemiel became the father.

The idea of the schlemiel as the parent presents an eighteenth-century answer to the dangers of satire. But the dangers that Jewish satirists, such as Euchel, perceived were clearly of a different order than those seen by Rabener. For the role of the Jewish father as the butt of the satire, as the epitome of blindness, substituted the seemingly harmless parent of the family for the leader of the state. In speaking to this issue, Euchel clearly was making the child perceive the parent as harmless. The idea of the parent as schlemiel, however, creates potentially greater difficulties for the question of Jewish identity. The schlemiel, always perceived from the perspective of the observer who is aware of the schlemiel's limitations, becomes the means by which the dichotomy between acceptable status, and its sign systems, and false status, with its attendant signs, is understood. The differentiation between the good Jew and the bad Jew is here the difference between the child and the parent. The use of language in Euchel's play merely confirms the readers' suspicions. As in the dramas presenting the image of the Jew on the German stage, the function of language is to categorize the Jew as Jew, but the Jewishness of the Jew here lies in the claim to status, a status assumed by the parent but denied by the reformers.

The creation of comic Jews speaking Yiddish on an internalized stage draws upon a series of values postulated by the reformers' reference group, the enlightened Christian. The image of the stage as the institution upon which the act of education can take place presupposes a fantasy theater, a theater that did not exist in reality within the German-speaking world of the time. This is, of course, the ideal theater, as Schiller observes, the theater as a moral institution. But this theater exists only within the mind. It is a theater of satire, since satire amuses and enlightens. Satire draws upon the comic as a device for teaching. The image of the comic Jew, speaking Yiddish, is isolated in the world of the text and removed from the daily reality of Jews such as Euchel and Wolfsohn. For the text is itself an icon of the Enlightenment, a world of books that serves as the surrogate for the political realities denied the writers of these books. Yiddish-speaking Jews are hidden in a new, enlightened ghetto which is to contain them and their corruption and which isolates them from the world of the "good," German-speaking Jew. The language of thieves, the spoken language of the Jew, is captured and controlled within the world of the book, the world of the imaginary stage. All of this is done in Yiddish, since Yiddish reveals the hidden nature of the Jew and therefore must be removed from the world of the enlightened Jew. The Maskil uses Yiddish to exorcise the image of himself as a speaker of Yiddish.

Euchel's claim is more than a claim that the children see better than their parents, that they are less encumbered by the traditions of Judaism and are therefore better able to function within the political state. Euchel sees in the conflict between parent and child, played out in the fantasy theater of the Yiddish world, the possible resolution of his own inner conflicts, taking place within his own inner world, a world in which the secret language of dreams was still Yiddish. The dream theater of Euchel's play is cast in a mold that is quite familiar, but in a context that causes this pattern to have quite a different importance, for Euchel's image of the parent as schlemiel is the further fragmentation of the self into yet more polar components, into qualities of language, of power, of status. Euchel does not focus on a specific location for this conflict. But, as can be seen, the implication of the Jews' language is that it is to be found more radically, less abstractly, within the more distanced world of the Eastern Jew.

V
Living Schlemiels

The first generation of German Jewish intellectuals who felt themselves to be liberated and tolerated bears some comparison with the generations of converts in the sixteenth century. Both groups felt themselves at home within their newly redefined identity, since this identity seemed to provide some type of shield against the animosity of the Christian world. And yet buried within this security was a nagging sense of self-doubt, of insecurity, which needed to have a locus, an identity separate from that of the one haunted by this self-doubt. This locus was found in the image of the Jews as limited, ignorant, and Eastern, bound by their hobbled language, whether Talmudic discourse or Yiddish. How this split in Jewish identity was articulated in the eighteenth century among the Maskilim, the followers of the Jewish Enlightenment, can be seen by examining the cases of three Jews. The three have certain features in common: they were all "Eastern" Jews, they were all deeply involved in the movement for Jewish intellectual emancipation during the age of Mendelssohn, and they all adopted modes of discourse of the German Enlightenment.

Moses Ephraim Kuh was born in Breslau in 1731 to traditional Orthodox parents.[91] His education followed a pattern common among the Maskilim. Coming from a merchant family of some means, he was introduced to Western letters only after an intense Jewish education which, according to his biographer Moses Hirschel, comprised "scholastic dogmatics, sophistic hypothesis, artificial subtleties, and other such nothings." Such a traditional rabbinic education provided Kuh with an extremely good command of Hebrew and the Talmud. His teacher was, however, a disciple of the German Enlightenment who also introduced Kuh into German rationalist philosophy. Kuh's training was as a bookkeeper, and his interests focused on foreign literature, especially British and French belles-lettres. After much effort he learned German, even though he felt that German did not possess the elegance and grace of either French or English, a view shared by many writers of his time, including Frederick the Great. After the death of his father, he went to Berlin in 1763, ostensibly to assume the position of bookkeeper in his uncle's gold and silver business. His primary reason for going to Berlin was to seek out the company of the new generation of German Enlightenment thinkers, such as Mendelssohn and Lessing. It was under their tutelage that Kuh for the first time turned seriously to the pursuit of German letters. He mastered the highly artificial style of the mid-eighteenth century, with its elaborate rules for prosody patterned after an eighteenth-century impression of classical poetry. His German quickly became polished under the direction of Karl Wilhelm Ramler, a friend of Lessing's and Mendelssohn's and editor of the periodical *The German Museum*, in which Kuh's early poetry appeared. All the while Kuh was spending his inheritance on "good works," supporting Christian as well as Jewish students, giving money to almost anyone who asked for it, with a sense of generosity that sprang from his newly found position in the German enlightened community.

In 1768 he left Berlin and undertook the classic European voyage to Italy. He toured the Netherlands, France, Italy, Switzerland, and the German states in the manner of any enlightened traveler of the late eighteenth century. Accompanying him on this long and arduous trip were three huge trunks full of books, the treasures of British, French, German, and Latin letters. On his return to Berlin, in 1771, a single incident occurred that altered his life completely. Jewish merchants alone were forced to pay a duty when they crossed any of the innumerable borders between the petty German states. Upon his return from Italy, Kuh crossed the border into Saxony and refused to acknowledge his identity. The scenario was described by one of Kuh's contemporaries a decade later: "[Kuh] dared to travel about eleven years ago as a simple human being and merchant without admitting to the customs officials his faith. He was discovered and had to pay duty, not on goods, but on the oldest faith in the world, a duty amounting to several thousand dollars."[92] Stripped of all his funds and much of his wardrobe by the customs officials, Kuh was forced to appeal to his family in Breslau for help, and thus he returned impoverished to his home.

In Breslau he began to write compulsively, poem after poem. His depression concerning his state, a depression that his contemporaries described with the fashionable eighteenth-century term *melancholia*, turned to mania. Kuh's madness, however, seen by his contemporaries as the result of "his thankless treatment by mankind," turned into a sense of being persecuted by the traditional Orthodox community in Breslau. He saw in his poetry, in his ironic comments, the reason for their hatred of him. Calling on his rights as a citizen of Prussia, he began to attack the Breslau Jewish community for persecuting him.

Kuh's madness and his attacks on the Breslau Jewish community brought forth a strong interest in him on the part of Christian missionaries, who saw in him a perfect subject for conversion. There began an intense attempt to bring him into the Protestant fold. Kuh's fixation on the persecution he was suffering from the Breslau Jews, however, did not permit him to take the attempt at conversion at all seriously, and he rejected all the advances made to him. He withdrew as much as possible from any contact with human beings, becoming phobic when approached by anyone. The form of his phobia was not unexpected. He saw in all strangers religious fanatics who were out to rob him of his freedom of conscience or, indeed, to murder him. Under close supervision by hired nurses, he saw them as members of this same conspiracy. He began to fixate on the danger that he felt from members of the Prussian garrison in Breslau, seeing in this uniformed authority a force that intended him bodily harm.

For six years Kuh labored under this paranoid delusion, and

he wrote compulsively. His contemporaries considered the four thousand to five thousand poems that he wrote during this period to be his best work, even though this seemed to violate for them the need for a rational basis for the creation of works of art. His ability to articulate his ideas in verse seemed even more surprising to those who knew him, since he seemed to have no such ability in normal conversation:

> In conversation where he was affected by external objects and disturbed, the course of his argument was easily lost. Concepts became confused. They no longer were clear and distinct, quali- ties necessary for any coherence, which is the essential quality of any conversation. If he could orient himself, link idea to idea, unaffected by external objects, and (so to say) withdraw into himself, such a break and confusion did not occur, through which the normal flow of ideas was affected or interrupted.[93]

Kuh sent his poetry to Lessing. Lessing, in turn, sent him to Mendelssohn, being in the midst of his own struggles with Chris- tian orthodoxy. Mendelssohn suggested that Kuh turn to forms such as moral example and to translations as a means of best using his poetic gifts. These poems were published in part by Ramler during the last few years of Kuh's life. Kuh died in April of 1790 after a long illness.

If one turns to the selection of poems published posthumously by his friends, one is struck by the very few texts that deal with his paranoia. Indeed, with few exceptions, the poems deal with classical themes and are written in a form typical of German neoclassicism, the epigram. The exceptions are the few translations from the Hebrew and Kuh's versions of Martial's epigrams, as well as a very small number of texts that reflect a personal level of experience.

In Kuh's poetry the literary persona, the voice, is that of Martial. It is ironic, dealing in witty bons mots with issues that are universal in nature—the relationship between the sexes, the nature of soci- ety or at least social position, external nature, and the beautiful. The ironic voice, usually occurring within a mock dialogue, is a literary artifact. It is the artificial tone of accepted Enlightenment discourse. When one looks at Kuh's life—at his education, his fascination with the literary masterpieces of the Western tradition, his philanthropy, and finally his trip to Italy—the model of self- education for German classicism, the sense of the model of the literary man that Kuh has selected in order to shape his self-iden- tity, becomes evident. Kuh needed to become a literary man, since it was in this form that the German Jew seemed to have access to Western (or at least Berlin) society.

The implications for an eighteenth-century Jew of becoming a literary man, one who writes and is written about, are clear. While court Jews had been welcomed (or at least tolerated) in the numerous German courts during the seventeenth and eighteenth centuries, they fitted nicely within the Christian model of the Jew as merchant or usurer well known from the late Middle Ages. The new prestige associated with the writer (or critic) in the eighteenth-century German bourgeois world provided another redefinition for the Jew. He could become a writer, for being a writer did not rely on class or capital.[94] The writer was the first truly mobile member of German society since the medieval monk, who could one day become an abbot. Social mobility, prestige, and the resultant stability of his position in society would result from the role of the literary man.

The Enlightenment's sanctification of the book as the most holy relic of human society was clearly tied to the disenfranchisement of the intellectual in eighteenth-century Europe. Unable to undertake a meaningful role in shaping the world about him, ofttimes powerless and penurious, the intellectual projected his impotence into the world of books, a world in which he became imbued with power. How much weaker were the Jews of the Enlightenment, who were perceived even by the intellectuals as incapable of commanding Western discourses. Mendelssohn, in his *Jerusalem* (1783), bemoaned the replacement of "the wise man" with his books: "We do not need the man of experience; we only need his writings. In a word we are *literati, men of letters*. Our whole being depends on letters; and we can scarcely comprehend how a mortal man can educate and perfect himself without a *book*."[95] Mendelssohn's condemnation of the replacement of a man by the cult of the book, and his own inclusion in this cult, was rooted to no little extent in the role of the myth of the hidden language of the Jews as undermining the Jews' participation in the generation of this world of books. The world of books had isolated itself from the people of the Book, and Mendelssohn, like his model Spinoza, wished to reintegrate them.

The denial of a sense of the aesthetic to the Jew becomes a problem to those writers about aesthetics in the eighteenth century who are themselves Jewish. The primary example of this is the physician-philosopher Marcus Herz, whose study *On Taste and the Grounds for Its Difference* (1776) contains one of the basic Enlightenment discussions of the relationship between taste and human nature. Herz was generally unoriginal, relying on aestheticians such as Johann Georg Sulzer for most of the basic concepts in his work. And yet he is constrained to discuss the influence of culture on the education of taste. He selects three moments in culture that he sees as affecting the education of taste: freedom of thought, religion, and ethics. Under the second of these major influences on the creation of taste, Herz distinguishes between the role of natural religions, which are not capable of creating a God that can be grasped by the human senses, and revealed religions, which insist on reducing God to qualities that can be comprehended through the senses. He dismisses Michelangelo's image of God (on the ceiling of the Sistine Chapel) as causing the greatest repugnance in him, thus identifying with the Protestant's rejection of Catholic iconography. He writes: "*My* God the Father escapes the moment of my comprehension as soon as I begin to perceive him through representational perception."[96] Such a view, while well within the rejection of Raphael during the Enlightenment, also has a hidden dimension. Herz is arguing that Jewish iconoclasm is the model for his rejection of Christian art. It is not that the Jews have no sense of the beautiful but rather that, in this case, their manner of comprehending the beautiful is that of natural religion. Herz's stress on the personal ("*My* God the Father") is but another way of claiming a special, perhaps even higher, status for the aesthetic nature of the Jew.

There was one major problem in assuming this role. Eighteenth-century aestheticians refused to ascribe a sense of beauty to any group they believed to be marginal. Whether black or Jew, the outsider was perceived as inherently unable to sense, and therefore to produce, the beautiful.[97] The sense of the beautiful became one of the major touchstones distinguishing between the civilized and the barbaric. And the Jews were among the barbarians. Moses Hirschel, in his introduction to Kuh's poetry, cites Kuh's works as proof of the great progress made at the close of the eighteenth century:

> It is not a useless task to undertake such a biography and preface it to literary work written by a Jew, that is, by a member of that nation that had been denied any sense of the beautiful, good, noble, or in short, for all arts and sciences out of intoleration, fanaticism, deceit, superstition, and prejudice up to our age. (30)

In becoming a writer in the eighteenth century, the Jew flaunted the inherited tradition of his incompetence in the creation of the beautiful. By creating works of art, he placed himself, at least in his own estimation, on the same level as all other creative individuals, no matter what their group affiliation.

Kuh began to write under the tutelage of Ramler. His poetry is totally indistinguishable from that of other minor poets of the mid-eighteenth century. It is neither better nor worse than that of non-Jewish poets of the time. It covers the spectrum of possible forms and poetic genres from the epigram to the fable. And then Kuh undertook his trip to Italy. The importance of such a trip, given the German mythology that grew up around the glories of Rome promulgated by writers such as Winckelmann, is self-evident. It meant retracing the supposed tracks leading to the intellectual world of the eighteenth century. For a Jew to see in the classical world the model for his present definition of self, to undertake a trip to Italy to explore those sights that inspired Christian writers such as Lessing, meant an attempt to redefine himself as a writer in the neoclassical mold.

Kuh then returned to the German states. And at the border at Sachsen-Gotha he was stopped by the custom authorities. They made inquiries as to whether anyone had anything to declare. Kuh did not answer. They then inquired of the passengers in the coach whether any were Jews, for Jews had to pay duty upon crossing the Saxon border, just as other objects must have duty paid on them. Kuh did not answer. After examining them and further asking about destination and objects of travel, the guards identified Kuh, dressed like a gentleman, much as Lessing's traveler must have been dressed, as a Jew. We must ask ourselves how the guards at the border knew Kuh was a Jew, and the evident answer must be through the nature of his language. Kuh's mother tongue was Yiddish, and he learned German fairly late in life. One can assume that he spoke good German but with a Yiddish accent. Language was the key to Kuh's unmasking as a counterfeit, as a Jew in intellectual's dress. Stripped of his money and his clothes, Kuh was forced to fall back on the aid of his non-enlightened, Orthodox family in Breslau.

The classic double bind situation results in an inability to deal with reality and collapse. Society has stated, through its literary institutions, Become like me—speak my language, think within my constraints, express yourself within my forms, undertake the same search for origins as I do—and you will become one with me. The state says, If you speak like a Jew, you are treated like an object; I can see beyond your superficial attempts to disguise yourself as a member of the intelligentsia and identify you.

In one of the very few biographical poems written during the resulting madness, Kuh recapitulates his experience at the Saxon border:

The Custom Official in E. and the Traveling Jew

Official: Hey you, Jew, you have to pay three dollars.
Jew: Three dollars? So much money? Why, sir?
Official: You ask me? Because you're a Jew.
        If you were a Turk, a heathen, an atheist,
        We wouldn't want anything from you.
        But as a Jew we must collect from you.
Jew: Here is the money! Does your Christ teach you this?

(1:187)

The custom official's tone—he addresses the Jew in the familiar—is that of the state addressing the Jew. But the harsh tone of the official is clearly in response to the Jew's having identified himself as a Jew. His toll or custom is that levied against the Jew upon crossing the Saxon border. Kuh's refusal to identify himself resulted in the confiscation of all his money and goods. The poem replays the situation as an alternative to having undergone the humiliation of being revealed to be a Jew and being forced to turn to his family for aid. Kuh's poem, in restructuring the incident, has the Jew win the confrontation. For unlike Martial's open-ended epigrams, this one concludes with the lesson the writer needs to have his readers draw from his text. True Christians do not—cannot—act like the custom official, like the state. But, of course, they do, and their brutality exceeds that of the situation portrayed by Kuh.

Kuh's reaction to the betrayal by the Christian world is to focus on the evils of orthodoxy, both in the world of the Jews and in the world of the Christians. Kuh's attacks on the Breslau Jewish community and his sense of being endangered by them point to his transference of fear of the Christian world to fear of the Jews. Like Spinoza, he sees himself condemned by his brethren for his attempts to enter the world of the non-Jew. This sense of alienation from the world of the Jews, a world from which he consciously separated himself in language, thought, and action, was increased when pressure was placed upon him by the Breslau Christian community to convert. Two of Kuh's brothers had already converted, one even marrying a Lutheran wife. The pressures on him to complete his identification with the Christian world were great, but his shattering experience at the Saxon border had revealed to him the limitations of the Christian world. He writes in another epigram aimed at the conversion of Elector August II of Saxony:

The Polish Jew, Who Became a Christian

A great noble, who is not threatened by anything
Denies his religion
To aspire to a new title, a new throne:
And I—lacking roof and bread—
You mock with bitter laughter.

(1:157)

Conversion is, for the "Polish Jew," the European equivalent to the Hottentot, a possibility. Of course, Kuh is himself a "Polish Jew"; he too is indigent, he too may well have been tempted by conversion. But Christians destroy:

To the Portuguese Inquisitors

It is true! One must call you humane;
Even envy must admit it,
For you never shed blood;
You take only from the innocents their possessions,
And then burn them alive.

(2:28)

They destroy Jews. First, they strip them of their worldly possessions, and then they destroy them. Conversion is of little help, for the Jews whom the Iberian inquisitors are burning are converted Jews, accused of having reverted to their ancestral religion.

Both Christians and Jews are dangerous. They conspire to destroy those who refuse to acknowledge their control over them. Or so it seems in Kuh's madness. He sees in the claims of a natural religion, a religion freed from his sense of the oppressiveness of social structures and institutions, the religion of the noble savage, the alternative to the religions of his world. In one of the last epigrams in the edition of his works, "The Guyennesse Indians," he writes:

You wild ones do not share our faith
You know no laws, which threaten in punishment of God;
yet you, honorable ones, never kill
The enemy with your poisoned arrows,
You kill only wild animals.
O! If Jews and Christians, who often, in spite of their faith,

permit themselves to do everything against their enemy,
Were as human as you!

(1:249)

Kuh manages to localize the source of his sense of persecution in the idea of orthodoxy. Shared equally between the Jews, from whom he attempted to escape, and the Christians, who did not permit him to escape, the idea of orthodoxy became a focus for the anxiety felt by Kuh. Here Kuh had incorporated into his system the Enlightenment's opposition to any type of rigidity (except its own), seeing in the orthodox the antithesis of its own demand for rationalism.

Kuh's anxiety is, however, an internalized one, projected in terms acceptable to the model of the idealized Jew onto the society that surrounds him. For Kuh's break with reality comes when the uniformed representatives of the state question his new, fragile identity. The state for the Prussian Jews was not merely an abstract. It was personified in the Prussian monarch, Frederick the Great, who stated that "in my kingdom everyone can be blest, according to their fashion." The state was Frederick II, and Frederick II was toleration epitomized. Confronted by a state that refused to acknowledge him as an equal member, Kuh, who had restructured his identity in the model of the literary man, for whom Frederick the Great also served as the primary representative, could only fall back onto the distinction between good Jews and bad Jews, between enlightened Jews and Orthodox Jews, between the rational and the orthodox. This was, of course, no more a representation of the reality of the world as he perceived it than were the older dichotomies. In his internalized world he was both part of the permanent world of the outsider, lacking any claim to that which he had shaped himself into, and a counterfeit of those accepted into the world of letters from other classes. The mechanical use of the epigrammatic style of Martial in writing thousands upon thousands of epigrams was an attempt to prove through the very act of writing that he too possessed a sense of the beautiful, that he too could articulate his sense of self through language. It was the highly polished language of German neoclassicism, a language that masked rather than mirrored Kuh's inner concern with that central flaw he perceived in his own character, his Jewishness. And the most evident outward manifestation of this Jewishness was his language. Thus he fled, in his madness, into a world of poetry, a fictive world that he had created for himself before his collapse and that presented the sole acceptable outlet for his sense of ruptured identity after his illness became manifest. Kuh is the Jew driven mad through the constraints of the Enlightenment, driven into a mode of self-hatred which he projects onto the world about him.

After the death of Mendelssohn in 1786, Ephraim Kuh was visited by the second of our trio of Eastern Jews, Solomon Maimon, who requested succor from him.[98] Maimon, born at Nesvij, Lithuania, in 1754, ranked as one of the most visible of all the Eastern Jews who were attracted to the Haskalah during its first generation. Maimon, a philosopher whose works received some acknowledgment from Kant himself, became, as did Mendelssohn, exemplary for the Christian as well as the Jewish world of the late eighteenth century. But in Maimon's case, it was not his life that served this myth-building function but his autobiography, published in its entirety under the editorship of Karl Philipp Moritz in 1792 and 1793. For an entire generation of Germans of all religious identities, Maimon's autobiography served as the most accurate representation of the nature and image of the Eastern Jew.

Maimon belongs to that group of Maskilim who completely replaced traditional Jewish identity with the Enlightenment's image of rationalism. For him, the only possible identity one could have was as a rationalist, an individual whose religious identity was as a follower of the religion of reason. Or at least so his autobiography would have one believe. Maimon's autobiography is one of the main sources for understanding the deformation that Jewish identity underwent during the late eighteenth century. Like all autobiographies, it is as much poetry as truth, to use the title of Goethe's autobiography. The structures that Maimon generates and the rationale and model upon which these structures are based, as well as the contrast with the historical figure of Solomon Maimon, provide a key to the alterations of Jewish identity in Germany during the Enlightenment, especially as it was reflected in the altered perception of those whom the Maskilim saw as the most "degenerate," to use Mendelssohn's term, of all European Jews.

Maimon's life can be sketched quite quickly. Born in Lithuania, he was educated within the strictures of European orthodoxy. He learned Hebrew, studied the Talmud, and was employed as a tutor in an Orthodox home. He discovered the teachings of the Haskalah after laboriously teaching himself to read the German alphabet. He journeyed to Berlin, became a disciple of Mendelssohn, and wandered throughout Germany as a scholar. He wrote prodigiously, contributing to learned journals and corresponding with intellectuals of the caliber of Kant and Goethe. At the conclusion of his life, having followed the principles of rationalism, he died supported by a Christian nobleman who had admired his work.

So goes the legend of Solomon Maimon. It is, however, truly a legend, and a legend built on a specific eighteenth-century model of the fictional representation of the inner biography of an individual, an individual who, however, was raised within the traditions of the Protestant world. For just as Kuh adapts the epigram of Martial as a means of articulating his newly created identity as a man of letters, so Maimon adapts a major model of the fictionalization of identity from his contemporary Karl Philipp Moritz. Indeed, what is striking in looking at Maimon's German work, a work aimed at the idealized German audience, an audience of enlightened thinkers, is the paucity of material dealing with his Jewish identity. For even though historians of German philosophy, such as the nineteenth-century critic Kuno Fischer, considered Maimon a quintessential Jewish exponent of Kant, very little in Maimon's written work in German presents any specially Jewish interpretation of Western philosophy.[99] Quite the contrary: except for his autobiography and a short piece translated from Maimonides, his German writings are devoid of any discussion of the Jews. So we must here turn, as we did with the works of Kuh, to those aspects of his works in which he reflects quite consciously on his self-image. The aporia of such texts provides the reader with the inherent contrast between the seeming insight of the poet and his true blindness. Maimon's autobiography forms one of the central references for both German and German Jewish images of the enlightened philosopher, and yet these images rest on the complex use of a literary model.

Extracts from Maimon's autobiography were initially published in the *Journal for the Practical Knowledge of Psychology*, founded by Karl Philipp Moritz and edited, in the final volumes, by Moritz and Maimon. In the same journal appeared fragments of Moritz's greatest work, the novel that was to appear in 1790 under the title *Anton Reiser: A Psychological Novel*.[100] The novel chronicles the life of a poverty-stricken boy in the world of repressive sectarian pietism. Often ill, he falls into the habit of reading voraciously to escape the daily realities of his life. Although talented in school, he is apprenticed to a hat maker. He draws attention to himself through his transcriptions of sermons by an enlightened pastor and eventually wins the sponsorship of a noble patron, who enables him to continue school. Because of his lack of self-respect, he flees from the competition of the schoolroom back into the world of fiction. He becomes the friend of the future actor Iffland and is led by him to the world of the theater. He sees in the theater the means to establish an independent life, and he becomes a member of one of the wandering troupes of actors who travel across Germany. At the close of the novel, his troupe is about to go bankrupt, and it seems that he will be forced out of the fantasy world of the theater.

Moritz's novel is the first major attempt to fulfill the demands of eighteenth-century aesthetics for a "realistic" novel that reflects the inner life of its hero. But the very verisimilitude of Moritz's portrayal of the fictional world of his hero caused even his contemporaries to take it as a thinly disguised representation of his own life. In the figure of Anton Reiser the fictive hero and the real world appear to mix, and at least through post–World War II studies of the work little interest was shown in distinguishing the fictional structure of the novel from the actual life of the author. They were seen to be the same, having the same ends, the representation of the contradictory demands of the world and of art as perceived through the eyes of a marginal member of society. There is a basic flaw in seeing any autobiography, especially a fictionalized one, as representative of the demands of the real world. *Anton Reiser* is the first attempt in Germany to present the internal life of the psyche as molded by life events. In order to do so, Moritz creates life events traumatic enough to mark his character's progress.

With slight alterations, Maimon's life story is that of Moritz's fiction. Substitute orthodoxy for pietism, philosophy for literature, and one has the autobiography of Solomon Maimon. Like Moritz's novel, Maimon's text remains a fragment. It ends with a clearly fictional chapter, an allegory on the nature of philosophical speculation, which underlines the hidden fictionalization of Maimon's life story. Noteworthy also is that Maimon, like Moritz, provides little of the superficial chronological structure expected in the eighteenth-century autobiography. Rather, like Moritz (or Rousseau), he relies on the recounting of a series of incidents that are shown to shape the inner nature of the central character.

In adapting the external structure of the psychological novel, Maimon endeavored to present the inner rationale for the development of his life to an audience whose aesthetic demands would be fulfilled by such a text. The German enlightened reader was confronted with a text that seemed to be a seamless representation of the inner life of the hero. The present-day reader is faced with a series of questions. How does the report of the realities in Maimon's autobiography relate to other accounts of his life? What are the primary junctures in Maimon's text that may provide some understanding of those realities? And finally, why is it that Maimon's autobiography was so widely accepted as the most accurate inner portrait of the Eastern Jew?

Maimon begins by dividing all of the population of Poland into six parts: "the superior nobility, the inferior nobility, the half-noble, burghers, peasantry, and Jews."[101] Maimon's world works based on this pecking order. His grandfather, he recounts, was a tenant of the most noble of that superior nobility, Prince Radziwill, of the leading family in Poland. One day the prince appears with members of his entourage in Maimon's village, and the boy is struck by the magnificence and splendor of the court. The extraordinary beauty and the costumes and decoration of a princess impress the boy, who is told by his father that in the afterlife such nobles will be forced to kindle the fires of the Jews, just as he had been forced to kindle one for them. This caused the lad to feel pity for those "doomed to such a degrading service." The boy is suddenly fascinated by the woodcuts in the various books in his father's library, especially one in a volume of astronomy. Thus the appreciation of beauty leads to art, and art to science. All the while the child has begun to learn the Talmud and Talmudic disputation. He describes this study as "eternally disputing about the book, without end or aim. Subtlety, loquacity, and impertinence here carry the day. This sort of study . . . has fallen into decay. It is a kind of talmudic skepticism, and utterly incompatible with any systematic study directed to some end" (48). Indoctrinated in Talmudic lore, he becomes a tutor to a family that lives in the most primitive conditions. Indeed, they are described as being so primitive that they "did not even understand the Jewish language, and made use therefore of Russian" (39). Not only do they not know Hebrew but they do not even know Yiddish. They speak Russian. They are, of course, in Russian Poland, where the nobles spoke Polish. The order of languages is thus established: Polish, Hebrew, Yiddish, Russian.

Prince Radziwill appears in one of the chapters. He is described as a vicious, stupid man whose primary occupation seems to be getting drunk. Maimon tells a series of anecdotes about the prince's drunken appearance at the inn run by Maimon's in-laws. He is deposited at the inn by his retinue, and when he awakes in a drunken stupor, he arranges a great feast, with golden plates and cups. During the preparation for the festivities he spies Maimon's wife and attempts to seduce her. Maimon reports that members of the court "became solicitous for the honor of my wife, and they gave her a hint to clear out as soon as possible. She took the hint, slipped silently out, and was soon over the hills and far away" (87).

Maimon reports on his learning to read German and his subsequent involvement with a group of Jewish mystics, Chasids, who base their newly revitalized faith on a reading of the Cabala. Like the Maskilim, Maimon portrays the followers of Chasidism as fellow opponents of the deadwood of rabbinic Judaism. He sees, in retrospect, "the Kabbalah [as] nothing but an expanded Spinozism" (105). The Chasids are opposed to the "fiction of a method" (117) in the *pilpul*, and attack "the abuse of rabbinical learning" and "the abuse of piety on the part of the so-called penitents" (161). This is a Chasidism that appears very much like the ideals of the Berlin Enlightenment, including Moritz. And, like the Berlin Enlightenment's, its rhetoric is clearly Protestant. For when Maimon gives examples of the abuses of Talmudic interpretation, he footnotes his text with exegesis from a Catholic theologian, showing how equally absurd Catholic interpretation can be.

Maimon appears in Berlin speaking "a language [which is a] mixture of Hebrew, German, Polish and Russian" (189) and eventually is presented to Mendelssohn, "who was not a little amazed, that a Polish Jew, who had scarcely got the length of seeing the metaphysics of Wolff, was already able to penetrate their depths so far" (215). Maimon begins to evolve his philosophic system, writing his exposition of Kant's philosophy. This creates enmity on the part of the Jewish community, which hounds him from town to town, threatening him with excommunication as they had Spinoza (260 ff.). For the third time he returns to Berlin, where he becomes involved with the circle of writers around the Hebrew journal *The Collector* and with Karl Philipp Moritz. Maimon concludes his autobiography with a detailed discussion of his contribution to the various journals during this period in Berlin and a final chapter that seems inexplicable, an allegory called "The Joyful Ball." Maimon ascribes this final chapter to "a friend" and calls it an allegory of the history of philosophy. It portrays a ball in which all schools of philosophy compete for the lovely Miss Metaphysics. She is finally captured by the masked stranger, whose name no one knows, and led off. Maimon footnotes the fact that one does not have to be an Oedipus to guess the name of this stranger. It is, of course, Kant.

The capture of Miss Metaphysics leads to the question of what Maimon's life was actually like. What were some of the realities hidden behind the text? As for his reception in the world of European philosophy of his time, Kant himself dismissed his work as inexplicable and "typical of Jews who like to better themselves on others' costs."[102] For Kant, Maimon's work is typical of the Jews' lack of originality. His life seems to have been one in which the claim to originality was an important one. He saw his contributions to philosophy as the sole rationale for his own existence. His contemporaries said, however, that his work was superficial, shallow, inexplicable.

Of his life one can observe that he was an alcoholic.[103] Indeed, it was said that he wrote his autobiography on an alehouse bench. When drunk, he became violent. Violence became the normal response to any disruption in his life, even to losing a chess match. When angered, he began to curse in Yiddish, seeming to forget his enlightened persona completely. The compulsive nature of Maimon's personality is perhaps best illustrated by a recurrent dream that he recounted to his biographer:

> He often dreamt that he found himself in Poland again and was robbed of all his books and writings. I believe that Lucien, changed into an ass, was in no worse a situation. "In this fear," said Maimon, "I am usually awakened through pure anger, and the joy that it was but a dream, is indescribably great."[104]

The linkage between his writing and his "escape from Poland" is absolute in Maimon's mind, but his status, the status of the philosopher as writer, is tenuous. Maimon describes days in which he cannot think. His reaction to those moments is the same fear that he felt in his dream of being robbed of his books and writings.

He seems to have been totally dependent in his relationship to other individuals. He begged and borrowed his way across Germany. Always short of funds, he seemed unable or unwilling to fulfill the ideal of the Enlightenment, the hard-working Jew. Unkempt, unwashed, his clothes usually in rags about him, he lived in lodgings that were filthy. He refused to permit anyone to enter in order to clean his rooms and would not touch them himself.

The contrast between the images of Maimon the seeker and Maimon the alcoholic is the contrast between the image of the hero as complex but comprehensible psychological fiction and the reality of daily life. For Maimon his entire life was as the outsider within the world of the German Enlightenment. His appearance, his actions, and his writings also served as biting correctives of the writings and thoughts of the insiders. Even in his correspondence with Goethe there is the tone of knowing better. But this attitude was coupled with the ultimate pattern for Maimon, the pattern of the acceptable, powerful Christian, the figure of Radziwill. For Radziwill's drunkenness, his treatment of Maimon's wife as a sexual object (just as Polish merchants had treated Maimon's mother in his youth), and the degradation under which Maimon thus lived provided for him the ultimate model, the drunken philosopher.

Here the persona was not fictive. Maimon's life became focused about the incident in his youth when the prince's retinue appeared in Maimon's home and he admired the beautiful Christian girl, unapproachable but destined to serve him in the next world. Here is the model for Miss Metaphysics, and Kant, as Maimon's double, captures her. Philosophy has been forced to serve the Jew and has given him, at least in his own eyes, the status of the nobleman. And yet Maimon was never accepted by the German establishment except as an interesting, if difficult, outsider. When Maimon decided that he might as well convert to Christianity, it was because he was tired of being persecuted by both Jews and Christians. His attempt to convert, like that of David Friedländer, was rejected, since it was based on a rationalist philosophical reason rather than a new faith.[105] The Church saw Maimon as outside its sphere, as did he himself. He was neither Christian nor Jew in his own estimation. To the Christian world he remained the Jew. The capture of Miss Metaphysics, with all its sexual overtones, was not sufficient to eradicate this stigma. And thus drunkenness, which was the mark of the highest stratum of society, became Maimon's mode of self-definition. It was a self-definition that came from a failed striving to achieve the status of the philosopher, the pure mind beyond racial designation. He remained the Jew as philosopher.

If the hierarchy of language that Maimon knew and accepted in his native land ranged from the language of the prince to the language of the peasant, from Polish to Russian, then his own scale of languages as an adult spanned an analogous range. For the highest rank was given, not to a language determined by geography, but to a language determined by function (and therefore by status), the language of the philosopher. The eighteenth century placed such language, the strict discourse of philosophical discourse, as the highest good. Indeed, philosophical discourse came to have an ethical implication. For argument according to the strict laws of Western philosophical discourse possessed moral value. Unlike the "fiction" of the *pilpul*, with its pointless argumentation for argumentation's sake, philosophical discourse, according to Maimon, had meaning and purpose.

The philosopher was the philosopher-prince in the eighteenth century. Like the man of letters, to whom he was closely related, the philosopher possessed status. One could take for example another follower of Kant, the Berlin physician Marcus Herz, whose philosophical speculation so interested Frederick the Great that the monarch awarded him the honorific title "professor." But, of course, Herz already had two major advantages over Maimon. He was a physician—Maimon makes light of his own attempts to fulfill this role in the Jewish community in Poland—and he was a "German" Jew, at least in terms of his sense of self. Maimon remains the Polish Jew, and his peregrinations through Europe bear some evidence of this mode of self-definition. His contemporaries commented on his seemingly congenital inability to settle down. In the autobiography Maimon describes Jewish penitents, including one Simon of Lubitsch, who "had also practised *Golath*, that is, a continuous wandering, in which the penitent is not allowed to remain two days in the same place" (133). Maimon observes his filthy, bedraggled state and his death by starvation. The status of the self-castigating holy man and that of the philosopher-prince both demand inclusion within a structure that allows status. Maimon's self-imposed exile from all camps created an unbridgeable conflict. As a philosopher he was perceived as a Jew; as a Jew he was attacked as being a philosopher.

His outward demeanor recapitulated the most evident outward manifestations of the prince in his drunkenness; of the penitent in his wandering and self-abnegation. When his outward facade, even his ability to win a game of chess, was in any way challenged, the conflict that underpinned his sense of identity released his original and hidden self, the Yiddish-speaking Jew of the Polish provinces. The rational philosopher vanished and was replaced by precisely that persona that he attempted to exorcise in his autobiography. By showing the psychological development of Salomon Maimon, a name he acquired only after his arrival in Germany to honor his intellectual model Maimonides (his actual name was Solomon ben Joshua), from the crudities of Polish Jewry to the heights of Enlightenment speculation, he wished to show a progressive model for the development of the psyche from darkness to light. Solomon Maimon is, of course, as much a fictional persona as is Anton Reiser. As with Reiser, the basic conflictual structure of the psyche is shown in the life events of the hero. Unlike Reiser, whose life story remains a fragment, Maimon desperately wishes to tie up the ends of his tale. But the inherently contradictory aspects that he drew upon to compose his sense of identity do not permit him this final synthesis. Like Moritz's novel, Maimon's autobiography, that fiction of the Eastern Jew, remains a fragment.

It was the very fragmentary nature of the autobiography, coupled with the superficial sense of progress that it generates, that made the work so very attractive to both Jew and Christian during the nineteenth and twentieth centuries. It seemed to prove that even Polish Jews could become civilized members of a Western culture.

Indeed, Maimon states that Polish Jews are even more likely to become enlightened than are German Jews, since they have so far to come (194). But the fiction of this progress and its reason, Maimon's own sense of being perceived as an outsider no matter what he undertook, reveal that the reception of Maimon's autobiography was owing largely to the need to see the status of Western Jewry as innately higher than that of some other group. This group was, however, not random. It was the Eastern Jew, the Jew living on the peripheries of civilization, among the barbarians of the East.

The third and final example taken from the Eastern Jews attracted to the German Enlightenment is Isashar Falkensohn Behr, born in 1746 in Salatin, Lithuania, "in a sad little corner of the world among his repressed and half-wild coreligionists," at least according to his German contemporaries.[106] Concerning Behr and his life in enlightened Germany, there is a series of major documents that chronicle his acculturation. The first and most revealing one is a detailed letter from Karl Lessing to his brother dated July 11, 1771, in which Karl Lessing records his meeting with Behr. He recounts that Behr had by then been in Berlin for about three years, having fled there not speaking a word of German. Bad business choices in Königsberg had isolated him in that city, and he had decided to remain there and study at the university. He had begun to learn German there from a mathematical textbook. In Königsberg he had been recommended to Mendelssohn and thus had appeared in Berlin. Lessing notes that he could not speak any German and that he was forced to communicate with him by means of the bits of Latin that he knew. "Now he writes a good German, understands Latin and French, and is no stranger in Mathematics, Philosophy, and Medicine. If he continues, he will accomplish much."[107]

Indeed he did. He continued his studies in Leipzig and then in Halle, where he received his doctorate in medicine in 1772. In that same year, he published one of the most visible works written by an Eastern Jew in the Germany of the late eighteenth century, the volume *Poems of a Polish Jew*. This volume of poetry, much like Maimon's autobiography two decades later, attracted the attention of his contemporaries, an attention to which we shall presently return. Behr's poetry, unlike that of Kuh, was the product of his leisure hours. It formed his escape from his medical studies and was, therefore, not the single focus of his self-definition. But like Kuh, he saw in his poetry the means to establish himself as a man of letters. Indeed, his poetry had been published anonymously in the *Almanac of the German Muses* (1771), where the editor had greeted it as possessing "naiveté, gentleness, and delicacy."[108] It is the first of this trio of attributes that will concern us. Even though Schiller was later to restructure the nature of aesthetic perception into "naive" and "sentimental" modes, the term *naive* had, for the mid- and late eighteenth century, something both attractive and pejorative. The simple songs of the peasant were the product not only of their naiveté but also of the fact that they could not avail themselves of more complicated literary forms. Here the image is of the noble savage writing in the forms of civilized man. During the eighteenth century, black writers in Europe and North America were often labeled naive. Eastern Jews were naive and had the capability to be reshaped within civilized and civilizing structures.

His poems having been received with this positive reaction by writers such as Ramler, it was evident that Behr would publish his poetry. He could have published these poems simply as *Poems*, but he chose quite the contrary: to unmask himself in the title he selected, *Poems of a Polish Jew*. In addition, Behr prefaced the collection with a long and detailed account of his intent in publishing such poems at this time under the title that he had selected. The preface, cast in the form of a letter to a friend and the friend's answer, summarizes the conflict that Behr perceived in his poems.[109] It is a conflict between the intent of the author, a Polish Jew, and the banality of the poetry. How can a Polish Jew, he writes in the introduction, write German poetry? The very title of his volume presents concepts "which have not stood together for a thousand years," that is, Western poetry and the Eastern Jew. He asks the reader to dismiss the stereotype of the Eastern Jew, "clad in black, face obscured, dark of mien, and raw of voice" (9), and read his poems. It is not in "raw" Yiddish that his poems are written, but in poetic German. Behr also adapts a very specific, though formulaic, image of his ideal reader. She is the "gentle readeress." And the poet asks for her acceptance for this volume of poetry dealing with love and flirtations, composed in the rococo mode. His sole goal is to please her. He is able to do this in spite of his barbaric nature:

> You gentle one,
> Have no false image!
> I am not wild,
> But perhaps even beautiful!

(11)

Echoing other eighteenth-century images of the voices supplied to other marginal men, such as William Blake's little black boy, who complains, "And I am Black, but O! my soul is white," this is the voice of the living stereotype of marginality. For Behr cloyingly casts himself in the role of the inarticulate noble savage, the savage for whom the European author usually supplied the voice.

Behr's poetry is consciously conservative. He avoids the new literary tradition of his immediate contemporaries such as Herder, Hölty, or Klopstock and recalls in his verse the older rococo tradition associated with Halle, that of Uz, Gleim, and Götz. These poets, to whom Behr makes reference in his introduction, were viewed as hopelessly old-fashioned by 1772. Their pale pseudoclassical images of shepherds and shepherdesses at play in the groves of arcadia were seen by their contemporaries as out of style. Behr calls upon this older tradition, even while using terms and ideas— such as his fascination with Frederick the Great—that were much more those of his contemporaries, since through accepted modes of expression he felt that he could be accepted within the tradition of German letters. He wished to be identified, not with the young radicals in German poetry, but rather with the staid and accepted tradition against which his contemporaries strove. He calls his persona Menophilus, the lover of song, in the classical tradition, setting himself apart from the tradition that denies the Jew aesthetic sensibility. Status for Behr would have been acceptance, by his fabled female reader, as part of the older tradition of German poetry. As the conservative German poet Boie wrote shortly before the publication of Behr's poetry: "The poems of the Lithuanian are now to be published. You are right, the Jewish Nation promises much, if it once awakens."[110]

Behr's poetry is indistinguishable from other mediocre poetry written in imitation of the masters of the German rococo. But Behr intended it to be so, as he states in his introduction. Three poems stand out as texts that could not have been written by Behr's models. They are an ode to Mendelssohn, one on his native province, and an ode, "modeled after a Hebrew ode," on the arrival of the Prussian Prince Heinrich in Königsberg. These three texts differ in content from the rest of Behr's verse, which deals, as rococo verse does, with the flirtations of paper figures. The ode to Prince Heinrich simply repeats the strong identification that Behr (and other Jewish writers of the period) had with the institution of the Prussian state. The ode to Mendelssohn, dated April 15, 1770, provides the Maskilim's image of Mendelssohn as the unconquerable hero braving the "thorns" of Christian bigotry as none of his coreligionists had ever dared to do. The ode presents the apotheosis of Mendelssohn as one of the immortals of Olympus, an image that fits well with the status accorded Mendelssohn in the German enlightened pantheon. The third ode, to Courland, stresses the German contribution to the life of that Baltic province. What is striking is that even such topics, which would seem to demand a specific opinion from the "Polish Jew" of the title, pass by with comments identical to those of Behr's non-Jewish models. Behr's claim that he is offering no more than "old wine in old bottles" holds up to critical scrutiny. And yet one must ask why Behr's program is so constructed and why his poems are so limited to the literal fulfillment of his program.

Behr was a "Polish Jew" who desired the status of a German intellectual. He also desired the economic status of a profession—medicine—for which he trained in Halle. The great lights of German poetry, prior to the revolution begun by Klopstock and the Göttingen brotherhood, were inhabitants of Halle. They also represented the establishment of a tradition of letters. Become a member of one establishment, undertake the training for another, and you will become a member of the inner circle. And yet such an acceptance would demand that Behr disguise his poetry as that of a man of letters, not that of a Polish Jew. Here the category of naiveté again comes into play. Behr could demand a position within the status of the German men of letters, if, like the black poets of his day, he could argue that he had entered into the world of letters a blank slate upon which the muse had written. The idea of the natural man who acquires the tools of expression and then presents works of great beauty runs quite counter to the traditional view of eighteenth-century aesthetics, which denies the wild man any sense of the beautiful at all.

Behr's poetry was read by his contemporaries as the work of the naive poet *par excellence*. A contemporary critic, K. A. Kütner, commented that Behr's poetry had the "old German tone of our best poets of songs, laughing pictures and coyness and innocent naiveté."[111] But it was in a review published in the *Frankfurt Intelligencer* shortly after the volume's publication in 1772 that Behr's volume came to serve an exemplary function. For the volume was reviewed by the young Johann Wolfgang von Goethe, and his essay on the volume was to become one of the most telling (and most often quoted) statements on the nature of aesthetic acculturation in the eighteenth century.

Goethe's critique of Behr is based almost exclusively on a polar reversal of the image of the Eastern Jew found in the Haskalah.[112] It is a reversal made possible by the existence of a counterstereotype in the form of the noble savage. But, of course, the noble savage also has his problems. Goethe expects "a fiery spirit, a feeling heart" that perceives the world quite differently than does the normal inhabitant of Germany. Like the blind boy suddenly given sight, the favorite analogy of eighteenth-century aesthetics, the Polish Jew coming to the West must see the realities of the world in a different perspective than do those who are constantly at home in this world.[113] And yet, Goethe complains, none of this unique perspective is to be found in Behr's poetry. On the contrary, the poems read as if they had been written by a Christian student of belles-lettres. He mocks the self-description of the poet, in the poem whose first stanza is quoted above, as wearing a powdered wig, having a shaven face, and clothed in a green coat with gold trim. Here is the Jew as poet in disguise as Lessing's traveler! But the core of Goethe's review, the section to which no commentator has made reference, is an elaborate aside. Condemning the faded colors of Behr's poetry, its paean to a weak, unemotional idea of love, Goethe launches into a description of the true relationship between man and woman. It revolves around the intense attraction of one for the other, has its locus in the home, and is the ideal of romantic love set in bourgeois terms. Goethe attacks Behr as not naive enough to see the inherent truths of such relationships, as spending his time and effort describing a world that cannot and should not exist. Goethe's stress on the healthful rather than the artificial, on the modern rather than the accepted, is but another manner of indicating that noble savages should stick to that which they know best, the naive. For Goethe sees Behr's poetry not as naive but as jaded. He demands that the Jew perceive the world in a new manner, a manner different from that of the Christian West. It is true that he casts this demand within new Lockean aesthetics, which see aesthetic perception as learned rather than intrinsic (thus his oblique reference, in the opening line of the review, to learning to see). The charge is still the same, however: Jews, especially those who come from the barbaric East, perceive the world differently. Goethe's critique of Behr is not a philo-Semitic one, as some have claimed, attacking the artificiality of Behr's surface acceptance of antiquated literary standards; it is simply the old canard in new dress.[114]

Behr's life, like that of Kuh and Maimon, follows a negative trajectory. He returns to the East, to Courland, where he practices medicine. But he makes at least one more attempt to enter the refined world of German intellectual company. In 1781 he moves to St. Petersburg and attempts to enter the closed world of German expatriates, who, like the German merchant-poet Ludwig Heinrich von Nicolay, had established an enlightened circle on the fringes of the Russian court. Nicolay writes to a correspondent in Germany at the beginning of May 1781 that "for a little while we have had here a third German poet, a Jew, Dr. Isaschar Behr, who has a very naive character but, as can be imagined, has little experience of the world."[115] Soon thereafter Behr leaves St. Petersburg and the role of the pet noble savage behind and vanishes into history. No trace can be found of his future life except that he returned to his native province, where one can assume that he continued to practice medicine.

Behr's problems in creating for himself a new and workable identity out of the status of the physician and that of the gentleman-poet were manifest. Central to these problems was the question of the nature of the Jew's perception of the world. Since according to Enlightenment dogma it is only cultural differences that divide men, bridging these differences would provide even such rare finds as the poetry-writing Eastern Jew (or black) with access to a new, culturally approved identity. But the problem was that early training so predisposed one's perception that in later life one still remained outside of acceptable standards; one remained naive or, in Goethe's view, became banal. Behr's verse was seen primarily as the work of one whose differences were so insurmountable that they themselves became interesting. Behr's flight back into the world of the Eastern European Jew was an attempt to create for himself a niche in a society where he would appear to the indigenous inhabitants to be the epitome of the physician-poet in the Enlightenment model. Perhaps he accomplished this. In the German circles in St. Petersburg, however, he again became the Jew masquerading as the German poet.

Kuh, Maimon, and Behr were three Eastern Jews who accepted the German as well as the German-Jewish promise of acculturation as a means to social acceptance and status. All three articulated their desire for this status within the norms of literary expression of their day: Kuh in using the strict form of neoclassical verse; Maimon in adapting the psychological novel for his own ends; and Behr in selecting the conservative form of German rococo verse (and its implicit world view). The mode of articulation was in each man's case determined by the demands of the world about him. It ranged from the most avant-garde (in Maimon's autobiography) to the most conservative (in Behr's poetry). But all three attempted to use the status attached to the form of their literary production as a means of cementing their position in German and German-Jewish society. All failed. Kuh lapsed into madness, Maimon into alcoholism and poriomania; and Behr fled back into that world in which the fragility of his new persona would not be evident. All three represent failed attempts to craft an integrated identity out of fragments of the German-Jewish self. These attempts failed, for the German Jews had, by the closing decades of the eighteenth century, localized the source of their anxiety about their own status. It was located in the East, where the Eastern Jews were seen as the reification of the German anti-Semitic stereotype. When living examples of Eastern European Jewry suddenly materialized and took on the appearance, attitudes, and language of Germans, this caused a slippage in the localization, a slippage that was corrected by labeling these cases as permanent outsiders. And it is to this double sense of status anxiety, in German as well as in German-Jewish society, to which the Eastern European Jews, such as those discussed, reacted.

CHAPTER FOUR

The Drive for Assimilation

I

The Secret Tongue of the Jews

Within a generation of the granting of civil emancipation to the Jew, German society had created a new language that it attributed to the Jew. Neither Hebrew nor Yiddish, not even the fantastic Hebrew-German mixture in which the Jews' oaths were written, it was called *mauscheln*. The early nineteenth-century Germans used *mauscheln* (sometimes called *jüdeln*, "to jew") to characterize the manner in which they heard Jews speaking with a Yiddish accent. *Mauscheln* is a German word based on the proper name Moishe.[1] It appeared as early as the Thirty Years' War in a 1622 broadside directed against *Christian* minters of bad coins. In its first use (as with the first uses of the word *jüdeln*) this word referred specifically to the actions of Jews. In the 1622 broadside Christian coiners were said to speak in *mauscheln* when they took bills of exchange. Here *mauscheln* clearly means to extort usurious interest *in the manner of a Jew*. By the beginning of the nineteenth century its meaning had shifted and referred to the discourse as well as the actions of the Jew. The language of the Jew began to serve as a *pars pro toto* for the Jew. The Jews' language, which became symbolic for their perceived essence as liars, falsifiers, and merchants, was captured in *mauscheln*.

What, then, is *mauscheln*? It is the use of altered syntax and bits of Hebrew vocabulary and a specific pattern of gestures to represent the spoken language of the Jews. What is stressed is the specifically "Jewish" intonation, the mode of articulation as well as the semantic context. This understanding of the way that Jews speak (and therefore act and think) can perhaps best be seen in the plays of the popular Berlin playwright Julius von Voss.

Voss used Jewish characters throughout his work and presented their macaronic language as a means of evoking laughter. Nowhere is this more telling than in his literary parody of Lessing's *Nathan the Wise*, published in 1804.[2] Where Lessing's Nathan speaks the language of reason, without any need for the corrupt language of human and therefore prejudiced society, Voss's Nathan speaks within the tradition of the newly assimilated Jew—in *mauscheln*. But the language that Voss attributes to Nathan is quite remarkable. His *mauscheln* is broken German spoken with a stage Yiddish accent, with bits of Hebrew thrown in for effect. Such a language would have been completely incomprehensible to his German audience, so Voss supplies footnotes for each Hebraism. The idea of special knowledge, here on the part of the playwright, gives him special status in interpreting the language of the Jews (and also the language of the Jews' actions, for Nathan is a complete parody of the selfless figure in Lessing's play).

The use of dialect is not limited to the Jews. In a conflict between two sharp traders in Voss's one-act comedy *The Jew and the Greek*,[3] both Jew and Greek speak with a heavy accent and with some use of foreign words. These phrases are thrown in for effect and in no way affect the audience's comprehension of the speakers' message. Voss's Lessing parody clearly was written as a drama to be read—thus the footnotes—while his later drama of the feuding merchants was meant to be performed. But in neither case was Voss's intent "anti-Jewish," at least not consciously. For he writes in the long introduction to his *Nathan*: "I ask only of the right good company of the Jews: that just because I have parodied Lessing's *Nathan*, that I not be considered among their enemies. The *loschon kaudesch*' ['holy language'] and certain uses of the home cannot be objected to by Israelites, for they are but leavings of their fathers" (xiii).

Voss is careful to remove himself from the charge of being reactionary in regard to the emancipation and acculturation of the Jews. He labels their signs of difference as "leftovers" from the age before emancipation. But what are these signs? They are primarily the language of the Jews, their magical language, which still served to characterize them in 1804. In Voss's later work, such as his *Joel Potsdammer's Flight from the Pigtail to the Royal Medal* (1817), he stressed the Jews' linguistic malleability, their naturally given talent to mimic the language (and the rhetoric) of the world in which they find themselves.[4] For Voss and his world, the world of the first generation of Germans to have to deal with Jews who spoke, acted, and thought like themselves, it was necessary to maintain a stage German Jew who was inherently different and whose difference was centered in language and discourse. Within the course of Voss's career, the qualities ascribed to the Jew, as seen from the perspective of those who perceived themselves as liberal on the issue of Jewish emancipation, were altered from the stereotypes of the stage Jew from the past. Figures such as Voss's Nathan or his Jewish merchant could no longer exist even within the fictionalized world of German Jewry if the author were to consider himself a liberal. Voss's last play again takes up Jewish characters, all of whom speak in *mauscheln*, but it takes place in the East, in Cracow.

Mauscheln was a quality of language and discourse that Jews perceived as a major problem in their true and total acceptance within the German community. In a work written in the most flowing academic German, the prolific popular philosopher and educator Anton Ree commented on the language of the Jews (1844).[5] Ree's book, written during the striving for acculturation at mid-century, provides a case study of the strength that the idea of *mauscheln* had for the German-speaking Jew. Initially, Ree was confronted with the question of what to call this problem. He recognizes that "Jews speak their mother tongue in such a way so as to make them noticeable as Jews" but searches for a name. He never mentions the terms *mauscheln* and *jüdeln* (except to say that there are "insulting terms" for this manner of speech). So Ree settles on "the Jewish dialect," paralleling Jewish speech to other German dialects, such as Low German, and therefore condemning them.

For the striving in the nineteenth century was for uniformity, at least in language, as long as political unification was not achieved. Ree states quite baldly that it is Germany, not Prussia or Hannover or Hamburg, that is the "fatherland" and that German, not regional dialects, must dominate. It is only with a shift away from *mauscheln* that Jewish economic and social status will be improved, that the Jews will achieve "culture." For according to Ree, *mauscheln* is a "sick" language (15), and it is language that determines the true nature of the human being. Thus the Jews are "sick" as long as they speak in *mauscheln*. And Ree takes this quite literally. He sees in the pronunciation of German by the Jews a pathognomic sign of a "specific modification of their organs of speech" (78). Thus Jews mispronounce Hebrew as well as German. This maladaptation of the organs of speech is the result of the isolation of the Jews; it is an acquired characteristic that can be altered once the Jews are treated like everyone else, once specifically Jewish schools are eliminated, once Jews are integrated into society. Then Jews will begin to speak correctly, and this will alter the physical basis for their *mauscheln*.

This rather bizarre attempt from the Jewish point of view to comprehend the nature of *mauscheln*, a creation of the German perception of the Jew, places the source of this "inability" to speak correctly in the isolation and inbreeding of the Jews and sees its solution in the integration of the Jews into German society. This comes from the pen of a Jew who was clearly integrated into the German world, a writer who saw in the perceived misuse by his coreligionists of German a source, if not *the* source, of their status as cultural pariahs. Ree's view, especially his theory of the Jews' malformed organs of speech, is clearly a radical attempt to see the hidden language of the Jews as the result of the isolation of the Jews. It is merely a "scientific" restatement of Hamann's view of the biological origin of the "hidden language" of the Jews. It places it, however, in the world of physical illness, which can be cured.

The basic structure of Ree's perception of the "hidden language" of the Jews dominates the discourse about the Jews' language in the mid-nineteenth century, not merely within the anti-Jewish rhetoric of the period but also within the philo-Judaic text. Julius von Voss's quasi liberalism is but a qualified conservative position; Ernest Renan must be viewed as a true liberal in terms of the pre-1848 definition of the term. However, Renan's prize-winning monograph *The History of the Semitic Languages* (1847) is dominated by the concept that Hebrew was the inviolable reflex of the innate nature of the Jews.[6] It is unimportant that Renan glorifies this relationship, seeing in Hebrew that language which best expresses the "monotheism of the desert." In his essay on the origin of language (1848) Renan provides the theoretical underpinning for his views. He sees language as the articulation of the intuitive creation of the collective rather than the individual. Hebrew is thus the reflex of the Jews, but the Jews of the desert, not of the city. Renan thus postulates an unstated alienation of the Jews' language from its wellspring, seeing in Christianity the present-day completeness of the language of the Jews. Unlike Ree, Renan does not provide for any agency that would permit the adaptation of the Jews into the world of the present except as speakers of the discourse of the Christian.

It is in the discourse of those Jews who have identified with the Christian attitudes toward the hidden language of the Jews that the assumption concerning the absolute relationship between perception and the articulation of perception takes place. In a pamphlet written in the 1830s and evidently aimed at a German-speaking Jewish audience, for the edification and conversion of the reader the tale is told of the remarkable conversion of a Jewish pawnbroker.[7] A student goes to the Jew and pawns two books: a Hebrew Bible and a Greek New Testament, which is printed with a facing German translation. The Jew takes the books and reads the New Testament in German in order to reify his "enmity against Christ" so that he can go to the synagogue and mock him. In reading the German text he is converted and is suddenly aware of having been "blind, simple, and stupid." He reads the text three times, eventually purchases the book from the student, and converts. The German book serves as the means of conversion, and through the power of the text the Jew moves from being a mocking, blind reader to being a seeing reader. This exemplary conversion is accomplished through the power of the book and shifts the rhetoric of the Jew from mockery to sympathy for the crucified Christ. He leaves the discourse of the synagogue, that inherent to the world of the Jew, and enters into the discourse of the New Testament. And yet the pamphlet ends with an overtly "Jewish" act, the purchasing of the New Testament from the student, who initially believes this to be yet another "Jewish trick." The Jew cannot alter his manner of seeing the world as consisting of purchasable commodities, including faith. This aspect of the discourse of the Jew is retained and turned, through a rhetorical device, into an acknowledgment of the power of Christianity. The Jew has been moved part of the way to insight through the exposure to the magic of the German text; it is presumed that he can make the entire conversion. And yet there remains the association of the older language of the Jew, the language and discourse of commerce, within the image of conversion. That remains untouched.

If we turn to an account of the actual conversion of a Jew during this period, we find a complexity of self-definition that is rooted in the idea of a hidden language of the Jew. August Lewald, born in 1792, published his *Memoirs of a Banker* in 1836.[8] In it he recounts his conversion to Catholicism in Vienna through the influence of the Jewish convert Johann Emanuel Veith. Lewald tells of the intellectual reasons for his conversion and links his conversion to Catholicism with his decision to abandon trade and become a writer: "Why did I become a Christian? Why did I give up trade? Why did I push myself into a strange caste, buy a fine, great house, undertake travel, seek acquaintances, make contacts? Why all this? I wanted to become someone else, but did I succeed?" When Lewald seeks to answer this question, the metaphor that springs to mind is that of language: "'As long as you think German, you will never speak like a Frenchman' is the rule of the language teacher, and as long as you think like a Jew, you will never be Christian." Lewald's ambiguity about his linguistic identity was raised only in the sphere of his identity as a Jew. He spoke German as his first language. And yet Jews do not speak German; they have a "hidden" *mauscheln* which is the reflex of their being Jews. When Lewald thinks of being Jewish, it is in these terms, terms that contradict the image of himself as a German writer. He links his Jewish identity, his role as a banker, his Jewish discourse, and his thinking like a Jew and sees them as immutable, even through the act of baptism. While he has removed himself from the world of the Jews, he still sees himself as being perceived as part of that world. When he no longer can withstand the pressures and capitulates to his identification of himself as a Jew, he takes himself to a "so-called German-Israelite Temple," one of the reformed synagogues in Germany that had patterned their language and the structure of their service after that of the Evangelical Church:

> What I found here could be called great progress: I heard an illuminating talk, in pure German, and listened to lovely music from voices and instruments. What a difference between this impression and that confusing, deafening noise of my childhood, the impression made upon me by the unintelligible humming of the Jewish service. . . . The decorous congregation, in the most attractive holiday clothing, the fine tone, which was to be found throughout, contributed to raising the effect of the entire service measurably.
>
> Only the religiosity was missing! . . . Your old Jehova understood you for centuries and was not tired hearing you when you prayed to him. But no matter how powerful German is, and how good it sounds in the modern ear, you should not have sacrificed the old language of the Lord.

Being Jewish and sounding Jewish are linked with acting Jewish. In Lewald's description the synagogue bears a close resemblance to the stock market. The language of trade and the language of the Jews are linked, and the German author, August Lewald, distanced himself from both. He also distanced himself from the charge that the Jews have simply retained their inherent nature while choosing a new linguistic mask, that of the Christian service. Jews should remain Jews, especially in their language, since their language and their discourse are one. Lewald sees all of this through a discourse mired in a sentimental nostalgia for a world from which he has consciously distanced himself. Only in understanding this world as distanced, both in the past (and replaced in the present by a new, "Christianized" world) and geographically (in Germany, not in Vienna), can he see it as nostalgic. It is nostalgia for a world that Lewald wishes would vanish completely. He gives us his earlier impressions of the language of the Jews as represented in what is for him the most Jewish of structures, the communal services, and sees the conversion of this discourse into German as unsuccessful, but unsuccessful only in the sense that it is inappropriate. He has projected his own sense of the true language of the Jews onto these unconverted Jews and uses his own text, his "autobiography of a banker now a writer," to show that he has been divorced from the false rhetoric of the synagogue. His conversion, from merchant to writer, from Jew to Catholic, is a real conversion, and yet there remains always in his description a hidden doubt. Much like the converted Jew in the pamphlet, converted by the power of a German book, Lewald is a convert through the power of language; he is a convert from an unacceptable discourse to another, more acceptable one, and yet the traces of the former discourse remain and are projected onto another world of Jews. This step, unnecessary for the Christian pamphleteer, marks the Jewish reaction to the act of conversion.

Another shift in the metaphor for the language of the Jews appears in the early nineteenth century. *Mauscheln*, while it changes from a term used to characterize the actions of the Jews to one used to characterize their language, retains its sense that the Jews both perceive the world differently and articulate this difference through their language. In the role of the Jew as writer this metaphor is continued. It is not in the world of higher letters, in the writings of a Herz or Mendelssohn, that one has the image of the Jews' writing as decadent and lying (though the reviews of these writers are often laced with surprise at their intellectual ability and honesty); rather it is in the rise of journalism at the beginning of the nineteenth century that the image of the Jew and the image of the journalist begin to be intermingled.

The image of the Grub Street journalist, the individual who will write anything for payment, appears in the German-speaking lands at the beginning of the nineteenth century. Certainly no German would have considered labeling Goethe a liar because he edited a journal. But the journals of the mid-nineteenth century were quite different from their predecessors. They were more involved in the politics of cultural life and court intrigue and were more open to external financial pressures. There grew up an image of these newspapermen as dishonest, bribable, liars, and Jews. The journalist, like the Jew, does not have an aesthetic sensibility. Indeed, journalistic language is the antithesis of the beautiful; it is the ugly, the base. It is like the comic macaronics of *mauscheln* but even more so, for as Georg Simmel has pointed out, in the dialectical relationship between journalists and their audience lies the wellspring of modern journalism. Like the magician, journalists manipulate their audience through their command of language. While they may appear to be shaping their audience, they are base in that they pander to it. They direct opinion, but only by undertaking to guess "what the tendencies of the multitude are."[9] For the German reader of the early nineteenth century the journalist and the Jew were identical, and indeed they merged in the best-known figure of popular journalism of the opening decades of the century, M. G. Saphir.[10]

Saphir was born in 1795 in a village near Pest. His first language was Yiddish, which he learned in a Hungarian milieu. In 1806 he was sent to study the Talmud in Prague, a study that he later attacked as the combination of "intellectual ability and ignorance, of cleverness and superficiality, of knowledge and frivolity."[11] In Prague he was introduced to German (and Western) letters by a Jesuit, so that by the time of his return to Hungary he had a command of German as well as French. His life became a series of wanderings, first to Vienna, then to Berlin, and then to Munich. He founded and edited newspapers and journals, worked as a free-lance critic, and was constantly in conflict with the higher literary world. In Berlin there was a much-publicized exchange with the literary lights of the city, including Willibald Alexis and Friedrich Baron de la Motte Fouqué, concerning the persecutory tone of Saphir's theater reviews. What his contemporaries loathed in his writing was its Jewish tone, which they defined as nihilistic satire. In the major pamphlet attacking him the charge was made in a transparent rhetoric: "This confusion of languages is much worse than the insults aimed at individuals of honor. Criticism has fallen into the hands of those who have *nothing to lose.*"[12] The italicized phrase represents yet another way of labeling the journalists as Jews, whose language lies outside of the accepted system of discourse and whose sole desire is to destroy the cultural discourse that they can never truly join. These critics are linguistic revolutionaries (the pamphlet labels Saphir one of the "literary sansculottists"), echoes of the identity of that other world, the world of the French Revolution, with which the Jews are also associated. Their very claim to linguistic parity with the Germans is viewed as destabilizing in the sense of the superior attitude of French culture toward the cultural discourse of the Germans.

Saphir became the Jewish journalist *par excellence*, the writer for "lying newspapers," able to be bribed, attacking for the pure pleasure of his Jewish vindictiveness. During the 1820s Saphir was trying to enter the mainstream of the German cultural scene. He attempted to convert to Protestantism but was rejected, as Pastor Theremin wrote, because of his editorship of "satiric journals," since such writing ran contrary to the "love and belief" demanded of true Christians.[13] After a four-year delay, Saphir was baptized, in 1832, and from Moses Saphir he became Carl Friedrich Moritz Gottlieb Saphir.

Saphir considered his Jewishness, like that of his contemporaries Börne and Heine, with whom he associated himself (and with whom he is often associated), as a "birth defect," which he righted as quickly as possible. This birth defect, like Ree's congenital speech defect of the Jews, was an error of nature, one that, however, could and would be corrected by humans. Saphir perceived the Jews' language as *mauscheln*.[14] Here is the creation of one labeled as a Jew, whose punning criticism was understood as the writing of a Jew, writing in a specifically Jewish mode of satire, attacking the rootless and languageless Jews as beings quite separate from himself. As a journalist, however, Saphir remains the Jew as writer. When Saphir writes his memoirs, his mother and his beloved grandfather retrospectively speak perfect, literary German. The idealized figures of youth, who spoke Yiddish, now speak literary German; the stereotyped Jews, in their rootlessness, speak *mauscheln*. This is, of course, a reversal of Saphir's own biography. For it is Saphir, the literate, converted, cultured journalist, who is forced to wander. It is of little surprise that one of the pamphlets directed against the Jew Saphir, written by the German Romantic critic Friedrich von den Hagen, calls Saphir, Heine, and Börne "wandering Jews."[15] They are wandering Jews not only in their apparent rootlessness but, what is more important, in their lack of a national language, for as Jews they may speak and write German, but their true language is journalese, which relates to literary or aesthetically pleasing German in the same way as does *mauscheln*. They are but two faces of the debasement of language.

The beginning of the nineteenth century saw the development of a further characterization of the Jews' language. On the more primitive level, Jews speak *mauscheln*. Their accent or intonation reveals them as Jews. This association remains throughout the nineteenth century. At mid-century A. Bahn, a popular dramatist, has one of his comic Jews say about Italians: "They all look nebbich eppes Jewish and whatabout by pronunciation of de language, by God, they don't note by birth at all. The best christ Germans don't speak no better than me."[16] This, of course, all in the heaviest *mauscheln*, but without the use of Yiddishisms, which had driven Voss, forty years earlier, to present a scholarly apparatus with his parody of Lessing's *Nathan the Wise*. The association of the various labels of the discourse of difference associated with the Jews is clear during the early nineteenth century. Bahn's use of an idiolect labeled Jewish is no more powerful in labeling the discourse of the Jew than the use by Saphir's opponents of the label "nihilistic satirist." Both set the Jew apart from the language of the world of acceptable German discourse. What has happened over the fifty years since the first generation of emancipated German Jews is that the sense of exoticism stressed by Voss has given way to a general assumption of the inherent difference of the language of the Jews, a difference not to be defined in terms of the inexplicable or magical nature of the Jew but tied to the Jews' familiarity. It is the contempt for the Jews' desire to become a part of the system, to abandon their difference, their exoticism, their magic, that dominates the discourse of anti-Semitism during the beginning of the nineteenth century and determines to a specific degree the response of Jews who employ the societal definition of the limits inherent in the language of the Jews in their definition of themselves as German writers.

II
The Rhetoric of Self-hatred: Börne

The dividing line between the first generation of emancipated Jews and the second is a historical accident.[17] In 1796 an artillery shell fired by besieging French troops breached the walls of the Frankfurt Ghetto, and like the walls of Jericho, the walls, which maintained the Jews within a strict definition of Jewish identity imposed by the Christian world, fell. But just as the emancipation of the first generation of Jews was for some a faulty adjustment to a fictional world, so, too, the liberation of the German Jews by the military forces of France turned out to be chimerical. Not only were the French extremely hesitant to grant the Jews under their dominion civil rights, as they were slow to grant them to the Germans, but the eventual fall of the French domination over the Rhineland caused extremely retrogressive attitudes on the part of the reconquering German troops. For even though the Jews in the occupied areas for the most part strongly identified with their "German" identity, the overall image of the Jew was as a radical, a Jacobin. The association of the Jews, already branded as foreign in the German consciousness, with the foreignness of the French complicated the question of identity, coupled as it still was with the sense of language. For as German was to have vanquished French in the German Enlightenment, no matter what Frederick the Great thought of German, the militant power of Germany vanquished the effete French on the battlefield. But the Jews—the Jews who had begun to speak German rather than Yiddish as their primary language—and their language were seen as "Frenchified."

The struggle for a German linguistic identity for the German Jews can be seen in the careers of three major literary figures of the next generation of German Jews, three figures who strove through assimilation and conversion to adapt themselves to the demands of the German-speaking world for an acceptable identity. These three—Ludwig Börne, Heinrich Heine, and Karl Marx—provide detailed case studies of the power that the double bind had in the early nineteenth-century evolution of a German-Jewish identity. It is clear from the masses of material on these three writers that a long monograph would be necessary to deal with the complexity of each of these figures. Here, three aspects of the creative lives of Börne, Heine, and Marx have been selected that amply illustrate the shifts in identity and the centrality of language in the shaping of the definition of self.

Ludwig Börne was born Judah Löw Baruch in the Frankfurt Ghetto in 1786, the son of a "court Jew" who functioned as a banker in the Rhineland.[18] His language was Yiddish, although he evidently learned German from tutors as a child. At sixteen he traveled to Berlin and lived in the home of Marcus Herz, the physician-philosopher. His studies took him to Heidelberg, where he was suddenly struck by the disparity between the promise of emancipation and the reality of life as a Jew in a Christian setting. At seventeen he mused on the strength of his native language and the value it might have for the Germans:

> The Jewish words *mies* ["rotten"], *schlemiel*, and more cannot be expressed in German. One should accept them and give them citizenship. It would cost much effort for those who have no contact with Jews to explain the concepts that relate to these words. I do not know how one could.[19]

These musings, jotted down at six o'clock in the morning, reveal how closely the negative and the positive sense of self are related to the sense of language. Börne selects two words, *mies* and *schlemiel*, both of which had been accepted into the German thieves' cant by the eighteenth century, as indicative of the power of Yiddish to express things unexpressible in German. But what things—the rottenness of life in the ghetto and the essence of the Jew. It is precisely these qualities that the young Börne wishes to see "civilized," given citizenship in the only true German state, the German language. And Börne relates the essence of language to the essence of the Jews, for one cannot understand the very concepts represented by these words, these negative labels for Jewish identity, if one does not relate these terms to the Jews and their worlds.

In 1807, four years after writing the diary entry cited above, Börne wrote a detailed essay on the Frankfurt Ghetto (1:7–11). The young Börne returns to the scenes of his youth and is struck dumb with horror by the nature of the ghetto. Everything is so dark and closed and limited. After seven years away from the Jewish quarter of Frankfurt, seven years spent in cities with emancipated Jewish populations or in university towns where large numbers of Jews did not live, Börne returns to his home city and to the image of the Jew and the Jews' language, which he had begun to articulate in the diary entry cited above. In that entry there was still a sense of ambiguity, seeing in the language of the Jews, in the reflection of their essence, some value, even if the value revealed itself to be a negative one. The darkness and blindness of the Frankfurt Jews, as perceived by Börne in 1807, permitted no such positive evaluation. Darkness is the theme of his essay "The Jews in Frankfurt." Their streets are dark, and this is a "symbol of the spiritual culture of the Jews." But the darkness of the former ghetto in Frankfurt is present in one specific quality, in the language of the Jews. Börne makes a specific distinction between the language of the younger Jews, his contemporaries, and the language of the elders, a distinction that is more than slightly reminiscent of the split in sign value of language in Euchel's *Reb Hennoch*. For the younger Jews he meets are "witty." They are "the young sons of Mercury" over whose lips stream "wit and witty observations." Even the young cousin whom Börne wishes to impress with his medical knowledge "wishes to find a satiric sense" in that which he says.

But it is the superficiality of these "witty" youngsters in which Börne revels. One young man is remarkable because he has read Anacharsis and Gibbon but has never read Lessing's *Nathan the Wise*: "This is the book that every Jew who makes any claim for education has read a dozen times and raises to the heavens as the most beautiful work of art even if he does not understand a word of it and bores himself in reading it" (1:10). Jews have no sense of the beautiful. Whether reflected in their assumption of the languorous pose of the dandy, with his witty repartee, or in the acceptance of standards of the beautiful promulgated by the Christian Enlightenment, the Jews' claim for a new manner of seeing the world is but the acceptance of new lenses ground by a Christian lens grinder. They are not reflections of their inner beings.

Börne contrasts this "wit" and "satire" with the extraordinary seriousness of the elders, who are called together to judge a question of ritual. As with the charges brought against the young scholar in *Reb Hennoch*, the rituals revolve around the question of *kashruth*, ritual purification, especially of food. In *Reb Hennoch* the question is the flaunting of established order through the *public* eating of unclean food; in Börne's essay the elders are debating whether food prepared for Passover is ritually clean if it has come in contact with an object—a playing card—which itself has come in contact with ritually unclean food. The rabbi is asked for his decision, and he presents a *pilpul* in establishing his answer. He argues that the nature of the surface of the object determines the ritual purity of the object: if the printed side of the playing card has touched it, it is clean, since the ink shielded the food from contact. The result is that one of the servants surreptitiously turns over the card.

The contrast in the modes of expression presented in Börne's essay is the key to his understanding of the Jews in the Frankfurt Ghetto. The elders speak in a mode of argument that is serious. This very fact reveals it to be false and the object of satire. Even the serving girl, with her peasant wisdom, knows this and reverses the card. It is the youths who are "witty" and "satiric," like the author of the piece himself. But they are also idle. Here the major distinction between Börne's evolving self-definition and this image of the Jews that he projects into the Frankfurt Ghetto can be seen. For Börne, himself studying medicine and then applied government and political science, sees himself as the antithesis of both the old order and the newly evolving Jews whose central manner of self-definition is their opposition to their elders. In Börne's correspondence with his father during this period there is a remarkable exchange. Börne's father wished his son to study medicine, seeing in this profession the necessary status to remove his son from the stigma of moneylending, his own profession and the hallmark of German Jewry, at least in the eyes of the Germans. Börne begins to study medicine but then decides to continue his studies in political science in order to escape from the ghetto completely. For studying medicine meant practicing among the Jews. Even Marcus Herz, the most prominent example of the Jewish physician admitted to the inner-most circles of Berlin enlightened thought, practiced medicine in the Jewish Hospital in Berlin. Börne wishes to escape the idea of the ghetto, an idea that he accepted from the first generation—a ghetto of the spirit, a ghetto of language and thought—and flee into the "real world," the world of politics. Napoleon's reforms had enabled some Jews to begin to consider the political sphere, and the universities were slowly being opened to Jews who wished to study applied political science. The "real world" was the world of the Christian political establishment. Not the hothouse atmos-phere of the enlightened debating societies of Berlin but the real-ities of actual political life were to be Börne's milieu.

In 1807 Börne decides that he must turn from the study of medicine to the study of government; during the same period he writes his essay on returning to the Frankfurt Ghetto. One must observe that the irony and wit of the essay are a clear indication of the double bind in which he found himself once he returned to the ghetto. In the world of the university he is "Baruch the Jew," as he himself writes.[20] He is clearly differentiated from his Chris-tian fellow students as a Jew. In the Jewish milieu he is a youngster successfully rebelling against his father's demands for his future. He rejects the patriarchal demands for authority over him, both in terms of his own father's wishes and in terms of the Jewish commu-nity's patriarchal demands for obedience. The conflation of these two images in the comical figures of the elders in his essay would seem to necessitate a positive presentation of the youthful figures whom he meets in the ghetto, especially in the light of his use of the same rhetorical mode—satire and irony—that they are using. He perceives them, however, as part of that which he wishes to reject. His younger Jews are idle; their wit is simply an excuse for avoiding any meaningful occupation. It is the same as the *pilpul*, idle intellectual activity that results in no profit.

Börne actually attempted to influence the course of events in the Frankfurt Jewish community. He prepared, at the behest of his father, a document on the proposed new regulations for the Frank-furt Jews.[21] He argued in this document, written in 1807, that even though the Jews did tend to suffer from a "hyperthymia of the merchant and profit addiction," this was the result of their histor-ical situation, and any specific laws aimed at the Jews would only tend to perpetuate this situation. Here Börne picks up a thread in the medicalization of the Jews that existed in Christian attitudes toward the Jews from the Middle Ages through the Enlightenment. Börne argues for the necessary assimilation of the Jews into the body politic (in which he himself wishes to be included) as a cure for this illness. For, he writes, "this is an unusual illness which carries within itself the basis for its own cure." Börne's use of the image of the Jew as patient is not merely hyperbole. He sees in the illness of the Jew the cause of the illnesses of the state, and the emancipation of the Jews as the cure for both parties.

The Enlightenment, as has been discussed, also saw the Jews as especially prone to illness. Like Börne, it also saw this illness as the result of a specific locus, the enforced isolation of the Jews in society. In F. L. de La Fontaine's medical survey of the Prussian provinces of Poland (1792) a separate chapter is given to the medical status of the Jews of Poland.[22] The filthy environment of the Jews, their food, and sexual practices all lead to a catalogue of illnesses from which the Jews suffer, which range from syphilis to conjunctivitis. For La Fontaine's study labels the Jews as ill, more ill than their Christian neighbors. He is able to distinguish between Christian and Jew based on the nature of their patterns of illness. The central etiology for La Fontaine for the illnesses of the Jews is the "all too early marriage in their thirteenth, fourteenth, or fifteenth year with their weak bodies. This takes from them the necessary fluid of life of lasting health. Therefore, a Jew here at forty looks much older than a healthy peasant or citizen at sixty or seventy." It is the sexualization of the Jews that, for La Fontaine, is the source of their illness. Börne sees in the Jews' economic addiction to profit an illness that has its roots in the special role allocated to the Jews. Thus Börne, too, distinguishes between the illnesses to which the Jew and the Christian are prone. He labels certain categories of Jews as diseased and localizes these diseased Jews outside of his definition of self. Unlike La Fontaine, he localizes them not in the East but within a specific class. But the association of the Jews' illness with sexuality, while not overtly present in this text, is present in the subtextual association of illness and sexuality. This will be a major factor in enabling Börne to project the charges of anti-Semitic rhetoric onto yet another group later in his career.

The course of Börne's own attempts to achieve some type of status within the world of politics met with failure. When the French-supported government of Frankfurt fell in 1814, Börne was dismissed from his position in the city civil service. Börne began a life, not as a member of the political establishment, indeed in the service of the city police, but as one defined by the state as an outsider. Already bound by a sense of no longer belonging to the Jewish community, whose world he saw limited by the blindness of the elders and the weakness of the youth, Börne entered that field left open to—in fact defined as the refuge of—the outsider: journalism.[23] The enlightened man of letters functioned within the establishment and received his sense of status from his use of language within the definition of that establishment; the journalist functioned within the broader framework of the establishment, serving as a critic, but a critic within the permissible bounds of censor and court. The first half of the nineteenth century saw a flight of German-Jewish intellectuals into the area of journalism, an area that permitted, indeed encouraged, the use of specific modes of language, including satire and irony, in the overall service of society. Again the limits self-imposed by the satirist in the Enlightenment had become the official policy of the state. But the use of polemical language, language that caught the eye of the reader, was rewarded within this world. Not the *pilpul*, not the wit of the younger Jews, but the ironic polemic of the political journalist becomes the accepted mode of discourse following the fall of the Napoleonic reforms. The fine line between negative aggressiveness and positive criticism is the discourse of the journalist.

In 1816, as a free-lance journalist, Börne authored an essay entitled "For the Jews" opposing the reactionary actions of the Frankfurt city council in attempting to return the Jews to the political status that they had had prior to the French conquest of the city.[24] The Frankfurt Council had abolished the rights of the Jews as "French institutions." Börne argues in this essay that the wars fought to liberate Germany from the French had been fought by Jews as well as Germans. (Indeed, the political orientation of the German Jews was quite opposed to their inherent best interest. They generally supported the German positions, even though ideologically it would have served their cause better to have supported the French. Indeed, the German cause would have been impossible had it not been for the financial support of the Frankfurt Rothschild family.) In this polemic, Börne equates the German loss of freedom under the French (paralleling Fichte's position) with the Jews' loss of freedom.[25] The loss of freedom on both sides makes it imperative that the Jews be granted the same freedom as the Germans. One must remember that arguing a seemingly patriotic line contradicted the inherently anti-Semitic rhetoric of exactly those patriotic writers, such as Fichte, whose views Börne is echoing. In 1816 he wishes to perceive the goals of Germans and Jews as identical, a view not shared by his Christian audience.

Four years later Börne, still called Baruch, attempted to establish his identity as a Jewish journalist writing in German for German (i.e., Christian) audiences. His polemic, only a small part of which has anything to do with the Jews, is directed at exactly those objects that were viewed as appropriate by his Christian counterparts. In 1818 two events occurred that defined Börne's Jewish identity. At the beginning of that year he appealed to the Frankfurt Council for permission to change his name, giving as his reason his desire to write for political and literary periodicals "in a way which would make my religious affiliation unrecognizable, a fact [which has been] standing in the way of my public relying on my writing."[26] The change from Baruch to Börne takes place, and on June 5, 1818, he is baptized as a Lutheran.

A new individual now exists, one on whom the public can rely because he is not immediately perceived as a blind and lying Jew. Indeed, he is no longer a Jew; he is the Lutheran journalist Ludwig Börne. In 1818 yet another moment in Börne's life forces his new identity to seem even more unreal than it did when he accepted it. To understand the background of this moment it is necessary to trace what had happened to the figure of the schlemiel from its appearance in Euchel's play through the post-Napoleonic era.

By the beginning of the nineteenth century *mauscheln* had assumed a specific quality within German consciousness, the comic.[27] With the civil emancipation of the Jews, more and more Jews were coming into social contact with Christians and were speaking German, but with a recognizable accent. This accent became the hallmark of the comic Jews. The contrast between the father and the son in Euchel's play became paradigmatic for the condemnatory attitudes of the Christian intelligentsia toward both the Orthodox (patriarchal) and the assimilationist strands perceived by them as existing among the Jews. Suddenly a literature written in mock Yiddish began to appear. Published in roman letters (not, as Yiddish is, in Hebrew letters), for a Christian audience, this dialect poetry had as its central rationale the presentation of the Jew as the comic figure. It is the same type of satire found in Wolfsohn and Euchel but, of course, with quite a different purpose. For the comic presentation of the Jew has as its intent the undermining of any sense that the Jew could change from that image which dominated the Christian consciousness. The older tradition that language was the marker for the essence of the Jew was continued here. The language was overtly Jewish in that the authors used a mock Yiddish in their writings. Friedrich Freiherr von Holzschuher, writing under the pseudonym Itzig Feitel Stern, authored a series of volumes that, according to Ave-Lallement, represented the first major reappearance of Yiddish in the nineteenth century.[28] The subject matter of all of his works is identical: the narrow-

minded blindness of the Jew. The comic intent of all of these works
was the creation of a Jewish persona, Itzig Feitel Stern, who reveals
his inner nature, his limitations, through his language. His language
is a mock Yiddish, much like the language of the "Jew's sermon"
ascribed to the youthful Goethe.[29] It is written in roman letters
and is stripped of most of its Hebrew elements. What Hebrew
elements are preserved are those that Yiddish shared with the thieves'
jargon, words that would have been available in the common patois
of the fictionalized criminal of the German adventure tales.

In 1815 a play entitled *Our Crowd*, by the Breslau physician
Carl Borromäus Sessa, was performed in Berlin.[30] Sessa's play uses
the mock Yiddish of Stern in a context more than slightly reminiscent of Euchel's comedy. First performed in 1813 in Breslau, the
drama received notoriety only with the Berlin production starring
Albert Wurm. Wurm was an actor who had made his reputation
starring in roles as the comic Jew. His command of the stage Yiddish
dialect made him representative of the actors who mimicked the
accent or language of the Jews. His personality became a central
feature in the exchanges concerning Sessa's drama. For Wurm was
a homosexual, and it was the linkage of the nature of comic representation of the Jew with the concept of perverse sexuality that
provided yet another nexus for Börne's mode of self-definition.

Our Crowd was a clear attack on the nature of the Jew, whether
conservative or assimilationist. Like Euchel's play, it condemned
both the older and the younger generation. Unlike the Yiddish
drama of the Maskilim, it had an institutional locus. For it was
written for the traditional German popular stage, the stage of the
comic one-act play, the *Posse*. Such dramas, like the British melo-
drama or pantomime, were aimed at the entertainment of the
broadest populace. They made little claim on the enlightened demand
that drama educate while entertaining. And yet Sessa's play, which
is the representation of the German image of the conflict existing
within the Jewish family of the period, was perceived, at least by
its Jewish viewers, as having polemical—that is, educative—intent.

The play depicts the education of the son of an "old clothes
Jew," who is sent into the world to make his fortune. His father's
language is clearly what Sessa imagines Yiddish to be. But it was
so presented as to be completely understandable to his German
audience. Such mock Yiddish works, such as those by Stern, would
pass as representative of the language of the Jews to the German
audience but were in no way truly Yiddish. Indeed, they were much
closer to the general accessibility of the thieves' jargon, with its
Yiddishisms, than to Western Yiddish. The son is portrayed as

speaking a stilted German laced with Yiddishisms. His desire is to become a writer of "pastoral sonnets and a library of tragedies in iambic verse." Indeed, the key to his character is found in the line, spoken in the broadest *mauscheln*, "I wish to toss the Jews aside. I'm enlightened—I've nothing Jewish about me" (202). Here the aesthetic pretensions of the Jews, such as Behr, are given literary form for a German-Christian audience. The adventures of the son, his relationship with the assimilated Jewess Lydie Polkwitzer, whom he wishes to marry, and his friendship with Isaschar, now Isidorius Morgenländer, all hinge on the use of language. Lydie reveals her inner nature when she is roused to anger and lapses into mock Yiddish. Isidorius, a student, breaks into mock Yiddish when he senses that his plans to marry Lydie may be thwarted by Jakob. The comedy concludes with the collapse of Jakob's fantasy world, a world that revolved about his having won a lottery, and his return to the world of the Jewish barterer. Little is left of his aesthetic pretensions when he turns to the audience at the conclusion of the play and asks: "Have you anything to barter?"

Sessa's play was a marginal success in its first performance, projecting as it does many of the Germans' fears of their own inadequacies onto the image of the Jews. Such fears are articulated, not only on the right, as in Sessa's play, but also on the left. Theodor Mundt's *Madonna* (1835) mocks both the "Itzig father" and the "Itzig son" because of their false emancipation and their broken language.[31] Mundt also continues the older argument that Jews by their very nature cannot have any sense of the beautiful. While Mundt's book had a limited and exclusive audience, Sessa's play was to be performed in the public arena in Berlin. The Berlin Jewish community pressured the liberal Prussian Chancellor Karl August von Hardenberg to ban the drama, which he did in 1815. At the end of that year a public outcry forced Hardenberg to rescind his order. This demand, which is preserved in the form of a series of pamphlets, had more to do with the image of the Berlin Jewish community's exercising its political power than it did with the quality of the play. Indeed, when the play was finally performed in Berlin, it was a *succès d'estime*, with the audience being quite bored by what was received as a not terribly imaginative presentation of the comic Jew. The overall success of the drama, which was widely played throughout Germany in the next few years, came almost exclusively from the publicity attendant upon its banning in Berlin.

In 1815 an anonymous pamphlet appeared that attacked *Our Crowd* from the standpoint of the German liberal. What is of specific interest is that the author centers much of his discussion on the language of the figures. He begins by observing that "if this comedy is indeed a drama of characters, it can only be so if all Jews are common Polish Jews."[32] Here the liberal separation of the "good" Jews, the German-speaking Jews in Germany, and the "bad" Jews, the Yiddish-speaking Jews in Poland, is presumed. But the author, in attempting to understand the wellsprings of the violently anti-Jewish attitudes of his Christian compatriots, dismisses language as the basis for difference: "About the language of the Jews, if one listens to common Swabians, Pomeranians, or similar people, one would laugh even more about them, if they appeared on the stage, than about the Jews in *Our Crowd*" (20). In separating hatred from laughter the author attempts to minimize the evidently commonly held view of the special status of *mauscheln*. Yet the relationship between hatred and laughter is present in the reception of the play. The theater was an institution where it was permitted or even encouraged to articulate one's deep-felt sense of anxiety about the mobility of the Jews in German society, a mobility that the audience in its bourgeois sensibilities felt impinged on their own exercise of power, their own control of their seemingly closed and stable world. This is yet another fantasy acted upon by the mob. For the repressive nature of German society after the Napoleonic Wars, the fantasy of the freeing of this society from yet another accented foreigner, one whom the Germans had endowed with the aura of greater and more profound culture and language, meant that it was possible to reverse all of these qualities in the image of the Jew. And this transference of images took place in the institution of the highest culture, the theater.

In 1818 the newly baptized and renamed Ludwig Börne wrote a long and detailed review of the Sessa play within the context of a series of drama reviews that he was writing for various German newspapers and journals. The review itself is one of the central documents of Börne's sense of self, written during the time when he was converting to Christianity.[33] Unlike the earlier works, the juvenilia, or the later discussions of the civil and political rights of the Jews, this review comes at a specific point in Börne's restructuring of his identity. It is a review of a literary work, it is a literary work written in a satiric idiom, it is a satire that presents the German image of the Jew, and it is an anti-Semitic satire that centers on the immutability of the Jews' mode of discourse. All of these factors, and more, make the review of *Our Crowd* a touchstone in comprehending the double bind of Börne's newly created persona.

Börne begins his review with a direct and pointed reference to Wurm's homosexuality. Wurm had been accused of homosexual activity by the mother of one of his lovers after the Berlin production of the Sessa play and had been convicted. He then had published a pamphlet, *Declaiming in a Jewish Mode*, which both defended his reputation as an actor and attacked the conspiracy that he perceived as having brought about the charges against him, a conspiracy led, needless to say, by the Berlin Jews. Wurm's use of *mauscheln* as a set piece, both on the stage and in salons, stressed the problem of sexual identity and perversion linked to the Jew. For Wurm's set piece was to declaim one of the classic works of German classical poetry, Schiller's ballad "The Diver," as a *nouveau riche* Jewess "dressed in an off-the-rack silk gown." As the poem became more and more emotional, his persona began to mix more and more of her *mauscheln* (in both sentence order and intonation) into her declamation.[34] Börne equates the "directionless passions" of homosexuality with the illness of the crowds that flock to performances of *Our Crowd*. These crowds are attracted to such excesses because they are composed of "neurasthenic individuals." They are amused by the performance because they bring a "pathological prurience" with them to the theater. It is not the Jews who are ill, who show the basis for their degeneracy through their sexuality, but rather the anti-Semites. The reversal of the claims of exactly that cadre of polemicists who supported the production of Sessa's play results in Börne's being able to claim that it is the anti-Semite who is deviant.

The claim of sexual deviancy as a means of categorizing the inner nature of the Other has, of course, political and institutional ramifications. The segregation of the deviant as a special subclass in nineteenth-century Germany began early in the century. Homosexuality, while still perceived as the result of childhood masturbatory practices, came more and more to be considered a primary sexual deviancy.[35] It was also one of the few "sexualized" crimes that were punished under German law. The labeling of the anti-Semite as homosexual, and his followers as merely sick individuals who were compelled by their illness to seek out his company, moves the nature of anti-Semitism from the level of a conscious, willful act to that of an automatic, pathological response. Like the innate blindness of the Jews, which like their illnesses is the result of their Jewishness, the blindness of the anti-Semite is the result of inherent qualities and is triggered by the actions of a seducer, here the homosexual as actor. The pathology would otherwise be latent.

Central to Wurm's characterization of himself—indeed, implicit in the very title of his defense—is his ability to speak mock Yiddish. This he perceived as the reason for the enmity of the Jews, for it revealed their hidden nature through the mimetic craft of the actor. Börne's reaction to this aspect of Wurm's craft as well as of Sessa's play is most revealing. He comments that the basis for all comedy is contradiction and that the use of an "unusual or corrupt accent" is only funny when there is, within the drama, some direct contrast to normal language. Sessa, however, writes his entire drama in a "disgusting jargon," which creates only boredom. "For listeners who know the Jewish dialect it is of no surprise and can, therefore, not please; for those who do not know it, it is incomprehensible." And yet the audience, not only in Berlin and Frankfurt but throughout Germany, evidently does understand the drama.

Börne is making a claim to the special language of the Jews, but it is a claim based on his rejection of this language as corrupt. Sessa's audience not only could but did understand the play. And they understood it because it was written, not in Yiddish, but in stage Yiddish, a dialect created to characterize the Jews on the stage rather than to reflect their reality in the society. And yet Börne's claim is that only those who know Yiddish can understand (and therefore be bored by) Sessa. Börne's claim is extraordinary: that the corruption of Yiddish has even corrupted those anti-Semites who indulge in excesses such as Sessa's drama. They are no better than the Jews who speak Yiddish; in fact, their very corruption is signaled by their ability to understand the play. Their mock Yiddish is like their homosexuality: it is pathological and contagious, at least among weak, enervated individuals.

The idea of Yiddish as a source for public corruption had moved by the beginning of the nineteenth century from the followers of the Haskalah into public debates on the status of the Jews. In a most remarkable, official letter from the Conference of Jewish Schools in Baden, dated 1834, there is a striking summary of this view, which by the beginning of the nineteenth century had assumed dogmatic proportions:

> One of the most necessary duties of our time is the gradual elimination of those qualities of the lower classes of Jewish coreligionists that have nothing to do with religion and are the result of their former political state. . . .
> Language is a jewel of mankind, the band of peoples, the seed and the fruit of education, and not without great import for the inner, ethical character of mankind. It determines the

positive or negative impression that one has on one's fellow man. . . .

It is a well-known fact that in earlier times a degenerate so-called Jewish-German dialect established itself. It is characterized by, among other things, incorrect, often disgusting pronunciation and intonation, incorrect constructions, admixture of corrupt Hebrew words (by which the Holy Language is often dishonored . . .) . . . the constant use of oaths, etc.

The greater part of the Jewish community has, through acquiring education, abandoned this, and only a part of the lower classes has preserved it. Experience teaches us not only that such individuals are the object of mockery on the part of followers of other religions but also that they create a sense of disgust in their coreligionists.[36]

Thus, the condemnation of Yiddish and its residue in German, *mauscheln*, is not only a question of acculturation but also the outward sign of moving away from the lower class into the bourgeoisie. In the 1825 guidelines for the instruction of pupils at the Free Jewish School in Hamburg, much is made of the need for the learning of "language," language not merely in the sense of national language (although that too is stressed) but in the sense of discourse, the cultural function of language.[37] Language is seen as that which determines (rather than is determined by) the manner in which the individual sees the world. In altering the nature of discourse, one alters the "human soul" (8). This view was shared by Jews in their perception of the function of language in other public institutions in addition to the school. In 1832 a major sum was offered by an anonymous woman in Vienna to pay for the institution of German-language sermons in synagogues in Vienna and Pest.[38] The broadsheet in which this offer was stated condemned the "degenerate wildness" of the present-day discourse among the Jews and encouraged the improvement of this through the alteration of the source of the corruption, the language used by the Jews in their synagogues, Yiddish. All of these proposals had as their hidden agenda the improvement of the Jews' social and economic position. Börne sees in the crowds that attend Sessa's play the mob, and he sets himself up as the arbiter of standards who sees their illness and its cause. The lower classes, like the Jews, are corrupt, and they show their corruption through their language.

And yet it is Börne/Baruch whose native language is Yiddish. It is he who wishes to distance himself from this barbaric misuse of German but who can, as one sees in his review, follow and understand the drama, perhaps better than most. There is more to this abnegation than merely the rejection of his "Jewish self" and the language with which even the Christian community associates him. For the clue, one must return to Sessa's play. The meeting between Jacob and his beloved Lydie comes as the young woman is on her way to church to sing. When Jacob, dressed clearly as a Jew, attempts to enter the church, the janitor bars his way, noting that the church is already full to overflowing with Jews. The Church is "being taken over by Jews." Börne's baptism, his attempt to enter into the economic mainstream of German life through his writing (language), his rejection of his Jewish persona—all are in vain. For as the Christian figure in Sessa's play observed, the Church is already too full of Jews. Later in his life, during his exile in Paris, Börne is still amazed at his inability to mask his Jewishness:

> It is like a miracle! I have experienced it a thousand times, and it still is eternally new to me. Some accuse me of being a Jew; some excuse me for being one; some even praise me for being a Jew. But all think about it. We are as if we were banished into this magic circle. None can escape. And I know full well from whence this evil magic comes. The poor Germans! Living on the bottom floor, oppressed by the seven floors of the upper classes above them, they resolve their feeling of anxiety by speaking about people who live even further below them, in the basement. Not being a Jew consoles them for not having been born a noble. (3:510–11)

Class and language are the markers of the Jew. The evils of anti-Semitism are projected onto these qualities. Yet this in no way explains Börne's sense of transparency. Why does he feel himself always seen as a Jew? Why can he not hide even in the Church? Because he is inherently a Jew, at least in the eyes of the Christian world. And he is a Jew because he bears the stigma of the new language of the Jews, not Yiddish but irony. In rejecting the language of the Jews, even the stage language attributed to the Jews, as incomprehensible, he has accepted a new mode of discourse for himself, but it is precisely this mode of discourse that becomes identified as Jewish. It is the ironic tone of the observer, but the observer as foreigner.

In 1819 Börne reviewed Richard Cumberland's eighteenth-century drama *The Jew*, which was the first drama to present a positive image of the Jew on the British stage. The review concludes with a condemnation of the actor who played the title character for having used "a half-strange language, in which one could neither think nor feel, and whose impression on the viewer would be difficult to imagine and, finally, the mix of the comic, which the Jewish dialect evokes [makes the central character into merely a] representation of Christian fantasy" (1:289). Again it is the nature of the Jews' language that Börne considers the marker of the Christian attitude toward the Jews. Even in a positive portrayal of the Jew, Börne hears the hidden language of the Christian anti-Semite saying that the immutable nature of the Jews is mirrored in their language.

The sexualization of the Jews and the nature of their language reflect the preoccupation with that inner Jew which Börne has attempted to exorcise. It is not merely that the world does not permit him to do this but that the reaction of the real world is mockery and violence. For in 1819 there occurred the worst anti-Semitic riots in memory, the "Hep-Hep" riots, named after the cry of the anti-Semitic mob. Triggered by the economic difficulties experienced in Germany during the post-Napoleonic era, the mobs turned their wrath against the Jews in the age-old cry against Jewish usury and exploitation. They also attacked the social climbing of the Jews and their pretensions to culture. Börne was shocked at the violence of the riots, more because they undermined his sense of stability than because of their rationale. Indeed, after the July revolution brought Louis Philippe to the throne, Börne left Germany for Paris, where he began a series of "Letters from Paris," which established his literary reputation in Germany.[39] One of the themes in these letters is the venality of the Frankfurt Rothschild family, parvenus who are the worst examples of German Jewry.

One of the undercurrents of Börne's critique of the Rothschilds is their use of a deviant form of rhetoric, the rhetoric of trade, and the fact that they reduce everything in the world to this rhetoric. Börne's critique sees this rhetoric as international, or rather non-nationalistic, just as he characterizes the Rothschilds as "speaking all foreign tongues with the same Yiddish accent."[40] The Rothschilds manifested their Jewishness in their use of language and used "Jewish" language in their trade. Samuel Bleichröder's first letter to the London house of Rothschild "ended with a postscript in Hebrew letters; the language of the letter and postscript was German, but this was German as Samuel Bleichröder spoke it— with a heavy Yiddish accent. From time to time, Samuel—and Gerson after him—would resort to the same method which simultaneously assured the confidentiality of the message (censors were thought to be primitive in those days) and reiterated the special kinship between the correspondents."[41] Börne's attacks are not merely attacks on the support of the Rothschilds for the autocratic regimes of Europe; they represent a clear association with the very theme of the "Hep-Hep" riots. Börne's journalism distinguishes the "good" Jews as opposed to the "bad" Jews. And these "bad" Jews are the Rothschilds, who, like Börne's father, are to be identified with status achieved through money, and the lower-class Jews, who are identified as petty usurers through their very language.

In making his distinction between the "good" and the "bad" Jew in society, Börne created a dichotomy that reflected his own basic sense of self. Just as he condemned the Rothschilds for being lackeys of the pope, he condemns the Germans (who attack him) as lacking style.[42] The idea of style in Börne—indeed, in all of the Jewish writers of this generation—is closely associated with their identification with France and with the importance of style in defining a writer's status. While there had long been German authors in Paris, as early as the Enlightenment, there had never been the set of associations that existed in the German mind after Napoleon. For popular German writers this linkage was "Paris-Revolution-Jew-Satiric Prose."[43] Writers such as Saphir and Börne became emblematic for this linkage. But an additional element was present, even though it was only rarely articulated. For all of this was a pose. The Jews' new language was merely window dressing for their old blindness and inherent inarticulateness. All of the Jews' claims, including the claims to style, were but a sham.

The nature of the new language and rhetoric of the Jew at the beginning of the nineteenth century is clear. It was bounded by a sense of the mission of language in freeing mankind from the intoleration of conventional society. It expressed itself in polemic, satire, or irony. It therefore had multiple levels of meaning. Liberal in its ideology, seemingly influenced by French Enlightenment discourse in its choice of modes of expression, this language became the hallmark of the social outsider as social critic. And it was closely associated with the Jew. Peter Hohendahl describes this as a loosening of the German Latinized style, an abandonment of Kantian conceptual language, and a mixing of levels of style.[44] It is also an abandonment of the style associated with the first generation of Maskilim, the followers of Kant in the Jewish camp. It is the new, post-Enlightenment language of the Jew with the new liberal ideology of post-Revolutionary France. It becomes bound to the image of the Jew, and the only question that remains is how it is articulated.

The semantic field designated by contemporary Christian usage as the new language of the Jews is quite complex. One specific quality can be seen in the fact that the Young German movement, seen by writers such as Wolfgang Menzel as "Young Palestine," is referred to in the conservative press as "jeune Allemagne."[45] This "Gallomania" links the idea of France—revolution, sexual excess, political turmoil, aggressive politics, a liberal concept of human rights—to the idea of the Jew. What is striking is that the qualities found in the image of France are the same as those that reify the stereotype of the Jew as traditionally found in Europe. Since the images of both the French, especially in the late eighteenth century, and the Jews are traditionally linked with their language, it is not surprising that the other qualities feared by the Germans become indelibly linked to the idea of language. So much so that writers such as an anonymous editorialist in the *Munich Political Newspaper* in 1835 can simply link Heine, Karl Gutzkow, Heinrich Laube, and other liberal writers as "disciples of the Israelite confessions [who wish to overthrow the] Christian-religious and political status quo in Germany [through their] propaganda of a public immorality."[46]

Wolfgang Menzel, in his programmatic essay "Recent Literature" (1836), lists four qualities of "jeune Allemagne" that make this group of "Jews" dangerous: the idea of a universal concept of man that opposes nationalism; the advocacy of a revolutionary future for Europe aimed at the destruction of the class system; opposition to religion and stress on materialism; and immorality.[47] All of these qualities are inexorably linked to the idea of France and to the writings of the Jew. The new language of the Jews is related in both form and content, a point that opponents of Menzel, especially in the Jewish camp, are at pains to point out. Writers such as Jakob Weil and Gabriel Riesser stress over and over again that such views, and the style in which they are expressed, are not representative of the greatest number of Jews in contemporary Germany.[48] Indeed, Weil goes as far as to argue that writers such as Börne and Heine are *not* Jews. He stresses their baptism as the act that differentiates them from Jews who remain steadfast to older, more conservative models of discourse. The defenders of the Jewish position thus tended to isolate writers such as Heine and Börne, who were attacked and libeled as Jews, as more representative of the Christian than of the Jewish world. Weil states that since Börne's moral and religious views reveal nothing about the nature of the Jews, there is no reason why his political views should be considered as representative of them. Jewish public opinion is determined to distance itself as much from the charges of moral and political deviancy as possible. It desires to accept the model of bourgeois respectability that it believes itself to have been offered, at least by implication, by mid-century. Writers such as Heine and Börne become neither Christians nor Jews, and yet they continue to serve in both communities as representatives of the inner nature of the outcast Jews as articulated through their language.

Börne spent much of his career countering attacks on him, attacks that he saw as having been precipitated not only by the content of his writing but also by its style. And this was precisely the charge that he lodged against his opponents, whether his actual political opponents or those Jews, such as the Rothschilds, whom he viewed as his antithesis. These individuals did not have style. Rothschild was willing to kiss the pope's ring, acting like a false convert; Menzel was willing to prostitute his liberal heritage. In all these cases, the basis for Börne's critique was precisely the charges lodged against him, that he was artless, without any style whatsoever, and that he used the illusion of style, which he borrowed from others, as a mask.

At the very end of his life Börne again attempted to radically restructure his persona. He had become Börne the journalist, but the very concept of "journalist," especially "liberal journalist," had become synonymous with "Jew." The Young Germany group of liberal writers was a school created by the denunciation of the Federal Diet in 1835. It included Heine and others of a liberal persuasion who were in fact mutually unsympathetic, if not hostile to each other. The Austrian envoy to the Vatican even commented on the "Talmudic" nature of these writers.[49] The idea that the Jews were transmuted into liberal journalists and were in league with the political enemies of Germany, specifically the French, had become a leitmotif of attacks on Börne by both Jews and Christians. Without a doubt the most vicious attack came from Wolfgang Menzel. Menzel, who had been a supporter of Börne, turned violently against him in the mid-1830s. In 1835 Menzel attacked the liberal Karl Gutzkow for the publication of his novel of sex and emancipation, *Wally, the Doubtress*. Menzel attacked the novel, which presents among other incidents a marriage between a Christian and a Jewess, as immoral. Börne, against whom Menzel had begun to write, supported Menzel in this condemnation, for it was on the level of the moral, especially the sexualization of the Jew, that Börne was the most rigid.[50] His stringent morality, even on questions of fictional sexuality, marks his new persona. For Börne is moving ever closer to the Catholic Church, especially the social activism of the French priest Félicité-Robert de Lamennais. In his last and perhaps his major work, *Menzel, the Eater of the French*,

Börne accepts the idealism of Lamennais's Catholicism as his new self-definition, seeing the Germans as the Jews of Europe and arguing Christian charity toward them as fellow sufferers from anti-Semitism. Menzel, who had reduced liberalism to a Jewish-French conspiracy, was countered with a burst of Christian socialist economic determinism. But more than that, Börne sees Menzel as a renegade from liberalism. Menzel is a convert to conservatism; he is the "pharisee of liberalism" who has betrayed his cause as Judas betrayed Christ (3:938). Menzel becomes a double for the seeking Börne, the Börne who moved from the Talmudism of the Frankfurt Ghetto (it was the Pharisees who wrote the first Talmud) to the wittiness of the university, to the Lutheranism of his role as journalist and commentator, to the Catholicism of Parisian intellectual circles. Menzel was Talmudic in his support of the liberals; he has now become Judas in his betrayal of his earlier principles. Börne's death in 1837, the year of the publication of his essay on Menzel, brings to end a life riddled with inner contradictions. But Börne becomes for his age emblematic for the new Jewish discourse, so much so that other Jews in similar circumstances use Börne as the touchstone for their attempts at defining their own identity.

III
The Farceur: *Heine's Ambivalence*

Of all the Jewish writers for whom Ludwig Börne served as a model none responded more deeply to him than did Heinrich Heine.[51] Heine was born to a merchant family in Düsseldorf in 1797. His life, as well as his development of what becomes identified as his highly personal literary style, is centered about the conflicts in his sense of identity. In no text is the relationship between life, style, and identity better articulated than in Heine's memorial volume for Börne, published in 1840. The threads of Heine's inner conflict are played out in terms of his attempt to understand Börne as a double who, however, chooses many of the wrong options open to him and whose life, therefore, is riddled with mistakes in judgment.

Heine begins his work with a reminiscence of his first sight of Ludwig Börne. It was 1815. Heine's father had taken the young man with him to a Masonic lodge, where they had spied Börne across the room. Heine's father had whispered: "That is Dr. Börne, who has written against the comic actors."[52] This is the entire report of Heine's first sight of Börne, and as it has often been remarked, it is evidently full of mistakes. For in 1815 there was no Dr. Börne. Börne's conversion and baptism took place in 1818. And the reference to the comic actors is clearly to Albert Wurm and the scandal about *Our Crowd* which occurred in that same year. Heine begins his memoir of Ludwig Börne before the creation of the subject about whom he is going to write. He sets this first meeting in 1815, the date of the first performance of the Sessa play, a play that seemed to him to have created the context for the "Hep-Hep" riots against the Jews in 1819. He also sets the theme of his analysis of Börne's life and times. Börne is seen as the creator of a specific type of language, a language that grows out of his inner self and is reflected by his actions. Heine connects this theme with the attack that Börne launched against Wurm and Sessa, an attack revolving around language and its relationship to human nature.

Heine's discussion of Börne's nature, in the opening paragraph of his study, begins with this enigmatic opening, an opening that to any German-Jewish reader of the 1840s who had lived through it would have immediately recalled the Wurm scandal and its sexual overtones. The readers of the 1840s, however, were then presented with a series of innuendos concerning Börne's sexual life, specifically the *ménage à trois* he supposedly had with Solomon Straus and his wife Jeanette Wohl. These innuendos were direct enough that Heine was forced to fight a duel with Straus, who chose to defend his wife's honor. Heine's comments, however, related to his attempt to sketch the nature of the polemical critic. From the very opening to the very close of the work, Börne is, in Heine's eyes, the quintessential polemicist. Indeed, Heine quotes extensively from Börne's works, especially his attacks on Heine, throughout the memoir, letting Börne's own rhetoric condemn him. For even if what Börne says may be true, the aggressive and negative manner in which he casts his argument reveals his nature. Heine also supplies the reader with examples of "good" discourse. Interspersed within the chapters on Börne are Heine's famed "Letters from Helgoland," romantic reveries on quasi-philosophical subjects that provide antithetical texts to the extensive quotations from Börne. Börne's criticism is but a reflex of his inner nature, and this nature is represented by his perverse sexuality. Here Heine's ironic comments on Jeanette Wohl serve as beacons for the reader. And yet the reader does not simply make the jump from the aggressive anti-Jewish polemic of the homosexual actor, Wurm, represented in the Jews' language, to the polemical language of Börne and his sexual perversities. The difference lies in Heine's own conflictive sense of the difference between heterosexual and homosexual "perversions." Heine's strong homophobia is closely linked to his fear of anti-Semitism. Indeed, the most famous case, Heine's attack on August von Platen, a minor German Romantic poet, is rooted in the association of Platen with German attitudes toward the Jews. Platen mentioned Heine only in passing in his *The Romantic Oedipus*, but most negatively, calling him the "pride of the synagogue" and stating that "I would be his friend, but not his lover; for his kisses stink of garlic."[53] Heine's reaction was excessive. In 1829, in *The Baths of Lucca*, Heine attacks Platen as both a poor poet, one relying on old and hackneyed forms, and a homosexual. Heine imagines, at the end of his attack on Platen, an ideal performance of Platen's *Romantic Oedipus*. Starring in the title role is Albert Wurm! Homosexuality is linked expressly with anti-Semitic polemic. Börne's heterosexual peccadillo is not condemned; it is merely made the brunt of ironic laughter. Heterosexual activity becomes the mark, not of the anti-Semite, but of the liberated Jew. Heine's long association with his French, Christian mistress clearly colored this implication. But Börne's sexual life was thus linked to Börne's Jewish identity.

For Heine, Börne was neither Jew nor Christian. In one of the most famous passages in the book on Börne, Heine comments that all men are either "Nazarenes" or "Hellenes." Both Jews and Christians are "Nazarenes," since they reveal an ascetic, iconoclastic, theoretical mind, while the "Hellenes" are "full of life, realistic, and proud of their capacity for development" (7:76). Now, this aesthetic distinction, rooted in German Romantic philosophy, with all of its anti-Semitic tendencies, is more than merely a distinction between the dry scholasticism of the Jews and the joyful science of the Greeks. It is a clear attempt to place both the Christian and the Jew in the same camp, showing both of their traditions as identical and claiming superiority for the world of the Greeks, a world crushed by the rise of Christianity. This view is a dominant one in German nineteenth-century thought, articulated best in the rationalist thinker Voltaire, whose views on the Jews permeated Heine's thought. For a Jew to make this claim, however, is quite a different matter from a Christian's claiming the eventual superiority of the Greeks. For in linking the Jews and the Christians as decadent forms of aesthetic perception, Heine attempts to reduce the Christian to exactly that position in which he had found himself for so many years, as one denied aesthetic sensibility. Both Christian and Jew are deficient in their view of the world; only the Greek can be trusted to have true aesthetic insight.

But Börne is more than the essential Nazarene; he is also the true Christian for Heine. For the real condemnation of Börne is not as a fictionalized composite Christian and Jew but in terms of the ideological rhetoric of Heine's own time. Heine states that Börne was a "born Christian, whose spiritualistic direction must have rebounded into Catholicism when . . . he allied himself with the Catholic Party" (11:103). For Heine, Börne is more than merely a Christian; he is a Catholic. And who, for Heine, is the quintessential Jew? No one other than Wolfgang Menzel! Menzel, perhaps the first modern literary anti-Semite, is for Heine the true Jew, the self-hating Jew. Heine not only labels Menzel—as Menzel labels everyone he attacks—as a Jew but characterizes him in a passage quite devoid of irony as one who peddles his Germanness, "like the peddler-Jew peddles his plunder" (11:101). What Heine reflects here is not a confusion; it is not chaos nor an abandonment of terminological clarity. The seeming confusion between Christian and Jew, between anti-Semite and philo-Semite, is a realization of the closeness of both to Heine's internalized image of the "bad" Jew from which he wished to escape.

Heine also provides the image of the "good" Jew within the Börne book, the "good" Jew as Greek. The book closes with the sleeping Heine dreaming of his meeting with a group of black-haired, black-eyed, bare-breasted nixes, one of whom asks the poet if she can sleep while resting on his knee:

> While she lay on my knee and slept, she sometimes murmured, like one dying, in her sleep, muttered to her compatriots all sorts of conversations, of which I understood but little, for she spoke Greek quite differently than I had learned it in school and from Wolf's grammar. . . . I understood only enough to know that she complained about the bad times and feared that they would get even worse, and she intended to flee even further into the forest. . . . Then suddenly, in the distance, a cry of coarse plebian voices was raised . . . she cried, I no longer know what. . . . Between, there was a Catholic mass-bell.
>
> And my beautiful nixes became evidently paler and thinner, until they completely dissolved into mist, and I awoke yawning. (11:131–32)

Thus Heine concludes his memoir of Börne. His nixes speak a Greek much like the German spoken by his mother, with a heavy accent redolent of her Yiddish. But this Greek, this icon of aesthetic truthfulness, can be vanquished by the coarse plebian voices of all polemic, including that which sees itself as both liberal and Catholic. Heine had supplied the reader with a new language of the Jews in the text, the Romantic revery, in the "Letters from Helgoland," but he wanted to be very sure that his message was not lost. Thus the very conclusion of the work repeats the message again, and again reappears the image of the sexualized Jew, but in a genteel and accepted form. For the clearly sexualized image of the Greek demigods who visit Heine's dreams evoke neither ironic laughter nor revulsion, since they are presented as aesthetic objects, beautiful objects to be admired, not to be possessed. And they eventually show their immaterial nature by fading away. Unlike the language of Börne or Wurm, Heine's language is associated with the image of noncorporeal sexuality and is therefore saved from debasement.

Polemic, sexuality, and language are linked by Heine in drawing the portrait of his double. These qualities, in Heine's mind, are the difference between himself and Börne, between the good Jew and the bad Jew, and seem to supply Heine with a necessary sense of his own self. Theodor Adorno observed that Heine's

> sense of communicative fluency and self-evidentness is the antithesis of a homely assuredness in a language. Only he rules over a language like an instrument who is not, in truth, in it. If he would have been totally within his language, he would not have been able to express the dialectic between his own words and those already existing, and the smooth, linguistic merging would have been lost. For the subject, who uses the language like a consumed thing, the language is always strange. Heine's mother, whom he loved, did not have a good command of German. His lack of opposition against popular usage is the imitative excess of the outsider. The assimilator's language is one of unsuccessful identification.[54]

Would that the issue were quite that simple. For Heine, unlike the writers of the first generation of German Jews who saw themselves as emancipated, was reacting not only against a Christian image of the Jews' language but against the new language of the Jews, the new polemic of the left, with which he felt himself associated because of his identity as a Jew. Indeed, what is most complex about Heine is his seeming need to separate out the sense of nostalgia, which he often associates with Yiddish (and the attendant artifacts of Jewish identity such as food and ritual), and the association of this language pattern with polemic and aggression. It is not merely, as Adorno observed, that Heine wishes to use Romantic language and thus fails because he cannot accept its conventions. Unlike Kuh, Heine has yet another layer of linguistic identification with which to combat, another type of polemic against which to contend. It is this polemic that he sees as "Nazarene" and that he locates within the work of both Börne and Menzel.

The complexity of Heine's understanding of himself and his language within the world of letters, a world in which he created the sense of status he needed, has its roots in Heine's youth. As Adorno mentioned, Heine's family spoke Yiddish in Düsseldorf. Yiddish was Heine's first language, and his youthful friends recount Heine playfully translating bits of Homer and Ovid into Yiddish.[55] But Heine also was raised speaking German. For Heine's parents may have spoken Yiddish but would have insisted that their children use German as their primary language of social intercourse with their peer group. Yiddish becomes associated with the language of the home, and the home with the image of the mother. This positive image would also have been contrasted with its antithesis, with the missing image of the father in Heine's work. Again, one must remember that it is the image of the father that Heine brings into the context of Börne and Wurm at the beginning of the Börne book. Heine's mention of his father in his fragmentary memoirs (1854) is generally positive, but his description reveals a clearly feminized image: "The beauty of my father had something soft, something without character, almost feminine" (7:482). This is contrasted with the masculine nature of his uncle. The father's feminine traits, his passivity, as opposed to the activity of his rich uncle, presents a link in the images of the homosexual and the Jew that Heine incorporates into his self-image.

One further image with which Heine would have had to come to terms is the locus of the bad Jew. Heine's contemporary Karl Gutzkow, one of the leading German Christian liberals, recalls the understanding of the image of the Jew that he had as a young man. He writes in his autobiography that "Christian-Germanic anti-Semitism was already present in the fraternity system. In school I got to know the Jew as a traitor and a braggard. What was feared by all was a hunchbacked monster from Poland, as vengeful as Shylock."[56] The image of the Polish Jew—crippled, vindictive, boastful—had become the standard fare of German political anti-Semitism, an anti-Semitism lodged in institutions such as the universities. And it was in the service of these very students that Börne risked arrest to return to speak to them at the famed meeting at Hambach that opposed German conservative politics. Börne's rhetoric, Heine writes in his memorial to the writer, was clearly in support of the wrong cause. Heine's association of "bad" Jews parallels Gutzkow's Christian association of the Jew with the image of the Eastern Jew, except that Heine associates them with "bad" language and discourse, as when he labels one Joseph Friedländer "a Jewish *Mauschel*."[57] It is Friedländer's discourse (specifically about Heine's literary work) that raises Heine's ire.

Heine's initial confrontation with the negative image of the Jew was not, however, in an Eastern context. It was on the trip in 1815 when he first, according to his account, spied the not-yet-existent "Dr. Börne." For that incident was placed by Heine during his first trip to Frankfurt, where he accompanied his father on a business trip.[58] It is in the former Frankfurt Ghetto, still primarily occupied by Jews, that he sees the dirt, crowds, and costumes of the ghetto Jew, that he first smells the stench of tightly packed humanity, and that he hears Yiddish spoken, not as a language of the kitchen, but as a language of trade and commerce. Even the Rothschilds spoke Yiddish among themselves. And it is his father, the liberal father who belongs to the Masonic lodge, who speaks the language of trade—in contrast to the mother, who speaks the language of the home—who takes him into this world. Both worlds are articulated in the same tongue, Yiddish, but they have separate and contradictory implications for the young man. For it is precisely from the world of trade, from the trade school, that he wishes to free himself, and it is that world that remains associated with his father (and his father's family) for the rest of his life.

In 1819, as a result of the "Hep-Hep" riots of the summer and fall of that year, seven Jewish intellectuals in Berlin founded the Association for the Culture and Science of the Jews.[59] The president of the group was Eduard Gans, a lawyer and disciple of Hegel. The organization had as its goal the study of the state and history of the Jews in order to provide access to Jewish tradition within the cultural context of European life. This meant the abandonment of specifically Jewish modes of discourse, the use of acceptable European languages, and the eventual acculturation of the Jews in Germany. Under the auspices of this group, Heinrich Heine actually undertook a trip to the Eastern provinces of Germany. In his report on this trip, *On Poland* (1822), he devoted a much greater segment to the Polish Jews than their presence in the population seemed to warrant, at least according to contemporary Polish sources.[60] The basic tenet of Heine's study, one that tied in with contemporary Christian views, concerned the economic value of the Jews in their present state. Heine seems to argue that if the Jews and the peasants were better treated, then the Jews would become peasants toiling the land and would, therefore, acquire a value for the

Polish provinces. Heine's image of the Eastern Jew is a clear prefiguration of a linkage between the anti-Semite and the Jew found in his book on Börne:

> A sense of horror overcomes me when I remember how, beyond Meseritz, I first saw a Polish village inhabited mainly by Jews. The Wadzeck Weekly Chronicle, cooked into a porridge, could not have nauseated me any more than those rag-bag figures of dirt; and the high-minded speech of a third-former enthusiastic about gymnastics [a reference to the nationalism of *Turnvater* Jahn] and Fatherland could not have martyred my ears so excruciatingly as the Polish Jew-Jargon. However, this disgust was soon replaced by pity, after I observed these individuals at closer range and saw the pig-sty-like holes in which they lived, spoke bad German, prayed, haggled—and were miserable. Their language was a German sprinkled with Hebrew and decorated with bits of Polish. . . .
>
> But they evidently did not progress with the rest of European culture and their spiritual world sank into a morass of unedifying superstition, which was forced into them by a sophistic scholastic in a thousand miraculous forms. . . . I still prefer the Polish Jew with his dirty fur, with his lousy beard, with his garlic breath, and his bad German to many others in the state-paper majesty. (7:192–93)

This is Heine in 1822. It is a Heine who localized the image of the bad Jew in Poland, or at least in what remained of Poland under German rule. The Polish Jews speak a false, degenerate language; they articulate their base thoughts in a false and corrupting rhetoric and logic. In other words, they are really no better than the "German-Christian" patriots, with their nationalistic rhetoric and overblown German. The world of the Polish Jew is characterized by a corruption of qualities and language that were pure. But even so, they are better than the assimilated Jews who have forgotten their identity. And lastly, these Jews smell.

The smell of the Jews, the *foetor judäicus*, is the medieval mephitic odor always associated with the Other.[61] For the Jews, it is a quality ascribed to them by the medieval anti-Semite that is linked with the sexualized image of the goat. For Jews, like the Devil, are horned like goats and have a goat's tail and a goat's beard. Their smell is but a further quality of this image. It is linked to the illness of the Jew by many writers against the Jews. But by the eighteenth century the stench associated with Jews is not seen as supernatural. Rather, pamphleteers such as J. G. Schudt comment that the smell of the Jews is the result of their uncleanliness and their immoderate use of garlic. But it is a quality associated with Jews and becomes an important marker for the image of the Jew in the nineteenth century. Needless to say, it was precisely this quality that Platen ascribed to the Jew Heine. And it was exactly this quality that Heine had used in distancing the image of the corrupt Jew to the outermost provinces of Prussia. Heine's vituperative attack on Platen may now be seen as part of a defense of Heine's persona against the charge of being one of the bad Jews, speaking badly, using bad rhetoric, being sexually perverse—all indicated by the omnipresent stench of the Jew.

Thus in *The Baths of Lucca*, a text in which Heine excoriates Platen, Heine also provided an image of the "bad" Jew that seems to glorify him:

> Thus an old Jew with a long beard and a torn cloak who cannot speak an orthographic word and is a bit mangy feels himself happier than I do with all my education. There lives in Hamburg . . . a man called Moses Lump ["rogue"], also called Moses Lümpchen, or Lümpchen for short. He runs around during the entire week, through wind and weather with his pack on his back, in order to earn his couple of marks. When he comes home on Friday evening, he lays down his bundle and all his cares, and sits down at his table with his misshapen wife and yet more misshapen daughter, partakes with them of fish cooked in garlic sauce, sings the most splendid psalms of King David, rejoices wholeheartedly at the exodus of the children of Israel from Egypt, rejoices also that all the miscreants who behaved wickedly toward them died in the end, that King Pharaoh, Nebuchadnezzar, Haman, Antiochus, Titus, and all such people are dead, while Lümpchen is still alive and partaking of fish with his wife and child.—And I tell you, *Herr Doktor*, the fish is delicious, and the man is happy, he does not have to worry about culture, he sits wrapped contentedly in his religion and green dressing-gown like Diogenes in his tub, he gazes cheerfully at his candles. . . .[62]

This ambiguous image of the Jew, with his garlic smell and misshapen family, resting in the arms of his religion, a religion that spares him worry about culture, is the antithesis of Heine's earlier image of the Jew. Heine both envies and disdains Moses Lump. Here Heine has moved the mythic world of the "bad" Jew from the East to Hamburg; he has reversed the implications of all of the qualities ascribed to him. This is in the context of both his attack on Platen and his critique of the assimilated Jew, the "Count Gumpelino." Heine stresses the sexual conservatism of the Jew; his family life and the garlic-flavored fish serve as signs of that normal life. But again this seemingly positive quality is undermined by Heine's adaption of the *foetor judäicus*. For Heine stresses the so-called "lower" senses, taste and smell, as opposed to the "higher" aesthetic senses, sight and sound. The arts and the world of aesthetic creation, what Heine refers to in the passage as "culture," are not involved in the sybaritic indulgences of the Jew. For the Jew relates to the world, not through the world of aesthetics, as the Christian often enough claims, but through the material nature of existence, through the world's smell. Heine thus responds to the anti-Jewish image of the Jew as one lacking any type of aesthetic sensibility. By glorifying the "lower" senses, as opposed to those to which the "higher" arts appeal, Heine provides an ironic glorification of the "crude" Jew, the Jew lacking all aesthetic sensibility. True aesthetic sensibility lies in those areas otherwise denigrated by the aesthetician as low, and this is where the true transvaluation of the aesthetic for the Jew takes place. All of this shifting from the "high" to the "low" senses, of course, is embedded in the highest and most esoteric of literary forms, which by its very production shows the world in which the author truly belongs. Heine does not cook gefilte fish; he writes poems about it.

The Baths of Lucca, written in 1829, looks back on an episode in the life of the young Heine that took place in 1825. In that year Heine completed his law studies, and shortly thereafter he converted to Christianity. Heine's conversion was seemingly *pro forma*.[63] He needed to acquire the official designation as a Christian in order to be able to compete for governmental positions, such as a teaching position at a university. But Heine's was not the only conversion that took place in 1825. Heine's conversion took place in June; in December, Eduard Gans, the president of the Association for the Culture and Science of the Jews, converted in order to accept a professorship at the University of Berlin. In his memoir of Ludwig Marcus, Heine recalls this incident as an "unforgivable felony," and shortly after Gans's conversion, Heine writes the poem "A Renegade," which although not published in his lifetime seems to summarize his attitude toward Gans's act.[64] He condemns the act of one who shortly before had rejected Christianity, and he sees the source of Gans's opportunism in his reading of "Schlegel, Haller, Burke." This triad of thinkers, the reason for Gans's conversion, is quite revealing. For all three stand in an intellectual tradition that stressed the close relationship between belief and political life.

Friedrich Schlegel, convert to Catholicism and the husband of Moses Mendelssohn's daughter, was one of the masters of the new Romantic and Catholic prose style; Karl Ludwig von Haller was the apologist of the Restoration and the most prominent creator of its rhetoric; and Edmund Burke was, for Heine, the great convert to ultraconservative politics and the betrayer of his former political associates. Gans has become a Christian, and becoming a Christian means abandoning the new Jewish language, a language neither Romantic nor conservative and in which belief has been separated from politics.

But if this is true of Eduard Gans, what of the newly baptized Johann Christian Heinrich Heine? Is the world of Harry Heine no more? Clearly Heine's reaction to Gans's conversion provided the poet with a means of articulating his own inner sense of insecurity concerning his baptism. Heine, like Börne, converted in order to enter the economic mainstream of German life. Jews had no value unless they had an economic role to play within the creative life of a society, so the anti-Semites, and Heine, wished to accept this role. There are numerous rumors of professorships that he desired or positions that he would have liked to fill. But Heine missed the moment—experienced by Börne—when he could have become a member of the integrated economy of the state. He remained outside, limited to the world of culture, a world open to him at least in terms of there being publishers willing to enter the marketplace to sell his works. It is this world of culture that the marginal Jew Moses Lump does not "have to worry about." But it is exactly that world in which the new language of the Jew is embedded. Thus when Heine writes in his aphorisms the oft-quoted bon mot "The baptismal certificate is the entry ticket to European culture," his irony is evident.[65] For Heine, access to culture was expressly *not* through his entry into the Lutheran Church. His banishment from acceptable society into the world of "culture," into the world viewed by German society as the realm of the outsider, of the Jew, was his fate. Heine envies the Hamburg Jew with his simple pleasures, with his nonorthographic language, not only because he is not concerned with the daily cares viewed by the Christian world as important but also because he is free from the new language of the Jews and is able to rely on the escapism offered by religion. The pressure of "culture," as John Murray Cuddihy has amply illustrated, becomes a leitmotif for nineteenth-century European Jewry.[66] It is important to understand, however, that this striving for culture is but an altered form of older modes of adaption and that *culture* itself is but a code word for language and rhetoric. Heine's "entry ticket" proves itself worthless as a means of entering German society. His further transformation from Johann Christian Heinrich Heine to Henri Heine does not help. Indeed, Heine's role, and his language, remains limited to an extremely artificial sphere. Not perceived as a German, since he is seen as a Jewish journalist (a tautology?) writing from Paris, nor as a Frenchman, since his works were identified as non-French by their language, Heine is condemned to a highly artificial world of intellectual limbo. Because he belongs to all worlds and yet is not accepted by any, Heine's language and rhetoric come to be understood as "international" or "cosmopolitan," two code words that come to have specific semantic connotations on both the left and the right. Isolated from what the creators of status considered the mainstream, Heine becomes aware of his role as the outsider and uses that role to create his own persona. He is Heinrich Heine, Henri Heine, the double who is not a double but the embodiment of the critical consciousness. For Heine, all segments of his persona merge and are necessary to create his sense of self, a sense quite independent from the acceptance of the world, since the world, in Germany and in France, will certainly never accept him as one of its own. Thus, Heine's baptism did not provide him with any of the outward symbols of status, as it did, at least momentarily, for Ludwig Börne. In accepting baptism, he became an outsider from yet another group that offered status through the command of its language and rhetoric, the Jews. But he also cut the bonds to his family. Indeed, one of the reasons why Heine wished to keep his baptism secret was fear of the censure of his family. Heine's ambiguous relationship to his family, reflected in the language and image of the Jew, is reflected in the nature of the language that he ascribes to the Jewish figures within his literary works.

Heine wrote a number of works containing Jewish figures, but very few of them center about the image of the Jew. His fragmentary novel *The Rabbi of Bacharach* (1840) presents a tale of the Jewish reaction to a charge of ritual murder. The rabbi of Bacharach and his beautiful wife speak a German carved out of the marble of Isaac of York's English. Only when they flee to the Frankfurt Ghetto is the shadow of the future of their language cast upon the work by the introduction of Jäckel the Fool, who speaks in a mock Frankfurt dialect which the reader is to take as proto-Yiddish. The idea that in the Middle Ages the Jews living in the Rhineland spoke the same German as did their German neighbors, that Yiddish was merely an aberration growing out of the ghettoization of the Jew, had been articulated in Heine's youthful report on the status of the Jews in

Poland. Leopold Zunz, one of the most productive members of the Association for the Culture and Science of the Jews, evolved a theory that Jews in Germany spoke German until the seventeenth century![67] But it is in a series of three late poems, the Byronic "Hebrew Melodies" (1851), which conclude his *Romanzero*, that the inner conflict surrounding Heine's crisis of identity and language is most manifest.

What is puzzling about these poems is that they, like the opening of Heine's Börne memoir, are full of "mistakes." Everyone has been at pains to point them out. They all seem to have to do with Heine's knowledge of Judaism and have been used to show that Heine's use of Jewish material is but the surface manipulation of literary themes. But as Leopold Zunz observed, "Who learns history from Heine?"[68] Perhaps no one, but what can be learned from him is the creation of a world of myth as a means of exorcising the inner conflicts existing within his sense of identity, even at the very end of his life.

"Princess Sabbath," Heine's reworking of the tale of Moses Lump, is the recreation of the world of the marginal Jew, and yet Heine begins the poem by evoking *The Thousand and One Nights*.[69] It recounts the tale of the marginal Jew, damned to a dog's life, except on the Sabbath, when he becomes a prince of Araby. This magical transformation is heralded by the singing of the Sabbath hymn written by Jehuda ben Halevy, "Lecho daudi likras kalle, come, my friend, meet the bride" (1:433–89). The poem closes with the *Havdalah* and the shaking of the *bessamim*, the ritual spice container, containing the aroma of the Orient, with which the Sabbath ends.

The error has been noted almost from the first publication of the poem: the hymn quoted by Heine does not happen to be by Jehuda ben Halevy. Why, then, mention him after citing the opening line of the poem in the original Hebrew? For Jehuda ben Halevy is one of the very few figures of the mythical age of Spanish Jewry whom even the least knowledgeable reader would have automatically associated with the golden age of Spanish Jewry, the high Middle Ages. If he had mentioned the actual author of the hymn, the sixteenth-century Galilean poet Solomon Alkebets, who would have associated his name with any specific world of myth? For by the middle of the nineteenth century, European Jewry had evolved a myth that created a parallel between their own world and a past world in which the status of the Jew had been unassailable. Often this parallel world was sought in the early Middle Ages, seen also by the Christian Romantics as the world in which a total integration of world and spirit had been possible. But even more frequently, European Jews sought out the world of Moorish Spain, a world in which Jews had had unassailable status, a status that had ended with the establishment of Christian hegemony over the Iberian Peninsula. This golden age was bounded by Jehuda ben Halevy and Solomon ibn Gabirol in the eleventh century and Maimonides in the twelfth. It ended with the beginnings of the persecution of the Jews during the late fourteenth century and the final expulsion of the Jews from Spain in 1492.

Heine was working from an actual source, Michael Sachs's 1845 history of the religious poetry of the Jews in Spain. The introduction of the figure of Jehuda ben Halevy was quite conscious and contradicted his source. But the very use of this poet links the world of the synagogue, the world of the daily life of contemporary Jewry, with the golden age of Spain. It is an ambiguous linkage, since it contrasts the "stench of the dung," experienced by the Jew during the week, with the spices of the Orient, a contrast based on the odors experienced by the Jews, rather than their own smell. The linkage to the tradition of the *foetor judäicus* is clear, however, and Heine's creation of the "Princess Sabbath" as an ethereal but sensual image is another link to the sexualization of the nature of the Jew.

It is not really too surprising that the second of the "Hebrew Melodies" is devoted to Jehuda ben Halevy. Heine begins the poem with an elegant German translation evoking the lamentation of the Psalmist: "If I forget thee, O Jerusalem, let my right hand forget its cunning" (Psalm 137). This passage is a cathexis deeply rooted in Heine's sense of Jewish identity. He quotes it in a letter to Moses Moser during 1824, the time when he was most deeply involved with the Association for the Culture and Science of the Jews, and it reappears in a letter written to Moser after his baptism (April 23, 1826).[70] Using this quotation, Heine also creates the image of the true language of poetry. Heine has already introduced the idea that Hebrew is the pure poetic language, the language of the true poet. But it is Hebrew that is made immediately equivalent to German within the structure of the poem. Heine creates the idealized poet, the Spanish Jew writing in Hebrew, as his alter ego, but it is a double fraught with ambivalencies and contradictions. Heine's biography of Jehuda ben Halevy can serve as an internalized biography of the idealized poet *in nuce*. Heine begins his account with the poet's education, and it is, of course, an education within the tradition of Jewish education experienced by Heine himself. At its center stands the Talmud. But Heine defines the Talmud as possessing two distinct moments, the pedantic, hair-splitting legalistic text and the myths and legends, Halachah and Haggadah. This contradictory model provides both training for the mind and a refuge from such training. All of this is cast in the special language of the Jews. And Heine stresses the sensual aspects of this language. Hebrew's "fat gutturals" are sung by the youthful poet. But the linguistic model that Heine evokes is the model of Germany. For in addition to the Hebrew learned by this Spanish Jew, his other language is Aramaic, the language of the Talmud. Unlike Hebrew, Aramaic is presented not as sensual but as vaguely comic. Heine sees it as equivalent to Low German and Swabian, the two comic dialects in nineteenth-century Germany. The analogy is quite clear. Yiddish is to "real" German as Aramaic is to Hebrew, as Low German and Swabian are to High German. It is vaguely comic, somewhat degenerate, and spoken by groups seen by the powerful, defining group as marginal. And it is not a language of poetry; it is rather a language of lower expression.

Yet Jehuda ben Halevy's flights of fancy, his refuge in the legends of the Talmud, turn him into the poet of the Romantic's dreams. He is the master of the dream world of poetry, "a poet of God's grace." He is, indeed, a poet as great as his contemporaries, the troubadours. And Heine draws the parallel quite literarily. The only difference between the Jewish poet and the Christian troubadours is that Jehuda ben Halevy worships not the distant beauty of an unapproachable lady but "Jerusalem." And as the wandering minstrels go off in search of the woman who will inspire their lines, so, too, Jehuda ben Halevy wanders to the Holy Land, where he is killed by an Arab soldier. And his dying words are, "Lecho daudi likras kalle, come my friend, meet the bride." At this point Heine concludes the tale of Jehuda ben Halevy, the inspired poet, and shifts the scene to contemporary Paris. He moves from the image of the Jewish poet singing the praises of the ethereal "Princess Sabbath" to his own wife, complaining about the poem he had just written.

Heine's movement from the Romantic poet of the golden age of Jewry in Spain to the world of contemporary European Jewry, inhabited by Heines and Rothschilds, grounds the image of the Jewish poet in Heine's own persona. Heine counters his wife's criticism of the poem by remarking that poets such as Jehuda ben Halevy and Solomon ibn Gabirol are unheard of in European culture because of the bias of that very culture. Jewish poets, especially those who write in Jewish languages, such as Hebrew, are simply not known as part of the European cultural tradition. He suggested that she learn Hebrew rather than spend her time in theaters and concerts; then perhaps she will learn to appreciate great poetry. The world of the language of the Jews is seen as submerged by the weight of European "culture." Here Heine means culture in the most limited sense of the arts. For poetry, especially the poetry of the Jews, is drowned by the more trivial and accessible media, the theater and music, in which the means of communication is easily acquired. The language of the poet is difficult and complex, like that of a foreign tongue.

Heine wants to believe in the magical world that he has begun to conjure in "Princess Sabbath." It is a world of myth, too pure, too willing to have its idealized poets accepted and honored in their own time. Heine chooses to represent the language of this world either by exquisite German translations from the Hebrew or, indeed, by the original Hebrew itself, never in the "comic" accents of Yiddish or Yiddish-accented German. When, in the draft of the poem, Heine incorporated a Yiddishism in the poem, he deleted it in the published version. But one Yiddishism does remain in the poem, and indeed, the entire Parisian segment of the poem seems to take shape around it. In describing the life of Solomon ibn Gabirol, Heine recounts his capture by the Khan and his being granted freedom once the Khan heard him sing. He recounts his eventual murder and the punishment of his murderer, but in telling the reader this tale, Heine sees in Gabirol the poet as schlemiel, who chases after the white bodies of the nymphs and winds up with the laurel. The sexualization of the Jewish poet is linked to the word *schlemiel*, and Heine provides a detailed discussion of this word, a word that, however, he sees, not as part of a Jewish linguistic tradition, but as one that has been subverted by its absorption into the world of the Christian or Christianized German.

Heine cites as his source for the word the German Romantic poet Adelbert von Chamisso, who had published his parody of the Faust legend under the title *Peter Schlemiel's Lovely Tale* (1814). For Chamisso the image of the schlemiel had very specific sexual reference. In a letter to his brother he observes: "Schlemiel, whose name has become proverbial, is a person, about whom the Talmud tells the following tale: 'He had intercourse with the wife of a rabbi, was caught, and killed.'"[71] Heine provides a variation on this theme in the poem. He refers to the biblical figure Schlemiel ben Uzry Schadday, who is killed accidently when "Pinchas" attempts to kill the "noble Simri," who is having sexual relations with "a woman from the tribe of the Caananites." Illicit sexuality is the cause of the schlemiel's downfall, but in Heine's version the schlemiel is the innocent bystander, not the one involved in the sexual act.

The word *schlemiel* thus implies, for Heine, a sexual relationship between parties where a ban has existed forbidding it. It is this mismatching to which he refers back when he discusses Chamisso's source for the term, Julius Eduard Hitzig, originally Itzig. Heine sees the very use of the word *schlemiel* as a sign of the assimilation of the comic aspects of the Jew into German society. He parallels this to Hitzig's own conversion and his intimate relationship with the conservative German Romantics. Indeed, when in the poem the poet presses Hitzig, born Itzig, for the meaning of the word, the convert can only flee into "Christian excuses," until the poet loses patience and forces him to recount the version reported earlier. The function of this tale and the very use of the word *schlemiel* is to distance the word into the world of the Christian.

As with Heine's parallel between the troubadours and the Hebrew poets of Spain, it is only a partially successful act. For Heine sees in this parallel something that is indeed accurate. Hidden within this parallel is the fact, which Heine mentions, that at one point Spain begins to burn her Jews; the tale of the schlemiel also contains a similar moment in which the literary world of the poet becomes transparent, revealing the sand upon which the poet has built his persona. For the spear that Pinchas used to kill the first schlemiel "has been preserved / and we hear it constantly whirling above our heads." The status anxiety experienced by the poet is tied, first, to his perception of his language; second, to the nature of the reception of his language in the literary world; and third, to his simple existence within society. What is for the converts of the sixteenth century a real possibility—their physical destruction at the hands of their new Christian coreligionists—has become by the middle of the nineteenth century the material of poetry. It is an immolation that takes place only within the world of the text, or at least so the poet hopes.

The world of the text and the world of language are intermingled in Heine's portraits of Jehuda ben Halevy and Solomon ibn Gabirol, and yet Heine attempts to differentiate between these two Jewish poets writing in a Jewish mode. For both of these poets, no matter what the external parallels to the poets of the Christian world, are perceived—indeed, labeled—by Heine as Jewish poets writing in a Jewish language. Heine distinguishes between them by introducing a quote from Jehuda ben Solomon Alcharisi that characterizes Gabirol as the thinker, ibn Ezra as the artist, and Jehuda ben Halevy as both. When one turns to Heine's contemporaries, it is clear that the initial distinction was made by them to distinguish between two writers whom they viewed as Jewish writers, Börne and Heine. In lectures on contemporary letters delivered at the University of Kiel in 1833, the liberal critic Ludolf Wienbarg distinguished between the reflective nature of Heine's style and the unreflected nature of Börne's work.[72] The eighteenth-century distinction between the language of nature and the language of artifice is used to draw the distinction between the poet whose rhetoric seems direct and untrammeled and the writer whose works appear to develop along preordained paths. Heine sees the distinction drawn between Börne and himself, as the two representative Jewish writers of their age, at least in the eyes of the German reading public, as flawed, for true writers are those who integrate both aspects in their work and are, in addition, "the beloved of all mankind." This universality is Heine's goal, and yet this could never be achieved within the limitations of his discourse. Rather, he would always be the outsider, cast by fate into the role of one who, by accident, like the schlemiel, would never quite achieve his own goals. The poet then becomes the Jew in terms of his status within the "culture" in which he lives. He can never quite be integrated into his own world and thus lives in perpetual fear of his world's collapsing. Heine has made the poet into the Jew, a role that he uses to project his own anxiety at being both a Jew and a poet. Unsure of his own language, he becomes more and more aware of the pitfalls within it. His insecurity stems not so much from his bilingualism as from the new language of the Jews, the language of witty rhetoric and political engagement, with all of its implications, which he has assumed.

The seemingly positive image of the Jew in the first two poems of the "Hebrew Melodies" is radically undercut and relativized in the final poem of the triad, "Disputation," which actually concludes the volume entitled *Romanzero*. "Disputation" is set in Christian rather than Moorish Spain, after the beginning of the decline of the golden age. A debate is to be held before Pedro II, "the Horrible," and his exotic wife Donna Blanka, the former Blanche de Bourbon, between a Father José, a Franciscan monk, and a Rabbi Juda of Navarre. At this fictionalized debate the mendicant preacher begins with a proselytizer's invective against the Jew. The rabbi's answer is full of "good taste." He refuses to become embroiled in the monk's invective and invokes the manner in which the leviathan will be prepared for the true believers on the Day of Judgment, with a "white garlic sauce." The contrast between the raging rhetoric of the monk, with his clearly political goal of defaming the

Jews, and the tempting, cajoling rejoinder of the rabbi is stark. This ironic contrast, which seems to place the rabbi's rhetoric on a higher plane than that of the monk, continues until the monk, in one of his tirades, lashes out against the "Tauves-Jomtof." The rabbi's reaction is at first angry puzzlement and then vituperation. "For if the Tauves-Jomtof is not sacred / what is?"

What has caused the radical turn in the rabbi's rhetoric? What is the "Tauves-Jomtof"? As early as the first critical editions of Heine's work, the scholarly editors pointed out that here, too, Heine erred. For the *Tosefot Yom Tov* is a commentary of the Mishna, not a detailed commentary but rather a series of scholarly footnotes written by Yom Tov Lipmann Heller, a rabbi in seventeenth-century Vienna, Prague, and Cracow. As each editor of Heine's works has repeated, this text appeared some three or four centuries after the events depicted in the poem (depending on whether you take Heine's date or the actual date of the debate upon which this fictionalized account was modeled). No one has asked the evident question, Why does the mere mention of the text so alter the rabbi's rhetoric? Why does it turn it from its "gustatory" reasonableness to a pitch of anger reminiscent of the monk's diatribe?

It is clear that Heine is satirizing the scholastic nature of Talmudic legalism, a satire that he had already evoked in his description of Jehuda ben Halevy's education. In such legalistic systems, once any authority is attacked, no authority is safe. For Heine, the idea of an authority that was a footnote to a commentary of a fragment of Scripture must have seemed a trivial one at best, but especially if it stemmed from a pen wielded by an Eastern Jew, writing in his corrupt Hebrew, rather than from the pen of a writer of the golden age. For Heine equated his (and even Börne's) German to the Hebrew of the golden age; it was the new, free, poetic language of the Jews. It was the conservatives, like "the Jew Menzel," who were like the Eastern Jews in their corruption of language.

Heine was certainly aware of the locus of Heller's commentary, for his autobiography appeared in German. Indeed, in a letter of September 8, 1825, Heine had observed that Moses Moser, "bank official, scholar and disciple of Hegel," to use S. S. Prawer's description, muttered Homer to himself, "as our ancestors muttered the Tosaphot Yomtob."[73] And even if he had been totally unaware of its detailed content, which has no bearing on the poem, he could have used its very reference as a means of evoking the anti-world to the world of the golden age. It is the Eastern Jew, the Jew of the ghetto, who appears in the "Disputation" in the guise of the Spanish Rabbi of Navarre. And he is indeed a schlemiel, even by Heine's redefinition of the term. He strives for a status that is undermined by his very language and rhetoric, and he is struck by a lance aimed at another. The reaction of the official audience caps the poem. Pedro asks his wife to judge the disputation. Out of "her ruby, magical lips" comes the decision: "I do not know which one is right / but it appears to me / That both the Rabbi and the Monk / They both stink." Both Jew and Christian stink! Heine's reference to the *foetor judäicus* has not at all been prepared in the text. From the erotically described lips comes this rank conclusion.

Heine's synesthesia is damning of the type of legalism that links Jew and Christian. It is the emotional, polemical rhetoric shared by Jew and Gentile alike; it is the counterpoint to the language of the true poet. But the removal of the poetic language from the world that is integrating aspects of the language of the Jew into attacks on the nature of the Jew means abandoning the world of the ghetto. For Heine begins the "Hebrew Melodies" with the odor of the "manure and garbage" of the streets from which the Jew escapes into the world of the Sabbath and Hebrew, that is, Jewish, poetry. He concludes the poems with an attack on the scholasticism of polemic that is cast in a rhetoric reminiscent of the odor of the streets. But the language of the streets is the Yiddish or Yiddish-accented German of the world of Heine's youth, the world of the merchant haggling in Yiddish. It is not a world that admits the poet who writes in its own language; for this world, poetry exists in its own ghetto and in a language far removed from daily cares. This double bind is one in which the poet is forced to recreate a new language from the language of daily experience, a language that mirrors the self-contained world of poetry. And yet this self-same language must reflect and perhaps even strive to alter the world from which it has been banned.

The association of Christianity and the religion of the Talmudic Jew through their common stance runs like a red thread through Heine's imagery. As early as a letter written to Immanuel Wohlwill on April 1, 1823, Heine presents a critique of Christianity that draws this comparison:

> I do call Christianity an idea, but what sort of one? There are dirty families of ideas who have embedded themselves in the cracks of this old world, in the abandoned bedsteads of the divine spirit, like the families of lice in the bedsteads of a Polish Jew. If one stamps out one of these idea-lice, it leaves a stench that can be smelled for centuries. Such a louse is Christianity, which was crushed some 1800 years ago.[74]

With Platen's attack, Heine was no longer able to separate the "good"-smelling Jews from the "foul"-smelling Jews. Rather, there were only Jews as perceived by the Christian world. At that moment he found himself embedded in his own metaphor, the rank Jew as perceived by the Christian world.

Heine's concerns throughout his lifetime revolved around the problem of the establishment of a poetic discourse not contaminated by a rhetoric that he sensed was inimical to his own interests. Such a poetic language could not exist in German unless one consciously distanced oneself from the implications of the metaphoric language used by the poet. In creating the very idea of the Jew as poet, Heine was forced to draw boundaries between his idea of the poet's function in the world and the language of the Other. The Other was partly the discourse of the anti-Semite, partly the language evolved by other writers who shared with Heine the label "Jew." These boundaries were, however, extremely flexible and were shifted each time a new antithetical force was felt. Touchstones, such as the model Heine evolved for the function of language, also seemed to change as they were adapted to new situations. Throughout Heine's creative life these problems remained. They were not problems in aesthetics but problems in the necessary restructuring of Heine's sense of self. They were problems in the creation of the persona of Heine the poet, not Harry Heine, Johann Christian Heinrich Heine, Dr. Heinrich Heine, nor even Henri Heine. They were problems in the underlying structures for the creation of a persona unaffected by the shifts in fortune to which the Jew was exposed. And yet the persona created within the world of language was that of the poet, whose only status is within the world that the poet creates, a world that is ephemeral and as much based on the whim of the world as is the status of the Jew. Heine's double bind is articulated within the new language that he has created and is both its source and its goal.

Within the closing three poems of *Romanzero* Heine presents *in nuce* his perception of the conflicts as well as their apparent resolution. The conflict between the worlds in which Jews could find themselves is resolved so as to remove the "little Jew" from exactly that conflicted world of "culture" in which Heine found himself (and in which he clearly was not made welcome). Religious identity thus provides an aesthetic alternative to this closed, Christian world of culture. The identity of the poet as a Jewish poet, again in the eyes of the readers and critics, be they Jewish or Christian, is stressed in Heine's paean to the Jewish poets of Moorish Spain. Heine's conclusion is that true poetry transcends religious identity but that Jewish poets, because of their language, are always bound to be seen as Jews. For Heine, this language of Jewish poetry is represented by Hebrew, and it is in fact the language in which Heine (together with his liberal contemporaries) writes. But Heine also attempts to differentiate himself from inclusion in this liberal, journalistic language.

In the final poem, "Disputation," Heine distances himself from the polemical nature of parochial dispute, whether of the left or right, whether by Jews or Christians. With this attempt Heine signals his awareness that he has been mechanically included, by friend (Wienbarg) and foe (Menzel) alike, in the same mode of discourse practiced by writers such as Börne. Whether he used or adapted their mode of discourse is, of course, unimportant. He saw himself, in works such as his biography of Ludwig Börne, as consciously using different modes of discourse, a different literary language. He perceived his language and his rhetoric as much closer to the tradition of his teacher August Wilhelm Schlegel, whose status as a gentleman-scholar-poet was best expressed by his appearance in the lecture hall at Bonn accompanied by his servant, who held his gloves while he lectured. This, for Heine, was the epitome of both culture and style, and it was this he saw distanced from the language, culture, style, and rhetoric of the Jew. His ambiguous relationship to this world of Romantic high culture can perhaps be best seen in his attribution of Eduard Gans's conversion, the mirror of his own, to the seduction into high culture by thinkers such as August Wilhelm Schlegel. Heine's reaction is best summarized in a letter to Moses Moser written in 1826: "I am now hated by Christian and Jew alike. I am truly sorry that I permitted myself to be baptized. I do not see that my lot has improved; rather, since then I have had nothing but ill luck."[75] In another letter to Moser, Heine spells it out even more clearly. His "personal suffering" is that "never removable Jew" which he is and which he remains no matter what discourse he employs.[76]

IV

The Child Convert: Karl Marx

In the writings of Börne and Heine the reader can trace the shifts in self-definition that resulted from their decisions, as adults, to assimilate into German society. Their identification of their conversion (and its resulting disappointment) with the weaknesses of the Jews illustrates the projection of all faults onto that source perceived by them as the reason for their failures, their Jewish identity. Thus both the "Eastern Jew" and the Westernized, assimilated Jew represented for Börne and Heine flaws in the nature of the Jew. They attempted to create a locus for their own persona somewhere outside of these two models and, of course, again failed. With Karl Marx the situation was somewhat different. For Marx found himself perceived as a Jew even though his level of Jewish identity was minimal.

Karl Marx, born in 1818, was converted to Christianity when he was six years old.[77] His father had converted the year before his birth; his mother was to convert a year after his own conversion. Much interest has been devoted to the relationship between the young Marx and his parents, especially his relationship with his father. Heinrich Marx, born Heschel Marx, was typical of the acculturated Jews who saw conversion as the natural next step in entering German society. He had strong emotional ties to his sense of "Germanness," opposing Napoleon and supporting the German position during the "War of Liberation." This identification with the German society was heightened by the family's life in Trier, a city perched on the linguistic border between German, French, and Dutch. Of all the cities in Loter, the ancient settlement of German Jewry, Trier was the one in which the level of awareness of the political and social implication of language was the highest. Marx's language as a child was German. His father identified himself with the Prussian state and thus with the German language and its concomitant rhetoric. When the young Karl Marx began to write poetry, his father encouraged him to write an ode that "should glorify Prussia and afford an opportunity of praising the genius of the Monarch [Frederick William III] . . . patriotic, emotional, and composed in a Germanic manner."[78] Good language for Jews is thus the antithesis of the new language of the Jews, the language of the Gallomanes, of Börne and Heine. It is "Germanic" rather than French, patriotic rather than critical, and emotional rather than polemically enlightened. It is bound to the metaphysical world enclosed by the very concept of Germany, a concept that transcended the merely earthly quality of the nation/state and drew on the transcendental implication of patriotism for the Germans, a people, like the Jews, without a true national state.

The idea of the Jew's language as the antithesis of the language of the Germans is found throughout early nineteenth-century thought. And nowhere is it more compelling and more influential than in the works of G. W. F. Hegel. For Hegel there was a clear distinction to be drawn between the legal and the structural definition of the Jew.[79] Like Voltaire, who was opposed to the institution of slavery, Hegel saw the civil definition of the Jew as inviolate. Jews, like blacks, had an inalienable right to their civil status within the modern state—in spite of their nature. For the Jews are for Hegel much like blacks. They are an ahistorical people, living outside of the progress of Western civilization. They lack self-consciousness, and their religious creed is materialistic. Hegel accepts Kant's and Michaelis's view that Judaism is not a true religion but rather a body of laws and that these laws, incorporated in the Talmud, reveal the innate blindness of the Jews. The Jews separate the essential spirit from life and thus are the antithesis of the Greeks, in whom the union of these two forces is the wellspring of creativity. Moreover, Judaism is a lesser form of revelation than Christianity, separating as it does the idea of God from the world of the senses. Here Hegel reflects the older view that the Jews are unable to present a synthesis of a higher order because of their manner of perceiving the world. In his aesthetics Hegel presents the clearest argument for the separation between the idea of the Jew in biblical terms and contemporary Jews. While Hegel praises the epic breadth of the Bible, he also limits the idea of Jewish creativity to the period of time when the Jews had a true role in Western civilization. Hegel sees this moment as existing at the shift from the Oriental world in its decline to the rise of the Western world. Only when the Jews had a role in the historical process did their works reveal a flame of creativity. In contrast, the post-biblical existence of the Jews, which did not at all fit into Hegel's concept of the progress of history, is symbolized in Hegel's writing by the legalist language of the Talmud.

One could argue that Hegel moved from a primitive anti-Semitism in his early theological writings to a more sympathetic understanding of the Jews in later works, such as his philosophy of history. In fact, the object of his concern shifted. Since he was constrained to support the civil liberties of the Jews based on his own rational understanding of the nature of the state, he shifted his perspective, seeing only in the biblical Jews, long vanished, Jews worthy of such integration. Hegel's creation of a mythology of the Jews, tied to their discourse, provided the background for much of the radical critique of Judaism to be found in the young Karl Marx.

Marx wrote his best-known critique of Judaism in 1843, about the time of his marriage to Jenny von Westphalen, the Protestant daughter of Marx's noble friend from Trier.[80] Published in the *German-French Yearbook*, in the sole issue of that journal edited jointly by Marx and other German radicals, it was not an independent essay but rather a review essay prompted by two pieces by Marx's then friend and ally, the radical theologian Bruno Bauer. Bauer had attracted Marx with his radical atheism during Marx's studies in Bonn. Indeed, Marx had planned to collaborate with Bauer on a series of pamphlets centering around their reading of Hegel's condemnation of religious (i.e., Christian) art. Of Bauer's essays the first is the most theoretical.[81] In it Bauer argued that emancipation of the Jews was an impossible goal, since no one living in an absolute state could be truly emancipated. Prejudice against the Jews would vanish, and emancipation become a possibility, when the nature of the state was altered. Any attempts to grant the Jews civil rights at this point in history would be impossible because of the nature of the state.

The second essay, "The Capacity of Present-Day Jews and Christians to Become Free," published by Bauer in *Twenty-One Sheets from Switzerland*, a short-lived journal edited by the radical poet Georg Herwegh, was a much more complex presentation of the idea of the Jew.[82] Bauer saw a dialectic difference in the natures of Jews and Christians. Christianity completed the Jewish program; Jews therefore had to come to terms with Christianity before they were truly liberated. In simple, theological terms, Bauer perceived Judaism as necessarily completed within Christianity. Thus, to achieve true emancipation in the future ideal state, Jews would have to pass through Christianity on their way to true freedom. This was, of course, the goal of evangelical Christianity, with the new suspension of all religion tacked on for radical consumption.

Bauer's language in this second essay bears examination. Bauer echoed Christian, evangelical rhetoric throughout the essay. He created an image of the Jew—most specifically of the language and rhetoric of the Jew—that stood in the long tradition of the Christian understanding of the limitation of the Jews' perception of the world, and he made this category an absolute one. At the very beginning of the essay, Bauer attacked the idea that Jews have the potential for citizenship in the state because of "the excellence of their religious ethics" (56). This shorthand for the writings of the Jews, for the Talmud, led Bauer to present the Jew talking to his audience:

> Well! one says, and the Jews say it themselves, Jews should not be emancipated because they are Jews, because they have such an excellent and generally humane ethical principle; rather, the Jew will disappear behind the citizen and be a citizen even though he is and remains a Jew. That is, he is and remains a

Jew in spite of the fact that he is a citizen and lives in general
human conditions: his Jewish and limited essence always overcomes his human and political duties. (57)

How did this limited, Jewish essence manifest itself? Again, Bauer
adapted the older rhetoric of the blindness reflected in the Jews'
perception of the world: "Jewish Jesuitism is the mere cunning of
sensual egoism, common craftiness, and with all of that, it remains
raw, gross hypocrisy, as it always deals with natural, sensual needs"
(60). Hegel's more esoteric critique of the Jews is placed into the
crudest materialistic form. Jews deal with the realities of the world.
When they appear to be dealing with anything more theoretical it
is a mask. And Bauer continues throughout the essay this old, anti-
Talmudic diatribe. Indeed, he even cites "the Jewish casuist, the
rabbi," giving advice as to the ritual cleanliness of food as an example of the "simple foolishness and insulting consequences of religious limitations" (61). All of Judaism is mere cunning, aimed at
the satisfaction of the sensual needs of the individual. But it is not
merely the religious Jews who are trapped within this model of the
Jew. Even the "enlightened Jews" (65) are caught within this Jewish
mode of seeing the world. Christianity, especially Protestantism,
is the closest religion to the total suspension of religious practices,
and the Jews, under no matter what guise, are the furthest away.
Thus the Christian must only follow through on the implications
of the tradition of Christianity, its "suspension," in order to become
that which the true Christian can become, no longer a Christian.
The Jew has a more complicated path to follow. Jews must strive
against the "fantastic, bottomless laws" that bind them; they must
break with their essence.

Marx turns to Bauer's two essays as the focus through which
he defines and shapes his understanding of the Jew, and he does
this in a specific medium. The *German-French Yearbook* was one
of a series of journalistic enterprises undertaken by German radicals during the 1830s and 1840s. Fritz Schlawe notes that the Young
Hegelians managed to turn out some twenty thousand pages in
their various journalistic undertakings. The very history of these
short-lived newspapers and periodicals is a history of the continuation of the "Jewish" language of journalism among yet another
group perceived by official social institutions (and themselves) as
outsiders.[83] Like the earlier journalists, they had as their primary
focus each other. And their discourse was limited to the analysis
of the faults and errors of their fellow writers. Unable to find an
outlet for their political interests within the arena of German poli-

tics until the late 1840s, and unable to publish their works, except sporadically, within Germany, they acquired their sense of status only with the printed word of the "movement" itself. This stage was limited to the authors who shared a manner of perceiving the world. And this manner of seeing the world was labeled as Jewish and foreign.

In October 1843 Marx moved to Paris, thus associating himself with the German-writing, Jewish liberals living there, such as Heine. Contemporaries, both allies, such as the co-editor of the *German-French Yearbook*, Arnold Ruge, and ideological opponents, such as Eduard Müller-Tellering, saw Marx's writings as the product of a Jew.[84] For Marx was linked in the popular mind with other "Jewish" radical writers, such as Moses Hess. Hess advocated an eclectic anarcho-socialism which came to interest the young Marx.[85] Indeed, Marx evidently used an unpublished essay by Hess in formulating his answer to Bauer. The strength of the association between Bauer and Hess, between the idea of the Jew and the radical, is not only to be found in Hess's unpublished paper on the question of the nature of money, for Marx's essay "On the Jewish Question" is also his first attempt to deal with materialist categories of history. And within *Twenty-One Sheets from Switzerland* there is a programmatic essay by Hess on "Socialism and Communism." "On the Jewish Question" is thus to be read in this complex matrix of Marx's striving to provide his own understanding of the Jews and their world within the highly esoteric world of his, a journalism labeled Jewish.

"On the Jewish Question," published in 1844, rejected the abstractions in which Bauer clothed his argument but accepted much of the basic structure of that argument. Marx accepts Bauer's characterization of the nature of the Jew, of the Jews' lack of a place within the historical process, and Bauer's rejection of Jewish particularism. But what is most important, he accepts Bauer's view of Judaism as a cult of egoism. Marx reflects Ludwig Feuerbach's heightening of Kant's refusal to see Judaism as a religion. Feuerbach sees Judaism as a gastronomic cult, since Jews perceive the world through their stomach.[86] When Marx turns to the essay by Bauer in the Herwegh anthology, his rhetoric takes a marked turn. Marx offers his own reading of the nature of the Jew based on Bauer and Feuerbach.

The discourse of the Jews is "haggling."[87] It is the "secular cult of the Jew" that articulates their egoism. True emancipation for "our age" would be the "emancipation from haggling and money" (110). Western society has already become Judaized in that it has accepted the role of money as the basis for social order. Thus the Jews have emancipated themselves in turning society into a cult of money. "The god of the Jews has been secularized and has become the god of the world. Exchange is the actual god of the Jew. His god is only the illusion of exchange" (112). This illusion is the Jew's answer to the creativity of the non-Jewish, Western world: "What lies abstract in the Jewish religion, a contempt for theory, art, history, man as an end in himself, is the actual, conscious standpoint, the virtue of the money man. The species relationship, the relationship of man to woman, etc. becomes an object of commerce! Woman is bartered" (112).

Marx begins his argument based on the difference between economic and civil emancipation within the modern (German Christian) state. He concludes by seeing that state not as German Christian but as Jewish. And the Jewishness of that state is manifested in the language ("haggling"), the aesthetics ("contempt for theory, art, history"), and the sexualized nature of the Jew ("Woman is bartered"). Marx sees his own life, his recent marriage to his Protestant, noble wife; his writing, especially this very essay; and his poetic creations as the antithesis of this image of the Jew. He sees himself not as a bookkeeper but as a creator of books. And he sees himself as the antithesis of the money Jew, for it is in the "practical Jewish spirit, Judaism or commerce" that the this-worldliness of the Jew is manifest. Marx's economic determinism begins, then, with the pun inherent in the German use of the concept "Jew," a term that by analogy had come to mean commerce in the vilest and basest sense.

But Marx adds a further implication to the idea of Jewishness. In "On the Jewish Question" Marx is responding to an essay that posits the rhetoric of the Jew as immutable until converted into Christianity. Marx sees all of Christianity as already converted into the basest nature of the Jews. But he also sees Bauer's argument as reflecting the type of attack lodged against the writings of Jews, or those labeled as Jews. Marx adapts Bauer's own rhetoric to criticize that world with which, by implication, Bauer has associated him, the world of Jewish language. "Jewish Jesuitry, the same practical Jesuitry that Bauer points out in the Talmud, is the relationship of the world of selfishness to the dominant laws whose crafty circumvention forms the chief art of this world" (113). But Marx's argument is not identical to that of Bauer. It avoids the theological underpinning of Bauer's hierarchy of religions, placing Christianity on the same (low) plane as Judaism. And Marx consciously avoids the abstraction of Bauer's writing.

The idea that Bauer's fault lies within his need to abstract and that Marx is providing a concrete presentation of the economic basis of the nature of the Jew lies at the center of the shift in rhetoric. It also may explain the extraordinary power of Marx's essay and its influence. For Marx uses specific, worldly examples and a language that is bound, not to the flights of theological fancy found in Bauer's essays, but to the reflection of the nature of the Jew in this world. In the *German Ideology* Marx (together with Engels) defined "good" language in regard to its reflection of reality:

> For the philosopher it is one of the most difficult tasks to descend from the world of thought to the real world. The immediate reality of thought is language. Just as the philosophers made thinking autonomous, so they also had to transform language into an autonomous realm. This is the secret of philosophic language in which thoughts, in the guise of words, have a content of their own. The problem of descending from the world of thought to the actual world turns into the problem of descending from language into life.[88]

Here is the line between the "philosopher" Bauer and the "journalist" Marx. For Marx uses language correctly; that is, he uses language as a reflection of the "manifestations of actual life" rather than as the "distorted language of the actual world," the language of philosophy. And such philosophy is coterminus with theological discourse, as practiced by writers such as Bauer, who adapt such a discourse for their philosophical writings.

Marx's essay "On the Jewish Question" served as a means by which he was first able to articulate that program which later became identified as "Marxian." Julius Carlebach enumerates the points in Marx's essay that reappear in expanded form as the fulcrum of Marx's later thought:

1. the criticism of civil, i.e., bourgeois society;
2. a materialistic approach to history;
3. the analysis of "the rights of man" as inadequate;
4. the call for a revolution even more profound than the earlier ones; and
5. the vision of a "perfect" society.[89]

All of these points appear when Marx is constrained to deal with that world with which he finds himself identified. He embeds this criticism in a text the theme of which remains the Jews' inability to alter themselves: "Thus it is not only in the Pentateuch and the Talmud that we find the essence of the contemporary Jew: we find it in contemporary society, not as an abstract but as a very empirical essence, not as the limitation of the Jew but as the Jewish limitations of society" (114). The Jews do not themselves possess the potential for altering their essence. Indeed, what they alter is their environment, which becomes infected by their presence. The means by which they pervert their surroundings is through the language of commerce, "haggling."

Marx thus agrees with Bauer on the nature of the Jews' blindness and even its manifestation in language. What he breaks with is Bauer's philosophical discourse, choosing instead a language that directly reflects this question. But in doing so he chooses a language that is Jewish. For Bauer's criticism of the Jews' articulation of their perception of the world is that they see it too concretely, that they separate the abstract from the real, thus negating both. Marx, in choosing to counter the abstract nature of Bauer's discourse, was forced to present his argument in a form that would have been recognized immediately as Jewish. Even a cursory glance at the essay by Moses Hess, included in the same volume as the second essay by Bauer, illustrates that Marx had adapted the concrete tone of Hess's argument. For although Hess was known as someone whose normal discourse was highly philosophical, the essay "Socialism and Communism," with its opening bemoaning the present division between theory and praxis, provides a concrete antithesis to the mode of argumentation present in the Bauer piece. Hess, identified by his ideological supporters and detractors alike as a Jew, becomes a source of Marx's new rhetoric and eventually his new ideology.

But Marx's essay "On the Jewish Question" demanded a major reshaping of Jewish rhetoric; his discourse may have been influenced by Hess, but it articulated itself around the nooks and crannies of Bauer's understanding of the Jew. For no matter how Marx wished to distance himself from the idea of the Jew and no matter how radically he defined the Jew as his antithesis, the world about him still saw him as a Jew. And thus in the first major joint effort by Marx and Friedrich Engels, *The Holy Family* (1845), a critique of Bauer and Feuerbach, Marx himself rewrites "On the Jewish Question."

Stanley Edgar Hyman has characterized *The Holy Family*, or at least large segments of it, as representing the corruption of ideas through the corruption of language: "Reichardt misuses foreign words, which are quoted at length; Faucher creates German words on English principles of work-formulation; Edgar Bauer mishandles Proudhon's French, which is unlike German, 'the language of politics and thoughtful observation'; Szeliga mixes his metaphors; Bruno Bauer writes a hopeless jargon of apology and qualification."[90] In rewriting "On the Jewish Question" in *The Holy Family*, Marx makes himself aware of the distinctions that he drew in his earlier essays, distinctions that led to his movement toward Hess's position, not in terms of the "Jewish Question" but in terms of the more general question of the role of ideology in society. *The Holy Family* is a critique of the circle around Bruno Bauer and his brother Edgar, a circle enmeshed in the liberal ideology of the Young Hegelians. This critique is stated in a rhetoric that, as has been shown, relied heavily on traditional Christian modes of expression.

In rewriting his essay, Marx stresses the fact that Bauer et al. have learned "the popular language of the mass and transfigure[d] that vulgar jargon into the high-flown intricacy of the dialects of Critical Criticism" (11). Bauer's language thus gives the appearance of abstraction but is in fact merely the "vulgar jargon" of the streets. It is not German—"Critical Criticism does not give a single thought in German" (38)—but rather a mix of foreign (French and English) elements in bad and confused German grammar. And this mangled language of the mob is the reflection of Bauer's religious perception of the world: "That relation discovered by Herr Bruno is, in fact, nothing but a Critically caricatured consummation of Hegel's conception of history, which in turn is nothing but the speculative expression of the Christian-Germanic dogma of the antithesis between Spirit and Matter, between God and the World" (85). Within this context, Marx begins to alter some of the basic views that he had seemed to accept from Bauer. Rather than conclude that the political nature of the state is determined by the presence of Jews, he moves from the social significance of Judaism to the political nature of the state. And Judaism no longer stands as negatively emblematic for *all* religion. The focus of the essays in *The Holy Family* is not the nature of the Jews but the nature and expression of Bauer's perception of the Jews. Marx even uses a Jewish source, Gabriel Reisser's critique of Bauer, as one of his authorities in analyzing Bauer's misuse of the image of the Jew. And finally, Marx modifies the idea that Jews are defined by their role within the system of exchange. Indeed, in *The Holy Family* Marx attributes all of the negative qualities that he (following Bauer) had associated with the intrinsic nature of the Jew to the Young Hegelians. For Bauer is nothing but a Christian in radical's clothing: "He could not have any inkling of [the true nature of the Jew] because he did not know the Jew as part of the real world but only as part of his world, theology; because he, a pious, godly man, considers not the active everyday Jew but the hypocritical Jew of the Sabbath to be the real Jew" (109). Bauer's perception of the world is determined by his books, volumes of Christian theology, and therefore he can never truly know the realities of the world, only the realities reflected in his language.

What Marx maintains is the association of Jews with the world of finance. This association, present in the image of the Jew in the writings of Börne and Heine, is Marx's basic distinction between his language and the language of the Jews. And in labeling Bauer and the Young Hegelians with the same qualities that he ascribed to the Jews, Marx also distanced himself from that faulty abstraction that revealed itself to be the language of the streets. He sees in Bauer the "Sabbath Jew" of Bauer's own critique, a Christian Talmudist whose abstractions reveal themselves to be bits of Christian trivia. Marx thus eliminates both categories as potential labels for himself. In his own definition of his persona he is neither the "Sabbath Jew" nor the "finance Jew."

Why does Marx find it necessary to distance himself so radically from these two models of the Jew? What would have been the markers of "Jewishness" for his contemporaries and therefore for Marx himself? Unlike in the cases of Börne and Heine, where the complexity of this question is increased by their adult redefinitions of their Jewishness, the locus of Marx's idea of the Jew must lie within his formative experiences, experiences that he had before his baptism and that colored his manner of perceiving the Jew even after he felt himself no longer to be one. For the caesura must seem much more radical for a child than for an adult, seen as it is in terms of absolute rather than relative reasons for conversion. For the child this break with the old seems total, and the promise of becoming a new person, unblemished by one's past sins or identity, an absolute promise.

The distance between the conversion of his father and siblings and the conversion of his mother may give some clue to the origin of Marx's internalized image of the Jew. Marx's father has been the subject of much scrutiny. He appears in retrospect to be a fairly typical example of the German Jew who accepted on face value the promises of the European Enlightenment about "the rights of man." His orientation, both intellectual and linguistic, was German. And it is clear that Marx held him to be a model of that which he wanted to become. The conversion of his family to Christianity was therefore only the final, rational step in their integration into German society. Marx's mother is quite another matter.[91] Her maiden name was Pressburg, and she was the daughter of Isaac Pressburg, a rabbi in Nijmegen. But her name gives one further clue to her identity. Her father's family had come from Pressburg, Hungary, to Holland, and evidently maintained their Eastern European identity, at least their linguistic identity, even while living in Holland. Heinrich Marx's father, grandson and brother of rabbis in Trier, had an impeccable "German" tradition behind him. Indeed, his first language appears to have been German. His wife, coming out of a Yiddish-speaking home in Holland, never acquired a native command of German. She was literate in neither Yiddish nor Dutch. Her letters reveal a Yiddish-tinged German, with sentence patterns clearly influenced by spoken Yiddish structures and a hesitant vocabulary.[92] If one could extrapolate from her written German, her spoken language would have been German, but with a marked Yiddish accent and perhaps numerous Yiddishisms.

Within Marx's home, then, there would have been two models for the language of the Jew. His father, with his liberal support of the Prussian state, would have been associated with German. Marx's youthful enthusiasm for German letters may well be associated with his father's sense of the nature of the German language as an expression of German patriotism. On the other hand, Marx's mother had little interest in such literary expression. Her reading would have been limited to tractates, and her world, as David McLellan has formulated it, would have been "almost totally limited to her family and home, rather overanxious and given to laments and humourless moralizing."[93] Yiddish-accented German would have been associated with the world of the home, and the contrast between the two would have stressed the parochial implications of the language associated with the mother. This sense would have been highlighted by the contrast between the integrated world of his father's family and the image of his mother's family as intruders from the East. When one turns to Marx's discussions of his family, it is not surprising that his mother seems to vanish from his perception.

The world associated with the mother had its presence on the streets of Trier. For while some of the Trier Jews may have been as well integrated into German society as was Heinrich Marx, a lawyer and a member of one of the German political clubs of his day, most of the Jews of Trier, according to the mayor of Trier in 1828, "belonged to the lower levels of society" and had been in Trier only for the past few decades.[94] These Jews would have spoken Yiddish as their primary language and would have been a very visible presence in the world of the youthful convert Karl Marx. The tenfold increase in the number of Jews in Trier in the first two decades of the nineteenth century would have made the town even more aware of the differences between the assimilated or acculturated Jews of Trier and those "belonging to the lower classes." Thus a pattern is established: language, gender, and class all contributed their qualities to the young Marx's image of the Jew. Yiddish-accented German, women, and the lower class merged with the image of the "peddler Jew," living off of his haggling in public places, to create the image of the Jew in Marx's early thought. The polar distinction between this image and the German-speaking, masculine, middle-class image of his father, earning his living from service, provides the model for the "bad" and the "good" Jew. And Marx categorizes the "good" Jew as that Jew who was not a Jew. The idea of conversion was also inherent in the young Marx's understanding of the Jew. Conversion was the ability to remove oneself completely from any association with the "bad" Jew, to no longer possess the stigma of belonging to a group any definition of which would include the qualities ascribed to the "bad" Jew.

When one turns to the older Marx's understanding of what makes up the essence of the Jew, the role of the Jews' discourse appears over and over again. In Marx's correspondence Jews are often characterized by their "bad" German. One often cited example of this is in a letter Marx wrote to Engels on April 10, 1856, after Heine's death:

> You know that Heine is dead, but did you know that Ludwig Simon of Trier had pissed on his grave—I meant to say, passed water—in the New York *New Times* [edited by] the former lion of the retired Parliament of the German Nation. The poet or troubadour of the Jew-broad high-shit, high-ash, or high-lime of Frankfurt on the Main discovers, of course, that Heine was no poet. He had "no soul," he was "full of meanness," and he did not only insult Kobes the First but also Börne's lady friend, the great Börne's mouse, or muse or cunt, Mrs. Strauss.[95]

All of the concluding few lines are written in what Marx in another context calls a "Jewish-nasal" style.[96] It is the language of the Jew and is countered by Marx's own language. What is remarkable about this passage is the contrast between the "high" language represented in Marx's Yiddish-accented paraphrase from Ludwig Simon's memoir of Heine and the sexual crudity of Marx's own language. But the associations in this letter may well explain Marx's extraordinary venom. For Simon is associated with Trier, with the world of Marx's youthful image of the Jew, and is linked with the world of the Jew as woman. Marx links this association through

Heine's use of Börne's sexuality in his memoir of the writer to his own sexualization of the Jew as critic. Thus the only position left for Marx is as the anti-Semitic rhetorician using the comic language of the Jew to reveal the inner falsity and transparency of the Jew's message.

Marx's sense of the position he must take vis-à-vis the language of the Jews is underwritten by his friend and colleague Friedrich Engels. In 1848 Engels had joined the public debate centering around the Poles' attempts to free themselves from Prussian and Russian domination and to reestablish their own state. The Prussians had claimed cultural hegemony over Poland because of the Jews' presence in the Prussian provinces of Poland. For do not Jews speak German? Suddenly, Yiddish, long viewed as a sign of the corruption of the Jews by Germany, was being used as a sign of their inclusion within the greater German cultural community. Engels attacks this argument in attempting to support the Polish claim to autonomy. It was presented in the Frankfurt Parliament by Adolf Stenzel, who called the language spoken by the Jews in Poland "German."[97] Engels counters with the ironic argument that these "peddler Jews, their lice, and their dirt" can be forgotten because they want to be Germans. And how do they show themselves to be Germans? They speak German in their homes. "And what a German!" Engels mocks Stenzel's claim that this "German" should be considered a sign that these Jews (and therefore the Polish territory in which they live) should be seen as belonging to Prussia. For the Jews have "German" as their language throughout the world, according to Engels. And thus perhaps the Prussians can lay claim to all of Europe and half of America because "German"-speaking Jews live there (5:323–25).

Engels's mocking of the idea that Yiddish could in any way be understood as German is linked to the idea that the mere acceptance of language is a sign of the acceptance of a culture. Linguistic differences are mirrors of the differences implicit between the Jews and the Germans. The Jews are not Poles, nor are they Germans. They speak a language that is non-national in nature and reflects the inner being of the Jews, their "haggler" essence. Confronted with an understanding of Yiddish in this way, Marx would have found his earlier impressions of the language and nature of the Jew reified by a non-Jewish authority, Engels, and would have been able to place himself on the side of the defenders of a "liberal" cause by accepting this view. Marx and Engels placed themselves on the side of the Polish-speaking aristocracy who had spearheaded the 1830 revolt and who stood ready to reinstate the Polish throne.

Again the pattern repeats itself: the Yiddish-speaker, the "Eastern" Jew as haggler, is opposed to the upper class, speaking a language integrated into an acceptable national image.

When one turns to Marx's major work, *Capital*, a work that in its various drafts concerns him his entire adult life, the extremely marginal presence of the Jew is at first surprising. And yet when the few references to the Jew are examined, the reader is struck by the continuity of Marx's flawed sense of self as projected in the qualities of the Jew. The beginning of the first volume of *Capital* defines the nature of "commodity" using the well-known example of the manufacture and sale of a coat. In an aside, Marx turns to the "language of commodity": "Let us note, incidentally, that the language of commodities also has, apart from Hebrew, plenty of more-or-less correct dialects. The German word 'Wertsein' (to be worth), for instance, brings out less strikingly than the Romance verb 'valere,' 'valer,' 'valoir' that the equating of commodity B with commodity A is the expression of value proper to commodity A. *Paris vaut bien une messe!* [Paris is certainly worth a mass]."[98] The language of haggling, the language of the Jews, is Hebrew, not Yiddish. It is the idealized language of the Jews when they supposedly had a role in the historical process, or at least, to refer back to Heine's mythology of language, when they lived at one with their Moorish neighbors during the golden age of Spanish Jewry. Hebrew is like other languages of trade—not German, for German is not as good a language of commodity as, let us say, French. But why French? Marx provides the answer in the example he chooses for the verb *valoir*. In 1593 Henri IV converted to Catholicism to assume the French throne and was reported to have said that "Paris was worth a mass." The conversion for gain, false conversion such as that practiced by the speakers of the Jews' language, is but another sign of the relationship between the realities of the world (commerce) and their mode of articulation.

But Marx, of course, distances himself from this charge. For his conversion, not to Protestantism, but away from Judaism, was a true conversion, since he was a speaker, not of Hebrew or the French associated by Germans with "Jews" such as Heine, but of the more truthful German, a language that poorly expresses the language of commodity. The true speakers of "Hebrew," the "correct dialect" of commodity, are the Jews in Poland. They are the "trading nation" *par excellence*, living "in the pores of Polish society" (1:172). Marx's reference to the Polish Jews comes in his discussion of the role of religion as an articulation of value within the concept of commodity. Christianity is posited as the "most fitting form of religion," since it reflects this materialism most directly, but not all Jews are likewise condemned, only the Polish Jews, as representatives of the "trading nations." The Polish Jews speak Yiddish, as Engels is at pains to point out, not Hebrew, so the "dialect" to which Marx refers in his discussion of the language of commodity is clearly the real language of the Jews, neither Hebrew nor Yiddish but haggling. In his later discussion of the transformation of money into capital, Marx brings the example that the value of money in circulation cannot be changed by any alteration in the "distribution [of wealth], any more than a Jew can increase the quantity of the precious metals in a country by selling a farthing from the time of Queen Anne for a guinea. The capitalist class of a given country, taken as a whole, cannot defraud itself" (1:256–57). The Jew as moneychanger is the prototypical Jew, who speaks a language of commerce that is deceptive but immutable. The national language of the Jews may shift. They may articulate their nature in English or German or French, but the national language that they employ is but camouflage for the true language in which they dupe their prey, "haggling." And this is unalterable.

The specialized language of the Jew as a mirror of the Jews' nature seems to remain an abstract in Marx's later writings. And yet at a moment when Marx stands at one of the central markers in any human being's life, at the brink of his fiftieth birthday, the childhood association of the specific language of the Jew, the language of his mother and the world of finance, reappears. He writes to Engels on April 30, 1868: "In a few days I will be fifty. When that Prussian lieutenant said to you: 'Twenty years in service and still a lieutenant,' I can say: 'A half a century on my back and still a pauper!' How right my mother was: 'If Karell had made capital, instead of....' "[99] The association of the mother's spoken language, here reflected in the "Jewish" pronunciation of his name with the idea of "capital," links the abstract language of commodity back to the specific, Yiddish-accented language of the Jews.

In the third volume of *Capital* Marx returns to the nature of the system of exchange that characterizes capitalism. The "illusion of exchange" for the younger Marx in "On the Jewish Question" was the Jew's God. In discussing the nature of systems of circulation as described by the London banker David Chapman, Marx returns to the nature of bills of exchange: "Alongside of banknotes, wholesale trade has a second and more important means of the circulation of value: the bill of exchange. Mr. Chapman has shown us how essential this is for the regular course of business in that good bills of exchange are accepted for payment everywhere and under all circumstances. 'For if the Taubes Jontof is not sacred, what is!' " (3:473).

Heinrich Heine's image of the Jewish scholastic from his poem "Disputation" returns to characterize the faith that makes inherently worthless bits of paper, bills of exchange, assume the aura of inviolable value. The capitalist system is thus the Talmud written in the language of the Jews, haggling. Marx's reference to this central text by his intellectual compatriot Heinrich Heine locates for the reader the place of the "bad" Jews and their language, and yet especially during the period of his drafting of the various volumes of *Capital*, Marx was himself seen as the polemical Jew, the Jew as revolutionary publicist. That Marx had to continue the distancing of his language from the language of the Jews is not surprising. He found it necessary to retain a clear and overt distinction between how he expressed himself and that mode of expression which he attributed to the Jew. It is little wonder that he turned to the final expression of Heine's ambivalence concerning his own Jewish identity for the source of this means of distancing himself and his language from the haggling of the Jews. In his reading of the "Hebrew Melodies," Marx rejects the image of the "Sabbath Jew," whom he had already categorized as merely a subtype of the Jew in his early writings, and he rejects the image of the Jew as poet, exposed to the whims of history. For Marx retained his image of himself as a "poet," an image that he had polished as a young man under his father's tutelage. His new language of expression, the language of revolution, the language of the prophet, was but a continuation of the idea of a language different from that of the Jew, and yet it was precisely this language that was seen by his contemporaries as quintessentially Jewish.

The Jews' language is a reflex of their essence, an essence formed by their historic and economic circumstances but an essence that becomes imprinted on the Jew as the outward mark of Cain. Much interest has been devoted to Friedrich Engels's supposed radical attempt to integrate Marxist thought (in terms of a model of economic determinism) with the new Darwinian evolutionary model.[100] Engels's late writings, many of which are fragmentary and all of which were written after Marx's death, seem to reflect his desire to explain physical characteristics of humanity, such as the development of the human hand, in terms of concepts such as the means of production, but as implemented through the mechanism of Darwinian evolution. This is merely new rhetorical window dressing for the typology that Marx had introduced into the first volume of *Capital* when, in explaining the capitalist character of manufacture, he presented the case that workers in the modern capitalist state can only sell their labor when they are employed within the factory, since labor only has value in this context: "Unfitted by nature to make anything independently, the manufacturing worker develops his productive activity only as an appendage of that workshop. As the chosen people bore in their features the sign that they were the property of Jehovah, so the division of labor brands the manufacturing worker as the property of capital" (1:482).

Marx's view of the negative adaptation of human beings to their surroundings had its roots in the formulation of the concept of degeneration by the physician B.-A. Morel during the 1840s.[101] Morel used very similar illustrations of the physical disabilities caused by poor working conditions, especially in the mines, to those that Marx brings to show the "degenerate population" of workers such as the potters (1:355). Indeed, this very formulation, as well as the detailed description of the potters' pathological physiognomy, is cited by Marx from a medical report on the conditions in the British potteries. But Marx's reference to the "features" that brand the "chosen people" as the "property of Jehovah" is of a clearly more primitive nature than the idea that economic conditions moderate human appearance. The Jews bear in their physiognomy the sign of their being possessed, owned, by their religion. Their outward appearance, like their language, is an indicator of their true nature. But what is it in the language of their physiognomy that reveals this fact? Why is Marx constrained to make this argument about the outward sign of the absence of free will?

Marx's view on the outward signs of the essence of the Jew has a parallel that may help to explain this seemingly gratuitous reference. Marx's great opponent within the revolutionary movement was the socialist Ferdinand Lassalle (1825–64), whose charismatic personality and early death in a duel created a myth about him as the swashbuckling advocate of liberal reform. Lassalle was also a Jew who saw the Jews as degenerate:

> I do not like the Jews at all, I even detest them in general. I see in them nothing but the very much degenerated sons of a great but vanished past. As a result of centuries of slavery, these people have acquired servile characteristics, and that is why I am so unfavorably disposed to them. Besides, I have no contact with them. There is scarcely a single Jew among my friends and in the society which surrounds me here [in Berlin].[102]

When Marx writes about Lassalle, however, he perceives him as the essential Jew. Lassalle is the "most unGreek of all the water-pollack Jews." He is "Itzig."[103] His books stink of garlic. But mainly he is that "Jewish nigger, Lassalle."[104] In a letter to Engels, Marx presents his impression of the external nature of the Jew as typified by Lassalle:

> Always this constant babble with the falsely excited voice, the unaesthetic, demonstrative gestures, the didactic tone. . . . And also the uncultivated eating and the horny lust of this "idealist." It is now completely clear to me that, as his skull shape and hair prove, he is a descendant of those Blacks who accompanied Moses on the exodus from Egypt. (If his mother or grandmother on his father's side did cross with a nigger.) Now this combination of Jewishness and Germanness upon the Black basic substance must bring forth a strange product. The pushiness of this fellow is also nigger-like.[105]

This letter, written in a mock scientific language, reflects much of the debate concerning the mulatto that took place during the mid-nineteenth century.[106] Marx's use of the Anglo-American term *nigger* throughout his discussions of Lassalle's physiognomy refers back to this idea of the mulatto as the degenerate product of two otherwise pure races. The qualities ascribed to the mulatto were those of cleverness and adaptability, but the mulatto was also seen to be sterile, unable to reproduce his or her own kind. The sexualization of the outsider, the individual who belongs to neither group, the outsider's outsider, distances the mulatto from consideration as a human. But, of course, Marx ascribes to the outsider Lassalle all of the traditional qualities associated with the Jew: a false language and rhetoric, bad manners, sexual aggressiveness, pushiness. And this to an individual whose public position distanced him from the sense of his own Jewishness.

The parallels to Marx's own sense of self are striking when one reads his condemnation of Lassalle. For Marx, too, took a strong position vis-à-vis the nature of the Jew, distancing himself from their capitalistic essence. Also, Marx was attacked for being too Jewish by revolutionaries such as Bakunin.[107] And what is more important, Marx shared, at least in terms of his own self-perception, Lassalle's physiognomy. Marx's nickname was "the Moor."[108] Indeed, upon first meeting Marx, Engels characterized him in a comic poem as "a dark form from Trier."[109] And Marx's letters are full of references to his darkness. Most striking are the letters from his young wife, for whom his exotic darkness has strong sexual connotations.[110] The implied contrast between the "red-haired, bright-blue-eyed Germans" and the "black Jews," a contrast that stressed the "ugliness" of the Jews, had already been stressed by Ludwig Börne.[111] Marx's "blackness" was a constant sign of his "Jewishness," for his lover, his friends, and his enemies. The implications of the "blackness" must not be ignored, for it is a pathological sign. In a long tradition of European medicine and folk belief that can be traced back to Greek humorial theory, the image of dark skin was understood as a sign of illness. It is a sign of the disease of Jewishness, which relates the Jew to the world of black slavery. In labeling Lassalle as black, Marx projects his own internalized sense of conflict onto Lassalle. For hidden within Marx's sense of self is the internalization of the German-Christian world's identification of him as a Jew. Lassalle is thus seen not as a Jew but rather as a hybrid, neither Jew nor black. His skin bears the sign of his pathology and distances his perversities from Marx's definition of himself. But Marx projects onto the figure of Lassalle all of the negative qualities ascribed to the Jew by contemporary society. Thus he can define himself as different from this "black Jew." For even though he shares the language of physiognomy with Lassalle, he sees himself as different (and better). He sees himself as the "good" Jew, the Jew as convert. But the strength of the idea of conversion is that all of the qualities of the Jew are nullified, and he becomes accepted into the privileged class. Marx is a convert, not to Protestantism, but to a world view where even the external signs of the Jew would vanish, the ideology of revolution. Marx, as an adult, still believes in that instant of conversion when all the outward signs of the Jews, such as the system and language of capitalism, will suddenly vanish. And at that moment the one sign remaining that he shares with the Jews, his blackness, will cease to have any significance.

It is at this point that Marx's image of the Jew returns full circle. For in 1863 Bruno Bauer, the catalyst of Marx's early, programmatic state on the nature of the Jew, published his study of the Jew in the Diaspora, in which he argued that the Jew was but a "white Negro" whose racial identity made spiritual baptism impossible and conversion thus unthinkable.[112] Bauer's views blocked any alteration of the nature of the Jew. Marx's own views thus are the articulation of a point of view held by one perceived by the world as a Jew, and thus unchangeable. Marx must argue that the Jew has the potential for change, a potential that he ascribes to the dialectic of history. And yet, hidden within his reference to the Jew in the third volume of *Capital*, in his reference to the physiognomy of the Jew, is the rhetoric of writers such as Bauer, who see the signs of Jewishness as immutable. In the double bind of the conflict, torn between models of conversion and of immutability, Marx incorporates contradictory aspects of both systems in his image of the Jew and his antithetical self-image: thus his confusion and the vehemence of his own rhetoric when confronted by the contradictory aspects of that "Jew" which he sees within himself.

CHAPTER FIVE

The Science of Race

I

The Linguistics of Anti-Semitism

In the shift in the rhetoric applied to the Jews from religious to "scientific," the idea of the special language of the Jews became one of the salient markers of the new "science" of race.[1] To understand the continuity of the labeling of the Jews as possessing only their own, base discourse, we can begin with the passage that, although predating any "scientific" discussion of the difference of the Jews, so shaped all of the later perceptions of the Jew, Richard Wagner's discussion "Jews in Music." In 1850 Wagner, a spoiled liberal, turned to the question of the nature of the Jews' aesthetic sensibilities as a result of his conflict with the popular Franco-Jewish composer Giacomo Meyerbeer. Wagner denied the Jew any ability to create aesthetically valid works of art, such as musical compositions, by denying the Jew access to civilized discourse:

> By far more weighty, nay, of quite decisive weight for our inquiry, is the effect the Jew produces on us through his *speech*; and this is the essential point at which to sound the Jewish influence upon music. The Jew speaks the language of the nation in whose midst he dwells from generation to generation, but he speaks it always as an alien. As it lies beyond our present scope to occupy ourselves with the cause of this phenomenon, too, we may equally abstain from an arraignment of Christian Civilization for having kept the Jew in violent severance from it, as on the other hand, in touching the sequelae of that severance we can scarcely propose to make the Jews the answerable party. Our only object, here, is to throw light on the aesthetic character of the said results. In the first

place, then, the general circumstances that the Jew talks the
modern European languages merely as learnt, and not as mother
tongues, must necessarily debar him from all capability of
therein expressing himself idiomatically, independently, and
conformably to his nature in any higher sense. A language, with
its expression and its evolution, is not the work of scattered
units, but of an historical community; only he who has unconsciously grown up within the bond of this community, takes
also any share in its creation. But the Jew has stood outside the
pale of any such community, stood solitarily with his Jehova in
a splintered, soilless stock, to which all self-sprung evolution
must stay denied, just as even the peculiar (Hebraic) language of
that stock has been preserved for him merely as a thing
defunct. Now to make poetry in a foreign tongue has hitherto
been impossible, even to geniuses of highest rank. Our whole
European art and civilization, however, have remained to the
Jew a foreign tongue; for, just as he has taken no part in the
evolution of the one, so has he taken none in that of the other;
but at most the homeless person has been a cold, nay more, a
hostile onlooker. In this Speech, this Art, the Jew can only
mimic and mock—not truly make a poem of his words, an
artwork of his doings.[2]

Wagner's prime example for this abuse of language is Heinrich
Heine, the poet who epitomizes the moment "when our poetry
became a lie" (99). Needless to say, Wagner also condemns those
composers who set Heine's poems to music. But it is the superficiality and lack of expression, the Jewish tone, that Wagner sees
in Heine as well as in all of the creative endeavors of the Jews.
While later, in his essays "What Is German?" (1865) and "Notes
on Religion and Art" (1881), Wagner abandons his "liberal" critique
of Christian society as the source of the Jews' isolation (and therefore their falsity of language), he never changes his view of the
Jews' mode of expression. The Jews have no community; they
therefore can have no true language. Hebrew is a nonfunctional
language, unable to express the range of experiences and aesthetic
perceptions of European experience.
　　Wagner denied the Jew any aesthetic sense, any ability to create
true art. This rejection must be read in light of the continuing
rumor that haunted Wagner's entire creative life, that he was the
son of his mother's Jewish lover.[3] With his attack on Meyerbeer
he distances himself from his "Jewish" self by seeing himself as
the creative genius *par excellence* as opposed to inherently inferior

Jewish composers. But what is more important, he links the Jewish artist with the French and, through his condemnation of Heine, with the Jewish journalist. The pattern, which had dominated the discourse about the nature of the Jews' language, continued in Wagner's essay. Published anonymously, it had a great role in focusing the question of the relationship between discourse and race. This theme repeats itself over and over within the "scientific" and "pseudoscientific" writings about the Jews at the close of the nineteenth century.

When Wilhelm Marr, himself the son of a baptized Jew, formulated the shift from an anti-Jewish rhetoric couched in religious terms to one couched in "scientific" language, he was able to use the sense of the alien nature of Jewish discourse as one of the centerpieces of his new science of "anti-Semitism." Marr, a polemicist who evidently coined the term, used the rhetoric of nineteenth-century anthropology, itself permeated with the rhetoric of race, to create the illusion of a new, powerful, objective manner of seeing the Jews.[4] As Hilary Putnam has pointed out, the strength of the rhetoric of science lies in its claim to be "free from the interminable and unsettling debates that we find [and were found] in religion, ethics and metaphysics."[5] Marr based his rhetoric upon this claim.

It was no longer the conflict between the truth of Christianity and the lies of the Jew but rather the contrast between the idea of a Germanic race, inherently truthful, and the perverted and perverting nature of the Jew. The shift from a rhetoric of religion to a rhetoric of race introduced the question of the Jews' language into the very center of scientific discourse, which throughout the late eighteenth and early nineteenth centuries had been preoccupied with race owing to the interest in the question of black slavery. Beginning in the 1860s, Marr continued the nineteenth-century tradition of linking the Jews with their language through the medium of the newspaper. Marr was fixated with the idea of the Jews' press. It runs through his work, especially his widely read pamphlet of 1879, *The Conquest of the Jews over the Germans*. The Jew controls the newspapers; the newspapers, therefore, lie, and that which they advocate proves the conquest of the Jews over the Germans.[6] This process repeats itself and is but a mid-nineteenth-century replication of the *topos* of the lying language of the Jews. Marr's pamphlet elicited a number of answers, from Jews as well as non-Jews. One of the most interesting was by the non-Jewish author Moritz von Reymond, who entitled his piece *Where Does "Mauschel" Hide?*[7] Reymond states his advocacy of assimilation and his opposition to the isolation of the Jews, of *Mauschel.* He seems, in his title and the tone of his piece, to credit Marr himself with all of the qualities ascribed to *Mauschel,* especially in Marr's qualification, buried in the pamphlet, that "if I were a Jew . . ." (37). With Marr, the son of a baptized Jew, the language of the new science, of the concept of a polygenetic origin of mankind, enters into the idea of the special language of the Jews. For parallel to the skin color of the black, the new science of racism, of anti-Semitism, to use Marr's coinage, is the special and hidden language of the Jew. Marr's importance for the shift of rhetoric from religious to scientific cannot be underestimated. The very term "anti-Semitism" itself was a formulation that Marr's contemporaries perceived as shifting the grounds of Jew hatred onto the basis of the "appearance of science," or so the *General Newspaper of German Jewry* stated in commenting on Marr's use of this term.

The idea of the cultural contribution of the Jews, of the Jews' aesthetic language as the indicator of their Otherness within a new science of race, appealed to those Germans who were still attempting to create a political as well as cultural identity out of the chaos of the German states. Here they could banish the Jews from sharing the newly coined culture of the nascent empire, a culture rooted in the written word and not much older than the history of Jewish civil emancipation itself. Eugen Dühring, the theoretician of German anti-Semitism, condemned Jewish participation in German culture.[8] He stressed the importance of Heine and Börne out of all proportion to his sense of their importance in German culture (a discrepancy that he himself remarks on) and followed his condemnation of the shallowness and self-seeking of the Jew as writer with a detailed discussion of the "Jewish and Marxist press." Dühring denies the Jew any aesthetic sensibility, stating quite baldly that "the Jew is lacking any free and selfless activity of the spirit, which alone can lead to disinterested truth and beauty" (77). Jewish language is merely parody. Even the seemingly "deep" emotions of a writer such as Heine are borrowed (in this case from Byron) and used to manipulate his Christian audience. This observation stands at the center of Dühring's presentation of the scientific nature of the Jew.

Such scientific discourse, especially when applied to race, affected all who were exposed to it. The rhetoric of science seemed so new and convincing to the writers and thinkers of the late nineteenth century that they perceived it as a break in the tradition of German racism. They saw a discontinuity between the myths of the Other which dominated German thinking during the first half of the nineteenth century and their own view of a biology of race rooted in empirical science. No longer was the perception of the Other to be the stuff of legend; it had become the focus of a science, with the extraordinary strength that the very word *science* had for the late-nineteenth-century mind, supporting its claim for objective status.

What was the claim made for the nature of the Other by late-nineteenth-century science? It was the basic claim for all of the various offshoots and parallels of scientific discourse during the latter half of the century: that human nature and the psyche are but reflexes of biology and that it is this that determines humanity's place in the world. All of humanity's tools and attributes, including language, are but materialistic reflexes of their biology.[9] The biological paradigm was rich in variations on the mechanisms through which humanity developed, but all these variations saw the totality of one's being as a reflex of that process.[10] Whether Darwinian or Lamarckian, whether Herbert Spencer's social Darwinism or Ernst Haeckel's biological recapitulation, all the variations on the biological model used their paradigms to explain the nature of human difference. For unlike Kant's view, it is not merely that the rational explains the natural but that the biological explains the rational. Language, with its long tradition as the primary marker for the special nature of humanity, undergoes a none too subtle biologization during the late nineteenth century, a process that makes it a reflex of human biology. When this concept is converted into the paradigm of race, it makes the special language of the Other a sign of the innate, biological difference inherent in the very concept of race.

The abyss between the perceiver and the object in concepts of race is total. It is a complete form of distancing. Placing the Other beyond the pale by stressing an unchanging sense of self provides an image of the Other that is the antithesis of self. This chimera of Otherness is, of course, the result of projection. The need to perceive the gulf as unbridgeable underlines the closeness of the image of the Other to the image of self. Yet the power of the scientific model, which rests on the dichotomy between subject and object, between "scientist" and "specimen," forces the Other, if one is to use the paradigm of race, into an absolute position, parallel to the illusion of absolute difference implicit in the model itself. When this occurs among Jews in the late nineteenth century, they generate a series of variations of the concept of a biology of language to enable themselves to write as scientists rather than as specimens. The acceptance or rejection of the scientific model, of the relationship between the Jews' language and their biology, forms a leitmotif for the understanding of the development of Jewish identity during the late nineteenth century.

The echoes of this "scientific" *topos* are found throughout the discourse about the Jews' special nature. In the historian Heinrich von Treitschke's initial attack on the Jews, published in his journal *The Prussian Yearbooks* at the close of 1879, this view defines his "image of the Jew."[11] There are "good" Jews, such as those who live and function in Western Europe, descendants of the Spanish Jews; and there are "bad" Jews, such as those who live in Germany, descendants of Eastern Jews. But even this superficial dichotomy, based on Treitschke's Western reaction to the idea of the Eastern Jew as corrupt and possessing a corrupt language, vanishes when he examines the Jews' language. Misquoting Tacitus, who called the Jews the filth of mankind, Treitschke observes that "there will always be Jews who are nothing more than German-speaking Orientals." It is this view, dominating Wagner's image of the hidden discourse of the Jews, which defines the Jew for the "racial" anti-Semite. Treitschke sees in the assumption by the Jews of Western language merely a mask to disguise their Oriental wiles, which are inculcated into them through "Jewish education." These dominate Jewish discourse among their Jewish contemporaries. Again there is a program that permits change (Become totally assimilated, and you will be accepted) but foresees such change only as a future event. Contemporary Jews, the Jews with whom Treitschke must deal on a day-to-day basis in Berlin, are tainted by the corruption of their discourse.

Treitschke's claim is read by his contemporaries, both Jewish and non-Jewish, in the light of Treitschke's status as a historian. Indeed, he lays claim to this status in terms of the very language that he uses to categorize his Jewish contemporaries. It is this claim to a scientific discourse about the Jews that gives his work so much power. Unlike Marr, whose polemical pamphlets were outside all of the institutions in which power was invested in Germany, Treitschke represented the privileged group, the academy, and he laid claim to the rhetoric of scientific objectivity in his work. This claim was assumed when he entered into the debate about the nature of the Jew. But even if the rhetoric of history laid claim to the status ascribed to science, its claim was dependent upon the objectivity attributed to the "real" sciences that dominated the nineteenth century, biology and anthropology.

Nowhere is the discussion of the special nature of the discourse of the Jews more pointed than in Theodor Billroth's 1876 handbook of nineteenth-century scientific education, *On the Teaching and Study of the Medical Sciences in the German Universities.*[12] Billroth, professor of surgery at the University of Vienna and one of the dominant figures of nineteenth-century medicine and culture (one of Freud's teachers and one of Brahms's closest friends), presented a detailed overview of the nature of medical education, commenting on the nature of the Jew as a potential candidate for admission to schools of medicine. The relationship between Jews and medical discourse, as has been illustrated, is a longstanding one. It relates to the Jews both as potential healers and as potential subjects of medical treatment. Billroth described in great detail the "problem" of Eastern Jews from Galicia and Hungary, who "have absolutely nothing, and who have conceived the insane idea that they can earn money in Vienna by teaching, through small jobs at the stock exchange, by peddling matches, or by taking employment as post office or telegraph clerks in Vienna or elsewhere, and at the same time study medicine." The "insane" student dominates Billroth's image of the Jewish medical student. He only has "a dictionary knowledge," that is, he is merely "a scholar, a Talmudist," who has no inherent intelligence, only the ability to memorize and repeat, an *idiot savant.* But what is most important, these Jews possess no language whatsoever: "They often understand so little German that they can grasp neither the language nor the sense of the questions, and they are quite incapable of expressing their thoughts, either in German or in any other tongue." Billroth's refusal to grant the Jews (here the Eastern Jews) any language, any form of acceptable discourse, stems from the image of Yiddish as a "non-language," a language beyond the pale of all the social conventions of culture. In doing so Billroth becomes aware that he has trodden extremely close to the position espoused by Marr and other anti-Semitic pamphleteers outside of the academy. He adds a long, multipage footnote (missing in the later English translation) to his discussion of the Eastern Jew as medical student which provides his scientific theory of "race."

In the footnote Billroth begins by distancing himself from the "Jew mockers" of his own time. He establishes his position, based on the evidence of the Jewish medical student, within a "scientific" theory, that of race. And race is closely tied to language. The basis for Jewish attributes lies in the "degeneration" of the Jews through their constant intermarriage, which is especially prevalent among Eastern Jews. The result is a specifically Jewish personality, one that sets off on a career without sufficient capital and trusts to luck. Such an individual is bound to be aggressive. Thus, the typical Jew for Billroth is one who exhibits a faulty view of his own position in society, a schlemiel.

The other aspect that dominates Billroth's image of the Jew is the Jews' racial inability to become part of that nation in which they dwell:

> It is a rather generally accepted error to speak of the Jews as Germans, Hungarians or Frenchmen, who happen to have a different confession than most of the other inhabitants of Germany, Hungary or France. One often forgets that the Jews are a distinctively delineated nation and that a Jew can no more become a German any more than a Persian, or Frenchman, or New Zealander, or African. Those who are called "Jewish German" are only those who happen to speak German, happen to have been raised in Germany, even if they speak and think more beautifully and better in the German language than many Teutons of the purest water. (153)

Billroth's prime criterion for difference is language. Like Treitschke, he is daily confronted with Jews who do not meet his model of the Eastern Jew, the Jew who has "no language," who is thus reduced to the level of the beast. He is confronted with Jewish students from his native Vienna, who seem to speak, act, and think like himself. He must be able to draw the line between himself and them. He admits their ability to "speak and think more beautifully and better" than the Germans but denies them access to the inner sanctum, the nature of German discourse, the language that reveals the German soul.

Scientific discourse can no longer rely on the Jews' sounding different, using different intonation or, indeed, a different vocabulary. The science of race discovered that it is the essence of language that the Jews can never possess, for they must remain mired in their Jewish discourse, which is seen as the present state of the Jews. Friedrich Ratzel, professor at Munich and Leipzig and the founder of political geography, codified this view of the Jews in his extraordinarily influential *History of Mankind* (1885–88), the model for all of the contemporary handbooks on physical geoanthropology.[13] This illustrated panopticon of the great chain of being provided two discussions of the Jews for its German, middle-class, nonscientific reader. The first is found in his survey of the "Red Sea Group of Races." There the Jews "are distinguished above the Arabs by deeper feeling and richer fancy; and both excel Hamites and Indo-Germans in the great energy—narrowness, if you will—of their

religious perception. Violence and exclusiveness, fanaticism in short
. . . are in general distinctive of the Semites" (3:183). It is the image
of the zealot, of the Eastern mystic, that contaminates Ratzel's
perception of the Jew.

The category of "fancy," an aesthetic category, is, however,
central to his distinguishing between Jewish discourse and that of
other Semites, such as the Arabs. Even though they are violent and
exclusive, the Jews do possess a "rich fancy." When Ratzel turns
to the Jews in Europe, he presents quite a different image. Ratzel
dates the entry of the Jews into European culture to "the political
collapse of the Jews": "The misfortunes of the national ruin, however,
brought about a purification which in a race aesthetically deficient,
but spiritually proud and austere, tended to strengthen the conception of a deity all-powerful and all-knowing, and at the same time
jealous and severe" (548). Jews in the Diaspora are characterized
as aesthetically deficient, as opposed to those Jews who remain in
their initial geographic status, who have a "rich fancy." Here is
Hegel's distinction between the creativity of the biblical Jews and
the paucity of creativity among his own Jewish contemporaries.
Ratzel simply translated chronology into geography. He retained
the image of the Jew as inherently different, as possessing a "Semitic disposition," in opposition to the "Greeks, who are funda-
mentally Aryan, [and] . . . who . . . had gone through a process of
spiritual refinement in truth, knowledge and beauty." When the
Jews come into contact with the Greeks, what dialectally results
is, of course, Christianity, the ultimate thesis. The Jews remain
without the sense of the beautiful, since this is now reserved for
Christians, as it had been reserved for the Greeks.

Scientific rhetoric of all levels limits or reduces the language
of the Jews to the damaged and hidden discourse traditionally ascribed
to them. It is of little surprise that the political anti-Semites who
draw on this new scientific restatement of an older anti-Jewish
view continue in this direction. Thomas Frey argued in his *Anti-
Semites' Catechism* of 1887 that "all Jews of all nations and all
languages" work for the Jewish domination of the world.[14] The
Jews' language is the language of lies, of perjury. This language
dominates the press and leads to the "moral decay" of letters (17).
All of these bromides are found throughout the literature published
by the political anti-Semites. Frey's "catechism" is of interest
because, like the older literature on the nature of the Jews, he
provides on the last page of his book a "list of often-used Jewish
words"—including such words as *acheln* ("to eat"), *Memme*
("mother"), and *trefe* ("unclean"). The primitive nature of this list

recalls the historical moment when the Jews did possess some type of distinguishing features in their language. Just as Billroth needed to dispossess the Eastern Jew of language, Frey needed to see in the hidden language of the Jew the overt marker of the difference of their discourse. In Gottfried zur Beek's edition of the *Protocols of the Elders of Zion* this theme is repeated. Beek repeats the canard that "the language of thieves and robbers is taken from Yiddish and Hebrew. Perhaps Hebrew will be introduced as the language of international diplomacy. This would be easy, since most of the ambassadors, ministers, and consuls are Jews or are advised by Jews. But there are secrets in the history of the Jews that are not safe even when written in Hebrew characters."[15] The magical nature of the Hebrew alphabet conceals the hidden plans and the nature of the Jews. The damaged discourse of the Jews was the occasion, in 1894, of a court case when J. Rethwitz, the editor of the *Hanover Post*, was accused of defaming the Jews because he claimed in print that the *Kol Nidre*, intoned on the Day of Atonement, freed all Jews from their oaths.[16] All Jews were free to take any oaths, since none were felt to be binding. This position had been the official one in the German states and had led to the introduction of the oaths made by Jews before a court would hear a Jew's testimony. Prussia was the last state to abolish the oath, in 1869. But in 1895 the view that Jews always lie reappeared; indeed, it had never been completely silenced.

The popular image of the Jew in the late nineteenth century and the early twentieth century presented the language of the Jew as distinctive and significant. Not only are the "bad" Jews distinguished from the "good" Jews in the popular novels of Felix Dahn and Gustav Freytag through their language, but the portraits of Jews on the stage are characterized by language that is "thickly guttural" or indeed "no dialect, only rarely the singing tone of the stock market broker."[17] Dietrich Eckart, later to become one of Adolf Hitler's mentors, simply characterized the language of his Jewish characters as "soupy."[18] On the stage, the figure of the Jew was marked by some alteration of the manner of speech. Indeed, if a Jew was presented without such a marker, this very fact played a role in the shaping of the character. Language, within the conventions of the literary world, served as a reflex of the hidden nature of the Jews' discourse. Again, it was a purposeful confusion, one that continued the *topos* of the hidden language of the Jew throughout the period of the domination of the science of race.

"Scientific" racism could speak of the damaged discourse of the Jew, of the "German-speaking Oriental." When this view was incorporated within the world of literary stereotypes, the subtleties of such shades of discourse were impossible to translate into literary devices. Thus literary representations of Jews still retained the overt markers of the difference between acceptable and unacceptable discourse in the use of corrupt language. The sign of unacceptable discourse was the corruption of language indicated by *mauscheln*. Here an older literary stereotype was continued even though the reference for it in society had all but vanished. The greater mass of German Jews had lost all of the overt linguistic signs attributed to the hidden language of the Jews. These signs—intonation, vocabulary, and grammar—were, however, still possessed by Eastern Jews, Jews present in great numbers within the Austrian Empire (in Hungary and Galicia) and within the Eastern provinces of the new German Empire. The movement of these Jews into metropolitan centers such as Berlin and Vienna and the extraordinary migration of Russian Jews through Western Europe after the assassination of Czar Alexander II in 1881 provided a real focus for German-speaking Jews, who began to associate the anti-Semites' image of *Mauschel* not with themselves, as the anti-Semites had intended, but with the mass of Yiddish-speaking Eastern European Jews.

II
Toward a Philosophy of Language

As German Jews internalized and began to respond to the new science of race, it was evident that they also continued to internalize and respond to the image of the faultiness of their own discourse. In doing so they created a number of theoretical responses, all of which centered about the question of the nature of language itself. These Jews evolved models dependent on or in response to those models of language that labeled them as different because of the limitations on the nature of their discourse. Moritz Lazarus, the founder of ethnological psychology, employed the older, Romantic association between race and language but denied any basis of this association through a biological definition of race. Rather, Lazarus, a believing Jew and the author of a detailed work on Jewish ethics published in German, created an image of a community based on a shared language as the basis for race. Into this community all who spoke the shared language were welcome. While this view was the basis for a new rhetoric of anthropological science, it did not remain limited to the arena of the academy. After the publication of Heinrich von Treitschke's broadside against the "German-speaking Orientals," Lazarus held a public lecture at the College of Jewish Studies in Berlin in which he attempted to counter Treitschke's defamation of his Jewish contemporaries as inherently foreign to German culture.

Lazarus's response centers about the question of language. Indeed, he answers the question that he poses in the title of his talk, "What is national?" by observing that what is national is the shared language of the nation.[19] Lazarus is not alone in this mode of response. Many of the Jews who responded to Treitschke touched on this point at one time or another in their answers. Lazarus, however, centers his answer about this question. He begins with the statement, "We are Germans, and must speak as Germans" (5). He then undertakes a long and detailed explanation of his nonbiological understanding of race, a position that stresses morals, territory, and religion. He places language at the center of any concept of race, since it both reflects and shapes our perception of the world. But the acquisition of language is an individual affair; by acquiring language one becomes a member of a subjectively defined group called a "race." Having laid the basis for such a definition of race, Lazarus continues to ask to what race the Jews present in his audience belong, and his answer is straightforward: "Gentlemen, we are Germans, nothing but Germans; when we speak from the concept of nationality, we belong to only one nation, the German." This is opposed to Fichte's claim that the Jews form a "nation within a nation," that is, that they possess a hidden discourse, which sets them apart from the mode of perception and understanding of the Germans. Lazarus bases his claim on the contribution of German-speaking Jews to German culture. From Moses Mendelssohn to his Jewish academic and literary contemporaries, according to Lazarus, the Jews' acceptance and use of German are the primary indicators that they belong to the German nation. Jews thus no longer possess their own nationality; rather, they belong to that nation whose language they speak. This fact shapes the very understanding of what being a Jew is:

> The Jews no longer have their own nationality. They are simply Jews who possess only a Jewish spirit. Therefore they necessarily draw from all the national spirits which they have become part of and in turn influence them. Even in the most basic and unique areas, in their religion, they have become individuated according to the nations in which they reside and can thus evolve their receptive role in the culture into a productive one. Philo wrote Greek; Maimonides, Arabic;

Spinoza, Latin; Munck and Dernburg, French; Mendelssohn, German. (44)

In this the Jews are like any other group that adapts itself to the world in which it lives. In fifty-eight pages, Lazarus attempts to answer Treitschke's charge that Jews are merely German-speaking Orientals, Poles in Western disguise. Treitschke had again linked the language of the Jews in Germany with the language and Talmudic discourse of the Eastern Jew. As many of the other Jewish commentators on his essay also remarked, he had his history backwards. The Polish Jews were descended from the Rhineland Jews—rather than the other way around. What is most fascinating is that this charge—that the Jews in Germany were part of the dark, fearful world of the East and that their discourse was not "European" but "Asiatic"—does not surface overtly in Lazarus's pamphlet. This charge is a powerful one, since it ties the culture of the Jew in the West to the perceived barbarism of Jewish mysticism and irrationality in the East. What Lazarus provides for the reader of his pamphlet is an appendix in which he details the immigration and emigration of Jews in Prussia. The point of this appendix is that since 1843 more Jews had emigrated from Prussia than immigrated into Prussia. Thus, hidden within the rhetoric of statistics is the rebuttal that Prussian Jewry was merely an extension of Polish (and other Eastern) Jewish communities. In fact, argues Lazarus, the real number of Jews may be increasing in Prussia, but they are members of the linguistic community of German-speaking Jews rather than Yiddish-speaking interlopers from a different "nation."

But Lazarus's attempt to eliminate the special status of the language of the Jews from his image of race did not provide an answer to those Jews who accepted the anti-Semites' premise that their discourse was indeed damaged. The answer to this charge was present in almost all of the self-critical presentations of the "Jewish problem" by Jews. The so-called assimilated or acculturated Jews (those who converted or who retained a marginal affiliation with their Jewish identity) were all torn by "the unceasing struggle with ourselves," as Conrad Alberti stated in 1889.[20] It was a struggle especially for writers such as Alberti, who saw themselves labeled both as radical members of the avant-garde and as Jews. In his essay published in the leading German liberal periodical, *The Society*, Alberti comes to terms with the charge of a special Jewish discourse in a most subtle manner. First he sees the Jews as a social group (rather than a religious one) that began to disintegrate with the beginning of emancipation. He takes on the anti-Semites' attack on the Jews as a religious group whose books (again it is the Talmud) sanctify all types of antisocial behavior. He frees the Jews of the charge of having a special discourse, of inherently knowing the rhetoric of the Talmud, by citing Victor Hugo's Communard, who stated "I can't read" as his defense for having burned the libraries of Paris. For the Jews, Alberti states, cannot read even the Old Testament written in Hebrew, let alone the difficult and complex language of the Talmud.

Alberti sees attacks such as those of the anti-Semites as the sole cause of the perpetuation of the Jews: it gives them a focus for their self-definition. His definition of the Jew is merely the reflex of that of the anti-Semite. "The younger Jewish generation was only to be freed as quickly as possible from the superfluous and destructiveness of Judaism." This can best be undertaken by ending rather than increasing the rhetoric of the anti-Semite. Yet Alberti sees this "freeing" of the Jews from their Jewishness as a slow process. He uses modern science as his model. The laws of genetic change and evolution work slowly, and the Jews will change only slowly. What change quickly, and have already changed among the "younger generation of Jews," are the "external features such as the "*mauschel* language" of the Jews. "Already today," he writes, "there are Jews of large stature, who, at least by their hair, nose, language, and posture, cannot be distinguished from a good Teuton" (1729). Alberti's prose, incorporating all of the expected scientific references to Darwin, Spencer, Nietzsche, and Wundt, is the model of the acceptable discourse of the German avant-garde, a pseudo-scientific discourse into which he fits without any hesitation. He crafts his argument to show his existing integration into the literary world of the periodical in which he publishes, to show his German literary persona rather than his hidden (or in his argument, lost) Jewish one.

Walter Rathenau, in his parodically entitled essay "Hear, Israel" (the opening of the Jewish doxology, the *Shema*), wrote in a similar vein for Maximilian Harden's periodical *The Future*.[21] Published in 1897, when Rathenau was thirty, the essay defines the "Jewish Question" as a cultural question. But Rathenau signals his readers, through his parodic title, that he will be speaking as an "insider," as one who knows the hidden language of the Jews.

> . . . the cultural question. Whoever wishes to hear its language
> can go any Sunday through the Thiergartenstrasse midday at
> twelve or evenings glance into the foyer of a Berlin theater.
> Unique Vision! In the midst of a German life, a separate,

strange race, lustrous and impressively costumed and with hot-blooded, active gestures. On the sands of the Mark Branden-burg, an Asiatic horde. The forced humor of these people does not betray how much old, unsatiated hatred rests on their shoulders. They do not imagine that it is only living in an age that has controlled all natural violence that has rescued them from that which their fathers suffered. In close relationship among themselves, in strict rejection of all that comes from outside—thus they live in a half-willed, invisible ghetto, not a living part of the people (*Volk*) but a strange organism in its body. (454)

Rathenau uses the language of science—here pathology—to characterize the Jews. Their most evident quality, their "language," represents their inherent difference. Rathenau, the heir of the founder of the German electrical industry, toyed with conversion, but unlike his friend Maximilian Harden, who had converted to Protestantism at the age of sixteen, he never undertook the actual step. It is clear that this essay was his attempt to separate himself from the anti-Semites' image of the middle-class Jew with cultural pretensions. Much like Alberti, he sees as the sole cure the integration of the Jew into German education (*Bildung*), quite the opposite of the "Jewish" education that Billroth had condemned. German education, the central force in the shaping and integrating of the German middle class, is the Jews' mode of access into German society. But this change, following Darwinian evolution, will be slow and cannot be hurried. Rathenau sees in the contemporary Jews' assumption of the externals of German culture and language merely Darwinian mimicry, the imitation of the insect. He sees the physical deformities of the Jewish male—his "soft weakness of form," his femininity—as the result of his oppression. He sees the Jews' ability to use language, especially the language of society, in only the most superficial manner as an ingrained fault that can only be overcome through the passage of time. It is this latter, the language of the Jews, the specific manner of their language as the reflection of their patterns of thought (459), that Rathenau sees as central to the image of the Jew. This must be altered if the Jew is truly to become part of the culture of Germany. Rathenau's views on his own Jewish identity change as he grows older, but the image of the Jews' language that he presents in this early essay reflects the scientism of the late nineteenth century.

Other Jews writing in German periodicals aimed at the German middle class repeat this image of the language-damaged Jews, who must, at least in the future, alter their language to become part of the German cultural community. Jakob Fromer, the librarian of the Berlin Jewish community, repeats this image in an essay in *The Future*, as well as in his autobiography, using his own persona, the Eastern Jew who has come to cultured Berlin, as an illustration.[22] In *The Prussian Yearbooks*, the pseudonymous Benedictus Levita wrote about the "spiritual degeneration" of the Jews which manifests itself in the sharp distinction between the "physical being, the language, the mode of living and of thought" of the Christians and of certain groups of Jews.[23] In this the author was clearly not including him- or herself in the group of Jews who possessed a damaged language. The answer, as in all cases, is for the Jew to assimilate, to become part of the German, if not the Christian, world. Jewish authors such as Ludwig Jacobowski, whose *Werther the Jew* (1892) was a best-selling novel in Germany and throughout Europe, translated this image into the conflict between the generations, seeing the younger generation as possessing the damaged discourse inherited from their elders. Only in the future could such a discourse be abandoned. This model reappears in Karl Ludwig Franzos's bestseller, *The Pojaz* (1905), in his contrast between the Eastern Jewish establishment, with its damaged, Talmudic discourse, and "modern," Westernized Jews in the East. Indeed, writers a generation earlier, such as Leopold Kompert and Berthold Auerbach, who had attempted to enter the mainstream of popular German writing through their use of peasant themes, had already established the paradigm of the "good" and "bad" discourse of the Jew, in Auerbach's *Poet and Merchant* (1840), for example. This model of acceptable (i.e., Western) and unacceptable (i.e., Eastern) discourse defines the literary stereotype of the Jew within the works of German Jewish writers.[24]

Moritz Goldstein, trained as a literary scholar and employed as an editor, articulated his pessimism more clearly than most when he wrote in a leading German cultural periodical, *The Artguard*, during 1912 that the only possibility for a Jewish culture would be for a future Hebrew culture.[25] A German Jewish culture was impossible, and the best that contemporary Jewish writers condemned to write in German could do was to write about their own Jewish experience in Germany as a transition to the return to the true language of Jewish experience, a language uncontaminated by the endemic presence of anti-Semitism. Goldstein's polemic centered about the role played by Jews in German culture. His central thesis is direct: "We Jews administer the cultural possessions of a people who deny us the right and the ability to do so." This conflict between the presumptions of the German cultural institution and the desires of the Jews is played out in the ambiguity of the role assigned to the Jew. The anti-Semites simply brand everything that comes from this society as Jewish, while the Jews functioning within the cultural mainstream do everything to disguise their Jewish identity. For these Jews (and many others) the very designation "Jewish" possesses a pejorative connotation.

Goldstein's essay, presented in a public, non-Jewish forum, called forth a stream of answers, a selection of which the liberal editor Ferdinand Avenarius published in the *Artguard*. Goldstein did the unforgivable: he pointed out the ambiguity of the Jewish role in German society in a public forum. The anti-Semites rejoiced. They saw in the distinction made between Jewish and non-Jewish strands within Germany a necessary first step to cultural apartheid.

The assimilated Jews who responded, represented by the essayist Ernst Lissauer, saw the present state of Jewish identity and its evident confusion as the result of being in transition from the ghetto to another "cultural community."[26] Lissauer's remarks are a camouflaged attempt to distinguish between two types of Jews, on the one hand a more primitive (and for him historically distanced) type, on the other hand those Jews who can function on the same level as others in the "cultural community" in which they now find themselves. Religious identity is not nor has it ever been essential for the self-definition of the Jew. Rather, the Jew, like Nietzsche's Superman, is progressing from a more primitive stage of development, characterized by religious identity, to a higher stage of development, characterized by the present identification with cultural qualities of the German community, to eventually emerge whole and complete. This dialectic of development captured the ambiguity of the "antithetical" moment in which the Jews now found themselves.

All of these Jewish responses to the *topos* of the hidden language or damaged discourse of the Jew shaped and were shaped by the simple fact that their authors used German as their means of acquiring status within the sphere of German cultural life. In each case the need to defend oneself against such a charge resulted in the pinpointing of those Jews whose language was really different, whose discourse was truly damaged. In "the third year of the World War about German existence"—so the date is printed on the title page—Eduard Engel, head of the stenographic bureau of the German Reichstag, published his *Speak German!* Engel was the best-known proponent of a purified German, a German especially purged of that French influence that came to be seen as corruption, especially during the period following the defeat of France in 1871 and the establishment of the German Empire. With the decline of French political prestige, Engel, a Jew, became the arbiter of "Germanness" in language, a William Safire for the Second Empire. One of the striking aspects of Engel's work was the extraordinary popularity of *Speak German!* and his subsequent practical volumes on purging German of its foreign elements. But *Speak German!* also contained a detailed attack on other forms of bad German, including Yiddish and *mauscheln*. There is, of course, a difference between these two examples of "degenerate" language: the former is the independent development of a dialect of German, which Engel recognizes, while the latter is merely an accent with which German is spoken. Engel observes:

> In Germany there is no more despicable designation of a commonness of language than *Mauschelei*. Tell me, what difference is there between *mauscheln* and speaking a Frenchified German? The High German or Yiddish *Mauscheler* incorporates in his German *Gemauschel*, a mix of German and bits of Hebrew: Is Hebrew, the language of the Bible, less elegant than monks' Latin or Berlin French? If one asks about the need to create *nuances* in the otherwise *nuance-poor* German language, one must turn to those knowledgeable in this Yiddish mix to inquire whether such garlic blossoms on the rose bush as *nebbich, chuzpe, stike* are an increase in the richness of the language similar to that of Frenchified German? The disgustingness of *Mauschelei* is the result of the dirtying that infiltrates their slimy German. For one with a healthy, if not to say finely tuned, sensibility of language, every linguistic dirtying, like *Mauscheln*, appalls. I recommend in all seriousness that one use *Mauscheln*, if at least for the variety, often instead of the term "foreignization." It doesn't sound good—it is not supposed to sound good—but it rings true and is true.[27]

Engel's views reflect the sense of linguistic community desired by the German Jew. And yet at the very same time the anti-Semites, such as Adolf Bartels and Otto Hauser, were arguing, following and citing Wagner, that behind the finest German that any Jew can be taught to speak lurks the inner voice of the Jews, with their borrowed German.[28] And the reason for this is linguistic poverty among the Jews. According to Hauser, this is the direct result of three thousand years of sexual inbreeding!

Engel was primarily a language purifier. His interest was thus political. He saw in the "foreignness" of the language of the Jews, or at least the language attributed to the Jews, a marker that represented the implied inferiority of the Jew. Integration into the German cultural and social community meant distancing the "dirtyness," the "garlic," the "illness," and the "Frenchifying" attributed to the Jew. For Engel *mauscheln* becomes synonymous with all bastardization of language, since that manifestation of corruption is implicitly associated with the Jew. He sees in the language attributed to the Jew the most evident public sign of the Jews' difference and subsumes under the rubric of language all of the other negative qualities ascribed to the Jew.

Engel is in no way unique. Indeed, his very pedantic approach to the question of the special nature of the Jews' language reduces his comments to a critique on the most superficial (and therefore most easily altered) aspects of the Jews' language. He is not interested in any theoretical paradigm into which to fit the language of the Jews, except the most general designation of *mauscheln* as un-German. Other Jewish writers and thinkers of the turn of the century see in the *mauscheln* attributed to the Jew a much more sinister manifestation of the illness of language.

Of all the critics of language writing at the turn of the century none had as far-reaching an effect as the Bohemian Jew Fritz Mauthner.[29] Mauthner is an excellent example of an assimilated Jew whose self-definition was molded by the attitude of the world in which he lived toward his language. Mauthner, unlike Engel, was not merely a language purist; rather, he strove to evolve a scientific psychology of language in which he embedded his projection of the language of the Jew. Like Engel, however, he shaped his projection of the "bad" Jew on the anti-Semitic concept that Jews speak a special, materialistic language that marks them as members of an inferior culture.

Mauthner has been of considerable scholarly interest because of his direct influence on the development of analytic philosophy. Recently, J. P. Stern has attempted to place Mauthner's preoccupation with language in the greater context of language identity within the Austro-Hungarian Empire.[30] While such a conflict does exist among writers who lived in non-German-speaking sections of the empire, such as Prague, even these writers see their situation as analogous to the situation of the Jew. For the general paradigm is that of the language ascribed to the Other, which marks them as possessors of an essentially flawed, inferior culture. The essential Other for the German-speaking lands is the Jew, and thus the language of the Jew becomes the touchstone for all problems of language conflict. This is not to say that the other conflicts between socially and culturally acceptable language and liminal language do not exist. The struggle for the legitimation of Czech as one of the official languages of the empire shows that they indeed did exist. But even for speakers of Czech, the language of the Jews was an even more flawed mode of expression than their own tongue. The projection of inferiority for all minorities within the German-speaking world was embodied in their image of the Jews and their language. Among the Jews themselves the need was to create a subgroup of Jews whose language identified them as inferior. Engel therefore selects the Yiddish-accented Jew as the butt of his attack on the language of the Jew as the essential language of the Other. Mauthner's use of this mode of projection is even more complex, since he evolved a philosophy of language from a series of conflicts concerning the special languages of the Jew.

Mauthner's initial understanding of his Jewish identity, at least in retrospect, came from his association of being Jewish with the discourse of the Jew. He writes in the first (and only) volume of his autobiography, published in 1918, that "I was by parentage a Jew, and I never learned anything about the Jewish religion or Jewish ethics; at best as a German child I heard the Jewish manner of speech and the *mauscheln* expressions" (110). Being Jewish was, for Mauthner, speaking Jewish.[31] He sees this as the wellspring for his own interest in language:

> Much would have to be said about the special circumstances which intensified one's interest in a psychology of language to a passion. From my earliest youth this interest was very strong in me—indeed, I don't understand how a Jew who was born in one of the Slavonic lands of the Austrian Empire could avoid being drawn to the study of language. In those days [the 1860s] he learned to understand three languages all at once: German as the language of the civil service, of culture, poetry and polite society; Czech as the language of the peasants and servant girls, and as the historical language of the glorious kingdom of Bohemia; a little Hebrew as the Holy Language of the Old Testament and as the basis of the Jewish-German jargon [*Mauscheldeutsch*] which he heard not only from the Jewish hawkers, but occasionally also from quite well-dressed Jewish businessmen of his society, and even from his relatives.[32]

The fragmentation of language in the empire served as Mauthner's point of departure in drawing into question the relationship between language and reality. But one should see the underlying qualities that he ascribed to the various language groups. German is the language of higher literature and culture; Czech, that of nostalgia and service; and *mauscheln*, that of materialism. And he sees himself directly related to this latter group through his relatives, who speak the language of the hawker and the stock exchange. Even those businessmen who appear to be culturally acceptable reveal their inner nature through their language.

Mauthner fled from the world of the Jew and materialism to the cultural center of the German-speaking world, Berlin, where he became the theater critic of the *Berlin Daily News* and a popular novelist. As a journalist Mauthner quickly learned the close association in the public mind between the language of the Jew and the language of the journalist. It was no accident that even the German writer Gustav Freytag characterized the Jewish journalist Schmock in his *The Journalists* (1852) as unprincipled and willing to follow the latest intellectual fashions. Mauthner's novel *The New Ahasuerus* (1882) centers about a totally assimilated Jew who converts to Catholicism and finally to liberal Protestantism and his struggles within the growing anti-Semitic atmosphere of Berlin. While Mauthner underlines the constant anti-Semitism in Prussia, he also stresses its illogical focus on someone who is fulfilling all of the cultural (and religious) demands of German society in order to conform to this society's image of the good Jew. For Mauthner knew firsthand the ubiquitousness of the view that Jewishness was immutable. As a journalist he employed a discourse labeled as Jewish; as a novelist he used this theme as a means of distancing the charge of having no part in the dominant cultural discourse.

One of Mauthner's major undertakings as a journalist for the most important newspaper in Berlin, Rudolf Mosse's *Berlin Daily News*, was the writing of parodies. Collected in a series of volumes, the first entitled *After Famous Models* (1879), Mauthner's parodies explored the fissures in the official poetic (and political) language of his time. The very writing of parodies became a means of undermining the official German of Mauthner's time *within* acceptable structures. For Mauthner's parodies were no different in kind or tone than the other parodies of his age. Indeed, the object of his parodies, the language of the more or less official discourse in poetry and politics, was the object of most of the parodies of his day. However, since he was the quasi-official parodist for the most visibly "Jewish" of the Berlin newspapers, having both a Jewish owner and a Jewish editor, Mauthner's parodies became associated with his "Jewish" and "journalistic" persona. The idea of the parody as the assumption of the linguistic identity of another, here one who belongs to the world of acceptable and entrenched discourse, was seen as the presumption of the Jew who assumed the identity of a German, having none of his own, and debased the original. The act of parody was seen, therefore, as a means by which the Jew denigrated the German by undercutting his language. And Mauthner was perceived as the quintessentially Jewish parodist.

Mauthner's parodies laid bare the literary pretensions of "professional" writers, with their professional language of art. In one of his little known (and certainly little read) broadsides against this class of misusers of language, Mauthner uncovers the hidden agenda of "polite language," the language of art. Entitled *Schmock or the Literary Career of the Present*, the pamphlet echoes Freytag and is a clear attack on the pretensions of the literary journalist (a clan to which Mauthner himself belonged). Mauthner introduces his problem with the following parallel: "Just as polite individuals today use the word 'Israelite' in the presence of Jews, while they would not hesitate to use the term 'Hebrew' among themselves, so too the literary individual is called to his face an 'author,' while behind his back he is called a 'journalist.' " Mauthner never returns to the question of Jews and writers, even though his opening analogy strikes deeply at the inherently anti-Semitic nature of "polite language." His attack is indeed against the "journalists," just as the attack of polite society is against the "kikes." And yet he is both—Jew and journalist. The stigma attached to one is carried over in Mauthner's writing to the other. The *mauschelnd* title of Mauthner's work also points at this analogy, the word *schmock* ("jewel," "penis," "fool") having become part of the slang of the nineteenth-century German. For the journalist's German is the language of the *schmock*, of the sexualized fool, and is best designated by an indicator of the bastardization of "good" German.[33]

In 1907 Mauthner withdrew from the world of Berlin literary life and settled on Lake Constance, where he began to work on his studies of the nature of language. For like the hero of his early novel, he had left the community of Jewry but remained identified in the public eye as a Jew—a Jew as journalist, as novelist, as parodist. In 1901 and 1902 Mauthner had published his *Contributions to a Critique of Language*, in which he stressed the accidental nature of our knowledge of the world and the total reliance of such knowledge on language. Language is therefore the limiting factor to any epistemological system, and anyone who believes in a firsthand knowledge of the world thus falls into the trap of what Mauthner calls the "superstition of the word." And the best example of such "superstition" is the relationship of the Jews to language. Mauthner's discussion recalls Hegel and his discussion of fetishism, which Hegel documents with reference to the religion of the African and which here is used to characterize the nature of the Jews' language.

Precisely among the Jews has the fetishism of the word so developed as to be illuminating. They know the exact terms and melody for addressing the Jewish God, but they also recognize the uniqueness of the superstition of the word, by which they dare not speak the name of God for fear of punishment. They have also developed the equivalent contradictions so sharply that revealed religion appears to be the authentic word of God. Since the old cult, with its sacrifices, and so on, ended with the destruction of the Jewish state, Judaism has become a word religion, a religion concerned with the word of God. The scholastic concern with the word of the Bible and the Talmud, this religious devotion to learning and teaching, remains a quality of Judaism. Perhaps this has led to a certain one-sided sharpening of the Jewish mind, and perhaps from this tendency comes a certain tendency of so many Jews toward writing. We see in writing the fetish of the word in a new form. The real fetish in the temple aided through supernatural means because of the gifts that were brought, in Jerusalem as in darkest Africa. What the fetish ate the priests digested. The old fetishes have disappeared. One no longer sacrifices to the cherubim, the winged oxheads. The "correct" words of the Bible have replaced them, and Talmudic logic extrapolates from the phrase that one should not cook a kid in its mother's milk an entire system of dietary laws. The sacrifice of intelligence is brought to the new fetish, and there are none any longer who can digest it.[34] Mauthner summarizes in this basic discussion of the "superstition of the word" the "bad" Jews' language. He sees the "new" Judaism as an exact parallel to the older traditions of the temple and sees both as equivalent to the superstitions of darkest Africa, echoing Hegel. The Jew is the black, not in terms of race, but in terms of a primitive relationship to the realities of the "word." This radical materialism is embodied in the illogical nature of *pilpul*.

Hidden within his discussion of the materialistic nature of the Jews' discourse is a genetic argument concerning the nature of the Jewish mind, as journalist as well as Talmudist. Mauthner sees in the word fetishism of the Jew grounds for the "one-sided sharpness of the Jewish mind" and for the Jews' addiction to writing. Writing is the product of this primitive preoccupation with the "realities" of the world. But Mauthner continues his explication of the nature of a Jewish perception of the world. He sees the "Orthodox communities in Poland," who speak a "corrupt German," as the locus of this "superstition of the word" (158–59). But Mauthner then seeks to undermine the discourse of science, which is riddled with anti-Semitic undertones, by showing that Western "scientific" logic is as much an arbitrary "theology" as is the *pilpul* (159). Mauthner presents the argument that the logical inadequacies of the Jews' language are the result of the fossilization of their language of science on a primitive level. Our present language of scientific proof is no better than "the Talmudic concerns of Orthodox Jews," only historically more removed from them (159). Mauthner sees a scale of development, borrowed from Hegel, from fetishism to Protestantism, which, however, is also limited to present concerns and will itself fossilize and be replaced.

The image of Judaism as a fossil religion is taken from Hegel, but the idea that this fossilization is reflected in the Jews' language, their argument, their linguistic identity, is new to Mauthner. He sees in this pattern the forces that determine the very nature of the Jews' perception of the world. In his exposition of *"Weltanschauung* and language" Mauthner returns to the model of the Jews' language for his example of the alienation between the world in which the Jews live and their manner of expression. People are differentiated by their language, Mauthner states, and when they no longer wish to be seen as different, they must change their linguistic identity: "And if, e.g., the Jews in Germany would pay more attention to themselves, then they must recognize that they will continue to form a tribe as long as they continue, more or less, to speak a jargon, which is incomprehensible to non-Jewish Germans. The Jew will only become a full German when *mauscheln* expressions become a foreign language or when he no longer understands them" (492). Mauthner is himself on the level of one who does understand such expressions, even if he does not use them. By his very identity as one who speaks a Jewish language, the language of journalism, he is corrupted by the hidden *mauscheln* of the Jews. He is forced to restructure his identity to exclude such individuals from the community of modern, scientific thinkers. Mauthner's creation of a "psychology" of language is a complex answer to his own sense of living within the double bind of language. The scientific discourse that he proposes, built upon the criticism of language, would free the Jews from the curse of their own tongue by having the Jews serve as the prime example of the materialism of language and its fossilization. One can transcend this double bind through the awareness of the limiting nature of language, but one can never be sure that one has liberated oneself from this blindness. Is not the ultimate curse that of not knowing the limitations inherent in one's language, the true disparities between the real world and the functional limits of language? Thus the limitations of the Jews place them in a privileged position, for they can be made aware of the limitations of their language, while language critics can only suspect their own limits. Mauthner's linkage between language and the manner of seeing the world and his use of the Jew, of the projection of that which he found and rejected within himself, as its model has one more major parallel in late-nineteenth-century thought.

Karl Kraus, like Mauthner born in Bohemia, evolved a complex sense of the need for a strict critique of language as a means of providing the most detailed insights into the corruption of society.[35] Kraus's relationship to his Jewish identity and to his radical sense of language purity are closely linked to the parallel manifestation in Engel and Mauthner. Kraus, who converted to Catholicism in 1911 and then left the Catholic Church in 1922 over his opposition to Max Reinhardt's involvement in the Salzburg Festival, is one of the most complex examples of the creation of the Jewish Other as a substitute for the hatred of the self. For Kraus's self-selected enemies were Jews, and they represented the essence of the Jewish language. They were newspaper reporters such as Maximilian Harden and Alice Schalek, editors such as Moriz Benedikt and Imre Bekessy, or popular writers such as Alfred Kerr or Felix Salten. All are seen as the antithesis of Kraus himself, and all manifest this antithesis in the nature of their language. To this august company Kraus adds Heine, Freud, and Theodor Herzl.[36] The corruption of these Jews, as opposed to the good Jews, such as Otto Weininger, Peter Altenberg, or Else Lasker-Schüler, is their corruption of language, which reflects the foul nature of their perception of the world. Kraus selected his enemies wisely. He created them as the projection of that which he perceived in himself (or at least wished to see in himself). For all of these enemies are the essence of the "destruction of Austria by Jerusalem."[37] The dichotomy between the "good" Jew and the "bad" Jew is here played out on the stage of a specific *fin de siècle* understanding of the nature of language. But this understanding of the universals of language is rooted, at least for Kraus and many of his contemporaries, both Jewish and non-Jewish, within the model of the corruption of the language of Jews. Kraus attempts to distance his rhetoric from that of the Jewish, liberal journalist, whom he views as part of a conspiracy to alienate European Jews from their Western culture. He can thus designate these journalists as the "spiritual guardians of the gates of the Ghetto,"[38] which places them in proximity to—

but clearly apart from—the sense of isolation attributed to the Eastern Jew.

Mauthner's reaction to the double curse of speaking both the hidden language of the Jew and the Jew's new, public language, journalism, is echoed within Kraus's experience. His break with the press of his time, especially with the writers of occasional pieces (feuilletons), is more than simply an attempt to distinguish his mode of discourse, with its heavy reliance on parody and irony, from the didactic language of the journalists; it is the delineation of the line between "good," that is, non-Jewish, language and the "bad" language of the Jews. This is nowhere better illustrated than in two of Kraus's many literary feuds, one with Felix Salten, the author of *Bambi*, and one with the anonymous satirist who pilloried Kraus on the grounds of his *mauscheln*.

In an essay entitled "Yiddish-accented Hares," Kraus takes on Felix Salten's use of *mauscheln* (or as he refers to it here, *jüdeln*) in one of his novels presenting anthropomorphized animals.[39] Like most of Kraus's essays, this "exposé" centers about a quote, in this case a quote in which the hares discuss the fearful appearance of a man in the forest and which Kraus reads as an example of Salten's Yiddishisms. What is striking about Kraus's reading of Salten is that he sees Salten's language as breaking through the normal literary discourse of the children's book: "There is nothing more striking than the instincts of the animals. But that they have been so linguistically assimilated is surprising. Perhaps it is a mimicry to protect them against persecution? But that they are to speak with a Yiddish accent [*jüdeln*] only in the moment of danger, that one can easily accept; when they are among themselves they can speak German" (46). Kraus repeats here a motif that he evolves in developing the idea that the Jews possess a special, base language: that the language of the Jews is an artificial sign of their separateness from the European cultural community. Much as Americans view the Oxbridge accent as a British cultural affectation, so Kraus sees the *jüdeln* of the Jews as an affectation which he associates with their corruption. Salten is the writer who mocks the purity of language by introducing into a discussion of the universal sense of terror attributed to the animals of the forest the image of the Jews as perpetually terrorized by the world around them. According to Kraus, this faulty analogy can be exploded if one sees the conscious use of Yiddishisms as a sign of artificial separateness, and this as the origin of fear. And yet, Kraus senses that what he perceives as artificial is seen by the anti-Semite as a permanent marker for the Jew. Kraus accuses Salten of exploiting *jüdeln* to create a false effect. With this accusation he throws the charge that the Jews possess a baser, more materialistic language back into the face of the Jew, or at least the Jew who can use better language.

When Kraus returns to the image of the "Yiddish-accented hares" in a later essay, "Growing Up as an Altar Boy," he uses yet another set of quotations, this time from the Jewish weekly *Bokovina People's News*, published in the Eastern provinces of the empire.[40] He apologizes for using the quotations, because he feels himself hypnotized by the quality of the language of the text and drawn to it as a satirist, "defenseless, like the hare before the glare of the boa constrictor" (31). Kraus's metaphor is an ironic reversal. He, the satirist, becomes the aggressor. The "altar boy" in this essay is Felix Salten, who recounts his youthful education in Hungary, where he attended the compulsory Catholic religious instruction and indeed served as an altar boy. All of this Kraus recounts using the text that he cites from the newspaper written by Eastern Jews for Eastern Jews and that glorified Salten as one who had maintained his Jewish identity in spite of the pressures applied to him while he was growing up. Kraus's attack on Salten is of secondary importance: his barbs are aimed at the language of the report of Salten's visit to the East, where Kraus, too, was born, and the attitude of the Jewish newspapermen toward Salten. For Kraus's point is not that Salten, like Max Reinhardt, has proven the baseness of both the Jews and the Catholic Church but that it is in the language of these Jews that their perversity can be read, and read like an open book.

In 1913, shortly after the publication of his collection of aphorisms, *Pro domo et mundo* (1912), there appeared in a Viennese satiric journal a caricature of Kraus hawking his books and accompanied by a series of aphorisms written in a mock Viennese Yiddish accent.[41] The satire, entitled "Pro domo et loco," called forth a complex reaction. Kraus reprinted the entire page, with the caricature, and then proceeded to parallel the crude image of the peddler Jew with long citations from a text that glorified Kraus as one of the few writers to free German from the double curse of Jewish and journalistic language. The contrast between the mock Yiddish attributed to Kraus, which revealed the basest anti-Semitic stereotypes, and the quotations from Jörg Lanz von Liebenfels, one of Adolf Hitler's main sources of inspiration, point up Kraus's need to distance himself from the accusation of speaking in a Jewish mode, even if this was merely the accusation of his enemies.[42]

In the same year, Kraus published his answer to a correspondent who was subtle enough to pick up the implication of Kraus's use of Lanz von Liebenfels's essay and cited the racist dictum "One cannot leave one's race" in order to elicit Kraus's response. In this essay, entitled "He's Still a Jew," Kraus presents the theoretical presuppositions of his understanding of the essence of a Jewish language. Kraus relates the essence of language to its function in the society or group in which it is found. He does not argue with the fact that he is a "Jew," at least in the terms of the definitions offered by racist critics, but he sees a distinction between materialistic Jews and those Jews who reject materialism. Thus the language of the Jews is the language of materialism. "It is this intonation that accompanies the rolling of money. It is the language of the world, it is its desire, and we may—we must—address it as a Jewish tendency, for it was the mission of the Jews, thanks to their gift of persuasion, fortitude, and greater gift at making it in the world, to which these qualities were attached."[43] Kraus sees a specific language of worldliness, of commerce, as typical of the Jews. He also perceives certain Jews' ability to transcend this baseness. He has his category of Jews who speak a good German, including Peter Altenberg and Else Lasker-Schüler (and, of course, Karl Kraus). What makes their German good German, and not the language of the Jews, is that they use a language that is nonmaterialistic. Here is the clue to Kraus's sense of the validity of language. For the language attributed to his enemies is the language of lies, of the marketplace, of the Jew as dissembler. Thus Kraus, in tabulating the quality of a truthful perception of the world, observes: "I do not know whether it is a Jewish quality to find an old whiskey drinker in a caftan more cultured than a member of the German-Austrian Association of Authors in his tuxedo."[44] The Eastern Jew, with his whiskey and in his distinctive dress, is more truthful than is the hidden Jew disguised as a German-Austrian author. So, too, is his language. Kraus can thus cite a Yiddish review of his work, in Yiddish, without any of the ironic and critical comments about the language in which the reviewer, J. Solowinski, wrote.[45] But when he turns to the regional newspapers or, indeed, to the great newspapers in Vienna, the sense of the hidden Jewishness of their false discourse haunts him. For Kraus sees in the language of the West, in German, the antithesis, not to Yiddish, which for him is a language associated with a different cultural milieu, but to the mangled German posited by the anti-Semite as the language of the Jew. Thus when Kraus reports on a trial of Eastern Jews for usury in 1915, he sees in the very language used by those accused of economic crimes the proof of their guilt.[46] And Kraus parodies their

German in condemning them! For these Jews are the ultimate in corruption; even their *mauscheln* is corrupt. They bastardize German with their misuse and reveal their inner selves. But it is Kraus who uses their language to reveal this. He uses the *mauscheln* of the Jew, perverting his own German to stress their perversity.

The distinction between Yiddish (*Jargon*) and the corrupt language of the Jewish journalist, of the liberal politician, is stressed by Kraus in a short interpretation of a "High German" sentence from a speech by a "socialist representative in Parliament."[47] Kraus plays with the two uses of *Jargon* in German: first, as a designation for Yiddish; second, as a term meaning highly artificial speech. Yiddish is not as objectionable to him as the highly forced language of politics. This view, one parallel to that expressed in Heine's youthful comments in his essay on Poland, relativizes the language of the Jew only to a limited degree, for while political language may be worse than Yiddish, this evaluation still places Yiddish on a relatively low plane.

Kraus's sense of the conflict between the nature of his own language and his perception of the special language of the Jews has its roots in his earliest writing. In 1898 he published a virulent attack on Theodor Herzl and the idea of Zionism as merely another anti-Semitic movement.[48] For Kraus perceived Zionism as yet another attempt to distance the Western Jew from Western culture. While Eastern Jewry could possibly benefit from the Zionist concept of a Jewish homeland in Palestine, Western Jews would lose their ideological identification with the West (and Western languages) if such a program were instituted. Kraus strains at the idea that *all* Jews have a common discourse. He takes the reports of the first Zionist congress, held in Basel in 1897, as the material for his analysis of the attitudes of Jews toward their own language. He annotates the commentators' repression of the diversity of the Jews present. The differences in patterns of gesticulation, of intonation, of language and culture, are repressed in these reports by writers who wish to stress the homogeneity of the Jews at Basel. Kraus feels that this rejection of the pluralistic nature of the Jews is a falsification of the nature of the different roles assumed by the Jews in Western and Eastern culture. Kraus hangs his interpretation of the function of the Zionist idea on the false vowel used by one of the delegates, the sign of the diversity of the Jew, of the unbridgeable gap between the Eastern Jew and the Western Jew. And the fault is placed squarely in the lap of Theodor Herzl—not Herzl the political leader but Herzl in his original manifestation as a newspaperman, a writer of feuilletons, for Moriz Benedikt's *New Free Press*, Herzl the "king of the Jews" writing for the most Jewish of Viennese journals, according to Karl Kraus.

Kraus's attack on the language of Herzl is his first attempt to distinguish between the new language of the Jews, the nonmaterialistic language of pure criticism, and what Theodor Adorno has called Kraus's struggle against the "spirit of circulating capital," the essence of the Jewish spirit.[49] But Kraus builds his critique of Herzl's misuse of language on one of Herzl's own most striking attempts to distinguish between the true Jew and the false Jew through the medium of language. At the beginning of his essay "A Crown for Zion," Kraus equates the attitude of the Zionists, represented by Herzl, with that of the anti-Semites: "Recently a few essays in the Zionist central journal, especially that essay entitled '*Mauschel*,' have secretly brought the desired reconciliation of both groups [Zionists and anti-Semites]. The cry 'Out with the Jews!' has been moved from within the camp of the Jewish nationalistic student groups to that region where the ever-ready political passivity accepts this slogan with joyful understanding, and suddenly one sees the Jewish anti-Semites directed toward a goal with the vigor not found in Aryan anti-Semites" (298). It is Kraus, in his attack on Herzl, who begins to formulate the concept of "Jewish anti-Semitism," which reappears in a 1899 essay on Zionism.[50] There he differentiates between Jewish anti-Semites and anti-Semitic Jews, two categories of Jews from which he disassociates himself. For it is Herzl, and his essay "*Mauschel*," that provides Kraus with his model for the idea of the Jew as a virulent opponent of the Jew, an opponent built upon the identity of enemies with their language.

Theodor Herzl's essay "*Mauschel*," which appeared in the official Zionist newspaper *The World* on October 15, 1897, is an attack on the opponents of Zionism and of Herzl personally.[51] Herzl most probably had in mind opponents from within the official Jewish hierarchy, and he articulated his anger in a burst of what Amos Elon calls "a piece of anti-Semitic horror propaganda."[52] In this piece the "bad" Jew is the Jew who speaks with a Yiddish accent, the Jew as *Mauschel*. This *pars par toto* is perhaps the most significant index of the centrality that the idea of the language of the Jew had for the professional Viennese writer. For in this essay Herzl was both author and Zionist, both the Jew writing good German for the papers of Vienna and the good Jew representing the best interest of European Jewry. The qualities ascribed to *Mauschel* are the classic attributes of the negative stereotype of the Jew: crippled, repressed, scabby; living in constant fear; pursuing culture only for profit; the essential profiteer; a distortion of that which is truly human; the anti-Zionist. What is more, *Mauschel* is the result of a mixing of races, of a type of miscegenation, which took place at some point in the history of the Jews. For *Mauschel* is a distinctly inferior racial type:

> *Mauschel* is anti-Zionist. We have known him for a long time. We have always been disgusted whenever we looked at his face ... in a kind of romantic tenderness we tried to help him because he was a scamp. Whenever he committed an act of meanness we tried to hush it up. . . . As a type, my dear friends, *Mauschel* has always been the dreadful companion of the Jew, and so inseparable from him that they were always confused. The Jew is a man like all others, no better, no worse ... but *Mauschel* is a distortion of the human character, unspeakably mean and repellent. Where the Jew experiences pain or pride, *Mauschel* only feels miserable fear, or faces you with a sneering grin ... impudent and arrogant. The Jew aspires to higher levels of culture; *Mauschel* pursues only his own dirty business. . . . Even the arts and sciences he pursues only for mean profit ... he hides behind subversive opposition movements and urges them on, secretly, whenever he is dissatisfied with the existing order; or he escapes into police protection and squeals when-ever he becomes frightened. . . . It is as if in a dark moment of our history some mean strain intruded into and was mixed with our unfortunate nation. . . . In times of anti-Semitism *Mauschel* shrugs his shoulders. Honor? Who needs it, if busi-ness is good?[53]

Herzl's figure of *Mauschel*, with its equation between discourse and identity, is not aimed at those Jews who have become culturally integrated into Austrian or German society. While these Jews may not identify with the aspirations of Zionism, they must admire it as one of the new nationalistic movements. *Mauschel* is the Jew who does not possess the potential for ethical action and cannot admire anything that cannot be converted into profit or gain. Thus Herzl's attack is not aimed at the Yiddish-speaking Jews, the East-ern Jews, who form one of the strongest groups (even if one of the most complex ones) attending the Basel congress. Herzl uses the image of Jews who speak with an accent as the icon of the "bad" Jews, for they attempt to be something that they are not; that is, neither are they Eastern Jews nor have they yet become Western Jews. The qualities ascribed to *Mauschel* by Herzl represent the antithesis of his romanticized image of his own identity. He informed

Reuben Brainin, his first biographer, that he was the descendant of noble Spanish Marranos rather than, as was the case, of Bulgarian Jews. The romanticized image of the Spanish Jews, as seen in Heine, was proof that one was not an Eastern Jew, and could not possibly be *Mauschel*, but the heir to the discourse of the great Hebrew poets.[54]

Karl Kraus sees in this attack on *Mauschel* the reification of his own distinction between the "good" and the "bad" Jew. The "bad" Jew incorporates all of those Jews who are associated with the manufacturers of "bad," that is, "Jewish," language, such as the *New Free Press*, for which Herzl wrote, or the Viennese popular stage, for which Herzl also wrote. The cathexis of Kraus's sense of the importance of language lies in the hidden agenda attributed to the producers of Jewish language with whom he wishes not to be identified. He selects as his models for the ideal Jewish language writers such as Peter Altenberg and Else Lasker-Schüler, writers who avoid any association with the "official" (and thus in Kraus's mind's eye "Jewish") cultural institutions and thus can produce "good" German. Kraus himself undertook to create such an institution in his periodical *The Torch*, which was independent of all the existing, corrupting cultural and linguistic structures of his time. Kraus's desire to withdraw from the cultural marketplace only moved him to create yet another object for cultural consumption. This double bind situation was heightened by the constant attacks on Kraus as the Jewish writer *par excellence*. Kraus seemed to relish these attacks. He reprinted any number of them in *The Torch* with his own commentaries.[55] But the overall effect of these attacks and Kraus's responses was to generate an image of the author as a consciously non-Jewish Jew, a paradox that even Kraus sensed. In his polemic against Heinrich Heine, published in 1910, Kraus selects as his antithesis the one Jewish writer who both had been compared to him and had become the anti-Semites' image of the essential Jewish writer. Kraus is careful not to attack Heine directly as a Jew; rather, he uses the markers that for his audience pointed to the image of the Jews' language. Heine is the father of modern journalism. He is the great Frenchifier of the German language. Heine sexualized the language of poetry: "Heine . . . has so loosened the corsets of the German language that today every little merchant can fondle her breasts."[56] This attack on Heine using the rhetoric of the anti-Semitic views of the nature of the Jews' language is seen by Kraus to be a defense of "good" language, language that does not blur the line between ornament and philosophy, and an attack on the "bad" language attributed by Kraus and Herzl to the Jew. Kraus felt himself to be supported in his views by writers such as Herzl. As a measure of Kraus's success one should note that while Fritz Mauthner uses Heine as a negative example in his writings on the philosophy of language, published before Kraus's attack on Heine, he writes a defense of Heine, which he published in 1914, after Kraus's polemic appeared.[57]

Kraus is labeled over and over again as the "arch-Jew." With the rise of the Nazis in Germany (and Austria), he begins to see the attack on the language of the Jews for what it is, an attack on the idea of the Jews as separate and inferior. The publication of Theodor Herzl's diaries in the 1920s provided Kraus with what he perceived to be some insight into the nature of Herzl's character, and he revised his opinion of the man, his work, and, one presumes, his language. In Kraus's last work, *The Third Walpurgis Night* (1933), he ironically admits to using the language of the Jews. In the book he includes a mock letter to the West German Radio in Cologne, which had asked to review his book on Shakespeare's sonnets. In the letter, written in the complex style of official German correspondence and mocking this essentially Teutonic bureaucratic style, Kraus observes that they really do not want to review the book, for the translations of Shakespeare's sonnets published by Kraus are "really translations from the Hebrew."[58] Shakespeare's sonnets in German are Kraus's "Hebrew Melodies." This labeling signifies Kraus's ironic awareness that the charges leveled at the Jews for writing in their "Jewish manner" constitute but an attack on the Jews' ability to function in Western culture. Kraus's response followed the demand from official Nazi circles that all works written by Jews in German be labeled as translations. Kraus's desire to purge himself of the "bad" language of the Jew is replaced by his need to see this distinction as spurious. For Kraus the presence of the Nazis in Vienna, where the problem of linguistic and literary criticism played out in the city's journals was converted into street brawls, marked the necessary turning point in his self-awareness.

The most telling example of the linkage between the special language of the Jews and the language of the press comes in Adolf Hitler's *Mein Kampf* (1927).[59] The Jews' language "is not . . . a means for expressing his thoughts, but a means for concealing them. When he speaks French, he thinks Jewish, and when he turns out German verses, in his life he only expresses the nature of his nationality" (307). Elsewhere Hitler stresses the protean nature of the Jews' language: "A man can change his language without any trouble—that is, he can use another language; but in his new language he will express the old ideas; his inner nature is not changed. This is best shown by the Jew who can speak a thousand languages and nevertheless remains a Jew" (312). Hitler then turns to the ultimate example of the contamination of German through the presence of the Jews, the German press. He undertakes the leap of exemplifying the presence of the Jew within the language of the press through his own knowledge of the Jews' language (much as Luther does in the later pamphlets with his use of the word *goy*):

> And it is precisely for our intellectual *demi-monde* that the Jew writes his so-called intellectual press. For them their tone is chosen, and on them they exercise their influence. Seemingly they all most sedulously avoid any outward crude forms, and meanwhile from other vessels they nevertheless pour their poison into the hearts of the readers. Amid a *Gezeires* of fine sounds and phrases they lull their readers into believing that pure science or even morality is really the motive of their acts, while in reality it is nothing but a wily, ingenious trick for stealing the enemy's weapon against the press from under his nose. (245)

The word *Gezeires* is a Yiddishism meaning arbitrary decrees. Hitler evidently associates it with the German word for *decoration* (*Gezierde*). He must prove that he has access to the hidden language of the Jews, that he too can understand their masked discourse. In accepting the secret nature of their language, Hitler wishes to present one of the unchanging patterns of the language of the Jews that reveal their "inner nature." He thus places himself in the role, usually assumed by the Jewish anti-Semite, of the specialist on the inner nature of the Jew. For language may be but a disposable mask for the Jew, but there is also something within it that reflects the innermost nature of the Jew. The language of the press is thus but the jargon of the Jew, even if it does not appear to be on the surface. Karl Kraus's view of the *Jargon* of the newspapers (Jewish-owned newspapers, that is) and Hitler's view are not that far apart. Indeed, Hitler may well have adapted this view and its rhetorical presentation from Kraus's own prose. The striving among Jewish critics of language such as Engel, Mautner, and Kraus for a language purified of the curse of *mauscheln* embodies a specific mode of negative projection. By accepting the linguistic standards of German or Austrian society concerning minority or liminal languages, they created a situation in which they were writing in a "borrowed" tongue, since these racist views of language denied such groups the true ability to alter their modes of expression. The double bind that resulted forced such Jews to undertake the role of language critics for all of society and provided them with the hidden motivation to prove their ability to transcend that which was perceived as unalterable, their language.

This model of linguistic identity also served other writers, such as the German writers of Prague, as a paradigm for their own attempts to grapple with their German identity. But these non-Jewish writers always had a worse case, the case of Jews who were not only cultural exiles but pariahs unable to alter their inherent nature, a nature represented by the Jews' language. Nowhere is this more clearly seen than in the Prague German poet Rainer Maria Rilke's letter to Sidonie Nadherny, in which he skillfully dissuades her from marrying the Jew Karl Kraus, a man who must remain a stranger to her. Rilke never uses the word *Jew* in his letter, and yet one can easily extrapolate the polemic against the nature of the Jew, who is even more isolated from the world of German culture than the Prague German.[60] It is no wonder that writers such as Engel, Mautner, Herzl, and Kraus needed to create the evil-speaking Jew as an entity separate from themselves in order to purge their self-image of the charge of Otherness.

III
Toward a Psychology of Language

Walter Rathenau stressed the feminine nature of the Jew in his 1897 essay. The relationship between the feminine physique, which he ascribed to the Jewish male, and the Jews' discourse, with its feminine attributes, stands in a long tradition of perceiving the discourse of the woman as different and thus in many ways related to that of the Jew. In his *Anthropology from a Pragmatic Point of View*, Immanuel Kant stresses the "loquacity and passionate eloquence" of the woman, through which she is "the ruler of men through modesty and eloquence in speech and expression."[61] Arthur Schopenhauer sees this stress on the discourse of the woman as an accurate reflection of the central strength of the woman, but he also perceives it as a negative, superficial force. Schopenhauer sees in the limited intelligence of the female character the source of women's failing: "It arises immediately from the want of reason and reflection above alluded to, and is assisted by the fact that they, as the weaker, are driven by nature to have recourse not to force but to cunning; hence their instinctive treachery, and their irredeemable tendency to lying."[62] Here the view that the primacy of language among women is the reflex of their biology is expressed without hesitation. Women and Jews misuse language. They both lie. They are both to be identified by the false, manipulative tone of their discourse.

The linkage of misogyny and anti-Semitism during the latter half of the nineteenth century is not random. For as both Jews and women become more visible on the horizon of European consciousness through their articulated demands for emancipation, both legal and cultural, a natural association takes place. It also occurs with the third mode of categorizing the discourse of the Jews. Just as the physical liberation of the female, in terms of her sexual and political identity, had been a prime tenet of the Young Germany movement, so, too, did this liberalization become inexorably associated with the pattern Jew-liberal-woman. Thus in defining the identity of the Jew in turn-of-the-century Europe as one of self-hatred, the distancing process began to include this triadic structure, and the relationship among its members was perceived in their use of language.

The best example of Jewish self-hatred that grew out of the materialistic model of the Jews and the nature of their language is Otto Weininger and his widely read and highly influential study *Sex and Character* (1903).[63] Weininger, a student of the Viennese philosophers Laurenz Müllner and Friedrich Jodl, attempted to combine a biology of human sexuality with a philosophy of sexual identity. His work, in retrospect a tractate against the tenor of his times, had extraordinary success, attributable to no small degree to the suicide of its young author on October 4, 1903, only a few months after its publication. Weininger has been taken as one of the classic examples of Jewish self-hatred, but the linkage between his self-hatred and his misogyny has been little explored. His death, in the room in Vienna in which Beethoven had died, had for his contemporaries exemplary quality, but its implication as a reflex of his work has been quite ignored.

Weininger echoes Schopenhauer's views of the innate language of the woman. Whether whores or mothers (the two closely related categories of the female for Weininger), all women use the same rhetoric. It is a faulty rhetoric, since it does not follow the traditional rules of logic. "The most common defect which one could discover in the conversation of a woman, if one really wishes to apply to it the standard of logic (a feat that man habitually shuns, so showing his contempt for a woman's logic) is the *quaternio terminorum*, that form of equivocation which is the result of an incapacity to retain definite presentations" (149). Women do not think logically. Rather they "think" by association. "The logical axioms are the foundation of all formation of mental conceptions, and women are devoid of these. . . . This want of definiteness in the ideas of women is the source of that 'sensitiveness' which gives the widest scope to vague associations and allows the most radically different things to be grouped together" (190). Women lie intuitively, as a reflex of their language. "The impulse to lie is stronger in woman, because, unlike that of man, her memory is not continuous, whilst her life is discrete, unconnected, discontinuous, swayed by the sensations and perceptions of the moment instead of dominating them" (146). Woman "may be regarded as 'logically insane"' (149). The form of that insanity is hysteria: "This is why women so often believe themselves to have been the victims of sexual overtures; this is the reason of extreme frequency of hallucinations of the sense of touch in women" (194). Women are predisposed to illness, to hysteria, by the very nature of their biology, not because of their womb (*hysteros*) but because of their language. For their language reflects their manner of seeing the world, a manner that is inherently flawed. "It is true that woman has the gift of speech, but she has not the art of talking; she converses (flirts) or chatters, but she does not talk" (195). Language itself is part of the sexual nature of the female.

Now the parallels to the descriptions of the Jews' discourse are clear. Both women and Jews use faulty logic. (For Weininger the Jew is always the male.) The Jews use the *pilpul*, which is associative. The *pilpul* is but another, intuitive means of lying. And the Jews reflect the specific illness of their Jewishness. These are the parallels that one would presuppose that Weininger would see, yet he ascribes to the Jews another set of qualities which do not completely parallel his image of women's language.

In order to understand the contrast between Weininger's image of the woman and his image of the Jew, the rhetoric of Weininger's argument must be examined, especially within the structure of the overall argument. For the chapter on the Jews is the penultimate chapter. It follows, indeed summarizes, much of Weininger's earlier discussion of the nature of mankind and the special status of woman. But Weininger's image of the Jew is one of a more depraved creature even than woman. His argument seems to build ever more radical case upon radical case, and the most radical is the nature of the Jew, for Jews, like women, not only have no center within their perception of the world but do not have a center in the world itself. For the woman, the man is the center, a center she must find outside herself; the Jew has no such ability. The Jew is thus a degenerate woman! Weininger manages to see the quality of "Jewishness," however, as he sees the quality of "femaleness," as a factor whose presence is possible in any and all individuals. "I think of [Judaism] as a tendency of the mind, as a psychological constitution which is a possibility for all mankind, but which has become actual in the most conspicuous fashion only amongst the Jews" (303). Just as Weininger argues that there is a wide scale for the "female," ranging from the most feminine to the most masculine but still quite readily distinguishable from the antithetical scale of the "male," so, too, does he argue that all people have the possibility of being Jews but all Jews are distinguished by this quality.

What is it that distinguishes the Jews, if not as a "race" then as a "psychological constitution"? It is those qualities that Weininger has perceived in the woman. Weininger proceeds to argue from "analogy." The Jewish psychology has little "sense of personal property" (306). Thus Jews are Communists (not Zionists, for Zionism is a form of nationalism that is antithetical to the Jews). Jews are doctors who wish to remove the mysteries from medicine and replace them with the materialism of drug therapy (315). Women have no sense of place and are materialistic. But even more is to be found within the "analogy" that Weininger perceives in the nature of aesthetic perception among Jews and women. For both have no sense of humor; they express themselves in satire, which is intolerant and "congruous with the disposition of the Jew and the woman" (319). Both reflect a "want of depth," typified among Jews by Heine (316).

All of these qualities are shared by the Jewish male and the woman. And yet Jews are far worse than women. Unlike women, they have no center. "Neither believe in themselves; but the woman believes in others, in her husband, her lover, or her children, or in love itself; she has a center of gravity, although it is outside of her own being. The Jew believes in nothing, within him or without him" (321). Jews perceive the world in a manner quite different from women or from any other group: they see the world as "double or multiple" (323). This is the central "idea of Judaism." It is a "want of reality, [an] absence of any fundamental relation to the thing-in-and-for-itself. [The Jew] stands, so to speak, outside reality, without ever entering it. He can never make himself one with anything—never enter into real relationships." Here we find the recapitulation of the image of the *pilpul*. Jews see things differently; they perceive the world in a manner quite unique to themselves. This is the "psychological constitution" to which Weininger refers. It is not the result of education but rather a "natural quality" of the Jew. It is manifested in the tone of the Jews' language: "Just as the acuteness of Jews has nothing to do with true power of differentiating, so his shyness about singing or even about speaking in clear positive tones has nothing to do with real reserve. It is a kind of inverted pride; having no true sense of his own worth, he fears being made ridiculous by his singing or his speech. The embarrassment of the Jew extends to things which have nothing to do with the real ego" (324). Here Wagner's rhetoric reappears with linkage of the Jews' language and their congenital inability to express themselves aesthetically. For Weininger the Jews' language, in terms of both its content and its articulation, marks the Jew.

And yet it is clear that the very structure of Weininger's book is an attempt to exorcise the demon of the Jews' language. The rigid polar structure of Weininger's means of seeing the world is the mode of perception that he attributes to "the Aryan, [who] although he sees as widely [as the Jew] feels himself limited in his choice" (323). The limits are the limits of argument—to the tightness of the syllogism, not to the open-endedness of the *pilpul*. But *all* of Weininger's discussion of the nature of the Jews is presented in terms of their language. The Jews' nature is seen through the structure of analogy, and its basis of proof is the validity of argument from parallels. Weininger abandons his schematic presentation of the nature of the woman, with its detailed exposition of the polar opposites of female character, which reveal themselves to be but two halves of the same entity, when he turns to the Jew. This is of little surprise. Weininger's misogyny is but the continuation of the older, philosophical tradition of dealing with the nature of the woman, a tradition marked by the strictures of philosophical discourse applied to the nature of the Other. The discourse, whether in Kant or Schopenhauer, follows the strict guidelines of Western philosophical argument and thus, at least logically, must be right. Weininger merges this philosophical discourse with the language of science and the biological model, giving it even further credence, at least in terms of its rhetoric. The strength of Weininger's argument is that it is "scientific" as well as "philosophical"; in terms of both aspects it is the antithesis of the language and intelligence of the Jew.

Weininger was, of course, a Jew. The attempt to exorcise this Jew within through the writing of his work was a failure. In his aphorisms Weininger observes that "the hatred of the woman is always an unsuccessfully overcome hate of one's own sexuality."[64] The analogy did not occur to him, at least not in his published writings. For it is clear that the hatred of his own identity is projected onto the "psychological type" of Jew, the Jew who thinks and argues differently from other human beings. What is most revealing about Weininger's suicide is its location, in the death chamber of Beethoven, the quintessential German artist, whose works by the beginning of the twentieth century had become identified with the "German spirit." It was with this mode of aesthetic articulation that Weininger wished to identify, at least in death. His *Sex and Character* had been a failure, not in its public reception, but in its function as the means of exorcising the Jew within. Indeed, in the very chapter that was to undertake this distancing—this proof that the author was not a Jew in the way that he perceived the world—his very mode of argument, his use of analogy, revealed him to be the feminine Jew that he feared himself to be.

Weininger's identification of himself as the outsider is reflected in his conversion. Like Heine and Börne, Weininger converted at the same time that he received his doctorate, an act repeated frequently throughout the nineteenth century. The act of acquiring the doctorate, and the social and economic implications of the degree in German or Austrian society, made the act of conversion almost imperative. For writing a dissertation, whether in Latin (as was the case earlier in the century) or in academic German, was the supreme act of language mastery. Not only did the doctorate provide entrance into the economic world of Christian Europe but it symbolized the student's command of the language of European intellectual discourse. Weininger's conversion illustrated yet another factor in the evolution of his self-image, for he did not convert to the dominant religion of the state, the Roman Catholic Church, but to Protestantism, a religion that in Catholic Austria provided little status and much in the way of a definition of self as the essential outsider.[65] The linkage of the philosophical language of the Austrian intellectual scene with Protestantism is not fanciful: it was precisely in the sense of the rejection of the metaphysical language of the Church and its replacement with the new language of science that the conflict within the Austrian (or at least Viennese) intellectual world took place.

Weininger was not the only Jew at the turn of the century who used the structure of scientific discourse as a means of distancing his identification from the idea of the Jew. Two years ahead of Weininger in the Scottish High School in Vienna was a young man named Arthur Trebitsch.[66] Trebitsch, like Weininger, was one of the classic test cases for Theodor Lessing in his book *Jewish Self-Hatred*, which grew out of Lessing's own confrontation with his Jewish identity. But Lessing was not interested in the mode of discourse employed by Trebitsch and Weininger. Both drew on the power of the scientific discourse for the basis of their presentation of the image of the Jew. Trebitsch suffered from a paranoid delusion that he was being persecuted by the "Alliance Israelite." In denying his Jewish identity, Trebitsch centered his fixation on that group which emphasized the value of Jewish identity within the European context. In 1919 Trebitsch suffered a massive paranoid episode, during which this fixation with the world conspiracy of the Jews no longer formed one element in his perception of the world but dominated him. He felt himself pierced by electromagnetic rays beamed at him by this Jewish conspiracy and fled from house to house in Berlin seeking refuge from these eternally persecuting Jews. Since the Jews that he feared were hidden within him, everywhere that he fled he felt himself pursued. Trebitsch published his major work, *Spirit and Judaism*, in 1919, shortly before this paranoid episode.[67] It is a historical and philosophical exposé of the basic nature of the Jews and their conspiracy. Needless to say, Trebitsch was welcomed with open arms by the growing anti-Semitic movement that developed at the close of the nineteenth century and flourished after Germany's defeat in 1919. Here was the Jew who bore witness to the truth of the accusation that it was the Jews who caused Germany's defeat. Trebitsch was not alone among Jews who joined the conservative, anti-Semitic party during this period. One can mention writers and activists such as Paul Nikolaus Cossmann and Ernst von Salomon, implicated in the murder of Walter Rathenau.

Trebitsch, building on Weininger, provided a "psychology" of the Jews, a picture of the Jews' inherent psychological difference cast in the language of nineteenth-century biological science. Trebitsch argued that the Jews' psyche is pathologically unique. The Jews are not rooted in the realities of the world; rather, they see in the future coming of the Messiah the *deus ex machina* that will resolve their existence in the world. The Jews thus are "degenerate" in their "secondary perception" of the world (33–34). This basic defect, cast by Trebitsch in the most esoteric of pseudophilosophical and scientific language, is the basis for his rejection of the Jew. How does this defect manifest itself? Through the Jews' language. Trebitsch finds yet another means of articulating the special language of the Jews: he sees the typical Jewish language expressed not so much in tone or national language as in a pattern of gestures that all Jews have in common (37). For Trebitsch, gesture is the hidden key to an understanding of the defect of the Jews' language and its materialistic bias. Gesture, part of language, reveals the nature of the Jew in its egocentricity, an egocentricity found

even in texts written in perfectly good German. Trebitsch immediately focuses on Heine, and the ruptured sense of irony found in
his verse. Heine's verse reveals him as without depth, without
character, as well as consciously ambiguous about his Jewish identity. Trebitsch thus holds up the late poems by Heine, the poems
discussed above, as examples of Heine's transcendence of his
"secondary defect" (72). Heine is caught between a "first-stage"
gift of expressing his sense of inner loss and the "secondary stage"
of that loss. Heine is thus the "father of journalistic prose," a Jewish
prose in which precisely this dichotomy is best exposed (73).

It is Heine's "wit" that reveals his pathology. For Trebitsch
there is a specific Jewish "wit," which is manifested in the Jews'
love for wordplay, for an undermining of the surface meaning of
the word and an emphasis on the word rather than on the thing
that it represents. It is this love for wordplay that characterizes
both the nature of the Jews' wit and their misuse of language in
general. And this misuse of language is linked by Trebitsch to the
special nature of the sexuality of the Jews. They use this language
in haggling even in the realm of marriage. The "secondary spirit"
of the Jews is manifested in their sexuality, since their perversions
are a reflection of their inability to relate at all to primary experiences, such as love (83). The Jews are the inventors of mastur-
bation and homosexuality, both of which reveal their true nature,
as they are only mechanical sexual acts, acts without any true
relationship between the sexual partners. The Jews are thus perverse both in their use of language and in their sexuality, both of
which are linked through their psychology.

By 1919 Arthur Trebitsch was able to call upon the structure
of depth psychology which was in the process of being developed
by Sigmund Freud. Trebitsch's reference to the Jews' wit is a direct
reference to Freud's study of wit and its relationship to the unconscious, and his discussion of the sexuality of the Jews is related
closely to that "new science of psychoanalysis with its Jewish
provenience" (151). Psychoanalysis focuses on language and sex
because Jews themselves focus on these two aspects of self as the
most evident manifestations of their hidden nature. While the "new
science" may be able to cure some illnesses, it cannot cure the
total (i.e., non-Jewish) person, who, unlike the Jew, is composed
of multiple and complex elements.

Between Weininger and Trebitsch lies the neurologist and
interpreter of dreams Sigmund Freud, who was one of the most
avid readers of *Sex and Character* in 1903. Freud's reading of Weininger has been the subject of numerous studies, and yet all tend to

focus on what Freud found and used in Weininger rather than on what he found and discarded.[68] Freud found the idea of inherent bisexuality compatible with the view promulgated by his friend Wilhelm Fliess, and it became one of the building blocks for his theory of sexuality. Freud seems not to have responded to Weininger's self-hatred as the reflection of his identity crisis. When one examines Freud's sense of the psychology of the Jew, especially in the light of his repeated use of himself as his own best case study, one can see a subtle reaction to models of Jewish self-hatred and Freud's own confusion of identity as scientist and Jew.

In 1926, on the occasion of his seventieth birthday, Freud was honored by the Viennese lodge of the Jewish fraternal order of B'nai B'rith, a group to which he had belonged since 1895.[69] Illness prevented Freud from addressing the group directly, but he wrote a short speech which was read on his behalf. This speech is Freud's *confessio judäica*. Its terseness reflects Freud's attempt to summarize in less than two pages of print his sense of Jewish identity, and it provides the key to an understanding of his sense of the psychology of the Jews. Freud observes that he joined the lodge in 1895 because of the "loneliness" he experienced in his personal and professional life, a loneliness that Freud links to his initial insights into "the depths of the life of the human instincts" (20:273). Freud then proceeds to stress that he joined the lodge because it was an association of Jews and would accept him and his views. In the same breath he rejects Judaism as either a religious or a nationalistic movement. "Plenty of other things remained over to make the attraction of Jewry and Jews irresistible—many obscure emotional forces, which were the more powerful the less they could be expressed in words, as well as a clear consciousness of inner identity, the safe privacy of a common mental construction" (20:274). Not language but a "common mental construction," a Jewish mentality, is the hallmark of the Jews. This phrase would seem to be a code word for a more extensive sense of identity, an identity based on a common perception of the world rather than on religious, political, or ethnic identification.

In claiming a common mental construction Freud is claiming a common discourse for all Jews. Setting himself apart from the world of Vienna and the world of science, with their own privileged discourses, Freud begins to identify with a discourse ascribed to the outsider, the Jew, in his world. Freud had begun an exploration of this mode of expression, the special language employed by the Jews, at the very beginning of his scientific career, during the very years when he was formulating his own concept of a universal discourse, the discourse of the unconscious, which would subsume and negate the idea of a special language ascribed to the Jews. Freud examined the particular case in his detailed study of jokes and their relationship to the unconscious. However, in order to understand Freud's analysis, one must first continue the examination of the comic language of the Jews, a concept that, as has been shown, is one of the constituent elements in the idea of the "hidden" language of the Jews from the Middle Ages.

We begin with a parapraxis, a slip of the pen. In his autobiography, *From Berlin to Jerusalem* (1977), Gershom Scholem, a man whose life was defined by books, makes surprisingly few references to those books that helped form his attitude toward literature, as well as his Jewish identity. Scholem's life, played out in the scholarly world of texts, recreated the idealized world of the Jew as scholar in a Germany that had only rediscovered these values of traditional Judaism shortly before his birth, in 1897. He writes of his first encounter with "some Hebrew books somewhere on the back shelves as well as other Hebrew books from the estate of my great-grandparents. . . . Otherwise I remember only two Jewish works of fiction that were very popular at the time, Israel Zangwill's *The King of Schnorrers* and the collection *Jüdische Witze* [Jewish Jokes] by Herrmann Noël."[70] These two titles remained with Scholem for over sixty years as the first Jewish books that he had read. Zangwill's comic tales of London Jewry became classics among European Jews soon after they were published in 1894. They provided a comic romanticization of historic Western European Jewry similar to that which Shalom Aleichem provided for the contemporary Yiddish-reading public. But what of this "work of fiction," the Jewish joke book by Herrmann Noël? No such author, no such book exists.

Scholem's memory has restructured the title and author of the collection. It was written or, perhaps better, compiled by a late-nineteenth-century German Jewish newspaperman named Manuel Schnitzer, who published *The Book of Jewish Jokes* under the pseudonym M. Nuél in 1907.[71] Scholem Christianizes Nuél's name to Noël, giving him the quintessential German first name Herrmann. Scholem saw in this work, with its "German" author-compiler, a major force in shaping his Jewish identity. His parapraxis leads us to the somewhat unusual world of the German Jewish joke book as a source for the definition of Jewish identity and the nature of the language in which that identity is clothed. Scholem's reference makes us, almost a century removed, aware of the power that the ethnic joke has in shaping communal as well as individual identity. For that at which we laugh determines and is determined by our sense of self.[72]

Schnitzer's Jewish joke book evidently held a major place in the redefinition of the nature of Jewish humor, or at least the Jewish joke, after the turn of the century. In his introduction, Schnitzer comments that the "Jewish joke reveals the Jewish character, the weaknesses of which are the object of its mockery. But one must not forget that it is always the Jews themselves who chastise their vanities" (9). Schnitzer sees in his collection, however, not a compilation of the weaknesses of the Jews to be read by the non-Jewish world, but a "folkloric" anthology of those stories "learned at grandmother's knee" that reveal the foibles of Jews in earlier, less enlightened times (7). His audience is the ideal Jew of his time, who laughs not at his or her own "vanities" but at those of the past.

The program stated in the introduction to Schnitzer's collection of 1907 is expanded in the collection itself. The volume is divided into sociological categories that reflect an idealized, intact world of European Jewry, a world ascribed by 1907 to the Eastern Jew. For the Eastern Jew had come to fill the position of the "primitive" in the popular anthropology of Western Jewry. By observing the *Ostjude*, says the Western Jew, we can learn where we have come from, just as Hegel uses the African black as the sign of the progress of European civilization. But also the *Ostjude* has preserved, better than we, an independent sense of self. Thus Schnitzer recounts tales about "important and unimportant rabbis," "students and pupils," "merchants and traders," "marriage brokers," and "beggars" (*Schnorrer*). In all of these tales and jokes the language is clear, unambiguous German. Indeed, when he uses a Yiddishism in his tales, he provides footnotes explaining it to his Jewish audience:

> The son of a famous German jurist, who, although a baptized Jew, held the highest judicial posts and was ennobled, became engaged to the daughter of a banker, who likewise, even though in another area of endeavor, came from a famous Jewish family. He, too, the papa of the young bride-to-be, had been born Christian, for his father had been baptized. The mother of the bride-to-be was especially happy about this match, and said to her prospective son-in-law:
> "You know, I had always wished for a son-in-law exactly like you. . . . "

"And what should he have been like?" he asked smiling.
"You know . . . just a nice Christian young man from a
*bekoweten** Jewish family." (59–60)

Schnitzer's note explains to his Jewish reader that *bekoweten* means
"honorable." This joke is typical of the entire volume. It presupposes absolutely nothing on the part of its audience; indeed, it
creates the assumption that the audience would perceive Yiddishisms (even terms such as *goy* ["non-Jew"] or *gannef* ["thief"], which
had established themselves in German slang long before the turn
of the century) as totally unintelligible. Schnitzer rejects any particularism in the discourse of the Jews. His folkloric collection, which
is supposedly retrospective (and thus includes some Yiddishisms
of the type "learned at grandmother's knee"), provides the image
of his ideal reader as removed from any language that could be
classified as Jewish. Thus Schnitzer is at pains to point out that
much of the comedy in the oral tales relied on the "tone-fall and
gesture" of the speaker, both of which are lost in the written form
and must, according to the compiler, be supplemented by a greater
amount of narration (10).

Schnitzer's ideal reader is one who is an exclusively German-
speaking Jew, one who speaks German but does not have a Yiddish
accent (*mauscheln*) and does not use Yiddishisms. Indeed, in the
sequel to his collection, Schnitzer provides an extensive series of
jokes about "the struggle for language and education," in which
Eastern Jews are portrayed struggling with German, providing comic
relief as they inevitably lose their struggles. The home of bad, comic
German lies to the East, in Poland, in Galicia. Schnitzer begins the
section with the following quotation from an apocryphal letter
from a German teacher who is called to Posen to teach in a Jewish
school there:

> If they wish to say *breit* ("wide"), they say *braat*; if they wish
> to say *Braten* ("roast"), then they say *Broten*; if they wish
> to say *Brot* ("bread"), then they say *Braut*; and if they really have
> to say *Braut* ("bride"), then they say *Kalle*.[73]

Kalle is the Yiddish word for bride, but it is not Yiddish that is the
butt of these tales but *mauscheln*. By the turn of the century Yiddish
had come to have a specific locus in the consciousness of Germans
as the primitive pidgin spoken by the Eastern Jew, as it was seen
in the writings of the German Jewish language reformer Eduard
Engel; or it could be understood as the true roots of a primitive,
nonrational discourse, as German Jews such as Martin Buber

perceived it. In either case it was exotic, distanced from the daily world of the German-speaking Jew. *Mauscheln*, the use of a Yiddish accent, intonation, or vocabulary items, was the mark of Eastern Jews who wished to acquire the cultural status of German speakers but by attempting to achieve this status revealed themselves as the Jews as outsiders. These Jews posed a threat to the integration of German-speaking Jews in the West by accentuating their "hidden" difference. The Eastern Jew was distanced by the German Jew into the world of the comic or the fictions of storytelling. They were thus placed in the past or at the fringes of Western "culture."

By 1907 Schnitzer has eliminated one aspect of the Jewish joke book, an aspect that only becomes evident when one examines other Jewish joke books of the period. For not only is the language of his Jewish jokes cast in acceptable German, the language of his reference group, but his stories are hygienically "clean." If we turn to the most widely read collections in the late 1890s, we find quite a different image of the ideal reader. Written for a Jewish audience, these collections are, as the subtitle of one of them reads, "nothing for children": they stress sexual double entendres; they are anthologies of "dirty" Jewish jokes. The most widely circulated of these collections were compiled by Avrom Reitzer, who published four collections just at the turn of the century.[74] Schnitzer's collections were evidently a reaction against volumes such as those published by Reitzer. All of Reitzer's jokes are told in *mauscheln*. The language of the jokes is labeled as the language of the Jews. There is absolutely no attempt to create a pseudoscientific matrix for the collection of the stories. Reitzer does not provide any "scholarly" apparatus that would label his collections as "folkloric." Finally, these tales stress the sexual. An example is the first tale in Reitzer's 1902 collection, entitled *Solem Alechem*:

> Avrom Boschel and Schmule Josel leave the temple Friday evening. In the heavens a star [*Stern*] is shining. "Look at the lovely fixed star," says Avrom. "What do you mean?" says Schmule. "Dats not a fixed star, dats got a tail [*Schwaf*], dats a comet-star." "Na, na," says Avrom, "that I really like to know for sure. I'll tell you what. Come home with me, we'll ask my Elsa. She's educated, she'll tell us." "You're right, let's go." When they arrived home, Avrom called his daughter Elsa. "Tell me, my child, what is the name of the star [*Stern*] that has the long tail [*Schwaf*]." "Papa, that's Ephrain Stern from Leopoldstadt."[75]

The play upon the double meaning of *Schwaf* ("tail" and "penis") in Yiddish is typical for this collection. What may not be clear from my translation is that the entire story, including the narrative intrusions, is written in *mauscheln*. Reitzer's tales presuppose an audience that can comprehend the double entendres presented in a German heavily laced with Yiddishisms. However, the actual knowledge of Yiddish in these jokes is limited to those words and wordplays that exist in German, either because of parallel linguistic features in both languages or because of borrowings into colloquial German from the Yiddish. In other words, it is in no way necessary to understand Yiddish (either written or spoken) to understand the jokes in Reitzer's collections. However, to the Jewish reader, the language appears to be transparent, for even those readers (i.e., Jews) who claim no Yiddish can understand the Jewish language of the joke. It is unimportant that the non-Jewish reader of German, especially one who speaks the slang of cosmopolitan areas such as Berlin, Vienna, or Frankfurt, could also understand these stories. For Jewish readers sensitive to their linguistic status as speakers of German, it would have seemed that there was some truth to the charge that no matter what the surface polish, Jews spoke a secret language. The idea of a secret language would have been especially powerful when stated within the limitations placed upon the professional use of language. We have seen how this structured the self-understanding of writers who were forced to use a language that it was claimed they could never truly master. But the charge of the secret language of the Jews was also aimed by the science of race at those primary or ancillary practitioners of the biological sciences themselves. As one of Freud's teachers, Theodor Billroth, had observed in a volume read by every medical educator and potential health care practitioner, the Jews were ill-fitted for the practice of medicine because of their inability to use the accepted discourse of civilized society. It is *mauscheln* that marks the Jew as the outsider (in German), especially in the eyes of those Jews, such as doctors, who perceived themselves as having achieved status in a German community that defined itself by the cultural implication of its language. In the Jewish joke book this sense of the Jews' language as different was then linked to that other hidden language, the language of sexuality.

Before we examine further the function of the Jewish joke as a means of defining the special language of the Jews at the turn of the century, it is important to observe that the history of the Jewish joke book does not begin with the *fin de siècle*. The first books of jokes about Jews intended to be read by Jews appear in Germany during the first generation after civil emancipation. The first seems to be L. M. Büschenthal's *Collection of Comic Thoughts about Jews, as a Contribution to the Characteristic of the Jewish Nation* (1812).[76] Six years later Sabattja Josef Wolff, the first biographer of Salomon Maimon, published a similar collection with an introduction by Büschenthal.[77] In both of his introductions, Büschenthal uses the eighteenth-century concept of *Witz* ("humor") as the basis for his rationale in presenting this material. Humor calls upon the rational mind, and the Jews, Büschenthal comments, have long been noted for their rationality. It is this that the jokes reveal. But the Jews have been damned as well as praised for this characteristic. Their jokes reveal that hidden within the seeming rationalism may be yet another quality, a response to "centuries of persecution":

> Necessity and weakness—this the female sex teaches us—give rise to deception, and deception is the mother of humor. Therefore one finds this much more frequently among persecuted and poor rural Jews than among rich ones. (iv)

Büschenthal argues that what in the past has passed for rationality, for the intense life of the mind among Jews, is simply the reaction to the persecutions that they have undergone. This false rationality can be revealed in their humor, which, like the language of the woman, as Kant observed, is the language of deception. The joke thus reveals the truth of the language of the Jews, that it is a weapon they use to defend themselves against the attacks of the Christian world.

Büschenthal's jokes are quite different from what his program would lead us to imagine. In the first joke in the collection, which uses direct discourse, we can examine the spoken language attributed to the Jew and its implications:

> A young Jewess sat in a loge in the theater in B——. A young rake entered and approached her in a familiar and aggressive manner. "Sir," said the young girl, "you evidently take me for someone else." "God forbid," he replied, "I can see very well that you are a young girl." He then became ever more impolite and finally brazen. The young girl, very upset, used her tongue, as only a young girl can. "Now, now," the rake cried, "don't eat me up!" "Sir, have no worries," she quickly replied. "I am a Jewess, and we are not allowed to eat pork." (5)

The story is told, as are all of the jokes in both early nineteenth-century collections, in the most cultured German. Indeed, the author-compiler is so sensitive to the linguistic implications of his text that when he uses the word for pork, *Schweinefleisch*, he prints it as *Schw——fleisch*, since the term *Schwein* ("pig") has a much greater pejorative connotation in German than in English. He thus spares his readers seeing a word that would be perceived as doubly offensive and must, of course, have that implication in the context of the joke. This sensibility is not a Jewish linguistic sensibility but a German one. The joke has a sexual component that the author uses to illustrate his theme: that Jews, when oppressed, can attack only verbally. In this they are like women, whose lack of strength is compensated for by their wit.

Büschenthal's collection, as well as Wolff's, also provides an image of the reader as a speaker of German. In these collections of stories written for a Jewish audience no reference is made to dialect, for in this first generation after civil emancipation *mauscheln* was still a widespread marker of the real difference between Jews and Germans. During the first decades of the nineteenth century the entire non-Jewish literature, which was aimed at satirizing the Jews, used *mauscheln* as a means of characterizing the inherent nature of the language of the Jews. Büschenthal wishes to distinguish his "speaking" Jews from the image of the Jews' language that dominated both stage and fiction. Indeed, it provided an explanation for the characteristics ascribed to the Jews, their rationalism, while distancing them from the language used to present these characteristics. Drawing on David Hume's concept of national characters, he wishes to show that the specifically Jewish character is but a direct response to the way the Jew was treated in the past. His analogy is that of language. For he writes his anecdotes in the best possible German, showing that he has moved completely from the language associated with Jewish oppression (Yiddish) to the language of true emancipation (German). Similarly, he implies in the very collecting of this material that such "national characteristics" as the Jews' wit will soon vanish with emancipation, with the result that the Jew will become as dull and boring as the German.

The parallel between 1800 and 1900 should not be overlooked: at both times a large group of Jews was identified by the nature of its language as different. In 1800 it was the Western Jew, who still heard Western Yiddish within the walled ghetto; in 1900 it was the large number of Yiddish-speaking Eastern Jews, who fled the pogroms in Russia and settled in Germany and Austria. At both times a Yiddish accent was the sign of a despised, incomplete symbiosis with the dominant common culture. The visibility of the Jews, especially in terms of the nature of their spoken language, recalled the old charges of a hidden language of the Jews. Both periods saw rampant and organized anti-Jewish movements in the German-speaking countries. After the defeat of Napoleon, riots caused the same type of insecurity in a Jewish community still very much insecure of its status as did the rise of political anti-Semitism in the late nineteenth century. In both periods the joke book served as a means of defusing this anxiety. It presented in softened and refined tones what the mobs in the streets were shouting about the Jews, and it gave focus and distance to this discourse by placing it within the covers of a book, a symbol of the higher culture. When, however, such books come too close to revealing the hidden, inner fears of their readers, when their mimetic quality reflects the wellsprings of their readers' anxiety, if only in distorted form, then even the book comes to be perceived as dangerous, as threatening. Such was the *fin de siècle* response to the Jewish joke book as a reflection of the hidden language of the Jew, especially in the case of the best-known study of the Jewish joke, published by Freud in 1905.

Much of the recent discussion on Sigmund Freud's Jewish identity has centered about the role that his father, Kallamon Jakob Freud, played as the source of Freud's understanding of what it meant to be a Jew. Freud's father was a Galician Jew who married into an established Austrian family and eventually moved to Vienna, the center of Austrian intellectual life. Freud never quite felt at home, even though he had moved to Vienna at the age of three.[78] This sense of ambivalence which manifested itself in many areas of Freud's personality evidently was heightened by his work with Josef Breuer. Older than Freud and more established in the Viennese intellectual and professional scene, Breuer contributed what came to be the paradigmatic case study, that of Anna O., to their joint *Studies in Hysteria* (1895). In this case study Breuer presents a reading of the "hidden" language of the Jew that may have provided the matrix for Freud's own examination of this language in his later study of the Jewish joke. Breuer, like Freud's father born in the provinces, is struck by Anna O.'s lack of religious feeling, for she came from a religious household.[79] This fact seemed important enough for Breuer to note it in his case notes. Thus according to the observations of her physician, one aspect of Anna O.'s illness is her loss of identity as a Jew — a Viennese Jew. Other symptoms of Anna O.'s illness had to do with various types of physical impairments, such as the paralysis of her hand, but Breuer's description of this case focuses again and again on the severe disruption of her language: during her illness Anna O.'s German began to disintegrate.

Bertha Pappenheim, Anna O.'s actual identity, lost her command of German. She began to communicate with her family and her physician, Breuer, exclusively in English, seemingly unaware that she had substituted English for German. In Breuer's case notes there is a letter written by her in the most stilted academic English, which indicates that her English was neither fluent nor even comfortable for her. She had associated German with her father—with his long and intense illness, with his death cries. English, a purely academic tongue, had none of these associations for her; it was foreign to her, both literally and figuratively. Breuer reports that the central crisis in her illness occurred when she perceived herself threatened by a "snake." In her delusion she tried to pray, but all that came to her was an English children's rhyme. The prayer that Bertha Pappenheim could not remember would have been in Hebrew. Hebrew, the religious language of the Jews and of her father, was repressed, forgotten, and replaced by a rote rhyme in a tongue with no overt associations. Breuer stresses in his case notes that Anna O. was "completely without belief." The loss of belief and the loss of language are one. Bertha Pappenheim repressed German and Hebrew, the two languages that she would have associated with the world of her father. This is neither surprising nor unusual. What is interesting is that the career of Bertha Pappenheim following her failed analysis with Breuer took her into the world of Eastern Jewry. She became highly involved with combatting the white slave trade, organizing a group that rescued young Eastern European Jewish women from the brothels. During this period, the 1920s and early 1930s, she also published a series of German translations from some of the major Yiddish popular works, such as the *Maasebuch*, a collection of folk tales, and the *Tsena Uranah*, the Yiddish Bible written for Jewish women. She became involved in the world that identified the Jew as a speaker of Yiddish, not German or Hebrew, and as female and a sexual object.

If Breuer's case study of Anna O. refers to her Jewish identity, if obliquely, it manages to avoid any discussion of her sexuality. Indeed, both the case study and Breuer's notes on the case comment that the patient seems to lack any overt sexuality. Breuer also avoids reporting his final confrontation with Anna O., during which she attributed the cause of her hysterical pregnancy to him. What is present in Breuer's case study is a detailed description of the collapse of Anna O.'s language. Breuer, the provincial Jew as Viennese doctor, heard her German collapse into *mauscheln*. The syntax wavered, the conjugation of the verbs began to disappear, until finally she used only incorrect past tenses created from the past participle. This is, of course, a fantastic form of Yiddish, the language of the Jew that is neither German (the language of the assimilated Jew) nor Hebrew (the language of liturgy). Breuer sees this decay of German into Yiddish, labeling it as *Jargon*, the pejorative term that German speakers used when referring to Yiddish.[80] He associates the collapse of language with the loss of a Western Jewish identity and the sexual Otherness of female discourse, but only on a subconscious level.

It was Sigmund Freud who made these associations overt. It was Freud, according to his own retrospective account, who saw the sexual etiology of the collapse of Anna O.'s language. It was Freud who understood the sexual dimension of "hysteria" and the role of language in its cure for the first time. Freud's recounting of this central discovery, one of Frank Sulloway's "myths of psychoanalysis," links language and pathology.[81] But just as Breuer repressed the question of Anna O.'s sexuality, Freud represses the relationship between her illness and her rejection of her Jewish identity. In *The History of the Psychoanalytic Movement* Freud tells two stories about his linkage of sexuality with the etiology of neurosis (14:13–15). During his stay in Paris, Freud hears the great neurologist Jean Martin Charcot recount a similar case, and Freud quotes Charcot directly as to the source of the young woman's illness: "Mais, dans des cas pariels c'est toujours la chose genitale." He also recounts a case for which he was called in on a consultation by the Viennese neurologist Rudolf Chrobak; he quotes Chrobak directly: "He is not good if he can't cure her after so many years." The sole prescription for such a malady, Chrobak added, is familiar enough to us, but we cannot order it:

Rx. Penis normalis
    dosim
    repetatur!

Freud brings these examples as proof that while the idea of a sexual basis for neurosis was evident, it had been treated as a joke the punch line of which everyone knew. But Freud's recountings of these two sexual jokes have an identical structure. Both stories are told in German, and the punch line, always a direct quote, is presented in a foreign language, either French or Latin. On the surface, such a recounting may lead to the illusion of verisimilitude or the slightly crabbed sensation that one gets from reading Krafft-Ebing's work on sexual pathology, in which all of the sexual references are presented in Latin. Both of these qualities may be present, but a third dimension provided the paradigm for Freud's sexual jokes, namely, the missing link of the Jewish joke and its role in defining Jewish identity in the 1890s.

In his correspondence with Wilhelm Fliess in 1897, Freud reports that he had already compiled a "collection of profound Jewish stories."[82] Not merely jokes but *Jewish* jokes, and this at the time when Freud is also collecting the reports of dreams that will form the basis for his seminal study of the language of dreams.

The centrality of the Jewish joke to Freud's thought at this early point in his development cannot be underestimated, nor should the relationship of the Jewish joke to *mauscheln* be ignored. As early as July 14, 1894, and October 31, 1895, Freud used Jewish jokes as commonplaces, repeating only their punch lines, in letters to Fliess, like Freud an acculturated Jew. Evidently such jokes served as common ground for both men whether in Vienna or, in Fliess's case, in Berlin. In the case of the punch line used in the October 31, 1895, letter, the joke actually reappears in its full form in Freud's study on the nature of humor. Freud's admission in his letter of June 22, 1897, that he had begun to collect "profound" Jewish jokes followed a period of intense interest in Jewish humor. Indeed, this very statement concludes a paragraph in his letter to Fliess in which Freud compares himself and Fliess to two figures in the punch line of a Jewish joke, "two beggars, one of whom gets the province of Posen" (p. 254). In this letter Freud uses a Yiddishism for the first time. (He employs the word *Schnorrer* for beggar.)

After his initial admission of his interest in the Jewish joke as a source for the nature of psychopathology, Freud laces his letters with Yiddishisms for comic effect: *meschuge* = crazy (December 3, 1897; December 29, 1897; March 23, 1900); *Parnosse* = sustenance (December 12, 1897); *Dalles* = poverty (June 9, 1898); *Knetscher* = wrinkles (December 5, 1898); *Tomer doch* = maybe? (August 20, 1898); *Stuss* = bunk (September 6, 1898); *Shigan* = craziness (November 9, 1899; March 23, 1900). What is striking about all of the Yiddishisms employed by Freud in his exchange with Fliess is that they are part of the urban slang of the period. They serve, however, as a sign of his emotional bonding with Fliess, as they both see in the shared joke about Jews a common external focus for their own anxieties about their status in German or Austrian society.

Without a doubt, the most telling moment in the exchange between Freud and Fliess is the letter of September 21, 1897, in which Freud acknowledges that his earlier seduction theory of the origin of neurosis was wrong. He casts his sense of loss in "a little story from my collection . . . 'Rebecca, take off your gown, you are no longer a bride'" (p. 266). This rather enigmatic punch line has been interpreted in a number of different ways. What is important, however, is that Freud uses a punch line from a "Jewish joke" shared between himself and Fliess as the appropriate discourse in which to clothe his sense of disappointment in his abandonment of the seduction theory and the promised status that he believed such a theory would have brought him. The punch line is made even more telling by the use of the Yiddishism *Kalle*, which is itself a sexual double entendre meaning both "bride" and "prostitute."

Freud makes a distinction between his own comic use of Yiddish and that of the Eastern Jew (which distanced the Other as the speaker of corrupt German in the shared joke) when in his letter of April 27, 1898, he refers to his brother-in-law Moriz Freud (a distant cousin who married his sister Marie) as a "half-Asian" who suffered from "pseudologica fantastica" (p. 311). He was a "half-Asian" because he was an Eastern Jew. (He was from Bucharest.) "Pseudologica fantastica" is the psychiatric diagnosis for those mythomaniac patients who lie in order to gain status. For Freud it was the damaged, comic discourse of the Eastern Jew that approximated the anti-Semitic image of the lying Jew. His representation of the discourse of the "good" Jew and the "bad" Jew continued in Freud's scientific work and was based upon his "collection of profound Jewish stories."

His collection can be reconstructed, at least in part, from the jokes published in Freud's *Jokes and Their Relation to the Unconscious* (1905). These stories reveal much of Freud's interest in presenting *mauscheln* in a scientific, i.e., German, context. While the overall intention of the books seems to be an analysis of the nature of the joke (*Witz*), Freud actually limits most of the study to those jokes that he labels as Jewish. Freud sees these as fulfilling the prime purpose of the joke in that "they are capable of making us laugh and . . . deserve our theoretical interest. And both these two requirements are best fulfilled precisely by Jewish jokes" (8:49). Freud analyzes the joke about two Jews meeting near a bath house ("Have you taken a bath?" asked one of them. "What?" asked the other in return. "Is one missing?") in terms of its use of *mauscheln*. He is aware that the shift in stress from *taken* to *bath*, which provides the ambiguity in the joke, is a quality of *mauscheln*. The origin of the displacement of meaning is thus in the language of the comic Jew, in his use of *mauscheln*. Freud analyzes a number of such jokes, all of which revolve about the juxtaposition of "bad" German, *mauscheln*, to "good" German, the German in which

Freud embeds the joke. The structure of the joke, as Freud describes it, is fulfilled in the very text that Freud is writing.[83] The teller of the joke is Freud. He not only recounts the joke but uses the form of the joke similar to that found later in Schnitzer's book of jokes. The joke is told in correct German. If there is any use of *mauscheln*, it is limited to that part of the joke that is clearly delineated as the direct speech of the comic character.

The object of the joke vanishes in the telling of the joke. The object is the Eastern Jew who is trying to achieve status by speaking German but who reveals himself through the nature of his language. Freud allies himself with a reader, whom he expects to be conversant with the "modern" scientific discourse on the unconscious, that is, Freud himself. This is, of course, a projection that reveals to us the identification that Freud, the provincial, has with those Eastern Jews who speak only in *mauscheln*. Freud's Galician father would have had at least a provincial accent which would have set him apart from Viennese Jews. His father, as Freud himself stated, served as his model of the persecuted Jew. He would also have been the model for the Jew who revealed his nature through the difference of his speech. The hidden language of the Jew has another, major dimension for Freud. It is not merely that provincial Jews speak comically but that this comic speech reveals their other hidden difference, their sexuality. The language of the Jewish joke is the language of sex. Marie Balmary centers her extraordinarily insightful reading of Freud's early life about the "hidden fault of the father," Kallamon Jakob Freud's unknown third marriage and Sigmund's birthdate, which, in reality, was two months earlier than his acknowledged date of birth.[84] The *Ostjude*, whether Jakob Freud or not, speaks a sexualized language, a language that reveals hidden truths in comic form. Kallamon Jakob's death in 1896 is seen by most critics (including Freud himself) as the catalyst for Freud's self-analysis, which led to the formulation of the new language of psychoanalysis. The actual language of his father, born in Tismenitz, Galicia, certainly played a role in the formulation of his image of the father, as did his association of this language with covert sexuality.

This paradigm is embedded in the nature of collections of Jewish jokes available to Freud during the period 1897–1905. In his work Freud mentions one specific contemporary source for his material (if we ignore his literary sources, such as Heine's works). He refers to the Munich periodical *Flying Pages*. This periodical, a sort of German *Punch*, was consciously apolitical. It contained few dialectal jokes, almost no Jewish jokes, and no sexual double entendres. And yet this selfsame periodical republished in 1890 an 1877 collection of Jewish jokes written in *mauscheln*.[85] This collection does not differ much in quality from the anthologies of Avrom Reitzer, except, of course, that it was directed at a non-Jewish rather than a Jewish audience. Freud would have had access to all of these collections of jokes, those written for a Jewish audience (such as Reitzer) as well as the collection published by *Flying Pages*. He makes reference to none of these collections, however; rather, he creates a new, scientific model (not unlike that later used by Schnitzer), in which he embeds these tales in an overtly scientific discourse. This scientific context heightens the difference between Freud's language, the language of the Jew as writer of scientific German, and *mauscheln*, the language ascribed to the Jews in the jokes that Freud presents.

In his study Freud dismisses the use of *Jargon*, that is, Yiddish, as a source of humor. First in an analysis of jokes about marriage brokers (*Schadchen*) and then later in a discussion of a joke about Jews and alcohol, he observes that *Jargon* weakens the effect of the joke, since the tale relies on the effect of the language rather than the content of what the language expresses (8:108, 114). In dismissing the use of Yiddishisms, or *mauscheln*, Freud undercuts the basis of those jokes that he labels as Jewish. For it is not merely the self-deprecating content of the jokes that makes them Jewish, as Freud claims, but also the very use of language, which Freud then rejects as superficial. The Jews in Freud's jokes speak an easily identifiable language. This is true in the joke that Freud relates about the *Schadchen* (with its punch line, "Do you call that living?") as well as in the joke that he cites from Heine's *The Baths of Lucca*, in which Heine's Jewish upstart Hirsch-Hyacinth boasts of his relationship with the Rothschilds: "And as true as God shall grant me all good things, Doctor, I sat beside Solomon Rothschild and he treated me quite as his equal, quite *'famillionairely'* " (8:16). The intonation of the first punch line and the punning misuse of German in the second are both qualities ascribed to the Jew speaking in *mauscheln*.

Freud provides the reader with a major case study of laughter as a means of expiating Jewish self-hatred. The case is scattered throughout the study in some dozen and a half references. It begins in the first paragraph of the study, when Freud, picking up a reference to Heine from the aesthetician Theodor Lipps, cites Heine's creature Hirsch-Hyacinth, the lottery agent and curer of corns, speaking about his "famillionaire" relationship to the Rothschilds. Heine, and indeed this story, becomes one of Freud's authorities for Jewish humor and its social function. Freud uses the story to illustrate the principle of condensation and returns to it again in his theoretical discussion of wit. He uses the joke again to illustrate Heine's own sense of rejection by his wealthy family. Freud draws the parallel between Hirsch-Hyacinth and Heinrich Heine because of the former's conversion to Christianity and his "Jewish" act in keeping the same last initial because he already had an *H* engraved on his seal. Freud remarks: "But Heine himself effected the same economy when, at his baptism, he changed his first name from Harry to Heinrich" (8:141). Freud not only uses Heine as his prime example of Jewish humor but also labels him as one who rejects his identity as a Jew. One must remember Freud's comment that he understood "Judaism" to be the intellectual community of Jews. In shifting his name from the Jewish Harry to the Christian Heinrich, Heine indulged in the rejection of his Jewish identity through Christian onomastics, which had some parallel in Freud's own case. For Freud's first name was that of his grandfather, Schlomo Sigismund Freud, who died a few months before his birth.[86] In rejecting Schlomo, or at least in relegating it to his Jewish or private self, Freud followed the pattern set by Heine, not in terms of conversion, but in the terms of separating himself from that world of Jewry rejected by the anti-Semite, whether the political or the scientific anti-Semite, and maintaining only his cultural affiliation. Freud's sensitivity to this question, his reference to the persons behind the character, is a reflection of his use of Heine as a stalking horse for his own ambiguities concerning his own Jewish identity.

We are thus left with a complex set of paradoxes that need to be resolved. Freud begins to collect "Jewish jokes" after his father's death, at a time in his career when he is trying to define his basic program. He collects jokes recorded in a very specific way: they are labeled by him as Jewish, they are written in good German, and they contain direct or indirect discourse that uses *mauscheln* to characterize the speaker as a Jew. At the same time Freud discovers, according to his own account, the basis for the neurosis of his friend and colleague Breuer's star patient in three jokes, all of which share the same structural devices as the Jewish jokes that he retells in his book on humor: they are told in good German, contain direct or indirect discourse, and use a foreign language to characterize the secretiveness of the speaker's *pointe*. All of this is against a background in the German-speaking world in which the dominant image of the Jewish joke, at least in the 1890s, when Freud is writing and collecting his material, is that of the off-color, or "blue," story.

In his study of the nature of humor and its relationship to the unconscious Freud separates two modes of storytelling, one that he illustrates with his "Jewish" jokes and the other, the sexually aggressive, which is almost without illustration. The model discussed above for the Jewish joke is, however, not the model that Freud perceives in his discussion of his "Jewish" jokes; rather, I have adapted the model of the sexually aggressive joke told as part of the verbal seduction of the woman. It is the joke that causes the object of the story to vanish in the identification of the male story-teller with his male listener. The Jew in the structural presentation of the "Jewish" joke in Freud's retelling thus becomes the woman and vanishes in the presence of the idealized German self as both raconteur and listener, turning the teller's desire for identification with his reference group into hostility toward the outsider, himself, who does not permit this. Freud rejects the very tales he tells as not real Jewish jokes, because they are told in dialect, a dialect that reflects his own insecurity about his status as a provincial Jew in society. He is a provincial, one who speaks a different tongue, not only because of his "hidden" Jewish language but because this language is sexual and reveals the true nature of the speaker as the same as that of the language of the caricatured Jew in the sexually suggestive Jewish joke. It is this model against which Freud reacts.

The idea that the humor of the Jew is identical to that of the woman is at least as old as Büschenthal's 1812 anthology of Jewish humor. But it is polemicized by Otto Weininger, who draws the analogy between the discourse of the woman and that of the Jew as proof of their inherently different mode of perceiving the world and the interrelatedness of their perspectives. Couched in Wein-inger's laborious pseudoscientific German is, following a detailed discussion of the relationship between the sexuality of the woman and that of the Jew, a discussion of the humorlessness of the Jew. Weininger juxtaposes sexuality and humor. He defines the source of all humor as the ability to transcend the empirical world and thus denies the Jew the ability to possess true wit (318). According to Weininger, "Jews and women are devoid of humor but addicted to mockery" (319). Thus the tone ascribed to the Jew as writer, with Heine serving as the central example, is also the tone of the language of women. Jewish discourse and feminine discourse merge and overlap in the world of satire, for true humor is possessed only by men.

Freud read and used many of Weininger's views. One view that he seems to have accepted was the need to draw a distinction between the language of science used by him and the language attributed to the Jew. This hidden language, the language that Viennese society used to characterize the Jew, was the language of the outsider. It was part of the hostile labeling of the Jew as different. But Freud projects this universal labeling of the language of the Jews as different onto a subset of Jews. He characterizes the *mauscheln* of the Jew attempting to enter Austrian society from the East as the true sign of the different, hidden language of the Jew. It is a public indicator of the Jew's difference and of Freud's own identification with the non-Jew rather than with the non-Jew's caricature of the Jew.

Freud wishes to stand outside of the limited world view attributed by this caricature to the Jew. He wishes to speak a different language. This is, of course, echoed much later in Freud's creative career in his description of the basis for Moses's slowness of speech: "Moses spoke another language and could not communicate with his Semitic neo-Egyptians without an interpreter" (23:33). Freud, like his "Egyptian" Moses, speaks a language other than that of the image of the Jew that he rejects. It is the language of scientific discourse. Yet that discourse, as it manifests itself in Weininger, is itself contaminated. Freud's scientific German, at least when he sits down to write his book on humor, is a language tainted by Weininger's anti-Semitism. Thus even in this seemingly neutral medium of writing about Jews, Freud finds himself confronted with a new, hidden language of the Jew, the language of the Jew as anti-Semite, in which all of the charges brought against the Jew come home to haunt the author and lead him to the only possible escape, self-destruction.

In this medium Freud creates a language for himself that is neither the language of women nor the language of Jews. Freud embeds both images in the new language of the unconscious. It is a language present in all human beings, one that is unmarred by the sexual or anti-Semitic politics of his day, or at least Freud hopes. The exercise of collecting and retelling Jewish jokes, of removing them from the daily world in which Freud must live to the higher plane of the new scientific discourse, that of psychoanalysis, enables Freud to purge himself of the insecurity felt in his role as a Jew in *fin de siècle* Vienna. He exorcises this anxiety by placing it in the closed world of the book and placing himself in the privileged position of the author employing the new language of psychoanalysis for an audience newly taught this discourse. It is no wonder that when Freud comes to remember his "discovery" of the sexual etiology of neurosis, the wellspring of this new language of psychoanalysis, his memory casts the source of his discovery in the structure of "Jewish" jokes. The very structure of the joke embodies the distancing of existing attitudes and their replacement by a new discourse, that of psychoanalysis.

Freud's new discourse is universal, but the distinction between the "civilized" language of the Egyptians and the language of the Jews still haunts it. This contradiction points up the lifelong double bind experienced by Freud in regard to his own sense of self. He is Moses, speaking a new language to those mired in the language of race. This world, the world of the Jews in Egypt, is in fact the world of Christian Europe in the 1930s. Freud's sense of his potential destruction at the hands of his disciples was not all that wrong in the light of Jung's anti-Semitism. But in reversing the qualities, in making himself into the outsider who speaks the civilized language and who has to learn the barbaric language of the Jews in order to teach them the truths of his own religious experience, Freud is creating a topsy-turvy world in which he is no longer the Jew as outsider speaking the Jews' language. For by the 1930s, psychoanalysis and the psychoanalytic discourse had been labeled by European anti-Semites such as Trebitsch as the new language of the Jews, a language that reflected the Jews' preoccupation with the material, the sexual, the perverse. Freud positions himself outside the world of the Jews, outside the arena of the Jews' language. Here the fascination with the language of the Jews as encapsulated within the Jewish joke is further distanced: Freud rejects the language of the Jews and sees himself as the creator of a new discourse. This myth of creation is parallel to his own early rejection of *mauscheln*, of the Yiddish-accented language of the provincial Jews, and his attempt to purify scientific discourse of its racist implications. The language of the Jews is comic, and the language of science is racist. He attempts to create a new language, which comes to be labeled as quintessentially Jewish and thus negates all his attempts.

Sigmund Freud can be seen as standing between Otto Weininger and Arthur Trebitsch, not only in that the former helped shape his views toward the language of the Jew and that Freud's own writings on Jewish language proved a reification of the latter's self-hatred; Freud was also captured by the rejection of aspects of Judaism, not as a religion but as a manner of perceiving oneself and one's sense of the importance of aspects of one's Jewish identity. The pathological intensity of Weininger's and Trebitsch's self-hatred caused their destruction; Freud was able to deal with many of the same aspects of self-questioning and rejection in a creative manner. Indeed, whether or not one accepts the argument put forth as early as the 1920s that Freud was essentially a "Jewish" thinker, it is clear that at least some of the conflicts that he perceived within his attempt to shape his own identity had their roots in conflicts with himself concerning his Jewish identity.

IV
The Invention of the Eastern Jew

One of the most successful ways to distance the alienation produced by self-doubt was negative projection. By creating the image of a Jew existing somewhere in the world who embodied all the negative qualities feared within oneself, one could distance the specter of self-hatred, at least for the moment. But a surprising turnabout occurred in the late nineteenth century. Until then the Eastern Jew had provided the touchstone for the exorcism of feelings of insecurity for the Western Jew.[87] With their language, their religious expression, their appearance, dress, and dietary practices, the Eastern Jews became the essential "bad" Jews. But within late-nineteenth-century debates about the nature of the Jews and their perception of the world, a surprising shift took place in the Western Jew's attitude toward the Jew in the East. The negative image of the Eastern Jew was displaced by the image of the nonassimilated Western Jew (or at least the Jew in the West), by *Mauschel*. This image was no longer associated with the Yiddish-speaking Eastern Jew but with the Western Jew, with his Jewish affectation. The mode of distancing was, however, the same: in both cases a negative stereotype was created to separate the implied value of the self from that within the self which was sensed to be without value. At the close of the nineteenth century, after the model of the assimilated Jew had become the standard self-image for the Jew in Western Europe, a slow shift in the model used to distance the sense of anxiety, of the slipperiness of the Jew's precarious position, took place, for the status quo became the model of social and linguistic acculturation rather than a real or remembered striving toward this state. Thus the splitting of the identity of the Jew into polar opposites took place in an antithetical manner that mirrored the division of the perception of self into "good" and "bad" aspects.

Reacting against the definition of the good Jew as the mirror-image of the enlightened German, Jews at the end of the nineteenth century discovered a new model for the "good" Jew in those very qualities despised by the Enlightenment.[88] The late-nineteenth-century German Jews created a new stereotype through which the anxiety as to the divisive nature of their self-definition was distanced and called it "the Eastern Jew." This image became the new definition of the "good" Jew, and it was contrasted with the assimilated or acculturated Jew, who became the prototypical "bad" Jew. This resulted in a series of classic double bind situations, since this stereotype was invented by Western Jews, who articulated their sense of self within a Western understanding of the realities of the Eastern Jew. The conflicts that the refunctioning of the Eastern Jew caused within late-nineteenth- and early-twentieth-century German and Austrian Jews provide a rich field for understanding how a model of self-hatred must provide some type of external articulation for the sense of self-abnegation. The essentially neutral projection of the Eastern Jew, a projection that is seen as positive, is used by radically different ideologies or movements as a means of articulating their own discomfort with the status of Western Jewry. The image of the Eastern Jew becomes a touchstone for an understanding, not of the Eastern Jew, but of Western Jewry.

In 1888 Ahron Marcus wrote in the first volume of his study of Chasidic thought:

> I assert that while the occidental, civilized Jews, insofar as one can speak of a Jewish science existing at all among them, possess only a rationalistic, watered-down continuation of Spanish, Aristotelian-Scholastic theology; the Jews of Eastern Europe, on the other hand, written off as enemies of civilization, separated by a Great Wall of China from modern culture, possess a lively science which verifies the legitimacy of their alleged origin as the age-old inheritors of the prophets by means of the simple fact that they stand on a level with the modern cosmology, which has been evident for centuries.[89]

Such a claim would not come as a surprise from the followers of Eastern Jewish mysticism, who saw themselves diametrically opposed to the forces of the Enlightenment. But Ahron Marcus was an acculturated German Jew, raised in Hamburg. In 1861 he moved to Cracow, and from there to Radomsk, where he remained from 1862 to 1866 as a disciple of the Chasidic miracle rabbi of Radomsk. Marcus felt himself drawn to the faith and ideology of the Eastern Jew as an antidote to the radical rationalism that permeated German (and Western) Jewry. Marcus thus reversed the accepted dichotomy created between the negative image of the Eastern Jews, their religion, and by implication their language, and the ideal of the Western Jew. For Ahron Marcus, the Eastern Jew became the idealized self-image of the Jew, containing all of the positive qualities that Marcus felt were lacking within his own community and his definition of self. As late as 1903, in a talk given in Hamburg, Marcus observed:

> Law and justice are the products of governing, balancing reason; love and sensitivity are the activities of feeling, which unite in loyalty and recognition as faith and knowledge.
>
> This union was able to arise, however, solely in the process of revelation; it was only able to survive through transmission and was only able to regain its original greatness by means of revelatory recognition, the prospect of which was projected into the future.
>
> The truth of this statement, the cornerstone of our religion, has been contested by scholasticism from Aristotle all the way down to Mendelssohn. Without wanting to do so, Kant supplied the proof for the truth of the latter.
>
> Judaism has had to fight a battle on two fronts since Abraham: against faith and knowledge, i.e., against blind faith and blind science. The concepts of paganism and religion are still all too frequently confused, even today.[90]

Marcus's comments are directed against the Haskalah, but his rhetoric, linking "scholasticism" and the negative image of the Jew, is taken directly from traditional attacks on Jewish logic, a logic attributed by the Haskalah to the Eastern, or Orthodox, Jew. What Marcus stresses is the role of an inherently Jewish mode of understanding, revelation, as opposed by rationalism. He posits the inherent opposition to this Jewish mode of understanding, a tradition that runs from Aristotle to Kant, as "Western." The dichotomy that he creates between the sense of the text, of language, among the Eastern Jews and that held by Western Jewry becomes one of the touchstones for the creation of the image of the Eastern Jew as the essential Jew during the *fin de siècle*. But Marcus uses the rhetoric of contemporary, "modern" philosophy, that of Eduard von Hartmann, to give his "Chasidic" insights form (and make them palatable to the German reader). His lectures and books are written in the densest academic German, which was totally inappropriate for capturing the spirit of that which he was describing but which provided authority to that which he wrote. His language was that of the German philosopher, and it attempted to translate the irrationality of the Chasidic brand of mysticism into the highly structured, rational language of the Western philosophical tradition, a tradition that he viewed as inimical to Jewish self-expression.

The most widely read exponent of a positive projection of the Eastern Jew, and thus a negative evaluation of the Western self-image of the Jew, was Martin Buber, born in 1878.[91] Buber, who was moved from his family home in Vienna to his grandparents' home in Lemberg after his mother abandoned her family, was raised in two worlds: first, the cultural world of the Austrian provinces, where German remained the primary language; and second, the Orthodox world of his grandfather, the famed midrashic scholar Salomon Buber. Buber's path to a productive definition of his own Jewish identity necessitated that he distance one pole or the other, but as can be imagined, the complexity of their interrelationship contaminated both facets of Buber's definition of self. Even if he were able to label one of these traditions as flawed, some qualities of this flawed tradition would remain within the positive definition of self.

The rise of political Zionism gave Buber his focus on his Jewish identity. In an essay written in 1917 for a magazine written for Jewish youth, Buber traces his "Path to Hassidism":

> Zionism gave the first stimulus to my liberation. I can only allude here to what it meant for me: the restoration of the context, the renewed rootedness in the community. No one requires the redeeming link with nationhood as much as he who has been seized by a spiritual quest, a youth abducted by the intellect away to the skies; but among the youths of this nature and with this destiny no one needs this link with nationality as much as the Jewish youth does. The others preserve the bond, deeply inherent, transmitted over millennia, to the native soil and to the racial inheritance of dissolution; the Jew, even he who has acquired a feeling for nature and perhaps a cultivated appreciation of German folk art and customs only yesterday, is directly threatened by it, has surrendered to it, provided that he does not find his way back to it. And for him who has disassociated himself from his society, the most glittering treasure of intellect, the most prolific, illusory productivity (only he who is bound can be truly productive) are not able to compensate for the holy insignia of humanity, rootedness, association, totality.[92]

The antithesis between acculturation, which Buber views as a surface phenomenon, and the true roots of Jewish identity, perceived by him as inherent in the Jew, is but the standard paradigm of Jewish uniqueness presented by racial anti-Semites given a positive value. In another essay from about the same period, "On the Spirit of the

Orient and the Jews," Buber stresses the racial identity of the Jew, attributing to this identity a specific mode of perceiving the world.[93] He states that the Jews can serve as the link between Eastern (or Oriental) perceptions of the world and Western (or German) perceptions and that even though German culture and language are not the best mode of expression for the Jew, they do have a special role in this process. Buber stresses the symbiotic relationship between German culture and the Jew but denies the Jew a functional role in this world. The Jew remains, for Buber, an outsider whose position is reified by the tenets of Zionism.

But Buber's reputation as the creator of the positive image of the Eastern Jew does not rest on his theoretical writings. In 1906 he published *The Tales of Rabbi Nachman* and in 1908, the *Legends of the Baal Shem Tov*, two books that fixed the image of the Eastern Jew for German Jewry. These tales, written in a striking German, document the dichotomy perceived between the official cultural tradition of the Austro-Hungarian Empire and that of Eastern Jewry, a tradition that the young Buber projects back into his own childhood:

> As a child, I experienced this in Sadagora, the filthy village of the "swarthy" Hassidic horde, which I was observing at that time—how a child experiences such things, not as thoughts but rather as images and feelings: that it has to do with the world for the sake of the complete human being and that the complete human being is no other than the true helper. The Zaddik is now primarily concerned with the alleviation of truly worldly sufferings, but is not he, nevertheless, according to the possibility, still that which he once thought he was and set himself up to be: the helper in spirit, the teacher of the world's meaning, the conductor of the divine spark? . . . Somehow, in a childish way, these questions dawned' on me already at that time. And I was able to make a comparison: on the one hand, with the district official, whose power rested upon vain customary coercion; on the other hand, with the rabbi, who was an upright and God-fearing man but an employee of the "directorate of the cult." Here, however, was something different, something incomparable; here was, degraded but intact, the living double-concern of humanity: true community and true leadership. There was something ageless, primeval here, something lost, longed-for, recurring.[94]

It is split between the Westernized ideas of Judaism, as an extension either of the state or of Western concepts of religion (cult), and the implied purity of the Eastern Jewish tradition, a tradition that in fact was no older nor more hallowed than the Haskalah, which Buber embeds in his retelling of the tales of the Chasids. That the Baal Shem Tov, the founder of modern Chasidism, was a contemporary of Moses Mendelssohn is lost in the attempts by Buber to create an "ageless, primeval . . . longed-for, recurring" model for the language of the Jews.

The method that Martin Buber describes in his account of writing the Chasidic tales reveals the inner struggle of a Western Jew, writing in a Western language, attempting to adapt cultural artifacts from a totally different milieu for the needs of his positive projection of the Jew. Buber uncovered the tales that he included in his first volume in, for him, a corrupt state:

> Among all those books, the collections of maxims of the Zakkidim and of legends from their life, there was a quite unusual one, different from the others and, moreover, the most folkish of them: the "Sippure Massiyot," "The Tales of the Events," stories of Rabbi Nachman of Bratzlaw, a great-grandson of the Baal Shem, which he delivered to his students and which one of them wrote down and published after his death in a clearly distorted form. These stories—partly pure fairy tales, partly creations of a special kind—these symbolic and sometimes slightly allegorizing stories, were woven from the distillation of mystical experience and the web of a constructive imagination. In common they had a trait that was not exactly didactic but rather instructive; Rabbi Nachman himself had called them the clothing of his tenets, and from the hands of scholars a comprehensive commentary had developed. But distortion also adhered to them all; the distortion of the content through all kinds of utilitarian and vulgar-rationalist touches, the distortion of the form through confusion of the lines and dulling of the pure colors as one infers them to be from the less affected parts. (969–70)

Buber sees in the "distortions" of the tales of Rabbi Nachman the work of the rationalistic and vulgar materialistic mind, that is, the mind of the "bad" Jew, a mind that he associates with the world of the scholar. Buber begins to restructure the tales, and what he omits is most striking: he deletes from the tales not those elements that one would associate with the falsification of the mystic by the rational but precisely those qualities that were perceived as suspect, as markers of the "bad" Jew, the irrational. In one tale, "The Simple Man and the Clever Man," Buber condemns the intellectual subtleties of the "clever" man which do not allow him to acknowledge the realities of the world.[95] The tale as Buber found it concludes with the introduction of the supernatural and the salvation of the "clever" man by the intercession of the Zaddick. Buber reworks the tale into a condemnation of Jewish cleverness and the praise of the "simple" approach to reality. He excludes the supernatural, as one would expect from a German writer steeped in the rational tradition, while claiming to reflect the antirationalist tradition within Judaism. What is more, he casts these tales, which are to be the reflection of the truly Jewish mode of discourse, in a language that is itself quite unique.

In 1904 Buber had translated into German a play by the Yiddish dramatist David Pinski. Buber had been struck by the extraordinary difficulty that he was having in capturing the essence of Pinski's language in German. In his foreword to the play, Buber comments on the special nature of both Yiddish, which he sees as a language of Jewish ethnic identity, and the German into which he translated the drama. Abraham Joshua Heschel has suggested that in order to understand Buber's style, one must appreciate the influence that Yiddish had on it.[96] There is indeed much more to it than this. For Buber, in undertaking the translation of Pinski's *Eisik Scheftel*, began to shape a language, a *mauscheln*, not the stage Yiddish accent with its comic overtones, but a literary *mauscheln*, which mirrored the positive qualities ascribed to the Eastern Jew. It was a language and a rhetoric that was created by Buber out of whole cloth. In its conscious simplicity and rejection of the irrational, it is related most closely to the language of the bourgeois fairy tales of the late nineteenth century, the fairy tales of Ludwig Bechstein and Hans Christian Andersen, which make the genre acceptable to the middle class. Buber's translation of *Eisik Scheftel*, with the creation of a language within German that could present the difference and yet the similarity between German and Jewish perceptions of the world, was successful precisely because it was completely within the cultural presuppositions of the German Jew.

In 1919 Buber attempted to refute Hugo Bergmann's emphasis on Hebrew as the sole acceptable language for the Jew.[97] Buber stressed that it was not the national language that he perceived as central to the definition of self but rather that which the language communicated. The abandonment of his attempts to create an idiom for the German Jew is not marked by the admission; rather, Buber merely reflects his desire to remain a German-speaking advocate of the Jew. German has a special function in Buber's self-definition. In translating the tales of Rabbi Nachman, he noted that the imperfections of the text became more evident in his German translation. German illuminates the text, a text clouded by Yiddish scholasticism.

Buber's lifelong concern with German, and the creation within German of an appropriate discourse for the Jew, is in fact a reflection of his own insecurity as a Western Jew. Chaim Weizmann describes the young Buber in Geneva at the turn of the century and comments: "We were good friends, though I was often irritated by his stilted talk, which was full of forced expressions and elaborate similes, without, it seemed to me, much clarity or great beauty. My own inclinations were to simplicity."[98] Buber's striving for his own discourse—a discourse that was clear, simple, mystical, and yet acceptable to the German self-censor hidden within him—presented him with an unbridgeable gap. In his description of the Jewish mystic, Buber stated that "the word is an abyss through which the speaker strides." When Buber created his idealized Eastern Jews and provided them with a specific form of discourse, he adapted those qualities that Jews such as Ahron Marcus have placed within their image of the Eastern Jew, qualities that on the surface are the antithesis of the self-definition of the Western Jew but in fact are those qualities given value by them.

In his often quoted *Major Trends in Jewish Mysticism*, which is to no little degree a "scholarly" answer to Buber's *Hassidic Tales*, Gershom Scholem stresses the close relationship between the language of the Jews and their definition of self:

> . . . something more precious than an adequate instrument for
> contact between human beings. To them Hebrew, the holy
> tongue, is not simply a means of expressing certain thoughts,
> born out of a certain convention and having a purely conven-
> tional character, in accordance with the theory of language
> dominant in the Middle Ages. Language in its purest form, that
> is, Hebrew, according to the Kabbalists, reflects the fundamen-
> tal spiritual nature of the world; in other words it has a mysti-
> cal value. Speech reaches God because it comes from God.
> Man's common language, whose *prima facie* function, indeed,
> is only of an intellectual nature, reflects the creative language
> of God.[99]

Thus the very nature of humanity is defined by language. Language is the true link with God. And this is for Scholem a real, national language, Hebrew (or the parallel language of the Jews, German), rather than the ineffable "dialogue" to which Buber wishes to reduce language.

Buber's attempt to create a specific discourse for the Jew and to place this discourse within the world of the Eastern Jew resulted in a major shift in interest in Eastern Jewry. This interest was to no little degree the result of the political conflicts in Europe immediately before and during the First World War.[100] For the idea that Yiddish was but a dialect of German, that the Eastern Jews shared the basic ideological interests of the German cultural community, reappeared with the sense of a growing alienation between Russia and the German-speaking countries. German and Yiddish came to be paired, as in the title of a projected pamphlet by Nathan Birnbaum, the German-speaking founder of the scientific study of Yiddish, which was to appear under the title *The German Language of the Polish Jews*. Needless to say, the Yiddish-speaking Jews of Eastern Europe, especially those in Poland, felt themselves at considerable risk owing to the claims of German Jews to a close cultural (and implied political) bond. For they remained Russian citizens under the political control of the czarist empire. Also, they considered the Germans' attitude toward them a romanticization of Yiddish and a stress on those elements in Yiddish culture that were viewed by most Yiddish writers as outside of the mainstream of Yiddish letters as that tradition had developed within the nineteenth century.

Buber, in the first issue of his periodical *The Jew* (1919), published an extraordinarily large number of essays on Eastern European Jewry (twenty-three essays out of eighty-eight), all written by Western or Westernized Jews. Typical of the contributors writing on the idea of the Eastern European Jew was Moses Calvary, a German Jew, who authored the essay on Yiddish in the first volume of *The Jew*.[101] Calvary contrasts Yiddish poetry with poetry written in other German dialects, attempting to demonstrate that Yiddish poetry possesses an independent discourse, while poetry in other dialects, such as Low German, simply adapts the cultural presuppositions concerning the appropriate literary discourse existing in High German. A look at the qualities that Calvary attributes to Yiddish can give the reader some sense as to why Yiddish writers rebelled at the German characterization of the nature of their literary language. In characterizing a poem by the Yiddish writer Morris Rosenfeld about the exploitation of workers in the New York sweatshops, Calvary comments: "I don't mean to imply that these hazy, gentle half-tones cannot be recaptured in Yiddish, but they are characteristic of Yiddish, a Yiddish raised to a form of its own." It is the intonation of Yiddish that captures its essence for the German listener, not the language itself. It is the implied *mausch-*

eln of the Yiddish-accented Jew. Indeed, in defending Yiddish, Calvary sees the Yiddish accent as a specific quality of the Yiddish-speaking Jews that permeates their discourse no matter what language they speak:

> Well, we know next to nothing about the laws that shape an intonation in a specific climate, or in a specific nation; however, I doubt that High German, for example, would essentially modify the accent. Not even the Hebrew language could be an antidote: In Palestine, I have often encountered an ardent opponent of Yiddish retorting with a "madua lo" (why not?) in the loveliest Yiddish accent. It is a risky business to condemn any language as being unattractive. Romance speakers regard the dynamic accent of Teutonic as extremely unattractive. In any case, I must confess that I have often enough listened with sheer delight to women and children chattering in Yiddish. (33)

Yiddish is a sign, a mark on the language of the child and the woman, of cultural nostalgia for a world that would be simple and direct, as is the language of the Eastern Jews. Needless to say, during this very period, Yiddish literature entered the age of modernism with a flourish, producing modernist poets and novelists of world rank. Their language was not the language of the simple, primitive Eastern Jews. On the contrary, Buber and his cohorts had created a mock Yiddish which they ascribed to these Jews, a *mauscheln* that they could use within their own cultural framework to define their own identity in a positive manner. For they found it necessary to have a language of their own that was marked by them as essentially Jewish rather than as part of either the acceptable literary discourse of their time or the language attributed to the Jew by the anti-Semites. What these writers then did was take an older, anti-Semitic model of nonacceptable Jewish language, a model that still had its echoes among the Jewish community in its negative image of the Eastern Jew, and transform it into a positive image. This could only be done by attributing to it those qualities that were seen as positive within the German cultural community.

One of the most striking reflections of the myth building concerning the Eastern Jew is to be found in the early-twentieth-century illustrations of Eastern Jews. The images of Hermann Struck and Ephraim Mose Lilien, artists of quite different political views, place the Eastern Jew within the iconography of the exotic.[102] The parallels between these positive images of the Eastern Jew and the use of very similar images in Ratzel's *History of Mankind* illuminate the close relationship between positive and negative stereotypes. This is especially interesting because the traditional caricatures of the Jew in imperial Germany, such as on anti-Semitic postcards, linked the appearance of the Jews to their language.[103]

That the glorification of the Eastern Jew was not limited to Jews existing within one specific language tradition can be seen within the life and work of the Czech poet Jiří Langer. In 1913 Langer, like Calvary, went to Palestine, and upon his return to the Westernized world of Prague Jewry, he fled into the East, both literally and metaphorically. For Langer, Prague had become the internalized image of the West, and Belz and the court of the Rokeaher Rabbi, the East. His return to Prague from Belz did not mean a return to the West. His brother František later wrote:

> Father told me with a note of horror in his voice that Jiří had returned. I understood what had filled him with dread as soon as I saw my brother. He stood before me in a frayed, black overcoat, clipped like a caftan, reaching from his chin to the ground. On his head he wore a broad, round hat of black velvet, thrust back towards his neck. He stood there in a stooping posture; his whole face and chin were covered with a red beard, and side whiskers in front of his ears hung in ringlets down to his shoulders. All that remained to be seen of his face was some white, unhealthy skin and eyes which at moments appeared to be tired and at others feverish. My brother did not come back from Belz, to home and civilization; he had brought Belz with him.[104]

Langer devoted the rest of his life to the composition of his spiritual autobiography, *Devět Bran* (*Nine Gates*), published in 1937. In it he records his movement from a negative model of the Eastern Jew, with his sense of isolation, of "ignorance, backwardness and dirt," to the blinding revelation of the sublimity of the "saint of Belz." Langer's autobiography is a striking document of the attraction of the reality of Eastern European Jewry for the Westernized Jew, whether German or Czech, and yet the very language of Langer's autobiography must raise certain questions. Langer, like Marcus and Buber, uses a Western language (in his terms) to catalogue his abandonment of his Western identity. This is highly problematic, for Langer, who had become a real rather than a fabled disciple of a miracle rabbi, chose to express his sense of community with him in a language that had become one of the cultural languages of Europe by the 1890s. Czech writers and intellectuals had demanded and had eventually received the official recognition they sought as spokespeople for a culture that assumed a parity with German. Indeed, in his autobiography, Langer undertook much the same

program as did Buber—to create for Czech a language of the Jew,
the mirror image of the Yiddish-intoned German that Buber fanta-
sized he was creating for German.[105] Into this web of language spun
by Langer came many of the same ambiguities concerning his own
position as an intermediary between two worlds he felt as antitheses,
the world of Prague and the world of Belz.

Langer's spiritual autobiography is as highly conscious of its
role in providing Western Jews with an idealized image of the pure
Jew as are Buber's tales. Within Langer's world at least two Prague
Jewish writers—Franz Kafka and Max Brod—reflected much of
the same ambivalence about their Jewish identity in their confrontation with the Eastern Jew. Brod, influenced by Buber and his
writings, created a clear antithesis between his own identity and
that of the acculturated Western Jew, while trying to create "Jewish"
works in German. Kafka was never able to create an antithesis
stable enough to allow him such an undertaking. On September
14, 1915, Jiří Langer took his friends Franz Kafka and Max Brod to
visit the court of the rabbi of Belz. Kafka wrote in his diary:

> September 14th. Saturday, with Max and Langer at the home of
> the miracle-performing Rabbi. Zizkov, Harantova ulice. Many
> children on the pavement and on the stairs. A guest house.
> Completely dark upstairs, a few steps blindly with hands
> stretched out in front. A room with pale half-light, grey-white
> walls, a few little women and girls, white head scarves, pale
> faces, are standing around, little movements. Impression of
> bloodlessness. Next room. Everything black, full of young men
> and young people. Loud praying. We squeeze into a corner.
> Scarcely have we looked around a little then the prayer ends,
> the room empties. A corner room with two window walls, each
> with two windows. We defend ourselves. "But you are Jews,
> too, aren't you?" The Rabbi cuts the strongest paternal figure.
> "All rabbis look wild," said Langer. He was in a silk caftan,
> underpants visible beneath it. Hairs on the bridge of his nose.
> Cap trimmed with fur, which he constantly shifts backwards
> and forwards. Dirty and clean, the peculiarity of people who
> think intensely. Scratches his beard, reaches into the food with
> his fingers—but when he rests his hand on the table for a
> moment, you see the whiteness of his skin, a kind of whiteness
> that you feel you have seen only in childhood fantasies. Of
> course, at that time even your parents were pure.[106]

Kafka plays out his own internalized conflict with his father within
the structure presented to grasp the nature of the difference between

the Western and the Eastern Jew. The rabbi's hand is both dirty and pure simultaneously. This image possesses both sets of qualities, those of the "bad" Jew, following the traditional image, and those of the "good" Jew, following Buber's romanticization.

Kafka's fascination with and repulsion by the world of the Eastern Jew, a world that encompassed and defined his own cultural identification with the language of German culture, seems to have had a major influence upon the structuring of his literary language. Many critics have commented on Kafka's recreation of the humor of Yiddish theater in his works. But Kafka's works were also consciously placed within the world of the German cultural avant-garde. Unlike Langer or Brod, Kafka seems to include no overt discussion of the problems of his (or anyone else's) Jewish identity within his literary work. And yet one exception to this statement is important for understanding how Jewish writers, confused about their identity as German-speaking Jews, used the *topos* of the hidden language of the Jews. In 1916 and 1917 Kafka published three of his tales in "Jewish" publications edited by Martin Buber. Kafka had listened to Buber lecture on Jewish mysticism in Prague in 1913 and had become interested, as had his friend Brod, in his own Jewish identity to no little extent through Buber's model, even though he was later to break with Buber.

One of the stories that Kafka published in Buber's *The Jew* was "A Report to the Academy," the tale of how an ape, ripped from the jungle, acquires the most human of all attributes, language, and thus becomes a member, if a marginal one, of human society.[107] Without language, the ape has no consciousness; he simply exists in the jungle. The analogy to the image of the Eastern Jew, existing outside of history and consciousness, is clear. Once captured, the ape makes a decision to acquire language, grasping the chance to become "like them," but "no one promised me that if I became like them the bars of my cage would be taken away" (179). The ape imitates human beings "because I need a way out." It is language that gives him this way out, and yet, of course, he remains an ape, both in his own eyes and in the eyes of human society. Kafka's irony is that the ape tells his own story in the language of civilization, German. The ape has acquired the tools with which to escape from his "apedom," but in terms of his innate nature, his sexuality, he is still attracted to other apes. Language does not free him from his essential self. And yet he narrates this conflict in the most elegant and accurate parody of academic discourse, a discourse aimed at the all-knowing academy. The parallels between the fate of the ape and that of the Jews, at least Jews who accept and internalize the *topos* of their own damaged discourse, is clear. Kafka reacts by presenting this image to the world of German-speaking Jewry. His parody points out the double bind that he recognizes (and Buber represses) in writing in a language that is viewed as foreign (German) in order to present a discourse that is Jewish. This double bind, Moritz Goldstein's answer for the transitional generation of German-speaking Jews before their children begin to write in Hebrew, provided Kafka with the material for his tale. It is material that can only be understood within the context of Buber's journal and his equation between his own German and the mystical discourse of the *Ostjude*.

The awareness of this *topos* and the attempt to rebut it go hand in hand among German Jewish writers. Lion Feuchtwanger presented the opposite side to Kafka's awareness of the double bind in which these writers found themselves when he wrote, "I have studied with care the works of German authors of Jewish descent in order to find some linguistic marker that indicated their Jewish ancestry. In spite of intensive study of the great German writers of Jewish descent, from Mendelssohn to Schnitzler and Wasserman, from Heine to Arnold and Stefan Zweig, I have been unable to discover such a marker."[108] The need to deny a Jewish component to the language of the Jews stems not so much from the anti-Semites' claim that they perceive such a quality as from the feeling among Jewish writers from Buber to Kafka and Lissauer that there is something "Jewish" hidden within their discourse, something that conflicts with their writing in German and produces a specifically Jewish tone, a *mauscheln*. Feuchtwanger's attempt to repress such a feeling of the uniqueness conflicted directly with his own sense that "my brain thinks cosmopolitan, my heart beats Jewish."[109] But language, the tool of the writer, had to be perceived as value-neutral if Feuchtwanger were to claim his social status as a German writer rather than as an outsider.

The dichotomy, or at least the confusion concerning this apparent split, reappears in a letter from Kafka to Brod written in 1921, in which he discusses Karl Kraus's essay "Literature." Kafka sees Kraus as the essential representative of a "German Jewish literature," a literature characterized by wit and truth. The wit that is the hallmark of this literary manifestation of Jews writing in German is "primarily *mauscheln*, and no one can *mauschel* like Kraus, in spite of the fact that none in this German Jewish world can do anything but *mauschel*."[110] Kafka presents the widest concept of *mauscheln*, seeing it not merely as a dialect but as a mark of the "self-tormenting usurpation of foreign possessions." This dichotomy is present not in the conflict between Eastern and Western concepts of the Jew but in the resolution of the conflict between "paper German" and the "language of gesture." Here, of course, Kafka has translated the stereotypical perception of the dichotomy existing between the idea of the Western Jew and the image of the Eastern Jew into more abstract terms. The "paper German" is the official language of the state; the Eastern Jews, as one can see in the above passage from Kafka's diary, are visible because of their patterns of gesture. The image of the gesturing, gesticulating Jew is coterminus with the image of the Eastern Jew as "bad." But one must also understand that Kafka's sense that *mauscheln* is an intermediary stage, a mediated stage between two cultures, is more or less identical to Buber's view of the function of German as the cultural mediator. His sense that *mauscheln* is a corruption of the language of the state (a fact that he does not view as totally evil) incorporates much of the traditional objections to the presence of the Eastern Jew within Germany. And often this objection is linked to the sexualized nature of the Eastern Jew:

> The Russian Jews have multiplied in Germany like frogs . . . ;
> they serve as cantors, functionaries, etc. But they do not know
> the language of the state and therefore evoke the justified
> German hatred for the Jews. . . . The first and true cause of
> German anti-Semitism is known to all, but no one dares to
> reveal it: It is the coming of foreigners . . . to Germany.[111]

This pastiche of quotations from various German Jewish sources of the *fin de siècle* can give a sense of the negative stereotype against which and with which Kafka is operating. Kafka moves, in his letter to Brod, from the ambiguity of the language of the Jews to the question of the other new language of the Jews, psychoanalysis, and comments that the Oedipus complex is the result, not of the innocent father, "but of the Jewishness of the father. Most who begin to write in German want to flee from Judaism, often with the unclear agreement of the father (and it is this unclarity which is aggravating)." Kafka has centered in on the cathexis between his own personal conflict with his assimilated father and the overall role played by the abstraction of "Jewishness" in the formation of the identity of writers.

Kafka projected this conflict onto the political stage, identifying the world of the father, with his damaged and accented language, with the unacceptable East. Yet the East is also the locus, according to Buber, of the purity of Jewish discourse. Kafka is thus caught in a double bind between the rejection and the glorification of the

discourse of the essential Jew, the *Ostjude*. One manner of resolving this is to flee into the world of books. Kafka's "Report to the
Academy" is *not* about Jews. It stands, as Patrick Bridgwater has
so ably shown, in a long literary tradition of educated apes. It was
this flight into literature, a literature supposedly closed to Jews
and doubly closed to Eastern Jews, that provided the context for
Kafka's exposition of the myth of the damaged language of the
Jews. Yet Kafka continued to associate this damaged discourse with
the sexuality of the Eastern Jews, with their innate difference. Even
the invention of this positive stereotype, the *Ostjude*, as the coun-
terbalance to the negative image of the Jew is permeated with the
self-doubt of the Jewish writer, a self-hatred that cannot be completely
projected onto the world of the new exotic, the Eastern Jew.

The German experiments in creating or "re-creating" a Jewish
discourse freed of the taint ascribed to the German discourse of
the Jews mark much of the creative writing by German Jews from
the late nineteenth through the early twentieth century. Acknowledging the correctness of the "scientific" charge brought against
the Jews that they were inherently different, that they spoke a
different, "hidden" language, Jewish writers sought a model for
their self-consciously "Jewish" discourse in that reification of the
anti-Semites' nightmare about the Jews, the *Ostjude*. The *Ostjude's*
discourse was perceived to be the epitome of "Jewishness." It was,
of course, also perceived to be monolithically homogenous, a fancy
that ignored the replication of Western European literary movements and controversies among writers in Yiddish.

The idealized discourse of the *Ostjude*, the true "hidden"
discourse of the Jew, was then adapted into German to give the
German Jews their own true voice. But this "hidden" discourse
stemmed from the anti-Semites' understanding of the Jew filtered
through the literary representations of the Jew in the West. By
reversing the stereotypical image of the discourse of the Jew, by
glorifying difference rather than viewing it with abnegation, the
German Jews, aware of the double bind of language in which they
were caught, imagined that they had found an escape back into
their own identity. This acceptance of the contaminated fiction of
the Jews' language, even in its polar image of the "good" Jew as
possessing a different discourse, collided with the simple fact that
Jewish writers, no matter what their subject matter, wrote within
the accepted literary discourse of their time and culture. When
Max Brod adopts the mode of the historical novel to examine "Jewish"
topics, his fictions are indistinguishable from those that he uses
to portray the world of sixteenth-century, Christian Prague. When

German writers suddenly discover the writings of the Eastern Jew, when they have Sholom Asch translated into German, they believe themselves to have rediscovered a "truly" Jewish literary discourse, one that speaks deeply to their newly aroused sense of Jewish identity. What they have discovered, of course, is that modern Yiddish letters are inherently Western in their choice of literary models. Sholom Asch's great historical novels owe more to the Western literary tradition than to any indigenous form of Yiddish narrative. Some of the writers of the early twentieth century are aware of this fallacy and try to ignore it; most accept the positive reevaluation of the literary discourse of the *Ostjude* as a momentous rediscovery of their own lost roots. Embedded in the Western "rediscovery" of the Eastern Jew is the use of this reevaluation of Yiddish to lend a positive cast to the self-image of the Western Jew as writer, a writer lacking confidence in his own mode of discourse because of its anti-Semitic contamination.

V
The Development of the Concept of Self-hatred

"Self-criticism" had, for German Jews, a strongly positive connotation well into the 1880s. Moritz Lazarus could speak pridefully of the Jews as the classical people of "self-criticism" in his pamphlet *What Is National?* And Emanuel Schreiber, the rabbi of the Bonn Jewish community, in 1881 published an entire book on the "self-criticism of the Jews," in which this quality is glorified and exemplified by his own attack on the neo-Orthodox Breslau Rabbinical Seminary.[112] It is only with the increase in virulent, public anti-Semitism, with its concomitant identification among German Jews with the Eastern Jew as an idealized image of the "good Jew," that the concept of "self-criticism" is replaced by the pathology of "self-hatred," an illness attributed to Jews. We have seen how the association of Jews with medical discourse, first as healer and then as part of that group most at risk from disease, reaches back into the Middle Ages. The merging of the image of the self-critical Jew with that of the mad Jew produced, in the final decades of the nineteenth century, the image of the self-hating Jew as part of the rhetoric of race.

A half-century after the French Revolution, within the confines of the Parisian Anthropological Society, the question of specifically Jewish tendencies toward illness, their form and frequency, was raised again. It was at the time of the most visible demands of French Jewry for a share in the power of the bourgeoisie, who had attempted to exclude them in the Third Republic.[113] In the *Bulletin* of the Anthropological Society, M. Boudin commented in a letter from Vichy concerning "idiocy and mental illness among German Jews" based on German census statistics. The focus of this short paper was on the much higher frequency of psychopathologies among Jews in Germany than among Catholics or Protestants in the same population. For example, in Bavaria one mentally ill individual was found for a population of 908 Catholics and 967 Protestants but for only 514 Jews. This led Boudin to observe that psychopathologies are "twice as frequent among the Jewish population as among the German population." Boudin attributed this to "the frequency of marriage between blood relatives."[114] Statistics as a means of quantifying insanity as a sign of Otherness had been used following the 1840 American census. In the interpretation of that data the anti-abolitionist forces, headed by John C. Calhoun, had argued that blacks suffered more frequently from mental illness when free than when enslaved; thus, freedom promoted psychopathology.[115] For Boudin, inbreeding, the exclusivity of the Jews, was the pseudoscientific origin of the Jews' tendency to psychopathology. The contemporary demand for legal equality was translated into its antithesis, the desire for psychopathology. Boudin also focused on the problem in Germany, rather than in France, distancing it even more. For the French, the German Jew became the Other. Boudin concluded his paper with a critique of the view that the etiology of psychopathology among the Jews could be traced to their "cosmopolitanism." The idea that the Jew is associated with modern civilization and the decadence of city life was introduced here, if only to be rebutted. What for La Fontaine had been a general predisposition to illness had become by the mid-nineteenth century a predisposition for mental illness. The Jews were seen as covertly ill, in a manner that provided observers with proof of their own emotional and intellectual superiority.

The statistics brought by nineteenth- (and indeed twentieth-) century writers on the topic of the mental instability of the Jews do not, of course, reflect any specific predisposition of the European Jewish community for mental illness. Indeed, this view has recently been labeled one of the "misconceptions" about the genetic disorders that befall the Jews.[116] The statistics, cited over and over by mental health practitioners during this period, most probably reflect the higher incidence of hospitalization of Jews for mental illness owing to their concentration in urban areas, which, unlike rural areas, were not as conducive to the presence of the mentally ill within society. Also, urban Jews had developed a better network for the identification and treatment of illness, including mental illness. The sense of community, coupled with the impression that the mentally ill were unable to function within urban society, may have led to more frequent hospitalization and thus to the higher statistical incidence of psychopathology among the Jews.

By the 1880s the linkage of the Jew with psychopathology was a given in anthropological circles. In the Parisian Anthropological Society the Prussian census of 1880 was the point of departure for an even more detailed debate on the psychopathologies of the Jews. Again statistics were used to stress the greater occurrence of mental illness among the Jews. The comments on the etiology of the mental illness are more diffuse. M. Zabrowski laid it at the feet of the ecstatic preoccupation with mysticism and the supernatural, a clear reference to the Eastern Jews, whose presence was being felt even more in Paris following the assassination of Alexander II in 1881 and the resulting forced immigration.[117] He and M. Sanson also stressed the curative role of agricultural employment and the absence of Jews in this field. The "cosmopolitanism" of the Jews, the pressure of the fields in which they were occupied, formed part of the reason for him. But M. Blanchard simply stated that "hysteria and neurasthenia are more frequent among the Jewish race than all other races." Thus it was no longer simply mental illness, itself a delimitation of La Fontaine's more general view of Jewish predispositions for illness, but rather "hysteria and neurasthenia" that were typical of the Jew. The source, according to M. Sanson, is endogamous marriage.

The view that all Jews were especially prone to hysteria and neurasthenia through inbred weakening of the nervous system appeared in canonical form in Jean Martin Charcot's *Tuesday Lesson* for October 23, 1888.[118] Charcot, Freud's teacher, described "a case of hysterical dysnie. I already mentioned that his twenty-year-old patient is a Jewess. I will use this occasion to stress that nervous illnesses of all types are innumerably more frequent among Jews than among other groups." Charcot attributed this fact to inbreeding.[119]

By 1890 Charcot's view had become a commonplace in European psychiatry. Standard German textbooks of psychiatry such as those by Schule, Kraeplin, Kirchhoff, and Krafft-Ebing cited Charcot. Krafft-Ebing can serve as typical for the general tenor of these observations:

> Statistics have been collected with great care to show the
> percentage of insanity in the various religious sects, and it has

been shown that among the Jews and certain sects the percentage is decidedly higher. This fact stands in relation with religion only insofar as it constitutes a hindrance to marriage among those professing it; the more when its adherents are small in number, and there is consequent insufficient crossing of the race and increased inbreeding.

This is a phenomenon similar to that observed in certain highly aristocratic and wealthy families, whose members, whether from motives of honor or money, constantly intermarry, and thus have many insane relatives. In such cases the cause is not moral, but anthropological.[120]

For Krafft-Ebing the "anthropological" cause of the greater incidence of insanity among the Jews is their endogamous marriages which he, as a liberal, compares to the degeneracy found in the inbred upper class. But it is mysticism, as in the image of the Eastern Jew, that he contrasts with the rationality of the Western religion. The result of this stress of inbreeding and mysticism is to focus on the exclusivity of the Jews. The form of this insanity has sexual implications:

> Very often, excessive religious inclination is itself a symptom of an originally abnormal character or actual disease, and, not infrequently, concealed under a veil of religious enthusiasm there is abnormally intensified sensuality and sexual excitement that lead to sexual errors that are of etiological significance.[121]

The disease of the central nervous system to which Jews are most prey is neurasthenia. It is in the description of neurasthenia in Krafft-Ebing's study of the illness that the image of the Jewish man is to be found. He is "an over-achiever in the arena of commerce or politics" who "reads reports, business correspondence, stock market notations during meals, for whom 'time is money.' "[122] The association of the Jew with the "American illness," through the use of the English phrase "time is money," presents the cosmopolitan Jew as the quintessential American. This conflation of two personifications of Otherness underlines the political implications of seeing in the "cosmopolitanism" of the Jews, in their function in the modern city, the source, on one level, of their neurasthenia. Yet this integration of the Jews into the negative image of modern civilization is contradicted by the view of the exclusivity of the Jews in their sexual isolation from Western society.

The image of the neurasthenic as Jew is not found as widely within Krafft-Ebing's text, however (even though he elsewhere in the same text stresses the special proclivity of the Jew for neurasthenia) (54). Rather, this analogy is taken from one of the discussions of the psychopathology of the Jews written from the Jewish point of view. The quote was used in Martin Engländer's essay on *The Evident Most Frequent Appearances of Illness in the Jewish Race* (1902). Engländer was one of the early Viennese supporters of Herzl and the Zionist movement. He discussed the cultural predisposition of the Jews to neurasthenia as a result of the "over-exertion and exhaustion of the brain . . . among Jews as opposed to the non-Jewish population." "The struggle, haste and drive, the hunt for happiness" have caused a "reaction in their central nervous system."[123] Neurasthenia is the result of the Jewish brain's inability to compete after "a two-thousand-year Diaspora" and "a struggle for mere existence up to emancipation." Engländer thus attempted to dismiss the etiology of neurasthenia as a result of inbreeding, citing the Americans as an example of a "race" in which neurasthenia predominates and in which exogamous marriages are common. The cause of the Jews' illnesses is their confinement in the city, the source of all degeneracy; the cure is "land, air, light" (46).

Engländer's views are not idiosyncratic. For him the madness of the Jews is a direct result of the Jews' political and social position in the West. Cesare Lombroso, whose name is linked with the concept of "degeneration" which he helped forge, was also a Jew. After authoring a number of studies on the degeneracy of the prostitute and the criminal, Lombroso was confronted with the charge that Jews, too, were a degenerate subclass of human being, a class determined by their biology. Lombroso's answer to this charge, *Anti-Semitism and the Jews in the Light of Modern Science* (1893), attempted to counter the use of medical or pseudoscientific discourse to characterize the nature of the Jew. But Lombroso also accepted the basic view that the Jew was more highly prone to specific forms of mental illness. He quotes Charcot to this effect, but, like Engländer, he sees the reason for this tendency not in the physical nature of the Jew but in the "residual effect of persecution."[124] Both Engländer and Lombroso accepted the view that some type of degenerative process, leading to the predominance of specific forms of mental illness, exists among all Jews. The only difference from non-Jewish savants that they saw was the cause of this process. In rejecting the charge of inbreeding, Jews such as Engländer and Lombroso also rejected the implications that they indulge in primitive sexual practices that violate a basic human taboo against incest. The confusion of endogamous marriage with incestuous inbreeding was a result both of the level of late-nineteenth-century science and of the desire of this scientific discourse to have categories with which to label the explicit nature of the Other. The Jews are thus mentally ill, they manifest this illness in the forms of hysteria and neurasthenia, and the cause is their sexual practice or their mystical religion or their role as carriers of Western cosmopolitanism. All of this is represented by their corrupt discourse.

The relationship between mental illness and the disruption of discourse has its roots in late-nineteenth-century medicine. The neurologist who listened to his hysterical patient or who diagnosed "general paralysis of the insane" owing to the patient's monomaniacal tirades and the psychiatrist who was able to characterize the discourse of the patient suffering from "dementia praecox" as "word salad" centered their perception of illness on the nature of the patient's language. Alterations in the nature of discourse were understood to be basic signs of pathology. Indeed, in the course of the closing decades of the nineteenth century they came to have the weight of the primary signs of psychopathology. How a patient spoke was important, and incompetent discourse was a sign of psychopathology.

It is in this context that Max Nordau's often cited call for the Jews to become "muscle Jews," published in 1900, must be read.[125] The connection of Jewish nationalism in the form of Zionism with German nationalism through the code of *mens sana in corpore sano* is evident. But, of course, this earlier call by the father of German nationalism, *Turnvater* Jahn, had been heavily overladen with anti-Semitic rhetoric. Nordau's call, like Rathenau's comments on the feminism of the Jew, is yet another attempt from within the Jewish community to co-opt the underlying premises of anti-Semitic rhetoric and use its strong political message for their own ends. Nordau's call for a "new muscle Jew" is based on the degeneration of the Jew "in the narrow confines of the ghetto." But not only the Jews' muscles but also their minds have atrophied in the ghetto. Implicit in Nordau's call is the equation of the "old Jews" and their attitude toward life. Zionism demands that the new, muscle Jew have a healthy body and a healthy mind. Thus he condemns his critics as having not only weak bodies but weak minds! This charge must be read within the inner circles of the Zionist movement, in which (as has been seen) the opponents of Zionism are viewed as merely Jews possessing all of the qualities ascribed to them (including madness) by the anti-Semites.

Neurasthenia, the American disease, the disease of modern life, is also the disease of the Jews, modern people incarnate. Degeneration was the result of sexuality and was symptomized by deviant sexuality. If the best authorities were to be believed, and at least in Germany the best authorities argued that inbreeding was the cause of the neurasthenia of the Jews, there is more than a slight implication of incest. Indeed, Engländer expressly defends the Jews against the charge of "racial inbreeding" while condemning the provisions of Mosaic law that permit marriage between uncle and niece. He thus gives evidence to the implicit charge that runs through all the literature on the insanity of the Jews: that they are themselves the cause of their own downfall through their perverse sexuality and that their degeneracy is the outward sign of their fall from grace. The sexuality of the Other is always threatening. With the implicit charge of incest, one of the ultimate cultural taboos of nineteenth-century thought is evoked. Inbreeding is incestuous and is a sign of the "primitive" nature of the Jews, of their existence outside the bounds of acceptable, Western sexual practice.[126]

The discourse of decadent civilization, of the city, is inexorably linked with the sexual exclusivity of the Jew. Nowhere is this linkage made more evident than in Thomas Mann's novella *The Blood of the Walsungen* (1905). This tale of brother-sister incest ends, at least in the first version, with an emphasis on the sexual exclusivity of the Jew. The brother has just consummated his relationship with his sister, and she ponders the fate of her German fiancé. Mann concludes the unpublished first edition with two Yiddishisms, a sign of the damaged, sexualized discourse of the siblings. Mann's father-in-law, Alfred Pringsheim, so objected to the inclusion of Yiddishisms ("We robbed [*beganeft*] the non-Jew [*goy*]") as a sign of the siblings' ethnic identity that Mann suppressed the planned publication of the story.[127] The novella, which Mann re-edited in 1921 to eliminate the Yiddishisms, echoed the sense of the corruption of both "modern life" as typified by the Wagner cult and the Jews. The Jews, through their lack of redemption, are morally weak, and this manifests itself in the most primitive manner, through incest. Indeed, Adolf Hitler, never the most original of thinkers, simply summarized "Jewish religious doctrine" as "prescriptions for keeping the blood of Jewry pure" (306). The view that within the Jews' sexuality is hidden the wellspring of their own degeneration haunts the overtly sexual imagery of anti-Semitic writings from the end of the nineteenth century. The Jew, the most visible Other in late-nineteenth-century Europe, is also the bearer of the most devastating sexual stigma, incest.

Even those Jews who accepted the idea that the Jew was predisposed to some form of mental illness, a concept articulated in the rhetoric of racial science, could not accept it as applied to themselves. Rather, they projected the idea of an innate tendency to psychopathology onto other groups of Jews, the "bad" Jews, with whom they refused to identify. Parallel to the invention of the Eastern Jew as the image of the ideal Jew, separate from the corruption of all Western traditions, there arises the image of the self-hating Jew as the necessary product of this Western tradition. In 1904 Fritz Wittels continued the argument of writers such as Conrad Alberti that those Jews who accept the value systems of German society are condemned to self-hatred.[128] In his pamphlet *The Baptized Jew* he adopts the entire *topos* of the hidden language of the Jews as presented in the rhetoric of science. Baptized Jews are, for Wittels, simply Jews who have "perjured themselves for base reasons"; they are lying Jews. One of the primary groups from which these baptized Jews stem comprises those who are born with "the pathology of the baptized Jew." The idea that these Jews are predetermined to such actions—that they suffer from "pseudologia phantastica," that they are congenitally unable to distinguish truth from lies— is yet another restatement of the corruption of Jewish discourse. Here, however, it is applied to one specific subset of Jews, those who have chosen assimilation into German culture. These Jews have the capacity to become "anti-Semitic" Jews. We have already seen that Karl Kraus used the concept of "Jewish anti-Semitism" in speaking of the Zionists. He postulated his perception of a "correct" Jewish identity as the basis for any definition of the "good" Jew and saw in Herzl and the Zionists the antithesis: they were Jews who hated other Jews and, by definition, themselves. For Fritz Wittels, the ultimate form of the baptized Jew is the Jew who hates his or her own race. Wittels, a follower and biographer of Freud, began to outline in his pamphlet the psychosis of self-hatred.

Some saw self-hatred as a necessary attribute of the "good" Jew. Weininger uses a primitive understanding of the concept of projection in describing the process of self-hatred:

> Thus the fact is explained that the bitterest anti-Semites are to be found amongst the Jews themselves. For only the quite Jewish Jews, like the completely Aryan Aryans, are not at all anti-Semitically disposed; among the remainder only the commoner natures are actively anti-Semitic and pass sentence on others without having once sat in judgement on themselves in these matters; and very few exercise their anti-Semitism first

on themselves. This one thing, however, remains nonetheless certain; whoever detests the Jewish disposition detests it first of all in himself; that he should persecute it in others is merely his endeavour to separate himself from Jewishness; he strives to shake it off and to localise it in his fellow-creatures, and so for a moment to dream himself free of it. Hatred, like love, is a projected phenomenon; that person alone is hated who reminds one unpleasantly of oneself. (304)

Weininger's awareness of projection as a psychological mechanism is but another adaptation of the rhetoric of science, here the science of psychology, to the psychopathology of the Jew. Both Wittels the psychoanalyst and Weininger the philosopher employ the model of the self-hater as one who embodies all of the essential negative qualities ascribed to the Jew. Weininger and Wittels have created a subclass for the psychology of the Jew which points toward self-hatred as the marker of the Jew most closely identifying with the double bind inherent in Western culture. Both Wittels and Weininger see the self-hating Jew as the apogee (or nadir) of this iden-tification. But both present this as a problem in the psychology of race. This shift in the rhetoric of science, or at least the contin-uation of the biology of race into a biological psychology of race, represents the very beginnings of an explanatory model of self-hatred rooted in a dynamic psychology.

With the gradual replacement during the opening decades of the twentieth century of the biologically determined model for psychopathology with that of a psychodynamically oriented one, one would have expected the image of the madness of the Jew to have vanished. With Freud's reorientation of psychopathology, any particularistic attribution of specific patterns of mental disease to any group, especially on the basis of a presumed group-specific sexual aberration, should have been impossible. But Freud's views of the universal patterns of human sexuality, especially in regard to fantasies of incest, could not destroy the image of the Jew as predisposed to mental illness. This view continued, not only in the theoretical writings of Wittels and Weininger but in the clinic where the most radical rethinking of the etiology of mental illness was being undertaken.

In Eugen Bleuler's Burghölzli, the clinic in which Freud's dynamic psychopathology was being applied in a hospital setting, Rafael Becker, a young Jewish doctor, was given the assignment of comparing Jewish and non-Jewish patients to determine whether the work done by earlier investigators could be validated with the psychoanalytic approach. Becker first presented his findings before a Zionist organization in Zurich during March 1919.[129] He began with the statistics upon which everyone had based their assumptions and thus predetermined his own findings. The Jews do indeed suffer from a more frequent rate of mental illness than that of the non-Jewish population, but not because of inbreeding. Indeed, inbreeding has led to the Jews' becoming less frequently infected by various illnesses, such as smallpox and cholera, since they "acquire immunizing force through inbreeding and the purity of the race" (6). Becker also denies that there is any specific "psychosis judäica," any specific form of mental illness that affects only the Jews, any more than there are any specific anthropological signs that determine the inferiority of the Jews (8). Mental illness for Becker (as for Bleuer) was not brain illness but psychic illness. Becker dismisses the increase in luetic infections and their results, as well as senile dementia, among the Jews as merely social artifacts; these are the result of alteration in society in general—the spread of syphilis in the former case and the increased life expectancy provided by better social conditions in the latter.

Becker denies any specific increase in mental illness because of a special proclivity of the Jews but sees in the increase in the rate of other forms of psychopathology the direct result of the acculturation of Western Jews. Even though Jews in earlier times suffered more greatly from oppression, their strong faith preserved their sanity. Only with the decline in Jewish identity in the nineteenth century has there been an increase in mental illness. Becker picks up a thread in late-nineteenth-century anti-assimilationist Jewish thought that places the roots for the moral decline of the Jew at the doorstep of Jewish emancipation and acculturation. He introduces Alfred Adler's newly coined concept of "inferiority" to give a dynamic dimension to his assumption that Jews are more frequently driven into madness than their non-Jewish persecutors (49). It is the "assimilated Jew" who is diseased, self-hating, and thus self-destructive.

Becker outlines the steps in the etiology of Jewish psychopathology. He denies any role to degeneration caused by inbreeding. He observes that because Jews are forbidden de facto the practice of certain occupations, many Jews marry very late. As a result, they have fewer and fewer children. (This is a substantial change from the charge made in the eighteenth century that the Jews' illnesses came from their early marriages and their large number of children!) As a result the normal sexual development of the Jew is stunted because of the lack of an appropriate sexual outlet. Becker provided his audience with a solution that they would immediately have accepted as correct. He sees an alteration of the social structure that caused such illnesses as the appropriate "therapy." Provide appropriate occupations, resolve the sense of inferiority that results from being unable to enter the profession that one desires, and earlier marriages will occur, which will remove the direct cause of the psychopathologies. In the meantime, Jews can avoid the causes of overstimulation of sexuality by avoiding alcohol and sharp spices ("so beloved in the Jewish cuisine") and by exercising, following Nordau's prescription. This was Becker's presentation before a Jewish lay audience in 1918; the next year he published the results of his scholarly researches in the Burghölzli, which repeat many of his earlier views.[130] He provides a case study of the inferiority complex of one of his patients, a thirty-eight-year-old merchant. The case study provides Becker with an illness that he now sees as the result of the position of the Jew in Western society. Not a "psychosis judäica" but rather, using the new rhetoric of psychoanalysis, "the Jewish complex." The Jewish complex in this patient, illustrated by long passages from the patient's own biographical account, is marked by the sense of inferiority brought about by his treatment in society from the age of four, when "at the market day in Altstätten I alone of all the children was mocked. . . . I felt the humiliation that the Jew as a human being must feel in society" (28). Becker's patient continues to describe his life in terms of the social inferiority that he perceived as a Jewish child in a Christian world. Even though Becker records a fairly detailed description of the patient's sexual life, he sees in all of the anomalies of his sexuality only the product of the social inequality that led to his sense of inferiority. Thus Becker is able to avoid any relationship between the inborn sexual perversities ascribed to the Jew and his psychosis.

It is important to observe that Wittels, Weininger, and Becker all use the rhetoric of psychology to avoid any reference to the charge of incest, a charge that underlies and reinforces the anti-Semitic rhetoric about the nature of the Jew within the discourse of science. Self-hatred thus becomes not only attributable to certain limited groups of Jews but separate from any discussion of the sexuality of the Jew. With Becker, this separation determines the very selection of the psychoanalytic model that he applies to his patient. It is a way of diverting the discussion of the inherent psychopathology of the Jew in different directions. Self-hatred becomes a means of internalizing and projects certain basic assumptions about the pathology of the Jew onto groups (such as merchants) quite separate from the author.

The theme of Jewish self-hatred reappears in the language of psychoanalysis in 1923 when Josef Prager writes an essay for Martin Buber's *The Jew* entitled "Repression and Breakthrough in the Jewish Soul."[131] Seeing Freud as an essentially Jewish thinker, Prager attempts to use the concept of repression as a tool for understanding the shaping of the "Jewish soul." He sees the conflict as existing between the norms of society and the ability of the Jew to adapt to them. When the society attaches negative evaluation to being Jewish, Jews who desire to be assimilated must repress these attributes, and in repressing them, they come to have a centrality for them. Now Prager sees this repression as being a quality of the drive for assimilation, and he sees in the articulation of one's Jewishness the first step to a "healing of the sick Jewish soul." Prager picks up the thread of a specific Jewish illness, an illness of the Jewish soul in Western society, which is "self-hatred." It is not the Eastern Jew but rather the Westernized Jew who is sick, and the illness is one of the psyche. Here the process of projection is complete. Articulated through the new "Jewish" language of psychoanalysis (the Viennese answer to Hebrew as a cultural language), Prager's argument implicitly presents the Eastern Jew as one free of such ills.

In 1924, E. J. Lesser provides another case study: Karl Marx as self-hater.[132] But Lesser hits on a new tack, seeing in Marx's self-hatred his Jewishness. Marx's language is that of the Jew in that he uses the *pilpul* in his argument. His Jewish identity even appears when he is damning the Jews. No matter what he undertakes, he remains the "full-blooded Jew." What is interesting is that other discussions of Marx's self-hatred in this period came to the same conclusion.[133] They return to Buber's model of a conflict between Jewish identity and Western civilization to explain the aberration of self-hatred. Self-hatred is thus the denial of the essential Jew within; it is the dialectical process undertaken within the psyche. The essential Jew in conflict with the values of the West produces the self-hater, that individual who typifies the Jew in the West.

In 1921 Hans Kohn, later to be one of the seminal figures of the German Jewish intellectual presence within the United States, had articulated the problem of Jewish self-hatred in an essay entitled "The Cultural Problem of Modern West-Jewry," published in Buber's *The Jew*.[134] The very fact that Kohn sees Jewish self-hatred as a problem of the cultural life of the Jew in the West is rooted in Kohn's denial of his identity as a racial Jew. He thus picks up two figures, Heine and Weininger, in whom the conflict is articulated between the sense of belonging to the German cultural sphere and their Jewish identity. "This land is dear to us like no other— and yet it is not our land." "What never leaves us is the sense that we have a second homeland." The rhetoric of Kohn's essay plays on the identity between national culture and identity promulgated by a number of late-nineteenth-century movements, among them Zionism and Teutonism.

Kohn sees this as a universal truth, however, and sees in Heine and Weininger identical forms of self-hatred stemming from the denial of this "racial" identity. That within "each of us there is this primal Jewish, this strange element" is for Kohn what the self-hater has denied. This "primal" Jewishness articulates itself in the language of the Jews, in Hebrew, and results in the creation of truly Jewish art: "Then the new Judaism will fill in the spiritual world with Jewish elements: the Jew will listen to the deep melancholy and sentimental humor of Eastern Jewish folksongs, the books that surround him will be Jewish, he will desire Jewish games, fairy tales, and theater, he will fill with life that which he finds to be real among the festivals and laws." This rebirth of a Jewish spirit will drive out the demons of self-hatred through the intercession of Zionism. But, of course, such a romanticization of the idea of the Jewish cultural object (as focused on the image of the cultural life of the Eastern European Jew) is but another projection of the inner anxiety of the German Jewish writer. While Kohn, unlike Buber, sees Hebrew as the "new language" for the Jews, the language in which they will be able to articulate their repressed Jewish cultural identity, he sees the content and structures of that culture in the split between the "good" Eastern Jew, the happy primitive, with folk songs cut in Herder's mode, and the "bad" Western Jew. Yet his model preserves much of the inner doubt of the Western Jew, preserved from the older dichotomy of the "good" Western Jew versus the "bad" Eastern Jew, for his idealized, culturally integrated Jews will be able to pick and choose from the religious aspects of Judaism those factors that mean the most to them. The means of selection is for Kohn "the stormy Jewish heart," the essence of a racial definition of the Jew as inherently different. In glorifying this difference, Kohn seeks out those who attempt to deny it, not because he seeks negative case studies, but because he knows that their internalized conflict mirrors his own. Just as they relied on the split between the two images of the Jew for their definition of the self, so, too, does Kohn.

Arnold Zweig saw self-hatred as a specific disease of the Austrian Jew:

> The so-called Jewish self-hatred, that specific Austrian form of ego denial, the Jewish *Weltschmerz*, Jewish doubt, the passionate drive to denial of one's own being, appears primarily there where the life of the non-Jewish society produced or mirrored real attraction, color, magic, and a humane humanity. We Jews of the German Reich, in what were we to lose ourselves? In the world of German books and music, of dead isolated geniuses, and that we did. But one must already be fairly confused within one's self in order to see in the Junker (of the Mark Brandenburg), in the Prussian officer, in the German industrialist or civil servant, a type of human being whose value is so convincing that one sacrifices one's self under all circumstances, that one finds oneself under all circumstances worthy of abnegation.[135]

Zweig's comment, written in 1927, comes after his confrontation with the world of the integrated, whole, complete Jew, the world of the Eastern Jew as perceived by the Western Jew, during the First World War. Zweig captured his impressions in a volume, undertaken with Hermann Struck, entitled the *Eastern Jewish Face* (1919), which presented the Eastern Jew, not from the standpoint of the desire for the Jew as the essential mystic, but rather as the essential proletariat. The tone of the volume can be seen in the following paean to the Eastern Jew as worker:

> Work is in every sense the antidote to care; in the Eastern Jew trust in God's aid never degenerates into rejection of work; on the contrary, work and its fruits are the carriers of divine assistance. And only he who can no longer work, who must beg, is truly desolate and poor. . . . In connection with this it scarcely need be mentioned that the work of the Jew is sincere and honest achievement. To have learned what one does, and to accomplish that which one has learnt as well as possible: this craftsman's temperament, which only needs to be raised to a higher sphere to be close to the spirit of the truly creative man, to the artist, is alive in the Eastern Jew in every craftsman; it too is grounded in religion and is sacred.[136]

Zweig's socialist romanticization of the Eastern Jew is the parallel image to his sense of the rootlessness of the Western Jew. Thus self-hatred as a model presupposes the existence of a whole, healthy

Jewry, integrated in its sense of self. The healthy Jew, whether seen as the epitome of the Jew as mystic or of the Jew as worker, exists in the never-never land of myth. The components used to construct this Jew, those qualities defined as healthy, are taken from the German idea of the whole, of the healthy, of the integrated, and projected on the Eastern Jew. In seeing the Western Jew as fragmented, as ill, as disassociated, the German Jewish writers of the early twentieth century have begun to articulate their own sense of distance. Yet it must be observed that the use of rhetoric and example always distances the self-hating Jew from the writer. Kohn sees Vienna as the center for self-hatred among the Jews; Zweig, the German Reich. Neither places himself within the damned circle of the self-hater; each perceives himself as standing outside this world, able to free himself from the conflicts that haunt him.

Zweig's idealization of the Eastern Jew, of the Jew without self-hatred, is linked to an understanding of the identity of the Jews as defined by their discourse. The discourse of the Eastern Jew is honest and straightforward; it represents the true nature of Jewish discourse. When Zweig turns to yet another subset of Jews, the Jewish actors, he sees in this group, as in the Eastern Jew, a specific type of Jewish discourse.[137] As Mediterraneans, the Jews possess a special discourse represented in their language—its tempo, its intonation, its gesture, even its special mode of humor. Jewish actors are inherently different from their German counterparts. Indeed, Zweig's adaptation of Ratzel's geographic categories reaches to the point that he understands the Jews' partiality to garlic and onions as a result of their Mediterranean nature. Given the fact that anti-Semitic biologists such as Gustav Jaeger had labeled the *foetor judäicus* as one of the natural signs of Jewish difference, this glorification of the difference of the Jews must be read within the rhetoric of racial science.[138] The actor is representative of the potential for an independent, Jewish discourse, a discourse, however, that has high social prestige within German culture. The Jewish actor becomes for Zweig a surrogate for the Eastern Jew, seen within the culture of the West. Thus difference in discourse, the fiction of the language of the Eastern Jew represented by the cultured German of writers such as Buber, is transferred to the stage, where the difference is played out within the same tongue. The fiction is eliminated, while the difference is maintained.

No better example of the desire to distance a sense of self perceived to be inadequate can be found than in the person of Theodor Lessing, the author of the paradigmatic study *Jewish Self-Hatred* (1930).[139] In another context Lessing had employed a devastatingly negative image of the Eastern Jew, an image that repeated all of the older images of the Eastern Jew as degenerate, while examining the process of irreconcilable inner conflict among Western Jews. In an account of a trip to Poland in 1906, Lessing, in a series of articles published in the most important German Jewish newspaper, excoriates the Eastern Jews as filthy and corrupt, willing to sell their daughters, while all the while claiming a false piety masked by scholastic quibbles. Lessing's view of the Eastern Jew was so much in line with the anti-Semitic caricatures of his time that sections of his reportage appeared in various anti-Semitic journals, and Binjimun Segel wrote a pamphlet condemning Lessing for providing such materials for the political anti-Semites.[140] Lessing based his series of essays on the political repression of the Eastern Jew, but the focus of the series was not the source of the Jews' degeneracy but rather its manifestation.

When Lessing, a Protestant convert who had become by 1930 a supporter of German Zionism, turned to the Western Jew, he applied much the same paradigm. At the turn of the century Lessing had begun to discover Zionism "and stumbled onto a self-proclaimed principle for cultivating esteem. I certainly was not mistaken about my essentially Germanic character, but I sensed that it was in bad taste to want to be German. I definitely felt that people excluded and ostracized me."[141] This reversal of the earlier model of identification with German culture provides one of the answers to Lessing's negative evaluation of both the Eastern Jew and the assimilated Western Jew. If status is to be had among the peer group by identifying with it rather than rejecting it, and one senses that one really does not fit the model of the peer group, one feels anxiety. This is especially true when the peer group has taken precisely those qualities that one identifies with ("Germanic character") and has accepted them but altered their labels. For the "good" Jew remains the "good" Jew, but the label on the "good" Jew has shifted from an acculturated or assimilated Jew to the separatist Jew even though the qualities ascribed remain constant. The "good" Jews are intelligent, hard-working, and rational, while their antithesis remains limited, scholastic, parasitical, and irrational.

When Lessing turns to the problem of the "bad" Jew in the West, he seeks those examples (Weininger, Trebitsch, Paul Rée, Maximilian Harden) who can be classified in this manner. For Lessing the category of "self-hatred" includes only the pathological extremes resulting from the internalizing of the conflict felt by Jews in the West. He does not see his own struggle with the "bad" Jew, the self-hater, as a mode of projection. Lessing does not see the Eastern Jew as the whole or healthy Jew. Rather, he sees in a rejuvenated, Western Jew a Jew integrated into a new world, the ideal countertype. Theodor Lessing is not merely a Jew who used pre-fascist models of "blood and earth" to characterize the nature of the Jew in the West. He is a Western Jew who, through the paradigm of "self-hatred," attempts to isolate certain qualities that he perceives within himself. The slipperiness of the implied antithesis into which the images of the Eastern Jew and the self-hating Western Jew are fit can be seen here. It is a false dichotomy. Neither the idealization of the Eastern Jew nor the self-castigation of the Western Jew provides an integrated model for the Jew. Both models point up the confusion present within Western Jewry as to their sense of identity.

In a 1918 letter to his mother from Warsaw, Franz Rosenzweig, who was later to attempt to create yet another language for Jewish experience in his *Star of Redemption*, captured the complexity of this mode of projection:

> Now I have observed how the *communis opinio* of the German soldier concerning the "Jewess" arises: you see, they cannot distinguish her from a Polish woman and consider it possible that a Jewess would lie and say that she was a Polish woman— which none would be so degenerate as to do. Unconsciously, the German soldiers are ascribing to the Eastern Jews that which they find to be a matter of course in the Western Jews— the denial of Jewishness. But it is exactly that which is the difference between "Eastern" and "Western" Jews—that the former would never dream of doing such a thing.[142]

The idealization of the Eastern Jew presented by Rosenzweig, which ignored the many faces of Eastern Jewry in 1918, captures the essence of the model of projection, a model here ascribed not to the Western Jew (i.e., Rosenzweig) but to the non-Jewish German. Again, while the model is correctly understood, the use of this model within German Jewish identity formation is a means of distancing the self from the "bad" Jew as the acculturated Jew.

With the rise of the Nazis, the image of the "self-hating" Jew, the self-critical Jew, became a touchstone for the political anti-Semites. Robert Weltsch, in an editorial in the *Jewish Panorama* of May 5, 1933, still called for the need for "self-criticism, in spite of everything."[143] While rejecting the type of biologically defined self-hatred exemplified by Weininger, as well as German Jewish critical overcompensation, he called for an introspective evaluation of Jewish identity. He sees the striving for assimilation as an illness that led to these forms of self-hatred. The Jew must have a "Jewish national sense," which must arise through "self-criticism." Weltsch's observations rely on a dichotomy between healthy self-criticism and diseased self-hatred. Healthy are those who reject their acculturated identities and see themselves primarily as Jews; diseased are those who remain mired within the corruption of a primarily German identity. Again it is the label of the Other, here the acculturated German, as self-hating and thus diseased that creates categories of the acceptable and the unacceptable Jews. Weltsch's Zionist orientation sees the "new Jew" as consciously rejecting the model of identity that predominated among German Jews during the late nineteenth and early twentieth centuries. His glorification of a separatist Jewish identity is parallel to the stress on national identities present throughout Europe. Just as the Nazis claimed that being consciously German was "healthy" and being Jewish was "diseased" (a metaphor that dominates Hitler's Mein Kampf), so, too, it was necessary for Jewish political ideologists to distinguish between "healthy" and "corrupt" Jewish identities. What is evident is that their own sense of self provided the model for the "healthy" Jew; that which they rejected, the model for the "ill" Jew.

The German model for the formation of a "healthy" Jewish identity had some influence on the other side of the Atlantic. Given the great prestige of German medical science in the United States, it is of little wonder that the American medical establishment, or at least American Jewish psychiatrists, took interest in the psychopathology of self-hatred. In 1920 A. Myerson, at the Boston State Hospital, attributed the psychopathology of the Jew to "social" rather than "biological" heredity.[144] Like Becker, he sees in the Jews' isolation from appropriate forms of work one of the major sources for their psychopathology. Myerson also sees in the rejection by the Jews of "sports and play" one of the sources of the illness of the Jew. Again following Nordau's image of the "muscle Jew," here redefined as the "all-American athlete," Myerson provides yet another theoretical restatement of this myth:

> Sports and play . . . form an incomparable avenue of discharge for nervous tension. They breed confidence in oneself. Being [extensor] in their character, they allow for the rise of pride and courage. Circumstances excluded the Jew from their wholesome influence, and the children of the race grew up to be very serious, very earnest, too early devoted to mature efforts, excessively cerebral in their activities, and not sufficiently strenuous physically. *In other words, the Jew, through his restrictions, was cheated out of childhood.* (96)

Myerson, like Becker, needs to localize the baneful influence on the Jews outside of the Jews themselves. He locates it in another society, Eastern Europe, not America with its reevaluation of older, foreign values. Indeed, the very fact that a large number of Eastern European Jews were manual laborers, under the most primitive conditions, relegates his condemnation of the image of the inactive Jewish child into the world of myth. For Myerson, the "bad" Jew as sick Jew resides in the East, is the Eastern Jew, the most evident representative of the stereotype of the Jew in post-First World War America.

The polemic attached to the idea of self-hatred as the pathological underpinning of the "bad" Jew continued in the United States throughout the mid-twentieth century. In Kurt Lewin's 1941 essay on Jewish self-hatred, Lessing's thesis was examined within a social psychological model.[145] Lewin, until 1932 professor of psychology at the University of Berlin and then the leading exponent of the study of group dynamics in the United States, was the major link between German concepts of self-hatred and American analysis of Jewish anti-Semitism. Lewin recognized, at least superficially, the false antithesis between the "bad" Eastern Jew and the "good" Western Jew in the German Jews' paradigm for the projection of their self-hatred. However, Lewin wishes to shift the discourse from one that sees self-hatred as an individual problem of adaptation, as in Lessing, to one of group dynamics. It is not the individual's need to compensate but rather the response of the group that is the source of self-hatred. Lewin believes that he is abandoning the labeling of the Jew as ill; instead, he is extending the idea, as in the older model, from a limited (though representative) number of Jews to the entire category. "In fact, neurotic trends in Jews are frequently the result of their lack of adjustment to just such group problems." Neurosis is the result, not of inbreeding, but of group dynamics. It is, however, not only the privileged group's pressure on the minority that induces this sense of inferiority for Lewin; if this were the case, would self-hatred not manifest itself among groups such as American Catholics? Assuming that this statement is empirically valid, Lewin seeks the etiology of self-hatred and finds it in those "Jewish" institutions associated with the Eastern Jew:

> To build up such a feeling of group belongingness on the basis of active responsibility for the fellow Jew should be one of the outstanding policies in Jewish education. That does not mean

that we can create in our children a feeling of belongingness by *forcing* them to go to Sunday school or *Heder*. Such a procedure means the establishment in early childhood of the same pattern of enforced group belongingness which is characteristic of the psychological situation for the negative chauvinists and it is sure to create in the long run exactly this attitude. Too many young Jews are driven away from Judaism by too much *Heder*. (199)

Lewin contrasts the German ideal of *Bildung*, education, with the institutional structures in traditional Judaism that have been viewed since the Enlightenment as antithetical to true education. Indeed, when G. E. Lessing's quintessential Jew Nathan the Wise educates his adopted daughter Recha, he turns her out so that she may learn from nature instead of educating her within "Jewish" structures such as the *heder*, or Hebrew school. Lewin's insights about the nature of group dynamics still revolve about the hidden agenda of the nature of subgroups of Jews. Under the mask of the "self-hating" Western Jew still lurk presuppositions about the mythic Eastern Jew, presuppositions present within American Jewry just as they are within German Jewry. The sick Jew is the Eastern Jew.

In 1939 the Austrian psychologist Bruno Bettelheim was released from Buchenwald and emigrated to the United States. Based in Chicago, Bettelheim began to write a series of essays on his experiences in the concentration camps. One of these essays, incorporated in 1960 in his wide-reaching study of the Jewish response to the Holocaust, *The Informed Heart*, was a study entitled "The Dynamism of Anti-Semitism in Gentile and Jew."[146] Bettelheim sharpened the category of Jewish self-hatred in this essay and provided an elaborate model of self-hatred as the rationale for the inability of Jews to survive the camps. In contrast to Lewin, he locates the source of self-hatred in the assimilated Jew. He sees the loss of autonomy in the camps as parallel to the overall loss of autonomy in modern society, indeed as the reason for the fragmenting of personality within the camps. The Jews depend on the values of the society—on rank, position, status—to define themselves. When these are removed, when they are reduced to the level of the beast in their own eyes, their identities are destroyed. This is the red thread that is present in Buber and in Weininger: that the Jews in the West have no center, that they have replaced it (if indeed it ever existed) with the outward trappings of Western society, articulated in the political or economic discourse of the West. Bettel-

heim analyzes the reactions of the Jews, the "adaptive mechanisms" that they used to cope in the camps, as "neurotic or psychotic
mechanisms," had they been manifested outside of the camps.

The Western Jews' actions are "insane" because they are in
response to an "insane" world. The Jews have no center; they are
insane. These responses internalize the anti-Semitic image of the
Jew and project it onto another subset of Jews, the Jews in the
camps. Indeed, Bettelheim's initial "speculation[s] on the extermination camp" provide a five-point list of factors that "explain"
the "docile acceptance of the situation in the camp." First, the
prisoners are aware of the "tenuous" nature of their psychological
"emergency measures"; second, they lose "libidinal energy" in
maintaining their "fictions"; third, they identify with the enemy,
which provides them with "gratification in being overpowered by
the enemy"; fourth, they perceive the world as a psychotic delusion
that can be maintained only by being passive, and avoiding any
direct confrontation with reality; fifth, in identifying with the
"enemy" "they were able to 'destroy' delusionally their enemy by
their own death." This pattern is, of course, the pattern of self-
hatred developed within the rhetoric of the psychology of race
during the early twentieth century. Self-haters know that their own
self-hatred is but a coping device, they focus all of their energy in
maintaining this device, they identify with the rhetoric of anti-
Semitism, they use this rhetoric as a means of avoiding any
confrontation with the reality of anti-Semitism in the streets, and
finally, they so identify with the anti-Semite that they must end
in suicide or madness.

The power of Lewin's and Bettelheim's contradictory models
dominated the understanding of self-hatred following the war. The
self-hating Jew is the "mad" Jew, and this Jew is the antithesis of
the self-definition of the observer. In a 1951 dissertation entitled
"Identification with the Aggressor," Irving Sarnoff attempted to
document this type of identification through the use of standard-
ized tests.[147] Drawing on the work of Bettelheim, Erikson, Anna
Freud, and Lewin (all German Jews), Sarnoff sees adult maladaption
(which he labels Jewish anti-Semitism) as a direct result of childhood insecurity. This was yet another attempt to create categories
of "healthy" and "diseased" Jews based, as with Lewin and Bettelheim, on social rather than biological causes. The problem with
Sarnoff and all of the other psychologists and sociologists who
followed this model for "self-hatred" is that they made specific
assumptions about what is "healthy" and what is "sick." To label
entire categories of identity as "diseased" is to indulge in the type

of polemic that lies behind the very concept of self-hatred, for, as has been shown, the double bind of identity formation may have a productive as well as a destructive outcome.

What is more, the strict polar definition of identity implied by the label "self-hatred" rests on a specific set of historical presuppositions about the structure of identity. This German model, if one may so label it, sees a simple and direct relationship between the internalization of a negative image of the Jew and the resultant shaping of the Jew's identity. This was valid within a culture that postulated an absolute polarity between "German" and "Jew." The "Germans," since they did not exist as an entity, needed some means of defining their fictional homogeneity. They did so by defining it negatively. We are Germans, which means that we are not Jews. This definition existed within Germany as a powerful and unbridgeable abyss between the fiction of the homogeneity of the "German" people and the assigned role of the Jew as the litmus test of difference. Once it became evident to the German Jews of the late nineteenth century that they had fallen into the double bind of this self-definition, they attempted to postulate other models for their own identity. These models were often simply negations or adaptions of the anti-Semitic image of the Jew. Either the Eastern Jew became the idealized image of the Jew, but an image shaped out of the fictions of Western Jewry, or the Eastern Jew remained as the antithesis of the healthy Jew. In defining and sharpening the idea of self-hatred as a category of illness, German Jews were able to relegate those Jews viewed as unsuccessful in their adaptation to a separate class, the diseased. They incorporated into this category all of the negative qualities with which they were labeled and from which they wished to distance themselves. The protean category of the self-hating Jew was thus developed. It placed the "bad" Jews within an accepted and recognized category of the anti-Semitic science of race, the psychopathology of the Jew, and separated them from the Jewish identity of the observer.

The "insane" Jew, the Jewish self-hater, was defined within a world in which there were specific limits on the concept of difference. When this concept emigrated to the United States, before and during the Holocaust, clothed in the status of German science, it was adopted without any question—this in a society in which the complexity of the definition of difference eliminated any simple polar definition of the Jew. Even though the myth of the "hidden language" of the Jews existed in American anti-Semitism, there was already a central racial marker for difference in the United States: the black. Class distinctions in the United States had more to do with defining difference for the Jew than did racial distinctions. Because of this, the very concept of the "Jew" as a label for difference was fragmented, especially after the Holocaust and the establishment of the state of Israel.

But most important was the power of myth. In defining difference, the Germans defined themselves as monolithically German until 1945. This was the central myth about the definition of German identity. It had nothing to do with reality; if anything, it attempted to transcend the realities of a pluralistic group, itself politically and culturally fragmented. The central myth of twentieth-century America, especially after the Second World War, was the myth of American heterogeneity—not the melting pot but the ability to possess multiple identities.[148] The power of this myth, itself fraught with the potential of the double bind, undermined the definition of the "self-hating Jew" within the model provided by German psychology. This model, based on valid psychological principles such as identification and projection, nevertheless reflected its historical origins. When applied to the American Jewish experience, it provided a working label for the signification of specific modes of divergence, modes that eventually turned upon the ideological implications of "Jewish self-hatred." For "self-hatred" among Jews is not the special prerogative of any specific group of Jews: it is the result of the internalized contrast between any society in which the possibility of acceptance is extended to any marginal group and the projection of the negative image of this group onto a fiction of itself that leads to "self-hatred" or self-abnegation. The German experience of the early twentieth century localized this general psychological truth in the experience of the assimilated Jew in Germany and thus endowed the overall experience of projection and identification with a specific ideological bias. Within all worlds of privilege this pattern repeats itself, but always with specific historical variations. The development of the concept of self-hatred within the experience of German Jewry led to a narrowing of the focus of the concept and to its interpretation within the specific contours of German Jewish experience. It was the tension between this more rigid, limited understanding of self-hatred (with its concomitant glorification of the difference of the Jew) and the post-Holocaust experience in the United States that provided yet another double bind through the American perception of Jewish identity formation after the Holocaust.

CHAPTER SIX

The Ashes of the Holocaust and the Closure of Self-hatred

I

The Language of Silence

On May 10, 1933, the official organization of students in Germany arranged for public bonfires to be held throughout the country. Into these fires were thrown books representing the intellectual patrimony of the Weimar Republic. In preparation for this action, the student organization had posted "twelve theses" on posters throughout Germany announcing their opposition to the "anti-German Spirit." The fifth of these twelve theses stated:

> The Jew who can only think Jewish but writes German lies. He who is German and writes German but thinks anti-German is a traitor. The student who speaks anti-German and thus writes anti-German is thoughtless and is untrue to his obligations.[1]

The program suggested to correct the lying of the Jews is stated in the seventh thesis:

1. We wish to take the Jews seriously as strangers, and we wish to respect the idea of race.
2. We therefore demand from the censor:
3. That Jewish works appear in Hebrew. If they appear in German, they are to be labeled as translations.
4. The strongest control of the use of German script.
5. That German script be used only by Germans.
6. That the anti-German spirit be removed from public libraries.

Jews are to be denied the use not only of German but even of the "German" typeface.

The response to these posters, which went up at the beginning of April 1933, was quite hostile, at least on the part of the German

Jews who still did not quite believe that the Nazi ideology could be translated into a program of action. Even the rector of the Berlin university ordered the removal of the posters because of these two theses. Rector Kohlrauch was in no way philosemitic, but he objected to their exaggeration. An anonymous author, however, presented a parody of these theses in which the "seventh thesis" states that during the First World War "we were able to determine that the Jews of Galicia and Russia were the flag bearers of the Old High German tongue."[2]

The Jews had been seen as the speakers of the true German. Now they were seen as not speaking German at all. It was this thesis more than any other that attacked at the very roots of German Jewry's identity. Max Herrmann, professor of the history of the theater at Berlin, stated in a letter to the ministry of culture on May 1, 1933, that he would not enter the university as long as the posters were displayed: "My honor is offended . . . by the reference to that group with which I am associated by birth, and about which it is publicly stated that the Jew can only think Jewish; that if he writes German, then he lies. . . . I write German, I think German, I feel German, and I do not lie."[3] Herrmann was removed from his post in the summer of 1933 along with the other Jewish professors in Germany and died in 1942 in Theresienstadt.

The importance of the poster announcing the basis for the book burnings in May 1933 is that it directly stated that the Jews' language was not to be considered German. Hitler had already presented his objections to acculturation in *Mein Kampf*.[4] He saw in the possibility of any group "becoming" German by merely learning the German language the eventual conquest of the majority through the insidious power of the minority:

> It is a scarcely conceivable fallacy of thought to believe that a Negro or a Chinese, let us say, will turn into a German because he learns German and is willing to speak the German language in the future and perhaps even give his vote to a German political party. . . . Only too frequently does it occur in history that conquering people's outward instruments of power succeeds in forcing their language on oppressed peoples, but that after a thousand years their language is spoken by another people, and the victors thereby actually become the vanquished. (389)

The German Student Union in their book burnings carried out Hitler's dictum that "a man can change his language without any trouble—that is, he can use another language; but in his new language he will express the old ideas; his inner nature is not changed. This is best shown by the Jew who can speak a thousand languages and nevertheless remains a Jew" (312). The Jews' use of the language of the people among whom they dwell has but one purpose:

> For . . . [the Jew's language] is not a means for expressing his thoughts but a means for concealing them. When he speaks French, he thinks Jewish, and while he turns out German verses, in his life he only expresses the nature of his nationality. As long as the Jew has not become the master of the other peoples, he must speak their languages whether he likes it or not, but as soon as they have become his slaves, they would all have to learn a universal language (Esperanto, for instance!), so that by this additional means the Jews could more easily dominate them. (307)

Hitler's racial linguistics is based on the image of hidden infiltration, a paranoia echoed elsewhere in *Mein Kampf* in his use of the image of the Jews as the cancer hidden within the German body politic. But it is the reality of the language of the Jews that permits them to burrow within. Like the blacks, they will never be able to hide their true nature, and thus like the blacks, they can never become truly German. Their mask has only one purpose: the eventual destruction of the host culture and its language. The language that the Jews will use to control the enslaved peoples is not Hebrew or Yiddish but Esperanto, an artificial tongue, a hybrid with no roots in any culture that is the product of a Polish Jew, Ludwig Zamenhof. The Jews still retain their hidden language for themselves, robbing those whom they conquer from within of all language and culture.

The program of action according to which the Jews in Germany would be able to publish in only Hebrew or Yiddish (or present their works as translations) was a natural consequence of Hitler's reasoning. The fact that somewhat less than 6 percent of German Jews even had a rudimentary knowledge of Hebrew did not faze the German Student Union.[5] The Nazis did translate this view of the special language of the Jews into practice. They ordered "Jewish" writers to be published only by a limited number of "Jewish" publishing houses. (Thus Kafka's novels were published posthumously by the Jewish publishing house operated by Zalman Schocken.) But what is more, they denigrated the ability of the writers of Jewish descent to express themselves in "good" German, relegating all such authors to the intellectual ghetto of the Cultural Association for Jews, founded in 1933.

The Nazis' racial linguistics was a continuation of the long tradition of viewing the Jews' discourse as polluted. Hitler's racial mentor, Julius Streicher, the publisher of *The Attacker*, is the link between the view of the Jews' language in *Mein Kampf* and the racial science of the early twentieth century. In 1928 Streicher published a long, pseudoscientific essay by "Dr. B" on the racial characteristics of the Jews. In the essay the language of the Jews is described in detail: "Speech takes place with a racially determined intonation: *Mauscheln*. The Hebrews speak German in a unique, singing manner. One can recognize Jews and Jewesses immediately by their language, without having seen them."[6] In the children's book *The Poison Mushroom*, a child's introduction to Jew hatred published by Streicher in 1938, this is the concluding sign in the "scientific" catalogue of the Jew's difference: "When the Jew speaks, he gestures with his hands. One says that he '*mauschelt*.' His voice often breaks. The Jew almost always speaks through his nose."[7]

But Streicher did not rely merely on the rhetoric of science; he called upon the Jews' own testimony about their difference. As late as 1941 he cites Abraham Schwadron, one of the most articulate Zionist supporters of Hebrew, in a passage written in 1916: "Thus you appear to me: you have no language. You *mauschel* in all languages; you are bereft of language."[8] Schwadron was engaged in a debate about the appropriate language for the projected Jewish state. Herzl had visualized the Jewish state as multilingual, rather on the model of Switzerland, a confederation of the European languages spoken by the Jews (except for that *Jargon* of the prisons, Yiddish, which, like dead skin, would be shed). He was opposed by such thinkers as Eliezar ben Jehuda, who argued that Hebrew was the necessary linguistic vehicle for the creation of a Jewish state.[9] When Streicher quotes Schwadron, it is, however, with the intent of isolating the Jew from all "civilized" language, especially from German. He attacks Yiddish as a "mix of Middle High German and Hebrew" but demands that the Jews avoid the use of German, even in this form, and rely only on Hebrew.

Streicher quotes "Jewish" sources for all of this, seeing in them a specific proof of the validity of his views.[10] If Jews state among themselves that they have no true language, then this must be the case. Jews lie, as Streicher stresses over and over again, but they lie only to the non-Jew; among themselves they speak the truth. Their polluted discourse is presented in Streicher's newspaper throughout the 1920s and 1930s in the cartoons of Jews, cartoons drawn by Philip Ruprecht, who signed himself "Fips." What is notable about these "talking" caricatures of Jews, from their first appearance in 1924 to the demise of the paper and the Third Reich in 1945, is that they are made to speak in *mauscheln*. Like the visualizations of the Jews in the caricatures of the late nineteenth century and like the presentation of the language of the Jews on the stage, when the Jews "speak" within the fictions of the anti-Semites, they speak with a notable accent. This accent, *mauscheln*, is the external sign of the difference of the Jews.

When the Nazis sought out examples of the universal, cosmopolitan discourse of the Jews, they used a canon of "Jewish" writers that had been developed in the late nineteenth century. The central figure in this canon was Heine. Typical for the Nazis' application of their sense of the special language of the Jews is the following extract from an essay by Otto Klein published in the *West German Observer* on March 1, 1936:

> It was a typical Jewish characteristic of him, this tendency to lying and to a criticism of everyone and everything, this inner drive to take every positive emotion in him, once he expressed it, and turn it into a dirty and low negation. . . . Josef Nadler [professor of German at Vienna] called him "the master of the dirty *Jargon* of the street". . . . What Heine was as a man, he was also, of course, as a poet.[11]

Heine spoke the "dirty *Jargon* of the street," the language of the Jews. Not Yiddish or even *mauscheln* but "Jewish-Oriental eroticism," according to Klein. The language of the Jews is thus connected with the metaphor of seduction, as well as metaphors of infiltration and contamination. This is yet a further strand in the Nazis' image of the hidden language of the Jews. Heine becomes the paradigm for the Jewish writer, as he had been during the late nineteenth century for critics as different as Karl Kraus and Adolf Bartels. Contemporary writers were measured against this model and were also found to be Jewish if they were so labeled. For the model was of universal dimensions and could be expanded at will. Thus Kurt Tucholsky was a new Heine, as was Heinrich Mann. The model for the hidden language of the Jews was the model of the writer as the carrier of infection, and the use to which this model was put was the distinction between the acceptable and the unacceptable, the human and the bestial, the ennobling and the corrupting. The power of this model lies to no little degree in its long, unbroken tradition within European thought.

By the time of the Weimar Republic it became necessary for the anti-Semites to create the image of the corrupt discourse of the Jew on as many different levels as possible, for the assimilated Jew in Germany bore no overt sign of "racial difference," especially not in terms of language. It was necessary to create both an external sign (accent) and the fantasy that this sign could be internalized (in the Jews' discourse) and thus not be immediately recognizable. Thus one's German-speaking Jewish neighbor was associated by analogy with the image of the Yiddish-speaking Jews in the big cities, who themselves were being assimilated into German culture by the 1920s.[12] The power of this association for those under the Nazis cannot be underestimated. Rudolf Augstein, one of the rebuilders of the German news media after the Second World War ended, recounts a schoolroom episode from 1934. He was asked by his German teacher to give a sentence using *m*'s:

> What example did I choose: "Mieze *mauschelt* with Simon." Great laughter. The teacher did not say a word. *Mauscheln*— that was the language of the murderous Nuremberg newspaper *The Attacker*, which you perhaps know about. Do Jews *mauschel*? Naturally not.[13]

What is indicative of Augstein's memory of his seduction by the rhetoric of German anti-Semitism is that this sentence seemed to occur to him spontaneously, even though his parents, Rhineland Catholics, were politically opposed to the Nazis. If we take the counterexample, that of the Jewish child in school in Germany during the late 1930s, we are struck by the parallelism of the experience. Marcel Reich-Ranicki, one of the most notable book reviewers in modern West Germany, observes that his experience as a Polish-born, German-speaking Jew in school during the early years of Nazi domination pointed up the contradictions of German racial theory. The most perfect "Aryan" types in his school, chosen by the biology teacher as examples of pure race, turned out to be Jews, indeed in one case an Eastern Jew: "No, instruction in racial science was not a great success in our class—especially since the fastest 100-meter runner and the best German students were Jews."[14] Reich-Ranicki learned the lessons of Nazi racial science all too well: Jews are physically weak and have no command of German, since language and blood are inexorably linked. Here the memories of writers such as Augstein and Reich-Ranicki return to the labeling of the language of the Jew as different, as foreign. The impact of this image in the internalized rhetoric of both Jews and non-Jews about the difference of the Jews was of great import. Bertolt Brecht, sitting in his Danish exile and writing against the Nazis, was sent a piece on the nature of the historical process by the German Jewish essayist Walter Benjamin. Brecht and Benjamin were intellectual sparring partners, with Benjamin usually the winner of their matches. Brecht, impressed by what he read, entered into his notebooks his praise of the essay as "clear and clarifying (in spite of all the metaphorics and Jewishisms)."[15] Jews speak differently, think differently. This is a view shared across the political spectrum but also a view held by many Jews themselves. If their German is corrupt, then Hebrew or other languages of intellectual discourse are the answer. Or they project this change onto other groups of Jews, onto groups of Jews labeled as speaking differently.

The Holocaust did not result from the Germans' perception of the Jews as speaking a different tongue, but this perception contributed to the overall impression of the Jews as essentially different from the Germans. The Jews spoke differently—especially the Eastern Jews. The German associated the image of the Eastern Jews and the *Jargon* spoken by them with the image of the Eastern (now Communist) barbarian and treated the Eastern Jew as a subhuman. This was quite the reverse of the glorification, albeit temporary, of Yiddish as the original German which followed on German incursions into Russian territory during the period following 1914. Thus one of the underlying images of the Jews in the Holocaust was the image of their inarticulateness, their inability to speak and think rationally. In his statement in prison before his trial and execution, Adolf Eichmann praised his own ability to speak the language of the Jews.[16] He had attempted to learn Hebrew so that he could have true insight into the mind of the Jew. This is the underlying claim of the Nazis in their perception of the language of the Jew. It is the branding of their language as inherently different, and thus the language serves as a marker for their eventual extermination.

On the surface the situation in the Anglophone world during the first half of the twentieth century appears similar. The representation of Jews on the stage, especially as comic figures, was linked to their use of dialect. From comics like Potash and Perlmutter to stage representations of the Jew such as in Anne Nichol's *Abie's Irish Rose* (1922) to recordings such as Joseph Hayman's "Cohen on the Telephone," the discourse of the Jews became a marker for their image. The major difference was that such a representation was not unique. The "speaking" Jew was but one of a series of representations of the "hidden" language of difference ascribed to the outsider. Without a doubt the most representative figure was that of Sambo, who spoke the "hidden" language of blackness. The black, represented on the stage by whites in blackface (who thus proved themselves knowledgeable of the "hidden" language of blackness), spoke in dialect. It was this language, the language of the black as comic figure, that marked the image of difference in the United States from the late-nineteenth-century minstrel shows to *Amos and Andy.*[17] But almost all groups seen as outsiders generated such images of their language. T. A. Daly's *McAroni Ballads* (1919) presented the "comic" language of the Italian immigrant to a world that viewed the Southern European Catholic with fear.

The internalization of the idea of a "hidden" language ascribed to the outsider occurred as well in the United States. However, the special role of any specific group in defining difference was relativized by the presence of other groups against whom similar charges were made. The Jews were thus in a rather unique position. In Germany the myth of the damaged discourse of the Jew absolutely defined the Jews' difference in society. In the United States it appeared that such a distinction also existed, except that it was paralleled by a number of like images of other groups. When American Jews internalized this image, they had to resolve the conflict between the special role of the Jew in European anti-Semitism and the subordinate role of this myth of difference in the United States. The attempts to deal with the charge of the particular discourse of the Jews illustrate many of the same strategies, but often with some awareness of the American situation.

Henry Roth's *Call It Sleep* (1934), one of the major pre-Holocaust representations of the Eastern Jewish immigrant experience in America, creates a pattern of linguistic equivalents: Yiddish is represented by colloquial American speech; English spoken with a strong New York City accent represents the language of the world outside the home.[18] But for Roth the positive value of the home (which is the world in which his mother lives) is contrasted with the world of the street (in which his father must struggle for existence). The positive value given to Yiddish is exactly the opposite of the value given to it on the street, where only "greenhorns" speak Yiddish. Both of these worlds of language are, of course, embedded in a literary language, that of Roth's novel. With this use of the two worlds of the discourse of the Jew, Roth increases the gap between the world of American Jewish experience and fears associated very specifically with the language of the Jews. Henry James, in his *The American Scene* (1907), had despaired of the future of English because of the "Hebrew conquest of New York," where the "East Side cafes" have become "torture rooms of the living idioms."[19] The Jew perverts the language of art. Thus in accepting his role as an American writer, Henry Roth turns this charge of corruption into the focus of his text. What is the real corruption, he asks—the world of the speakers of Yiddish, autonomous and comforting, or the world of the streets, with its bestial language? In putting this into literary perspective in a novel of undoubted competence and power, Roth shows the American choice, for the American Jew not only must choose between intactness and corruption, a linguistic choice inconceivable for the German writer, but then must prove an ability to transcend the latter and become, at least at one remove, the Henry James of the American Jewish experience. With Roth, the conflict of language, as played out within the fiction of *Call It Sleep*, has a productive outcome in the creation of the work of art.

In the United States the confusion about the value of the language of culture and its relationship to the language of the Jews assumed many of the same forms as in Germany. Samuel Roth, a small-time publisher and pornographer, published his *Jews Must Live* (1934) with the explicit dedication: "To the First Generation of Jews That Will Learn How to Pronounce My Name Softly."[20] Roth's virulent attack on Jews echoes much of the European debate concerning the "hidden" language of the Jews. His dedication points toward this, as does much of his discussion of the function of language in defining the nature of the Jew:

> Do thousands of French families in the United States compel their children to study French after school so as to preserve with them the inheritance of French culture? Or is there any reason to believe that the French think less of their culture than the Jews think of theirs? . . . The preservation of Jewish religion and culture are merely excuses for something else, a smoke-screen. What the Jew really wants and expects to achieve through the instrumentality of the Hebrew school is to cultivate in his son the sharp awareness that he is a Jew and that as a racial Jew—apart from all the other races—he is waging an old war against his neighbors. (91)

Roth's claim to authority is that he is a Jew: "But what sort of speech is this for a Jew, you are probably asking yourself, by this time? I can see the question half-glimmering in your eyes. . . . I am myself a Jew, I know it. But I am a Jew who has been brought to the point where he so loathes his people that he thinks in terms of their destruction" (55). Roth's language is the language of European self-hatred which internalized the language of the anti-Semite about the discourse of the Jew and seemed to separate the self-hating Jew as writer from all other Jews.

All of Roth's discussions of the Jew, from his condemnation of Jews as lawyers and doctors to his discussion of the lying of the Jews (and its relationship to the *Kol Nidre*), centers about a European image of the discourse of the Jew as damaged and corrupt. Roth, who functioned on the margins of the literary world of New York as the American publisher of, among other works, a pornographic sequel to D. H. Lawrence's *Lady Chatterley's Lover* as well as James Joyce's *Ulysses*, saw his failure as a publisher, as a member of the literary establishment, as a result of the financial manipulations of the "Jews." His own involvement with language, an involvement that he glorifies and ascribes to the world of culture, is contrasted with the damaged, materialistic discourse of the Jew. In his view, it was this conflict with the Jews that destroyed him and that he wished to revenge in his *Jews Must Live*.

Roth's book is typical of the European discourse of self-hatred. Roth's image of the Jew as outsider, a view from the standpoint of an *Ostjude* born and raised in Austria and Poland who wishes to become part of the New York intellectual world, is tied to the stereotyped image of the Jew in European anti-Semitism. He concluded his book with a long appendix entitled "Do Jews Emit a Peculiar Odor?" The book and this chapter end with a translation of Heinrich Heine's poem "Disputation." Roth offers this text as his final proof of the difference of the Jews' discourse. He cites a central literary text, a text by the quintessential Jewish author, at least according to the anti-Semites. Heine seems to tell the "truth" about the Jews in spite of writing in German. Roth placed his own text parallel to the role he assigned to Heine. Heine is the essential Jewish writer for the anti-Semites and therefore has wide readership. This role is one to which Roth could only aspire.

Roth begins his book with a dedication that makes explicit reference to the "hidden" language of the Jews, and he ends it with a bow toward the ambiguity of Heine's position as Jew, cultured European, and popular author. Samuel Roth is not unique. Similar rejections of a "Jewish" identity as incompatible with cultured discourse can be found among Jews of German ancestry in America, such as Gertrude Stein and Walter Lippmann, as well as Eastern Jews such as Samuel Roth and Bernard Berenson. Roth's virulent rejection of his Jewish identity, and his fantasy about the destruction of the Jews, is much less subtle than Stein's encoding of her rejection of her Jewish identity in her complex poetic production or, as Meyer Schapiro has indicated, Berenson's rejection of his Eastern European background, his claim that German (not Yiddish) was his mother tongue and his response to the "puzzling character" of the Jews.[21] Related to the rejection of language by such writers is their rejection of the Jews as the bearers of culture. Roth and Berenson see the Jews as incapable of any aesthetic sensibility. All of these responses to the internalization of anti-Jewish attitudes toward the relationship of Jews to the discourse of culture and its mode of production were shifted when the fantasies of the destruction of the Jews became the realities of Auschwitz.

The Holocaust has been the most momentous force to shape modern Jewish identity.[22] Its force was felt not only among those Jews who directly experienced it but among all individuals who could even remotely perceive themselves as Jews. The translation of what had become abstract patterns of anti-Semitism into a program for action based on the Western stereotype of the Jew meant that all "Jews" could be at risk. Neither the high cultural attainments of the society in which one lived nor the acculturation or even assimilation of the Jew into that society precluded the possibility of individuals being identified as Jews. The treatment of a segment of society as Jews (whether Jewish or not) caused all those who had even the remotest sense of identification with the Jews to restructure their sense of self. The anxiety generated by this process of rethinking, especially among writers undertaking their redefinition of self in the public sphere, was to no little degree the reaction to the function that the Jews' language had had in defining what was essentially Jewish. Following the defeat of Hitler's Thousand Year Reich and the creation of the State of Israel, writers and thinkers who had been forced to come to terms with their often newly found Jewish identity began to deal with the idea that the Jew possessed a special language.

According to German Jewish commentators writing after the Holocaust, something ineffable died in the death camps. Theodor Adorno provided the label for this when, in 1949, he stated, in a formulation that he later regretted, that "to write poetry after Auschwitz is barbaric. And this corrodes even the knowledge of why it has become impossible to write poetry today."[23] The loss of poetic diction, of the voice expressing the self after having survived the camps, is the result of such a view. For Adorno, only the comfortable realities of a bourgeois poetry of progress died; for other critics, such as George Steiner, born in Paris of German Jewish parents, language *per se* died. "The thing that has gone dead is the German language. . . . Something immensely destructive has happened to it. It makes noise. It even communicates, but it creates no sense of communion."[24] German is damaged, and the damage has come from the banalization of the language of Goethe, Heine, and Nietzsche (Steiner's triad) through the Nazis. Descriptions of language as "barbaric," as mere "noise," as "creat[ing] no sense of communion" recycle the Nazi charges against the language of the Jews. The German now speaks the corrupted and corrupting language ascribed to the Jew. Indeed, following the war there appeared a spate of books about the irreversible decay of the language of German culture through the Nazis. The most famous of these was by the Berlin professor of French Victor Klemperer, who had spent the war years at forced labor, having been spared the death camps only because of his marriage to a non-Jew. He reported that he had saved his sanity by collecting with philological accuracy examples of how the Nazis had corrupted German.[25] The image of language as the indicator of corruption—indeed, as its truest indicator—is extraordinarily powerful. But it was not only the murderers but also many of the victims who were thus condemned to using this medium.

The implication that the survivors were as damaged as their persecutors, if not more damaged, is implicit in this image of the Jew in the postwar world. Adorno and Klemperer wrote in German, Steiner in English and French. None considered *his* language impaired, but see in the damaged discourse of the murderers a statement about the muteness of the victims, for the victims are perceived as speechless, both in dying and in death. If the murderers can still speak, the victims are forced into silence. The image is quite explicit. The Jews, especially the German Jews, have been using a language that is not only not their own (or merely a mask) but in the death camps turned on them, made them the victims of those speaking their adopted tongue. Unlike in the earlier images of the hidden language of the Jews, once these Jews were exposed to the fact that it was impossible to "be" Jewish and "speak" German, they were condemned to a life of silence. Germans, as the debate in Germany following the publication of Steiner's essay in 1959 stressed, could still create art from the rubble of the zero hour (the fanciful but widespread metaphor for the creation of a new German culture from nothingness following the war). Jews, dead in the camps, exiled abroad, had no such capability.

This inability to perceive language, especially German, as a medium for the expression of the Jewish experience resulted in the casting of a new, postwar language for the Jew, that of silence or inarticulateness. The Jews, whether they experienced it or not, are the essential survivors of the Holocaust and are so labeled by the world. But surviving, especially when one was never part of the world of destruction, means that one is forced to account for or bear witness to one's survival. For the dead are truly mute, and only the living can articulate their loss. But the survivor is seen as a *silent* witness to the horrors of the Holocaust. This silence is tied to the death of language in the camps—of poetic expression, of language in the cultural or poetic mode. Here is the double bind of post-Holocaust Jewish identity, at least as incorporated by those who see themselves both as Jews and as writers.

It is evident that the image of the death of language is merely a revitalization of a literary conceit that haunted *fin de siècle* writing. The psyche is so fragile that no poetry can capture its fragility. Rilke, the young Hofmannsthal—indeed, most of the modernist poets of the early twentieth century—expressed this inherent inexpressibility in the most delicate of poetic languages.[26] This trope was an affectation, a reaction against a literary theory, realism, which saw all experience as expressible and recordable. The major difference between the poets of the *fin de siècle* and those of the post-Holocaust generation is that after Auschwitz this poetic trope of inexpressibility had become internalized as a Jewish response to the Holocaust. The literary trope had become the measure of experience, and traced the perceived limits of expression. But like the poetry at the turn of the century, this trope led, not to silence, but to the creation of the image of silence within the writing of the Jewish poet, such as Paul Celan, born Paul Antschel in Czernowitz, Romania, in 1920. Raised in a Yiddish-speaking milieu in the new state of Romania, writing in German and, after he survived the camps, living and teaching first in Vienna and then in Paris, until his suicide in 1970, Celan is representative of the Jewish writer who internalized the image of the death of language and made it productive. In *Nobody'srose,* a collection of his poetry published in 1963, he wrote:

> If one came
> if a person came,
> if a person came into the world today, with
> the glowing beard of
> the patriarchs: he would be able,
> if he would speak of this
> time, he
> would be able
> only to babble and babble,
> again and again.[27]

Elsewhere, in the collection *From Threshold to Threshold* (1955), he wrote more explicitly:

The words that you speak—
you thank
destruction.[28]

The poet cannot speak, and yet he must speak. He speaks in a damaged medium, a medium that can no longer carry its message. The trope of the Viennese *fin de siècle* has become the identifying sign for the language of the Jew as poet.

Adorno's dictum, however, was in no way limited to the language of the Jews. For him, all poetry written in the false poetic discourse of the postwar world was doomed to failure. Celan's answer was to preface one of his poems in *Nobody'srose* with the quote from the Polish poet Marina Zwetajewa that "all poets are Jews" (85). Thus the silence ascribed to the Jews is turned about and made the universal of poetic discourse. Celan stated this in 1958, in the speech he made when he accepted the literary prize of the city of Bremen, when he said that "language remains unlost, in spite of everything. But it must transcend its own inanswerability, its own horrible silence, its thousand darknesses of death-bringing speech."[29] Silence is not the specific attribute of the language of the Jews but rather the quality that forms all poetry after Auschwitz.

The rejection of the particularity of the language of the Jew as poet is to no little degree the rejection of the enforced particularity of the language of the Jews as carried out by the Nazis. The experience of the language of the Jews as productive rather than destructive gives the poet as Jew (and the Jew as poet) the ability to undertake the writing of poetry. And yet there remains the inherent double bind. The experience of the Jews is at once particular to the Jew who has survived the camps, who has heard German used by the camp guards and the response of the Jews in a spectrum of languages including German. It is, however, also universal. The inherent meaninglessness of the world of the camps and its babble of tongues had to be given meaning by the poet. The experience of the Holocaust and its statement had to be understood as a universal rather than as yet another example of Jewish particularism. The curse that the Jews spoke and thought differently was turned into the claim that the particular fate of the Jew was the ultimate fate of all humanity. The language damaged in the Holocaust was the universal language of humanity, not merely the language of the Jews. The rebirth of Hebrew in Israel was no antidote.

Celan is representative of an attempt to externalize the sense of difference inherent in being treated as a "bad" (i.e., mute or without language) Jew in the camps into a universal of human experience. His roots are in a world in which the sense of a special language of the Jews was inherent in the daily realities of life in the former Austrian imperium.[30] It was a conglomerate of national languages where the pressure upon linguistic minorities was immense after the dissolution of the empire in 1919. Celan stemmed from a world in which the language of culture was German; of the state, Romanian; of daily life, Yiddish; of religion, Latin and Hebrew; and in which Hungarian was heard on the streets as often as the Slavic tongues of Poland and the other new Eastern states. The sense of identity as a Jew became closely linked with the unraveling of this maze of languages. Speaking a "Jewish" language set one apart. The answer was to see in the very mix of languages the claim to a universal position beyond the confines of all national languages.

Thus the Holocaust continued many of the older models of the "hidden" language of the Jew and added to them the image of the silence, the muteness, of the Jew. Like the older tropes about languages, this image is taken from a discourse that has no specific relationship to the Jews and is perceived as a special quality of the Jews. Jewish writers after the Holocaust, like those before it, must prove their ability to command a common literary discourse. But after the Holocaust, they must claim their right to speech, for incorporated in the image of the silence of the Jew following the Holocaust is the silence of the dead, the myriads who indeed were robbed of language, identity, and life and whose mute presence haunts the survivor.

In texts written by American Jewish writers after the Holocaust, the image of the fractured discourse of the Jews, of Jews' silence after the Holocaust and the writer's need to conquer it, reappears at one remove from the historical realities. Cynthia Ozick prefaced her 1977 story "Usurpation" with the statement, "It came to me that if only I had been able to write . . . in a Jewish language— Hebrew or Yiddish, or, say, the Ladino spoken by ibn Gabirol's descendants—it would have been understood instantly."[31] This is the need for a "Jewish" discourse, a discourse unblemished by the Western charge of the damaged discourse of the Jews and redolent of an intact, fictional world of Jewish discourse before the Holocaust, the world of ibn Gabirol. Ozick is a writer who has attempted to recreate a "Jewish" discourse in American prose fiction similar to that of Henry Roth. This illusion of a "speaking" Jew, a Jew who is able to possess her own discourse, unpolluted by the charges brought against the Jews' language, is central to her construction of an American Jewish discourse.

Quite at the other end of the pole of a "Jewish" identity in post-Holocaust America from Ozick, who created a religious identity for herself to define herself as a Jew, is Anne Roiphe. In her *Generation without Memory* (1981), Roiphe, a thoroughly assimilated "ethnic" Jew, attempted to recreate the world of language of which she was no longer a part.[32] For her a central "part of the Jewish experience is language" (195). But the Jews' language is either the "mysterious" Hebrew, which is "in part like a child's made-up language, more wonderful because it is private and marks the speaker as a member of select group," or the "vulgarity" of Yiddish, a vulgarity associated with her parents' rejection of Yiddish. Roiphe sees herself shut out of this world of language: "I don't speak either Hebrew or Yiddish. I am a provincial, caught in a modern time, a prisoner perhaps of limited education" (81). Forgetting the past, forgetting the language of the past, is the great fault of American Jewry. This language acquires value only after the Holocaust. The romance of the language of the Jews, part of the loss of meaning for Roiphe, becomes one with the destruction of those Jews who spoke the forgotten language of the Jews.

The demand to reconstruct and understand the "hidden" language of the Jews in the light of the Holocaust is also the demand to avoid "self-hatred":

> This taboo had its legitimate base in the desire not to deliver ammunition into the hands of the anti-Semitic enemy. It was originally not paranoia, but group protectiveness. The trouble with this taboo is that it crossed, clashed, with equally strongly felt modern demands on the modern writer, the artist, the journalist, to tell the truth as one sees it about one's world, becoming a witness to the universal experience by examining honestly one's own space. (198)

What Roiphe sees is the conflict within the writer, the artist, the journalist—the aesthetic double bind perceived within the manipulator of language. Self-hatred exists linked to the discourse of the Jew about the Jew. Self-hatred is part of the examination of the damaged language of the Jew, of the English-language equivalent to the Hebrew "romance" and the Yiddish "vulgarity" of the language of the Jew. Self-hatred is the language of the Jew as author of books in English about the strains of the American Jewish experience. This "taboo" subject was the very origin of Roiphe's own book. Following an article about the presence of a Christmas tree in her home, published in the *New York Times*, there was a vituperative outpouring against her. Her position as an assimilated Jew became, according to her critics, that of the self-hating Jew. Roiphe is trapped in the double bind that results from her simultaneous needs to understand her position as a Jew in a society that labels itself heterogeneous and to understand herself as a "survivor" of the Holocaust: "Our particular relatives having been desperate or hopeful enough, we escaped the Holocaust" (11). Roiphe's struggle with her sense of the "different" language required by the Jew, and the relationship of this language to the role of an author who considers herself "Jewish" in the post-Holocaust world, mirrors the confusion of older models of the Jew with contemporary ones. The struggle with these confusions marks many of the writers of the post-Holocaust period. Their attempts to create worlds of words that draw this confusion into perspective will be our concern in this chapter.

II
The Language of Survival and the Projection of Self-hatred

From the world of the survivor as author, I have selected four writers who share certain common features. All shifted from their "original," pre-Holocaust language to another tongue as their literary mode of expression and focus on the "hidden" language of the Jews at one point or another within their writing. They represent two quite distinct generations: an older one, who experienced the charges about the hidden language of the Jews as part of the anti-Semitic rhetoric associated with the Holocaust, and a younger one, whose experience of the Holocaust itself was as children and who learned of the "secret" language of the Jews from daily experience. All of these writers translated their understanding of the "hidden" nature of their own discourse, magnified by their having moved from one language of experience to another language of narration, into a discussion of the language of "good" Jews and "bad" Jews. In this mode of projection, it is the "bad" Jew, the Jew as different, whose language is damaged, who is mute, who is the antithesis of the "good" Jew, the Jew as author in the cultured language of the West.

No writer of the post-Holocaust era has captured this sense of the relationship of the language of the Jews to the development of a literary identity better than Elias Canetti. Born in 1905, he exemplifies the post-Holocaust writer whose roots in the linguistic confusion of the Austro-Hungarian Empire served as the mainspring for his creative effort. For like Celan, Canetti is the Eastern Jew articulating the understanding of the fate of the Eastern Jew through his literary works. And yet Canetti is the Eastern Jew with a difference, for Canetti's first language was not Yiddish but Ladino, or Spaniola, the language of the Iberian Jews exiled in the fifteenth century, who settled throughout the Mediterranean basin. The center of Canetti's preoccupation with language and its function is embodied in his autobiography. His relatively small literary production and his major work on the nature of crowd psychodynamics can serve as glosses on his autobiography.[33] And this autobiography, now in three volumes, serves as the most detailed account existing in post-Holocaust letters of the formation of a Jewish identity out of an incorporation of the special language of the Jews. The first volume of Canetti's autobiography, *The Tongue Set Free* (1977), begins with an epiphany, the earliest memory of childhood, which is indelibly linked with language, sexuality, and violence:

> My earliest memory is dipped in red. I come out of a door on the arm of a maid, the floor in front of me is red, and to the left a staircase goes down, equally red. Across from us, at the same height, a door opens, and a smiling man steps forth, walking towards me in a friendly way. He steps right up close to me, halts, and says: "Show me your tongue." I stick out my tongue, he reaches into his pocket, pulls out a jackknife, opens it, and brings the blade all the way to my tongue. He says: "Now we'll cut off his tongue." I don't dare pull back my tongue, he comes closer and closer, the blade will touch me any second. In the last moment, he pulls back the knife, saying: "Not today, tomorrow." He snaps the knife shut again and puts it back in his pocket.
>
> Every morning, we step out of the door and into the red hallway, the door opens, and the smiling man appears. I know that he's going to cut it off, and I get more and more scared each time. That's how the day starts, and it happens very often.[34]

The image, as he is able to reconstruct it later, is of his nanny, a Bulgarian woman who was brought to tend him as a two-year-old while the family was on holiday at Karlsbad. The threat of the loss of language, of the linguistic castration of the child, haunts all of Canetti's later works. For Canetti saw himself at home in a language—Ladino—that he equated with the security of the family. Bulgarian, here represented by the threats of the nursemaid's lover (she herself only spoke Bulgarian), is the language of the outsider. And for Canetti, Ladino is equivalent to his own sense of the discourse of Jewish identity, at least in his retrospective recreation of his own childhood:

The loyalties of the Sephardim were fairly complicated. They were pious Jews, for whom the life of their religious community was rather important. But they considered themselves a special brand of Jews, and that was because of their Spanish background. Throughout the centuries since their expulsion from Spain, the Spanish they spoke with one another had changed little. A few Turkish words had been absorbed, but they were recognizable as Turkish, and there were nearly always Spanish words for them. The first children's songs I heard were Spanish, I heard old Spanish *romances;* but the thing that was most powerful, and irresistible for a child, was a Spanish attitude. (5)

Here the division between the extended family and the image of the mother already begins to segment the identity of the writer. For the German of the mother's enthusiasms is the language of culture, and this becomes one counterpole to the image of the threatening world about the child. The world in which Canetti finds himself also possesses a "magic language." (This is his own formulation.) It is Hebrew, and Canetti associates Hebrew with the distanced world of ritual and family observance rather than with institutional observance or political identity. When he was a young boy the family moved to England. Thus Canetti learns English in a local grammar school, and yet another layer is added to the associations of language with self, for in England the author recalls his first childhood relationship to the opposite sex and the death of his father. Language becomes the web in which the author sees himself captured. He wonders whether he does indeed have a true identity or whether his world, like that of his maternal grandfather, consists of fragments of reality:

He tried to speak to all people in *their* language, and since he had only learned these languages on the side, while traveling, his knowledge of them, except for the Balkan languages (which included his Ladino), was highly defective. He liked counting his languages off on his fingers, and the droll self-assurance in toting them up—God knows how, sometimes seventeen, sometimes nineteen languages, was irresistible to most people despite his comical accent. I was ashamed of these scenes when they took place in front of me, for his speech was so bristling with mistakes that he would have been flunked by Herr Tegel in my elementary school, not to mention our home, where Mother corrected our least errors with ruthless derision. On the other hand, we restricted ourselves to four languages in our home, and when I asked Mother if it was possible to speak seventeen languages, she said, without mentioning Grandfather: "No. For then you know none at all." (87)

Reality for Elias Canetti in the 1970s is closely connected with the truth of language. His great puzzle is how a true identity can exist separate from a "pure" language. Canetti sees himself as having consciously grown out of an amalgam of Ladino, German, Hebrew, and English (with Bulgarian thrown in for good measure). This combination assured him of being perceived, and of perceiving his world, as cosmopolitan. This is the very charge brought against the Jews by the anti-Semites Canetti fled when he left Austria for England in 1939.

Canetti limits this application of the image of the polyglot Jew to a positive one, the image of the writer as a young European. He places in a central position in this first volume of his autobiography an image of disgust that encapsulates and projects his unarticulated sense of displacement:

> A train was standing there, it was stuffed with people. Freight cars were joined to passenger cars; they were all jammed with people staring down at us, mutely, but questioningly. "Those are Galician— — —," Schiebl said, holding back the word "Jews" and replacing it with "refugees." Leopoldstadt was full of Galician Jews who had fled from the Russians. Their black kaftans, their earlocks, and their special hats made them stand out conspicuously. Now they were in Vienna, where could they go? They had to eat too, and things didn't look so good for food in Vienna.
>
> I had never seen so many of them penned together in railroad cars. It was a dreadful sight because the train was standing. All the time we kept staring, it never moved from the spot. "Like cattle," I said, "that's how they're squeezed together, and there are also cattle cars. . . . But I stood transfixed, and he, standing with me, felt my horror. No one waved at us, no one called, they knew how unwelcome they were and they expected no word of welcome. . . . I wanted the train to start moving, the most horrible thing of all was that the train still stood on the bridge. (110)

The Eastern Jews, the Yiddish-speaking Jews, are inarticulate. They are essentially different. They are animal-like. What Canetti wishes to mirror in this passage, of course, is not the nature of the Jews but the treatment of the Jews which causes them to become the way they are. And yet the images that he incorporates are exactly those of the mute Jews on their way to the death camps. It is impossible to read this passage, set in Vienna during the First World War, and not see projected over it the newsreel images of the freight cars packed with Jews on their way to the death camps. The very force of the image demands this association. Canetti thus distances himself from the Eastern Jew, as different both from the Western "man of culture" that he has become and from the survivor that he undoubtedly is.

At the close of this first volume Canetti records how he became a writer. Choosing a neoclassical theme, he composed a tragedy in heroic verse. In this manner he adopted the cultural values of the West, of his mother's image of the correct world, and repressed the Eastern Jew within. The degree of this repression is complete. Canetti records that he had great difficulty in school learning shorthand:

> I was used to the existence of different languages since my childhood, but not to the existence of different scripts. It was annoying that there were Gothic letters along with the Latin ones, but they were both alphabets in the same realm and the same application, fairly similar to each other. The shorthand syllables introduced a new principle. (230)

The image of a world comprising numerous languages but only one alphabet is of a world devoid of Jews. At least two, if not three, of the languages to which Canetti was exposed as a child were written in Hebrew script (Hebrew, Ladino, and Yiddish). The image of a foreign script as magical and undecipherable again relates the internalized image of the Jew as something foreign to the special nature of the Jews' language, a language that is hidden, uncultured, essentially mute.

This image is carried through into the second volume of Canetti's self-exploration. Here Canetti contrasts the muteness of the Eastern Jew with the new language of the Jew which permits him to become a "real" writer, that is, a writer within the strictures of the Western image of the use of language. Canetti presents the image of the Eastern Jew Backenroth:

> I never knew his first name, or else it has slipped my mind. He was the only *beautiful* person in our laboratory, tall and slender, with very bright, deeply radiant eyes and reddish hair. He seldom talked to anyone, for he knew almost no German, and he rarely looked into anyone's face. But if he *did* ever look at you, you were reminded of young Jesus as he is sometimes

shown in paintings. I knew nothing about him and felt timid in his presence. I knew his voice; he spoke Yiddish or Polish to his two fellow Galicians. And when I noticed him talking, I automatically drew closer, in order to hear his voice, though I understood nothing. His voice was soft and strange and extremely tender, so that I wondered whether it was the twittering sounds of Polish that feigned so much tenderness. But his voice sounded no different when he spoke Yiddish. I told myself that his, too, was a tender language, and I was no wiser than before.[35]

The male Eastern Jew is a feminized pet. Only the sounds of his inarticulateness make him seem tender, not the meaning. His physiognomy reminds Canetti of the antithesis of the Eastern Jew, of Western religious art. But this figure with but half a name becomes a fascination for Canetti and his "Russian friend from Kiev," Eva Reichmann. She, too, is an assimilated Jew who spoke Russian at home and then went to school in Czernowitz, where she learned German. She speaks no Yiddish. "I had the impression that this language was as alien to her as it was to me; she regarded it neither as something special, nor with the tenderness one feels toward a language which is about to vanish" (188). Inherent in the image of Yiddish is the Holocaust looming in the future for the persona in Canetti's work but central in his reconstruction of this lost world. Neither Canetti nor his friend dares to speak to this "beautiful" but mute object. Neither admits to possessing a language with which he or she could possibly communicate with him:

> "But in what language?"
> "That's not hard. I can communicate with people who don't know a word of German. I learned that from my grandfather."
> She laughed: "You talk with your hands. That's not nice. It doesn't suit you."
> "I wouldn't do it normally. But that's how we'd have broken the ice. Do you know how long I've been wanting to talk to him?" (190)

The world of the grandfather, the polyglot world which does not possess a true language, the gestures of the Jews, their overt language—all are seen as potentially providing a key for unlocking the secret of communicating with Backenroth. At that moment the head of the laboratory in which they all work comes in and solemnly announces: "Herr Backenroth poisoned himself with cyanide last night. . . . He seems to have been very lonely. Didn't any of you notice anything?" (191). The Eastern Jew's silent, self-imposed death by cyanide (one of the means of murder in the death camps) causes guilt and anger in Canetti: "When I hear her sentences again in my memory, the sentences whose strange tone enchanted me, I feel anger, and I know that I failed to do the one thing that would have saved him: instead of toying with her, I should have talked her into loving him." This level of displacement reveals Canetti's creation of a surrogate self, the non-Yiddish-speaking Eastern Jew as the female Other, onto whom he places the guilt for not having cared enough to have saved the Eastern Jew, the inarticulate Jew. Had he but served as this Jew's voice, had he given him language, he would have been saved. It is thus his guilt but also that of the Eastern Jew. For his death is self-inflicted, the result of his rejection by the Westernized Jew. The key is hidden within the language of the Eastern Jew. It is the language of death, of silence, of the Holocaust. But it is also a parochial language, the language of the *Eastern* Jews, the language of a world that the Ladino-speaking (but German-writing) Canetti sees as distinct and different from himself.

The true language, the universal, nonparochial language of the Westernized Jew, is, however, not German. German is but the surrogate for that true language implicit in the title of the second volume of Canetti's autobiography, *The Torch in My Ear*. The Torch is Karl Kraus's one-man periodical, and Canetti becomes Kraus's adept during his year in Vienna. Canetti's creation of his "true" and universal language, the answer to the confusion of tongues about him (and their identification with his own Jewish identity), is the rejection of language as spoken medium and the emphasis on Kraus's sense of language as something to be listened to. The ear of Canetti's title stresses the false objectivity that he ascribes to the listening subject:

> And since the issue was the combination—in all variants—of language and person, this was perhaps the most important dimension, or at least the richest. This kind of hearing was impossible unless you excluded your own feelings. As soon as you had put into motion what was to be heard, you stepped back and only absorbed and could not be hindered by any judgment on your part, any indignation, any delight. The important thing was the pure, unadulterated shape: none of these acoustic masks (as I subsequently named them) could blend with the others. (220)

This "school of hearing" removed the speaking Jew from his world; he became the passive, listening Jew, reveling in the universal ability to analyze and dissect. Nothing could be hidden; nothing could be understood as special or private. Everything was open to analysis, to understanding. Canetti's analysis of his own coming to this awareness is his mode of distancing his complex relationship to this lost world, the world of childhood, the world of the destruction of the Holocaust. He cannot simply present the Eastern Jew as the internalized image of the self as Other but rather must incorporate into this image the realities of this world that has vanished. He presents as an answer his "school of hearing." Language becomes only the object of study, not the medium for analysis. But it is clear that Canetti listens to himself speak. He speaks in German, a language that mirrors both the universalism of Karl Kraus's Vienna and the particularism of the Vienna of Adolf Hitler, with its stress on the special nature of the Jews' language. Part of this special nature is the acidic criticism, the destructive analysis, always associated with the literary language of the Jews. Thus the very act of hearing, modeled after a Jew who saw himself as but another member of the Western intellectual world, Karl Kraus, becomes a positive reconstruction of the anti-Semite's understanding of the particular nature of the Jews' language. Canetti's choice of German as his medium of communication during his long exile in England placed him squarely within the double bind present in the image of the language of the Jews.

The alternative position does not provide any better resolution to this dilemma. Arthur Koestler, who was born in Budapest in 1905 and died in London in 1983, moved from the intellectual world of Kraus's Vienna to that of postwar Britain with seemingly greater ease.[36] Koestler's major works, such as his coming to terms with his communism, *Darkness at Noon* (1940), and his numerous works on the moral and scientific dilemmas of postwar society, all avoid any direct discussion of Koestler's own Jewish identity. Koestler had been involved in Zionist politics as a student at the university in Vienna and had made his first trip to the Near East in 1926. It was only after his disillusion with communism that he again saw in Zionism some type of ideological answer to the political persecution of the Jews. In his novel *Thieves in the Night* (1946), which was to be the first volume of a trilogy of the rise of political Zionism, he began a detailed portrait of the position of the Jews in the Middle East during the 1920s and 1930s. But Koestler portrayed the figures in the novel as inherently unable to act, as able only to react. Indeed he sees these Jews as self-hating Jews: "I do not even love my people. I rather dislike them. Self-hatred is the Jew's patriotism."[37] The response to this novel (and to his history of Zionism, *Promise and Fulfillment* [1949], written after the founding of the state of Israel) was immediate and telling. Koestler was identified with Joseph, the hero of his novel, and was branded a "self-hating Jew."[38]

Koestler's call for the radical assimilation of the Jews into the culture in which they found themselves or into the new integrated Jewish state (a state of Jews and Arabs) was keyed to the idea of language, for assimilated Jews spoke the national language of the country in which by historical accident they found themselves (as Koestler went from German to French to English), or they spoke Hebrew, stripped of all religious overtones. Joseph is condemned by the religious figures in the novel because although he has a very good command of the language, he does not have any knowledge of the religious tradition of the Jews, as he writes: "I became a socialist because I hated the poor; and I became a Hebrew because I hated the Yid" (279). In a later preface to the novel, Koestler summarized his view: "If power corrupts, the reverse is also true; persecution corrupts the victim, though perhaps in subtler and more tragic ways. In both cases the dilemma of noble ends begetting ignoble means has the stamp of inevitability."[39] The idea of the inevitable response of the Jews as victims internalizing their own persecution is the model for the self-hating Jew. Koestler, however, needs to separate this world of persecution and self-deprecation from the world of status in which he finds himself.

In 1976 Koestler published a major study of the Jews in the East entitled *The Thirteenth Tribe: The Khazar Empire and Its Heritage*.[40] The theme of the book is quite straightforward. Koestler argues that Eastern Jewry was not descended from the Diaspora of Jews from the Jewish kingdoms of the Near East but was the product of the conversion of a tribe of Oriental nomads. Koestler's argument places the Eastern European Jewish tradition as separate and unique from that of the Western Jew. It is evident from Koestler's long historical explanation that he associates this Eastern tradition with all of the barbarism inherent in the Western image of the East. In Koestler's work this is reified by his own association of this image with the Stalinist and post-Stalinist Soviet Union, the Russia of the gulags. It is a world of horror and brutality, and it was out of this world, rather than out of the world of Western civilization, that the Eastern Jew stemmed.

Koestler's greatest difficulty in making this point is that these Eastern Jews *seem* to be speaking a language that looks and sounds much like another Western language, German. It is, of course, the German that Koestler abandoned upon being freed from prison in Loyalist Spain and upon coming to England. For Koestler the history of Yiddish gives credence to his thesis concerning not only the Eastern origin of the Yiddish-speaking Jews but also how Jews acquire language (or at least how barbaric Jews acquire a barbaric language). Yiddish is one of the Jabberwockies that "the American grandchildren of immigrants from Eastern Europe . . . find rather comic." It evolved out of the domination of German culture in Poland and the primacy of German as a cultural language in the East in general:

> One can visualize a *shtetl* craftsman, a cobbler perhaps, or a
> timber merchant, speaking broken German to his clients,
> broken Polish to the serfs on the estate next door, and at home
> mixing the most expressive bits of both with Hebrew into a
> kind of intimate private language. How this hotchpotch became
> communalized and standardized to the extent which it did, is
> any linguist's guess. (156)

These Eastern Jews adopted the language of the culturally superior world about them: "Among the later immigrants to Poland there were also, as we have seen, a certain number of 'real' Jews from the Alpine countries, Bohemia and eastern Germany. Even if their numbers were relatively small, these German-speaking Jews were superior in culture and learning to the Khazars, just as the German Gentiles were culturally superior to the Poles." Eastern Jews are, by definition, culturally inferior to Western Jews. Indeed, these Eastern Jews are basically illiterate: "The evolution of Yiddish was a long complex process, which presumably started in the fifteenth century or even earlier; yet it remained for a long time a spoken language, a kind of *lingua franca*, and appears in print only in the nineteenth century. Before that it had no established grammar" (154). The manner of the growth of the language of the Eastern Jew is itself of interest: "Thus Yiddish grew, through the centuries, by a kind of untrammeled proliferation, avidly absorbing from its social environments such words, phrases, idiomatic expressions as best served its purpose as a *lingua franca*" (154).

Koestler's portrait of the special language of the Eastern Jews is an externalization of the charges brought against German-speaking Jews that their language was contaminated. The language of the Eastern Jew is a non-language. It grows by functioning as a parasite on the host cultures. It lacks any true structure, adapting itself to the needs of the moment. Needless to say, none of this has anything to do with the history of Yiddish, but it has much to do with Koestler's image of the inappropriateness of the Eastern Jew's language. Not only are there medieval Yiddish manuscripts that reflect the existence of a written tradition as early as that for many other European languages but the absence of a written grammar for Yiddish is paralleled in other European languages. Yiddish had a systematic grammar some forty years before Dutch, for example. But it is more important to note the cultural relativism that Koestler uses. People accept new languages because they are better than the old ones. Yiddish is the worst of all possible languages, since it is merely a shadow of German and is a "private" rather than a public language at that. Koestler thus distances himself from what was to a Hungarian Jew the language closely associated with the anti-Semite's image of the Jew, Yiddish, and relates Yiddish to another tongue, German, as only a pale and defective copy of a cultural language. All of this is perceived through the model of the value of language in defining the Jew, which he focuses through the experience of the Holocaust. Yiddish is defined by Koestler as the "popular language of the Jewish masses, spoken by millions before the Holocaust, and still surviving among traditionalist minorities in the Soviet Union and the United States" (152).

This view points to the underlying political agenda in Koestler's book and to the function that this agenda has in shaping his image of the Jew. For Koestler the textual history of the Diaspora Jews "is either not specifically Jewish or not part of a living tradition." The only answer to the paradox of the Jew is either "emigration to Israel, or gradual assimilation to their host nations." In Israel Hebrew had become the new language of the Jews, with the ideology of success (not of victimization) associated with it. And the image of the host nations refers back to this image of parasitism which Koestler has adapted from anti-Semitic rhetoric. For Koestler's radical solution is the result of his reassessment of Sartre's definition of the Jew: "The Jews of our day have no cultural tradition in common, merely certain habits and behavior-patterns, derived by social inheritance from the traumatic experience of the ghetto, and from a religion which the majority does not practice or believe in, but which nevertheless confers on them a pseudonational status" (198). The stigma that Koestler associates with the "old" Jew— the Jew as speaker of Yiddish, the Eastern Jew as cultural barbarian—is the stigma of the destruction of the Jews.

As a survivor not only from the horror of his own imminent execution at the hands of the Spanish Loyalists but of the Budapest Jewish community, Koestler sees his own intellectual integration into the cultural world of the West as the primary answer to his own sense of guilt. It is of little wonder that it is within this quite remarkable book that Koestler presents his most complex image of the Jew, the Jew as the essential outsider become insider. For when one asks where the assimilated, Hungarian-speaking Jewish community would fall in Koestler's division between "real" Jews (his term) and the Eastern Jew, it is clear that it would fall with the latter.[41] Koestler's story of the life and death of the Jewish state of the Khazars is the history of the Eastern Jew *in nuce*. It is the story of Koestler's own intellectual milieu and results, as does Canetti's, in the creation of a "bad" Jew, speaking at very best a "hotchpotch" rather than a real language. All of this is understood through the eyes of the post-Holocaust survivor, himself an Eastern Jew.

Two younger writers, Jerzy Kosinski, born in 1933, and Jurek Becker, born in 1937, both in Łodz, survived the Holocaust as children. Both chose to write about their experiences in a language other than their native Polish—Kosinski in English, Becker in German. In those of their works that deal with the image of the Jew and the experience of the Holocaust there is a clear attempt to answer the image of the "silence" of the survivor, to create a speaking Jew to rebut the mute Jew of postwar myth.

Lawrence L. Langer, in one of the first major studies of the texts that have examined the theme of the Holocaust, presented a detailed reading of Jerzy Kosinski's *The Painted Bird* (1965).[42] Let us put aside for the moment Langer's evident inability to distinguish between those works written by survivors, which attempt to shape their experience into a discourse that allows an explanation of their survival, and those written by authors who use the theme of the Holocaust as a means of commenting on the human condition. Langer's discussion of Kosinski makes two points that are of interest to us. First, *The Painted Bird* "is literally a speechless novel." In his comments on the novel, Langer quotes Kosinski: "Observation is a silent process; without the means of participation, the silent one must observe."[43] Second, Langer comments on the central character's "inability at first to speak or understand the local dialect, and perhaps chiefly . . . his appearance, for his swarthy skin and dark eyes mark him as a child of gypsy or Jewish origin (we are never told, nor does it matter)" (171). It does matter, of course; it matters in perceiving the function of the writing of the novel as a means of distancing and explaining the role of the survivor. The speechlessness that Langer senses in the novel, the absence of spoken passages, the inability to articulate ideas in a foreign tongue—all focus on the conclusion of the novel. Kosinski concludes the novel with his child hero restored to his family. He has him experience the world after the war, a world as incomprehensible as the world that he had survived. The child, mute, unable to speak in a world that has denied him language at all, finds that even the restoration to his family cannot provide the missing language for him. The conclusion of the novel, which is indeed the very beginning of the novel in terms of the perspective of the narrator, has the nameless child sent to a sanatorium in the mountains, where he learns to ski and, skiing alone, has an accident. He awakens from the accident months after it occurred:

> April sunshine filled the room. I moved my head and it did not seem to hurt. I lifted myself on my hands and was about to lie down when the phone rang. The nurse had already gone, but the phone rang insistently again and again.
>
> I pulled myself out of bed and walked to the table. I lifted up the receiver and heard a man's voice.
>
> I held the receiver to my ear, listening to his impatient words; somewhere a man like myself, who wanted to talk with me. . . .
>
> I had an overpowering desire to speak. Blood flooded my brain and my eyeballs swelled for a moment, as though trying to pop out onto the floor.
>
> I opened my mouth and strained. Sounds crawled up my throat. Tense and concentrated I started to arrange them into syllables and words. I distinctly heard them jumping out of me one after another, like peas from a split pod. I put the receiver aside, hardly believing it possible. I began to recite to myself words and sentences, snatches of Mitka's songs. The voice lost in a faraway village church had found me again and filled the whole room. I spoke loudly and incessantly like the peasants and then like the city folk, as fast as I could, enraptured by the sounds that were heavy with meaning, as wet snow is heavy with water, confirming to myself again and again and again that speech was now mine and that it did not intend to escape through the door which opened onto the balcony. (213)

This conclusion provides the entire voice of the novel. We have been listening not to silence but to speech, literary speech, of course, a convention, the first-person monologue, but to speech. We have not been isolated from the voice of the author, not exposed to the silence of the observer; quite the contrary, we have been listening to a living voice, the recaptured voice of the living witness. Kosinski sets out to record the experience of the child not in the form of a book but in the form of a monologue. This device enables him to give the child speech. The muteness of the child following the horrors inflicted upon him is the muteness of the survivor. Kosinski, unlike Celan, needs to restore the speech of his central character, and he does this in the conclusion of the novel. Speech, not the ability to write, is restored. Indeed, the mute child carries around with him a slate upon which he writes. This is his means of communicating with the world. The act of writing is thus simply a poor surrogate for "real" speech. The writing of books is merely a poor answer to the speechlessness of the survivor. The reality of the Holocaust comes when written language is converted into spoken language.

In *The Painted Bird* Kosinski gives us the illusion of speech, not its reality. But it is an illusion ascribed, as Langer quite correctly observes, to a nameless victim, portrayed as neither gypsy nor Jew. The victim is simply the child. Given Kosinski's rather late identification of himself with Jewry, an identification that came substantially after 1965, one must ask why the child remains unidentified. The simplest answer is that Kosinski wished to present a universal case, the child as victim, a child below the horizon of awareness of "Jewish" or "gypsy," the child victim. But if the recovered voice of the witness is the voice of the young adult bearing witness, he has created a fiction within the fiction. The witness, quite aware of the reasons for his persecution, turns his newly acquired speech to the task of providing an explanation for the horrors that the mute or speechless/languageless child experienced. Kosinski thus creates two personae: the speaking witness and the mute victim. Behind both looms the author, as Jew and as Pole, writing in English. In an early interview with George Plimpton, Kosinski stressed the distancing effect of moving from Polish, the language of experience, to English, the language of authorship: "English helped me sever myself from my childhood, from my adolescence. In English I don't make involuntary associations with my childhood. I think it is childhood that is often traumatic, not this or that war."[44] For Kosinski it is, of course, childhood that is identical with the experience of the Holocaust. The recovered voice is the new, uncontaminated voice of the American author. The world of the Pole and the Jew, of the muteness of the child and the spoken language of the witness, is distanced in the written text of the American author. The third level of the creation of the speaking Jew is reached, for Kosinski is able to distance both of his literary personae (the mute child and the Polish-speaking adult) as fragments of the "bad" Jew; he is able to create a new, English-speaking author, and it is this creation in his later works that has so perturbed contemporary critics.

In Kosinski's *Blind Date* (1978) the creation of the "new" Jew, the Jew as American writer, whom Kosinski calls Levanter (perhaps the man from the Levant, the wandering Jew), is the epitome of violence and destruction.[45] Themes from *The Painted Bird*, including the scene in which a cuckolded farmer gouges out the eyes of his wife's lover (and which is echoed in the closing passage of *The Painted Bird*), reappear in the image of an old man with his eye falling out in *Blind Date*. But what is most important, Kosinski returns to the image of the mute child. Levanter finds himself in a cab, and the cab driver reveals that he knew his family when Levanter was a child: "I saw him. He was crazy. No doubt about it." "As I remember him," Levanter said, "the kid was quite normal. . . . He was no crazier than you or I" (93). The irony is, of course, that it is Levanter commenting on himself as a child. But these moments, these epiphanies of a fictionalized reality, are held together by Levanter/Kosinski's telling of the story of his rape of a young woman and his eventual infatuation with her. The entire work, and indeed all of Kosinski's most recent work, is permeated with images of control and destruction. The victims are always women. Kosinski creates an image of the "new" Jew, the "good" Jew as the macho warrior. Thus the madness of the child, the image of the victim, becomes the "bad" Jew; the "good" Jew is the Jew as writer, for, like the image of the writer which looms over *The Painted Bird*, Kosinski creates a literary world, a world of words, in which he can shape the persona of the author as masculine and thus in control. He distances himself from his own history, creating for himself the image of the American author such as Ernest Hemingway or Norman Mailer.

Kosinski's pattern of creation illustrates one of the major problems with the double bind in which Jewish authors have found themselves. In accepting the image of what is the correct stance for an author and for a Jew from a society in which he perceives himself as an outsider, the survivor tends to use the text in a manner that may well undermine it. Thus when Kosinski comments on the "silence" of the witness or adopts the pose of the macho male, he is fulfilling the expectations of American society vis-à-vis the Jew. The first Jew is clearly the Jew as victim, the Jew robbed of language through the Holocaust. The victim is needed by the post-Holocaust world as a means by which to assuage the sense of guilt at having survived. Kosinski's child survives and recaptures speech to assure us of his survival. The macho pose is the alternative fantasy to the image of victim. It is the "super-Jew," the Jew as warrior, as the new Israeli, not the Jew as woman, as the essential victim. But here, too, there is a necessary distance. For Kosinski is not the "new" Jew, the Jew as warrior, but rather the American Jewish author who lives out all of his fantasies of superiority within the all too safe world of the text.

If the world of *The Painted Bird* is the world of the author as survivor, then the world of Jurek Becker's first novel, *Jacob the Liar* (1969), is the world of the victim.[46] Becker, who spent his childhood in the Łodz ghetto and then in the camps at Ravensbrück and Sachsenhausen, learned German in East Berlin. Like Kosinski, he writes in his adopted tongue. His first novel centers about the image of the Jew as victim coping with the world of the Holocaust. The eponymous hero, Jacob the Liar, invents the existence of a radio in the ghetto of the small town in which he lives. The radio becomes the source of hope for all those who are without hope. Jacob, who adopts a small child whose parents are deported, is torn between the lies that give comfort and the realization of the eventual destruction of himself, the child, and their world. In an extraordinary moment in the novel he takes the child into the basement, where she believes the imaginary radio to be hidden, and recreates, from behind a screen, a "fairy-tale" hour for her. The world of wholeness, of the normal, is recreated in the lies of Jacob, but they are lies that he consciously knows only ameliorate the world in which he and the child find themselves.

Becker, like Kosinski, has taken one of the strongest myths about the discourse of the Jew, the image of the lying Jew, and reversed it. Jacob lies as a means for survival, not out of any inborn desire to lie but because of the force of circumstance. In retelling the story of Jacob, Becker is forced to create a new discourse for the Jew, at least for the speaking Jew in the novel. He employs a narrator to retell the tale of Jacob's lies, but it is a narrator who is himself creating a tale, not the story of the heroism of the martyrdom in the camps (a literary perspective common to novels on this theme written in the German Democratic Republic), but the tale of the creation of a moment of near sanity through lies in a world gone mad. The success of Becker's undertaking can be measured in the very fact that the speaking Jews in Becker's novel are given a discourse that, for postwar German critics, seems to be an accurate reconstruction of the discourse of the Jew. Becker's use of the German literary devices, such as the intonation of the narrative voice, as well as the "local color" (through the conscious absence of any Yiddishisms) of the Łodz ghetto, creates, for the German reader, the impression of the speaking Jew. Becker's success in this undertaking permits the living Jew, the narrative voice, to recount the events of the "lying" Jew and thus give proof of his ability to command both a "Jewish" discourse and a "German" one. Kosinski's need to distance himself from the firsthand experiences of the Holocaust is paralleled by Becker's creation of a literary discourse for the survivor within German. The act of writing attempts to distance the charge of the silence of the Jews while putting to rest yet another calumny, the image of the lying Jew.

Becker's attempt to mirror the world of the victim, of the dead, in *Jacob the Liar* succeeds because we are confronted with the living voice of the narrator at the conclusion of the novel. The pendant to *Jacob the Liar*, Becker's *The Boxer* (1976), is a much more complicated novel; it presents the world of the child not as victim but, as in Kosinski's first novel, as survivor.[47] Like *Jacob the Liar*, *The Boxer* depends on the voice of the narrator to place the reader in a specific relationship to the world of the survivor, the created images of the "good" Jew and the "bad" Jew, of the acceptable solution and the unacceptable one to the problem of bearing witness. The plot of *The Boxer* is fairly straightforward. Aron Blank, who calls himself Arno to avoid being again identified as a Jew, has survived the camps and is searching for his son, Mark, who, before the Germans invaded, had been living with his divorced wife. He finds a child called Mark in a hospital for displaced children and identifies him as his missing child, even though the last name is not correct. He raises the child in the turmoil of postwar Germany, living, as did Becker and his father, in the Soviet zone of Berlin. The tale shows the shaping of both father and son by the postwar experience. Emblematic for this experience is the title vignette. The boy is beaten up by a group of toughs, and his father decides to teach him how to box. The new Jew, Arno, needs to have the tools to deal with the new world, tools that Aron lacked. The relationship between father and son, however, deteriorates as the boy grows up. Eventually Mark leaves home, wanders the world, and dies fighting as a Jew during one of the Arab-Israeli conflicts. The novel closes with the narrator, who had reconstructed Arno/Aron's and Mark's story from his interviews with Aron, becoming aware that Arno's fate was determined through his survival and that surviving can be as much of a hell as were the camps.

Becker's presentation of the survivor as victim and as the "new" Jew is yet another restructuring of the image of the writer. The pseudo-Yiddish tone of *Jacob the Liar* (which has been compared with Shalom Aleichem's romanticized reconstructions of *shtetl-life*) presented one language for the speaking Jew. It was not *mauscheln* but the intonation of the Yiddish speaker, an intonation that has its roots as much in the literary tradition of Jewish narrative presented by the premier Christian novelist of the German Democratic Republic, Johannes Bobrowski, and his *Levin's Mill* (1964) as it does in Yiddish.[48] The investigatory tone of *The Boxer* is quite different. The tone is taken from the world of socialist realism, of the narrator as investigative reporter. But the theme reported is quite the same: the special language of the Jews, the death of the Jews' language in the world of the camps. When Arno/Aron first meets Mark he asks: '"Did anyone tell you who I am?' The child says: 'No.' 'I am your father. . . . Then you are my son,' Aron says. 'Do you understand?' 'No.' For a few minutes Aron could not understand what Mark could not comprehend. The directress of the hospital had not said a word that he was *meschugge*. He said: 'What don't you understand?' 'That word.' 'What word?' 'The one you said.' 'Son?' 'Yes'" (64–65). The word son does not exist in Mark's world, since for as long as he can remember he has not been a "son," only a child. What is most striking about this moment in the narrative is that the author's use of indirect discourse embedded in the direct dialogue between father and putative son, a discourse that is to reveal to us the inner working of Arno's mind, is characterized by the use of a Yiddishism, one that is clearly part of German slang but in spite of this is also self-evidently Yiddish.

Arno is the Jew as survivor; his son, the child who must develop a new persona. The father's world is determined by his camp experience; the son's is also, but he at least has the potential for some independent growth and change. After Mark leaves, he writes his father a long letter explaining his action. The core of the letter is his charge that his father's silence had made any relationship between them impossible: '"You can say that I never spoke to you about this as long as there was a chance. Then I must charge you with having raised me to silence. I know that you are a rather intelligent person, I am evidently one also. Why then did we never speak about these important matters? It wasn't my fault that I can only guess what is going on in your head. I never heard from you'" (285). The silence is the silence between generations, but it is also the silence of the Jew as survivor.

Aron is unable to respond. He never answers any of his son's many letters. For seven years Aron receives his son's letters, one a month until June 1967, when the letters cease. What puzzles

Aron is how his son had become a Jew, a Jew who would live on a kibbutz and die fighting for Israel. Who could have "made a Jew out of him?" he wonders. Does not one have the right to choose? "A child of Catholic parents can choose when it comes of age freely to remain or not remain a Catholic. Why then, he asked me, are the children of Jewish parents denied the same right?" (298). But being a Jew denies the possibility of free will. The narrator presents Aron's questions as impossible, and he avoids the most evident of answers. Mark "becomes" a Jew, a "new" Jew because his father remains an "old" Jew, a silent Jew, a Jew condemned to the world that followed the camps. Mark's attempts to "speak" to his father through his letters and Aron's inability to respond are the metaphor for the difference.

Becker claims to incorporate many of his own wartime experiences into his fiction.[49] In an interview given during the late 1970s, Becker speaks about his father's search for him following the war, when he was seven. He reports that his earliest memories stem from this period. After he was found by his father, they went to live in the Soviet zone of Berlin for "reasons which I can only guess. For he would never speak to me of them" (11). Unlike the protagonists of his novel, Becker remained in East Berlin with his father until his father's death in 1972. His sense of identity was as a Jew in the new Communist state. He observes that "he does not know what the signs are which mark one as being Jewish. I know that others claim to identify such signs. I hear that a Jew is one whose mother is Jewish. . . . A human being is one who has human beings for parents, no more, no less" (13). While Becker rejects the particularism of any religious identification as a Jew, he sees himself within a larger literary tradition.

At the conclusion of this interview he observes that after *Jacob the Liar* appeared, reviewers placed him in the tradition of Shalom Aleichem and I. B. Singer. He had, however, only been exposed to Shalom Aleichem in the highly sanitized stage version of his work *Fiddler on the Roof* and had never read any Singer at all. "Now I can imagine, that someone will say after this bit of information: 'See, there we have it! It's the Jewishness in you which the critics recognize. And whether you admit it or not, it's there.'" Becker concludes by observing that perhaps there is a modicum of truth in this: "I don't feel myself as a Jew, but am one in a hundred ways. And so? Why should I try to solve this riddle? Would I be any the wiser? I am afraid not. I am afraid that I would uselessly try to solve the secret, a secret without which my life would be poorer" (18). The secret that Becker senses behind his "Jewish" identity, his identity as a Jewish writer, or at least a writer in a Jewish mode, is the secret language of the Jews, the overcoming of the curse of silence, of his father's silence, and his ability to write this silence out of existence in the fantasies of his prose. For he kills his alter ego, Mark, in defense of a Jewish world. Mark becomes the ideal of the "state of peasants and workers," the German Democratic Republic's motto, by working as a "peasant" (Aron's word) on a kibbutz, and he dies in the defense of that world, just as the heroes of all good socialist realistic novels are programmed to die in defense of the socialist fatherland. *The Boxer*, with its complex narrative mode, its mode of retelling, but a retelling, not through the spontaneous flow of language mirrored in the fiction of *The Painted Bird*, but through the probing voice of the questioner, is the exorcism of the silence of the father as Jew and the Jew as father.

Canetti and Koestler, Kosinski and Becker, form a most disparate group. Indeed, what relates them is their projection of the specific qualities of the discourse of the Jew onto a specific image of the Jew, the Jew as survivor. In some cases this alter ego is glorified, in others it is condemned. In all cases this fictional discourse is distanced from the world of the author, from the choice that he has made to move from a language contaminated with images of his inability to deal with the world of his own survival to the language that mirrors his new persona, that of the writer. Yet throughout the works written by this new persona in this new language there is the echo of the old, the world of the damaged discourse of the Jew. It reappears when the author turns to the image of the Jew as Other or self, for it is embedded in his unconscious reception of this image within the European Jewish experience.

All of these writers, whether writing in English or in German, reflect the older, direct model of internalization and projection. They take the charges made about the hidden or damaged discourse of the Jew and ascribe them to figures present in the world they believe themselves to have left behind, Jews belonging to the fictive world of their creators' former discourse. By shifting his language, the "self-critical" Jewish writer posits the negative image of the Jew in the world that he has left. The damaged discourse of the Eastern Jew in the works of Canetti and Koestler and the muteness of Becker and Kosinski's children are but further projections of the internalized image of the writer's own discourse. What remains is a world, admittedly within the fictions of the writer, in which the discourse of the Jew, damaged as it may be, is localized and distanced.

III

The Dead Child Speaks: Reading The Diary of Anne Frank

No single document written during the Holocaust riveted the attention of the Western reading public more than the diary kept by Anne Frank and published in extract by her father, Otto, in 1947.[50] Translated from the original Dutch into French in 1950, these extracts were initially read by a relatively small audience. Even the 1950 German translation had no resonance. It was only with its publication in the United States in 1952 that the diary was brought to the attention of a wider reading public. The English stage adaptation in 1955 inspired a republication of the German translation by the house of S. Fischer, and this caught the imagination of the German reading public. The German critic Philipp Wiebe, writing in the socialist *World of Work* in 1955, summarized the German response to the discovery that the Jews murdered in the Holocaust were not passive and silent about their fate: "When we read the publisher's note about her dreadful death, we feel a true pain about the tragic fate of this young Jewess, who, through her jottings, has become better known to us than our sister."[51] The Western reading public, in Germany as well as in the United States, came to measure the Holocaust through its identification with the individual fate of Anne Frank. Untangling the reading of this text presents some extraordinary complications, complications resulting from the fragmentary nature of *The Diary*'s publication as well as from its reception in the light of its dramatization. Anne Frank provided a ready-made definition of the Jew as author, and the Jewish author as mute victim after the Holocaust.

The complexity of reading *The Diary of Anne Frank* can be measured by its function in any number of studies of the Holocaust written by German Jewish survivors during the late 1950s. Theodor Adorno, in an essay on the reconstruction of the past, used an anecdote concerning the dramatization of *The Diary* to show the limitations of texts in uncovering the true nature of the Holocaust and its origin. He reports that he had been told of a woman in Germany who had seen the production of the stage version of *The Diary* and had said afterwards, deeply moved: "Yes, but *that* girl at least should have been allowed to live."[52] Adorno sees this as a tentative first step to an awareness of the nature of the Holocaust, but an awareness that, "although it seems to trivialize the dead," is limited by its focus on a single case and avoids any search for the cause of the tragedy. What Adorno does not read into this response is the inherent ambivalence of the statement, for it is possible to read it as stating: "We were in general right to kill them, but in this specific case we should have behaved differently." Adorno, himself a survivor who escaped Germany in 1934, sees here as faulty the focus on the individual as the means of escaping any search for the true roots of the Holocaust. He also shows how the Germans remain unmoved even by this individual fate to examine their own basic attitudes toward the Jews. George Steiner, in his essay on the "hollow miracle," echoes this view: "True, German audiences were moved not long ago by the dramatization of *The Diary of Anne Frank*. But even the terror of *The Diary* has been an exceptional reminder. And it does not show what happened to Anne inside the camp. There is little market for such things in Germany."[53] The drama based on *The Diary* provided the audience in Germany as well as throughout the Western world with a living victim. It provided the resurrection of one of the dead witnesses of the Holocaust, one who spoke and thus broke through the silence attributed to the victim.

The relationship between *The Diary* and the play is important for understanding the movement of the text from the world of the text to that of "realistic illusion," the world of the theater. It also provides the frame for one of the most striking images of the "self-hating" Jew to be found in post-Holocaust writing. In 1950 the Jewish-American writer Meyer Levin read the French translation of the diary. Levin, a lifelong Zionist, in 1931 had authored the first English novel dealing with the kibbutz movement. Convinced that *The Diary* was the living witness to the Holocaust, "the voice from the mass grave," he reviewed it in the *Congress Weekly*, the organ of the American Jewish Congress, and his review led to the publication of the English translation by Doubleday.[54] Levin thus received permission from Anne Frank's father, Otto, to write the stage adaptation.

When the dramatization was finished, it was passed on to the producer, Cheryl Crawford, who rejected it, at least in part on the advice of the dramatist Lillian Hellman, as unplayable.[55] The project eventually passed into the hands of Kermit Bloomgarden, who, again with the advice of Hellman, commissioned the husband-and-wife team of Frances Goodrich and Albert Hackett to write a new adaptation of *The Diary*, which was performed in 1955 and won the Pulitzer Prize. Starring Susan Strasberg, it was the hit of the 1955/56 Broadway season. In 1959 Millie Perkins was cast as Anne

Frank in George Stevens's film version of the play, with Joseph Schildkraut as Otto Frank. The success of the film imprinted the figure of Anne Frank as the image of the victim on international awareness. The motion picture, with all of its sense of the need for a commercial success among groups other than Jews, maintained the sanitized version of Goodrich and Hackett and added to it many of the banalities of Hollywood's post-Holocaust image of the Jew as victim. Anne Frank becomes a positive figure through being the essential victim in a manner parallel to that of the figure of Noah Ackerman (played by Montgomery Clift) in Edward Dmytryk's 1958 film of Irwin Shaw's *The Young Lions* or Danny Kaye's comic S. L. Jacobowsky in the film version of Franz Werfel's *Me and the Colonel* (1958). Jews are victims—positive victims but victims nevertheless. This short history of the creation of the dramatization is of importance only in that it sets the stage for one of the most complex creations of a projection of self-hatred by a twentieth-century Jewish writer. From 1953 to 1957 Meyer Levin instituted a series of lawsuits against the producer of the play as well as Otto Frank. In January 1958 Levin was awarded fifty thousand dollars in damages.

Levin's struggle with *The Diary*, a text that had a central position in his understanding of the Holocaust in the history of Western Jewry, and his projection of the "bad" Jew formed the basis for a novel, *The Fanatic* (1964), and the second volume of his autobiography, *The Obsession* (1974). The first volume of his autobiography, *In Search* (1950), ended with the founding of the state of Israel; the second volume, initially entitled "The Manipulators," dealt exclusively with *The Diary* and his role in presenting it to the world. This autobiographical text is remarkable, for, like Elias Canetti's memoirs, it is as much an attempt to provide a reading of a series of actions as it is an attempt to present them. The "frame" of the autobiography is Levin's psychoanalysis, which is aimed at his trying to understand the basis for his "obsession" with the diary. Levin sees his exclusion from participation in the presentation of *The Diary* to the living world of the theater as the result of a plot on the part of the German Jewish Communist intelligentsia. He focuses on Lillian Hellman, born in New Orleans of German Jewish ancestry, blacklisted under McCarthy, and one of the most visible representatives of American liberalism on the Broadway stage, as the essential "bad" Jew. He sees her as manipulating *The Diary* to stress its "international" rather than its specifically Jewish character. His dramatization of the diary was unacceptable, he believes, because it was "too Jewish." The "bad" Jew, that Jew which Levin wishes to distance from himself, is the German Jew, the international Jew:

> It was true . . . that although Otto [Frank] was entirely unpre-
> tentious, something of the aristocratic manner remained,
> despite even the experience of Auschwitz—and, nasty as this
> seems—I must put down that even on that day there arose in
> me a faint doubt as to his view of me, a doubt that I once
> suppressed with shame, as being due to my early Chicago preju-
> dices against German Jews, who persisted in their superiority-
> attitude toward us *Ostjuden* from Poland or Russia. . . . To this
> day I accuse myself of this counter-prejudice against German
> Jews, yet I cannot rid myself of the feeling that I am seen by
> them as a Yid. (42–43)

Levin uncovers the fact that the Franks were indeed a wealthy, highly assimilated family in Frankfurt before they emigrated to the Netherlands. Indeed, he further discovered that they were related to the Straus family (which owned Macy's) and that Otto Frank had spent a year in New York working for them. The German Jewish conspiracy is thus complete.

Levin's need is to mold Anne Frank and her text into a "Jewish"—that is, anti-assimilationist—model, for he sees in the assimilation of the German Jews, of Frank herself, a fault that can only be rectified by a return to his own sense of what is appropriate for the witness to the torment of the Jews. Frank must be made to speak as a Jew, and Jews, having been treated as different, must see themselves as positively different. The "Hellman-Hackett" version of *The Diary* (as Levin refers to it throughout the text) stressed the universalism of Anne Frank. Thus their text altered a passage that stressed the difference of the Jews ("Who has made us Jews different from all other people? . . . If we bear all this suffering and if there are still Jews left, when it is over, then Jews, instead of being doomed, will be held up as an example.") into one that stated their representative function as victims ("We're not the only people that've had to suffer. There have always been people that've had to . . . sometimes one race . . . sometimes another.") (29–30). For Levin this alteration, which made Anne Frank the representative of yet another example of humankind's inhumanity to humans rather than of specifically German persecution of the Jews, smacks of the assimilationist tendency that views him as merely a "Yid." The world of the German Jew is corrupt and degenerate. Levin reproduces this image in great detail in his best-known work, his novelization of the Leopold-Loeb murder case, in which he presents the world of Chicago's German Jewish community as one that produces unmotivated murders not unlike those of Nazi Germany. *Compulsion* (1956) was a work that he hoped would "show what those overproud German Jews, with their superiority and their exclusiveness, were like" (110).

Both the Hackett dramatization of *The Diary of Anne Frank* and Levin's seemed to present antithetical readings of a text in the light of two models of the Jew present in Eisenhower's America. The first was of the Jew as child, as victim, like all other children, like all other victims. The only answer to this image was the liberal answer: humanity must eliminate all suffering, and such suffering, too, would vanish. How? The underlying theme of the drama is certainly not a Marxist one. There is no intimation that anti-Semitism (or indeed any other persecution) is the result of a decaying world of capitalism. Rather the audience is left with the vague feeling that something must be done, even if no program is presented. Levin's reading presents a program. It is through the strong identification of Jews as political and religious Jews, defined in the light of the newly realized political ideal of Zionism, that such horrors can be prevented from happening again. *The Diary* itself, or at least the fragments that have been published, presents a mix of both views. But Levin's selective reading of these fragments reveals strikingly his wish to label Anne Frank as the "good" Jew, and thus the "good" Jew as writer, and his parallel wish to see in Hellman the "bad" Jew as writer.

One of the central proofs that Levin brought in his court suit against the Hacketts was the use of a specific scene placed at the conclusion of the second act: "Here, now, was the Chanukah scene, just as I had placed it, as the climax at the close of the second act. Anne, extremely excited, hurrying about distributing her little gifts, the excitement mounting and mounting—something seemed wrong to me. The way they had done it was more like Christmas" (121). Indeed, the Chanukah celebration is so presented in the Hacketts' play. But what is the parallel in the diary itself?[56] On December 7, 1942, Anne Frank records that Chanukah and St. Nicholas's Day fell almost together. Chanukah was celebrated, but "the evening of St. Nicholas's Day was much more fun." In December 1943 there are five separate entries recording her joy at the coming of St. Nicholas's Day and Christmas. It is on St. Nicholas's Day that good little boys and girls are rewarded with gifts, while bad children receive coals in their shoes. Anne Frank was typical of assimilated Jews, who adopted Christian religious observations without any religious overtones in lieu of a Jewish religious celebration. Both versions of the play thus create a speaking Jew, and being Jewish, at least in the world of the theater, is tied to the image of religion, if not to religion itself. The language that Anne Frank is made to speak is stage English, just as her diary was written in literary Dutch, so there is no specific linguistic marker for her identity.[57] She does not speak with a Jewish accent, does not mix bits of Hebrew in her discourse. The authors, no matter what their political persuasion, must give her some type of identification as a Jew. For the illusion is that the Jewish dead of the Holocaust are made to speak. This is, of course, merely an illusion. The dead remain mute; the living revivify them for their own ends.

Early in his recounting of his involvement with the dramatization of *The Diary*, Meyer Levin cites one authority whose work on the pattern of survival has become a standard in the past decades. Bruno Bettelheim, born and educated in Vienna, was incarcerated in Dachau and Buchenwald during 1938 and 1939. His study *The Informed Heart* (1960) was his attempt to see the Holocaust as an outgrowth of modern society. He views the inability of the Jews to respond to the world of the camps as merely another manifestation of the dehumanization of modern technological society. As early as 1943 Bettelheim expressed this view in one of the first psychological studies of the Nazi persecution of the Jews. But it was only in 1960, after the tremendous success of the dramatization of *The Diary of Anne Frank*, that Bettelheim produced a monograph on the Holocaust, a monograph that contained a study of *The Diary*. In it Bettelheim criticizes Otto Frank for putting his family into hiding and maintaining, in their hiding place, the idea that life must continue "as nearly as possible in the usual fashion."[58]

Bettelheim castigates the Franks for not hiding individually or providing themselves with weapons to resist their (for Bettelheim) inevitable discovery and deportation. Bettelheim's criticism of the reception of *The Diary* is aimed at those who wish "to forget the gas chambers and to glorify attitudes of extreme privatization, of continuing to hold onto attitudes as usual even in a Holocaust" (247). He sees the popularity of the book as a part of the denial "that Auschwitz even existed. If all men are good there was never an Auschwitz" (249). This is the final line of the Hacketts' dramatization. Meyer Levin cites Bettelheim as his authority on survival, since he survived the camp experience. He sees him as the "good" survivor whose work exposes the "bad" survivor, Otto Frank, whose actions caused the death of the "good" Jew, Anne Frank (39). Similarly, George Steiner sees in Bettelheim's study the inner truth of the Holocaust because of his claim to authentic personal experience: "Fiction falls silent before the enormity of the fact, and before the vivid authority with which that fact can be rendered by unadorned report" (389). Indeed, Bettelheim himself, in his 1979 collection of essays pointedly called *Surviving*, republished his 1960 essay "The Ignored Lesson of Anne Frank."[59] It becomes clear that Bettelheim too is responding to the "speaking" Anne Frank of the drama, at the conclusion of which she says, in a disembodied voice, "In spite of everything, I still believe that people are really good at heart." "This improbable sentiment is supposedly from a girl who had been starved to death, had watched her sister meet the same fate before she did, knew that her mother had been murdered, and had watched untold thousands of adults and children actually being killed. The statement is not justified by anything Anne actually told her diary" (250). Bettelheim implies that he knows that the opposite must have been true—that Anne Frank must have lost her individuality in the camps, that she, too, must have been dehumanized. Of course this is as much a subjective reading as that of the Hacketts.

Bettelheim's pessimistic reading of Anne Frank's fate is needed by him to explain her failure to survive. Indeed, in the 1960 essay, Bettelheim compares Anne Frank's diary with the autobiography of another survivor, Marga Minco, whose *Bitter Herbs* appeared in 1960.[60] Bettelheim is appalled at the "universal admiration of [the Franks'] way of coping, or rather of not coping. The story of little Marga who survived, every bit as touching, remains totally neglected by comparison" (250). It is the living survivor, Bettelheim himself, who is neglected, while the voices of the dead continue to haunt him. Bettelheim's reworking of the earlier excursus on Anne Frank in this later essay repeats many of the earlier claims. It lays directly on the doorstep of the "play and movie" the denial of the realities of the Holocaust: "If all men are good at heart, there never really was an Auschwitz; nor is there any possibility that it may recur" (251). Bettelheim has created in his image of Anne Frank the source of the denial of the Holocaust, of the father as the "bad" Jew, of the speaking witness as the lying witness.

In January 1959, while Bettelheim was writing his long essay on Anne Frank, a German schoolteacher named Lothar Stielau was charged with disseminating anti-Semitic propaganda. Stielau, a member of a neo-Nazi party in Lübeck, had claimed that *The Diary of Anne Frank* was a fabrication, created to defame the German people. Stielau's claims had been published in the party's newspaper in December 1958. He saw in *The Diary* a mix of sentimentality and pornographic sexuality aimed at showing the German people in the worst possible light. Stielau charged that the Holocaust, as portrayed in *The Diary*, simply had not happened. The court ordered him dismissed from the civil service and removed from his position in the school system. But this was in no way the end of the anti-Semites' denial of the reality of *The Diary*. In the United States in 1967 an essay repeating most of the charges made against *The Diary* appeared in what had become a shadow of H. L. Mencken's *American Mercury*. The author, Teressa Hendry, labeled *The Diary* a "fiction" and dismissed it as part of the libel against the Germans.[61] In 1979, the same year in which Bettelheim published his collection *Surviving*, Ditlieb Felderer published a slim monograph entitled *Anne Frank's Diary: A Hoax* with the virulently anti-Semitic Institute for Historical Review in California.

Felderer presents an interesting case. An Austrian Jew born in 1943, he emigrated to Sweden, where he became a convert to the Jehovah's Witnesses, who sent him to Germany after the war to document the Nazi crimes against their members who were persecuted as pacifists. His pamphlet on *The Diary* is one of the most widely circulated of the revisionist documents. Recently, in an appearance in Ithaca, New York, he further revealed his own indebtedness to the rhetoric of self-hatred. He wrote in a letter composed in his idiosyncratic English to the editor of the *Cornell Daily Sun* (March 13, 1985):

> Just as [there have been letters] . . . against censorship when that censorship applies to Zionist books like the faked "Anne Frank Diary." . . . When these methods are used against so-called "Jews" its McCarthyist horror. When they are used against "Nazis" it becomes a wonderfully moral exercise.
>
> I have been to study the Auschwitz camp 27 times. My forensic and archaeological studies revealed that there were no gas chambers for killing humans. Much of the camp is faked. I believe much of the testimony against Mengele is equally fabricated. Most of his accusers look quite healthy. I think Dr. Mengele was probably a humanitarian physician. The Khazars want us to believe that he is totally guilty based solely on Khazar "survivor" testimony.

Felderer's rhetoric in this text (as well as in his attack on *The Diary*) recalls the ancient charge that "Jews lie"! But these Jews are a special subgroup who have created the charge of genocide against the Germans—the Eastern Jews. Using Arthur Koestler's image of the Eastern Jews as false Jews, being merely converts, and associating this charge with the new Jewish discourse of the Zionists (into which he places *The Diary*), Felderer shields himself from the charge of being a lying Jew. He is the truthful Jew, the Jew as investigatory scientist, who reveals to all his special place within the world of the anti-Semite. He is neither a Khazar (a false Eastern Jew) nor a Zionist—he is the persecuted Jew, the Jewish anti-Semite.

Felderer's arguments, while more detailed than the others, are not very different from Stielau's and Hendry's. All were widely reported in the American press. The basis for all their charges was Meyer Levin's lawsuit against Otto Frank and his claim to have written the authentic version of *The Diary*—for the stage! This claim was twisted into a claim that Levin actually wrote *The Diary*: "*The Diary of Anne Frank* . . . has been sold to the public as the actual diary of a young Jewish girl who died in a Nazi concentration camp after two years of abuse and horror. . . . Any informed literary inspection of this book would have shown it to have been impossible as the work of a teenager" (27). So says Hendry, but this is the central thesis of all of the anti-Semitic readings of *The Diary*.

All of these accounts make detailed reference to Levin's court case and interpret the findings of the judge for Levin as "proof" of the fictionality of *The Diary*. Hendry calls *The Diary* fiction labeled as fact. Thus *The Diary* is for the anti-Semites further proof of the lying discourse of the Jews. Jews lie, and they lie to profit themselves through the claims of their own annihilation in their creation of "fictions" about themselves. Seen in this light, *The Diary of Anne Frank* is yet another failed Jewish novel. It fails because it is not a "real" representation of the hidden language of the Jews but rather a literary work that any "informed literary inspection" would reveal as a work of fiction written within non-Jewish literary conventions. Thus part of Levin's response to the struggle he has with his own Jewish identity is the fact that he has undermined the veracity of *The Diary* as testimony. In claiming to have authored the only valid reading of *The Diary*, he cast the veracity of the diary into doubt. This is Levin's implicit reading, which is then internalized and projected onto everyone involved with the dramatization of the work. It also becomes part of the readings of *The Diary* during the 1960s. What is clear is that the anti-Semitic readings of *The Diary* are but continuations of older charges of the dissimulation of the Jews. Since *The Diary* comes to have a central role in defining the nature of Jewish discourse, the pollution of its interpretation by the anti-Semitic reading causes the figure of Anne Frank to assume a central role in projections of Jewish self-doubt.

This is especially the case with *The Diary*'s role in defining the damaged discourse of the Jew as a force in shaping the identity of the writer who perceives him- or herself as Jewish.

The confusions surrounding the Jewish readings of *The Diary of Anne Frank* are examined and explained in the work of Philip Roth.[62] Roth's fascination with the double bind situation present within American Jewish identity dominates his writing. Beginning with his collection of short stories, *Goodbye, Columbus* (1959), which won the National Book Award for fiction, Roth comments on the decline of American Jewry under the pressure of the "American way of life." His early ideal for the Jew seems to be the introspective writer *manqué*, like the hero of the title story of that collection, the writer who has yet to prove himself but who separates himself from the commercial world of bourgeois Jewish values. The confusion that reigns among his early characters can best be judged in his tale "Eli, the Fanatic," from *Goodbye, Columbus*. The eponymous hero of the tale confronts the Jew in the form of a group of Eastern European Jews who come to settle in a suburban community. Their dress calls attention to them and thus, in the minds of the local Jews, to the idea of the Jew itself. Eli is sent to persuade the newcomers to change their appearance, their outer sign of identity, which they are quite willing to do. He, however, becomes obsessed with the idea of their difference and assumes their castoff garments, becoming a parody of those whose identity as Jews had so frightened and fascinated him.

According to Roth, *Goodbye, Columbus* earned him the label of "being anti-Semitic and 'self-hating,' or at least, tasteless."[63] This attitude was compounded, if anything, when Roth published *Portnoy's Complaint* in 1969. Peter Shaw, the associate editor of the Jewish conservative periodical *Commentary*, concluded his review:

> But if he has not been bad for the Jews, he has decidedly been bad to them—and at the expense of his art. For *Portnoy's Complaint*, in descending to caricature to get its effects, fails at the very point of imagination which raises a novel above a tract. Roth has been a positive enemy to his own work, while for the Jews he has been a friend of the proverbial sort that makes enemies unnecessary.[64]

Labeled as a "self-hating Jew," a label that arose to characterize the psychopathology of assimilation as represented by the discourse of acculturated Jews, Roth incorporated this charge in his fiction. If the author who writes about Jews in a critical manner is "self-hating," then one manner of dealing with this image is to create a persona, the author labeled as "self-hating Jew," in one's own fiction. Roth begins, in a trilogy about the Jewish-American novelist Nathan Zuckerman, to explore the psyche of a Jewish writer identified as writing like a Jew, but a negative Jew, a "bad" Jew, a "self-hating" Jew. Roth explores this psyche, as he had in *Goodbye, Columbus*, with the tools of the social critic, irony and satire. Zuckerman is not Roth or even a Roth surrogate; he is what his readers expect the author of *Portnoy's Complaint* to be. In a sense Roth creates a figure based on the paradigm of the Jew that he rejects: *"Jews are people who are not what anti-Semites say they are.* That was once a statement out of which a man might begin to construct an identity for himself; now it does not work so well, for it is difficult to act counter to the ways people expect you to act when fewer and fewer people define you by such expectations."[65] Roth wishes to explore how the author labeled "self-hating" arrived at his identity. He reverses the image and seeks after the definition of the Jews as people who are not what Jews say they are. He has more than adequate information to construct a "self-hating" identity for Nathan Zuckerman.

Nathan Zuckerman is one of the most complex representations of the Jew as author in modern prose fiction. He first appears in Roth's work as a character in the fiction of Peter Tarnopol, the protagonist of Roth's *My Life as a Man* (1974). Zuckerman is the literary figure whom the author Tarnopol uses to project all of his internalized sense of the "pain of life," having Zuckerman suffer, in the stories, from inexplicable migraines. The use of a character created by a fiction to represent the confusion between life and art, between the charges made in American society about being a Jew and a writer and their embodiment within the work of art, raises the problem of self-hatred and its relationship to the "damaged" discourse of the Jew to a new level of analysis. Roth sees the problem as one with the myths of Jewish identity imported from Europe, myths that are inappropriate to the formation of the identity of the American Jew, especially the American Jew as writer. He gives the reader the ultimate confusion between life and art, the confusion that he has his character's character, Zuckerman, experience quite against his logical perception of the world in the course of the trilogy.

The education of Nathan Zuckerman is portrayed in Roth's novel *The Ghost Writer* (1979).[66] In this novel Zuckerman meets the Jewish-American short story writer E. I. Lonoff, viewed as a "quaint remnant of the Old World ghetto" whose "fantasies about

Americans" some thought "had been written in Yiddish some-where inside czarist Russia" (13). Lonoff lives as a recluse in New England, married to a woman whose ancestry reaches back to the American Puritans. He divides his time between teaching at a women's college and drafting and redrafting his "brilliant cycle of comic parables" (17). Lonoff is the Jewish writer as establishment figure. Zuckerman arrives as a newly published author in 1955 to convince Lonoff to "adopt" him as his protégé. In Lonoff's home he meets Amy Bellette, who is ostensibly cataloguing Lonoff's papers for the Harvard Library, where they are to be deposited. A former student of Lonoff's and now his lover, Bellette is revealed in the course of the writer's fantasies to be Anne Frank, who survived the death camps and eventually came to the United States.

The juxtaposition of Anne Frank and Nathan Zuckerman to Lonoff provides Roth with the context in which he defines the Jew as writer. Anne Frank's central position in this definition is height-ened by Roth's use of the label "self-hating" for Zuckerman even at this very early stage of his career. Nathan has written a tale of the interfamilial squabbles over the inheritance left by one of his aunts. He sees the story as portraying the strength of character of some of the individuals involved as well as the pettiness of indi-viduals placed in a society without rigid ethical standards. His parents, especially his father, see the story as an attack on all Jews as moneygrubbing. He sees "himself and all of Jewry gratuitously disgraced and jeopardized by my inexplicable betrayal" (85). His father turns to a remote family acquaintance, a judge who had helped his son get into the University of Chicago, for advice. The judge writes Nathan a long letter, with an appended questionnaire, that points to the potential misuse of his work by a "Julius Streicher or a Joseph Goebbels" (91). The letter ends with a postscript: "If you have not yet seen the Broadway production of The Diary of Anne Frank, I strongly advise that you do so. Mrs. Wapter and I were in the audience on opening night; we wish that Nathan Zuck-erman could have been with us to benefit from that unforgettable experience" (90). It is the drama based on The Diary that defines Anne Frank. It is the image of the speaking, living witness, the dead come to life, the dead never having died, that provides the emotional clue to the inner life of the American Jew as critic.

Judge Wapter is the "bad" Jew; he attempts to manipulate Nathan by equating his world with that of Anne Frank, by equating the American Jewish experience after the Holocaust with that of Europe. Roth sees these two worlds as inherently different, sepa-rated not only by the difference in the structures of society but by the very occurrence of the Holocaust. In the United States the Holocaust, through its commercialization in works such as the dramatization of *The Diary of Anne Frank*, has provided all Jews with a homogenous history. Roth sees the need to provide autonomy for each individual's experience, to reverse Bruno Bettelheim's view that the camps were the ultimate loss of autonomy in a mass age. The dramatization of *The Diary* provided a history for all American Jews that was distant from their own private terrors. Zuckerman's father demands that Nathan respond to the judge's letter, but Nathan refuses:

> "Nothing I could write Wapter would convince him of anything. Or his wife."
> "You could tell him you went to see *The Diary of Anne Frank*. You could at least do that."
> "I didn't see it. I read the book. *Everybody* read the book."
> "But you liked it, didn't you?"
> "That's not the issue. How can you *dis*like it? Mother, I will not prate in platitudes to please the adults." (95)

The Diary of Anne Frank is the true experience, the Jew as writer in an appropriate discourse; it is the drama that provides the clue to the middle class's expropriation of fears that are not their own. What happened to the Jews of Europe a decade before became the pattern against which Roth's American Jews, those who so freely wield the label of "self-hating Jew" against the writer, measure themselves. But it is a trivial model; it is the world of the commercial theater or film, not the reality of Belsen, that defines their identity. Thus when Roth recounts to Lonoff Amy Bellette's admission that she is Anne Frank (and his seduction by her), it is in terms of the drama. She goes to New York from Boston to see "the dramatization of Anne Frank's diary":

> It wasn't the play—I could have watched that easily enough if I had been alone. It was the people watching with me. Carloads of women kept pulling up to the theater, women wearing fur coats, with expensive shoes and handbags. I thought, This isn't for me. . . . But I showed my ticket, I went in with them, and of course it happened. It had to happen. It's what happens there. The women cried. Everyone around me was in tears. Then at the end, in the row behind me, a woman screamed, "Oh, no." That's why I came running here. . . . And I knew I couldn't when I heard that woman scream "Oh, no." I knew then what's been true all along: . . . I have to be dead to everyone. (107–8)

It is evident even to Lonoff that she is creating a fiction, indeed a fiction patterned after her mentor's own stories. She recounts her life as Anne Frank, how she survived Belsen as a mute and passive child, how she took the name Bellette from *Little Women* (creating herself as a literary character), how she discovered her father's publication of her diary in an old copy of *Time* in a dentist's office, how she ordered and received a copy of the Dutch original. Roth's reading of *The Diary* through the eyes of Amy Bellette reveals the work as one of unselfconscious self-analysis, but a book that received its force through the writer's death: "But dead she had something more to offer than amusement for ages 10–15; dead she had written, without meaning or trying to, a book with the force of a masterpiece to make people finally see" (127). Roth plays this found work of art off against the craft of the play. And he, too, uses the example of religious celebration.

> As for celebrations, she had found St. Nicholas's Day, once she'd been introduced to it in hiding, much more fun than Chanukah, and along with Pim made all kinds of clever gifts and even written a Santa Claus poem to enliven the festivities.
> . . . How could even the most obtuse of the ordinary ignore what had been done to the Jews *just for being Jews*, how could even the most beknighted of the Gentiles fail to get the idea when they read in *Het Achterhuis* that once a year the Franks sang a harmless Chanukah song, said some Hebrew words, lighted some candles, exchanged some presents—a ceremony lasting some ten minutes—and that was all it took to make them the enemy. (124, 126)

Roth makes language, the Hebrew of the liturgy, into the means by which Amy Bellette defines the world of Anne's Jewishness. The "Jewishness" of the drama rings false in Roth's presentation, since it is the most superficial identification with Jewish ritual rather than with Jewish ethics. The Franks' Chanukah, in Roth's eye, is quite parallel to the Jewish wedding presented in the title novella of *Goodbye, Columbus*. It is ritual language without meaning.

It is not simply that Roth sees in the silence imposed on Anne Frank, on her role as the dead author speaking, the misreading of her text. Roth parallels the fate of Lonoff's two "children": Anne, the woman who seduces him, and Nathan, the man who wishes to become his "son." Nathan's upbringing is thus strikingly parallel to that of Anne:

In fact my own first reading of Lonoff's canon . . . had done more to make me realize how much I was still my family's Jewish offspring than anything I had carried forward to the University of Chicago from childhood Hebrew lessons, or mother's kitchen, or the discussions I used to hear among my parents and our relatives about the perils of intermarriage, the problem of Santa Claus, and the injustice of medical school quotas. (14)

Zuckerman's attraction to Anne, the idea of being "Anne Frank's husband," has some of its roots in his identification with her understanding of herself. Both see themselves as Jews in terms of the minimal identification with the special language of the Jews—not Hebrew, the language of liturgy, of the annual visit to the temple, but the Yiddish-tinged language of the Jewish writer, Lonoff. Lonoff becomes all Jewish writers for Zuckerman. He becomes (in Zuckerman's analogy) Kafka as well as Babel. And when he fantasizes Amy into the role of Anne Frank, a role that she created for herself out of the stuff of Lonoff's fictions and the Hacketts' play, he sees her as Kafka's "K": "Everything he dreamed in Prague was, to her, real Amsterdam life. . . . It could be the epigraph for her book. 'Someone must have falsely traduced Anne F., because one morning without having done anything wrong, she was placed under arrest'" (148). Anne is a fiction of Amy in Zuckerman's world. She is a fiction that Zuckerman wishes to use to prove that he is not a "self-hating" Jew: "Oh, marry me, Anne Frank, exonerate me before my outraged elders of this idiotic indictment! Heedless of Jewish feeling? Indifferent to Jewish survival? Brutish about their well-being? Who dares to accuse of such unthinking crimes the husband of Anne Frank!" (148).

For at this point, at the close of Roth's novel, Zuckerman knows that Amy is not Anne. "When the sleeve of her coat fell back, I of course saw that there was no scar on her forearm. No scar; no book; no Pim" (145). Amy's fiction of Anne Frank enables Zuckerman, the "self-hating" Jew, to perceive that his voice can be one apart from the fragments of European history that make up the world of Anne Frank. No scar, no book, only theater. The voice of the poet, of Lonoff as the master craftsman, is likewise revealed to be dry and cramped, destructive of art as much as the bourgeois theater in which *The Diary* is played. Zuckerman can go on to examine that world in which he has found himself, that world, according to Roth, of social accessibility and moral indifference, where one cannot always figure out what a Jew is that a Christian is not.

In Roth's reading of *The Diary of Anne Frank* the model of

self-hatred incorporated in American consciousness, based on the analogy of the American experience with that of Europe, is drawn into question. Bettelheim, Steiner, and, indeed, even Meyer Levin accept the polar definition of the "self-hating" Jew, one who internalizes the charges of anti-Semitic rhetoric, specifically about the nature of his own language, and projects these charges onto others labeled as Jews. For Bettelheim the villain is Otto Frank; Levin sees in him the same villain, the "bad" Jew, but for quite different reasons. Roth takes the idea of the Jewish writer in post-Holocaust American society as his theme. He wishes to examine how the very process of internalization and projection works in forming the consciousness and identity of his prototypical "Jewish" writer, Nathan Zuckerman.

Roth's point of departure is his fictionalization of the double bind in which writers such as Bettelheim, Steiner, Adorno, and Levin found themselves when "reading" *The Diary of Anne Frank*. They saw the work, especially when presented as a play or a movie, as a resuscitation of the Jew as victim, without acknowledging that such an action would draw into question the very role of the survivor. This double bind situation, the survivor's confrontation with the survival of the victim, a victim seemingly better able than the survivor-witness to articulate the horror of the Holocaust, becomes the stuff of Roth's fiction. In the education of Nathan Zuckerman, in his confrontation and fantasy about Anne Frank, is the very stuff of the double bind of contemporary readings of *The Diary of Anne Frank*, distanced through the use of satire and understood as part of the European inheritance that shapes the identity of the American Jewish writer. Roth wishes to distance himself from the world of Nathan Zuckerman, from the world of the Jew who internalizes the charge of the silence of the Jew as victim and the special role assigned to the articulate Jew as witness, the Jewish author as the creator of his own undamaged discourse. In the various readings of *The Diary of Anne Frank* one can see the function of such a text, especially in its form as play and movie, in providing the matrix for a discussion of the appropriate language of the Jew as survivor.

IV

The Language of the Mad

Of all of the models of the damaged discourse of the Jew found in the literature after the Holocaust none seems more all-pervasive than that of the language of madness. While this image of the Jews' discourse has been dismissed as merely the reflection of the incomprehensibility of the Holocaust as represented by the survivor's inability to adapt to the postwar world, the actual language ascribed by Jewish writers to the mad in their texts reveals the roots of this image as much deeper and more telling than has been imagined. We know that the roots of the image of the Jew as mad, as possessing a damaged discourse, are to be found in the pseudoscience of nineteenth- and early twentieth-century racist biology. This image was internalized by some Jewish writers and projected onto the assimilated Jew as the essence of the "bad" Jew through the development of the category "Jewish self-hatred." With the rise of the Nazi state and its reification of the image of the Jew as "diseased" or "mad" and through the creation of structures, such as the concentration camps, which parodied "medical" structures such as asylums, the Jew began to react against the very association of Jews with the concept of madness. With the Holocaust Jewish writers began to explore the association of Jewishness and madness, specifically the label "self-hatred," as a means of categorizing a specific madness of Jews.

The theme of the Jew as mad haunts much of post-Holocaust writing. It represents an attempt by writers who know that their discourse is unimpaired even though consciously Jewish to deal with the fancy that Jews are mad, because of their inherent nature, because of their shared experience, or because of their survival. Jewish writers in America begin to examine the charge of the difference of the Jew from the standpoint of the discourse ascribed to the Jew, the discourse of madness. The post-Holocaust understanding of madness is heavily colored by Freudian models of insanity, according to which madness is reflected in the language of the mad. These writers accept the basic premise that madness is reflected in the impaired communicative function of their characters and that this impairment is understood by their fictional characters and the world about them as somehow related to their Jewish identity. These writers use the theme of the "crazy" Jew to explore the dynamics of how Jews internalize a mad world. Using the mechanics of modern psychology, they examine the universals of human response to an incomprehensible world in the light of the attribution of this response as a typically "Jewish" one. Tied into their autopsy of the theme of the damaged discourse of the Jew is an examination of the "self-hating Jew" as one who believes the charges that the world has lodged against the Jew. The Jewish writer in the act of writing disproves the charge of the damaged nature of the Jews' discourse. In the fictions that are created one of the central themes is the exploration of this charge and an examination of how this belief becomes part of the deformation of Jewish identity following the Holocaust. The act of writing sensibly about mad Jews becomes the writer's proof of the intactness of the writer's Jewish identity.

The first major literary analysis of the implications of the nature of the Jews' madness as mirrored in a case of "self-hatred" came from the world of American Yiddish writing. Israel Joshua Singer, born in Bilgoraj, Poland, in 1893, the son of an Orthodox rabbi, had established himself in Warsaw following the First World War as one of the most rigorous of Yiddish realists. In 1933 he emigrated to America, where most of his great epics of Jewish life in Europe were written. His *The Brothers Ashkenasi* (1936), published simultaneously in Yiddish and English, assured him a major position in American Jewish letters, both Yiddish and English.[67]

I. J. Singer spent the 1930s and 1940s in America, observing events in Europe from the perspective of a Yiddish writer in American exile and safety. At the point when the first information about the Nazis' "final solution" for the Jews began to spread throughout the Allied nations, Singer turned to a re-creation of the now lost world of the German Jew as a means of understanding his own survival as an Eastern Jew in America. He began to explore the thread of the madness of the Jew as a means of understanding the Jewish response to the German experience. In his last major work, published shortly before his death in 1944, Singer explores the disease of self-hatred as a means by which Jews internalize the charge that they are essentially different, that they possess a damaged perception of the world. In doing this, Singer distances his own growing sense of alienation from a world in the process of destruction, the world of Yiddish culture, whose cultural intactness had provided a platform for his observations.

I. J. Singer's *The Family Carnovsky* (1943) appears to suffer even more than most novels of the early 1940s that presented contemporary events from a myopia imposed upon it by its place and time of creation. Read superficially, the work seems an attack on the German Jews for having brought the Holocaust upon themselves (and others) through their apostasy. Is this novel, given its date of composition and the bias of its author in favor of traditional Eastern European values, merely a crude tract against assimilation and intermarriage? Is it the vengeance of the *Ostjude* against the *Yeke*, the German Jew, for real or imagined slights?

Singer chose to recount the history, not of an indigenous family of German Jews, but of a family of Eastern Jews who emigrate to Germany in search of the ideals of the Jewish Enlightenment, the

Haskalah. David Carnovsky is a Lithuanian Jew, the stereotypical *Litvak*, the doubter of traditional values, who seeks the idealized world of Moses Mendelssohn at the center of the Haskalah, Berlin. But this is the Berlin of the 1920s, a city in moral collapse, a city of political street riots as well as the rising power of the Nazis. David attempts to raise his son Moishe Georg, called Georg in German as well as Jewish society, as "a Jew in the house . . . in the street a German."[68] This model of the individual as German and Jew, to paraphrase the title of Jakob Wassermann's 1921 autobiography, is indeed the model for the idealized image of the enlightened Jew, publicly the involved nationalist, privately the religious head of the family. The separation of state and religion, an Enlightenment myth never instituted in Europe, became part of the required model for the German Jew. Parallel to this model Singer introduces the family of Solomon Burak, with the same roots as those of David Carnovsky but with an abiding sense of his own identity quite separate from that assumed by the German Jews.

David Carnovsky's acculturation leads to the eventual intermarriage of his son, who is now accepted into German Jewish society because of his new social position as well as his abandonment of his Eastern European identity. Indeed, the German Jews are willing to accept him in spite of his racial stigma as an *Ostjude*. The Eastern Jew is seen by Singer's German Jews as "black." Georg is seen as a racial inferior by those German Jews who have accepted the racial standards of the majority.

Georg's marriage to Teresa, a member of the German middle class, is perceived by his father as a step toward apostasy; the German Protestant family of Georg's fiancée sees it as a marriage with a member of a different and lesser race, a black race. The offspring of the marriage between Georg and Teresa, Joachim Georg, called Jegor, illustrates the final break with the tradition of the Eastern European Jew. Jegor's existence on earth begins with his father's ambivalence about circumcising him. Georg moves from opposing the act of circumcision to performing it himself. Not only is circumcision the external sign of the traditional bond of the Jews but it is perceived by the Germans as a physical sign of the unique sexuality of the Jews. Georg's son seems the perfect mix of both parents' traditions. The idea of a genetic mix, of an individual falling between the races, is inherent in Jegor's image. It is the division of the two races, rather than their amalgamation, that is emphasized. Jegor's Christian uncle, the former *Oberleutnant* Hugo Holbeck, is both attracted and repelled by his half-Jewish nephew. An advocate of the *Dolchstosslegende*, which argued that German defeat in the First World War was the result of Jewish betrayal on the home front, Hugo fills Jegor's head with tales of battle:

> "Good night, Mutti," Jegorchen said, watching the last rays of light vanish. As soon as they faded, the terrible figures came back. The shapes on the carved ceiling came to life and began to dance. Although the lamp had been turned off, it continued to give off fiery rays of light. Circles whirled in front of his eyes—big circles, small circles, tiny ones. They spun so fast that they seemed to be playing tag. Jegor was ashamed to call his mother again but he was terrified of the darkness that was so full of sound and movement. His fear finally put him to sleep curled up in a ball and with the blankets drawn over his head. But even in his sleep the figures kept coming from every corner of the room, every crack in the door. All the dead soldiers about whom Uncle Hugo talked came together with torn, bloody bodies, without heads or legs. They swarmed around his bed. Now he was fully grown, like his Uncle Hugo. He wore high boots, a spiked helmet, and carried a sword. He was taller than everybody else and a lieutenant. The goddamn Frenchmen charged him, each of them a freak, a monster. He led his company in an attack and wreaked terrible havoc with his sword. They fell, one by one. But suddenly one leaped at him, a black man from Africa, the kind Uncle Hugo had described to him. He rolled the whites of his eyes, held a giant knife between his teeth, and leaped at him. Jegorchen held up his sword but the Negro caught the blade in his bare hands and tore at Jegorchen's throat. "Yay!" he screamed like the wind whistling through the chimney. (149)

Jegor's dream, the attack of the black, fits in well with the general fear of the black prevalent in Germany after the First World War. The Black Terror on the Rhine, the stationing of French colonial troops on the Rhine as part of the army of occupation, confronted the Germans with a reality that they had earlier only perceived through their colonialist myths. Part of the myth and thus part of the sublimated stereotype of the blacks is their aggressive hypersexuality. Indeed, the French colonial troops, only a small segment of whom were in fact Africans, were accused primarily of sexual misdeeds. Here the realities of the political myths about the blacks, which centered about their sexuality, appear in the context of normal childhood fears of castration and dismemberment.

For Jegor, the idea of being incomplete, of being black, is contrasted with the image of completeness offered by his qualified

acceptance by his uncircumcised, blond uncle. Jegor seems to internalize the "scientific" anti-Semitism of his uncle. Childhood sexual
competitiveness which rejects the father as the potential castrator
seems justified, since the father has permitted a type of dismemberment in allowing the child to be circumcised. The proven
castrating power of the father, at least as perceived by the child,
is contrasted with the protectiveness of the uncle and mother. The
confusions of evolving sexuality are thus given a locus in the blackness and Jewishness of the father and in the understanding that
this force is also present within the self. I. J. Singer's use of the
literary nightmare, the dream as the icon of the subconscious,
stresses the inner life of the child. The reader observes those conflicts
that would normally be played out within the psyche, hidden from
all consciousness, including that of the character. As the reader
sees, the fears of the child are articulated through images and stereotypes existing within the real world. These images are reinter-
preted to give form to the anxieties of the child. The sense of Jewish
self-hatred found in Jegor's image of himself is but a reflection of
the normal competitiveness existing between father and son. In
this case, however, an added dimension is the inherent polarity
between light and dark, Jewish and non-Jewish, which exists through
the presence of Jegor's uncle and his racial theories. Within his
fantasy Jegor can flee into a world polar to that of his father, a
world in which he becomes the epitome of light. In the real world
there is no such escape.

The reader's introduction to the political implications of the
racial theory that Jegor has amalgamated into his fantasy world
comes in the lecture of Dr. Kirchenmeier, one of Jegor's teachers
and a crass opportunist. He introduces Jegor's classmates to the
physical signs of the racial "degenerate," using Jegor as his unwilling model. He contrasts the "Nordic" and the "Negroid-Semitic"
types, forcing Jegor into the role of a "freak," a cross between both
"pure" categories (194–95). When Jegor is stripped to demonstrate
these views and his body is exposed to his classmates, his ambivalence concerning himself is underscored. With this act the linkage
of blackness, Jewishness, and aggressive sexuality has been made,
at least through Jegor's perception of his world. His reaction to his
degradation, to the exposure of his Jewishness and blackness, prefigures his attempted suicide at the end of the novel (197).

Singer does not permit the confusion of stereotypical perceptions of the Jew to rest here. He has stressed that this confusion,
while present in the dominant society, is perceived through the
adolescent mind of Jegor. The confusion concerning his own iden-

tity is compounded by the normal sexual competitiveness that he senses between himself and his father; however, this sexual competitiveness is articulated by Jegor in terms of the stereotypical structures of blackness and Jewishness, as well as the hypersexuality of the Jew:

> He was also terribly jealous of his mother, who each night was taken from him by this dark and malevolent Jew. He couldn't stand it when his father turned out the light in the dining room and retired to the bedroom with her, slamming the door in his face. She would then comb out her long, flaxen hair and put it up in braids. In her clinging nightgown she seemed to Jegor a vision, a divine yet voluptuous idealization of the perfect Aryan woman, the symbol of the New Order. He couldn't stand the lustful and rapacious way his father looked at her. Jegor used every excuse to disturb his parents in their bedroom and to keep them from being together. The women in his sexual dreams always resembled his mother and he often stayed in bed late to hide his shame from her when she came in to change his sheets. His father's medical library contained many volumes describing in clinical detail the sexual experience. There were books on anatomy, on venereal disease, on pathology, and on sexual aberration. Jegor studied these books for hours, lying in his pajamas in his bedroom. The books aroused such emotions in him that he often didn't hear his mother call him to the table. His eyes shone with an unhealthy glow, his cheeks broke out in blotches. He made copies of the forbidden pictures as well as all kinds of fantastic drawings of naked female bodies. He also copied drawings from newspapers and magazines that ridiculed the Jews.
>
> He hid these drawings carefully, but one day his father caught him at it. Jegor had drawn a blond angel being raped by a fat curly-haired *Itzick*. (205)

Even after the family Carnovsky left Germany for America the equation of sexuality, blackness, and Jewishness continued. Indeed, in America his inferiors, such as his Jewish cousins and the American blacks (speaking English), seem to have become his superiors, and being German as well as speaking German, at least German with the racial attitude of Jegor, is perceived in this new world as negative (255). Thus Jegor's values are confronted with a truly "new world," one in which he cannot function. He thus flees ever deeper into his "German" identity, for in Yorkville he seems more German than the Germans (274). His ultimate attempt to identify with the

German side of his divided self is seen in his letter to the Nazi officials in New York, in which he asks to be "allowed to return to his homeland where he was prepared to lay down his life for the Third Reich" (282). The letter reaches the desk of Dr. Siegfried Zerbe, an amalgam of Goebbels and Mephistopheles, who sees in the boy a potentially usable tool. Jegor begins to live on the fringes of Yorkville society until he strikes out across the country with his German-speaking friends in search of work. Unlike his Jewish cousins and the Buraks, Jegor is unable to function in the competitiveness of the New World. He returns to Zerbe filthy, hungry, a failure, and Zerbe attempts to seduce him:

> Jegor only stared at him through clouded eyes and Dr. Zerbe considered the matter closed. He poured two glasses of wine. "Here, let us drink to our new existence," he said, quaffed the wine in one swallow, and kissed Jegor full on the mouth.
>
> Jegor felt so revolted by the wet slime that he recoiled. Dr. Zerbe moved after him. *"Bube!"* he panted through drooling lips. His gnarled face had turned an unhealthy blue. His eyes were like tarnished pieces of dirty glass. His weak, eager hands clawed at Jegor's garments.
>
> Jegor's eyes opened wider and wider and suddenly saw double—two faces at once. One moment it was Dr. Zerbe's; the next, Dr. Kirchenmeier's. The wrinkles, the murky eyes and naked skulls, even the rasping voices seemed one and the same. He felt the tremendous surge of revulsion, hate, and strength that possesses one when facing a particularly loathsome reptile. From the bookshelf against which he cowered, an ebony statue of an African goddess with exaggerated breasts looked down on him. He gripped it in his hand and drove it with all his strength into the naked, sweating skull of the frantic little man before him. (331–32)

The echo of Mephistopheles' attempt to seduce the chorus of angelic boys at the close of *Faust II* is heard here. But even more evident is the linkage of Zerbe with the author of Jegor's first confrontation with his own sexual identity and distorted self-image, Dr. Kirchenmeier. I. J. Singer's use of the African fetish with its exaggerated sexuality as the murder weapon is an oblique reference to this earlier episode, with its linkage of blackness and sexuality. Jegor stumbles out of Zerbe's apartment and returns to his father's building, where he shoots himself. The novel closes with the family reassembled, the father attempting to save the life of his son and the sun beginning to dawn.

Singer's adaptation of the model of decay of the family from the European narrative tradition, with its rise in sensitivity and sensibility, is rooted in yet another paradigm. As has been shown, the late nineteenth century saw the degeneracy of the Jew as mad. The general etiology for the prevalence of insanity among the Jews was inbreeding: through inbreeding, the Jews had become ever more degenerate over the centuries. Singer argues quite the opposite: that the inbreeding of the Jew results in strength being built upon strength. It is only when an exotic strain is introduced that the problem of degeneracy becomes evident. Singer's image of race in *The Family Carnovsky* questions this entire equation of madness, self-hatred, and race. Singer's image of Jegor stresses the complex mix of confused self-perception and family ambivalence on all sides, as well as the universals of human sexuality. The metaphors selected by Jegor to express his inner conflicts are racial, not because of the reality of degeneracy and self-hatred among the Jews but because of the confusion of aspects of Otherness on his part. His father is identified with the negative facets of the Jew as outsider—his blackness and his aggressive sexuality, in polar opposition to the blondness and passive acceptance of his mother (and, by extension, her family).

The confusion arises in the introduction into the normal triad of authority figures other than the father. Kirchenmeier, Jegor's teacher in the gymnasium, and Zerbe, the representative of the New Order in New York, both manipulate the boy for their own ends. Jegor, who has identified with the values of his mother and her brother, with their blondness and *Kultur*, is almost destroyed by Kirchenmeier's use of him as the example of the prototypical Jew. Jegor still manages to identify his negative feelings toward Kirchenmeier with those directed against his father. It is only with Zerbe's attempted seduction at the close of the novel, a seduction that after 1905 would be viewed in medicolegal terms as a degenerate act, that Jegor is able to focus his negative feelings away from those elements in his own self-image that he has long associated with his father. Suddenly racial metaphors are no longer appropriate.

The father's association with punishing images of blackness and fear in the child's terror of the dark and of the mythical black is dissipated in Zerbe's final act. It is with Zerbe's murder with an artifact associated with blackness that the relationship of the father with the fearfulness of the black is eliminated. For Jegor, Zerbe becomes one with Kirchenmeier at the moment of his attempted seduction. The forces of evil are thus associated and removed from any relationship to the father and his Jewish identity. After Jegor's attempted suicide, the novel closes with "the first light of dawn" entering the room where Georg is laboring to save his son's life. The father has become a figure of light in the reader's eye rather than the stereotype of darkness.

Jegor's attempted suicide at his father's doorstep is not an act of madness; it is the ultimate acknowledgment of his abandonment of his own self-hatred and his expiation for it. With the destruction of those idols that he had created to establish an identity separate from that of his father a vacuum remains. As Nietzsche says at the conclusion of the *Genealogy of Morals*, the collapse of these idols results in "a will to nothingness, an aversion to life, a rebellion against the most fundamental presuppositions of life . . . man would rather will nothingness than not will."[69] Jegor is not mad; quite the contrary. His act is the final acknowledgment of his own confusion of identity and his abandonment of his earlier "madness," his self-hatred. It is his will toward nothingness.

Singer's novel is an attempt to draw into question the polar model of self-hatred. He does this within an elaborate fiction, the fiction of the family novel, with all of its literary complexities and its reference to a consciously German literary tradition. In the 1940s the figure of Thomas Mann, whose family novel *Buddenbrooks* was the source of his Nobel Prize, had come to represent the "good" German in the United States. Singer uses the literary reference within the tradition of Yiddish narrative prose in a conscious manner to point to his ability to examine the lives of the Jews as survivors within the model of accepted literary discourse, a discourse that had labeled such Jews as mad and damned. Concluding the novel with the possibility of Jegor's survival from his suicide attempt places the discourse about the self-hating Jew, present in works such as Theodor Lessing's widely read monograph, in question. Lessing's self-hating Jews died in madness, often by their own hands. This solution is dismissed by Singer, who sees the confusion between "normal" psychological tensions within a family and the internalization of anti-Semitic rhetoric as being at the heart of self-hatred.

The problem for I. J. Singer during the 1940s was to create an image of the Jew that began to rectify the Jewish acceptance of a self-image based upon anti-Semitic stereotypes. As we have seen in Philip Roth's later work, this need to separate the idea of the Jew from the reality of the Jew as perceived from an American perspective forms one of the strongest themes in post-Holocaust writing. It is not merely the question, Can it happen here? but the understanding that the world of the direct survivor is different from that of the tangential survivor, that the world of the camps is different from the world of America. It is in the works of Saul Bellow that this theme of the different levels of survival first begins to take shape.[70] Bellow's early works, written under the impact of the Holocaust and dealing with the question of survival, universalized this question problem. In *Henderson, the Rain King* (1939) Bellow places his survivor, the survivor of the ravages of bourgeois American society, in the jungles of Africa, where, like the Israeli as the "muscle-Jew," he overcomes all testing to show himself as a viable member of the degenerate world of the West. Henderson is clearly not Jewish. Indeed, Bellow selects for him an "Aryan" physiognomy that seems to be based on some idealized image of "Nordic man" taken from fascist ideology.

Herzog (1961) is quite a different tale. From the very beginning of the novel Moses Herzog is labeled as both Jewish and mad: "If I am out of my mind, it's all right with me, thought Moses Herzog."[71] So the novel opens. The linkage between the discourse of the mad and that of the Jew is manifest in this novel; as with Singer, the linkage is in the idea of the special language of the survivor. Herzog ruminates about the idea of his survival as an individual and as a Jew from the "demonic nihilism of Hitler" (75): "To realize that you are a survivor is a shock. At the realization of such election, you feel like bursting into tears" (75). Herzog's world consists in the compulsive writing of letters, which prove to him that he still survives and that he can still write. Bellow integrates the idea of the language of the Jew as mad with the idea of the Jew as failed writer. Herzog cannot write his magnum opus, his study of Romanticism; what he can write is a never-ending series of letters which he sends throughout the world to prove his existence to himself.

Yet the very language of these letters is the language of the Jew as mad. First, there is the real language, in which the letters are cast. Herzog remembers his experience in the navy, an experience that marks him because of his language as different. Bellow's Franco-Canadian roots, as much as his Jewish identity, provide the building blocks for Herzog. He is the author not in command of his own tongue, a lack that enables the non-Jew to label him as different:

> In the Service his mates had also considered him a foreigner. The Chicagoans questioned him suspiciously. "What's on State and Lake? How far west is Austin Avenue?" Most of them seemed to come from the suburbs. Moses knew the city much

better than they, but even this was turned against him. "Ah, you just memorized everything. You're a spy. That proves. One of them smart Jews. . . ."

. . . He believed his American credentials were in good order. Laughing, but pained, too, he remembered that a Chief Petty Officer from Alabama had asked him, "Wheah did you loin to speak English—at the Boilitz Scho-ool?" (159–60)

Herzog's difference is mirrored in his language, which in the novel is the language of the alienated madman, the dangling man, as Jew. But the Jew as Jew does not come off much better in this world. The language of the Jews is attributed to Herzog's nemesis, Valentine Gersbach, the man who cuckolds him. He speaks "phony Yiddish" (211) and reads Buber, the German philosopher who masquerades as an Eastern Jew (64). Indeed, in a flashback early in the novel Herzog recapitulates the moment when he is able to put Gersbach in his place. It is the moment when Gersbach mispronounces a Yiddish word (61) that he tosses into the conversation in order to establish his "Jewish" identity vis-à-vis Herzog. The perimeters are set. The madman-survivor speaks the true language of the Jew, giving insight into his own survival and his own helplessness in the light of it. This survival is also the survival of the Jew marked as different by his language in the jungles of New York, in the American university. It is not the survivor of the camps but rather the survivor of society who is labeled as mad.

In *Mr. Sammler's Planet* (1970) Bellow presents the world of the survivor of the concentration camps. The title character has survived, his self-created identity as an Anglophilic Pole of Jewish ancestry destroyed by his treatment as a Jew. And yet he maintains this damaged identity in New York after the Holocaust, since it is the only identity he has. He is a damaged survivor and a mad one. In spite of his experiences, his insanity is shown to be the only possible response to the Dantesque world of New York, a world that tests the survivor by daily making him survive. Artur Sammler, named after the anti-Semitic philosopher Schopenhauer, is surrounded by the insane, psychopaths who are Jews. His daughter, Shula, survived the Holocaust by being hidden in a convent. Her madness and that of her Israeli former husband are the direct result of their experience. He fought with the Russian partisans and was almost murdered by his fellow soldiers because he was a Jew. She has a truly "split" identity; she is sometimes the Jewess Shula and sometimes the Polish Catholic Slawa. Madness for both is, as Sammler observes, "also a masquerade, the project of a deeper reason, a result of the despair we feel before infinities and eternities."[72] Madness seems to be the appropriate response to survival. Sammler, "confidante of New York eccentrics; curate of wild men and progenitor of a wild woman; registrar of madness" (109), is the prism through which we see (and hear) all of these mad people speak. He is the Jew who has preserved his "Polish-Oxonian" facade (22) and is confronted with the language of the Jew as mad at every moment.

It is not merely that he sees the conflict between the German Jew and the Eastern Jew as a false fragmentation of Jewish identity in America. The German Jew (here the German Jewess) is either "romantic" (12) or a "WASP snob" (275), in both cases coming into an irreconcilable conflict with the *Ostjude*, which leads to a sense of fragmentation, the carrying over of the conflicts of the Old World into the New. But the madness of the Jew also extends into this world. Sammler's former son-in-law, Eisen, the survivor, comes to New York to establish himself as an artist. He "had been wounded at Stalingrad. With other mutilated veterans in Rumania, later, he had been thrown from a moving train. Apparently because he was a Jew. Eisen had frozen his feet; his toes were amputated" (25). Eisen's madness is directed at first against his wife, Sammler's daughter, and it is from his violence that Sammler rescues her and brings her to New York. Eisen learned engraving as a trade but then "discovered Art":

> Then he sent each member of the family a portrait of himself copied from photographs. Did you see any? They were appalling, Walter. An insane mind and a frightening soul made those paintings. I don't know how he did it, but by using color he robbed every subject of color. Everybody looked like a corpse, with black lips and red eyes, with faces a kind of leftover cooked-liver green. At the same time it was like a little schoolgirl learning to draw pretty people, with cupid mouths and long eyelashes. Frankly, I was stunned when I saw myself like a kewpie doll from the catacombs. In that shiny varnish he uses, I looked really done for. It was as if one death was not enough for me, but I had to have a double death. (62)

In Eisen's language of art is trapped the truth that the mad see: the double dying of the true survivor in the Hades called New York. But Eisen's madness is not merely the madness of the seer, for Eisen is the mad Jew as the violent new Jew. Eisen is "iron," his name in German and Yiddish, and his is an iron and an idea of art forged in the new Israel.

Eisen comes from Israel and brings with him samples of his new art form, medals made from the raw materials of the Holy Land, "iron pyrites, belonging at the bottom of the Dead Sea" (157). The fool's gold of Eisen's art is ornamented with "the usual Stars of David, branched candelabra, scrolls and rams' horns, or inscriptions flaming away in Hebrew: Nahamu! 'Comfort ye!' Or God's command to Joshua: Hazak!" (157). Eisen shows these medals to Sammler and to his nephew, Wallace, a ne'er-do-well who is ransacking his dying father's house looking for hidden caches of money:

> "Shouldn't these be ground smoother?" said Wallace. "And what is this word?"
> "Hazak, hazak," said Sammler, "the order God gave before Jericho, to Joshua. 'Strengthen thyself.'"
> "Hazak, v'ematz," said Eisen.
> "Yes, well . . . Why does God speak in such a funny language?" said Wallace. (157)

Eisen, like Israel, has strengthened himself, has become a "muscle Jew," unlike Sammler. This strength of the "funny language," of a Hebrew that Sammler knows and uses even within his self-hating "Polish-Oxonian" identity, is the language of the new Jew, of Eisen.[73] This sense of the hidden language of the Jew reappears at the climax of the novel, in the final confrontation between Sammler and the world of New York. Sammler spends most of the novel recounting his adventures in New York. One of the most striking is his observing the actions of a black pickpocket who worked the Broadway buses. At the climax of the novel the pickpocket is photographed in the act by one of Sammler's acquaintances. Sammler and Eisen come upon them as the pickpocket is attempting to wrest the camera away from him. Sammler implores Eisen to do something before real violence is done. Eisen pleads, "I don't know English," but eventually takes the bag in which he keeps his medals and beats the black to the ground with a violence that horrifies Sammler (262–65). It is the violence that he has held in check within himself, the violence based on the understanding that if you do not kill them, they will kill you. Eisen's madness, his violence, and his language are thus all tied together, but Sammler's language, too, is not freed from his madness.

Sammler survived the Holocaust by hiding in a tomb in a Polish cemetery. He buried himself alive in order to keep alive. His survival is thus a parody of survival, just as the tale of the Jew who ran the Łodz ghetto in the novel is an account of the parody of the normal world as a mad response to the destruction of the Holocaust. He escaped from a mass grave to hide in a tomb. The metaphor he chooses for his survival is striking: "In contraction from life, when naked, he already felt himself dead. But somehow he had failed, unlike the others, to be connected. Comparing the event, as he mentally sometimes did, to a telephone circuit: death had not picked up the receiver to answer his ring" (127). Death seems to be the only true communication—true speech, not the assumed languages of this world. Sammler's madness is that he cannot find an uncontaminated language in which to speak and thus must use a discourse that has proven ineffective. When he perceives the nature of death, he sees it as the unspoken word, as silence. This madness takes the same form in Sammler as it does in Eisen. "Fits of rage, very rare but shattering, laid him up with intense migraines, put him in a postepileptic condition. Then he lay most of the week in a dark room, rigid, hands gripped on his chest, bruised, aching, incapable of an answer when spoken to" (28). Sammler's answer is to return to the tomb, to repress the violence that his "British" self does not permit. Yet Sammler does seek after a new identity. He goes to Israel during the Aqaba crisis (225) and sees this act as an attempt to shape a new self; yet he goes as a reporter for a Polish news service, in his old guise as gentleman-traveler, not as Eastern Jew.

Bellow's creation of the world of the European survivor immigrant separates him from the American experience. Sammler's American niece and nephew can only wonder at his perception of the world. Their focus, like that of many of Philip Roth's American Jewish characters, is on money, sex, and status. Bellow, like Roth, separates the European Jewish experience from that in the United States. The Dantesque image of New York—not paradise but purgatory—is the world as seen through Sammler's eyes, the eyes of the madman-survivor. His language, damaged beyond any hope of resurrection, does not give him access to the world of America except as the outsider as observer. His silence is the silence of the madman-survivor. Bellow is thus creating an alternative *Ostjude* to the comic *Ostjude* of the tales written by Leo Rosten. There the fragmentation of language, especially the Yiddish-tinged English of Rosten's title character, Hyman Kaplan, serves the older, comic tradition of American dialect comedy.[74] Kaplan seems untouched by the Holocaust. His world is the world of the fantasy of the European immigrant in the year 1890, a world in which upward mobility is assured, at least to the children of the immigrant, and the comic discourse of the immigrant masks the innate good sense of the peasant. The mad in Bellow's world reveal truths that are hidden to others; the comic Jew in Rosten's world masks the horror of modern Jewry through the repetition of banalities cast in the superficialities of dialect. The damaged language is not that of Hyman Kaplan but that of Mr. Sammler. For Kaplan there is still the future of his family's assimilation into the American way of life; for Sammler's child no such prospect exists.

The language of the mad permeates the work of another Franco-Canadian author, Mordecai Richler, like Bellow born in French-speaking Canada and like Bellow a Canadian Jewish writer who uses the narrative fiction of the Holocaust world as a vehicle to explore the distinction between the world of the survivor and the world of the American Jew. In his novel *St. Urbain's Horseman* (1971) the questions of the language of the mad, the language of the Jew, and the guilt of postwar Jewry are linked. The protagonist of Richler's novel, the second part of the trilogy that began with *The Apprenticeship of Duddy Kravitz* (1959), is a Canadian Jewish director living and writing in London. Jacob ("Jake") Hersch is introduced to the reader standing accused of the rape and sodomization of a German *au pair* girl. His crime, as it is presented to us, woven within the retrospective strands of the novel, is that his "friend" Harry Stein assumed his identity and lived out the sexual fantasy, his attempt to deal with the Holocaust, that Jake had only described in one of his "film scripts." Running throughout the novel is the image of Dr. Mengele, the doctor of Auschwitz, who was still hiding in the South American jungle, and Jake's fantasies about capturing or killing him. Jake's fantasy concerns his cousin Joey, who was a grown man during the war years and about whom he has spun the most elaborate tales. Joey was a small-time criminal, actor, and gigolo who led the sort of life of real adventure that Jake can only imagine. He was involved in the Spanish Civil War and in the Israeli war of independence, and Jake imagines him searching for Mengele. He is for Jake "St. Urbain's Horseman," the knight of retribution coming from the main street that runs through Montreal's Jewish community:

> Out there, he had thought, resuming his place in the dock. Out there, riding even now. St. Urbain's Horseman. . . . Out on the steaming flood plains of the Parana, neck-reining his magnificent Pleven stallion with his bridle hand as he reaches into his goatskin saddlebag for his field glasses, searching the savannahs

below for the unmarked track that winds into the jungle, between Puerto San Vincente and the border fortress of Carlos Antonio Lopez, where the *Doktor* waits, unaware. . . .

How, Jake was asked again and again, as if it were perverse of him, could he still hate the Germans?

—Easily.

—Now look here—Nancy would reason sweetly—can you hate Günter Grass?

—Without any trouble whatsoever.

—Brecht?

—Unto the tenth generation.

Which Nancy, barely seven years old on V-E Day, could not comprehend. And so how could he tell her, without seeming psychotic, about his Jewish nightmare, the terror that took him by surprise in his living room, striking only on those rare evenings when he brimmed over with well-being, a sense of everything having knit mysteriously together for once. . . . Then, in Jake's Jewish nightmare, they come. Into his house. The extermination officers seeking out the Jew vermin.[75]

It is the personal involvement, the response to the label of the Jew, that captures Jake. Jake lives the vengeance against Mengele, not merely to revenge the Jews that Mengele killed but to ward off the repetition of this act. Joey becomes the "muscle Jew." He is a boxer, an actor in Western films. He is the Jew as soldier of fortune. He is also the seducer and sexual athlete. It is this fantasy that Jake takes as the ideal of the new Jew and incorporates into his fantasy.

It is, however, a fantasy that is captured within a double bind situation. For while he glorifies the new Jew, the "muscle Jew" of the new Israel, he is ashamed of the manifestations of the old Jews—their concern for worldly goods, their clannishness, their language: "As a St. Urbain Street boy he had, God forgive him, been ashamed of his parents' Yiddish accent. Now that he lived in Hampstead, Sammy (and soon Molly and Ben, too, he supposed) mocked his immigrant's twang" (13). And yet Jake consciously assumes the burden of his parents' language. When confronted with a young British homosexual who attempts to ingratiate himself with Jake ("I'm m-m-meshgugga for the things you've done on the telly") (167), Jake cuts him by correcting his pronunciation: "Meshugga." He fantasizes about his sexual rival, his wife's potential lover, who with impeccable British savoir-faire "tucked the car into the smallest imaginable space . . . without cursing the car ahead of him, or behind, in Yiddish" (181). Jake uses Yiddish as the marker for both the Jew and the victim. But he never acts upon any of his fantasies, except to follow Joey's exploits vicariously. Sharing the same name ("J. Hersch"), often he is confused with his cousin or is the butt of those who wish to find him. In one case, one of Joey's former mistresses comes to Jake in order to find Joey and recover the seven hundred dollars she has lent him. Her present boyfriend, Harry Stein, insists that Jake assume the responsibility of repaying the money. When Jake refuses, Harry, who is employed by Jake's accountant, begins to harass him, first sending taxis in the middle of the night and then revealing Jake's financial dealings to the Inland Revenue.

Harry Stein is a psychopath. Richler points this out over and over in the novel. He is the antithesis of Jake, since he puts his fantasies into practice. He has already been jailed for attempted blackmail and sexual harassment. He is the "little Jew" who, unlike Jake, cannot make it in this world. He experienced the war first-hand. He was an "evacuee" exploited by those to whom he was sent: "It was a bloody selection ramp . . . but, in lieu of Old Eich-mann, there were market farmers and shopkeeps to poke and prod us, choosing the healthiest lads" (25). Like Jake, Harry disliked being reminded of his Eastern Jewish identity: "'You're a born momzer,' Bloom said, knowing how it grated on Harry to be spoken to in Yiddish" (60). Unlike Jake, who speaks of madness only in the context of citing Samuel Johnson on the human condition (78), Harry has had at least one serious "breakdown" (300). Harry is the sociopath who lives out Jake's fantasies. The judge is puzzled as to how Jake became associated with Harry. Like Bellow's madmen, his condition is a necessary parallel to the apparent sanity of the hero.

It is only a seeming sanity, since Jake's madness is subsumed in art. He suffers from much the same deformation of his identity as does Harry, but he is able to capture and contain it in his crea-tivity. The question of his identity is multiple: Jake is a Jew and Anglophone in Catholic, Francophone Canada, a Canada described as viciously anti-Semitic. He flees to England, where, like Heine in Paris, he becomes merely an "outsider" rather than a Jew. But he carries the sense of his double bind which reflects his relation-ship to his origin: "As certain homosexuals pander to others by telling the most vicious anti-queer jokes, so Jake . . . shielded [himself] from ridicule by anticipating with derisive tales of their own. Their only certitude was that all indigenous cultural standards they had been raised on were a shared joke. No national reputation could be banded abroad without apology" (163). This is true of Jake's

Jewish identity as well as his Canadian one. He marries a non-Jew in England. He becomes as British as the British allow, remaining always the outsider. Harry is likewise the outsider, but he is even more self-consciously so because he places himself on the outside. He is the Jew as exile in his own land; Jake has chosen a world where his identity labels him as the outsider.

The use of the madman as the parallel to the creative figure in a comic novel provides Richler with the complex ability to distance the idea of the Holocaust as the source of Jewish guilt. It is clear that Jake focuses on the Holocaust as his articulation of the anxiety felt by all human beings, not merely Jews. Jake is a schlemiel because he lives out the struggles about his status anxiety in his creative imagination. Harry's sordid attempts to translate these fantasies into reality lead only to his punishment. For Harry, Jake is a "self-hater," not because of his Jewish identity, but because "when you direct something about working-class people it is obviously done for the rich to laugh at" (276). Richler's continuation of the trilogy, in his novel *Joshua Here and Now* (1980), provided yet another example of the use of the Holocaust as a means of defining the creativity of the eponymous central character. Joshua, like Jake, is caught in a web of sexual misadventures that translate his private fantasies into gross realities. For Joshua these fantasies are connected with the sexual debasement of the Germans as revenge for their degradation of the Jews. As in Philip Roth's *Portnoy's Complaint*, the private sexual fantasies of the central character of the novel are confused with other aspects of his identity, including his sense of himself as a Jew. Richler and Roth both point to the inability of their characters to separate specific aspects of their confusions about themselves, confusions that result from the definition that these characters see provided for them by the society in which they live.

In an autobiographic profile in the *New York Times*, Richler commented on the labeling of his work as "self-hating":

> I had to force two more novels through the hothouse before I found my own voice and wrote *The Apprenticeship of Duddy Kravitz*, for which the pillars of Montreal's Jewish community have never forgiven me.
>
> "Why," I was once asked, "couldn't you have given the boy an Italian name?"
>
> "Why," I was asked after I had lectured at a suburban synagogue, "does everybody adore Shalom Aleichim, but they hate your guts?"[76]

Richler's works, especially *St. Urbain's Horseman*, analyze the image of the self-hating Jew. Like Roth, Richler attempts to discover what makes self-hating Jews what they are perceived to be. Like Roth, Richler uses the image of the discourse of the mad as a means of delineating the comic discourse of his anti-hero. It is important to observe that all of the novels we have been discussing, including *Mr. Sammler's Planet*, are inherently comic novels. They attempt to provide a necessary distance between the author and the world that he is describing, a distance that is created by the alienating effects of comedy. We read Bellow, Roth, and Richler as a means of seeing the characters not as reflections of the authors' sense of self but as negative projections of that which they are perceived as being and from which they wish to distance themselves.

In the second volume of Philip Roth's trilogy, *Zuckerman Unbound* (1981), the figure of the obsessive madman is introduced in a manner parallel to that in Richler's novel. Zuckerman has just published his *Portnoy's Complaint*, a novel called *Carnovsky*, a clear reference to the confusion of identities in I. J. Singer's *The Family Carnovsky*. He is immediately attacked by the Jewish communal structure as a self-hating Jew:

> Plenty of people had already written to tell him off. "For depicting Jews in a peepshow atmosphere of total perversion, for depicting Jews in acts of adultery, exhibitionism, masturbation, sodomy, fetishism, and whore mongery," somebody with letterhead stationery as impressive as the President's had even suggested that he "ought to be shot."[77]

The confusion between Zuckerman and his character, Carnovsky, is profound. He himself seems to fall into this confusion periodically. But Roth places him carefully in juxtaposition to the mad Jew, Alvin Pepler, robbed of his chance to win in the television game shows because he is Jewish. The "Jewish Marine from Newark," Zuckerman's home town, comes to haunt Zuckerman throughout the novel. Like Harry Stein's, Pepler's obsession focuses on the success of the creative Jew, who achieves success through being "self-hating." Pepler attempts to use Zuckerman to publish his autobiography, part of his obsession about achieving his true value.

Pepler is the failed Jew, the Jew as victim, the self-made victim of the non-Jewish society in which he lives. Zuckerman is the self-hating Jew, the parody of the writer in search of himself. His search, like that of Portnoy, is largely sexual. As a new celebrity, Carnovsky has made him (or at least his character) a household name; he dates the Irish actress Caesara O'Shea for publicity reasons. His infatuation with her as a much-married sex symbol of the society in which he wishes to travel becomes a fixation after he learns that she started as an actress "playing Anne Frank at the Gate Theatre" (116). Again, Anne Frank as living image of the Holocaust impinges herself onto the creative consciousness of the author as his own fiction:

> He was thinking of Caesara starting at nineteen as the enchant-
> ing Anne Frank, and of the photographs of film stars like the
> enchanting Caesara which Anne Frank pinned up beside that
> attic bed. That Anne Frank should come to him in this guise.
> (116)

Anne Frank becomes part of Zuckerman's sexual fantasy, as she had in *The Ghost Writer*, but it is a fantasy that has its roots in the linkage between language, Jewish identity, and the sexual etiology of self-hatred. This theme reappears in the epilogue to the trilogy. When Zuckerman remembers his first sexual experience during a trip back to his old neighborhood, this becomes explicit:

> When they shut the garage doors he feared the worst—his
> mother had warned him that Thea was too "developed" for her
> age, and no one had to remind him that she was Christian. But
> all Thea made him do was to stand beside a big black grease
> spot and repeat everything she said. The words meant little to
> him but a great deal obviously to Thea and the grocer's daugh-
> ter, who couldn't stop giggling and hugging each other. It was
> his first strong experience of the power of language and of the
> power of girls. (283)

It is out of this matrix, which includes the childhood experience of the Holocaust as the formative definition of "being Jewish," or at least of not being Christian, that Zuckerman's own identity is formed. Alvin Pepler, Zuckerman's alter ego, is also Zuckerman's creation. Pepler is Carnovsky, since he shapes himself after this fiction: "Or would Zuckerman's imagination beget still other Peplers conjuring up novels out of his—novels disguising themselves as actuality itself, as nothing less than real?" (251).

Zuckerman's fiction of the Jew and Pepler's reality merge here. Roth is on the one hand parodying those (such as the writers in *Commentary*: "Are you trying to show them up in heaven and over at *Commentary* that you are only a humble, self-effacing ye-shiva *bucher* and not the obstreperous author of such an indecent book?" [156]) who identified Roth with Portnoy and yet on the other hand aware that even a fiction is real, since it functions in the real world. The book exists as part of the "real" world; thus the author must be responsible for his actions in creating the book. The work of art exists not merely as a creation: it also acquires a life of its own. Thus Zuckerman is confronted with his father's dying words, which condemn him for writing *Carnovsky*, and with his brother's rejection of him for the same reason. The father's ideal "Jewish" work of art is *Fiddler on the Roof*, in which the Jew is the object of kitsch. But his consciousness is part of the real world in which Zuckerman must exist.

Zuckerman is a writer who no longer fits the pre-Holocaust model of the Jew. Zuckerman's father was denied admission to medical school because he was a Jew; Zuckerman finds none of these barriers. Indeed, his literary agent sees Zuckerman as Kafka's ape, being educated into becoming culturally acceptable at the University of Chicago, that bastion of American liberalism:

> I can just imagine what an enchanting little baboon you were at the University of Chicago. Pounding the seminar table, scream-ing at the class that they had it all wrong—you must have been all over the place. Rather like the Nathan in this abrasive little book. . . . My point is that to turn a jungle baboon into a semi-nar baboon is a cruel, irreversible process. I understand why you won't ever be happy around the water hole again (154).

Franz Kafka, the introspective Jew, and Isaac Babel, the active one, stand at the poles of Zuckerman's ideal of the Jew as writer. But as we have shown, the tale of training the monkey to address the academy is a parable on the Jew achieving the ability to speak, to address the Western establishment in its own discourse, but it is a parable. Zuckerman, as a human being, achieves this also by being retrained, by ceasing to identify himself as a "Jew from Newark." This is the claim to fame of Alvin Pepler, whose label on the game show was "The Jewish Marine from Newark." All of his tutoring by high-school English teachers will never turn him into the writer he desires to be, for Pepler bases his identity on his real or imagined persecution by the establishment, which Pepler sees as a Jewish establishment. This establishment rejects the Jew because it does not want Jews to be too visible, at least according to Pepler. And they attempt to buy Pepler off and suggest to him that his sense of persecution could best be remedied by psycho-therapy—the wronged Jew as sick Jew (52).

For Pepler the fixing of the quiz show has become his single obsession. He wishes to use this as the basis for a novel or musical that would justify him and place him on the same level of status that he momentarily had and that he now associates with Zuckerman. In his obsessive behavior he comes to see himself as Zuckerman's creation, viewing Zuckerman as one who has stolen his persona and cast it into literary form (223). His vengeance is to shadow Zuckerman, much as Harry Stein did, and to attempt to blackmail him by threatening his mother with kidnapping, exactly the same sociopathic act that Richler attributes to Harry Stein. It is a mock threat, as was Stein's, stemming from the fantasy of the criminal. But Zuckerman feels himself threatened, not only by Pepler's act but also by the simple fact of his existence as his double. Pepler is that which Zuckerman was, "the Jew from Newark"; his is the personality of the ape taken from the jungle, but an ape untrained in the niceties of Western language and demeanor. In the course of the novel Zuckerman becomes aware that the act of writing has social repercussions. His brother condemns him for writing *Carnovsky*, because of its dark vision of what it is to be a Jew in America (at least as seen from Zuckerman's perspective as a reformed ape): "To you everything is disposable! Jewish morality, Jewish endurance, Jewish wisdom, Jewish families—everything is grist for your fun machine" (274). "You can't believe that what you write about people has *real consequences*" (275). "You and your 'liberating' book! Do you really think that conscience is a Jewish invention from which you are immune?" (276).

In the second volume of the Zuckerman trilogy, Roth explores the contradiction in the idea of self-hatred as the internalization of anti-Semitic rhetoric about the Jew. The association between madness and self-hatred is tied to the concept of assimilation. Writers such as Singer, Bellow, Richler, and Roth make this analogy overt. In creating characters who are labeled as writers and as self-hating, they expose this association. They create characters who have internalized the associations between their own discourse and the confusion that they feel in regard to their identity as Jews. These schlemiels see that this polar response is not sophisticated enough to explain the totality of their character. They turn to a more elaborate mode of explanation which relegates self-hatred to the position of a symptom rather than the cause of the character's fractured identity. What remains in the fictionalized psyche of the characters is the conviction that the source of their identity is their internalization of the anti-Semitism of the world about them. It is this misapprehension that lies at the root of the characters' often comic misinterpretation of the world.

V
Closure

In 1983 Woody Allen released *Zelig*, a film that chronicles the life of an individual robbed of any true identity who assumes the identity and physiognomy of anyone with whom he is confronted. Allen sets this film in the 1920s, before the Holocaust, and presents the adventures of a "madman," as he is seen by the world, which treats his ability as a psychopathology. Among his various transformations, Leonard Zelig becomes, at one point in the film, an Orthodox Jew with beard and accent, and later, a follower of Hitler on his way to seizing power in Germany. The frame of this film is the retrospective recreation of the "case" of Zelig through the fictional comments of those who knew him, such as his psychoanalyst and wife, Dr. Eudora Fletcher, and authorities, such as Susan Sontag, Saul Bellow, Irving Howe, and Bruno Bettelheim, who comment on the Zelig case from a mock-scholarly point of view. Bettelheim's inclusion in the film, and his comment that Zelig was an individual without a true personality who simply reacted to the world about him and internalized it, points to a conscious attempt on Allen's part to join in the chorus of writers who are trying to lay to rest the polar definition of self-hatred espoused by writers such as Bettelheim. *Zelig* is a parody of the psychoanalytic case study and has roots in the fictions of madness present in the American cinema (as in *I Never Promised You a Rose Garden*). It mirrors the awareness of the conflict presented in the association of universals of pathological behavior, such as Allen's "ahedonia," with specifically "Jewish" qualities ascribed to the self-hating Jew. It is this association that Allen draws into question.[78]

Philip Roth presents the destruction of the image of the special discourse of the self-hating Jew as mad in the closing volume of his Zuckerman trilogy, *The Anatomy Lesson* (1983).[79] Roth makes the confusions present within his "self-hating" writer, Nathan Zuckerman, manifest and reveals the hidden truth about "Jewish self-hatred"—that it is part of the human condition, that it is not a *psychosis judäicus* nor even a "Jewish complex" but part of the struggle of every human being with his or her sense of growth and eventual decay. *The Anatomy Lesson* is about pain, a pain that so dominates Zuckerman that he can do little but focus on it. This focus on pain, a physical pain, is not very different from the egocentricity that has characterized Zuckerman from his initial appearance in *The Ghost Writer*. Zuckerman sees this pain as a "penance for the popularity of *Carnovsky*": "The crippling of his upper torso

was, transparently, the punishment called forth by his crime: mutilation as primitive justice. . . . Who else could have written so
blasphemously of Jewish moral suffocation but a self-suffocating
Jew like Nathan?" (34). Zuckerman's pain is the pain of Jewish
self-hatred. Here Roth echoes Heine's "The New Jewish Hospital
in Hamburg," written in 1842:

> A hospital for poor, sick Jews,
> for people afflicted with threefold misery,
> with three evil maladies:
> poverty, physical pain, and Jewishness.

> The last named is the worst of all the three:
> the thousand-year-old family complaint,
> the plague they dragged with them from the Nile valley,
> the unhealthy faith from ancient Egypt.

> Incurable, profound suffering! No help can be looked for
> from steam-baths, showerbaths, or all the implements
> of surgery, or all the medicines
> which this house offers its sick inmates.[80]

Roth uses this theme, the idea of self-hatred as the illness of the
Jews, an illness that reveals their hidden corruption in ironic reversal. Anne Roiphe, in quoting Heine's poem, comments that the
Jewish poet often confuses "the emotional pain of his childhood
with the condition of his family religion. This is a common enough
error and even readers of American writers (Philip Roth, Joseph
Heller) may sometimes mix the failure in loving with the flavor
of the ethnic and religious experience. These things overlap but
are not quite the same" (35). This is a reading of Roth that ignores
the distance that Roth builds into his characters, especially Zuckerman. Zuckerman is not Roth. Indeed, Roth mocks the bad reader
in *The Anatomy Lesson* who wishes to dismiss the difference
between the writer and his character (85). Zuckerman is the American writer on Jewish themes who has begun to internalize the
charge of being a self-hating Jew, of having a corrupted, degenerate,
self-hating discourse. This is Zuckerman's equation of his physical
pain with his Jewishness. But it is a very specific form of Jewishness
that Zuckerman internalizes: it is the identity of the writer as the
self-hating Jew.

Pain must be a universal of human experience. Or so Zuckerman wishes to believe. The first antidote that Zuckerman describes
in the course of the novel is literature as therapy—not "Jewish"
literature but the literature of culture, the literature he read as an

undergraduate at the University of Chicago, George Herbert, the British "metaphysical" poet, literature as the "antidote to suffering through the depiction of our common fate" (5). This therapy is as useless as the myriads of other treatments, from physical- to psychotherapy, that he undertakes to lessen his pain. Zuckerman's pain is connected intimately with his definition of himself, with his identity as a middle-aged writer, the author of *Carnovsky*. The death of his father, reported in detail in *Zuckerman Unbound*, is tied to the novel and the theme of self-hatred. In *The Anatomy Lesson*, Zuckerman's mother dies, removing the final ties to his childhood and releasing all of the sense of loss that one has when confronted with this final break with the past. His mother dies of a brain tumor that first presented itself in what appeared to be a minor stroke. When she was readmitted a few months later, her neurologist asked her to write her name for him, "and instead of 'Selma' [she] wrote the word 'Holocaust,' perfectly spelled" (41). After his mother's death, it is this piece of paper that Nathan keeps as his inheritance from a mother who, according to Nathan, had never even been able to say the word (59).

The pain of the loss of parents, of the inevitable sense of aging, is linked by Zuckerman with his Jewishness, which in turn is defined by the Holocaust. Jewish self-hatred is a disease, a genetic error that will destroy the remaining Jews as well as its carrier. According to Zuckerman's fantasy, this is the origin of all evil, of the Holocaust, of the threat against the state of Israel. Shortly after the beginning of the 1973 war with the Arabs, Zuckerman's most virulent critic, Milton Appel, asks him to write in support of the state of Israel. Zuckerman's response summarizes his reading of Appel's attack on him: "In your view, it really isn't deranged Islam or debilitated Christianity that's going to deal us the death blow anyway, but Jewish shits who write books like mine, carrying the hereditary curse of self-hate. And all to make a dollar" (95). The self-hatred in a Jew is, for Zuckerman, the identity that he has accepted from the world about him and internalized. "I cracked a few jokes about playing stinky-pinky in Newark and you'd think I'd blown up the Knesset. . . . This is not my maiden appearance in the pages of *Foreskin* as their Self-Hating Jew of the Month" (100). Pain becomes associated with this specific type of Jewish identity for Zuckerman. He attempts to distance himself from this association. Just before calling Appel to answer his request, he thinks: "Appel has nothing to do with the pain. The pain predates that essay by a year. There are no Jewish evil eyes or double Jewish whammies. Illness is an organic condition. Illness is as natural as health" (159). But of course Zuckerman cannot persuade himself of the truth of his statement.

Zuckerman's focus is Milton Appel, the editor of *Inquiry*, a writer who first supported and then attacked Zuckerman's work. Appel saw himself as alienated from any Jewish experience. He, like Lonoff, had come from a Yiddish-speaking milieu. Zuckerman, on the other hand, had a father who was an English-speaking member of the Newark professional middle class. But Appel's early work, according to Zuckerman, although its subject matter was consciously non-Jewish, revealed the Jew under the skin. He wrote "about practically everything except the language in which his father had hollered for old junk from his wagon. But this was hardly because the Jew was in hiding. The disputatious stance, the aggressive marginal sensibility, the disavowal of community ties, the taste for scrutinizing a social event as though it were a dream or a work of art— to Zuckerman this was the very mark of the intellectual Jews in their thirties and forties on whom he was modeling his own style of thought" (73). After the Holocaust Appel returned to his earliest roots, to that mute world of Yiddish-speaking immigrants, and produced an anthology of Yiddish writing in English translation. From there he went on to become a vocal supporter of the state of Israel, a distinguished, chaired professor at New York University, indeed took on all of the marks of the acceptable Jew, the unself-hating Jew, against which Zuckerman measured himself.

Roth uses the "reality" of the attack on him in Norman Podhoretz's *Commentary*, an attack written by Peter Shaw, the associate editor of the conservative Jewish journal, as the text that Zuckerman internalizes. The centerpiece of Appel's charge against Zuckerman is his silence, his muteness on the question of the continued existence of the state of Israel:

> Maybe he has spoken up on this, but if so I haven't seen it. Or does he still feel, as his Carnovsky says, the Jews can stick their historical suffering up their ass? (And yes, I know that there's a difference between characters and authors; but I also know that grown-ups should not pretend that it's quite the difference they tell their students.) (85)

Shaw's actual statement illustrates Roth's method in incorporating the image of self-hatred within the figure of Zuckerman:

> For Portnoy's theory is that in repressing his natural instincts his mother was in effect acting as an agent of the Jewish tradition. All the don'ts of his childhood . . . teach that renuncia-

tion, self-control, and repression are all. In fury over this impo-
sition Portnoy turns on Jewishness itself:

> Jew Jew Jew Jew Jew Jew! It is coming out of my ears
> already, the saga of the suffering Jews! Do me a favor, my
> people, and stick your suffering heritage up your suffering
> ass—*I happen also to be a human being!*

> ... But wait a minute. What kind of "literary investigation" is
> this? A sustained cry of loathing for things Jewish in terms that
> perpetuate the most familiar stereotypes—how is this literary?
> (77)

Roth mocks the inability to separate the function of the literary
text (and thus the writer) in society from the realities of the society.
For Shaw the literary text is the mimetic representation of the
world as perceived by the author; for Roth the satirist it is a
consciously unreal representation that catches the hidden world,
the world unavailable to anyone's direct observation. This confusion is Appel's as well. He claims that the real fiction is the distinction drawn between the world and the work of art. He does not
see that the true reality is the function of the work of art in the
world, not its representation of the world. We teach our students,
Appel the critic comments, to distinguish between fictions and the
world, but we know better; we are the true readers of the texts
produced by this self-hating Jew, for we are secure in our Jewish
identity. We translate from the Yiddish, we support the state of
Israel, we have not written *Carnovsky*. We understand the damaged
discourse of the Jew. This position is rejected by Zuckerman but
also half believed by him. Appel, like Lonoff, had provided the
model for his literary persona, so his rejection of him is an attack
on himself. This double image of the Jewish writer, the self-satis-
fied and the self-hating Jew, is created by Roth as a representation
of what happens when the polar definition of self-hatred, the absolute distinction between the "good" and the "bad" Jew, is internalized by writers who see themselves and are seen by their readers
as "Jewish" writers other than writers who are Jewish and who
explore the contours of the Jewish experience in the United States
after the Holocaust.

But the villain of the novel is not Appel but pain. And Roth
presents the reader with Zuckerman as a character whose choice
is to confront his pain or flee from it. His association of his pain
with his own identity means that flight, even into drugs, alcohol,
and sex, is not possible, since these very experiences are thus colored

by these associations. Art also is not a possible outlet, for Zuckerman associates true art not with *Carnovsky*, his own work, but with the figure of the artist represented by his memory of Thomas Mann addressing the University of Chicago in 1949. Thomas Mann was "the Good European [teaching Zuckerman] how to speak [his] . . . own tongue" (178). Art is the civilizing of the Jew, Zuckerman as Kafka's ape. And his teacher is the German as "Good European," not the evil Nazi. Thus when Zuckerman seeks an outlet, it cannot be art, for art is also contaminated by the sense of the ineffectuality of the Jews' discourse, which is inherently inferior to that of the "Good European."

What Zuckerman seeks out as his cure is the study of medicine. He returns to Chicago with the intention of entering the School of Medicine. The sick are to cure themselves. This association of illness and medicine is again made through the image of a "Jewish" component—the Jew as doctor and as patient; the magic ability of the Jew to cure even himself. Zuckerman is received by his former college roommate, now a doctor, with great skepticism. He sees the madness of Zuckerman's flight from reality. Medicine is not an answer, no matter what the traditional relationship between "Jewish" discourse and the discourse of medicine. The medical model, the model of doctor, patient, and cure, is not applicable when doctor and patient are one; and the only cure is death. Moreover, the illness of "self-hatred," the disease from which Zuckerman imagines himself to be suffering, is itself an artifact of the medicalization of the Jew. Here again I. J. Singer's *The Family Carnovsky* haunts the background to Roth's trilogy. For the central figure is a doctor who can not "cure" the real illness of his son: his confused identity. He can only attempt to save him once Jegor has made that choice—suicide—which has resolved his confusion. Medicine and its discourse about the Jews is intimately tied to the "disease" of self-hatred, a disease that Zuckerman has convinced himself is the root of his own pain.

The conclusion of the novel links illness, pain, and a specific form of post-Holocaust Jewish identity. Zuckerman goes off with the father of his former roommate to take him to visit his wife's grave. High on drugs and alcohol, Zuckerman begins to hallucinate. He sees in the coffins in the Jewish cemetery the world that still dominates him: "We are the dead! These bones in boxes are the Jewish living! These are the people who are running the show!" (260). The Jewish dead are the confusion of Zuckerman's own dead parents with the dead of the Holocaust, the past that seems to control his future identity as a Jew. He falls onto one of the gravestones, smashing his jaw. He awakes, mute, his jaw wired, in the hospital. In the hospital he has an exchange with one of the residents. Signing and writing, he discovers that the doctor is in emergency medicine because of his own weakness, his dependency, his fear of failure. Medicine remains for Zuckerman as part of his fantasy, a fantasy of a new life, a new incarnation, free from his own failures, the neurosis that makes him Zuckerman.

In the hospital he begins to play at medicine: confronted with the most grotesque horrors, he incorporates them into his fantasy, as he has his struggle with Appel over his Jewish identity. Roth concludes the novel with the neutral voice of the narrator summarizing the case of Nathan Zuckerman:

> For nearly as long as he remained a patient, Zuckerman roamed
> the busy corridors of the university hospital, patrolling and
> planning on his own by day, as though he still believed that he
> could unchain himself from a future as a man apart and escape
> the corpus that was his. (291)

Roth's "anatomy lesson" is that Jews are human beings who cannot escape their own mortality. The universal sense of mortality has become linked in Zuckerman's consciousness with his role as a Jew and a writer. While Roth uses here a *topos* of twentieth-century letters, the author as the representative human being and the act of writing as the means of establishing meaning and order in life, he is also incorporating his examination of a parallel theme, that of the damaged discourse of the Jew and its externalization in self-hatred. Zuckerman's inability to cope with his own mortality becomes associated with his inability to deal with his identity as a "self-hating" Jew. Roth takes this identification as a sign of the American Jewish writer's confusion about his or her own relationship to the past as a Jew and an American. He takes the figurative structure of "self-hatred," with all of its historical associations to the "hidden" language of the Jews, and reveals it to be part of the fantasy life of the writer projected onto the world. He uses the devices of identification and projection as part of his construction of the psyche of his fictional characters. Thus Zuckerman shatters his jaw at the conclusion of a novel that is marked by the central figure's inability to write—an inability not merely to compose fictions but physically to commit these fictions to paper, because of the incessant pain in his arms and back.

The conclusion of *The Anatomy Lesson* provides silence as Zuckerman's discourse, or at least a crippled reliance on the written word as a poor substitute for a meaningful discourse. The satire that Roth aims at Zuckerman—as the writer who has accepted on a number of different levels the charge of possessing a damaged discourse—is rounded off in "The Prague Orgy," the novella-length epilogue to the trilogy. In this final statement of Zuckerman's search for an appropriate discourse for the modern Jewish writer, the writer heads for Prague, where authors are taken seriously— where they are jailed rather than allowed to date movie stars. There he undertakes a failed search for the unpublished stories of a dead Yiddish writer. He sees in the image of the city of Prague (rather than that of modern Israel, which left him impotent) the image of that used, abandoned city appropriate for Jews and writers. Zuckerman has come full circle from the middle-class, Jewish Newark of his childhood to the fantasy city of Prague, the city of the golem and of Jewish myth clothed in Yiddish, the appropriate language for the Jews. And yet these are a culture and a language that he can never command. This sense of alienation reifies his sense of the triviality and inappropriateness of his own discourse.

The silence, the muteness, the inexpressibility associated with the post-Holocaust Jewish writer in the West and the function of this device within fictions such as Kosinski's *The Painted Bird* is shown to be part of the writer's craft. For Zuckerman seems to become mute as a result of his internalization of "self-hatred" just as Kosinski's narrator seems to become articulate in his projection of this sense of alienation into his world of fiction. Zuckerman is unable to reconcile the pursuit of his art, the writing of works that express his experience as a writer and a Jew, since his art has placed him outside of the pale as a Jew. And being placed outside of the pale, to use this metaphor with all of its historical associations, means that as a Jew, here the self-hating Jew, he is fair game for all attacks, even those from within his own psyche. Roth also takes the metaphor of the decay of the body as the sign of mortality of all human creations and links it to the source of the concept of self-hatred, the medical model. His trilogy, especially the final volume, is a case study of what happens when a writer, insecure about his role in society, accused of writing in a damaged discourse, internalizes this charge, partially projecting it onto the world about him while still identifying with it. Zuckerman internalizes the writer's sense of alienation but defines it not as a universal human fear but as a specifically Jewish one.

Philip Roth and the writers of the 1970s and 1980s place a closure on the concept of the self-hating Jew. By creating a character who accepts a concept of identity formation foreign to his own experience, Roth shows us what happens when historically determined concepts of identity formation are viewed as universal. Zuckerman is a post-Holocaust Jewish writer in America. He is haunted by the double bind of pre-Holocaust models of anti-Semitism which have their historic roots in the experience of European Jews. The European experience, even when transferred seemingly intact to America in the form of American anti-Semitism, must be perceived differently in its new context because of the quite different social and ethnic matrix into which it is transplanted. American anti-Semitism is much more complex than German anti-Semitism. The history of Jewish self-hatred until the Holocaust is the history of Jewish responses to the double bind of German identity formation. The existence in the United States of a multivalent society, with many different Others, made it possible to project one's anxiety onto other groups, outside of one's own.

In addition, the establishment of the State of Israel, the rebirth of Hebrew as a national language, and the new, militant image of the Jew as warrior confront American Jews with an image of the Jew rooted in a newly acquired sense of national identity and thus parallel to the ethnic identity of may other groups in American society. This new image mitigated some of the anxiety felt by Jews in the diaspora caused by the charge that they were inherently different from their neighbors. It also highlighted that difference. For being Jewish, which meant having a "Jewish" *national* language, Hebrew, could be seen as a positive attribute, since the creation of the State of Israel and the reestablishment of its language provided an analogy to other ethnic groups within American society. But it also provided further proof of the charge that the Jews possessed a "hidden" or secret language as well as providing a new class of Jews, actually possessing a different language and discourse, on which to project the anxieties generated by their sense of difference. Thus one of the most recent forms of Jewish self-hatred is the virulent Jewish opposition to the existence of the State of Israel. The sense of the double bind exists in a new and complex manner. The older European form seems no longer to have validity. What is a daily experience within European, especially German, society from the Middle Ages to the mid-twentieth century becomes an inappropriate response to the world of contemporary America. European Jews had no other group onto which to project their own anxieties, certainly no group as visible and central to the definition of the Christian world of the Central European as the Jew.

In the United States other such groups, especially blacks, exist. It was (and is) just as easy, if not easier, to project one's anxiety onto groups perceived as lower in the estimation of the privileged group as it is to project one's hostility onto a fictional extension of one's own group.[81] Self-hatred moves from being a response in all of its subtlety to the sense of alienation inherent in the image of the Jew in Germany represented by the Jews' hidden language to a descriptive metaphor for the internalization of a false understanding of the role of a Jew as writer in the contemporary world. It is not that "self-hatred" has vanished. Given the existence of groups that wish to share power and groups that refuse to share power, self-hatred, with its double bind model of identification and projection, remains a part of the vocabulary of identity of human society. What may well have been destroyed is the particular case, the association of the language of the Jew as writer with a particular form of damaged discourse and the need for the Jew as writer to create an image of the "bad" Jew (and damaged Jewish discourse) from which he must distance himself. Writers from I. J. Singer to Philip Roth have shown that such a process accepts the charges of Jew haters about the essential nature of the Jew. Thus, after a thousand years this chapter of Jewish identity formation for the Jewish writer has been closed.

Notes

1. The literature on the nature of self-hatred is not as extensive as one might imagine. The phrase "Jewish self-hatred" was popularized by Theodor Lessing, *Der jüdische Selbsthass* (Berlin: Jüdischer Verlag, 1930), but is rooted in work done in Germany before World War I. (A discussion of this material, its origin, and its influence will be found in chap. 5.) The more recent theories devoted to the psychology of Jewish self-hatred are well summarized in Ronald M. Demakovsky, "Jewish Anti-Semitism and the Psychopathology of Self-Hatred" (Ph.D. diss., California School of Professional Psychology, 1978). Of the recent sociological studies, Hans Mayer, *Outsiders: A Study in Life and Letters*, trans. Denis M. Sweet (Cambridge: MIT Press, 1982), reexamines Lessing's categories using literary texts. More pedestrian but useful are Gordon Allport, *The Nature of Prejudice* (Garden City, N.Y.: Doubleday, 1958), 138–58; Jack Levin, *The Functions of Prejudice* (New York: Harper & Row, 1975); Robert Wuthnow, "Anti-Semitism and Stereotyping," in *In the Eye of the Beholder: Contemporary Issues in Stereotyping*, ed. Arthur G. Miller (New York: Praeger, 1982), 137–87; and Jack Nusan Porter, *The Jew as Outsider* (Washington, D.C.: University Press of America, 1981). Two historical studies that are thought-provoking but only skim the surface of the problem are Lionel Kochan, *Jewish Self-Hatred*, Noah Barou Memorial Lecture, 1970 (London: World Jewish Congress, 1970); and *Encyclopaedia Judaica: Decennial Book*, s.v. "Jewish Self-Hatred," by Jacob Neusner (Jerusalem: Keter, 1982), 551 (with a short bibliography of Neusner's other essays on the topic). Further literature on this topic will be discussed within the substance of this book.

2. For a detailed presentation of the implications of "double bind" theory for the study of human interaction see Carlos E. Sluzki and Donald C. Ransom, eds., *Double Bind: The Foundation of the Communicational Approach to the Family* (New York: Grune & Stratton, 1976). Here we

shall be differentiating mental representations of an object with special attributes from what D. Boesky has labeled "representational systems which parallel the ego in scope" (D. Boesky, "Representation in Self and Object Theory," *Psychoanalytic Quarterly* 52 [1983], 564–83).

3. These categories—"denial in art and word" and "denial in fantasy"— are taken from Anna Freud, *The Ego and the Mechanisms of Defense* (New York: International Universities Press, 1966), esp. 109–21.

4. Frantz Fanon, *Black Skins, White Masks* (New York: Grove Press, 1967), 188.

5. Prosper Mérimée, *Carmen*, trans. Walter F. C. Ade (Woodbury, N.Y.: Barron's, 1977), 42.

6. Houston Stewart Chamberlain, *Foundations of the Nineteenth Century*, trans. John Lees, 2 vols. (London: John Lane, 1910), 1:388–89. The intellectual context of Chamberlain's work has been outlined by Geoffrey G. Field in *Evangelist of Race: The Germanic Vision of Houston Stewart Chamberlain* (New York: Columbia University Press, 1981).

7. Cited in Fritz Stern, *Gold and Iron: Bismarck, Bleichröder, and the Building of the German Empire* (London: George Allen & Unwin, 1977), 498.

8. Paul Weber, *Geistliches Schauspiel und kirchliche Kunst in ihrem Verhältniss erläutert an einer Ikonographie der Kirche und Synagogue* (Stuttgart: Neff, 1894); and Paul Hildenfinger, "La Figure de la synagogue dans l'art du moyen âge," *Revue des études juives* 47 (1903), 187–96. The iconography of color in Germany is tied to the split image of the "dark" killer of the "fair" hero, as in the image of Hagen killing Siegfried. This image is absorbed into the image of the dark Judas who kills the "knightly" Jesus in early Germanic versions of the gospels. This association of "dark" and "fair" is present even into twentieth-century images of the Jews: see Karl-Joseph Kuschel, *Jesus in der deutsch-sprachigen Gegenswartsliteratur* (Gütersloh: Benzinger, 1978).

9. Adam G. de Gurowski, *America and Europe* (New York: D. Appleton, 1857), 177.

10. Erik H. Erikson, *Childhood and Society* (New York: W. W. Norton, 1950), 301, 311–15. For the context of Erikson's work and life see Robert Coles, *Erik Erikson: The Growth of His Works* (Boston: Little, Brown, 1970).

11. The relevant passages are to be found in Ralph Manheim's translation of *Mein Kampf* (Cambridge: Houghton Mifflin, 1943), 325, 624, 629. Erikson's reading of *Mein Kampf* is very clearly a post–World War II reading, presented in the light of the victory against Nazi racism. For a parallel reading by an anti-Nazi Social Democrat *during* the late 1930s see the recently published manuscript by Hans Staudinger, *The Inner Nazi: A Critical Analysis of "Mein Kampf,"* ed. Peter M. Rutkoff and William B. Scott (Baton Rouge: Louisiana State University Press, 1981).

12. E. D. Morel, "The Employment of Black Troops in Europe," *Nation* (London), 27 March 1920, 893.

13. Reiner Pommerin, *Sterilisierung der Rheinlandbastarde: Das*

Schicksal einer farbigen deutschen Minderheit 1918–1937 (Düsseldorf: Droste, 1979). For the contemporary view of the Nazis concerning the black and the relationship of this image to that of the Jew see F. Zumpt, *Kolonialfrage und nationalsozialistischer Rassenstandpunkt* (Hamburg: Hartung, 1938); and Walter Kucher, *Die Eingebornenpolitik des Zweiten und Dritten Reiches* (Königsberg: Graefe und Unzer, 1941). For an analysis see my *On Blackness without Blacks: Essays on the Image of the Black in Germany* (Boston: G. K. Hall, 1982).

14. Dr. B., "Die Rassenmerkmale der Juden," *Der Stürmer* 38 (1928), 2.

15. Jean-Paul Sartre, *Anti-Semite and Jew*, trans. George J. Becker (New York: Schocken Books, 1948); Albert Memmi, *Jews and Arabs*, trans. Eleanor Levien (Chicago: J. P. O'Hara, 1975).

16. Emil L. Fackenheim, *Encounters between Judaism and Modern Philosophy: A Preface to Modern Jewish Thought* (New York: Basic Books, 1973). See also Steven T. Katz, *Post-Holocaust Dialogues: Critical Studies in Modern Jewish Thought* (New York: New York University Press, 1983).

17. The centrality of the illusion of power as the wellspring for the functioning of projection was recognized not only by Freud but by Karen Horney in *The Neurotic Personality of Our Time* (1937). Freud's introduction of this concept into a model of social and cultural history in *Totem and Taboo* (1912–13) set the ground work for recent adaptions of this concept in the work of René Girard and Michel Foucault. See also Paula Heimann, "Certain Functions of Introjection and Projection in Early Infancy," in *Developments in Psychoanalysis*, ed. Melanie Klein et al. (London: Hogarth, 1952), 301. Concerning the assignment of categories to stereotypes of power and powerlessness see Howard J. Ehrlich, *The Social Psychology of Prejudice* (New York: Wiley Interscience, 1973).

18. The role of language has been stressed by the Cuban poet Roberto Fernandez Retamar in "Caliban: Notes towards a Discussion of Culture in Our America," *Massachusetts Review*, 1974, 7–72.

19. John Murray Cuddihy, *The Ordeal of Civility: Freud, Marx, Lévi-Strauss, and the Jewish Struggle with Modernity* (New York: Basic Books, 1974).

20. See the discussion of the "levantization" of the language of the Jews in Salo Wittmayer Baron, *A Social and Religious History of the Jews*, 19 vols. (New York: Columbia University Press, 1952–83), 7:8–10. The quote from Al-Jahiz is taken from Baron's discussion. Baron's views are complemented by the recent work of Paul Wexler, "Jewish Interlinguistics: Facts and Conceptual Framework," *Language* 57 (1981), 99–149. Baron and Wexler reject any conspiracy theory of language building, i. e., that the Jews evolved a pattern of discourse to serve as a means of hiding their true purpose from the non-Jewish world. See also François Grosjean, *Life with Two Languages: An Introduction to Bilingualism* (Cambridge: Harvard University Press, 1982). Some discussion of this question has appeared in Murray Baumgarten, *City Scriptures: Modern Jewish Writing* (Cambridge: Harvard University Press, 1982), 10–12, 25–31, 153–55.

21. Fanon, 17.

22. Richard Rodriguez, *Hunger of Memory: The Education of Richard Rodriguez* (Boston: David R. Godine, 1981).

23. George Eliot, *The Works of George Eliot*, Cabinet Edition, 24 vols. (Edinburgh: William Blackwood, 1878–85), vols. 3–5, *Daniel Deronda*, 3:323. For the context of her remarks see Elenor Shaffer, *"Kubla Khan" and the Fall of Jerusalem: The Mythological School in Biblical Criticism and Secular Literature, 1770–1880* (Cambridge: Cambridge University Press, 1975).

24. An insightful though limited study of the double bind in which Jewish women found themselves while aspiring to a role in German culture during the first generation after emancipation is Hannah Arendt, *Rahel Varnhagen: The Life of a Jewish Woman*, trans. Richard Winston and Clara Winston (New York: Harcourt Brace Jovanovich, 1974). For Arendt the only possible outcome of such a situation was Rahel's antagonistic attitude toward Jews.

CHAPTER TWO. THE DRIVE FOR CONVERSION

1. Haim ben Bezalel, *Sefer Ha-Adamah* (Cracow, 1593). A parallel account of the "miraculous" nature of Reuchlin's intervention is recorded in the diary of Josel of Rosheim, the titular leader of the Jews in the Holy Roman Empire during the Reuchlin-Pfefferkorn controversy. He wrote that "enemies and destroyers of our people have arisen seeking to suppress the Oral Law. But God performed a miracle within a miracle, and from among the sages on the nations arose a man to restore that Law to its pristine recognition. The community of Frankfurt sacrificed life and property and spent large amounts until the Lord saw our misery and saved us from the designs of the apostate" (cited in Salo Wittmayer Baron, *A Social and Religious History of the Jews*, 19 vols. [New York: Columbia University Press, 1952–83], 13:189).

2. Joshua Trachtenberg, *The Devil and the Jews: The Medieval Conception of the Jew and Its Relationship to Modern Antisemitism* (New Haven: Yale University Press, 1943), 88–97. Baron, 9:122 ff., stresses the magical nature of the Jews in his chapter "'Demonic' Alien." Trachtenberg and Baron are interested in documenting the mythology that surrounded the Jews and determined their public image. Guido Kisch, *The Jews in Medieval Germany: A Study of Their Legal and Social Status* (Chicago: University of Chicago Press, 1949), argues that canon law rejects any inherent difference between Jew and Christian (323–27). He sees class rather than mass as the source of medieval anti-Judaism and denies any "natural animosity" of the Christian toward the Jew. All of this may be true in the reading of his legal sources (especially the *Sachsenspiegel*), but it ignores the social realities, according to which the image of the Jew is determined as much by the myth building as by abstract legal codes. Of great value in outlining the myths about Jews (and their social ramifications) are: James Parkes, *The Conflict of the Church and the Synagogue:*

A Study in the Origins of Anti-Semitism (Cleveland: World, 1961); idem, *The Jew in the Medieval Community: A Study of His Political and Economic Situation* (London: Soncino Press, 1938); Ernest L. Abel, *The Roots of Anti-Semitism* (Rutherford, N.J.: Fairleigh Dickinson University Press, 1975); Andrew McCall, *The Medieval Underworld* (London: Hamish Hamilton, 1979), 250–84; Moses A. Shulvass, *The Jews in the World of the Renaissance* (Leiden: Brill, 1973); and Bernard Glassman, *Anti-Semitic Stereotypes without Jews: Images of the Jew in England, 1290–1700* (Detroit: Wayne State University Press, 1975).

3. Beryl Smalley, *The Study of the Bible in the Middle Ages* (Notre Dame, Ind.: University of Notre Dame Press, 1964), 156–72.

4. Benvenuto Cellini, *The Autobiography of Benvenuto Cellini*, trans. George Gull (Baltimore: Penguin, 1956), 121–22.

5. Moise Schwab, "Les Mots hébreux dans les mystères du moyen âge," *Revue des études juives* 46 (1903), 148–51. Recently work has been done by Bruno Klammer: "Dramatisches Sprechen im Bozner Passionspiel 1495," in *Virtues et Fortune: Festschrift für Hans-Gert Roloff*, ed. Joseph P. Strelka and Jörg Jungmayr (Bern: Peter Lang, 1983), 64–90. See also Raymond Chapman, *The Treatment of Sounds in Language and Literature* (Oxford: Blackwell, 1984).

6. Ms. Bodl. 482, fol. 1d; cited in Smalley, 171.

7. Ernst Cassirer et al., eds. and trans., *The Renaissance Philosophy of Man* (Chicago: University of Chicago Press, 1948), 226, 249.

8. Otto Kluge, "Die hebräische Sprachwissenschaft in Deutschland im Zeitalter des Humanismus," *Zeitschrift für die Geschichte der Juden in Deutschland* 3 (1931), 81 ff., 183 ff., 4 (1932), 100 ff.; Umberto Cassuto, "Wer war der Orientalist Mithridates?" *Zeitschrift für die Geschichte der Juden in Deutschland* 5 (1935), 230–36. See also Baron, 13:174. Still of use is the older study by Ludwig Geiger, *Das Studium der hebräischen Sprache in Deutschland vom Ende des XV. bis zur Mitte des XVI. Jahrhunderts* (Breslau: Schletter, 1870).

9. Baron, 13:167.

10. Ibid., 13:162.

11. Johannes Reuchlin, *Docter johanns Reuchlins tütsch missive, warumb die Juden so lang im ellend sind* (Pforzheim: Thomas Anshelm, 1505). This discussion of Reuchlin draws on the standard biographical material presented in Ludwig Geiger, *Johann Reuchlin: Sein Leben und seine Werke* (Leipzig: Duncker & Humblot, 1871).

12. Cited by Leon Poliakov, *The History of Anti-Semitism*, trans. Richard Howard, 3 vols. (New York: Vanguard Press, 1965–75), 1:151.

13. The literature on early modern and medieval converts is quite limited. By far the best and most detailed discussion of a single case of involuntary baptism is Solomon Grayzel, "The Confession of a Medieval Jewish Convert," *Historia Judaica* 17 (1955), 89–120. For more detailed bibliographic information see Guido Kisch, *Judentaufen: Eine historisch-biographisch-psychologisch-soziologische Studie besonders für Berlin und Königsberg* (Berlin: Colloquium Verlag, 1973), 3–5. Kisch deals primarily

with nineteenth- and twentieth-century converts. The question of the marginality of Christian proselytes has been explored in detail by Jacob S. Raisin, *Gentile Reactions to Jewish Ideals with Special Reference to Proselytes* (New York: Philosophical Library, 1953). A good comparative study of the different approaches to conversion in various parts of Europe is Stephen Sharot, *Messianism, Mysticism, and Magic: A Sociological Analysis of Jewish Religious Movements* (Chapel Hill: University of North Carolina Press, 1982). The more general background of the Church's attitude toward the Jews is to be found in Jeremy Cohen, *The Friars and the Jews: The Evolution of Medieval Anti-Judaism* (Ithaca, N.Y.: Cornell University Press, 1982). Most important is the recent book by Heiko A. Oberman, *Wurzeln des Antisemitismus: Christenangst und Judenplage im Zeitalter von Humanismus und Reformation* (Berlin: Severin & Seidler, 1981).

14. This discussion is based on the edition edited by Gerlinde Niemeyer, *Hermannus Quondam Judaeus: Opusculum de Conversione sua. Quellen zur Geistesgeschichte des Mittelalters*, vol. 4 (Weimar: Böhlau, 1963). Also of importance is the essay by J. Aronius, "Hermann der Prämonstratenser," *Zeitschrift für die Geschichte der Juden in Deutschland* 2 (1888), 217–31.

15. See Solomon Grayzel, *The Church and the Jews in the XIIIth Century* (New York: Hermon Press, 1966), 276.

16. Rudolf Cruel, *Geschichte der deutschen Predigt im Mittelalter* (Darmstadt: Wissenschaftliche Buchgesellschaft, 1966), 62.

17. Hyam Maccoby, ed., *Judaism on Trial: Jewish-Christian Disputations in the Middle Ages* (Rutherford, N.J.: Fairleigh Dickinson University Press, 1981), 159–60. See also David Berger, ed. and trans., *The Jewish-Christian Debate in the High Middle Ages: A Critical Edition of Nizzahon Vetus* (Philadelphia: Jewish Publication Society, 1979).

18. Friedrich Heinrich von der Hagen, ed., *Minnesinger*, 5 vols. (Leipzig: Barth, 1838–61), vol. 1, bk. 3, p. 342.

19. Compared with the literature on Reuchlin, the literature on Pfefferkorn is quite limited. Most important are the two essays by Ludwig Geiger, "Johannes Pfefferkorn: Ein Beitrag zur Geschichte der Juden und zur Charakteristik des Reuchlin'schen Streites," *Jüdische Zeitschrift für Wissenschaft und Leben* 7 (1869), 293–309, in which the question of the attitude toward Pfefferkorn as a Jew is first raised; and his discussion of sixteenth-century converts, "Die Juden und die deutsche Literatur," *Zeitschrift für Geschichte der Juden in Deutschland* 2 (1888), 321–27. Geiger's monograph *Die deutsche Literatur und die Juden* (Berlin: Georg Reimer, 1910), as well as his essays in the *Allgemeine Deutsche Bibliographie* on Pfefferkorn, add little to this material and to the material presented in his monograph on Reuchlin (see above, n. 11).

20. On the question of the original language and rhetoric of Pfefferkorn's texts see Meier Spanier, "Zur Charakteristik Johannes Pfefferkorn," *Zeitschrift für die Geschichte der Juden in Deutschland* 6 (1935), 209–28; Leonard Forster, "From the 'Schwabenspiegel' to Pfefferkorn," in *Medieval German Studies Presented to Frederick Norman* (London: University

of London, Germanic Institute, 1965), 292–95; and K. H. Gerschmann, "Zu Johannes Pfefferkorns 'Übersetzung der Evangelien,'" *Zeitschrift für Religion und Geistesgeschichte* 21 (1969), 166–71.

21. See Oberman, 42.

22. Johannes Pfefferkorn, *Der Juden Spiegel* (Cologne, 1508), Ev-Flr.

23. Johannes Pfefferkorn, *Ich bin ein buchlin der Judenveindt ist mein namen* (Cologne, 1509).

24. Victor of Karben's pamphlet exists in a Latin as well as a German version. Like Pfefferkorn's works, it most probably originally appeared in German, for while he knew enough Latin to cite the Vulgate, it is highly unlikely that he possessed the polished Latin style of the translation (*Hier inne wirt gelesen wie Her Victor von Carben . . .* [Cologne: Heinrich Quentell Erben, 1508]). Victor of Karben's work was popular enough that it was reprinted with additions as *Judenn Buochlein: Hyerinne würt gelesen / wie Herr Victor von Carben / welcher ein Rabi der Juden gewesst ist a zuo Christlichem glauben kommen . . .* (N.p., 1550).

25. For a discussion of this debate see Geiger's essay on the converts' attitudes, "Die Juden und die deutsche Literatur."

26. Karben, *Hier inne wirt . . .* , a4r.

27. Reuchlin reprinted this letter in *Augenspiegel* (Tübingen: Thomas Anshelm, 1511), 20a.

28. Ibid., 6a, 4a, 17b.

29. For the broader context of the understanding of Hebrew in the late Middle Ages and Renaissance see Arno Borst, *Der Turmbau von Babel: Geschichte der Meinungen über Ursprung und Vielfalt der Sprachen und Völker* (Stuttgart: A. Hiersemann, 1957–63).

30. Johannes Pfefferkorn, *Handspiegel* (Cologne, 1511), c2v.

31. Ibid., a3v. A detailed discussion of this incident and the charges of sacrilege on which it was grounded is given in Oberman, 128 ff., who reprints with a translation and commentary a contemporary broadside on the accusations.

32. Ibid., a2v.

33. Reuchlin, *Augenspiegel*, 22v.

34. Geiger, *Reuchlin*, 265.

35. Francis Griffin Stokes, trans., *Letters of Obscure Men* (New York: Harper, 1964), 200. The text has been compared to Eduard Böcking, *Epistolae obscurorum vivorum* (Leipzig: B. G. Teubner, 1858). Little of real interest has been published on the *Letters*. Rather they have been used, not as literary documents of the myths present in sixteenth-century Humanistic circles about the Church, but as quasi-historical statements about the Church. The complex irony of the text has been almost totally ignored. See, for example, the recent book by Reinhard Paul Becker, *A War of Fools: The "Letters of Obscure Men," a Study of the Satirized* (Bern: Lang, 1981).

36. Poliakov calls his chapter "The Birth of a Jewish Mentality" (1:83–90).

37. Kisch, *The Jews in Medieval Germany*, 204; Willibald M. Plöchl,

Geschichte des Kirchenrechts, 5 vols. (Vienna: Herold, 1953–69), 2:65–66.

38. Petrus Nigri is cited by Reuchlin as the only other authority in his lifetime to have condemned the Talmud. His attacks on Jewish Messianism and his authorship of one of the few Hebrew grammars available in the late fifteenth century made him a central figure in the movement to convert the Jews.

39. Eduard Böcking, ed., *Ulrichs von Hutten Schriften,* 7 vols. (Leipzig: B. J. Teubner, 1859–70), 5:345 ff.

40. Hutten's attitude toward Rapp is constantly cited as an anomaly in his writings, yet no one has seen his role in the creation of the double for Pfefferkorn. See Hajo Holborn, *Ulrich von Hutten* (Göttingen: Vandenhoek & Ruprecht, 1968), 50; and Thomas W. Best, *The Humanist Ulrich von Hutten* (Chapel Hill: University of North Carolina Press, 1969), 51.

41. David Friedrich Strauss, *Ulrich von Hutten* (Bonn: Emil Strauss, 1877), 74.

42. Johannes Pfefferkorn, *Brantspiegel* (Cologne, 1512), A2v.

43. Ibid., D3r.

44. See Geiger, *Reuchlin,* 270 ff.

45. Johannes Pfefferkorn, *Streydtpeuchlyn* (N.p., n.d.), E4b.

46. Johannes Pfefferkorn, *Ein mitleydliche claeg* (1521), H2r.

47. See the summary of the critical literature on this topic in C. Bernd Sucher, *Luthers Stellung zu den Juden* (Nieuwkoop: B. De Graaf, 1977), 125–99.

48. The major studies of Luther's and his contemporaries' attitudes toward the Jews, in addition to Sucher (n. 47), are Phillip N. Bepp, "Jewish Policy in Sixteenth-Century Nürnberg," *Occasional Papers of the American Society for Reformation Research* 1 (1977), 125–36; Selma Stern-Taeubler, "Die Vorstellung vom Juden und vom Judenthum in der Ideologie der Reformationszeit," *Essays Presented to Leo Baeck on the Occasion of His Eightieth Birthday* (London: East and West Library, 1954), 194–211; Johannes Brosseder, *Luthers Stellung zu den Juden im Spiegel seiner Interpreten* (Munich: M. Hueber, 1972); and Joachim Rogge, "Luthers Stellung zu den Juden," *Luther* 40 (1969), 13–24. See also Carl Cohen, "Martin Luther and His Jewish Contemporaries," *Jewish Social Studies* 25 (1963), 195–204; and Hayim Hillel Ben-Sasson, "The Reformation in Contemporary Jewish Eyes," *Proceedings of the Israel Academy of Sciences and Humanities* 4 (1971), 239–326. The best overall study is the discussion in Oberman, 125 ff.

49. See Paul Reiter, *Martin Luthers Umwelt, Charakter und Psychose sowie die Bedeutung dieser Faktoren für seine Entwicklung und Lehre: Eine historisch-psychiatrische Studie,* 2 vols. (Copenhagen: Levin & Munksgaard, 1937–41).

50. On the attitudes of the young Luther see Marilyn J. Harran, *Luther on Conversion: The Early Years* (Ithaca, N.Y.: Cornell University Press, 1983).

51. Luther's works are cited from Martin Luther, *D. Martin Luther*

Werke, 58 vols. (Weimar: Herrmann Böhlau, 1883–1972). Hereafter, *WA* refers to the edition of his writings; *WA Br,* to the letters; and *WA TG,* to his Tabletalk. Here, Luther to Spalatin, 5 August 1514, and Bucer to Luther, 23 January 1520, *WA Br,* 1:28 ff. and 614–17, respectively.

52. Luther to Spalatin, 15 February 1518, *WA Br,* 1:141 ff.

53. *Von der Winkelmesse und Pfaffenweihe,* in *WA,* 38:213.

54. *WA,* 53:419, 434. Here cited from *Luther's Works,* ed. Helmut Lehmann, vol. 47, ed. Franklin Sherman, trans. Martin H. Bertram (Philadelphia: Fortress, 1971), 139, 151.

55. Cited in Geiger, *Reuchlin,* 342.

56. *WA,* 53:636–37.

57. *WA TG,* 5327.

58. *WA,* 54:100.

59. Luther to Amsdorf, 23 January 1525, *WA Br,* 3:428 ff.

60. Luther to Spalatin, 16 April 1520, *WA Br,* 2:82 ff.

61. *WA TG,* 7038.

62. For the general background to Margaritha's life and times see Selma Stern-Taeubler, *Josel of Rosheim, Commander of Jewry in the Holy Roman Empire of the German Nation,* trans. Gertrude Hirschler (Philadelphia: Jewish Publication Society, 1965), 98–103; the present discussion draws primarily on the monograph by Josef Mieses, *Die älteste gedruckte deutsche Übersetzung des jüdischen Gebetbuchs aus dem Jahre 1530 und ihr Autor Anthonius Margaritha* (Vienna: W. Löwit, 1916); and Ludwig Feilchenfeld, *Rabbi Josel von Rosheim: Ein Beitrag zur Geschichte der Juden in Deutschland im Reformationszeitalter* (Strasbourg: J. H. Ed. Heitz, 1898), 27 ff.

63. See Haym Hillel Ben-Sasson, "Jewish-Christian Disputation in the Setting of Humanism and Reformation in the German Empire," *Harvard Theological Review* 59 (1966), 385 ff.

64. Antonius Margaritha, *Das gantz Jüdisch glaub* (Leipzig: Melchior Lother, 1531), Dd5r.

65. Ibid., F2v. Samuel Maroccanus's thirteenth-century *Epistola contra Judaeos* appeared as *Das Jhesus Nazerenus der ware Messias sey* (N.p.: W. Hemberg, 1536) with an introduction by Wenceslaus Lenck, and in an extended translation by L. Haetzer as *Gespräch zweyer Jüdischen Rabinen / von der Person Christi* (Heidelberg, 1583).

66. Paulus Staffelsteiner, *Ein kurtze underrichtung / das man einfeltig dem Herrn Jesu Christo nach wandern und in in volkummenlich und seinem wort glauben sol / und sich die Jüdischen Lerer / als ire Rabini / Schriffgelerte und Phariseer / heuchler und gleyssner / mit iren ungegründeteb erdichten Cermonien . . . untersteen . . .* (Nuremberg: Hans Guldenmundt, 1536), reprinted as *Von der Juden Ceremonien / so sie in Vermählungen der Kinder / und ihren Begräbnussen pflegen zu uben* (Heidelberg? 1583).

67. Paul of Prague, *Gründtliche und klare beweisung aus heimlichen verborgenen Wörter und Buchstaben heiliger Göttlicher Schrifft . . .* (Leipzig: Jacob Berwalds Erben, 1556).

68. Paul of Prague, *Mysterium Novum, Ein New herrlich / und gründtlich beweiss nach der Hebreer Cabala, dass eigentlich der Name und Tittel dess Herrn Jesu Christi Gottes Son, in dem fürnembsten Propheceyungen von Messia, verdeckt inn dem Hebraischen Buochstaben bedeutent ist* (Vienna: Michael Apfell, 1582).

69. Paul Weidner, *Ein Sermon / durch Paulum Weidner der Ertzney Doctorem / und in der Hochlöblochen Universität zu Wien Hebraischer sprachen Professoren: den Juden zu Prag Anno M.D. LXI den 26. Aprilis in ihrer synagoga gepredigt: dadurch auch etliche Personen zum Christlichen glauben bekert worden* (Vienna: Raphael Hofhalter, 1562).

70. Peter Gay, *Freud, Jews, and Other Germans* (New York: Oxford University Press, 1978), 3 ff.

71. *WA*, 53:417.

72. *WA*, 53:552.

73. *WA*, 53:648.

74. *WA*, 53:417. A major new presentation of the debate concerning the Jews is to be found in Mark U. Edwards, Jr., *Luther's Last Battles: Politics and Polemics, 1531–46* (Ithaca, N.Y.: Cornell University Press, 1983), 115–42. See also his recent essay "The Older Luther, 1526–1546," *Michigan Germanic Studies* 10 (1984), 48–64.

CHAPTER THREE. THE SPIRIT OF TOLERATION

1. Martin Luther, *D. Martin Luther Werke*, 58 vols. (Weimar: Hermann Böhlau, 1883–1972). Hereafter, *WA* refers to the edition of his writings; *WA Br*, to the letters; and *WA TG*, to his *Tabletalk*. Here, *WA*, 26:638, 648. The translation cited is *The Book of Vagabonds and Beggars*, trans. John Camden Hotten, 3 vols. (London: Hotten, 1860), 3:39. The present discussion of the perception of Yiddish as thieves' cant relies on the standard discussion by Friedrich Christian Benedict Ave-Lallement, *Das deutsche Gaunerthum in seiner social-politischen, literarischen und linguistischen Ausbildung zu seinem heutigen Bestande*, 4 vols. (Leipzig: F. A. Brockhaus, 1858–62), 4:313–19. Ave-Lallement argues strongly and convincingly that the association between these two languages of marginality does not show their identification. But he also shows that this identification had been assumed up to the time he was writing.

2. *WA*, 26:648; *Book of Vagabonds and Beggars*, 3:39. See also Eric J. Hobsbawm, *Bandits* (New York: Delacorte, 1969).

3. Ave-Lallement, 4:4 ff.

4. The most recent and most convincing study is the detailed essay by Paul Wexler, "Jewish Interlinguistics: Facts and Conceptual Framework," *Language* 57 (1981), 99–149. For the general background of the development of Yiddish the standard work remains Max Weinreich, *History of the Yiddish Language*, trans. Shlomo Noble (Chicago: University of Chicago Press, 1980). A valuable bibliography and overview is contained in Solomon A. Birnbaum, *Yiddish: A Survey and a Grammar* (Toronto: University of Toronto Press, 1979).

5. Ave-Lallement, 4:86–103.

6. Johann Christoph Adelung, *Mithridates oder allgemeine Sprachkunde*, vol. 2 (Berlin: Voss, 1809), 222–24.

7. Ave-Lallement, 3:214–39.

8. Johann Christoph Wagenseil, *Belehrung der Jüdisch-Teutschen Red- und Schreibart* (Königsberg: Paul Friedrich Rhode, 1699) (see Ave-Lallement, 3:218–20). See also Harry Zohn and M. C. Davis, "Johann Christoff Wagenseil, Polymath," *Monatshefte* 46 (1954), 35–39; Stephen H. Garrin, "Johann Christoff Wagenseil's *Belehrung der Teutsch-Hebräischen Red- und Schreibart*: A Significant Contribution to Yiddish Scholarship," *Michigan Germanic Studies* 9 (1983), 33–44; and, for a discussion of the parallels to the ideology of language present in German grammars of the same period, Wolfgang Huber, *Kulturpatriotismus und Sprachbewusstsein: Studien zur deutschen Philologie des 17. Jahrhunderts* (Frankfurt am Main: Peter Lang, 1984). Of interest in this context, though without any specific reference to the question of the nature of language as pollution, is Lionel Rothkrug, "Peasant and Jew: Fears of Pollution and German Collective Perceptions," *Historical Reflections/ Réflexions historiques* 10 (1983), 59–78.

9. Heinz Moshe Graupe, *The Rise of Modern Judaism: An Intellectual History of German Jewry, 1650–1942*, trans. John Robinson (Huntington, N.Y.: Robert E. Krieger, 1978), 53–55.

10. The general discussion of language and identity in Germany relies on the standard work by Eric A. Blackall, *The Emergence of German as a Literary Language, 1700–1775*, 2d ed., rev. (Ithaca, N.Y.: Cornell University Press, 1978). For a discussion of the attitudes of the Christian intellectual community to Hebrew as a surrogate for the Jews see Hans Joachim Schoeps, *Philosemitismus im Barock: Religions- und geistesgeschichtliche Untersuchungen* (Tübingen: J. C. B. Mohr, 1952), 134–62; and David S. Katz, *Philo-Semitism and the Readmission of the Jews to England, 1603–1655* (Oxford: Clarendon, 1982), 43–88. Schoeps discusses the Swedish attitudes, and Katz the British ones; both show the confusion between the image of Hebrew as a divine language and the image of the Jews.

11. See Weinreich, 103–4.

12. Wilhelm Christian Just Chrysander, *Jüdisch-Teutsche Grammatik* (Leipzig and Wolfenbüttel: Johann Christoph Meisner, 1750); see p. E2v.

13. Thomas de Cantimpré, *Miraculorum et exemplorum memorabilium sui temporis libro duo* (Duaci: Baltazris Belleri, 1605), 305–6; Heinrich Kornmann, *Opera curiosa I: Miracula vivorum*, 2d. ed. (Frankfurt: Genschiana, 1694), 128–29 (lst ed., 1614); Thomas Calvert, *The Blessed Jew of Marocco: or, A Blackmoor Made White Being a Demonstration of the True Messias out of the Law and Prophets by Rabbi Samuel* (York: Thomas Broad, 1649), 20–21. On Franco de Piacenza see Leon Poliakov, *The History of Anti-Semitism*, trans. Richard Howard, 3 vols. (New York: Vanguard Press, 1965–75), 1:143n.

14. Salo Wittmayer Baron, *A Social and Religious History of the Jews*, 19 vols. (New York: Columbia University Press, 1952–83), 11:1333. See

also the text of the drama in Adelbert Keller, ed., *Fastnachtspiele aus dem 15. Jahrhundert*, vol. 1 (Stuttgart: Literarischer Verein, 1853), 1–33.

15. M. Blakemore Evans, ed., *The Passion Play of Lucerne: An Historical and Critical Edition* (New York: Modern Language Association, 1943), 68–76.

16. The text of the play and this historical introduction are to be found in Karl von Amira, ed., *Das Endinger Judenspiel* (Halle: Niemeyer, 1883). See also Poliakov, 1:63, who, however, discusses the play without concern as to the actual dating of the text.

17. *Jüdischer Hertzklopffer* (Nuremberg, 1621). I am indebted to Professor Leonard Forster for this source; see his "Inter Bohemicum: A Report on German Baroque Literature in Czechoslovak Libraries," *Daphnis* 9 (1980), 315.

18. Christian Gerson, *Das Jüdischen Thalmuds fürnehmster Inhalt und Widerlegung* (Leipzig: Herbordt Kloss, 1685).

19. Johann Christoph Gottfried, *Jüdische Lügen / Welche aus dem Buche / so die Juden die Geschichte Gottes genannt, Heraus gezogen und ins Deutsche übersetzet sind* (Catzen-Ellenbogen, 1714).

20. Johann Friedrich Mentes, *Buch des Glaubens des Messias* (Hamburg: Johannes Neumann, 1720); Christoph Gustav Christian, *Bekehrung Israel* (Schwobach: Johann Michael Kuhn, 1723); idem, *Hebräisch- und Deutsche Vocabular und Wörter-Büchlein / so allen und jeden / Die mit denen Jüden / in Handel und Wandel / umgehenden Christen / sonderlich denen Studirenden Jugend / sehr nutzlich und profitabel seyn wird* (N.p., 1727); Paul Christian Kirchner, *Jüdisches Ceremoniel, D.i. Allerhand jüdische Gebräuche . . .* (N.p., 1720); Moritz Wilhelm Christian, *Kurtze Beschreibung einer wohleingerichteten Synagog, sammt einem Anhang von vielerley Jüdischen Curiositäten . . .* (Regensburg: Johannes Georg Hofmann, 1723); idem, *Schechitos Ubdikos; oder, Das Schächt- und Visitir-Buch, Welches diejenige So bey den Juden Schächten und Nachschen Profession machen will* (Regensburg: Johannes Georg Hofmann, 1724).

21. Adam Liebrecht, *Das hertzliche Vertrauen und demüthigste zuverlässliche Zuflucht zu allen frommen Christlichen Glaubens-Genossen / Samuel Jacobs / eines gewesenen Jüdischen Rabbi / jetzto Adam Liebrechts / und Moses Levi / eines Handelsmanns / nunehro Christian Gottlieb Hamburger genannt . . .* (Leipzig: Christoph Zunkel, [c. 1720]).

22. J.W., *Jüdischer Sprach-Meister; oder Erklärung was zwischen zweyen Juden, als einen Rabinen und Handelsmann, in einen Discours von unterschiedlichen Sachen, auf ihre gewöhnliche Redens-Art / abgehandelt wird . . .* (N.p., [1702]).

23. *Gründliche und wahrhaffte Abbildung des verstockten, und durch ihre eigene Bossheit verblendeten Judenthums* (N.p., 1749).

24. Johann Heinrich Callenberg, *Kurtze Anleitung zur Jüdisch-teutschen Sprache* (Halle: Jüdisches Institut, 1733).

25. Robert A. Kann, *A History of the Habsburg Empire, 1526–1918* (Berkeley: University of California Press, 1977), 185–86.

26. Alfred D. Low, *Jews in the Eyes of the Germans: From the Enlightenment to Imperial Germany* (Philadelphia: Institute for the Study of Human Values, 1979), 128.

27. J. J. Engel, *Schriften*, 12 vols. (Berlin: Mylius, 1844–45), 6:105 ff. The literature on the figure of the Jew in the eighteenth century centers on the appearance of the image of the Jew in texts by Christians, primarily theatrical ones, although Gellert's positive image of the Jew in his 1747–48 novel, *The Life of the Swedish Countess of G. . . .*, is always mentioned. See Herbert Carrington, *Die Figur des Juden in der dramatischen Literatur des XVIII. Jahrhunderts* (Ph.D. diss., Heidelberg, 1897); Helmut Jenzsch, *Jüdische Figuren in deutschen Bühnentexten des 18. Jahrhunderts* (Ph.D. diss., Hamburg, 1974); Wilhelm Stoffers, *Juden und Ghetto in der deutschen Literatur bis zum Ausgang des Weltkrieges* (Graz: Heinrich Stiasny, 1939); and, with the bias of Nazi racial politics, Elisabeth Frenzel, *Judengestalten auf der deutschen Bühne: Ein notwendiger Querschnitt durch 700 Jahre Rollengeschichte* (Munich: Deutscher Volksverlag, 1942).

28. See the presentation of selections from this text in Peter Gay, ed., *The Enlightenment: A Comprehensive Anthology* (New York: Simon & Schuster, 1973), 746 ff.

29. See Wilfried Barner, "Lessings *Die Juden* im Zusammenhang seines Frühwerks," in *Humanität und Dialog: Lessing und Mendelssohn in neuer Sicht*, ed. Erhard Bahr et al. (Detroit: Wayne State University Press, 1982), 189–210; and Karl S. Guthke, *Erkundungen: Essays zur Literatur von Milton bis Traven* (New York: Peter Lang, 1983), 49–102. The most complete overview is Wilfried Barner, "Vorurteil, Empirie, Rettung. Der junge Lessing und die Juden," *Bulletin des Leo Baeck Instituts* 69 (1984), 29–52.

30. Christian Wilhelm von Dohm, *Über die bürgerliche Verbesserung der Juden*, vol. 2 (Berlin: Nikolai, 1781–83), 300–346.

31. Johannes Andreas Eisenmenger's *Entdecktes Judentum* appeared in a series of reprints throughout the eighteenth and nineteenth centuries. On Dohm and Eisenmenger in terms of the context of their writing and Eisenmenger's central position in defining the image of the Jew see Jacob Katz, *From Prejudice to Destruction: Anti-Semitism, 1700–1933* (Cambridge: Harvard University Press, 1980), 13–62.

32. Ludwig Geiger presents all of the texts in his appendix "Zur Geschichte des Judeneides 1712–1869," *Geschichte der Juden in Berlin*, vol. 2 (Berlin: J. Guttentag, 1871), 265–80.

33. The importance of the literary representation of the Jews' language cannot be underestimated. Jews, especially those seeing the German bourgeoisie as their reference group, took the language of the Jews on the stage as a model for the correctness of language (and attitude) in daily life. Nowhere is this more striking than in Markus Herz's pamphlet *Freymuthiges Kaffeegespräch zweer jüdischen Zuschauerinnen über den Juden Pinkus* (1771). Pinkus is the hero of a drama by the contemporary German author Stephanie, who was in turn influenced by Cumberland's positive image of the Jew (and his language). Another text by a Jew of the period

in which Jews are presented speaking unaffected German is David Arnstein, *Eine jüdische Familienszene* (1782). The importance of a correct German for the Jew of the Enlightenment and the implications of a "cultured" vocabulary are outlined in Werner Weinberg, "A Word-List for Teaching Eighteenth-Century Jews Some Fine Points of High German," *Leo Baeck Institute Yearbook* 29 (1984), 277–94.

34. M. J. Landa, *The Jew in Drama* (London: P. S. King, 1926), 119.

35. Johann Georg Hamann, *Sämtliche Werke*, ed. Josef Nadler, vol. 2 (Vienna: Herder, 1950), 122.

36. George Steiner, *After Babel: Aspects of Language and Translation* (London: Oxford University Press, 1975), 74–77.

37. Johann Gottfried Herder, *Sämmtliche Werke*, ed. Bernhard Suphan, 33 vols. (Berlin: Weidmann, 1877–1913), 24:66–75. See Michael M. Morton, "Herder and the Possibility of Literature: Rationalism and Poetry in Eighteenth-Century Germany," in *Johann Gottfried Herder: Innovator through the Ages*, ed. Wolf Koepke (Bonn: Bouvier, 1982), 41–63; and F. M. Barnard, "National Culture and Political Legitimacy: Herder and Rousseau," *Journal of the History of Ideas* 44 (1983), 231–53.

38. See the discussion by Klara Pomeranz Carmely, "Wie aufgeklärt waren die Aufklärer im Bezug auf die Juden?" in Bahr et al., eds., 177–88.

39. On the history and implication of productivity as a sign of the value of the Christian as opposed to the valuelessness of the Jews see Tamar Bermann, *Produktivierungsmythen und Antisemitismus: Eine soziologische Studie* (Vienna: Europa, 1973).

40. The general discussion of the actual role of the Jew in German society has been simplified by the work of Selma Stern-Taeubler, especially her *The Court Jew: A Contribution to the History of the Period of Absolutism in Europe*, trans. Ralph Weiman (Philadelphia: Jewish Publication Society, 1950), and her *Der preussische Staat und die Juden*, 4 vols. (Tübingen: J. C. B. Mohr, 1962–75), vol. 3, *Die Zeit Friedrich des Grossen*. See also Nachum Gross, ed., *Economic History of the Jews* (New York: Schocken, 1975); and Katz, *From Prejudice to Destruction*, 34–73. For the most recent attempt to trace the social, political, and economic interactions that define the Jew in terms of the Jewish community see Calvin Goldschneider and Alan S. Zuckerman, *The Transformation of the Jews* (Chicago: University of Chicago Press, 1985). The background to this history is documented in Hans I. Bach, *The German Jew: A Synthesis of Judaism and Western Civilization, 1730–1930* (Rutherford, N.J.: Fairleigh Dickinson University Press, 1983).

41. Michaelis's critique and the attendant correspondence are reproduced in Julius Braun, ed., *Lessing im Urtheile seiner Zeitgenossen*, vol. 1 (Berlin: Stahn, 1884), 35–37.

42. Hans-Friedrich Wessel, *Lessings Nathan der Weise: Seine Wirkungsgeschichte bis zum Ende der Goethezeit* (Königstein: Athenäum, 1979).

43. All references to the published letter to Lavater are to the older collected edition, *Moses Mendelssohn's Gesammelte Schriften*, ed. G. B.

Mendelssohn, 7 vols. (Leipzig: F. A. Brockhaus, 1843–45), 3:37–49. On the debate with Lavater see Sylvain Zac, "La Querelle Mendelssohn-Lavater," *Archives de philosophie* 46 (1983), 219–54; and B. Mevorah, "Johann Kaspars Lavaters Auseinandersetzung mit Moses Mendelssohn über die Zukunft des Judenthums," *Zwingliana* 14 (1977), 431–50. The very fact that this controversy appeared to Mendelssohn's contemporaries, such as Lichtenberg, as an elaborate joke (see his 1773 satire *Timorus*, subtitled "A Defense of Two Israelites, Converted to the True Faith through the Power of Lavater's Proof and the Göttingen Sausages") makes his own response even more radical. Lavater, whose physiognomic theories had been lampooned by Lichtenberg, was simply not taken seriously except by those immediately involved in the debate.

44. Alexander Altmann, *Moses Mendelssohn: A Biographical Study* (University: University of Alabama Press, 1973). The idea that the conflict with Lavater formed the central experience in Mendelssohn's formation of his identity may first have been put forth by Meyer Kayserling, *Moses Mendelssohn: Sein Leben und Wirken* (Leipzig: H. Mendelssohn, 1862). See also Michael A. Meyer, *The Origins of the Modern Jew: Jewish Identity and European Culture in Germany, 1749–1824* (Detroit: Wayne State University Press, 1979), 29–56.

45. Lavater's diary entries are published in Leo Weisz, "Aus Lavaters Tagebüchern," *Neue Züricher Zeitung*, 21 March 1961.

46. Cited in Weisz.

47. The draft letter is cited in Mendelssohn, *Schriften*, 3:105–6.

48. Johann Georg Hamann, *Briefwechsel*, ed. Walther Ziesemer and Arthur Henkel, 7 vols. (Wiesbaden: Insel, 1955–79), 2:33.

49. Friedrich Wilhelm Schütz, *Leben und Meinungen Moses Mendelssohns* (Hamburg: Möller, 1787), 99; and Mendelssohn, *Schriften*, 5:573.

50. Moses Samuels, *Memoirs of Moses Mendelssohn* (London: Saintsbury & Co., 1827), 142.

51. Naphtali Herz Wessely, *Divrei Shalom Ve'emes*, vol. 2 (Berlin, [1782]), 12a. For the more general context of this statement see Moshe Pelli, *The Age of Haskalah* (Leiden: E. J. Brill, 1979), 48–72.

52. Mendelssohn, *Schriften*, 5:673.

53. Ibid., 5:206.

54. Cf. Walter Kern, ed., *Aufklärung und Gottesglaube* (Düsseldorf: Patmos, 1981), 25–50.

55. G. E. Lessing, *Sämtliche Schriften*, ed. Karl Lachmann/Franz Muncker, 23 vols. (Stuttgart: G. J. Göschen, 1886–1924), 19:320.

56. Joachim Gessinger, *Sprache und Bürgertum: Sozialgeschichte sprachlicher Verkehrsformen im Deutschland des 18. Jahrhunderts* (Stuttgart: J. B. Metzler, 1980). Gessinger presents the linguistic context in which Mendelssohn found himself but pays no attention at all to the peculiar situation of the German Jews (168).

57. For a detailed presentation of the incident see M. K. Torbruegge, "On Lessing, Mendelssohn and the Ruling Powers," in Bahr et al., 305–17.

58. Selma Stern-Taeubler, "The First Generation of Emancipated Jews," *Leo Baeck Institute Yearbook* 15 (1970), 38–39.

59. *Hame'asef* 4 (1788), 84. The best introduction to the Haskalah's attitude toward traditional values, including language, is Isaac Eisenstein-Barzilay, "The Treatment of the Jewish Religion in the Literature of the Berlin Haskalah," *Proceedings of the American Academy for Jewish Research* 24 (1955), 39–68. What is striking in all the literature on the role of the Jews in the Enlightenment and the role of the Enlightenment in the Jewish community is that these questions have rarely been treated in the same context, the context in which they existed. Thus Salomon Maimon is considered either a German or a Hebrew author, not one who is coping with two new languages.

60. Gottfried Selig, *Kurze und gründliche Anleitung zu einer leichten Erlernung der Jüdischdeutschen Sprache* (Leipzig: Christian Friedrich Rumpf, 1767), A2v. See also his *Geschichte seines Lebens und seiner Bekehrung*, 3 vols. (Leipzig: C. G. Hertel, 1775–77).

61. Gottfried Selig, *Lehrbuch zur gründliche Anleitung zu einer leichten Erlernung der Jüdischdeutschen Sprache* (Leipzig: Voss und Leo, 1792), ix.

62. See Jacob Katz, *Zur Assimilation und Emanzipation der Juden* (Darmstadt: Wissenschaftliche Buchgesellschaft, 1982).

63. Elias Ackord, *Die Juden oder die nothwendige Reformation der Juden in der Republik Polen* (Warsaw: Michael Gröll, 1786).

64. David Friedländer, *Über die Verbesserung der Israeliten im Königreich Pohlen* (Berlin: Nicolai, 1819). See also Meyer, 57–84.

65. Johann Gottlieb Fichte, *Beitrag zur Berichtigung der Urteile des Publikums über die französische Revolution*, ed. Reinhard Strecker (Leipzig: Felix Meiner, 1922), 114 ff. See also Katz, *From Prejudice to Destruction*, 57. The Jewish reception of this passage can be judged from S. Ascher's pamphlet *Eisenmenger der Zweite* (Berlin: Carl Ludwig Hartmann, 1794), 24–25, where the terror, which had just begun, is cited as the inevitable outcome of Fichte's views.

66. Karl Wilhelm Friedrich Grattenauer, *Über die physische und moralische Verfassung der heutigen Juden* (Leipzig, 1791).

67. Henri Grégoire, *Essai sur le régénération physique, morale et politique des juifs* (Metz: Lamort, 1789).

68. Karl Wilhelm Friedrich Grattenauer, *Bemerkungen über die Lehrart Jesu mit Rücksicht auf jüdische Sprach- und Denkungsart* (Offenbach: Ulrich Weiss, 1788).

69. See Mendelssohn's pamphlet *Or lantetive* (Berlin, 1783), [ix]. On Mendelssohn's own writings in Yiddish see Kh. Borodyanski, "M. Mendelson un zayne yidishe briv," *Historishe shriftn (YIVO)* 1 (1929), 297–346.

70. Mendelssohn, *Schriften*, 5:604–5. The translation is from Eva Jospe, ed. and trans., *Moses Mendelssohn: Selections from His Writings* (New York: Viking Press, 1975), 106.

71. See the essay "Über die Sprache," reprinted in Moses Mendelssohn, *Gesammelte Schriften*, vol. 6, pt. 2, *Kleinere Schriften II*, ed. Eva J. Engel (Stuttgart: Frommann, 1981), 3–24.

72. Lessing, 17:40. The best discussion of the problems of the image of Spinoza and the influence of his thinking in the works of the early Lessing is Karl S. Guthke, "Lessing und das Judentum oder Spinoza absconditus," *Das Abenteuer der Literatur* (Bern: Francke, 1981), 123–43.

73. Cited by Harry Austryn Wolfson, *The Philosophy of Spinoza* (Cambridge: Harvard University Press, 1934), 11–12.

74. *Hame'asef* 3 (1786), 92.

75. For an overview that is useful, if dated, and contains a good survey of the literature in its notes see Rudolf Hallo, "Christian Hebraists," *Modern Judaism* 3 (1983), 95–116. Initially published in 1934, it is still of interest.

76. See the discussion by Poliakov, 3:176 ff.

77. Immanuel Kant, *Gesammelte Schriften*, 28 vols. (Berlin: George Reimer, 1902–80), 6:125–28.

78. Immanuel Kant, *Anthropology from a Pragmatic Point of View*, trans. Victor Lyle Dowdell (Carbondale: Southern Illinois University Press, 1978), 101–2. See also Poliakov, 3:178 ff.

79. Samuel Hochheimer, *Über Moses Mendelssohns Tod* (Vienna: Johannes Jakob Stahel, 1789), 35 ff. The identification of the Eastern Jew as part of the sphere of the Slav rather than as a Jew can be seen as early as the eighteenth century. German Jews used the term "Polack" to refer to Eastern European Jews, specifically those from Poland (see Max Weinreich, "Two Yiddish Satirical Poems about Jews," *Philologische Schriften* 3 [1929]).

80. For a good survey of the function of satire see Wolfgang Promies, *Die Bürger und der Narr oder das Risiko der Phantasie* (Munich: Carl Hanser, 1966).

81. On Rabener see J. Jacobs, "Zur Satire der frühen Aufklärung: Rabener und Liscow," *Germanisch-Romanische Monatshefte* 49 (1968), 1–13.

82. Mendelssohn, *Gesammelte Schriften*, vol. 6, pt. 1, 137–41.

83. See Bernard D. Weinryb, "An Unknown Hebrew Play of the German Haskalah," *Proceedings of the American Academy for Jewish Research* 24 (1955), 165–70.

84. A good summary of the literature on Euchel in Hebrew and Yiddish is provided by Pelli, 190 ff., who, however, only mentions the play (229).

85. See my essay "The Flight of the Hero: Modalities of Reception in Yiddish Fiction," *Colloquia Germanica* 4 (1976), 336–52. See also Dan Miron, *A Traveler Disguised: A Study in the Rise of Modern Yiddish Fiction in the Nineteenth Century* (New York: Schocken, 1973), esp. 34 ff.

86. R. K. Angress, "The Generations in *Emilia Galotti*," *Germanic Review* 43 (1968), 15–23. See also Sol Gittleman, *From Shtetl to Suburbia: The Family in Jewish Literary Imagination* (Boston: Beacon, 1978).

87. Peter L. Berger, "Excursus: Alternation and Biography," in his *An Invitation to Sociology: A Humanistic Perspective* (Garden City, N.Y.: Doubleday Anchor, 1963), 60.

88. The text of Euchel's play is reprinted in M. Erik, ed., *Di Komoidis vun der berliner aoifklerung* (Kiev, 1933), 71 ff. These themes reappear in Joseph Herz's *Esther* (1828) (see Robert M. Copeland and Nathan Süsskind, eds., *The Language of Herz's "Esther": A Study in Judeo-German Dialectology* [University: University of Alabama Press, 1976]). What is interesting is that highly Germanicized Yiddish (*Daytschmersch*) becomes the stage language for serious drama until the late 1880s.

89. For the context of this use of language see Joachim Dyck, ed., *Minna von Barnhelm; oder, Die Kosten des Glücks* (Berlin: Wagenbach, 1981), 11 ff.

90. On the concept of the schlemiel see esp. Ruth R. Wisse, *The Schlemiel as Modern Hero* (Chicago: University of Chicago Press, 1971), 3-24. Wisse does not see the Enlightenment roots of the concept; she focuses instead on the nineteenth century.

91. The present discussion of Kuh is based on the biography by Moses Hirschel that prefaces the two-volume edition of Kuh's poetry, Ephraim Moses Kuh, *Hinterlassene Gedichte* (Zurich: Orell, Gessner, Füssli und Comp., 1792), as well as the later biography by Meyer Kayserling, *Der Dichter Ephraim Kuh: Ein Beitrag zur Geschichte der deutschen Literatur* (Berlin: J. Springer, 1864).

92. J. Kranz, *Über den Missbrauch der geistlichen Macht und der weltlichen Herrschaft in Glaubensachen* (Berlin, 1782), 14.

93. Hirschel, in Kuh, 1:114.

94. On the refunctioning of the concept of the writer in the eighteenth century see Hans Jürgen Haferkorn, "Der freie Schriftsteller: Eine literar-soziologische Studie über seine Entstehung und Lage in Deutschland zwischen 1750 und 1800," *Archiv für Geschichte des Buchwesens* 5 (1962-63), 523-712.

95. Moses Mendelssohn, *Jerusalem, or On Religious Power and Judaism*, trans. Alan Arkush (Hanover, N.H.: University Press of New England, 1983), 104.

96. Markus Herz, cited from *Versuch über den Geschmack und die Ursachen seiner Verschiedenheit*, 2d ed., rev. (Berlin: Christian Friedrich Voss, 1790), 159. See in this context Mark Boulby, "Marcus Herz the Psychologist," *Akten des VI. Internationalen Germanisten-Kongress Basel 1980* (Bern: Peter Lang, 1980), 327-32. The denial to the Jews of all aesthetic sensibility throughout the Enlightenment (except the ability to create naive works) is a commonplace. Friedrich Maximilian Klinger sees this as the salient mark of the Jew in the past and the present (*Betrachtungen und Gedanken über verschiedene Gegenstände der Welt und der Litteratur*, vol. 1 [Königsberg: Nicolovius, 1809], 237).

97. See my *On Blackness without Blacks: Essays on the Image of the Black in Germany* (Boston: G. K. Hall, 1982), 19-34.

98. The literature on Maimon as a philosopher is quite extensive: Samuel H. Atlas, *From Critical to Speculative Idealism: The Philosophy of Solomon Maimon* (The Hague: M. Nijhoff, 1964); Shmuel Hugo Bergman, *The Philosophy of Solomon Maimon*, trans. Noah J. Jacobs (Jerusa-

lem: Magnes, 1967); Francesco Moiso, *La filosofia di Solomone Maimon* (Milan: Mursia, 1972); Noah J. Jacobs, "Solomon Maimon's Relation to Judaism," *Leo Baeck Institute Yearbook* 8 (1963), 117–35. However, the biographical literature, such as J. H. Witte, *Salomon Maimon: Die merkwürdigen Schicksale und die wissenschaftliche Bedeutung eines jüdischen Denkers* (Berlin: H. R. Mecklenburg, 1876), simply accepts the autobiography as the literal account of his life. The major volume that presents supplemental material is Sabattja Josef Wolff, *Maimoniana, oder Rhapsodien zur Charakteristik Salomon Maimons* (Berlin: C. Hayn, 1813), from which all of the additional material on Maimon's life is taken.

99. Kuno Fischer, *Geschichte der neueren Philosophie*, 10 vols. (Heidelberg: C. Winter, 1897–1904), 5:7.

100. The best study of Moritz is Mark Boulby, *Karl Philipp Moritz: At the Fringe of Genius* (Toronto: University of Toronto Press, 1979). For a survey of the literature on Moritz and *Anton Reiser* see Hans Joachim Schrimpf, *Karl Philipp Moritz* (Stuttgart: Metzler, 1980), 49–55.

101. This and the following quotations are from the English translation by J. Clark Murray, *Solomon Maimon: An Autobiography* (London: Alexander Gardner, 1888), here, 1. All of Maimon's German works, including the *Lebensgeschichte*, are reprinted in Solomon Maimon, *Gesammelte Werke*, ed. Valerio Verra (Hildesheim: Georg Olms, 1965). I have used the English edition but refer to the German edition where sections have been omitted in the English. The general background to Maimon's times is supplied by William W. Hagen, *Germans, Poles, and Jews: The Nationality Conflict in the Prussian East, 1772–1914* (Chicago: University of Chicago Press, 1980).

102. Kant to Carl Leonard Reinhold, 28 March 1794, in Immanuel Kant, *Briefwechsel*, vol. 2 (Berlin: Georg Reimer, 1900), 476.

103. Wolff, 87 (Yiddish), 109–12, 140, 208, 212–13.

104. Ibid., 94.

105. The figure of Friedländer shows some of the internal and external pressures that were brought by the politics of acculturation. The prime disciple of Mendelssohn and his most evident successor, he made an unsuccessful attempt to convert in 1799 (see Meyer, 57–84).

106. Cited in the one scholarly essay on Behr, Daniel Jacoby, "Der Verfasser der 'Gedichte eines polnischen Juden,'" *Euphorion* 7 (1900), 238–46; and Kayserling, *Kuh*, 43–47. Recent references to Behr are based on Goethe's review rather than on Behr's own works (see, for example, Marcel Reich-Ranicki, *Über Ruhestörer: Juden in der deutschen Literatur* [Munich: Piper, 1973], 13–14).

107. Lessing, 20:156–57.

108. Cited in Jacoby, 241.

109. Isashar Falkensohn Behr, *Gedichte von einem pohlnischen Juden* (Mietau and Leipzig: Jakob Friedrich Hinz, 1772), 8 ff.

110. Cited in Kayserling, *Kuh*, 46.

111. K. A. Kütner, *Charaktere teutscher Dichter und Prosaisten* (Berlin: C. F. Voss, 1781), 494.

112. Johann Wolfgang von Goethe, *Werke*, 129 vols. (Weimar: Hermann Böhlau, 1887–1919), 37:221–25. See the polemical study by Mark Waldman, *Goethe and the Jews* (New York: G. P. Putnam, 1934), which remains the standard presentation.

113. See my *On Blackness*, 19–24.

114. The question of philo-Semitism as a model for identity formation has not yet been raised. The very idea of philo-Semitism is simply the polar opposite of that against which it often defends itself, anti-Semitism. See Alan Edelstein, *An Unacknowledged Harmony: Philo-Semitism and the Survival of European Jewry* (Westport, Conn.: Greenwood Press, 1982), for examples.

115. Jacoby, 240.

CHAPTER FOUR. THE DRIVE FOR ASSIMILATION

1. There has been much confusion about the origin of the word *mauscheln*, and an extremely large amount of bad scholarship about it has been copied from reference book to reference book (and cited in numerous studies). On these errors and their correction see Solomon A. Birnbaum, "Der Mogel," *Zeitschrift für deutsche Philologie* 74 (1955), 249. The oldest source for either *mauscheln* or *jüdeln*, a broadside entitled "Ein neues und zurvor nie an Tag gebrachtes Kipp- Wipp- und Münzer Lied" which is dated 1622, is reprinted in Julius Opel and Adolf Cohn, eds., *Der dreissigjährige Krieg* (Halle: Waisenhaus, 1862). In this poem there are two uses of the term, one as a verb (*mauscheln*) and the other as a noun (*Mauschel-Brüder*); the contexts of both make it clear that the reference is to Christians who act (not speak) like Jews.

2. Julius von Voss, *Der travestierte Nathan der Weise* (Berlin: John Wilhelm Schmidt, 1804). See also Heinrich Stümcke, *Die Fortsetzungen, Nachahmungen und Travestien von Lessings Nathan der Weise* (Berlin: Gesellschaft für Theatergeschichte, 1904). The nature of the language of the Jews within the literary representation of the figure of the Jew has been examined little. The two best essays are Peter Althaus, "Soziolekt und Fremdsprache: Das Jiddische als Stilmittel in der deutschen Literatur," *Zeitschrift für deutsche Philologie* 100 (1981), 212–30; and Kathryn Hellerstein, "Yiddish Voice in American English," in *The State of the Language*, ed. Leonard Michaels and Christopher Ricks (Berkeley: University of California Press, 1980), 182–201. Because of the very limited samples in these essays, they are only tentative in their conclusions. Neither goes much beyond the "U" versus "non-U" debate, and neither sees the relationship among the various types of discourse and dialects attributed to the Jews. See Alan S. C. Ross, "U and Non-U: An Essay in Sociological Linguistics," in *The Importance of Language*, ed. Max Black (Englewood Cliffs, N.J.: Prentice-Hall, 1962), 91–107, for the basis of their arguments. This stress on dialect as sociolect is, of course, only one part of the concept of the discourse of difference. It is most important to Ross because of his

British examples but is not even applicable to the tradition of British-Jewish use of dialect.

3. Julius von Voss, *Der Jude und der Grieche*, in his *Lustspiele* (Berlin: Johannes Wilhelm Schmidts Wittwe, 1811), 5:1–32 (each play separately paginated).

4. To be found in a volume supposedly edited (but actually written) by Voss entitled *Jüdische Romantik und Wahrheit von einem getauften Israeliten* (Berlin: Johannes Wilhelm Schmidts Wittwe, 1817), 3–64. This volume also contains a sympathetic biography of Maimon based on his autobiography.

5. Anton Ree, *Die Sprachverhältnisse der heutigen Juden, im Interesse der Gegenwart und mit besondrer Rücksicht auf Volkserziehung* (Hamburg: Hermann Gobert, 1844).

6. It is indicative of this stress that Henri Tronchon calls his chapter on Renan and the Jews "Les Voix d'Israël" (see his *Ernest Renan et l'étranger* [Paris: Les Belles-Lettres, 1928], 115–54).

7. The pamphlet, simply titled *Bekehrungs-Geschichte eines Israeliten*, is to be found in the Zunz Library, Jews' College, University of London.

8. August Lewald, *Memoiren eines Banquiers* (1836). The passages cited are from the selections reprinted in Guido Kisch's excellent study (with readings) *Judentaufen: Eine historisch-biographisch-psychologisch-soziologische Studie besonders für Berlin und Königsberg* (Berlin: Colloquium Verlag, 1973), 73–81. This should be read in the light of Eleanor Sterling's topology "Jewish Reactions to Jew-Hatred in the First Half of the Nineteenth Century," *Leo Baeck Institute Yearbook* 3 (1958), 103–21.

9. Georg Simmel, *The Sociology of Georg Simmel* (New York: Free Press, 1950), 185–86.

10. The best and most detailed study of Saphir's life in regard to the beginning of the movement of Jewish assimilation is Sara Friedländer, "Saphir Moric Gottlieb. Tanulmany a zsido assimilacios törekvesek kezdetereiröl," *Literaturwissenschaftliches Jahrbuch des deutschen Instituts der königlichen Ungarischen Peter Pazmany Universität Budapest* 6 (1940), 200–309.

11. M. G. Saphir, "Meine Memoiren," in *M. G. Saphir's Schriften* (Brno: Karafiat und Sohn, 1880), 23, 43.

12. See the pamphlet *M. G. Saphir und Berlin* (Berlin: Cosmar und Krause, 1828), 10. This pamphlet is signed by Friedrich Baron de la Motte Fouqué, Friedrich Wilhelm Gubitz, and Willibald Alexis. Saphir's response, not unexpectedly, simply ignores the central charge of a difference in the "hidden language of the Jews" and concentrates on the misquotations in the original pamphlet (see his *Der getödtete und dennoch lebende M. G. Saphir* [Berlin: L. W. Krause, 1828]).

13. Friedländer, 223.

14. Ibid., 237.

15. Friedrich von den Hagen, *Neueste Wanderungen, Umtriebe, und Abenteuer des Ewigen Juden unter dem Namen Börne, Heine, Saphir, u.a. Zum Besten der Anstalten gegen die St. Simonie ans Licht gestellt von Cruciger* (Wilhelmstadt: Friedrich, 1832).

16. Cited in Elisabeth Frenzel, *Judengestalten auf der deutschen Bühne: Ein notwendiger Querschnitt durch 700 Jahre Rollengeschichte* (Munich: Deutscher Volksverlag, 1942), 165.

17. See Eda Sagarra, *A Social History of Germany, 1648–1914* (London: Methuen, 1977), 304–23; Alfred D. Low, *Jews in the Eyes of the Germans: From the Enlightenment to Imperial Germany* (Philadelphia: Institute for the Study of Human Values, 1979), 243 ff.; and Friedrich Meinecke, *The Age of German Liberation, 1795–1815*, trans. Peter Paret (Berkeley: University of California Press, 1977). For the present chapter, Manfred Schneider, *Die kranke schöne Seele der Revolution: Heine, Börne, das "Junge Deutschland," Marx und Engels* (Frankfurt: Syndikat, 1980), has been of extreme interest.

18. On Börne's life and times see Erika Anders, *Ludwig Börne und die Anfänge des modernen Journalismus: Eine stilkritische Untersuchung* (Ph.D. diss., Heidelberg, 1933); Ludwig Marcuse, *Ludwig Börne: Aus der Frühzeit der deutschen Demokratie* (Rothenburg: J. P. Peter, 1967); Heinz Politzer, "Studies on Jewish Contributors to German Literature: Heine and Börne" (Ph.D. diss., Bryn Mawr, 1950); and Wolfgang Schimming, *Ludwig Börnes Theaterkritik. Die Schaubühne*, vol. 5 (Emsdetten: Lechte, 1932). Of importance for this study has been the essay by Charlene A. Lea, "Ludwig Börne: Jewish Emancipationist or Jewish Anti-Semite?" *Seminar* 16 (1980), 224–34, which, however, does not answer the question raised in the title.

19. All references to Börne's work are to the critical edition edited by Inge Rippmann and Peter Rippmann, *Ludwig Börne: Sämtliche Schriften*, 5 vols. (Düsseldorf: Joseph Melzer, 1964–68), here, 4:39. The best attempt to place this early essay into the historical context of its time remains Ludwig Geiger, "Zu Börnes Aufsatz 'Juden in Frankfurt,'" *Zeitschrift für die Geschichte der Juden in Deutschland* 2 (1888), 391–93. A detailed bibliography on Börne's image of the Jew is printed in Börne, 5:1158–62.

20. Börne to his father, 24 July 1807, in Börne, 5:606.

21. The proposals seemed to have had no effect whatsoever (ibid., 1:14–71).

22. F. L. de La Fontaine, *Chirurgisch-medicinische Abhandlungen verschiedenen Inhalts Polen betreffend* (Breslau: Korn, 1792), 145–55.

23. See Horst Albert Glaser, ed., *Deutsche Literatur: Eine Sozialgeschichte, 7: 1848–1880* (Reinbek: Rowohlt, 1982), esp. 47 ff. The best study of the nature of the literary and critical discourse is Hartmut Steinecke, ed., *Literaturkritik des Jungen Deutschland: Entwicklung-Tendenzen-Texte* (Berlin: Erich Schmidt, 1982).

24. Börne, 1:170–78.

25. Low, 103 ff.; Howard Morley Sachar, *The Course of Modern Jewish History* (New York: Dell, 1977), 65–70.

26. Cited in the biography appended to Börne, 3:998.

27. Steven M. Lowenstein, "The Yiddish Written Word in Nineteenth-Century Germany," *Leo Baeck Institute Yearbook* 24 (1979), 179–92.

28. Friedrich Christian Benedict Ave-Lallement, *Das deutsche Gaunerthum in seiner social-politischen, literarischen und linguistischen Ausbildung zu seinem heutigen Bestande*, 4 vols. (Leipzig: F. A. Brockhaus, 1858–62), 3:231.

29. See my *The Parodic Sermon in European Perspective* (Wiesbaden: Steiner, 1974), 88–93.

30. All references to Carl Barromäus Sessa's *Our Crowd* are to "Unser Verkehr," *Deutsche Schaubühne* (Augsburg: Jenisch, 1815), 195–242. The best discussion of the Sessa scandal is Charlene A. Lea, *Emancipation, Assimilation, and Stereotype: The Image of the Jew in German and Austrian Drama (1800–1850)* (Bonn: Bouvier, 1978), 78–86. On Albert Wurm and the Jewish dialect see Jacob Katz, *Out of the Ghetto: The Social Background of Jewish Emancipation, 1770–1870* (Cambridge: Harvard University Press, 1972), 86. Concerning the homosexual scandal see Frenzel, 93 ff.

31. Low, 252.

32. *Über die Juden: Auf Veranlassung der Posse: "Unser Verkehr"* (Königsberg: George Haberland, 1815), 4.

33. The review is published in Börne, 1:415–20.

34. Cited from Julius von Voss, "Über des Schauspielers Herrn Wurm jüdische Deklamation," in his *Jüdische Romantik*, 294.

35. See my essay "Sexology, Psychoanalysis, and Degeneration," in *Degeneration*, ed. J. Edward Chamberlin and Sander L. Gilman (New York: Columbia University Press, 1985), 72–96.

36. Translated from the original in Jacob Toury, ed., *Der Eintritt der Juden ins deutsche Bürgertum: Eine Dokumentation* (Tel Aviv: Diaspora Research Institute, 1972), 312–13.

37. *Bemerkungen über Sprache und Sprachunterricht, als Beförderungsmittel der allgemeinen Bildung* (Hamburg: F. C. A. Otto, 1825).

38. This broadsheet, headed *Aufforderung an israelitische Prediger* and dated 1832, is to be found in the Zunz Library, Jews' College, University of London.

39. See Börne, vol. 2, esp. pp. 3 ff. on the nature of the French language, and 3:3 ff. for the "Letters from Paris." Even though there had been a tradition, going back to the role played by Friedrich Melchior Baron von Grimm in the French Enlightenment, of German intellectuals in residence in Paris serving as conduits for French thought into Germany, Börne's position seemed unique. He was a German Jew writing, not in French, but in German, and for a German Christian audience. His role was thus as an outsider, with some of the prerequisites of an insider (locus) who was presenting the most modern aspects of life to politically and culturally more backward countrymen. It would seem that such a position would have given him status, but it also

implied a position of greater intellectual authority, such as that held by the French-speaking and French-writing Grimm, delegated to a more familiar German-speaking and German-writing Jew.

40. Fritz Stern, *Gold and Iron: Bismarck, Bleichröder, and the Building of the German Empire* (London: George Allen & Unwin, 1977), 6.

41. Ibid., 8.

42. See Börne, 3:342.

43. See Börne's tabulation of the insults hurled at him, 3:350–61. The linkage of Börne to Saphir was important, since Saphir was seen (quite correctly) as a journalist whose satiric talents could be purchased (and were) by the highest bidder, in his case Metternich.

44. Peter Uwe Hohendahl, *Literaturkritik und Öffentlichkeit* (Munich: Piper, 1974), 115.

45. Cited in Alfred Estermann, ed., *Politische Avantgarde, 1830–1840*, 2 vols. (Frankfurt: Athenäum, 1972), 1:295. On Menzel and the first application of the concept of race to the systematic analysis of literary texts see Erwin Schuppe, *Der Burschenschafter Wolfgang Menzel: Eine Quelle zum Verständnis des Nationalsozialismus* (Frankfurt: Schulte-Bulmke, 1952), 101–10.

46. Cited in Estermann, 1:295, from *Literatur-Blatt*, 26 October 1835, 440.

47. Cited in Estermann, 1:164–84, from *Münchener Politsche Zeitung*, 29 December 1835.

48. Cited in Estermann, 1:297–304, from Jakob Weil, *Das junge Deutschland und die Juden* (Frankfurt: Jäger, 1830).

49. Low, 252.

50. In Börne, 2:969 ff.

51. After the initial formulation of my views on Heine and Jewish language, S. S. Prawer's magisterial study, *Heine's Jewish Comedy* (Oxford: Clarendon, 1983), appeared. Prawer makes reference to the initial draft of this present chapter on pp. 598–99. I am indebted, as all Heine scholars must be, to Prawer's overview, which completes but does not replace my focus on Heine's need to deal with the idea of a hidden language ascribed to the Jews; see my review in the *Times Literary Supplement*, 2 December 1983. The best biography of Heine, Jeffrey L. Sammons, *Heinrich Heine: A Modern Biography* (Princeton: Princeton University Press, 1979), devotes relatively little space to the question of Heine's Jewish identity. On the more limited topic the best studies are Israel Tabak, *Judaic Lore in Heine* (Baltimore: Johns Hopkins Press, 1948); Hartmut Kircher, *Heinrich Heine und das Judentum* (Bonn: Bouvier, 1973); Ruth L. Jacobi, *Heinrich Heines jüdisches Erbe* (Bonn: Bouvier, 1978); and Ludwig Rosenthal, *Heinrich Heine als Jude* (Frankfurt: Ullstein, 1973).

52. All of Heine's works cited are in Heinrich Heine, *Sämtliche Werke*, ed. Ernst Elster, 7 vols. (Leipzig: Bibliographisches Institut, 1887–90), 7:15. Where volumes of the two new critical editions (being produced in Düsseldorf and Weimar) of Heine's works exist, the text and the notes have been checked against them.

53. August Graf von Platen, *Sämtliche Werke*, ed. Max Koch and Erich Petzet, 12 vols. (Leipzig: Bibliographisches Institut, 1910), 10:164–65.

54. Theodor Adorno, *Noten zur Literatur*, 3 vols. (Frankfurt: Suhrkamp, 1969), 1:150–51.

55. Cited in Kircher, 97; see also his references to Yiddish, pp. 99 and 111.

56. Karl Gutzkow, "Rückblicke auf mein Leben," in his *Werke*, ed. Peter Müller, 4 vols. (Leipzig: Bibliographisches Institut, n.d.), 4:65.

57. Heinrich Heine, *Briefe*, ed. Friedrich Hirth, 6 vols. (Mainz: Florian Kupferberg, 1950–55), 1:286–88. See also Prawer, 218–19.

58. Kircher, 97.

59. For the best discussion of the nature of the Association for the Culture and Science of the Jews see Walter Kanowsky, *Vernunft und Geschichte: Heinrich Heines Studium als Grundlegung seiner Welt- und Kunstanschauung* (Bonn: Bouvier, 1975), 182–89.

60. Sammons, 88–89.

61. Leon Poliakov, *The History of Anti-Semitism*, trans. Richard Howard, 3 vols. (New York: Vanguard Press, 1965–75), 1:142. On the social function of smell see Alain Corbin, *Le Miasme et le jonquille: L'Ordorat et l'imaginaire social XVIIIe-XIXe siècles* (Paris: Aubier Montaigne, 1982).

62. The translation is adapted from S. S. Prawer, *Heine, the Tragic Satirist* (Cambridge: Cambridge University Press, 1961), 192.

63. For a summary of the material on Heine's conversion see Prawer, *Comedy*, 33–35 and 206–7; and Kircher, 117–23.

64. Prawer, *Comedy*, 33–36.

65. Ibid., 16.

66. John Murray Cuddihy, *The Ordeal of Civility: Freud, Marx, Lévi-Strauss, and the Jewish Struggle with Modernity* (New York: Basic Books, 1974), esp. 3 ff.

67. See Leopold Zunz, *Haderashot biYsrael*, ed. H. Albeck (Jerusalem, 1954), 202 ff.

68. Cited in E. R. Malachi, *Mekubolim in Eretz Israel* (New York, 1928), 83.

69. On these poems by Heine see Gerhard Sauder, "Blasphemisch-religiöse Körperwelt: Heinrich Heines 'Hebräische Melodien,' " in *Heinrich Heine: Artistik und Engagement*, ed. Wolfgang Kuttenkeuler (Stuttgart: Metzler, 1977), 118–43; and Helmut Koopmann, "Heines 'Romanzero': Thematik und Struktur," *Zeitschrift für deutsche Philologie* 97 (1978), 51–70.

70. Heine, *Briefe*, 1:133.

71. Adelbert von Chamisso, *Werke*, 6 vols. (Berlin: Weidmann, 1864), 6:86.

72. Ludolf Wienbarg, *Aesthetische Feldzüge*, ed. Walter Dietze (Berlin and Weimar: Aufbau, 1964), 186.

73. Prawer, *Comedy*, 185.

74. Heine, *Briefe*, 1:63.

75. Ibid., 250.

76. Ibid., 284.

77. Marx's life and writings were among the major catalysts for the formulation of the concept of Jewish self-hatred (see E. J. Lesser, "Karl Marx als Jude," *Der Jude* 8 [1924], 173–81; and Gustav Mayer, "Der Jude in Karl Marx," *Neue jüdische Monatshefte* 2 [1917–18], 327–30). Recent discussions also have built upon this association. Of value in the present discussion have been the following studies: Arnold Künzli, *Karl Marx: Eine Psychographie* (Vienna: Europa, 1966), 65–72, 195–225; Julius Carlebach, *Karl Marx and the Radical Critique of Judaism* (London: Routledge & Kegan Paul, 1978), 331–43; Shlomo Avineri, "Marx and Jewish Emancipation," *Journal of the History of Ideas* 25 (1964), 445–50; Solomon Bloom, "Karl Marx and the Jews," *Jewish Social Studies* 4 (1942), 3–16; and Helmut Hirsch, *Marx und Moses: Karl Marx zur "Judenfrage" und zu Juden* (Frankfurt: Lang, 1980). Of the older, classical studies Edmund Wilson's *To the Finland Station* (New York: Atheneum, 1974) argues that Marx attributes to a fictive proletariat the qualities associated with the Jew. The most recent general study is Murray Wolfson, *Marx: Economist, Philosopher, Jew* (New York: St. Martin's Press, 1982). See also Poliakov, 3:380 ff.; Cuddihy, 119–50; and Schneider, 211–58. For the general context of the reception of Marx see Eric J. Hobsbawm, ed., *The History of Marxism: 1. Marxism in Marx's Day* (Bloomington: Indiana University Press, 1982).

78. Marx's works cited are the two standard editions: Karl Marx and Friedrich Engels, *Gesamtausgabe*, 18 vols. (Berlin: Dietz, 1978–82), hereafter cited as MEGA; and idem, *Werke*, 39 vols. (Berlin: Dietz, 1956–69), hereafter cited as MEW. Here, MEGA, sec. 1, vol. 1, pt. 2, 204, cited by David McLellan, *Marx before Marxism* (London: Macmillan, 1970), 31. McLellan's book is the best general introduction to the young Marx.

79. For a discussion of Hegel's image of the Jews see Low, 274–86; Shlomo Avineri, "A Note on Hegel's Views on Jewish Emancipation," *Jewish Social Studies* 25 (1963), 145–51; Robert S. Wistrich, *Socialism and the Jews: The Dilemmas of Assimilation in Germany and Austria-Hungary* (Rutherford, N.J.: Fairleigh Dickinson University Press, 1982), 15–24; and McLellan, 16–23.

80. On Marx's family background see Eugene Kamenka, "The Baptism of Karl Marx," *Hibbert Journal* 56 (1958), 340–51. See also Albert Massiczek, ed., *Der menschliche Mensch: Karl Marx' jüdischer Humanismus* (Vienna: Europa, 1968).

81. On Bauer and Marx see Zvi Rosen, *Bruno Bauer and Karl Marx: The Influence of Bruno Bauer on Marx's Thought* (The Hague: Martinus Nijhoff, 1978); David McLellan, *The Young Hegelians and Karl Marx* (London: Macmillan, 1969); and Nathan Rotenstreich, "For and Against Emancipation: The Bruno Bauer Controversy," *Leo Baeck Institute Yearbook* 4 (1959), 3–36. Bauer's essay "Die Judenfrage" was published in the *Deutsche Jahrbücher für Wissenschaft und Kunst* in November 1842. On the title see Jacob Toury, "The Jewish Question: A Semantic Approach," *Leo Baeck Institute Yearbook* 11 (1966), 85–106.

82. Georg Herwegh, ed., *Einundzwanzig Bogen aus der Schweiz* (Zurich

and Winterthur: Verlag des literarischen Comptoirs, 1843), 56–71; Moses Hess's essay "Sozialismus und Kommunismus" is to be found on pp. 74–91.

83. Fritz Schlawe, "Die junghegelische Publizistik," *Die Welt als Geschichte* 20 (1960), 30–50. Metternich's secret policy during the 1840s heard the voice of the journalist as the voice of the Jew (see Hans Adler, ed., *Literarische Geheimberichte: Protokolle der Metternich-Agenten,* 2 vols. [Cologne: C. W. Leske, 1977], 1:156).

84. Werner Blumenberg, "Eduard Müller-Tellering: Verfasser des ersten antisemitischen Pamphlets gegen Marx," *Bulletin of the International Institute of Social History* 6 (1951), 178–99.

85. On Marx's debt to Hess see Robert Tucker, *Philosophy and Myth in Karl Marx* (Cambridge: Cambridge University Press, 1961), 112; McLellan, *Young Hegelians,* 153–55; and Edmund Silberner, *Moses Hess: Geschichte seines Lebens* (Leiden: E. J. Brill, 1966), 192 ff.

86. Ludwig Feuerbach, *Essence of Christianity,* trans. George Eliot (New York: Harper, 1957), 114. See also Wistrich, 22.

87. MEW, 1:347–77; the translation used here is that by David McLellan, *Karl Marx: Early Texts* (Oxford: Blackwell, 1971), 85 ff.

88. MEW, 3:432–33.

89. Carlebach, 165.

90. Stanley Edgar Hyman, *The Tangled Bank: Darwin, Marx, Frazer, and Freud as Imaginative Writers* (New York: Atheneum, 1966), 90. For a detailed discussion of the literary critical method of *The Holy Family* see S. S. Prawer, *Karl Marx and World Literature* (Oxford: Clarendon Press, 1976), 86 ff. The text of *The Holy Family* is to be found in MEW 2:3 ff.; the translation used here is by Richard Dixon and Clemens Dutt in Karl Marx and Friedrich Engels, *Collected Works,* 50 vols. (New York: International Publishers, 1975–85), 4:7–211.

91. On Marx's mother see Künzli, 50–65; and McLellan, *Marx before Marxism,* 28–32.

92. MEGA, sec. 1, vol. 1, pt. 2, 187.

93. McLellan, *Marx before Marxism,* 31.

94. Hubert Schiel, *Die Umwelt des jungen Marx* (Trier: J. Lintz, 1954), 7. See also Heinz Monz, *Karl Marx und Trier* (Trier: R. Laufner, 1964).

95. MEW, 29:38–39.

96. Ibid., 28:304.

97. Ibid., 5:323 ff. See also Helga B. Whiton, *Der Wandel des Polenbildes in der deutschen Literatur des 19. Jahrhunderts* (Bern: Peter Lang, 1981).

98. MEW, 1:146. The translation used is from *Karl Marx, Capital,* trans. Ben Fowkes, 3 vols. (New York: Vintage, 1977), 1:144.

99. MEW, 32:75. The distance from the world of Western, Yiddish-speaking Jewry to the linguistically assimilated Jews of the first third of the nineteenth century must have seemed extraordinary for that generation. Unlike the later shift of language identity among Eastern Jews who moved to Germany during the last two decades of the nineteenth century,

the sense of alienation existing between generations could not be localized in the older generations' escape from another, foreign world. For the Jewish speakers of German, the gap between themselves and their parents would have been heightened by the sense that there seemed to be both a sense of continuity (in geographic locus) and a clear discontinuity in language identity. See in this regard Peter Freimark, "Sprachverhalten und Assimilation: Die Situation der Juden in Norddeutschland in der ersten Hälfte des 19. Jahrhunderts," *Saeculum* 31 (1980), 240–61.

100. The irony is that the older Engels, in the *Dialectic of Nature*, calls up the "Touves-Jomtov" to categorize the biological establishment's reaction to Darwin's thought. Thus all establishments, economic and intellectual, that rely on faith are really only Jews in disguise (see Marx's discussion of the nature of the Jews in this category in the essay by Diane Paul, "'In the Interests of Civilization': Marxist Views of Race and Culture in the Nineteenth Century," *Journal of the History of Ideas* 42 [1981], 115–38).

101. See Ruth Friedlander, "Benedict-Augustin Morel and the Development of the Theory of Dégénérescence" (Ph.D. diss., University of California, San Francisco, 1973).

102. Ferdinand Lassalle, *Une Page d'amour de Ferdinand Lassalle* (Leipzig: Brockhaus, 1878), 47–50. See also Robert S. Wistrich, *Revolutionary Jews from Marx to Trotsky* (New York: Barnes & Noble, 1976), 51–56.

103. MEW, 30:29 ff. Here the locus of the "bad" Jew is the world associated with Marx's mother, with the world in which Jews reveal themselves by their "bad" language, Yiddish, and live like subhumans.

104. Ibid., 29:234. Marx makes a more direct reference to the *foetor judäicus* in his attack in *Herr Vogt* when he addresses the nature of the "Jewish" press, with which he was, of course, usually linked (ibid., 14:601 ff).

105. Ibid., 30:254.

106. Joel Williamson, *New People: Miscegenation and Mulattoes in the United States* (New York: Free Press, 1980).

107. Wistrich, *Socialism*, 49.

108. Künzli, 71. See all of Engels's correspondence with Marx, in which he addresses Marx as "Dear Moor."

109. MEGA, sec. 1, vol. 1, pt. 2, 268.

110. MEW, Ergänzungsband 1:641 ff.

111. Börne, *Börne*, 1:876.

112. Bruno Bauer, *Das Judentum in der Fremde* (Berlin: F. Heinicke, 1863), 29. See also Carlebach, 147.

CHAPTER FIVE. THE SCIENCE OF RACE

1. The literature on the "Jewish problem" in the late nineteenth and early twentieth centuries is quite extensive. In addition to the studies cited throughout the notes, the following studies were of use: Alex Bein,

Die Judenfrage: Biographie eines Weltproblems, 2 vols. (Stuttgart: Deutsche Verlagsanstalt, 1980); George L. Mosse, *The Crisis of German Ideology: Intellectual Origins of the Third Reich* (New York: Grosset & Dunlap, 1964); idem, *Germans and Jews: The Right, the Left, and the Search for a "Third Force" in Pre-Nazi Germany* (New York: Grosset & Dunlap, 1971); Roderick Stackelberg, *Idealism Debased: From Völkisch Ideology to National Socialism* (Kent, Ohio: Kent State University Press, 1981); Marjorie Lamberti, *Jewish Activism in Imperial Germany: The Struggle for Civil Equality* (New Haven: Yale University Press, 1978); Richard Levy, *The Downfall of the Anti-Semitic Political Parties in Imperial Germany* (New Haven: Yale University Press, 1975); Donald L. Niewyk, *The Jews in Weimar Germany* (Baton Rouge: Louisiana State University Press, 1980); and idem, *Socialist, Anti-Semite and Jew* (Baton Rouge: Louisiana State University Press, 1971). On the general history of the science of race see James C. King, *The Biology of Race* (Berkeley and Los Angeles: University of California Press, 1981); and Nancy Stepan, *The Idea of Race in Science in Great Britain, 1800–1960* (Hamden, Conn.: Archon Press, 1982).

The most valuable recent study of the problem of Jewish identity in literature is the detailed study by Klara Pomeranz Carmely, *Das Identitätsproblem jüdischer Autoren im deutschen Sprachraum von der Jahrhundertwende bis zu Hitler* (Königstein: Scriptor, 1981). Carmely focuses on three models that she perceives as different means of self-definition among German and Austrian Jews—assimilation, socialism, and Zionism—without perceiving the inherent interdependence of various models of self-definition. A comparative study that is much more far-reaching than Carmely's but suffers from its lack of any central thesis is Leon Israel Yudkin, *Jewish Writing and Identity in the Twentieth Century* (New York: St. Martin's, 1982). Yudkin covers all of the major literary traditions of Western Europe and the United States, as well as Israel, in 166 pages, in what amounts to a useful survey.

2. Richard Wagner, *Richard Wagner's Prose Works,* trans. William Ashton Ellis, 10 vols. (London: Kegan Paul, Trench, Trübner & Co., 1912–29), 3:84–85. On Wagner's anti-Semitism see Leon Poliakov, *The History of Anti-Semitism,* trans. Richard Howard, 3 vols. (New York: Vanguard Press, 1965–75), 3:429–57. Concerning Wagner and the model of Jewish self-hatred among his followers see Peter Gay, "Hermann Levi: A Study in Service and Self-Hatred," in his *Freud, Jews, and Other Germans* (New York: Oxford University Press, 1978), 189–230. See also Jacob Katz, *From Prejudice to Destruction: Anti-Semitism, 1700–1933* (Cambridge: Harvard University Press, 1980), 175–94. The idea that musical style is racially determined does not stop with Wagner's comments on Mendelssohn and Meyerbeer. Mahler's music was described as *jüdeln* in Nicolas Slonimsky, ed., *Lexikon of Musical Invective* (New York: Coleman-Ross, 1953), 121. Mahler's response was to ask his wife to "stop him when he emphasized his speech with too much gesticulation"—this, of course, after his conversion to Catholicism in 1897 (see Egon Gartenberg, *Mahler: The Man and His Music* [New York: Schirmer, 1978], 47). This association almost always

has Wagner's formulation in mind. From D. Paulus Cassel's rebuttal of Wagner, *Der Judengott und Richard Wagner* (Berlin: J. A. Wohlgemuth, 1881), to Heinrich Berl, *Das Judentum in der Musik* (Berlin: Deutsche Verlags-Anstalt, 1926), defenses of Jewish musical creativity have made direct reference to Wagner.

3. See, for example, Martin Gregor-Dellin, *Richard Wagner: Sein Leben, sein Werk, sein Jahrhundert* (Munich: Goldmann & Schott, 1983), 310–14. Compare the pamphlet written by Friedrich Nietzche's brother-in-law, Bernhard Förster, *Das Verhältniss des modernen Judenthums zur deutschen Kunst* (Berlin: M. Schulze, 1881).

4. Reinhard Rürup, *Emanzipation und Antisemitismus: Studien zur "Judenfrage" der bürgerlichen Gesellschaft* (Göttingen: Vandenhoek und Ruprecht, 1975), 95–114, 103. On the perceived disjuncture through the introduction of "scientific racism" see Uriel Tal, *Christians and Jews in Germany* (Ithaca, N.Y.: Cornell University Press, 1974).

5. Hilary Putnam, *Reason, Truth and History* (Cambridge: Cambridge University Press, 1981), 185.

6. Wilhelm Marr, *Der Sieg des Judenthums über das Germanenthum* (Bern: Rudolph Costenoble, 1879). See also his pamphlet *Öffnet die Augen, Ihr deutschen Zeitungsleser, Antisemitische Hefte*, vol. 3 (Chemnitz: Ernst Schmeitzer, 1880). The background of Marr and his sudden popularity is given by P. G. J. Pulzer, *The Rise of Political Anti-Semitism in Germany and Austria* (New York: John Wiley, 1964), 49 ff. On Marr's background and family see S. M. Dubnow, *Die neueste Geschichte des jüdischen Volkes*, trans. Elias Hurwicz, vol. 3 (Berlin: Jüdischer Verlag, 1923), 10.

7. Moritz von Reymond, *Wo steckt der Mauschel? oder Jüdischer Liberalismus und wissenschaftlicher Pessimismus: Ein offener Brief an W. Marr* (Bern: Georg Froben, 1880), 60.

8. Eugen Dühring, *Die Judenfrage als Rassen-, Sitten- und Culturfrage* (Karlsruhe and Leipzig: H. Reuther, 1881), 53 ff.

9. This view of biology is true of a wide spectrum of thinkers, including Friedrich Nietzsche (see Friedrich Nietzsche, *Du sollst der werden, der du bist*, edited by Gerhard Wehr [Munich: Kindler, 1976]).

10. On the varieties of evolutionary models in general see William Provine, "Geneticists and the Biology of Race Crossing," *Science* 182 (1973), 790–96. On the varieties as understood in the late nineteenth century see Vernon L. Kellogg, *Darwinism Today* (New York: Henry Holt, 1907), which remains the best presentation of the diversity of biological paradigms in late-nineteenth-century biology. A very good presentation of the diversity of such views has recently been published by Ernst Mayr, *The Growth of Biological Thought: Diversity, Evolution, and Inheritance* (Cambridge, Mass.: Belknap Press, 1982).

11. Treitschke's essay and a selection of the replies (excluding that of Moritz Lazarus) are reprinted in Walter Boehlich, ed., *Der Berliner Antisemitismusstreit* (Frankfurt am Main: Insel, 1965); all of the references to Treitschke are to pp. 5–12. Treitschke mocked the "thin-voiced" Jews during his university lectures (see Richard Gutteridge, *Open Thy Mouth*

for the Dumb! The German Evangelical Church and the Jews, 1879–1950 [Oxford: Basil Blackwell, 1976], 13).

12. Theodor Billroth, *Uber das Lehren und Lernen der medicinischen Wissenschaften an den Universitäten der deutschen Nation nebst allgemeinen Bemerkungen über Universitäten: Eine culturhistorische Studie* (Vienna: Carl Gerold's Sohn, 1876), selectively translated by William H. Welch as *The Medical Sciences in the German Universities: A Study in the History of Civilization* (New York: Macmillan, 1924); the pages of the German edition concerning the Jews are 146–54. For the context see Monika Richarz, *Der Eintritt der Juden in die akademische Berufe* (Tübingen: Mohr, 1974), 28–43.

13. Friedrich Ratzel, *The History of Mankind*, trans. A. J. Butler, 3 vols. (London: Macmillan, 1896). The German edition appeared between 1885 and 1888.

14. Thomas Frey, *Antisemiten-Katechismus* (Leipzig: Theodor Fritsch, 1887), 14; the vocabulary list is on p. 203.

15. Gottfried zur Beek, ed., *Die Geheimnisse der Weisen von Zion* (Berlin: Auf Vorposten, 1920), 197. The history of this text is itself of interest, since it originates in the novel *Biarritz* (1868), by "Sir John Retcliffe," i.e., Herrmann Goedsche, and reflects an attempt to create a fictional representation of the "true" discourse of the Jews. The confusion between fictional representations and scientific ones is evident in the movement of the *Protocols of the Elders of Zion* from the world of the novel to its place as "evidence" in the science of race.

16. For a contemporary anti-Semitic evaluation see *Die Aufhebung der Juden-Emanzipation und ihre rechtliche Begründung* (Leipzig: Hermann Meyer, 1895), 4–17. For the context see Ismar Schorsch, *Jewish Reactions to German Anti-Semitism, 1870–1914* (New York: Columbia University Press, 1972), 129.

17. On the German anti-Semitic novel see George Mosse, "The Image of the Jew in German Popular Culture: Felix Dahn and Gustav Freytag," *Leo Baeck Institute Yearbook* 2 (1957), 226–27. For a more recent rereading of Freytag see Mark Gelber, "An Alternate Reading of the Role of the Jewish Scholar in Gustav Freytag's *Soll und Haben*," *Germanic Review* 58 (1983), 83–88. The quotations about the nature of the language of the Jews are taken from Otto Ernst, *Die Revolverjournalisten* (1902), and Karl Rössler, *Im Klubsessel* (1913), cited in Elisabeth Frenzel, *Judengestalten auf der deutschen Bünne: Ein notwendiger Querschnitt durch 700 Jahre Rollengeschichte* (Munich: Deutscher Volksverlag, 1942), 161–62.

18. Dietrich Eckardt, *Familienvater* (1904), cited in Frenzel, 161.

19. Moritz Lazarus, *Was heisst national?* (Berlin: Ferdinand Dümmler, 1880). Ismar Schorch's reading of Lazarus (60 ff.) seems to discount the central role that language played in shaping Lazarus's concept of Volk. See Lazarus's essay "Sprache," *Pädagogische Encyclopadie* 9:41–73, for a summary of his views. These views recur in his correspondence with his brother-in-law Hermann Steinthal, the author of a major monograph on the nature of language (see Ingrid Belke, ed., *Moritz Lazarus und Heymann*

Steinthal: Die Begründer der Völkerpsychologie in ihren Briefen [Tübingen: Mohr, 1971]).

20. Conrad Alberti, "Judentum und Antisemitismus: Eine zeitgenössische Studie," *Die Gesellschaft* 4 (1889), 1718–33.

21. W. Hartenau [Walter Rathenau], "Höre, Israel!" *Die Zukunft* 18 (1897), 454–62. On Rathenau and the problem of Jewish identity in the late nineteenth century see Rudolf Kallner, *Herzl und Rathenau: Wege jüdischer Existenz* (Stuttgart: Klett, 1976); and Leo Baeck, *Von Moses Mendelssohn zu Franz Rosenzweig: Typen jüdischen Selbstverständnisses in den letzten beiden Jahrhunderten* (Stuttgart: Kohlhammer, 1958). See a recent book by George L. Mosse, *German Jews beyond Judaism* (Bloomington: Indiana University Press, 1985).

22. Jakob Fromer, "Das Wesen des Judenthumes," *Die Zukunft* 47 (1904), 440–56, reprinted as part of his *Vom Ghetto zur modernen Kultur* (Heidelberg: Im Verlage des Verfassers, 1906).

23. Benedictus Levita [pseud.], "Die Erlösung des Judenthums," *Preussische Jahrbücher* 102 (1900), 131–40. The list of Jews in the public sphere during the nineteenth century who saw their discourse as inherently damaged is very long. Victor Adler, co-founder of the Austrian Socialist Party, for example, wrote to Karl Kautsky on August 21, 1886: "I do not have the calling for a quiet, scholarly occupation. I believe myself quite useful as a copier of the ideas of others. We Jews seem predestined to copy others' ideas" (Edmund Silberner, ed., *Sozialisten zur Judenfrage: Ein Beitrag zur Geschichte des Sozialismus von Anfang des 19. Jahrhunderts bis 1914* [Berlin: Colloquium, 1964], 292).

24. On these stereotypes and conflicts see Jacob Katz, "Berthold Auerbach's Anticipation of the German-Jewish Tragedy," *Hebrew Union College Annual* 53 (1982), 215–40; Joseph P. Strelka, "Leopold Kompert—Erzähler des jüdischen Ghetto," in *Die Osterreichische Literatur: Ihr Profil im 19. Jahrhundert (1830–1880)*, ed. Herbert Zeman (Graz: Akademische Druck- und Verlagsanstalt, 1982), 431–38; Egon Schwarz and Russell A. Berman, "Karl Emil Franzos: *Der Pojaz* (1905): Aufklärung, Assimilation und ihre realistischen Grenzen," in *Romane und Erzählungen des bürgerlichen Realismus*, ed. Horst Denkler (Stuttgart: Reclam, 1980), 378–92; and Mark Gelber, "Ethnic Pluralism and Germanization in the Works of Karl Emil Franzos (1848–1904)," *German Quarterly* 56 (1983), 376–85. What is noticeable is how the stress these Jewish writers place on the language and discourse of the Jews in their fictions differs. This is contrasted with the unselfconsciousness of Jews whose status in society does not depend upon language about their "hidden" language (see, for example, the autobiographical material published in Monika Richarz, ed., *Jüdisches Leben in Deutschland: Selbstzeugnisse zur Sozialgeschichte*, 3 vols. [Stuttgart: Deutsche Verlagsanstalt, 1976–82]). What is evident is the general lack of any comments on the "hidden language of the Jews" by mainly middle-class Jews. This is in the light of the stereotypical images of the Jews and their discourse in middle-class German periodicals (see Henry Wassermann, "Jews and Judaism in the *Gartenlaube*," *Leo Baeck Institute Year-*

book 23 [1978], 47–60). Compare the use of literary language and stereotypical images of the Jew (both positive and negative) in the Jewish periodicals of the period that relied heavily on the model of the image of the Jews and their discourse in the *Gartenlaube* (see Itta Shedletzky, "Some Observations on the Popular *Zeitroman* in the Jewish Weeklies in Germany from 1870 to 1900," *Canadian Review of Comparative Literature*, special issue, 9 [1982], 349–60).

25. Moritz Goldstein, "Deutsch-jüdischer Parnass," *Der Kunstwart* 25 (1912), 281–94. Goldstein also wrote an essay fifty-five years later presenting the background and motivation for his piece: "German Jewry's Dilemma: The Story of a Provocative Essay," *Leo Baeck Institute Yearbook* 2 (1957), 236–54.

26. Ernst Lissauer, "Deutschtum und Judentum," *Der Kunstwart* 25 (1912), 6–15, 225–61.

27. Eduard Engel, *Sprich Deutsch! Ein Buch zur Entwelschung* (Leipzig: Hesse and Becker, [1917]), 90. See also Joseph Wulf, ed., *Literatur und Dichtung im Dritten Reich* (Gütersloh: Mohn, 1963), 511.

28. Adolf Bartels, *Kritiker and Kritikaster: Pro domo et pro arte* (Leipzig: Eduard Avenarius, 1903), which associates an attack on journalistic criticism with his first attack on "Jewish language" in German literature; Otto Hauser's many works on the Jewish influence on German letters, which began to appear at the turn of the century, are summarized in his later pamphlet *Die Juden und Halbjuden der deutschen Literatur* (Danzig and Leipzig: Der Mensch, [1933]).

29. The literature on Mauthner is extensive. See esp. Joachim Kühn, *Gescheiterte Sprachkritik: Fritz Mauthners Leben und Werk* (Berlin: De Gruyter, 1975). See also Gershon Weiler, "Fritz Mauthner: A Study in Jewish Self-Rejection," *Leo Baeck Institute Yearbook* 8 (1963), 136–49.

30. J. P. Stern, " 'Words Are Also Deeds': Some Observations on Austrian Language Consciousness," *New Literary History* 12 (1981), 509–28.

31. Fritz Mauthner, *Erinnerungen. I. Prager Jugendjahre* (Munich: Georg Müller, 1918), 110. Cf. his *Muttersprache und Vaterland* (Leipzig: Dürr and Weber, 1920), 60 ff.

32. Cited in Stern.

33. Fritz Mauthner, *Schmock oder die litterarische Karriere der Gegenwart* (Berlin: F. and P. Lehmann, 1888), 9.

34. Fritz Mauthner, *Beiträge zu einer Kritik der Sprache*, vol. 1, *Sprache und Psychologie* (Stuttgart: Cotta, 1901), 158.

35. On Kraus and his Jewish identity see Wilma Abeles Iggers, *Karl Kraus: A Viennese Critic of the Twentieth Century* (The Hague: Nijhoff, 1967), 33–36, 171–91; and Harry Zohn, "Karl Kraus: 'Jüdischer Selbsthasser' oder 'Erzjude'?" *Modern Austrian Literature* 8, nos. 1 and 2 (1975), 1–18. Kraus's association of the newspapers of Vienna with *mauscheln* may be based partly on the columns of Daniel Spitzer, who created the speculator Itzig Kneipeles as a stock comic character for the *Neue Freie Presse* during the late nineteenth century. Martin Buber, in a letter to Werner Kraft dated March 20, 1917, brings the association between Weininger and

Kraus full circle. He labels Kraus as a "Jew unhappy with himself" and states: "The introspective Kraus is named Weininger" (Martin Buber, *Martin Buber: Briefwechsel aus sieben Jahrzehnten*, ed. Grete Schaeder, 3 vols. [Heidelberg: Lambert Schneider, 1972], 1:487). On Kraus's ideas on language see Josef Quack, *Bemerkungen zum Sprachverständnis von Karl Kraus* (Bonn: Bouvier, 1976), 189; and J. P. Stern, "Karl Kraus's Vision of Language," *MLR* 61 (1966), 71–84. Given Karl Kraus's strong interest in the role of the erotic within his cultural sphere, it is striking that the linkage between sexuality (in the public sphere) and public anti-Semitism is not made by him. Indeed, it is only in Karl Bleibtreu's review of Otto Weininger's *Sex and Character*, published in *Die Fackel* 157 (1904), 12–20, that the parallel worlds of sexuality and anti-Semitism are explored. Bleibtreu sees the qualities of being a woman and being a Jew as universal potentials within all human beings. But Weininger's view that such qualities are the natural focus of the woman (or the Jew), i.e., the biological aspect of Weininger's argument, is repressed by Bleibtreu. Concerning the seeming abyss between Kraus's image of the woman and his image of the Jew, note the absence of any discussion of anti-Semitism in Nike Wagner's otherwise splendid *Geist und Geschlecht: Karl Kraus und die Erotik der Wiener Moderne* (Frankfurt: Suhrkamp, 1982). For more general background see Kari Grimstad, *Masks of the Prophet: The Theatrical World of Karl Kraus* (Toronto: University of Toronto Press, 1982).

36. On Kraus and his opposition to the new language of psychoanalysis see Thomas Szasz, *Karl Kraus and the Soul-Doctors* (Baton Rouge: Louisiana State University Press, 1976).

37. *Die Fackel* 378–79 (1915), 58.

38. Ibid., 17 (1899), 21.

39. Ibid., 820–26 (1929), 45–46.

40. Ibid., 847 (1931), 31–34.

41. Ibid., 381–83 (1913), 42–48.

42. See Gerald Stieg, *Der Brenner und Die Fackel: Ein Beitrag zur Wirkungsgeschichte von Karl Kraus* (Salzburg: Otto Müller, 1976), 255–60.

43. *Die Fackel* 15 (1899), 4; 386 (1913), 1–8.

44. Ibid., 6.

45. Ibid., 649–56 (1924), 141–42.

46. Ibid., 457–61 (1917), 1–19.

47. Ibid., 608 (1922), 17.

48. Karl Kraus, "Eine Krone für Zion," reprinted in *Karl Kraus: Frühe Schriften, 1892–1900*, ed. Johannes J. Braakenburg, 2 vols. (Munich: Kösel, 1979), 2:298–314.

49. Theodor Adorno, "Sittlichkeit und Kriminalität," in his *Noten zur Literatur*, 3 vols. (Frankfurt: Suhrkamp, 1965), 3:66.

50. *Die Fackel* 11 (1899), 1–6.

51. Theodor Herzl, *"Mauschel,"* reprinted in his *Zionistische Schriften*, 5 vols. (Berlin: Jüdischer Verlag, 1934–35), 1:209–15. For the context

see Gisela Brude-Firnau, "Der Toleranzbegriff Theodor Herzls," *Seminar* 19 (1983), 20–32.

52. Amos Elon, *Herzl* (New York: Holt, Rinehart & Winston, 1975), 251. On Herzl's attitude toward the language and accent of Vienna see Elon, 44–45.

53. Quoted in Elon, 251–52.

54. Ibid., 14–15.

55. See *Die Fackel* 531–43 (1920), 163–77.

56. Reprinted in Karl Kraus, *Untergang der Welt durch Schwarze Magie* (Munich: Kösel 1960), 188–219, here 193.

57. Mautner, *Beiträge*, vols. 2, *Zur Sprachwissenschaft* (Stuttgart: Cotta, 1901), 645, and 3, *Zur Grammatik und Logik* (Stuttgart: Cotta, 1902), 525; idem, "Heinrich Heine," in his *Gespräche im Himmel* (Munich: G. Müller, 1914), 59–91, which is directed against Bartels but with clear reference to Kraus.

58. Karl Kraus, *Die Dritte Walpurgisnacht* (Munich: Kösel, 1952), 139.

59. Adolf Hitler, *Mein Kampf*, trans. Ralph Manheim (Cambridge: Houghton Mifflin, 1943). For a detailed background to the text see Werner Maser, *Adolf Hitlers Mein Kampf* (Munich: Bechtle, 1966).

60. Ilse Blumenthal-Weis, "Rilke and the Jews," *Jewish Frontier* 26 (1959), 18. The internalization and projection of such anti-Semitic attitudes toward the "foreignness" of Jewish discourse can be seen in writers admired by Kraus. Peter Altenberg, for example, after his conversion to Catholicism in 1900, attacks the Zionists as "these 'Jewish' *Goim*, who are the most dangerous race! They have their inborn brutality and our own 'audaciousness.' " Indeed, in a letter written in 1914 he characterizes the Zionist writer Ludwig Ullmann as writing a "jüdelnde" diction, seeing in his ideology a reflection of the innate "Jewishness" of his language (see Camillo Schaefer, "Peter Altenberg: Ein biographischer Essay," *Freibord*, Sonderreihe, 10 [1979], 21).

61. Immanuel Kant, *Anthropology from a Pragmatic Point of View*, trans. Victor Lyle Dowdell (Carbondale: Southern Illinois Press, 1978), 217–19.

62. Arthur Schopenhauer, *Selected Essays of Arthur Schopenhauer*, trans. Ernest Belfort Bax (London: George Bell, 1891), 341. See also Annegret Stopczyk, *Was Philosophen über Frauen denken* (Munich: Matthes & Seitz, 1980); and Lorenne M. G. Clark and Lynda Lange, eds., *The Sexism of Social and Political Theory: Women and Reproduction from Plato to Nietzsche* (Toronto: University of Toronto Press, 1979).

63. Otto Weininger, *Sex and Character* (London: William Heinemann, 1906). All references have been compared to the original, now available in a reprint with commentary by a collective and appendix, *Geschlecht und Charakter: Eine prinzipielle Untersuchung* (Munich: Matthes & Seitz, 1980). The literature on Weininger that is of interest is quite limited: see Hans Kohn, *Karl Kraus—Arthur Schnitzler—Otto Weininger: Aus dem*

jüdischen Wien der Jahrhundertwende (Tübingen: J. C. B. Mohr, 1962), 30–46; and for a complete overview on the secondary literature, William Walter Jaffe, "Studies in Obsession: Otto Weininger, Arthur Schnitzler, Heimito von Doderer" (Ph.D. diss., Yale University, 1979). Perhaps the best study of Weininger is Jacques Le Rider, *Der Fall Otto Weininger, Wurzeln des Antifeminismus und Antisemitismus*, trans. Dieter Hornig (Vienna: Löckner, 1984). The association of the model of the woman with that of the Jew is usually negative. However, a reversal of this relationship is to be found in Theodor Lessing's *Weib, Frau, Dame: Ein Essay* (Munich: Verlag der ärztlichen Rundschau, 1910). Writing in response to Weininger, under the influence of feminism and Zionism, Lessing reverses the relationship, seeing it as positive but still making the basic association (see Julius Carlebach, "The Forgotten Connection: Women and Jews in the Conflict between Enlightenment and Romanticism," *Leo Baeck Institute Yearbook* 24 [1979], 107–38).

64. The aphorisms are reprinted in the new edition of Weininger's work, *Geschlecht und Charakter*, 626.

65. Kohn, 32.

66. The best overview of Trebitsch's life and career remains Theodor Lessing, *Der jüdische Selbsthass* (Berlin: Jüdischer Verlag, 1930), 101–31. On his mental illness see his "autobiographical" statement *Die Geschichte meines "Verfolgungswahn"* (Vienna: Antaios, 1923), which is quite detailed.

67. Arthur Trebitsch, *Geist und Judentum: Eine grundlegende Untersuchung* (Vienna: Ed. Strache, 1919). All references are to this edition.

68. The best study of Freud's reading of Weininger is the recent essay by Peter Heller, "A Quarrel over Bisexuality," in *The Turn of the Century: German Literature and Art, 1890–1915*, ed. Gerald Chapple and Hans H. Schulte (Bonn: Bouvier, 1981), 87–116, which summarizes the literature on Weininger and Freud.

69. All references to Freud are to *The Standard Edition of The Complete Psychological Works of Sigmund Freud*, 24 vols. (London: Hogarth Press, 1953–74), here 20:271 ff. Studies that focus on the question of Freud's Jewish identity are: Arnold Kutzinki, "Sigmund Freud, ein jüdischer Forscher," *Der Jude* 8 (1924), 216–21; Ernst Simon, "Sigmund Freud, the Jew," *Leo Baeck Institute Yearbook* 2 (1957), 270–305; David Bakan, *Sigmund Freud and the Jewish Mystical Tradition* (New York: Van Nostrand, 1958); John Murray Cuddihy, *The Ordeal of Civility: Freud, Marx, Lévi-Strauss, and the Jewish Struggle with Modernity* (New York: Basic Books, 1974); Marie Balmary, *Psychoanalyzing Psychoanalysis: Freud and the Hidden Fault of the Father*, trans. Ned Lukacher (Baltimore: Johns Hopkins University Press, 1982); Martha Robert, *From Oedipus to Moses: Freud's Jewish Identity*, trans. Ralph Manheim (London: Rutledge & Kegan Paul, 1977); Reuben M. Rainey, *Freud as a Student of Religion* (Missoula, Mont.: American Academy of Religion, 1975); Peter Gay, "Six Names in Search of an Interpretation: A Contribution to the Debate over Sigmund Freud's Jewishness," *Hebrew Union College Annual* 53 (1982), 295–308; idem, "Sigmund Freud: A German and His Discontents," in his *Freud, Jews and*

Other Germans (New York: Oxford University Press, 1978), 29–92; Marianne Krull, *Freud und sein Vater: Die Entstehung der Psychoanalyse und Freuds ungelöste Vaterbindung* (Munich: C. H. Beck, 1979); David Aberbach, "Freud's Jewish Problem," *Commentary* 69 (1980), 35–39; Dennie B. Klein, *Jewish Origins of the Psychoanalytic Movement* (New York: Praeger, 1981); Justin Miller, "Interpretation of Freud's Jewishness, 1924–1974," *Journal of the History of the Behavioral Sciences* 17 (1981), 357–74 (the best overview); Theo Pfrimmer, *Freud: Lecteur de la Bible* (Paris: Presses Universitaires de France, 1982); and Max Kohn, *Freud et le Yiddish: Le Préanalytique* (Paris: Christian Bourgois, 1982). The last is the first book-length study of Freud's book on humor. It badly confuses Yiddish with the image of the Yiddish-accented speaker in Germany. Following the completion of this study, there appeared a detailed study of Freud's humor, which does not place this humor in a historical context: Elliott Oring, *The Jokes of Sigmund Freud: A Study in Humor and Jewish Identity* (Philadelphia: University of Pennsylvania Press, 1984). All of the recent studies draw heavily on the anecdotal material presented in Max Schur, *Freud: Living and Dying* (New York: International Universities Press, 1972). Recently an essay on the relationship between the language of psychoanalysis and the implications of a language for German Jewish identity has appeared: Stanley Rosenman, "The Late Conceptualization of the Self in Psychoanalysis: The German Language and Jewish Identity," *Journal of Psychohistory* 11 (1983), 9–42.

70. Gershom Scholem, *From Berlin to Jerusalem: Memories of My Youth*, trans. Harry Zohn (New York: Schocken, 1980), 40. On Scholem and his relationship to the growth of German Jewish thought in the twentieth century see David Biale, *Gershom Scholem: Kabbalah and Counter-History* (Cambridge: Harvard University Press, 1979). Sholem was extremely sensitive to the use of *mauscheln* within German Jewish comic discourse. He viewed Kurt Tucholsky's use of *mauscheln* in his "Herr Wendriner" monologues (published during the late 1920s) as "sinister documents" (see Harold L. Poor, *Kurt Tucholsky and the Ordeal of Germany 1914–1935* [New York: Scribner, 1968], 219).

71. M. Nuél [Manuel Schnitzer], *Das Buch der jüdischen Witze* (Berlin: Hesperus, 1907). The influence of Buber's "model" of the Germanization of the tradition of Eastern Jewry can be seen in the structure of Schnitzer's later collection, *Rabbi Lach und seine Geschichten* (Berlin: Hesperus, 1910). Similar to Schnitzer's collection are Richard Schmidt, *O diese Juden!* (Berlin: Roszius, 1906); Simon Joseph Rügenwald, *Humor aus dem jüdischen Leben* (Frankfurt: Kauffmann, 1903); and Louis Böhm, *Lieder eines fahrenden Chossid: Humoristische Dichtungen für jüdische Geselligkeit* (Hildesheim: Louis Manasse, 1910), which bears an introduction by the state rabbi of Hildesheim and contains poetry for comic declamation written in High German with a few, untranslated Yiddishisms.

72. The only study of the image of the comic Jew that attempts to explore this image synchronically is Sig Altman, *The Comic Image of the Jew: Explorations of a Pop Culture Phenomenon* (Rutherford, N.J.: Fair-

leigh Dickinson University Press, 1971). This volume is marred by the lack of firsthand historical information on the tradition of the comic Jew in Europe. See also Theodor Reik, "Freud and Jewish Wit," *Psychoanalysis* 2 (1954), 12–20.

73. M. Nuél [Manuel Schnitzer], *Das Buch der jüdischen Witze: Neue Folge* (Berlin: Gustav Riecke, [1908?]), 98.

74. Avrom Reitzer, *Gut Jontev: Rituelle Scherze und koscher Schmonzes für unsere Leut* (Vienna: Deubler, 1899); idem, *Nebbach: Rituelle Scherze, Lozelech, Maisses und koschere Schmonzes für unsere Leut* (Vienna: Deubler, 1902); idem, *Solém Alechem. Nix für kinder: E Waggon feiner, vescher, safter Lozelach, Schmonzes, takef pickfeiner Schmüs für ünsere Leit* (Vienna: Deubler, 1902); idem, *500 Lozelech Maisses koschere Schmonzes pickfeine Schmüs für unsere Leut* (Vienna: J. Deubler, n.d.).

75. Reitzer, *Solém*, 3.

76. L. M. Büschenthal, *Sammlung witziger Einfälle von Juden, als Beytrage zur Characteristik der Jüdischen Nation* (Elberfeld: H. Buschler, 1812).

77. Sabattja Josef Wolff, *Streifereien im Gebiete des Ernstes und des Scherzes*, 2 vols. (Berlin: Ernst Siegfried Mittler, 1818–19).

78. Ernst Freud et al., *Sigmund Freud* (New York: Harcourt Brace Jovanovich, 1978), 53.

79. Breuer's case notes are published in Albrecht Hirschmüller, *Physiologie und Psychoanalyse in Leben und Werk Josef Breuers. Jahrbuch der Psychoanalyse*, supp. 4 (Bern: Hans Huber, 1978). Her loss of faith is mentioned in a letter to Robert Binswanger of November 4, 1881, reprinted by Hirschmüller; the case is described in Freud et al., 2:21–47.

80. Hirschmüller, 354.

81. Frank J. Sulloway, *Freud, Biologist of the Mind* (New York: Basic Books, 1979), 57 ff. See also Patrick Mahony, *Freud as a Writer* (New York: International Universities Press, 1982).

82. Sigmund Freud, *The Complete Letters of Sigmund Freud to Wilhelm Fliess, 1887–1904*, trans. and ed. Jeffrey Moussaieff Masson (Cambridge: Belknap Press of Harvard University Press, 1985), p. 249. All other references to Freud are to the *Complete Psychological Works* (see n. 69).

83. I rely here on two insightful essays: Jeffrey Mehlman, "How to Read Freud on Jokes: The Critic as Schadchen," *New Literary History* 6 (1975), 439–61; and Mary Jacobus, "Is There a Woman in This Text?" ibid., 14 (1982), 117–41.

84. See my discussion of Balmary's work in "Psychoanalyzing 'Psychoanalyzing Psychoanalysis,'" *Contemporary Psychiatry* 2 (1983), 213–15.

85. *Der jüdische Spassvogel, oder Jocosus hebricosus. Ahne Versammlung von aller mit ahner pauetischen Vorred*, 2d ed. (Munich: A. L. Berend, 1890). See also Freud, 8:57.

86. Freud et al., 46. Freud, of course, became quickly labeled as a "Jewish" thinker. For Jung the association of the study of humor and the study of sexuality was part of his characterization of Freud's Jewishness.

Thus he refers to the "obscene joke-psychology" of Freud's sexual theories (cited in Frederic V. Grunfeld, *Prophets without Honor: A Background to Freud, Einstein, and Their World* [London: Hutchinson & Co., 1979], 59).

87. The literature on the image of the Eastern Jew in the West has documented the complexity of the projections concerning the *Ostjude*. The first critical essay on this topic was my "The Rediscovery of the Eastern Jews: German Jews in the East, 1890–1918," in *Jews and Germans from 1860 to 1933: The Problematic Symbiosis*, ed. David Bronsen [Heidelberg: Carl Winter, 1979], 338–67. Steven E. Aschheim has published his dissertation on this topic: *Brothers and Strangers: The East European Jew in German and German Jewish Consciousness, 1800–1923* (Madison: University of Wisconsin Press, 1982). For more detailed historical material see Jack L. Wertheimer, "German Policy and Jewish Politics: The Absorption of East European Jews in Germany [1868–1914]" [Ph.D. diss., Columbia University, 1978]; and idem, taken from his dissertation, "The Unwanted Element: East European Jews in Imperial Germany," *Leo Baeck Institute Yearbook* 26 (1981), 23–46.

88. On the complexity of the Jewish perception of their cultural context see Sidney M. Bolkosky, *The Distorted Image: German Jewish Perceptions of Germans and Germany, 1918–1935* (New York: Elsevier, 1975); Michael A. Meyer, *German Political Pressure and Jewish Religious Response in the Nineteenth Century*, Leo Baeck Memorial Lecture no. 25 (New York: Leo Baeck Institute, 1981); and Sanford Ragins, *Jewish Responses to Anti-Semitism in Germany, 1870–1914: A Study in the History of Ideas* (Cincinnati, Ohio: Hebrew Union College Press, 1980).

89. Ahron Marcus, *Hartmann's inductive Philosophie im Chassidismus*, vol. 1 (Vienna: Moriz Waizner, 1888), 9. See also Markus Marcus, *Ahron Marcus: Die Lebensgeschichte eines Chossid* (Montreux: David Marcus, 1966).

90. Ahron Marcus, *Glauben und Wissen im Judentum. Vortrag gehalten am 2. November im israelitisch wissenschaftlichen Verein zu Altona* (Hamburg: M. Lessmann, 1903), 4.

91. The recent biography of Buber by Maurice Friedman, *Martin Buber's Life and Work*, 2 vols. (New York: E. P. Dutton, 1981–83), supersedes all of the older material on Buber. It is, however, just as much a hagiography as the earlier biographies even though it brings out much more material.

92. Martin Buber, "Mein Weg zum Chassidismus," *Werke III: Schriften zum Chassidismus* (Munich: Kösel & Lambert Schneider, 1963), 966. The relationship between Buber's concept of Jewish mysticism and other modern Jewish approaches is perhaps best captured in Gershom Scholem's criticism of Buber. One must remember, however, that Scholem has his own agenda concerning the presentation of Jewish mysticism to the Western reader.

93. Martin Buber, "Der Geist des Orients und das Judentum," *Von Geist des Judentums* (Leipzig: Kurt Wolff, 1911), 9–48.

94. Buber, "Mein Weg zum Chassidismus," 963–64.

95. Friedman, 1:104–5.

96. Ibid., 10–11.

97. Hugo Bergmann, "Das hebräische Buch und die deutschen Zionisten," *Der Jude* 4 (1919–20), 287–88. For the background see Friedman, 1:260. Cf. Jischak Epstein, "Israel und seine Sprache: Ein Fall sozialer Psychopathologie," *Der Jude* 4 (1919–20), 322–26.

98. Chaim Weizmann, *Trial and Error* (London: H. Hamilton, 1949), 86–87.

99. Gershom Scholem, *Major Trends in Jewish Mysticism* (New York: Schocken, 1941), 17.

100. See Zosa Szajkowski, "The Struggle for Yiddish during World War I: The Attitude of German Jewry," *Leo Baeck Institute Yearbook* 9 (1964), 131–60; and Emanuel S. Goldsmith, *Architects of Yiddishism* (London: Associated University Presses, 1976). Of great interest, of course, remains the fact that whenever the formation of a German Jewish identity was discussed by Jews, one of the central questions revolved about the hidden language of the Jews. In his 1934 dissertation, written under Karl Mannheim but defended after Mannheim's expulsion from the University by the Nazis, Jacob Katz stresses that the development of Yiddish was a cultural development, not a *biological* one. Race does not explain language for Katz (see Jacob Katz, "Die Entstehung der Judenassimilation in Deutschland und deren Ideologie" [Ph.D. diss., University of Frankfurt, 1934], reprinted in his *Zur Assimilation und Emanzipation der Juden* [Darmstadt: Wissenschaftliche Buchgesellschaft, 1982], 15).

101. Moses Calvary, "Jiddisch," *Der Jude* 1 (1916–17), 25–32, cited here in the translation by Joachim Neugroschel, in *Essays from Martin Buber's Journal Der Jude, 1916–1928*, ed. Arthur A. Cohen (University: University of Alabama Press, 1980), 31–44. Cf. the more balanced approach to Yiddish in the essay by J. Eljashoff of Kowno, "Uber Jargon ('Jüdisch') und Jargonliteratur," which appeared in the *Jüdischer Almanach 5663* (Berlin: Jüdischer Verlag, 1902–3), 56–61.

102. See, for example, Ekkehard Hieronimus, *Der Grafiker E. M. Lilien (1874–1925)* (Braunschweig: Städtisches Museum, 1974).

103. See, for example, Wilhelm Stöckle, *Deutsche Ansichten: 100 Jahre Zeitgeschichte auf Postkarten* (Munich: Deutscher Taschenbuchverlag, 1982), plates 11–12. On the background of this tradition see Judith Vogt, *Historien om et Image: Antisemitisme og Antizionisme i Karikaturer* (Copenhagen: Samieren; Oslo: Cappelen, 1978). A rich source for the images and self-images of the German-speaking Jewish community is the catalogue of a major exhibition held in Berlin in 1981, *Juden in Preussen: Ein Kapital deutscher Geschichte* (Dortmund: Harenberg, 1981).

104. František Langer, "My Brother Jiří," foreword to Jiří Langer, *Nine Gates*, trans. Stephen Jolly (London: James Clarke & Co.), xv.

105. Langer, 12. The negative attitude toward Langer as a Western Jew who abandoned the mode of his world can be seen even in the work of a contemporary writer who also glorified the Eastern Jew as the future hope for Judaism: see Max Brod's memoir, *Der Prager Kreis* (Stuttgart: Kohlhammer, 1966), 156–57. For the general historical background to the

problem of cultural and linguistic identity in Prague see Gary B. Cohen, *The Politics of Ethnic Survival: Germans in Prague, 1861–1914* (Princeton: Princeton University Press, 1981).

106. Franz Kafka, *Tagebücher, 1910–1923* (New York: Schocken, 1948), 478–79. For the general background see Fritz Strich, "Franz Kafka und das Judentum," in his *Kunst und Leben* (Bern: Francke, 1960), 139–51; Felix Weltsch, "The Rise and Fall of the Jewish-German Symbiosis: The Case of Franz Kafka," *Leo Baeck Institute Yearbook* 1 (1956), 255–76; Evelyn Torton Beck, *Kafka and the Yiddish Theater* (Madison: University of Wisconsin Press, 1971); Walter Sokel, "Language and Truth in the Two Worlds of Franz Kafka," *German Quarterly* 52 (1979), 364–84; Carmely, 101–69; and Hartmut Binder, ed., *Kafka-Handbuch*, 2 vols. (Stuttgart: Kröner, 1979), 1:21–39, 65–69, 390–94. Kafka's German-language attempts to recreate his impression of "Jewish" discourse, or at least the discourse appropriate to Jews, represents one of a number of complex cases from the early twentieth century. Two more complex German fictionalizations of the *Ostjude*, cast in the "travels in Poland" model introduced by Heine, are of similar interest, since they reflect a positive projection of the Eastern Jew. Alfred Döblin's 1926 *Reise in Polen* and Joseph Roth's 1927 *Juden auf Wanderschaft* both recreate the Eastern Jew with the positive image of an integrated society of Jews. Both works reflect their author's tortured relationship with his own Jewish identity (see David Bronsen, *Joseph Roth* [Cologne: Kiepenheuer und Witsch, 1974]; and Wolfgang Kort, *Alfred Döblin* [Boston: Twayne, 1974]). What is of interest is that Roth, the Eastern Jew who accepts the cultural values and status of the German-language writer, in a review of Döblin's work, the work of the middle-class professional who has converted to Christianity, observes that Döblin captured a "Jewish discourse" in his work. It is the idealized discourse of the fictionalized *Ostjude* perceived by the Western Jew alienated from German as the language of anti-Semitism (see Ingrid Schuster and Ingrid Bode, eds., *Alfred Döblin im Spiegel der zeitgenössischen Kritik* [Munich: Francke, 1973], 168–70). For a sense of the reality of the Eastern Jews' position at the same moment see Frank Golczewski, *Polnisch-jüdische Beziehungen, 1881–1922: Eine Studie zur Geschichte des Antisemitismus in Osteuropa* (Wiesbaden: Franz Steiner, 1981). For a somewhat later set of images see Efraim Frisch's 1937 account of his trip to Poland, reprinted in Guy Stern, ed., *Efraim Frisch: Zum Verständnis des Geistigen* (Heidelberg: Lambert Schneider, 1963), 248–53.

107. All references are to Franz Kafka, *The Penal Colony*, trans. Willa Muir and Edwin Muir (New York: Schocken, 1961), 173–83. See also Peter Bridgwater, "Rotpeters Ahnherren, oder: Der gelehrte Affe in der deutschen Dichtung," *Deutsche Vierteljahrschrift* 56 (1982), 447–62. For the biographical background see Ronald Hayman, *Kafka* (Oxford: Oxford University Press, 1982).

108. Lion Feuchtwanger, *Centum opuscula: Eine Auswahl*, ed. Wolfgang Berndt (Rudolstadt: Greifenverlag, 1956), 489.

109. Ibid., 388.

110. Franz Kafka, *Briefe, 1902–1924*, ed. Max Brod (New York: Schocken, 1966), 335–38. Concerning this letter see Carmely, 158.

111. Cited in Wertheimer, "The Unwanted Element," 37. He quotes from *Ha-Melitz* 134 (1895), 2–3; and *Ha Maggid*, 22 July 1891, 227–28, 236–37.

112. Emanuel Schreiber, ed., *Die Selbstkritik der Juden* (Berlin: Carl Duncker, 1880).

113. Stephen Wilson, *Ideology and Experience: Antisemitism in France at the Time of the Dreyfus Affair* (Rutherford, N.J.: Fairleigh Dickinson University Press, 1980).

114. M. Boudin, "Sur l'idiote et l'alienation mentale chez les juifs d'Allemagne," *Bulletins de la société d'anthropologie de Paris* 4 (1863), 386–88.

115. See my *On Blackness without Blacks: Essays on the Image of the Black in Germany* (Boston: G. K. Hall, 1982), 2–11. See also Ted Porter, "The Calculus of Liberalism: The Development of Statistical Thinking in the Social and Natural Sciences of the Nineteenth Century" (Ph.D. diss., Princeton University, 1981); and Ian Hacking, *The Emergence of Probability: A Philosophical Study of Early Ideas about Probability, Induction, and Statistical Inference* (London: Cambridge University Press, 1975).

116. Richard M. Goodman, *Genetic Disorders among the Jewish People* (Baltimore: Johns Hopkins University Press, 1979), 421–27.

117. M. Zabrowski, "A propos du procès-verbal," *Bulletins de la société d'anthropologie de Paris* 7 (1884), 698–701.

118. J. M. Charcot, *Leçons du mardi la Salpêtrière*, 2 vols. (Paris: Progrès médical, 1887–89), 2:11–12.

119. Charcot's influence was felt immediately. See "Sur la race juive et sa pathologie," *Académie de médecine* (Paris), ser. 26, no. 3 (1891), 287–309.

120. Richard Krafft-Ebing, *Text-Book of Insanity*, trans. Charles Gilbert Chaddock (Philadelphia: F. A. Davis, 1905), 143. A detailed summary of these views can be found in Alexander Pilcz, *Beitrag zur vergleichenden Rassen-Psychiatrie* (Leipzig and Vienna: Deuticke, 1906), 26–32.

121. Krafft-Ebing, 143.

122. Richard Krafft-Ebing, *Nervosität und neurasthenische Zustände* (Vienna: Hölder, 1895), 96. For the context see T. J. Jackson Lear, *No Place of Grace: Anti-Modernism and the Transformation of American Culture* (New York: Pantheon, 1981).

123. Martin Engländer, *Die auffallend häufigen Krankheitserscheinungen der jüdischen Rasse* (Vienna: J. L. Pollak, 1902), 12, 17. An overview of the literature on this topic from 1900 to 1932 is to be found in Rafael Becker, "Bibliographische Übersicht der Literatur aus dem Gebiete: 'Geistereserkrankungen bei den Juden,'" *Allgemeine Zeitschrift für Psychiatrie* 98 (1932), 240–76.

124. Cesare Lombroso, *L'Antisemitismo e la scienze moderne* (Turin: L. Roux, 1894), 83.

125. Max Nordau, *Max Nordaus Zionistische Schriften* (Cologne: Jüdischer Verlag, 1909), 379–81. The answer to Nordau and to the various

Jewish uses of this image of the Eastern Jew as the diseased Jew was very plate in coming (see *Hygiene und Judentum: Eine Sammelschrift* [Dresden: Jacob Sternlicht, 1930]). Recently it has been argued that the Eastern European Jewish community, at least in the United States, was *healthier*, rather than more diseased (see Jacob Jay Lindenthal, *"Abi Gezunt*: Health and the Eastern European Immigrant," *American Jewish History* 70 [1981], 420–41).

126. On the historical importance of incest in nineteenth-century thought see Herbert Maisch, *Inzest* (Reinbek: Rowohlt, 1968), 27–30. See also Mary Douglas, *Purity and Danger: An Analysis of Concepts of Pollution and Taboo* (Harmondsworth: Penguin, n.d.), 41–72, on the power of the symbols of defilement and taboo. See a recent book by George L. Mosse, *Nationalism and Sexuality: Respectability and Abnormal Sexuality in Modern Europe* (New York: Howard Fertig, 1985).

127. See Marie Walter, "Concerning the Affair Wälsungenblut," *Book Collector* 13 (1964), 463–72. For a summary of the reception of this text see Hans Rudolf Vaget, *"Sang réservé* in Deutschland: Zur Rezeption von Thomas Manns *Wälsungenblut," German Quarterly* 57 (1984), 367–75.

128. Fritz Wittels, *Der Taufjude* (Vienna: Breitenstein, 1904).

129. Rafael Becker, *Die jüdische Nervosität: Ihre Art, Entstehung und Bekämpfung* (Zurich: Speidel & Wurzel, 1918). On the nervousness of the Germans see Observator, *Uber die Nervosität im deutschen Charakter* (Leipzig: Neuer Geist, 1922). See also Jack Zipes, "Oskar Panizza: The Operated German as Operated Jew," *New German Critique* 21 (1980), 47–61, as well as Peter D. G. Brown, *Oskar Panizza: His Life and Works* (Bern: Peter Lang, 1983), especially 137–38 on Panizza's anti-Semitic image of the Jew and the Jews' language.

130. Rafael Becker, *Die Nervosität bei den Juden: Ein Beitrag zur Rassenpsychiatrie für Arzte und Gebildete Laien* (Zurich: Orell Füssli, 1919). The association of Semitic and decadent, in the medical as well as the cultural sense of the term, is made throughout the turn of the century (see, for example, Ottokar Stauf von der March, "Decadence," in his *Literarische Studien und Schattenrisse* [Dresden: E. Pierson, 1903], 13–30).

131. Josef Prager, "Verdrängung und Durchbruch in der jüdischen Seele," *Der Jude* 7 (1923), 675–81.

132. E. J. Lesser, "Karl Marx als Jude," ibid., 8 (1924), 173–81.

133. Cf. Gustav Meyer, "Der Jude in Karl Marx," *Neue jüdische Monatshefte* 2 (1917–18), 327–31.

134. Hans Kohn, "Das kulturelle Problem des modernen Westjuden," *Der Jude* 5 (1921), 281–97.

135. Arnold Zweig, *Caliban oder Politik und Leidenschaft: Versuch über die menschlichen Gruppenleidenschaften dargetan am Antisemitismus* (Potsdam: Gustav Kiepenheuer, 1927), 199–200.

136. Arnold Zweig and Hermann Struck, *Das ostjüdische Antlitz* (Berlin: Welt, 1922), 73. See also H. Z. Kamnizter, "Die Wandlung Arnold Zweigs: Zionismus, Psychoanalyse, Sozialismus," *Kürbiskern*, 1972, 106–22; and Carmely, 74–100.

137. Arnold Zweig, *Juden auf der deutschen Bühne* (Berlin: Welt,

1928), 22–25. This is in response to works such as Franz Josef Cramer, *Das antisemitische Theater* (Leipzig: Oswald Mutze, 1900).

138. Gustav Jaeger, *Die Entdeckung der Seele* (Leipzig: Ernst Günther, 1880), 106–9.

139. On Theodor Lessing see Solomon Liptzin, *Germany's Stepchildren* (Philadelphia: Jewish Publication Society of America, 1944), 165–69; Gay, *Freud*, 197–98; Herbert Poetzl, "Confrontations with Modernity: Theodor Lessing's Critique of German Culture" (Ph.D. diss., University of Massachusetts, Amherst, 1978); Lawrence Baron, "Theodor Lessing: Between Jewish Self-Hatred and Zionism," *Leo Baeck Institute Yearbook* 26 (1981), 323–40; and Hans Mayer, *Outsiders: A Study in Life and Letters*, trans. Denis M. Sweet (Cambridge: MIT Press, 1982), 357–63. Lessing's own interest in the psychopathology of self-hatred was understood as stemming from his own fragmented sense of self. Lessing had attacked psychoanalysis as a "typically Jewish abortion." In 1936 Freud recalled Lessing's attack on him and wrote to Kurt Hiller that Lessing's self-hatred was "an exquisite Jewish phenomenon" (cited in Gay, *Freud*, 195).

140. Theodor Lessing, "Eindrücke aus Galizien," *Allgemeine Zeitung des Judentums* 73, nos. 49, 51, 52, 53 (1909), 587, 610–11, 620–22, and 634–35, respectively; Binjimun Segel, *Die Entdeckungsreise des Herrn Dr. Theodor Lessing zu den Ostjuden* (Lemberg, 1910).

141. Theodor Lessing, *Einmal und nie wieder: Lebenserinnerungen* (Gütersloh: J. Bertelsmann, 1969), 396–97. The translation is from Baron, 331.

142. Franz Rosenzweig, *Briefe*, ed. Edith Rosenzweig (Berlin: Schocken, 1936), 323–24. On Rosenzweig's mode of expression see the introduction and selections in Nahum N. Glatzer, ed., *Franz Rosenzweig: His Life and Thought* (New York: Schocken, 1961), 251–60.

143. Robert Weltsch, "Selbstkritik, trotz allem!" in his *Ja-sagen zum Judentum* (Berlin: Jüdische Rundschau, 1933), 59–66. For the context of German Zionist rhetoric see Stephen M. Poppel, *Zionism in Germany, 1897–1933* (Philadelphia: Jewish Publication Society of America, 1977); Jehuda Reinharz, *Fatherland or Promised Land: The Dilemma of the German Jew, 1893–1914* (Ann Arbor: University of Michigan Press, 1975); idem, *Dokumente zur Geschichte des deutschen Zionismus, 1882–1933* (Tübingen: Mohr, 1981); and Lenni Brenner, *Zionism in the Age of the Dictators* (London: Croom Helm, 1983).

144. A. Myerson, "The 'Nervousness' of the Jew," *Mental Hygiene* 4 (1920), 65–72. Cf. *Medical Record* (New York), 16 February 1918, 269–75. The use of "scientific" rhetoric permeates into the recesses of Jewish identity, almost always to characterize the Other as psychopathological. Cf., for example, the essay by the Hungarian Jew Maximilian Schächter, "Assimilation," *Jahrbuch für jüdische Geschichte und Literatur* 9 (1906), 107–20.

145. Kurt Lewin, "Self-Hatred among Jews," reprinted in his *Resolving Social Conflicts* (New York: Harper Brothers, 1948), 186–200. See also Lewis W. Brandt, *Psychologists Caught: A Psycho-logic of Psychology*

(Toronto: University of Toronto Press, 1982), 226–34. One of the most important elements in Lewin's definition was his assumption that a positive relationship to the group to which one belongs (or is assigned) is a *necessary* prerequisite for individual mental health. The corollary to this view was, of course, that a discordant relationship (whatever its cause) was a sign of mental illness. This view became the dominant definition of positive group identification in the United States through the legal acceptance of Lewin's definition (as presented in the brief prepared by Kenneth B. Clark) as to the psychological damage suffered by black students in segregated schools. The court, in its findings in *Brown v. The Board of Education of Topeka* (1954), accepted Lewin's premise that such stigmatization causes psychopathology in the form of self-hatred. While there may be a pathological result to the discordance between group identity and self-definition, it is certainly not necessarily the sole form of identity formation that can result. But the power of "self-hatred" as a category was such that it could be (and was) used to label the only possible reaction to a dissonant sense of the relationship of the self to superimposed categories of identity. I rely here on the work done by William E. Cross, Jr., "Black Identity: Rediscovery of the Distinction between Personal Identity and Reference Group Orientation" (Paper presented at the 1981 Bi-Annual Meeting of the Society for Research in Child Development, Boston, 2–5 April 1981).

146. Bruno Bettelheim, "The Dynamism of Anti-Semitism in Gentile and Jew," *Journal of Abnormal and Social Psychology* 42 (1947), 152–68. For the literature on Bettelheim see the extended discussion of *The Informed Heart* in chapter 6.

147. Irving Sarnoff, "Identification with the Aggressor: Some Personality Correlates of Anti-Semitism among Jews" (Ph.D. diss., University of Michigan, 1951). Cf. R. Segalman, "A Test of the Lewinian Hypothesis on Self-Hatred" (Ph.D. diss., New York University, 1967). For the background of Lewin's thought see Alfred J. Marrow, *The Practical Theorist: The Life and Work of Kurt Lewin* (New York: Basic Books, 1969).

148. The classic work on ethnic identity formation following the Second World War remains Daniel P. Moynihan and Nathan Glazer, *Beyond the Melting Pot* (Cambridge: MIT Press, 1970).

CHAPTER SIX. THE ASHES OF THE HOLOCAUST AND THE CLOSURE OF SELF-HATRED

1. Translated from Gerhard Sauder, ed., *Die Bücherverbrennung. Zum 10. Mai 1933* (Munich: Carl Hanser, 1983), 92–93.

2. Ibid., 94.

3. Ibid., 101–2.

4. Adolf Hitler, *Mein Kampf*, trans. Ralph Manheim (Cambridge: Houghton Mifflin, 1943).

5. Sauder, 96.

6. Dr. B., "Die Rassenmerkmale der Juden," *Der Stürmer* 38 (1928), 2.

7. Ernst Heimer, *Der Giftpilz* (Nuremberg: Verlag der Stürmer, 1938), 10.

8. "Mauschelpredigt," *Der Stürmer* 6 (1941), 5. On Streicher and his anti-Semitism see Dennis E. Showalter, *Little Man, What Now? Der Stürmer in the Weimar Republic* (Hamden, Conn.: Archon, 1982); and Randall L. Bytwerk, *Julius Streicher* (New York: Stein & Day, 1983). By the 1920s, the myth of the Jews of Germany possessing a special language had radically parted from the social reality present in Germany. Yet in most of the anti-Semitic literature the theme of the "hidden" language of the Jews has been retained. Thus in the *Sigilla Veri* (2 vols. [N.p.: Bodung Verlag, 1929]), one of the numerous handbooks listing Jews (and thus documenting Jewish influence), the subtitle of the work states that it is a "lexicon of the Jews, their friends and enemies, of all times, with their . . . thieves' language, nicknames, secret organizations."

9. See the discussion by Shlomo Avineri, *The Making of Modern Zionism: The Intellectual Origins of the Jews' State* (New York: Basic Books, 1981), 83–87. The rise of modern Hebrew, especially after the Holocaust, introduces a new variable in the myths about Jewish discourse. Suddenly, there is a national language of the Jews which fulfills the first of Alfred Weber's criteria for nationhood; there is a special language of the Jews which contrasts with the languages of the diaspora. And this language is associated with a very different image of the Jew, the Jew as warrior rather than scholar. All of the modern discussion of the hidden language of the Jews is colored by the rise of Hebrew during the twentieth century as a national and a literary language. While this present study does not consider those writers who were raised speaking German and who adopted Hebrew as their literary language, such relationships present a different set of problems for the definition of the self. (See my *Difference and Pathology: Stereotypes of Sexuality, Race, and Madness* [Ithaca, N.Y.: Cornell University Press, 1985], 109–10.) Likewise, the presence of Hebrew (and the State of Israel) is a condition that authors writing in languages other than Hebrew, such as Philip Roth, must (and do) take into consideration.

10. Julius Streicher in *Der Stürmer* 12 (1941), 6.

11. Otto Klein, translated from Joseph Wulf, ed., *Literatur und Dichtung im Dritten Reich* (Gütersloh: Mohn, 1963), 466.

12. Jack L. Wertheimer, "Between Tsar and Kaiser—The Radicalization of Russian-Jewish University Students in Germany," *Leo Baeck Institute Yearbook* 28 (1983), 329–50.

13. Quoted in Geert Platner, ed., *Schule im Dritten Reich: Erziehung zum Tod? Eine Dokumentation* (Munich: dtv, 1983), 47.

14. Marcel Reich-Ranicki, ed., *Meine Schulzeit im Dritten Reich* (Cologne: Kiepenheuer & Witsch, 1982), 60.

15. Bertolt Brecht, *Arbeitsjournal*, ed. Werner Hecht, 2 vols. (Frankfurt: Suhrkamp, 1973), 1:294.

16. See the discussion of this tendency of German anti-Semitism to categorize the special language of the Jews in Manes Sperber, *Churban oder die unfassbare Gewissheit* (Munich: dtv, 1983), 55–56.

17. See Geneva Smitherman, "White English in Blackface, or Who Do I Be?" in *The State of the Language,* ed. Leonard Michaels and Christopher Ricks (Berkeley: University of California Press, 1980), 158–68.

18. See Kathryn Hellerstein, "Yiddish Voice in American English," in *The State of the Language,* ed. Leonard Michaels and Christopher Ricks (Berkeley: University of California Press, 1980), 182–201. The range of responses to the image of the Jew as multilingual can be judged in the series of statements in the symposium on "Hebrew and Yiddish Legacies" of Anglo-American Jewish authors published in the *Times Literary Supplement* (London) (May 3, 1985), 499–500. Among the writers who discuss the image of the Jew as possessing more than one tongue (and therefore perhaps none) are Cynthia Ozick and Philip Roth.

19. Henry James, *The American Scene* (London: Chapman & Hall, 1907), 129–31. See also Louis Harap, *The Image of the Jew in American Literature: From Early Republic to Mass Immigration* (Philadelphia: Jewish Publications Society, 1974).

20. All of the quotations are from Samuel Roth, *Jews Must Live: An Account of the Persecution of the World by Israel on All the Frontiers of Civilization* (New York: Golden Hind Press, 1934). See also Alvin H. Rosenfeld, "Inventing the Jew: Notes on Jewish Autobiography," *Midstream* 21 (1975), 54–67.

21. Meyer Schapiro, "Mr. Berenson's Values," *Encounter* 16 (1961), 57–65.

22. I am combining two concepts of the victim. One, sketched by Erving Goffmann, stresses the internalization of the sense of stigma associated with being the victim; the other, best outlined by C. B. Wortman, stresses the need for control felt by the victim and the creation of structures of control. I am arguing that both of these take place in writers who identify themselves as Jews and thus as potential (or actual) victims of the Holocaust. The victim senses him- or herself as guilty, bearing the stigma of the victim as well as needing often contradictory structures to deal with being marked. All of these control distance in this sense through fictions about the establishment of control or projections of the loss of control onto figures created within these fictions of control (see Erving Goffman, *Stigma: Notes on the Management of Spoiled Identity* [Englewood Cliffs, N.J.: Prentice Hall, 1963]; and C. B. Wortman, "Causal Attributions and Personal Control," in *New Directions in Attribution Research,* ed. J. H. Harvey et al. [Hilldale, N.J.: Erlbaum, 1976]). On the general function of images as a means of dealing with reality see Terrence Des Pres, *The Survivor: An Anatomy of Life in the Death Camps* (New York: Oxford University Press, 1976); Günther B. Ginzel, ed., *Auschwitz als Herausforderung für Juden und Christen* (Heidelberg: Lambert Schneider, 1980); A. Roy Eckardt with Alice L. Eckardt, *Long Night's Journey into Day: Life and Faith after the Holocaust* (Detroit: Wayne State University Press, 1982); Lawrence L. Langer, *Versions of Survival: The Holocaust and the Human Spirit* (Albany: State University of New York Press, 1982); and idem, *The Holocaust and the Literary Imagination* (New Haven: Yale

University Press, 1975). On the continuities of literary images in the writings about the Holocaust see David G. Roskies, *Against the Apocalypse: Responses to Catastrophe in Modern Jewish Culture* (Cambridge: Harvard University Press, 1984).

23. Theodor W. Adorno, *Prisms*, trans. Samuel Weber and Shierry Weber (London: Neville Spearman, 1967), 34.

24. George Steiner, *Language and Silence: Essays on Language, Literature and the Inhuman* (New York: Atheneum, 1967), 96. On the German response see *Sprache im technischen Zeitalter* 6 (1963), 431–506.

25. Victor Klemperer, *LTI: Notizbuch eines Philologen* (Berlin: Aufbau, 1947).

26. See George Steiner, *Extraterritorial: Papers on Literature and the Language Revolution* (New York: Atheneum, 1971), 71 ff.

27. Paul Celan, *Die Niemandsrose* (Frankfurt: S. Fischer, 1963), 24. On Celan and the problem of language see Robert Foot, *The Phenomenon of Speechlessness in the Poetry of Marie Luise Kaschnitz, Günter Eich, Nelly Sachs and Paul Celan* (Bonn: Bouvier, 1982), which also has a rather complete bibliography. See also Peter Mayer, "'Alle Dichter sind Juden': Zur Lyrik Paul Celans," *Germanisch-Romanische Monatshefte* 23 (1973), 32–55. It is striking that the experiments that attempted to create a "Jewish" discourse in German were often perceived as succeeding when they mirrored the ideology associated by Hebrew writers with Hebrew letters. Schalom ben-Chorin wrote of the German Jewish poetess Elsa Lasker-Schüler after her flight from Germany to Palestine that "in the soul of this poetess lives the Hebrew soul. Even though she knew not a word of Hebrew. . . . She read little, but knew much out of the depth of her soul." Similarly, the poet Uri Zvi Greenberg observed that Lasker-Schüler "wrote poetry in Hebrew with German words" (Schalom ben-Chorin, *Mein Glaube, mein Schicksal* [Fribourg: Herder, 1984], 93).

28. Paul Celan, *Von Schwelle zu Schwelle* (Stuttgart: Deutsche Verlags-Anstalt, 1955), 53.

29. Paul Celan, *Ausgewählte Gedichte*, ed. Beda Allemann (Frankfurt: Suhrkamp, 1972), 128.

30. J. P. Stern, "'Words Are Also Deeds': Some Observations on Austrian Language Consciousness," *New Literary History* 12 (1981), 509–28.

31. Cynthia Ozick, *Bloodshed and Three Novellas* (New York: Knopf, 1976), 11.

32. Anne Roiphe, *Generation without Memory: A Jewish Journey in Christian America* (New York: Linden Press and Simon & Schuster, 1981).

33. Dagmar Barnouw, *Elias Canetti* (Stuttgart: Metzler, 1979), 1–17. This volume also includes an overview of the literature on Canetti. Canetti's sense of the centrality of language as the definition of the sense of self is forged, according to his own account, during the Nazi period. He sees his obligation as one to preserve *German* (not merely language) from the corruption of the Nazis. In defining his goal, he uses the rhetoric of purification taken from the Nazis (see Elias Canetti, *Aufzeichnungen, 1942–1948* [Munich: Hanser, 1965], 110–11).

34. Elias Canetti, *The Tongue Set Free*, trans. Joachim Neugröschel (New York: Seabury Press, 1979), 3.

35. Elias Canetti, *The Torch in My Ear*, trans. Joachim Neugröschel (New York: Farrar, Straus & Giroux, 1982), 185.

36. On Koestler see Steiner, *Extraterritorial*, 181–85; Harold Harris, ed., *Astride Two Cultures: Arthur Koestler at 70* (New York: Random House, 1976); John Atkins, *Arthur Koestler* (London: Neville Spearman, 1956); Iain Hamilton, *Koestler: A Biography* (London: Secker & Warburg, 1982); Peter Alfred Huber, *Arthur Koestler: Das literarische Werk* (Zurich: Fretz und Wasmuth, 1962); and Sidney A. Pearson, *Arthur Koestler* (Boston: G. K. Hall, 1978), esp. 149 ff.

37. Arthur Koestler, *Thieves in the Night* (New York: Macmillan, 1946), 278.

38. On self-hatred see the review by Isaac Rosenfeld, "Palestinian Ice Age," *New Republic* 115 (1946), 592.

39. Cited in Pearson, 149.

40. Arthur Koestler, *The Thirteenth Tribe: The Khazar Empire and Its Heritage* (London: Pan, 1977).

41. See Andrew Handler, ed. and trans., *The Holocaust in Hungary* (University: University of Alabama Press, 1982), 36–42.

42. Jerzy Kosinski, *The Painted Bird* (Boston: Houghton Mifflin, 1965; New York: Bantam, 1972). On Kosinski see Norman Lavers, *Jerzy Kosinski* (Boston: Twayne, 1982); Stanley Corngold, "Jerzy Kosinski's *The Painted Bird*: Language Lost and Regained," *Mosaic* 6 (1972/73), 153–68; Byron L. Sherwin, *Jerzy Kosinski* (Chicago: Cabala Press, 1981); Paul Bruss, *Victims: Textual Strategies in Recent American Fiction* (Lewisburg, Pa.: Bucknell University Press, 1981); and Welch D. Everman, *Jerzy Kosinski: The Literature of Violation* (San Bernardino: Borgo Press, 1984).

43. See Langer, *The Holocaust and the Literary Imagination*, 168–91. Langer cites Kosinski's *Notes of the Author on "The Painted Bird"* (New York: Scientia-Factum, 1965).

44. Jerzy Kosinski, quoted by George Plimpton in *Paris Review* 14 (1972), 193–94.

45. Jerzy Kosinski, *Blind Date* (London: Hutchinson, 1978).

46. Jurek Becker, *Jacob the Liar*, trans. Melvin Kornfeld (New York: Harcourt Brace Jovanovich, 1975). (The German original, *Jakob der Lügner*, was published in 1969.) On this novel see Marcel Reich-Ranicki, "Das Prinzip Radio," *Die Zeit*, 20 November 1970, in the light of Reich-Ranicki, *Meine Schulzeit*, 60.

47. Jurek Becker, *Der Boxer* (Frankfurt: Suhrkamp, 1976). On this novel see Marcel Reich-Ranicki's complex reaction, "Plädoyer für Jurek Becker," *Frankfurt Allgemeine Zeitung*, 19 February 1977. On the topology of Jewish figures in German belles-lettres see Christiane Schmelzkopf, *Zur Gestaltung jüdischer Figuren in der deutschsprachigen Literatur nach 1945* (Hildesheim: Georg Olms, 1983); and Heidy M. Müller, *Die Judendarstellung in deutschsprachiger Erzählprosa (1945–1981)* (Königstein: Athenäum, 1984).

48. Leah Ireland, "'Your Hope Is on My Shoulder': Bobrowski and the World of the *Ostjuden*," *Monatshefte* 72 (1980), 416–30.

49. Hans Jürgen Schultz, ed., *Mein Judentum* (Berlin: Kreuz, 1979), 10–18.

50. On the reception of *The Diary* see Lawrence L. Langer, "The Americanization of the Holocaust on Stage and Screen," in *From Hester Street to Hollywood*, ed. Sarah Blacher Cohen (Bloomington: Indiana University Press, 1983), 213–30. See also Henry F. Pommer, "The Legend and Art of Anne Frank," *Judaism* 9 (1960), 36–46; and Alvin H. Rosenfeld, *A Double Dying: Reflections on Holocaust Literature* (Bloomington: Indiana University Press, 1980), 51–53.

51. Philip Wiebe, in *Welt der Arbeit*, 29 April 1955.

52. Theodor W. Adorno, "Was bedeutet: Aufarbeitung der Vergangenheit," in his *Eingriffe* (Frankfurt: Suhrkamp, 1968), 143–44.

53. Steiner, *Language and Silence*, 108.

54. All references are to Meyer Levin, *The Obsession* (New York: Simon & Schuster, 1973), here 35. On the trial see *New York Times*, 14 December 1957, 16; 7 January 1958, 31; 9 January 1958, 40. On the book see the review by Victor Nevesky in *New York Times Book Review*, 3 February 1974, 5; and the letters to the editor responding to it by Levin and Kermit Bloomgarden, 3 March 1974, 34–35.

55. On Lillian Hellman and the Jews see Bonnie Lyons, "Lillian Hellman: The First Jewish Nun on Prytania Street," in Cohen, *From Hester Street*, 106–22.

56. Anne Frank, *The Diary of a Young Girl*, trans. B. M. Mooyaart-Doubleday (Garden City, N.Y.: Doubleday, 1952); Frances Goodrich and Albert Hackett, *The Diary of Anne Frank* (New York: Random House, 1956). See also Anna G. Steenmeijer, ed., *A Tribute to Anne Frank* (Garden City, N.Y.: Doubleday, 1971).

57. *The Diary* reflects Anne Frank's own understanding of herself as a young writer, a writer in Dutch, not in her native German. The literary quality of *The Diary* certainly stems from this sense of distance. Cf. *Anne Frank's Tales from the Secret Annex*, trans. Ralph Manheim and Michel Mok (New York: Doubleday, 1984), a collection of her literary jottings at the time she was writing *The Diary*.

58. Bruno Bettelheim, *The Informed Heart: Autonomy in a Mass Age* (New York: Avon, 1971), 248. Two major readings of Bettelheim have appeared recently: Jacob Robinson, *Psychoanalysis in a Vacuum: Bruno Bettelheim and the Holocaust* (New York: Yad Vashem-YIVO Documentary Projects, 1970); and Langer, *Versions of Survival*, 33–54.

59. Bruno Bettelheim, "The Ignored Lesson of Anne Frank," in *Surviving and Other Essays* (New York: Alfred A. Knopf, 1979), 246–57.

60. Marga Minco, *Bitter Herbs* (New York: Oxford University Press, 1960).

61. Teressa Hendry, "Was Anne Frank's Diary a Hoax?" *American Mercury*, Summer 1967, 26–28. A complete clippings file on the Stielau affair is available at the Wiener Library, London, which also has a collection of so-called revisionist materials dealing with *The Diary*.

62. On Philip Roth see John N. McDaniel, *The Fiction of Philip Roth* (Haddonfield, N.J.: Haddonfield House, 1974); Bernard F. Rogers, Jr., *Philip Roth* (Boston: G. K. Hall, 1978); Glenn Meeter, *Philip Roth and Bernard Malamud: A Critical Essay* (Grand Rapids, Mich.: William B. Eerdmans, 1968); and Sanford Pinsker, *The Comedy That "Hoits": An Essay on the Fiction of Philip Roth* (Columbia: University of Missouri Press, 1975). On the question of Roth's "self-hatred" see Theodore Solotaroff, "Philip Roth and the Jewish Moralists," *Chicago Review* 13 (1959), 87–99; and Allen Guttman, "Philip Roth and the Rabbis," in his *The Jewish Writer in America: Assimilation and the Crisis of Identity* (New York: Oxford University Press, 1973), 64–76. In general, see Robert Alter, *After the Tradition: Essays on Modern Jewish Writing* (New York: E. P. Dutton, 1969).

63. Roth's comments are taken from his essay "Writing about Jews" (1974), reprinted in his *Reading Myself and Others* (New York: Farrar, Straus & Giroux, 1975), here 160.

64. Peter Shaw, "Portnoy and His Creator," *Commentary* 47 (1977), 77–79.

65. Roth, "Writing about Jews," 165.

66. All quotations are from Philip Roth, *The Ghost Writer* (Harmondsworth: Penguin, 1980).

67. The best overview of the life and writings of I. J. Singer is Clive Sinclair, *The Brothers Singer* (London: Allison & Busby, 1983). See also Charles Madison, *Yiddish Literature: Its Scope and Major Writers* (New York: Schocken, 1968), 449–78; Irving Howe, "The Other Singer," *Commentary* 41 (1966), 78, 80–82; and N. Mayzl, *Forgeyer un Mittsaytler* (New York: Cyco, 1946), 372–91.

68. All references are to the English translation of *The Family Carnovsky* by Joseph Singer (New York: Harper & Row, 1969), here 24. On the novel see the essay by M. Ravitsch in *Tsukunft*, March 1944, 87 ff., as well as the following reviews of the English translation: P. Adams, *Atlantic Monthly*, 223 (February 1969), 133; J. Bauke, *Saturday Review*, 22 March 1969, 66; A. Bezanker, Nation, 23 June 1969, 800; H. Roskelenko, *New York Times Book Review*, 16 November 1969, 72–73; and S. Simon, *Library Journal*, 1 January 1969, 97.

69. Friedrich Nietzsche, *The Genealogy of Morals*, cited in *Basic Writings of Nietzsche*, trans. Walter Kaufmann (New York: Modern Library, 1966), 599.

70. The best analysis of these figures is Dorothy Seidman Bilik, *Immigrant-Survivors: Post-Holocaust Consciousness in Recent Jewish American Fiction* (Middletown, Conn.: Wesleyan University Press, 1981). See also Malcolm Bradbury, *Saul Bellow* (London: Methuen, 1982); Jeanne Braham, *A Sort of Columbus* (Athens: University of Georgia Press, 1984); Daniel Fuchs, *Saul Bellow: Vision and Revision* (Durham, N.C.: Duke University Press, 1984); Jan Bakker, *Fiction as Survival Strategy* (Amsterdam: Rodopi, 1983); Irving Malin, ed., *Saul Bellow and the Critics* (New York: New York University Press, 1967); and John Jacob Clayton, *Saul Bellow: In Defense of Man* (Bloomington: Indiana University Press, 1979).

71. Saul Bellow, *Herzog* (New York: Viking Press, 1964), 1.

72. Saul Bellow, *Mr. Sammler's Planet* (New York: Viking Press, 1970), 136.

73. See Murray Baumgarten, "Language Rules," in his *City Scriptures: Modern Jewish Writing* (Cambridge: Harvard University Press, 1982), 112–35.

74. See, for example, Rosten's extraordinary justification of his use of dialect in Leo Rosten, *O Kaplan, My Kaplan* (London: Constable, 1979). One must compare this to the absence of dialect to characterize a subgroup of Jews in modern Israeli humor (see Elliott Oring, *Israeli Humor: The Content and Structure of the Chizbat of the Palmah* [Albany: State University of New York Press, 1981]). Rosten has come to be the touchstone for the "comic" Jew's use of *mauscheln* in English. See, for example, Philip Howard's column "For Liking Yinglish, I Should Apologize?" *The Times* (London), 18 June 1983, which sees *mauscheln* only as the sign of the "comic" Jew, the Jew as coward and materialist, the Jew as creator of different discourses, and closes with a reference to Rosten.

75. Mordecai Richler, *St. Urbain's Horseman* (London: Weidenfeld & Nicolson, 1971), 62 ff. See Victor J. Ramraj, *Mordecai Richler* (Boston: Twayne, 1983); Arnold E. Davidson, *Mordecai Richler* (New York: Ungar, 1983); George Woodcock, *Mordecai Richler* (Toronto: McClelland & Stewart, 1970); and G. David Sheps, ed., *Mordecai Richler* (Toronto: Ryerson Press, 1971). See also David Rome, *Clouds in the Thirties: On Antisemitism in Canada, 1929–1939: A Chapter on Canadian Jewish History* (Montreal, 1977).

76. Mordecai Richler, "Hemingway Set His Own Hours," *New York Times Book Review*, 11 September 1983, 48.

77. Philip Roth, *Zuckerman Unbound* (New York: Farrar, Straus & Giroux, 1981), 16.

78. On Allen see Mark Shechner, "Woody Allen: The Failure of the Therapeutic," in Cohen, *From Hester Street*, 231–45. On the context of the film see Lester D. Friedman, *Hollywood's Image of the Jew* (New York: Ungar, 1982).

79. Philip Roth, *The Anatomy Lesson* (New York: Farrar, Straus & Giroux, 1983). The epilogue, "The Prague Orgy," is published in the collected edition of Philip Roth's trilogy published under the title *Zuckerman Bound* (New York: Farrar, Straus & Giroux, 1985), 701–84.

80. Heinrich Heine, "The New Jewish Hospital in Hamburg," cited in the translation from S. S. Prawer, *Heine's Jewish Comedy* (Oxford: Clarendon, 1983), 433.

81. See esp. Steven M. Cohen, *American Modernity and Jewish Identity* (New York: Methuen, 1983). On the general context of anti-Semitism in America see Nathan Perlmutter and Ruth Ann Perlmutter, *The Real Anti-Semitism in America* (New York: Arbor House, 1982); Ernest Volkman, *A Legacy of Hate: Anti-Semitism in America* (New York: Watts, 1982); Bela Vago, ed., *Jewish Assimilation in Modern Times* (Boulder, Colo.: Westview Press, 1981); David A. Hollinger, "Ethnic Diversity,

Cosmopolitanism and the Emergence of the American Liberal Intelligentsia," *American Quarterly* 27 (1975), 133–51; and Glenn C. Altschuler, *Race, Ethnicity and Class in American Social Thought, 1865–1919* (Arlington Heights, Ill.: Harlan Davidson, 1983).

Index

456 INDEX

SANDER L. GILMAN is Professor of Humane Studies in the departments of German and Near Eastern Studies at Cornell University and professor of Psychiatry at the Cornell Medical College. Among his books are *Bertolt Brecht's Berlin*, *The Face of Madness: Hugh W. Diamond and the Rise of Psychiatric Photography*, *On Blackness without Blacks*, and *Seeing the Insane: A Cultural History of Psychiatric Illustration*.

THE JOHNS HOPKINS UNVERSITY PRESS

JEWISH SELF-HATRED

This book was composed in Trump Medieval by EPS Group, Inc., from a design by Martha Farlow. It was printed on 50-lb. Sebago Eggshell Cream Offset paper and bound in Holliston Payko by The Maple Press Company.